RUSTIC ARCHITECTURE

SEARCHING FOR AUTHENTICITY RUSTIC ARCHITECTURE IN AMERICA 1877-1940

EDWARD R. FORD

ORO
EDITIONS

ORO Editions
Publishers of Architecture, Art, and Design
Gordon Goff: Publisher

www.oroeditions.com
info@oroeditions.com

Published by ORO Editions

USA, EUROPE, ASIA, MIDDLE EAST, SOUTH AMERICA

Book Design: Pablo Mandel / CircularStudio.com
Typeset in Akzidenz-Grotesk Pro

10 9 8 7 6 5 4 3 2 1 First Editions

Library of Congress data available upon request.

ISBN: 978-1-957183-94-7

Color Separations and Printing by ORO Editions Inc.
Printed in China

ORO Editions makes a continuous effort to minimize the overall carbon footprint of its publications. As part of this goal, ORO, in association with Global ReLeaf, arranges to plant trees to replace those used in the manufacturing of the paper produced for its books. Global ReLeaf is an international campaign run by American Forests, one of the world's oldest nonprofit conservation organizations. Global ReLeaf is American Forests' education and action program that helps individuals, organizations, agencies, and corporations improve the local and global environment by planting and caring for trees.

Contents

8 Introduction

11 **THE OTHER LIFE**

13 The Malaise of the Overcivilized
19 English Origins
33 Downing, Vaux, and Olmsted: The Rustic in America

45 **THE ADIRONDACKS**

47 Thomas and William Durant
57 Grosvenor Atterbury
77 William Wicks and Augustus Shepard

87 **THE CHALET**

89 The Chalet: Kirtland Cutter in Chicago
99 The Log Chalet

105 **THE RAILROAD**

107 Railroads, National Parks and the Northern Pacific
112 Sublime Imperialism
115 Yellowstone: Building a Railroad, Building a Park

125 **THE RUSTIC**

127 Rustic Begins: Two Log Cabins
137 The Old Faithful Inn
165 The Longs Peak Inn
169 The Surreal

173 **THE FOREST RUIN**

175 Sacred Groves
183 The Portland Forestry Building: The Temple of Capitalism
199 Bernard Maybeck: The Grove of Redwoods

223 **THE MONUMENT AND THE CHALET**

225 The Great Northern Railroad
229 Louis Hill: Monuments and Chalets
234 The American Sublime
237 Glacier National Park: The Hotels
263 Glacier Park Chalets: Into the Wilderness
277 Kirtland Cutter in Montana

297 **GEOLOGY**

299 Geology and Ruins
305 The Santa Fe Railroad
309 Mary Colter: The Lookout Studio and Hermit's Rest
325 Geology: Herbert Maier and Gilbert Underwood
353 The Desert Watchtower: The Hopi, the Diné, and Mary Colter
362 Cultural Appropriation

365 **RATIONALISTS AND ROMANTICS**

367 Literary Rationalism
375 The Paradise Inn: Rationalist Prologue
388 Albert Good's Bible
391 Stephen Mather and the Log Cabin
397 Park Service Pragmatists: Gilbert Underwood, Daniel Hull and Fred Willson
427 Park Service Romantics: Thomas Vint and Ernest Davidson
443 Herbert Maier and the Roofless Museum

467 **CONCLUSION**

474 **ACKNOWLEDGMENTS**

476 **END NOTES/BIBLIOGRAPHY**

486 **DRAWING SOURCES**

494 **ILLUSTRATION CREDITS**

498 **INDEX**

INTRODUCTION

I wrote the paragraph that begins this book ten years ago. Its content has not changed and its location in the text has not moved. It is the story of Horace Kephart, who in 1904 abandoned a conventional life and home in the suburbs to pursue a "primitive" life in the backwoods of North Carolina in a primitive hut he built for himself. I thought this story contained a lesson about ourselves, perhaps about another version of ourselves than the one we know, and I thought it contained a lesson about a different kind of architecture than the one we inhabit.

Kephart's hut was a very small part of a much larger phenomenon, the emergence of a particular type of architecture between 1880 and 1910, the rustic. There was something about rustic architecture that sets it apart from other American stylistic interludes. To be sure the Greek revival and the Colonial revival had ideological foundations in addition to providing historic nostalgia, and the Gothic revival had a whiff of the exotic accompanying its piety, but rustic architecture was fundamentally different. The buildings were a mechanism for a transformation of the fundamentals of living, including the fundamentals of building.

Rustic architecture and those who pursued it were a manifestation of a particular condition of that same era, identified as the "malaise" of overcivilization. It was a desire for a life closer to nature, to escape the city for the country, to connect to our primal origins, to abandon the sophisticated present for the primitive past.

The rest of the text that follows that first paragraph has been in constant flux over those ten years. More was discarded than was included. Conclusions were abandoned and rehabilitated. Endless variations of countless paragraphs were explored. There were two problems. For many the primal experience was temporary and much shorter, the great mass of tourists for whom a three-day escape into the primitive could happily coexist with a conventional urban life. The connection between Kephart's dramatic, permanent life change and a tourist's one-week rustic vacation was not clear and it was not clear that there was a connection.

The rustic life was a much larger social phenomenon than a few hermits in the woods. What was unique to this era was not the desire to escape but the massive numbers of those who did so, the millions of visitors to the Adirondacks and the thousands of visitors to the national parks. It was mass tourism and it was hard to believe that the primitive qualities of Kephart's experience could be duplicated in massive numbers for short periods of time.

And rustic architecture was a much larger economic phenomenon than a few huts in the woods. It involved the production of large-scale, often highly industrialized architecture to accommodate the plethora of tourists in the years 1883-1940. It can be argued that much of this is glib and often pure fiction in terms of truly rustic experience. And it can be argued that the alternate architecture, like the alternate life, was an equally glib and shallow veneer.

But there was a larger problem still. Seeing this architecture solely in the context of the "malaise" is to not understand it at all. The era of 1865-1910 also saw the exponential growth, followed by the near collapse, of the transcontinental railroads, a massive, high-maintenance infrastructure that often lacked customers. The unneeded railroads needed markets. Tourism beckoned, and the desire for an escape from civilization, however short, provided a much-needed market. Those suffering from the malaise of over-civilization had to be seduced by mass marketing, and rustic architecture was the tool. The architecture was as much the product of capitalist greed as of existential angst.

However creative that architecture was, it was part of something much larger that was highly destructive. Rustic architecture was an integral component of nineteenth-century mass tourism; mass tourism was an integral component of the development of not just the West but the industrial exploitation of its forests, its prairies, and its deserts and the building of the railroads was at its heart.

The task it seemed was to find the connection between a widespread social and spiritual desire, a massive industry created to accommodate it, an apocalyptic economic movement that drove it all, and a form of architecture built to house it. I was tempted at times to conclude that the whole enterprise—the preservation of fragments of wilderness simultaneous with the destruction of much of the landscape, the expropriation by imitation of Native American cultures that were simultaneously being obliterated—were simply trophies of a colonial conquest that pretended to be uniquely American but were no different than similar colonial trophies in India and elsewhere.

I came to conclude that while all of this was at times true, there was something more than mere play-acting, however tainted its origins and however deplorable the actions of its builders, something that did manifest an alternative life and that took place in an architecture that was, at times, truly an alternative way of building, not just a pretense but a reality. There were many with a genuine desire for an alternative life closer to nature, there were many for whom it was a glib charade, and there were a much larger number that straddled the boundary between the two.

There was architecture that was genuinely rustic, built in a way closer to nature and there were veneers of pseudo-craft designed to hide the industrial realities below, and there was much architecture that at times did both, often in the same building. I hope I have made the case that there is great architecture in this body of work, but the line between the sham and the authentic, between preservation and appropriation, between greed and altruism, is decidedly blurred. The text that follows describes works of art as profound and creative as any American work of architecture but they coexisted alongside some glib and superficial work.

There is yet another problem—a conspicuous one. We are engaged at present in an intense evaluation and perhaps reinvention of the way we evaluate buildings, coming to terms with history, with clients that were flawed in ways we did not realize, with historians and theoreticians whose work is founded on beliefs we despise and practicing architects who were complicit in both.

This text is written with the assumption that buildings can embody a set of beliefs, which is not the same thing as being associated with a set of beliefs—and while the line between the two is not easy to locate it is a critical boundary. In the text that follows I will try to locate this boundary between the values, good or bad, that are inherent in these building and not merely assigned to them.

Despite all this, the architectural results remain significant. It is an architecture that, then and now, evokes a variety of reactions—nostalgia, awe, romantic allusion, and empathy with nature itself. Like any architectural style it contains some kitsch, some masterpieces, and a great deal that falls between. There is just below the surface the troubling consequences of the processes that produced it, that the architecture was achieved at a cultural, economic, and ecological price. But at its best it produced something truly original, something true to the best impulses of those who wished to experience it, if not necessarily always to those who built it.

Perhaps the truth is that it is not the rustic architecture that is glib and shallow, but rather the way we have come to understand it.

THE OTHER LIFE

THE MALAISE OF THE OVERCIVILIZED

What did you go out into the wilderness to look at? A reed being shaken by the wind? But What did you go out to see?[1]

Jesus' question to John the Baptist
Matthew 11:7-8

Horace Kephart was to all appearances a success. He was, in 1900, the head of the Mercantile Library in St. Louis, married, the father of five children, and beginning a career as a writer and editor. But 1904 found him a changed man,unemployed, abandoned by his family, recovering from bouts of alcoholism and depression, and living in a tent in the woods to the west of Asheville, North Carolina. Yet none of the problems of his family and career were the sole reason or even the primary reason for his changed circumstances. He later explained: "This instinct for a free life in the open is as natural and wholesome as is the gratification of hunger and thirst and love. It is Nature's recall to the simple mode of existence that she intended us for. Our modern life in cities is an abrupt and violent change from what the race has been bred to these many thousands of years."[2] He moved into a cabin with the inset of winter, but he never left the Smokies. He was not alone with these impulses.

John Burroughs owned a large, well-furnished house on the Hudson, but in 1896 he largely abandoned it and built a small log cabin for himself about a mile away. He wrote: "The work of reclaiming that wild land seemed to stir the aboriginal instinct in me and I found myself longing for a wigwam or cabin to which I might retire when I was in the mood and live a life of rude simplicity."[3] He stayed there twelve years. When he moved, he moved to another cabin.

In 1879, Frank Cushing was assigned by the US Department of Ethnology to spend three weeks at the Zuni Pueblo in western New Mexico. He spent five years there, learning their language, eating their food, wearing their clothes, learning their history and rituals. He was adopted by the tribe, and left only when the government forced him to.

All of these events took place between 1879 and 1904 and there are many similar stories from the same period of people abandoning not just their daily lives but the civilization that housed them for a life that was in some way archaic, following impulses they saw as intuitive, living the existence nature intended us for. It coincided exactly with Paul Gauguin's departure from Paris to live a "primitive" life in Tahiti. Gauguin died in the South Pacific. Kephart, Burroughs, and Cushing made a clean, long-term if not permanent break with over-civilization, but there were others for whom escape was temporary. The escape might be for a summer in the Adirondacks.

John Muir, writing in 1901 said: "Thousands of tired, nerve-shaken, over-civilized people are beginning to find out that going to the mountains is going home; that wildness is a necessity."[4] Writing in 1981, T. J. Jackson Lears used this same term, overcivilized, to describe a central condition of the period 1880 to 1920:

Toward the end of the nineteenth century, many beneficiaries of modern culture began to feel they were its secret victims. ... American anti-modernism, particularly in its dominant form—the recoil from an 'overcivilized' modern existence to more intense forms of physical or spiritual experience supposedly embodied in medieval or Oriental cultures.[5]

Opposite: Horace Kephart's first camp

Horace Kephart

John Burroughs at Slabsides

Thomas Eakins' *Portrait of Frank Cushing*

The result was a widespread search for what Lears calls "authentic" experiences and resulted in a variety of phenomenon, including the arts and crafts movement. At the same time this phenomena did not condemn the society that had produced it.

Kephart and Burroughs saw no compromise with turning their backs on civilization. Far more common were those who wanted to inhabit both worlds—the modern and the archaic. As Lears writes: "Anti-modernism was not simply escapism; it was ambivalent, often coexisting with enthusiasm for material progress. ... a complex blend of accommodation and protest."[6]

And there were many others whose wilderness experience was short lived or intermittent but no less sincere. In1897, the composer Edward MacDowell bought a large, comfortable roadside house for himself in rural New Hampshire, but he soon built a one-room log cabin for himself about a half mile away where he retired daily to work in solitude. In 1903, the painter Charles Russell built a cabin of logs (actually telephone poles) for himself in the backyard of his Queen Anne clapboard house in Great Falls, Montana. He retired there daily to work.

It was a phenomenon not confined to intellectuals and artists. The two founders of the Philips Petroleum company, Frank and Waite Phillips, did something very similar. Waite built a log cabin in the backyard of his first home and then when he built an Italianate mansion in New Mexico, built a number of log cabins in the surrounding mountains. His biographer surmises he was trying to recreate an idyllic time of his boyhood. His older brother Frank built a Palladian mansion in the city, built a log cabin mansion in the country and adjacent to the log mansion built a small replica of the log cabin he lived in as a child.[7]

Were the permanent impulses of Kephart, Burroughs, and Cushing profound and the temporary impulses of MacDowell, Russell, and the Philips brothers glib? It seems unlikely. The latter group were able to move back and forth between their two worlds, and there were the hundreds if not thousands who owned a home in the city, often a neoclassical one, and a log cabin retreat in the Adirondacks or elsewhere. One life needed the other. It was not indecision; it was necessity, a need of the "other," the creation of a life that is a mirror of the life one lives in which everything is reversed.

The idea that the end of the nineteenth-century malaise was a particular historical moment is convincing but an equally plausible explanation for the phenomenon of the rustic retreat that it is the result of universal, even archetypal, impulses. Kephart and Burroughs certainly saw the impulses that drove them as timeless, not the result of an end of the century malaise. The need to escape from the city is as old as the city. It is more than a question of escape from urban density but a reconnection to primal desires, which are even older.

Seneca, writing around 59 CE describes this:

Believe me, that was a happy age, before the days of architects, before the days of builders! All this sort of thing was born when luxury was being born,—this matter of cutting timbers square and cleaving a beam with unerring hand as the saw made its way over the marked-out line. ... For they were not preparing a roof for a future banquet-hall; for no such use did they carry the pine trees or the firs along the trembling streets with a team of drays—merely to fasten thereon panels heavy with gold. Forked poles erected at end propped up their houses. With close-packed branches and with leaves heaped up and laid sloping they contrived a drainage for even the heaviest rains. Beneath such dwellings they lived, but they lived in peace. A thatched roof once covered free men; under marble and gold dwells slavery.[8]

There were a variety of phenomenon driving the escape from overcivilization particular to its age—lifestyles disconnected from the natural world, a kind of boredom with conventional religion, a desire for a true spiritual experience, the rise of corporate capitalism, the increase in urban populations. All could be factors.

There are a variety of developments, generally specific to the period—the rise of camping and the publication of guidebooks to wilderness survival. Nessmuk's *Woodcraft* was a prominent one, but there were many others—Horace Kephart's *Camping and Woodcraft* (1917) or Dan Beard's *Shelters, Shacks and Shanties* (1914). The era saw the creation of the Boy Scouts, the Girl Scouts (1912), the Campfire Girls (1910), and the establishment of communities like Gustav Stickley's Craftsman Farms and the creation of a number of national parks.

So, the idea that the creation of the Adirondack camps and the national parks are symptoms of an end of the nineteenth-century malaise, characterized by a sense of being overcivilized, of being too far removed from the natural world, in search of authentic experiences, can explain a great deal, but in other ways it does not quite fit.

There is a third explanation, that the temporary wilderness experience was little more than a hollow ritual. Collis P. Huntington bought Camp Pine Knot in the Adirondacks in 1890 and began to spend a good deal of time there. J. P. Morgan owned a camp, Uncas, close by. Alfred Vanderbilt's family spent much time at Camp Sagamore in the Adirondacks. They went hunting and fishing with guides but there was little that was rustic about their lives other than the bark and log walls. There was an army of servants and staff to provide for their comfort and they frequently had large gatherings. There was not much solitude and it is not a life that can easily be seen as an "other." It was probably not devoid of authentic experiences, but Vanderbilt and Morgan did not think of themselves as overcivilized. It seems doubtful that their time in the woods was the product of a malaise.

Perhaps the most convincing explanation of the rusticated experience—the act of adapting for a short time a life the reverse of the norm—is that it is a necessary kind of "play." Isiah Berlin, quoting Schiller, characterizes the idea of romanticism in this way:

Schiller imagines that once upon a time there was a marvelous human unity, a golden age, where passion was not divided from reason, and liberty was not divided from necessity. Then something appalling happened: division of labor, inequality, civilization—in short, culture occurred, rather on the lines of Rousseau, and, as a result of this, ungovernable desires, jealousies, envies, men divided against other men, men divided against themselves, fraud, misery, alienation. How are we to get back to this original state without lapsing into some kind of innocence or childishness which is plainly neither feasible nor desirable? ... Schiller speaks about the Spieltrieb, 'play-drive'. He says that the only way in which human beings can liberate themselves is by adopting the attitude of games-players. What does he mean? Art for him is a form of play, and he explains that the difficulty for him is to reconcile on the one hand the necessities of nature, which cannot be avoided, and which cause stress, and on the other hand these rigorous commandments which narrow and contract life.

This play can take many forms, including cultural mimicry.

If we are children at play ... we can impersonate Red Indians, and if we imagine ourselves to be Red Indians, we are for these purposes Red Indians, and we obey the rules of Red Indians, without a sense of pressure; there is no pressure upon us because we invent the rules, and our parts, ourselves. Anything we make is ours, anything we make does not constrict us. ... if we can only do that, we are saved.[9]

A key point of course is what is thought to be authentic behavior is only being played at, then one must wonder if the architecture built to accommodate it is only a stage set.

Woolaroc, Frank Phillips cabin

Charles Russell cabin

Edward MacDowell cabin.

Pages from *Shelters, Shacks and Shanties* by Dan Beard

Architecture

But what was really unique about the search for the authentic rustic experience at the turn of the century was the sheer numbers of those participating—the quarter of a million people who visited the Adirondacks in 1900 or the 120,000 people that visited national parks in 1904.[10] Most stayed in tent camps, traveling in stagecoaches for a week or more. The more wealthy stayed in hotels. The more adventurous brought their own tents and made their own plans. Were they escaping an overcivilized world? Were they seeking authentic experiences? Undoubtedly some were.

But regardless of whether this age of reaction to overcivilization was a particular historic moment or the resurfacing of an old archetype, it was also something else. It was the age of the dramatic rise of modern rustic architecture. Rustic architecture was very old of course but this was rustic architecture as aesthetic intent not utilitarian necessity. The new architecture required the adaptation of the log cabin vocabulary not only to large houses, but to larger buildings—hotels, large recreational spaces, and exhibition buildings with long spans and complex structural requirements.

The Old Faithful Inn was begun in 1903. In 1905 a Swiss Chalet, El Tovar was built at the south rim of the Grand Canyon. The Great Northern Railway built two large rustic lodges and nine smaller chalets at Glacier.

Less visible but no less important were the log houses, one could say mansions, that were built for the wealthy between 1900 and 1910. Alfred Vanderbilt's primary residence in New York was a neoclassical marble palazzo, but his home in the Adirondacks was a log camp. E. H. Harriman and Louis Hill, controllers of the two great western railways, likewise possessed neoclassical and Renaissance private residences, but log houses in the West. Log rustic buildings were great attractions at the great fairs and exhibitions of the era—at Chicago in 1893, in Portland in 1905, and San Francisco in 1916.

The period that saw the rejection of overcivilization, of the pursuit of the authentic experience of the natural world,s was the same period that saw the rise of rustic architecture. Surely these are related phenomenon, if not the same phenomenon, but the two are not so neatly connected.

Authentic experience was about individuals. Rustic architecture was about masses of consumers. Given the numbers in search of authentic experience, what was an ideology became an economic opportunity. It became a tool of mass consumption. So how do the sentiments of a Kephart or Burroughs find their way into mass tourism and a week in the Adirondacks or Yellowstone, and how can all of these be embodied into the architecture that was to house them?

The Park Service did not exist before 1916 and the large rustic buildings constructed in the parks prior to that date are with few exceptions built by the railroads. Just as the beliefs of a Kephart or a Burroughs do not easily slide into the tastes of mass tourism or the lifestyles of a Morgan or a Vanderbilt. The building culture of axes and logs does not slide easily into the construction of hotels or mansions. The primitive architecture of Kephart and Burroughs may have stood outside the boundaries of normal society but the architecture of the railroads stood at its profit-driven capitalist center.

And if the masses of tourists and millionaires at times played at being rustic their architecture played at being rustic as well. It is an architecture that has its great moments. It produced some conceptually and formally uncomfortable hybrids, but it sometimes created a truly novel expression of a complex reality.

The rise of the middle class made the Adirondacks and Yellowstone accessible to multitudes, and of course it was the railroad which made it possible to access both. But the railroads were not passive participants in this architectural process. They promoted its creation, determined its organization, and manipulated both the economy and the government to do so, and ultimately did as much to determine the style as any pioneer craftsman with an axe.

Conclusion

Whether temporary or universal, the search for authentic experience is perhaps best explained by realizing that whatever its origins, the wilderness escape and the architecture created to accommodate it falls into the nebulous concept I will call the other, the other life housed in the other architecture. The life in the other house is usually temporary, because it is an existence that is not really open to us. It represents the other world we might live in, the different life we might have led, the different person we might have been, the sins we could have committed, the virtues we might have embodied, the alternative life. And it required a different architecture, of otherness, a radical alternative to the norm.

If the desire for alternative experience was a manifestation of a larger characteristic of the modern condition, or an archetypal phenomenon, rustic architecture can be seen in the same ways, something we inherited, not something we created. If the impulses were not new, nether was the architecture. It is a style closely associated with the wilderness, particularly national parks, but it did not originate there. Some of its forms came from the wilderness and some came from the great exhibitions of the period. Large parts of it came from the industrial/handcraft infrastructures the industrial forces in the West created. And just as the motives that produced it were hundreds of years old, so was the aesthetics that it employed.

There is a persistent thought not just in Western art but in Western culture that there was a time before this time, perhaps an ancient one, that was better. When life was simpler, more direct, more straightforward—a primitive life—where sophisticated technologies did not separate us from nature, where complex systems of thought did not cloud our analysis of simple problems, that there was a time when art was more natural, when it was not art at all. Problems of making, including problems of representation, were solved in a direct, vital, and straightforward way using what was at hand and unencumbered by the prejudices of precedent. It is of course one of the oldest archetypes, the loss of Eden.

F. M. Piper delin. 1779

ENGLISH ORIGINS

We are learning that harmony is more likely to result from a use of native materials. ... we incline to a humble respect for the past. We become aware of the unvoiced claims of those long-gone races and earlier generations that tracked the wilderness, plains, or desert before us. In fitting tribute we seek to grace our park structures by adaptation to their traditions and practices.[1]

So wrote Albert Good in 1938 in his three-volume, 6,000-page design manual *Park and Recreation Structures.* Almost all the work included was in the rustic style, buildings built in national and state parks, predominately in the 1920s and '30s. To Good, the rustic style is indigenous; it is regional; it had over long periods of time grown out of the land it occupies. It draws on multiple cultural heritages—English and Dutch settlers along the Atlantic seaboard, French fur traders along the Mississippi, Spanish settlers via Florida and Mexico. Good wrote: "Over the covered wagon routes the ring of the pioneer's axe is echoed in the efforts of today. The habits and primitive ingenuity of the American Indian persist and find varied expression over wide areas."[2]

The rustic architecture that appeared between 1885 and 1940 had its own unique qualities, but it came from more distant places and more distant pasts. It owed much to eastern America; it owed much more to Europe, particularly England. It drew from traditions that go back to Renaissance Italy and classical antiquity but it did so through an English lens. The immediate ancestors of rustic architecture came from the England of the romantic era, particularly its picturesque landscape traditions.

The leading English practitioners of this style were not untrained rustics, but writers, scientists, the leading architects of the period and the King's architectural tutor. Kephart, Burroughs, and Cushing had a great deal in common with them. They shared forms and techniques, but they also shared ideologies.

There was in eighteenth-century England an equally strong desire for the other life, however temporary, and there was an architecture to go with it. It was a life, an architecture, and an aesthetic that were the opposite to the traditional dwelling, the traditional lifestyle, and even the ideological norm.

Christopher Hussey characterizes the typical eighteenth-century English garden as a belt, as a sequential narrative, a series of events—evocative pavilions, structures, or views, along a path, often a loop.[3] These smaller buildings stood apart not just from the architectural language of the main house but the cultural norm and were meant to evoke another world, or at least another sensibility—the pagoda, the grotto, the ruin, the hermitage.

These buildings were anti-buildings, an alternative architecture, and to many an alternative life. The rustic aesthetic was always a kind of mirror—a reverse image—hidden in the garden, of the primary residence, just as American rustic architecture was to become a mirror of the architecture of the normal condition.

What follows are eight rustic paradigms, rustic prototypes, that, while they may have had short lives as fashionable English garden buildings, came to have many American descendants.

Opposite: The Root House, Stourhead

The Rustic Lodge:
Pavilion at Moor Park, c.1764

In the 1760s Robert Adam was working on the estate at Moor Park. His major focus was the large country house. It was huge, built of polished stone with a tile roof supported by Corinthian stone columns, all refined classical in form. He was also working simultaneously on another building at Moor Park, a lodge and tea pavilion. It was small and rustic, with a thatched roof supported by rough logs and suggestive of a rather crude Gothic building, different in every way from the main house and even more different from Adam's work as a whole.

This is a fairly universal type of eighteenth-century building—the garden pavilion that was built of an alternative architecture, usually as an outlying structure away from the main house. It was to be used only in certain conditions. The rustic buildings were a small part of something larger. This was very much about the architecture of the garden, particularly the narrative garden.

Such works were rarely part of the house and its immediate gardens. For Adam and many others this type of architecture was only appropriate in this context, as an alternative to the aesthetic norm. Uvedale Price wrote: "Near the house picturesque beauty must, in many cases, be sacrificed to neatness."[4] William Chambers thought this type of architecture had its place, but was only appropriate in certain circumstances and locations, it was always the architecture of the backyard garden pavilion: "Round the main habitation, and near all their decorated structures, the grounds are laid out with great regularity, and kept with great care. ... it [is] absurd to surround an elegant fabric with disorderly rude vegetation." But away from the main house, the mood changes: "When the buildings are rustic, the scenery which surrounds them is wild; when they are grand, it is gloomy; when gay, it is luxuriant."[5]

Many were critical of this kind of architecture; many are critical still, Adam's biographer Arthur Bolton despised this aspect of Adam's work calling it, "sham rusticity, a fashion which has a recurring tendency as we know to our own cost." It was to Bolton an act of rebellion: "The more highly organized the architectural tradition the greater will be the revolt, and the more passionate the insistence on the return of Nature, however difficult it may be to give a satisfactory philosophical basis to that enigmatical demand."[6]

But the difference between the norm of the main house and the eccentricity of the garden pavilion was about much more than architectural style. It could be a difference of craft—the archaic. It could be a return to the distant past to a life that was less refined.

The Temple of Logs:
A Return to Architectural Origins
Illustrations from "The Origins of Buildings and Orders," 1759

In 1759 William Chambers published his own theory of the primitive hut, "The Origins of Buildings and Orders," illustrated with two historical, hypothetical huts of his own invention. The first was a squared off temple of Doric-like wood shafts and capitals, and the second, the temple in ruins. Chambers' huts were simply historical rewinds, a small classical temple built with logs for columns. Chambers and Adam established the basic rustic methodology—taking a classical design, substituting logs for standard elements such as column shafts. Chambers' art historical process works in both directions from the primitive to the refined and from the refined to the ruin, from nature to architecture and back to nature.[7]

This became a standard methodology—a small classical temple in which the conventional materials of the temple were changed—to rusticated brick in place of polished stone, reed and plank with logs in place of classical columns, thatch in place of a traditional roof, and roughness in place of precision. It is clear from Chambers' writings that he meant this to be a model of the building in which the classical language was born. Chambers may have constructed or planned to construct a similar log temple at Kew about the same time. This model of the "other" architecture was the classical reenactment. Of course, the primitive hut did not originate with Chambers, although he originated the use of the term in English. Similar hypothetical constructions were made by Perrault, Blondel, and others. Chambers may have been aware of Laugier's drawings of the primitive hut of 1753 but his book was not published in English until 1755.

The rustic classical temple became commonplace. Adam designed several, and it appeared in the pattern books of the era. A 1767 example contained in *Grotesque Architecture or Rural Amusement* by William Wrighte illustrates a variety of grottoes and mosques. The first example is a primitive hut that Wrighte describes as a historical reenactment, "to be built with trunks of trees and irregular timber. The inside walls may be lined with moss, and covered on the top with thatch." Even in the popular press it retained its ideological content *as* Wrighte wrote: "It is intended to represent the primitive state of the Dorick Order, and is proper to be placed at the entrance of a wood, or on or on the top of a small eminence."[8]

This was the return to classical origins, but there were other architectural origins to return to.

The Section of MERLIN's CAVE in the Royal Gardens at Richmond.
as Design'd by Mr. Kent. J. Vardy delin. et sculp.

The Cathedral of Trees:
Merlin's Cave
Richmond, 1735

The theory that origins of Gothic architecture were imitations of the forest is as an idea as old as Raphael (c.1519) but Alexander Pope gave it its own life in the eighteenth century. Pope was something of a rock star in his day for his essays, poetry and influence on taste. But he was also a designer. He described an idea for a landscape design: "I have sometimes had an idea of planting an old gothic cathedral in trees. Good large poplars with their white stems, cleared of boughs to a proper height would serve very well for the columns, and might form the different aisles or peristiliums, by their different distances and heights."[9] Like Chambers' garden pavilion Pope's grove was to be a return to origins but not to classical ones. Its form was drawn from Gothic buildings but its real ancestor was rather itself, a grove of trees.

William Warburton, the bishop of Gloucester and the editor of Pope's collected works, shared with Pope the conviction that Gothic architecture originated in groves of trees: "For having been accustomed, during the gloom of paganism, to worship the Deity in Groves (a practice common to all nations) when their new religion required covered edifices, they ingeniously projected to make them resemble groves," not just the forms of Gothic but the details: "Nor could the Columns be otherwise than split into distinct shafts, when they were to represent the stems of clumps of Trees?"[10]

Warburton was not alone. William Stukeley was an Anglican cleric, but he was also a rustic architect, and a pioneer archaeologist. He studied Neolithic structures. He measured, and drew Stonehenge, which he thought, mistakenly, was built by Druids. He also saw Gothic as a literal as a copy in stone of a forest:

In British oak groves our old naturalists, poets & priest the Druids inculcated the precepts of religion, ... the groves were places more immoderately consecrated to the adoration of the supreme being. ... Thus the tall shaft of a column adorned with a capital of foliage work, is a fine imitation of the body of an oak trimmed up with a few loose leaves left at the top, ... Thus the body of the temple were crowded with long rows passed with numerous colonnades of pillars ... which perfectly resemble a chapel in a wood beset with alleys made by old hoary trunks of oaks.[11]

James Hall, Pages from *Essay on the Origin and Principles of Gothic Architecture, 1797*

For Stukeley the building of an "other" architecture became a stage for living an "other" life. Interest in Druidic culture led to obsession and then to imitation. He was not just a scholar; he was something like a reenactor. He may have performed Druidic rites at his own Druidic structures. And it was not just a return to Gothic, it was a return to nature—back to the uncorrupted origins of architecture.

Reconstructing pagan temples and reenacting Druidic rituals might seem odd activities for an Anglican clergymen but this was more than a return to the natural origins of architecture. It was a return to the origins of British architecture and the origins of British religion. There was a strong element of nationalism in this which helps explain most conspicuous and least likely member of this group, Queen Caroline, wife to George II. Having lived in Germany until she was thirty, it is easy to understand what appears to be a desire to connect ideologically to the origin of British character and culture. In 1735 she built her own Gothic temple emerging from a forest in the gardens of Richmond palace, Merlin's cave. William Kent was the architect, assisted by two of Stukeley's associates. Merlin's cave consisted of three conical thatched roofs supported by three vaulted spaces, Gothic in form but constructed of a rustic wood frame and plaster vaults. It was a national cultural memorial, with wax statues of characters from English history and library of key English books housed in rustic bookcases.

Examples of a truly Gothic garden pavilion, one that replicates the shafts, ribs, and vaults of Amiens or Lincoln are rare, no doubt because of the difficulty in finding geometrically suitable tree trunks and branches. But it fell to James Hall to prove the point by replicating the process by arranging a grove to resemble a cathedral. Since his constructions were more large-scale models than buildings using easily bent wood rods, he proved neither that it was possible nor that it had happened. This theory of Gothic origins has few adherents today, but if the idea was popular in eighteenth-century England, it became an epidemic in nineteenth-century America.

The Grotto: An Alternative Nature
Alexander Pope's Grotto, 1725-39

The grotto in the garden is an ancient tradition, common in Ancient Rome and the Italy of the 1500s as in the large one in the Boboli Gardens of 1583. Alberti wrote of the grotto extensively. But when Alexander Pope built his own in 1725-39 it became a must-have garden experience in England. A visitor describes it:

Cataracts of Water Precipitating over your Head, from impending Stones and Rocks, while saliant Sprouts rise in rapid Streams at your Feet: Around, you are equally surprized with flowing Rivulets and rolling Waters, that rush over airey Precipices, and break amongst Heaps of ideal Flints and Spar.[12]

Like the log temple it presumes a transformation of nature into architecture, but this time geological.

The plan tells a different story than the description of the phenomenological experience. It was dependent on its classical skeleton. Its shape is that of a traditional classical interior, composed of columns, domes, and exedras but all obscured by a rough-edged incrustation of shells and rocks—a structure that is not quite nature, but neither is it architecture.

A ruin of the same type—a ruin of transformed nature—is one of the best known of these grottoes and the best preserved; it was built in1746 at Stourhead. Like Adam's rustic work it is a classic form given a rough rustic surface. In this case a Pantheon-like space with a cave-like encrustation of stones that give the walls the appearance of being lava.

Like the log temple, it presumes a transformation of nature into architecture, but this time it is stone, not wood. Its intention is, in the same way of many rustic buildings, to blur the line between nature and architecture. But Adam's and Chambers' buildings are assembled of parts. The grotto was excavated. It was nature that was occupied. The eighteenth-century fascination with rustic architecture was in some ways the same phenomenon. Both involve the erosion of the human-made object of ideal geometry, turning it back into the materials of which it had emerged from. But if the building in the process of emerging from nature had an appeal, even more appealing was the building returning to nature.

A Return to Nature: Studley Royal, 1767

Incorporating ruins into gardens, particularly Gothic ones, was much the fashion of the day, so much so that the construction of pseudo-ruins was equally popular. One of the largest was created when William Aislabie extended the garden at Studley Royal to include the large crumbling, roofless walls of the ruins of the Fountains Abbey, built in the twelfth century.

Ruins appealed to a multitude of sentiments but there were two distinct types—the ruin as memory and the ruin as nature. William Shenstone saw ruins as memory—they were the monument to a past that has been lost, what he called, "that pleasing melancholy which proceeds from a reflection on decayed magnificence."[13] Shelley's poem *Ozymandias* is a familiar example.

William Gilpin saw it differently. The appreciation of ruins was not about nostalgia, or even about the past. It was about the eternal battle between human-made-architecture and the nature that will eventually reclaim it. He said of Fountains Abbey: "A ruin is a sacred thing. Rooted for ages in the soil, assimilated to it and becoming as it were a part of it. We consider it as a work of nature, rather than of art."[14]

Georg Simmel codified the view in his essay "The Ruin" in 1911:

Architecture is the only art in which the great struggle between the will of the spirit and the necessity of nature issues into real peace: that in which the soul in its upward striving and nature in its gravity are held in balance. ... Although architecture, too, uses and distributes the weight and carrying power of matter according to a plan conceivable only in the human soul. ... The ruin of a building, however, means that where the work of art is dying. Other forces and forms, those of nature, have grown; and that out of what of art still lives in the ruin and what of nature already lives in it, there has emerged a new whole, a characteristic unity.[15]

In the second school of thought the ruin was an analog of nature. It sought architecture that sat between the natural and the human-made—between a cave and a dome as in the grotto, between a forest and a temple as in the primitive hut, and it was important to be neither and at the same time both.

An Alternative Aesthetic: The Surreal
The Stourhead Root House, 1770

Stourhead is one of the best architecturally preserved gardens in England, but a key piece is gone—the Root House built in 1770 by Henry Hoare. It seems to have formed a pair with the nearby Grotto. Both were subterranean voids taking the form of a small domed interior something like the Pantheon, but in the case of the Root House this overall form is almost illegible beneath its incrustation of natural materials. The Root House walls were formed of tree trunks and branches and the individual parts—twisted, usually forked branches—were chosen for their irregularity to suggest the architectural emerging from nature or nature emerging from architecture. The logs begin to break free of the surface of the dome find their own more irregular form. It suggests a very different architecture than most of the contemporary hermitages and follies, one assembled from parts, not by subdividing a geometric form. I will categorize this impulse as the surreal.

The Root House is the surreal and not the classic version of the rustic. Many rustic buildings, like those of Adam, were simply bark-on-log versions of familiar precedents. Structures of this type departed only a little from classical forms. Columns, pediments, and entablatures were simply partially or totally made of logs. Proportions and classical forms—tholos, stoa, etc.—were unchanged. Buildings might draw on Gothic precedents, but the method would be the same. Adam's classic rustic buildings have far more repose and far less animation than the Root House.

The Root House suggests something altogether different, an alternative formal strategy, less symmetrical, un-balanced, fragmented, assembled from parts, made with irregular logs, and executed with a strategy of letting the assembly of those irregular forms dictate the overall form. In this mode each piece maintains its own visual identity, exhibiting an external character that is the result of inner forces. The geometric form of the totality almost disappears under the identity of its parts. The Root House transcended the roughened-up classicism of the typical garden pavilions to take on a more animated, non-geometric form.

The surreal goes beyond transformed classicism. It is a decidedly unclassical aesthetic implying that one might read these irregular twisting forms as having a kind of inner animation. Price describes this type as well:

There is often a sort of spirit and animation in the manner in which old neglected pollards stretch out their immense limbs, roads, and in every wild and irregular direction: on some, the large knots and protuberances add to the ruggedness of their twisted trunks. ... as the finest timber tree (however beautiful in other respects) with all its health and vigour, cannot exhibit.[16]

The Root House aesthetic to many seemed dangerous territory. Rustic buildings were not an alternative way of composing architecture, simply an alternative palate of materials. John Plaw, author of one of the many pattern books of the era, felt that all architecture should be:

constructed on the principles of symmetry and correspondence of parts ... I am aware some persons think Dwellings on a humble scale, and Cottages, ought rather to be irregular in their forms, and broken in their parts, taking certain structures for examples, which, in my opinion, should rather serve as beacons of danger, warnings of bad taste. What man of genius would think of building a new house, having the patchwork and bungling appearance of an old one?[17]

The qualities of the picturesque—decay and fragmentation—can be read as ruins and often are, as a kind of embodied history, but it can also be understood as the natural result of inner forces.

The two strands of rustic architecture, the classical world of externally applied form and the surreal world of form that comes from within, or if you prefer, the beautiful and the picturesque, and the tensions between them were to continue well into the twentieth century.

What I am calling the surreal is a quality that at the time was known as the picturesque. To Uvedale Price the otherness of the rustic was not beautiful but what he called picturesque, described in his *An Essay on the Picturesque, as Compared with the Sublime and the Beautiful* (1794). A well-preserved Greek temple was beautiful; a Greek temple in ruins was picturesque. The picturesque possessed the opposite qualities of the beautiful: roughness rather than smoothness, sudden rather than gradual variation, age and decay rather than youth and freshness. Price summarized, "qualities of roughness, and of sudden variation, joined to that of irregularity, are the most efficient causes of the picturesque." Irregularity in practice, usually meant asymmetry and incompleteness.[18]

F. M. Piper, Drawing of the Stourhead Root House 1770

A Return to Simplicity: John Nash: The Swiss Cottage, Cahir, Ireland, 1810

Some felt rustic architecture was particularly inappropriate at the higher strata of society. According to Richard Payne Knight one cannot transpose the architecture of the humble dwelling to the residence of the elite: "to adapt the genuine style of a herdsman's hut, or a ploughman's cottage, to the dwellings of opulence and luxury, is as utterly impossible, as it is to adapt their language, dress, and manners to the refined usages of polished society."[19]

But many came to disagree, and many of the wealthy sought the rustic experience as well, usually for a short time. An example of the temporary is the "Swiss" cottage built around 1810, probably designed by John Nash, in Cahir, Ireland. It is a small part of the estate of Richard Butler, Lord Cahir, only a few miles from his primary home, Cahir castle. It seems to have been used in the manner of a *ferme ornée* where the residents played at being simple farm folk during short visits from their nearby castle for which they brought along the cook and the servants. Legend has it that it was an imaginary return to his impoverished childhood origins.

The Swiss dwelling was becoming popular. A building called a Swiss chalet was built by Jeffry Wyatville for the Duchess of Bedford with a thatched roof and two-story porches supported by tree-trunk columns, Endsleigh Cottage in 1815, including an Alpine garden.

We would recognize neither of these as what we think of as a chalet. It is an idea more from literature than architecture, popularized by Rousseau. In his novel *Julie: Or, The New Eloise* he describes the idyllic condition where natural impulses are uncorrupted, a chalet in the Alps where the heroine works. Despite the formal differences between these two Swiss buildings, they have common themes. The inhabitants both played at the temporary pursuit of an alternative life-a simple life, a life that was more natural, a life that someone at considerably lower income might lead but with plenty of servants. Both suggest an element of return, to a lost time, to one with a simpler, more natural pre-industrial life, or something less more personal, to a bygone moment in one's life, perhaps a return to imaginary childhood.

Monuments of Conquest: The Ruins at Virginia Water Windsor, 1826

In 1816, large segments of a Roman colonnade from the ruined city of Lepis Magna in North Africa were brought to England and presented to the Prince Regent, who, in 1826, had Jeffry Wyatville assemble them as a massive, oversized monumental ruin in Windsor Park, now called Virginia Water. It has the historically evocative qualities of ruins like Studley Royal and it has the same ambiguous boundary between the natural and the human made.

It is picturesque. It convoys a romanticism about the past. It creates an ambiguous boundary between the natural and human-made but it does something else.

It is the ruin of a lost culture taken as a trophy by one that has survived. It is also spolia appropriated from a conquered culture. It is a monument of conquest—a demonstration of the colonial power of the British imperial machine. Its appeal owes much to another concept particularly associated with the eighteenth-century English landscape—the sublime, a strange simultaneous experience of humility and arrogance, a sense that one is powerless in the face of natural events but at the same time the instrument of their implementation, one that was to become an enabling device in both England and America for cultural appropriation.

The Sublime: The Mountains

Arguably American rustic architecture's greatest debt to eighteenth-century England is not a form but an idea, an idea without which there might have been no national parks. In a general sense it is the concept of the sublime. In a specific sense it is the idea that mountains, particularly Alpine mountains, are beautiful. An idea that before the Enlightenment was rare.

In a 1712 essay Joseph Addison, editor of *The Spectator*, put forth the revolutionary idea that Alps were, if not exactly beautiful, aesthetically enjoyable. To him there was nothing in Italy more delightful than the, "vast heaps of mountains ... thrown together with so much irregularity and confusion." He wrote: "The Alps fill the mind with an agreeable kind of horror."[20]

In a later essay he dreams he is wandering through the Alps, an experience that which while challenging, is profound:

I fancied myself among the Alps, and as it is natural in a dream, seemed every moment to bound from one summit to another, till at last, after having made this airy progress over the tops of several mountains, I arrived at the very centre of those broken rocks and precipices. ... till I had gained the top of these white mountains, which seemed another Alps of snow. I looked down from hence into a spacious plain, which was surrounded on all sides by this mound of hills, and which presented me with the most agreeable prospect I had ever seen.[21]

Addison called this quality "greatness." Examples of greatness included vast uncultivated desserts, huge heaps of mountains, high rocks and precipices, or a wide expanse of waters, a place, "where we are not struck with the Novelty or Beauty of the Sight, but with that rude kind of Magnificence which appears in many of these stupendous Works of Nature."[22]

Greatness was not just about size, it was about a sense of the infinite, an object so expansive we cannot comprehend its limits: "Our Imagination loves to be filled with an Object, or to grasp at anything that is too big for its Capacity." It had a spiritual component as well: "We are flung into a pleasing Astonishment at such unbounded Views, and feel a delightful Stillness and Amazement in the Soul at the Apprehension[s] of them."[23]

What Addison called greatness is now universally called the sublime after Edmund Burke defined it half a century later in *A Philosophical Enquiry into the Origin of Our Ideas of the Sublime and Beautiful* (1757). Burke's thinking was simple. Beauty was a quality that caused pleasure. The sublime was a quality that caused pain. What was new in this was, as Burke observes: "we have a degree of delight, and that no small one, in the real misfortunes and pains of others,"[24] that is, the sublime could be pleasurable if we are observing pain or something potentially painful but not experiencing it: "The passions which belong to self-preservation turn on pain and danger; they are simply painful when their causes immediately affect us; they are delightful when we have an idea of pain and danger, without being actually in such circumstances."[25]

The sublime in landscape and architecture was, again, the result of enormous size and succession—a form of the infinite. Burke's examples of sublime architecture are generic, the, "ancient heathen temple" or the, "old cathedral." Their principle sublime qualities were, "greatness of dimension" either by simply being huge or by having an apparently infinite series of repetitive parts. The aisle of a great Gothic cathedrals is a prime example. To Burke this was not something to be imitated. A good building needed to be comprehended from a single viewpoint and even the interior of the Pantheon was to Burke defective since one could only see half of it at one time.

There were three aesthetics at work in the eighteenth-century aesthetic theory, in the terminology of the day—the beautiful, the sublime, and the picturesque. While there are countless designs that sought to be beautiful, and countless designs that sought to be picturesque, there were few that aspired to be sublime. Most thought the sublime a quality best confined to nature. There were examples of sublime buildings described in the key texts of the day, but they were typically generic, non-Western or Gothic.

This was a common eighteenth-century view. Chancing upon a sublime experience in nature was one thing, to deliberately create one in architecture was another. To deliberately pursue either of these was a mistake. Burke wrote: "Designs that are vast only by their dimensions, are always the sign of a common and low imagination. ... to be otherwise is the prerogative of nature only." Uvedale Price agreed with Burke. Sublime architecture was a bad idea, "to create the sublime is above our contracted powers, though we may sometimes heighten, and at all times lower its effects by art."[26]

Addison saw no reason this could not be translated into landscape or architectural design: "Greatness, in the works of architecture, may be considered as relating to the bulk and body of the structure, or to the manner in which it is built. As for the first, we find the ancients, especially among the Eastern nations of the world, infinitely superior to the moderns."[27] Pyramids, the Great Wall of China and the Tower of Babel possessed greatness because of size, but the Pantheon exhibited greatness because its interior walls extended beyond the limits of one's vision.

The eighteenth-century view of the sublime became the framework through which the nineteenth century viewed the American Landscape, particularly the West, but for another reason, that the sublime experience was not just intimidating. It was elevating. From Yosemite to Niagara, it is the way we see the American landscape, but it has a dark side. The nature of the sublime experience was seen as not just the relief of observing but not experiencing pain. It was about the simultaneous experience of being overwhelmed at one's insignificance while at the same time feeling exalted and empowered. Immanuel Kant saw the sublime in this way, as intimidating but simultaneously enabling:

Sublimity, therefore, does not reside in anything of nature, but only in our mind, in so far as we can become conscious that we are superior to nature within, and therefore also to nature without us. ... Only by supposing this Idea in ourselves, and in reference to it, are we capable of attaining to the Idea of the sublimity of that Being, which produces respect in us, not merely by the might that it displays in nature, but rather by means of the faculty which resides in us of judging it fearlessly.[28]

Contemporary writers such as Robert Doran, agree:

The transcendent in art or nature induces a feeling of inferiority *or submission; on the other, it is precisely by being overpowered that a high-minded feeling of* superiority *or* nobility of soul *... is attained. The tension between these two poles of a single experience—of being at once below and above, inferior and superior, humbled and exalted—produces the special dynamism of the sublime."* [29]

This type of dual experience was particularly characteristic of the Anglo experience of the Western American landscape. And the sublime became a desirable characteristic of much of the architecture of the West, that developed its own expression of power and monumentality. It also became a justification for much of the "inevitable" damage caused by western expansion,

The sublime experience is still very much with us-from the horror movie to bungee jumping. Its application in architecture and landscape has evolved. William Cronin argues that the sublime had lost its meaning in American aesthetics by the end of the nineteenth century. Mountains were simply beautiful; no anxiety was required to enjoy them.[30] For those who built the West, this was not the case.

Conclusion

All of these rustic prototypes were to find their way into the rustic architecture of America, especially in the West.

- The ruined grotto, the form emerging from geology, reappears in Arizona.
- The Greek Temple built of logs, the return to origins, reappears in Portland.
- The church that grew out of a forest, the temple of the ancients, reappears in San Francisco.
- The Root House with its internal vitality reappears in Wyoming.
- The sublime oversized humbling log basilica reappears in Montana.
- The chalet appears from the Adirondacks to Chicago and beyond.

The otherness of the English garden—the other architecture and the other life becomes a national obsession, complete with a national tourist industry. The process of how they arrived there is perhaps due to direct influence. But it may be something else. The passion for rustic buildings, like the desire to lead a more authentic, natural life, can be seen as a particular or universal phenomenon. We can see Horace Kephart's story as an example of an end of the century malaise or the resurfacing of universal impulses and we can see the many manifestations of rustic design in the same way. That they are a series of something like archetypal buildings that reappear periodically in history, or as elements of the thread of direct influence, from England to New York to the Adirondacks to the West.

Perhaps it was some deeply buried subconscious universal architecture, some combination of the spirit of the age with the nature of the place. Perhaps a reflection of a particular historical moment. But as for the question as to how they came to America the answer is direct influence through an architect who was well acquainted with the theory and practice of the English garden, Andrew Jackson Downing.

DOWNING, VAUX AND OLMSTED: THE RUSTIC IN AMERICA

Opposite: Central Park, The Children's Shelter, 1866

Historians tell us that the1840 election, between William Henry Harrison and Martin Van Buren, was the first modern presidential campaign, thus providing us with the first campaign slogan, the first campaign songs, and perhaps the first "messages" to keep on or go off of. It has become popularly known as the "log cabin campaign."

It began when a newspaper, *The Baltimore Republican*, said of Harrison: "Give him a barrel of hard cider and settle a pension of two thousand a year on him, and take my word for it, he will sit the remainder of his days in his log cabin,"[1] implying that Harrison, a hero of the Native American wars, was an unschooled rustic. He was in fact a child of the Virginia aristocracy, born in a mansion on the James. But his supporters, rather than denying the falsehood of the uncouth frontiersman, embraced it, and log cabin banners, log cabin toy houses, and log cabin whiskey bottles appeared everywhere. Harrison was a man of the people and his non-existent log cabin birthplace was the evidence. Thus the log cabin began its journey to becoming the great American icon. The log cabin is more symbolically loaded than the English Root House and it possessed a genealogical significance as a point of influence for any "real" American architecture that imitated it.

But if the log cabin was politically correct it was for many not architecture and as a cultural artifact is had little value. A Newburgh New York nursery owner named A. J. Downing wrote of it:

A dwelling house, for a civilized man, built with no higher aspirations than these, we look upon with the same feelings that inspire us when we behold the Indian, ... these are only manifestations of the grosser wants of life; and the mind of the civilized and cultivated man as naturally manifests itself in fitting, appropriate, and beautiful forms of habitation and costume.[2]

Nevertheless, it was not long after this that he began to show an interest in rustic architecture, not because he thought it was particularly American but because of his debt to English landscape traditions of the eighteenth century. For Downing as for the English, rustic was the architecture of the other. Rustic architecture belonged only in the outlying buildings. It is an alternative architecture to escape from the norm of one's real life. But once you were away from the house in the woods, the picturesque became appropriate, including the rustic: "buildings of a more irregular outline, in which appear bolder or ruder ornaments, and a certain free and more rustic air in finishing, are those which should be selected to accompany scenery of a wilder or more picturesque character, abounding in striking variations of surface, wood, and water."[3] This type of building which he called, "an intermediate kind of architecture, originally a variation of the classical style, but which, in becoming adapted to different and more picturesque situations, has lost much of its graceful character, and has become quite picturesque in its outlines and effects."[4] This included "the Swiss cottage" but it also included logs.

Calvert Vaux, Uncle Tom's Cabin, project, 1855

For Downing, as for the English, there were two types of architecture and two aesthetics—the graceful and the picturesque. Because the former belonged with the cultivated it often was associated with the main dwelling, and because the latter belonged with the wild it tended to be at the perimeter. This was not always the case but it was true in the case of Downing's own house. As with his English counterparts, rustic architecture belonged only in the outlying buildings. It is an alternative architecture to escape from the norm of one's real life. The iconic significance of the log cabin continued to grow but in the Downing tradition is more focused on logs as natural elements rather than iconic images.

The primary impact of Downing's one and only visit to England in 1850 was that he hired Calvert Vaux as a partner. Vaux's English training and experience was Gothic, but once in America he took his cue from Downing's eclecticism. Rustic was to him one of a number of styles. Downing died in an accident 1852 and Vaux continued the firm and his rustic work as well. The rustic entered the mainstream of American architecture not through the pioneer log cabin but through the English garden shelter.

Initially, Vaux was more taken with the log cabin as an icon and began his independent career with one. An 1855 project included a log cabin on the grounds of the estate of Matthew Vassar called "Uncle Tom's Cabin," a reference to Harriet Beecher Stowe's 1852 book. This project is in truth out of character for Vaux. Like Downing he was more interested in logs as a material and how they could be used to create an architecture that hovered between the natural and the human made than he was in literary allusions.[5]

In 1857 Vaux took on Frederick Olmsted as a partner, and with their winning entry in the Central Park competition that same year, they entered history. It is a history that has been slow to credit Vaux who was a far more accomplished designer and far superior draftsman than Olmsted, and Vaux is clearly responsible for the rustic structures that followed.

Central Park

The role rustic architecture initially played in Central Park was in part the same as it played in the English garden—picturesque primitive structures located in the parts of the landscape that were also rough and primitive. Their rustic architecture was an analog of nature, open structures suggesting a tree or a grove of trees, not a nostalgic reference to a pioneer's log cabin.

Central Park was an escape in every sense of the word, composed of representations of certain geographic areas, some of which had little to do with the native ecology of Manhattan Island. One of these was the Adirondacks. In 1858 Olmsted wrote to the Board of Commissioners: "It is one great purpose of the park to supply the hundreds of thousands of tired workers, who have no opportunity to spend their summers in the country, a specimen of God's handiwork that shall be to them, inexpensively, what a month or two in the White Mountains or the Adirondacks is, at great cost, to those in easier circumstances."[6]

One might wonder why Olmsted and Vaux, with the multitude of natural landscapes with which they were familiar, chose to replicate the Adirondacks in Central Park, but in the years before Yosemite and Yellowstone had been popularized the Adirondacks held, at least for some, a special niche in the American imagination. In 1857, William Stillman, editor of the *Crayon*, led a party of ten to twelve of Boston's leading figures in art, literature and politics—including Louis Agassiz, Ralph Waldo Emerson, and James Russel Lowell—into the Adirondacks. This group was quickly identified as the Philosopher's camp. They spent August at Follensby Pond. Stillman describes their life there: "My camp was a shelter of bark, raised on poles, open in front to the morning sun, just sufficing to shed the rain, while my bed was a layer of the branches of the fir-trees that grew around."[7] This was something new. Emerson had taken many a walk in the woods but he had never slept in a lean-to.

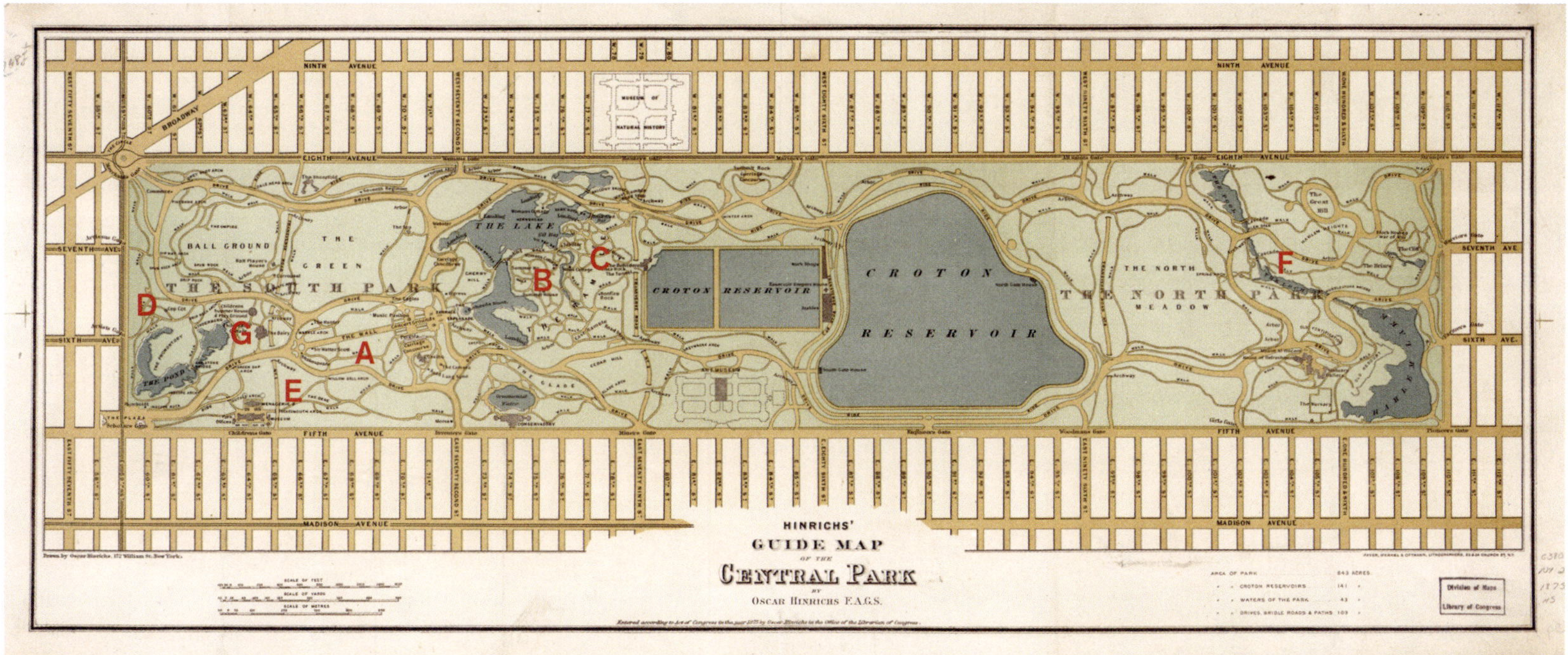

Olmsted and Vaux, Central Park plan, 1875

A Mall

B Ramble

C Rustic Summerhouse

D Cop Cot

E Dene Shelter

F The Ravine

G Kinderberg

Olmsted and Vaux's Central Park on a simple, conceptual level is an expanded English garden, an "other" landscape, with a path leading from the architecture of the norm to the architecture of the primitive. The plan has a similar polarity between the graceful and the picturesque to that of Downing's estate and a progression leading from one to the other. It occurs alone the long axis that extends from the southeast corner along the Mall to the Bethesda Terrace and the lake. The axis and the view ends in the distance with the Belvedere at Vista rock, but the route leaves the axis extending into a dense green labyrinth, the penultimate section is the area between the lake and Vista Rock, the Ramble, an irregular wooded network of curving paths. Vaux wrote: "We determined that the Ramble should be the picture that people come to see."[8]

From its inception the Ramble, built in 1859, was seen as a miniature version of the Adirondacks. Vaux wrote describing the artificial hills around the pond near the southeast entrance: "they will certainly not compare favorably with the Kaatskills or the Adirondacks, but they are all the suggestion of the Kaatskills or the Adirondacks that thousands of our fellow citizens will ever have an opportunity of studying." [9] On other occasions Olmsted wrote of the Ramble being inspired by his visits to the tropical forests of South America. As the English garden had zones of rustic informality so did Central Park in the Ramble and the Ravine.

Thus the Ramble, the miniature Adirondacks, was to have a different kind of landscape and a different kind of architecture. The Ramble is a dense forest of man-made landscape. The great concentration of rustic structures was there, containing thirteen rustic shelters, four bridges, and a cave. Other larger structures form shade arbors covering benches.

While there are rustic structures there are no log cabins, no log chalets; there are no Robert Adam-like classical buildings covered with bark. All of Vaux's structures larger than a bench or bridge are suggestive, with varying degrees of literalness, to a tree or a grove of trees.

Reconstructed rustic bridges

SUMMER-HOUSE IN RAMBLE NEAR THE BELVEDERE.

The Rustic Summerhouse in the Ramble, 1866

The most conspicuous and the most intriguing of the structures in the Ramble was the Rustic Summerhouse, elevated with an overlook, one of the largest and one of the few for which a drawing survives. Built in 1866, it was a central structure with a core of six tree-trunk columns and a large overhang on all sides. The plan is hexagonal, composed of equilateral triangles. The hexagonal ring of columns at the center supports the long cantilevers that flow outward to form the tree-like shelter. There are smaller shelters nearby such as a bench covered with an arbor imitating a tree or a pair of trees.

The North Woods, like the Ramble, is another miniature Adirondacks. It is defined by the Ravine, a crevice formed by the one real stream in Central Park, the Loch, that flows through the northeast corner of the park. The key architectural elements here were a number of rustic bridges. There are also a variety of bridges scattered throughout the park each following its own rules. They have a typology that spans from the engineered to the grotesque. Some are classical forms built of logs—an imitation in logs of the classic Roman x railing. Some take the form of conventional structural trusses—a log Howe truss. Some are surreal in the tradition of English Root House. All are built of cedar.

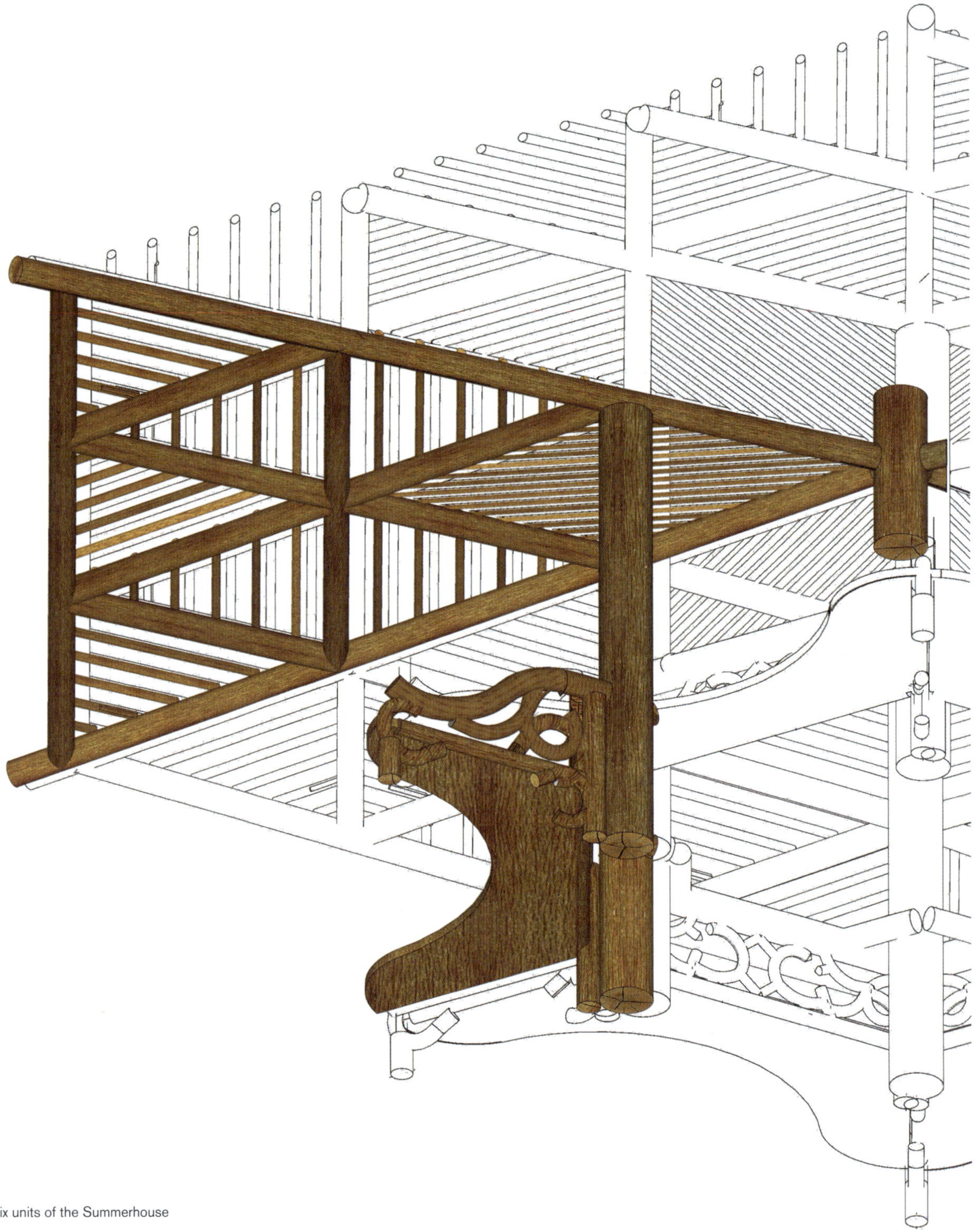

One of the six units of the Summerhouse

The Dene Shelter

Rustic elements were not confined to the two recreated Adirondacks. There are rustic structures outside the densely wooded areas such as the Ramble, especially on high promontories. As with Downing, an Olmsted and Vaux favorite is the rustic structure with a seat and a view. Two of the most visible sit on rocks along the edges of the park near entries, perhaps a preview of the ultimate destination. The originals are long gone, but they have been rebuilt. They follow the tree or tree grove model used elsewhere, a central cluster of columns in an octagon with cantilevered branches.

The Dene Shelter, also on top of a rock, near Fifth Avenue, is a smaller version of the double-roofed octagon, but with two projecting bays. The second is on a high rock outcrop near the artist's gate on the south edge at Sixth Avenue, is Cop Cot, which means "little cottage on the crest of the hill" in Scottish. Vaux's rustic shelters are typically circles, hexagons, or octagons. Cop Cot is an octagon in plan with perimeter columns and log brackets supporting a two-tiered pyramidal roof.

The Dene is a valley that runs south toward the Zoo. Both of these shelters are visible from outside the park and both give views back into the city to those who occupy them. Olmsted and Vaux vigorously opposed a proposal to give the park neoclassical gates, perhaps these shelters were their idea of a threshold.

Dene Shelter

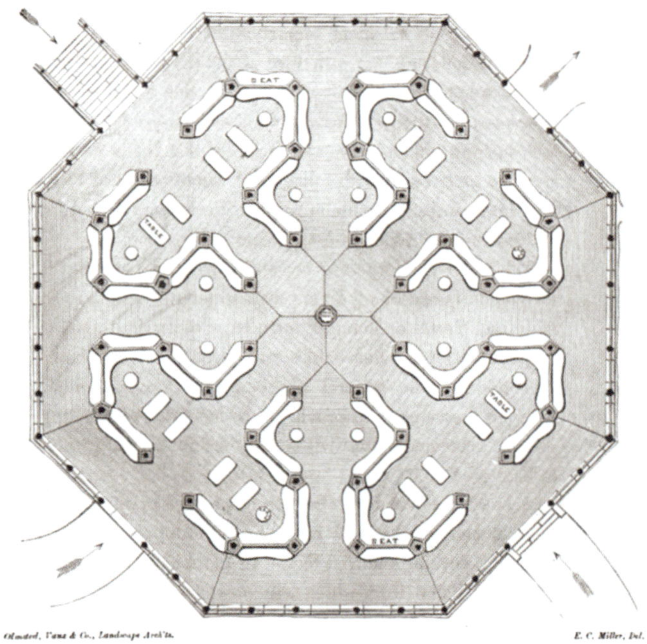

PLAN

ELEVATION

Children's District
The Kinderberg Shelter, 1866

There was a fundamental change of methodology in 1866. Rustic structures appeared in more conspicuous locations and dramatically increased in scale as a part of the creation of the Children's District near the park's southeast corner. This was a facility for mothers and children of the poor created at the insistence of the park's commissioners. Its largest element was the *Kinderberg* (Children's Mountain) Summerhouse built of unmilled cedar timber. It was another of Vaux's giant octagons, 110 feet across and composed of 48 interlocking "trees," set atop a hill with views and rustic furniture in which to rest (some of them reduced in size to accommodate children). Like Stukeley and Warburton's analogs of forests it was trees turned into architecture or perhaps architecture returning to trees.[10]

The Children Shelter, Prospect Park, Brooklyn

Ambergill Falls Shelter, Prospect Park, Brooklyn

Prospect Park, 1860-72

In 1860, Vaux and later Olmsted begin work on Prospect Park in Brooklyn. Here Olmsted is more explicit as to their objectives. His intent again was to bring the forest, perhaps the Adirondacks, to the city:

It is, of course, impracticable anywhere within the necessary limits of a city park, to make sure that visitors shall enjoy a sense of complete rural seclusion; but the inclination which influences those who are able to go far into the country for recreation, is often strong with thousands, who are in no position to leave their business and their families. While, therefore, results which would seem forced or improbable are to be avoided, it is desirable to meet this requirement on a scale that shall be adequate for the purpose.[11]

What the Ramble was to Central Park, the Ravine was to Prospect Park—the mountains brought to the city. Olmsted wrote: "Although we cannot have wild mountain gorges, for instance, on the park, we may have rugged ravines shaded with trees, and made picturesque with shrubs, the form and arrangement of which remind us of mountain scenery."[12] There were a variety of buildings in various architectural styles in the park and rustic structures were a key element in the imaginary journey to the forest beyond Manhattan. Smaller bridges were located at the west end of the Ravine. And there were the smaller elements, more than 50 rustic seats built of cedar and sassafras.

The area now known as the Vale of Cashmere was another natural ravine near the northeast entry that the designers filled with an irregular pond and a playground overlooked by a rustic arbor.

The Thatched Shelter, Prospect Park, Brooklyn

The Rustic Summerhouse, Prospect Park, Brooklyn

The typology of rustic structures was similar to that used at Central Park and there were a number of each type. There were rustic bridges, including the 35-foot-span of simple verticals and horizontals at the Binnen Falls Bridge crossing the stream atop a waterfall. There are rectangular linear trellises such as the one that shaded a portion of the walk north of the Children's Playground. The shelter above Ambergill Falls was a simple rectangular platform edged by a bench and railing. And again, all were connected with views. While the open structure of the tree turned into architectural form is common, actual rustic buildings, that is walled, enclosed spaces, e.g., log cabins, are almost unknown in Vaux's work. Most of the shelters are largely open with no walls and have much trellis covering as roof.

A new direction not present in Central Park was the 1874 Thatched Shelter, also called the "Swiss Thatched Cottage." It had an H-plan with a polygon at either end topped with steeply pitched roofs with dormers. While not enclosed it comes very close to being a building with walls and arched windows and in its way far more domestic and less interesting than the Rustic Summerhouse of Central Park. Only one of the Prospect Park rustic shelters survives, the rectangular, hipped-roof Landing Shelter near the Carriage Concourse.

Ultimately however Olmsted concluded that creating the Adirondacks with its rustic shelters was impossible. Some compromise, something more pastoral, was necessary:

We, therefore, abandon all ideas of contrasting the publicity of the city with the privacy of deep woods, mountains, lakes, and rocky fastnesses, and accept another ideal altogether, that of pastoral rural life, as the most valuable and universally available one for the purpose we have in view.[13]

Rustic Arbor, Boston

Echo Park, Los Angeles

Influence

The influence of these rustic structures was widespread. In 1886 a "unique rustic summerhouse" was constructed at the waterworks in Philadelphia's Fairmount park. A large curved rustic arbor was built in the Boston Public Garden sometime after 1865. Their influence is found in abundance on the West Coast, in Echo Park Los Angeles c.1898 and in rustic shelters in Golden Gate Park in San Francisco in 1880. In an 1870 article The *American Agriculturalist*, after praising Vaux and Olmsted's work at Central Park noted that:

It is probable that the successful introduction of rustic work at [Central] Park has done much towards popularizing it for we now seldom visit neighborhood where any attention is given to rural ornament that we do not see more or less ambitious attempts at this kind of decoration.

They warned, however, that: "A mere association of grotesque branches is not pleasing. There must be an architectural design."[14]

Few of Vaux's log buildings have walls, they do not enclose any space in the environmental sense, they mainly provide roofs and some do not even do that. This is no small point as the entire structure of each is completely exposed. There is no concealed milled lumber. There are no layers of fictive log construction. While they are structurally adventurous, they are straightforward down to their nailed joints. This is something that is not true of most of the rustic architecture that follows. Vaux's buildings have an authenticity that the Many Glacier Hotel does not. Vaux's rustic work had no primitive huts or Druidic Root Houses. It is not an association with history. They are analogs of nature, not of architecture. They were constructed trees and forests, not classic temples or chalets that had been rusticated. Yet there is an otherness. It was a concept that was endlessly extended and expanded in the next 50 years. The primitive fragment of nature became greatly enlarged and it still contained within it the alternative architecture of primitivism. What is most essential about them in terms of this narrative is that they establish rustic as the architecture of the other linking the architecture of the Adirondack retreat to the wildernesses of Central Park.

In the 1930s, rustic architecture, particularly national park architecture, was seen as indigenous to the West, the product of local vernacular traditions. Over time it was recognized that there was an influence from the Adirondacks, which there undoubtedly was, but Vaux's work predated the rustic architecture of the Adirondacks by many years and it was far more visible and accessible. Unfortunately, it was far less durable and the scarcity of surviving original may explain its neglect, but it was also in 1932 not something Albert Good and his friends wanted to think about.

Very few of Vaux's rustic structures remain in either park, although many are in the process of being reconstructed. At this moment a major effort is underway to rebuild many of the structures in Central Park including a large part of the Kinderberg Summerhouse. What might have been Vaux's last rustic structure was for himself, "Restawhile" an 1877 rustic summerhouse near his home atop the Palisades. But it is critical to remember that Vaux's rustic work was a smaller part of a much larger decidedly unrustic practice. It also was part of another life.

THE ADIRONDACKS

THOMAS AND WILLIAM DURANT

If Olmsted despaired at the possibility of recreating the Adirondacks in Central Park, he might have been encouraged by an article that appeared in the *New York Times* on August 9, 1864, titled "Adirondack." The paper announced that not only were the Adirondacks coming to Central Park; Central Park was coming to the Adirondacks: "Within an easy day's ride of our great City, ... is a tract of country fitted to make a Central Park for the world. The jaded merchant, or financier, or litterateur, or politician, feeling excited within him again the old passion for nature."[1] The occasion, in fact the news story, was the creation of the Adirondack Railway, that when finished would traverse the region from Saratoga to Canada and provide easy access to the wilderness. In the process New Yorkers were assured that after a morning's ride of a few hours they would be able to, "spend the afternoon in a solitude almost as complete as when the 'Deerslayer' stalked his game."[2]

It is a remarkably optimistic article. It points out that not only is the region filled with lakes and streams to rival Switzerland but with untold resources waiting to be developed and exploited, even announcing that the purpose of the railroad was to access "mines and forests." It was a remarkable vision; the wilderness will be simultaneously consumed and preserved: "The furnaces of our capitalists will line its valleys, and create new fortunes to swell the aggregate of our wealth; while the hunting-lodges of our citizens will adorn its more remote mountain-sides and the wooded islands of its delightful lakes. It will become to our whole community, on an ample scale, what the Central Park now is on a limited one."[3]

Readers are also assured that this endeavor could not be in better hands, those of Thomas Durant, "one off the ablest railroad men in the country." Durant is remembered today, not always with respect or admiration, as the father of the Union Pacific Railway, the eastern half of the great transcontinental railway of 1869. Durant's one-time partner said of him that he had neither, "a high sense of honor, sound judgment, [nor] financial skill." His activities included stock fraud, stock manipulations, and building large quantities of unnecessary track since he was compensated by the mile. Richard White is more blunt. He calls Durant, "Scheming and manipulative" and wrote: "He never took an ethical high road. He betrayed partners, and he betrayed strangers. When there was no low road, he blazed one."[4] But Durant and his son who succeeded him require examination if we are to understand rustic architecture. It was not an architecture that was indigenous to Western America but one that came there from England via the East, Central Park and the Adirondack camps and it was the railroad that brought it. Durant and his railroad were not the facilitators of that architecture but its creators and advocates.

So the escape to the farther reaches of the English garden that had become the escape to the farther reaches of Central Park became the escape to the Adirondacks, but what was different was not the distance but the numbers. The walk in the garden had become mass tourism and it had large consequences. It was to destroy a rustic life that was in many ways authentic and replaced it with one that was often a rustic charade.

But it was an event twelve years later in which the Adirondacks firmly established itself in national culture. By 1869 the railroad had been completed to The Glen, 40 miles north of Saratoga Springs.

Opposite: Thomas Durant on the route of the Union Pacific

Adirondack shelter, c. 1910

The same year William "Adirondack" Murray published *Adventures in the Wilderness; or Camp-Life in the Adirondacks*. It had an influence that is hard to measure but visitation to the Adirondacks simultaneously increased exponentially. Popular history tells us that the result was chaos, that the book sent a multitude of unprepared campers into a wilderness unprepared to receive them, being meagerly supplied with hotels, services or even roads. Murray did much to define what for many was the Adirondack experience. In explaining its essential quality, he says several times that: "Wherever the axe sounds, the pride and beauty of the forest disappear," and speaks of, "magnificent vistas 'untouched' by man's axe."

For "Adirondack" Murray the guides and the lean-tos they built were not just the essence of the experience, it was the essence of the place. The guides possessed a unique character born of the environment they inhabited. They are not overcivilized; quite the contrary they were, "uncontaminated with the vicious habits of civilized." They were inseparable from their place in the world:

A more honest, cheerful, and patient class of men cannot be found the world over. Born and bred, as many of them were, in this wilderness, skilled in all the lore of woodcraft. ... Bronzed and hardy, fearless of danger, eager to please, un- contaminated with the vicious habits of civilized life, they are not unworthy of the magnificent surroundings amid which they dwell.

They were in fact the product of that geography: "Under the base of these overhanging mountains they were born. ... The wilderness has unfolded to them its mysteries and made them wise with a wisdom nowhere written in books."[5]

But the phenomenon Murray's book ultimately made happen was another piece of technology that was to both create and destroy the Adirondacks simultaneously, the railroad.

After the arrival of the railroad the Adirondacks of Murray was not to disappear, but it was to be radically transformed. The temporary camp became a permanent one; the permanent camp became the lodge, complete with separate dining hall and rec room. The tour through the lakes with a guide became the summer stay in the lodge. The venison cooked at the campfire became the venison, still local, served by the waiter on the silver tray. The guides remained but they were often outnumbered by the servants. There was less authenticity and far more playing at being rustic.

Early visitors to the Adirondacks traveled by guideboat with guides and as the English garden required a rustic otherness so did the Adirondack camp. They often stayed in bark or pine-bough shelters, often in temporary camps. The bark or brush shelter and the small log hut was well established tradition that provided little more than simple shelter. It was in popular lore the ancestor the Adirondack camp. This quickly evolved into something larger, more permanent and elaborate. Camp is a misleading term; the life within was hardly rustic. The generic Adirondack camp was large and permanent typically a group of buildings in which housing, dining, and kitchen were likely to be in separate buildings.

And the building culture changed with it, following a similar path, from the rustic to the industrial, from the bark shelter to the lodge. The lean-to built by the guide became the lodge built by the contractor from Lake Placid. The handyman guide was supplanted by the immigrant carpenter. The aesthetics did not change, the rustic remained the same, at least on the surface. Life in the Adirondacks became a series of veneers and so did much of the architecture.

The arrival the railroad began a historical divide in Adirondack culture. Emerson and Agassiz sleeping on pine boughs in open bark lean-tos were rustic. The Vanderbilts or Huntingtons would bring countless servants to the lodge in addition to the large staff already there. For them the Adirondacks meant a change of clothes. There was fishing and hunting and boating but is not an escape from an overcivilized world. For J. P. Morgan who rarely visited his camp at Uncas it wasn't even that. By 1904, according to the *New York Sun*: "There is just the faintest idea of the old camp life perpetuated in the camp of a Vanderbilt, or a Carnegie, or a Lewison or a Morton. The hunter's shack, the bivouac of fresh bark and saplings, has been taken as a model, but the simplicity of the rough camp has been elaborated until now the new structures are more like Indian bungalows. Swiss chalets, French and Dutch houses or colonial cottages than like a hunter's shack."[6]

A far more serious actor was Timothy Woodruff who lived at Camp Kill Kare: "He adheres in a large degree to the primitive ways of camp construction, and sleeps in an open camp himself. This is a structure of logs, chinked with mud, mortar and moss. It faces great campfire and its beds are made of balsam boughs." In fact, Woodruff had a reputation for extravagance, exemplified by elements such as the gondolas imported from Venice plying the lake or the bears kept as pets. And he could not cut the cord. It was connected to the main lodge by electric call bells.[7]

The way of life idealized by Murray, the author/guide was transformed as well. In 1892 the Adirondack Forest Preserve was created, and the state began to assemble land where logging would not be allowed. A number of larger private preserves were created at the same time, the largest being the Adirondack League Club. Strangely, the creation of the preserve did not preserve the Adirondack way of life but in the eyes of many completed its destruction.[8]

The Durants

But let us return to Thomas Durant who the *Times* had called, "one off the ablest railroad men in the country," and his railroad.

In the end Durant's railroad did not get very far. Finished in 1871, it reached only as far as North Creek, a fraction of its intended length. But the profit to Durant was huge. He acquired an enormous area of land in the Adirondacks from the state—if not free, close to it—for five cents an acre, with no subsequent property taxes. The State like the Federal Government promoted the building of railroads through massive land grants. He added to this over the years by buying clearcut areas sold at auction. So 1871 found him a man who owned a very short railroad but over 650,000 acres of forest.

But the central character in this narrative is his son William who joined him In 1876, and took over his affairs after his death in 1885. William is credited with a number of accomplishments-the invention of the Adirondack style, the development of the Adirondacks into a tourist destination and attracting the wealthiest Americans to establish summer residences there, and to a degree he deserves credit for all of these. Durant's early biographers credited him with the design of a number of camps but design may not be the right word, and recent scholarship has established the involvement of architects with many of these. Craig Gilborn describes Durant as an "artistic director" rather than an architect. Although his name is mentioned in association with other hotels and camps, it is only his involvement with them that is documented, not a role in the design.

William is often portrayed as a visionary but he does not seem to have a plan for his life, which ended in bankruptcy. He began as one of the wealthiest residents of the Adirondacks and its largest landowner, and played a key role in its environmental destiny, but not as an architect or even a builder. Even the designs that he may have been responsible for are vastly inferior to other work going on nearby. His greatest accomplishment was in constructing his own legend following his financial collapse. If rustic life was merely acting and rustic architecture merely a rustic veneer on an industrial reality then William was its greatest practitioner, perhaps its inventor.[9]

In any case the Durants were not building hotels or resorts. They were selling the land for buildings—large parcels for hotels, large parcels for hunting and fishing clubs, and large parcels for the evolving institution of the Adirondack Camp. And they were providing much of the lumber. They were also building a transportation system that serviced the developing hotel industry. It began with the railroad, then stagecoaches to the interior, then steamers on the lakes. The course of development of the Durant transport system was from North Creek to Blue Mountain Lake and from there to Raquette Lake, where a number of camps were under construction and where they built their own, Pine Knot.

Maid's Cabin, 1877
First phase: Solid log wall construction

Spruce Lodge, 1880
Second phase: Sawmill siding on saw-milled frame

Durant Cabin, 1889-92
Third phase: Log and bark facing on milled frame

Pine Knot Chalet
Left: 1878 Chalet
Right: Chalet with 1882 addition

In 1879, Durant's transport system began to take shape and with it a new building culture as it developed. That year he founded the Blue Mountain and Raquette Lake Steamboat Line with connections by stage from North Creek to Blue Mountain Lake, four steamers on Blue Mountain and Raquette Lakes, and wagons between the two lakes for baggage services and construction equipment and materials. The damming of the Raquette River provided access to Lake Utowana and provided Durant with the power for a sawmill. Travel to the area increased dramatically as did construction of accommodations. At the same time they were building the new Adirondacks they were destroying the old one, as we will see.

Pine Knot

There are three distinct phases of architecture at Pine Knot based on the extent of its connection to the industry beyond the Adirondacks and three languages of wood construction to go with them.

First were the true log cabins, built before the navigable river and sawmill, when the main connection to the railroad at North Creek was by canoe. It was a building culture of axes and solid logs—the language of rustic log buildings, built of solid logs and filled with twiggy furniture. These have a rustic authenticity, largely out of technological necessity. It included five buildings constructed as they appeared to be, straightforward log buildings of solid log construction, usually spruce. Also built was a larger cabin, the primary residence, now called the Chalet. The was the true rustic phase of construction, of genuine log construction, and it was short lived.[10]

Changes in the transport system and the creation of the sawmill enabled the second phase of building at Pine Knot c. 1880, one that included sawmill lumber and access to shipped materials. These nine utilitarian buildings were conventionally framed of milled lumber and covered with sawn siding. They were service buildings, built in the most economical way. As always, here was a direct link between the system of transport and the culture of building.

Having disposed of a truly rustic system he created a fictive one. The third is a hybrid of the two, in which the logs and bark rustic first phase is veneered over the sawmill frame of the second. The buildings of this phase are clad with a rustic narrative that is largely ornamental, draping the frame with nostalgic veneer, first of bark then of half logs.

The central building, the Chalet, is an illustration of a technology in transition. Thomas' lower story of solid logs was built before the dam and steamship service. William's top story, the structure of rustic veneer of stretched bark on milled lumber (some of it brought from Virginia), was built after, an incrustation of indigenous rustic coating on a standard industrial frame from the sawmill. The top half of Durant's Chalet at Pine Knot is largely a fiction, yet it is the best evidence for its architectural significance of Pine Knot and the architectural contributions of Durant.

In general Pine Knot gets more critical attention than it deserves, but the Chalet, however confused its construction, was a key moment in rustic history. This was not just a chalet; it was a rusticated chalet, one of many to follow.

The origins of Durant's chalet design are uncertain. Harold Hochschild reports that it was inspired by a music box Durant owned. Sheila Meyers argues convincingly that the chalet owes something to a building William must have known well from his time in England, the Swiss cottage of the royal family at Osborne House.[11] The Pine Knot Chalet does have the cantilevered second floor, wide broad low slope roof, and gable of the chalets illustrated in well-known books such as Gladbach's *Der Schweizer Holzstil*, but it has little of the paraphernalia of the chalet—board profiled rails, scroll brackets, and elaborate bargeboards. What is different about Durant's building of course is that all these elements were made of logs.

A key Pine Knot building in the new rustic veneer style was Durant's own cabin (1889-92) using a system of log trim and stretched-cedar-bark, encrusted wood-frame construction. The bark sheathing is divided horizontally by belt courses formed of half-round bark-clad poles. None of this is structural and the bark and log design has nothing to do with the configuration of the sawmill frame behind. The porch columns are bark-clad posts supporting rectilinear milled beams with bark cladding running structurally the wrong way. It does have a scissor-truss log-roof structure supporting a bark-clad interior roof deck—a rare example of Durant using exposed structure that was real. For the most part Durant's architecture is one of surface. There are two types of brackets in traditional chalets such as those illustrated in Gladbach. One is a series of parallel squared logs each of which projects beyond the one below, or a single square timber at an angle of about 45 degrees, braced against the wall. Durant uses both of these but he makes them of logs, not squared timbers. A series of projecting parallel logs support the second floor. A series of 45-degree brackets support the projecting roof. This was a practice followed by many who came

Recreation Hall (Metcalf Hall), c. 1898
Wall of pine boards on milled studs

Pine Knot, Durant Cabin, 1889-92
Scissor truss and log facing on sawmill roof frame

after. There were a few real log buildings built at Pine Knot in this era such as Metcalf Hall, but they were the exception.

What the new third style gained in imagery it lost in authenticity. There is little at Pine Knot that is spatially or structurally rustic or inventive. It has a great deal of rustic decoration that was influential such as in the *chinois* railings found at nearby Camp Scott and rustic screens, but it was a veneered architecture for a veneered life. Both life and architecture were literally superficial. This was perhaps a key moment in the history of the rustic. Rustic reality had given way to the rustic illusion, and a decidedly non-rustic technology was the vehicle. Durant's architecture at Pine Knot is for the most part cosmetic.

Not only was it not truly rustic; it was not sustainable. The president of the Adirondack League Club argued that the practice of using branches and tree trunks as ornament was wasteful and harmful. Renewing spruce trim was required every three to seven years to prevent the bark from delaminating, and a single building could consume six wagon loads of poles.[12]

Durant's use of sheets of bark was even more problematic and ominous. It is a methodology that was both an old Adirondack tradition and a new, destructive technology—peeled bark. Hemlock was plentiful in the Adirondacks and its bark was easily peeled to yield large sheets. A common temporary Adirondack shelter was the bark lean-to—a frame of small logs covered with bark sheets looking something like a tent. It is a fairly horrifying proposition for the modern environmentalist given that it requires the destruction of entire trees in order to use a tiny fraction of their wood for temporary use, but bark lean-tos were a tiny fraction of a larger environmental problem. Hemlock bark was used as a source of tannins for tanning leather. By 1890, one million acres of forest had been cut over for bark and more than half the Hemlocks were gone.[13]

So if we are looking for evidence that the rustic life was genuine or that rustic architecture was authentic Durant is a poor witness on both counts. His life in the woods with his hunting and fishing guides resembled an English aristocrat visiting a country estate, not a return to primitive origins, and his architecture wall so much rustic wallpaper on an industrial frame.

In 1889-90 things began to unravel in Durant's life. He was subject to a different malaise, primarily financial. The tax exemption on his land had expired. A divorce and the loss of a lawsuit brought by his sister eliminated much of his cash.

The changes in Durant's fortunes coincided with some much larger ones as 1892 was a pivotal year in Adirondack history as well.

In 1884, William Stillman revisited the site of the Philosopher's camp at Follensby Pond. He found it unrecognizable due to logging. He wrote: "The very scene of our acting and thinking has disappeared down to its geological basis, pillaged, burnt, and become a horror to see." Unfortunately, this is an inaccurate observation. Much of what is now the Adirondack Forest preserve was substantially intact in 1884. The massive, industrialized destruction was about to begin.[14]

Previously, timber had been cut in much of the Adirondack Forest but selectively, mostly spruce trees of intermediate size. Much of the forest remained but much of the spruce had been harvested.[15] But after 1892, construction of railroads along the Adirondack perimeter improved access and transport. The introduction of the crosscut saw improved efficiency. But most importantly the market shifted from lumber to wood pulp, and for this any size tree would do and the clear cutting began. Fortunately, this coincided with the birth of the Adirondack preservation movement. In 1892 the Adirondack Forest Preserve was created, and the state began to assemble land where logging would not be allowed.

In this process Durant was more on the side of the exploiters than the preservationists. Financial problems forced him to sell Pine Knot in 1895 and this event coincided with another. Durant began to sell his land, and he was the largest landowner in the Adirondacks. Again, the idea that there was a strategic plan is by no means certain or even likely. Whether the result of vision or by default, the environmental balance sheet on William West Durant is this. In 1885, the year of his father's death, he owned over 650,000 acres

Pine Knot Chalet
Swiss-style stepped log bracket at the chalet

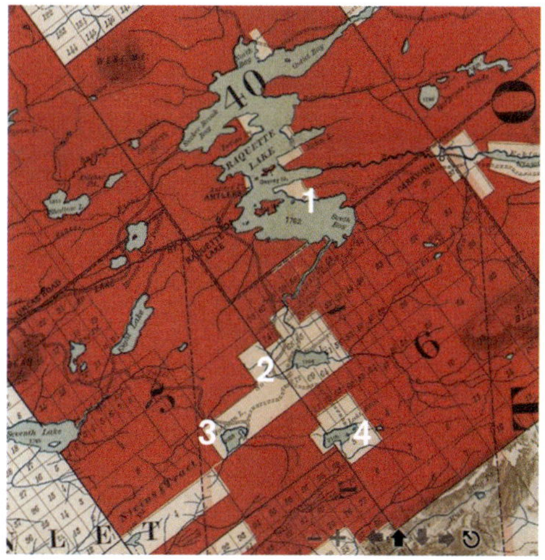

Adirondack Preserve in red

1 Camp Pine Knot, Raquette Lake
2 Camp Sagamore
3 Camp Uncas, Mohegan Lake
4 Camp Kill Kare, Lake Kora

Pine Knot, Metcalf Hall, 1898

of Adirondack forest, an area equal to all the public owned acres in the Adirondack preserve. In 1910 he owned zero. He gave nothing away.

It was all sold. Most of the remaining land was sold to lumber companies, railroads, and in some cases individuals, and the vast majority of it probably logged. The largest single parcel was 400,000 acres sold to a lumber syndicate in 1899.[16] Durant did create a small preserve for his own rustic life, but he did so by destroying a much larger area of forest. The area of forest that he destroyed to his own profit was twenty times the size of what he preserved. In 1904 Durant left the Adirondacks and declared bankruptcy.

At this point in the narrative, it might seem we have encountered an oddity, a strange character pursuing two mutually exclusive ideologies of environmental destruction and wilderness tourism, but Durant is not an eccentric character. He is in fact the prototype for those who created both rustic architecture and the national parks.

The creation of the Adirondack style was the end point of much larger process, one that was repeated and in fact had already taken place in some locations throughout the West following a relatively similar script.

A railroad is built financed by the government through large land grants.

A timber industry is created or transformed as a result—partially to provide timber for the railroad, and to provide timber for the railroad's customers.

The indigenous building culture of the axe and the log is destroyed, replaced by the sawmill. A large quantity of forest is destroyed as a result. A smaller quantity of forest is preserved.

A desire appears to recreate the architectural culture that was lost, perhaps by creating fragments of that lost culture but more commonly by cladding an industrial frame with a veneer of the architecture of the axe and the log that are being displaced.

This was to be the process of rustic architecture in the West, in the national parks, or elsewhere.

In a much smaller transaction of much larger architectural consequence Durant sold about 24,000 acres to the Forest Preserve. The area surrounded three parcels totaling about 4,500 that he set aside for camps, creating a buffer where no timber would be cut, and within which he was to build two more camps.

Durant's architectural significance was to be as a client not a designer. His personal problems were about to multiply but his rustic architecture was about to become authentic. Just as the veneered nostalgia of Pine Knot seemed to be in ascendancy there was a dramatic reversal.

Big boom at Glens Falls on the Hudson River, circa 1890
A barrier set up to stop logs on the river

GROSVENOR ATTERBURY

There were of course many camps made with real solid logs in the early days. The first phase of Pine Knot with its straightforward unpretentious solid-log buildings was constructionally typical of much that was being built nearby, particularly two camps built by Thomas Durant's nephews—Camp Fairview (1879-1880) built by Frederick Durant on Raquette Lake, Camp Cedars (1880) built by Charles Durant at nearby Forked Lake, and Camp Echo (1880) built by Phineas Lounsbury on Raquette Lake. All of them, like the first phase of Pine Knot, were built of solid spruce logs. Portions of some of the three camps were built with log siding and milled lumber, indications of the building culture that was to come, the log veneers that characterized the latter Pine Knot buildings. There soon developed a prejudice against solid buildings as we will see, but around 1890 solid-log construction saw something of a revival.

Between 1890 and 1905 several large camps were built in the Adirondacks that used solid-log walls as primary enclosure—R. H. Robertson's Camp Santanoni (1893), William Wick's Camp Rabbit Wild (1892), and the William Read Camp (1906).

One of the most conspicuous of these real log buildings was Camp Uncas. Before selling Pine Knot, William Durant had begun work on another camp nearby, Uncas, a name taken from *The Last of the Mohicans*. It has little in common with Pine Knot other than bark. It returns to the old solid unlayered log wall. It was different in every way and the reason was its designer, Grosvenor Atterbury. If Pine Knot was shallow and glib, Uncas was solid and deep.

Grosvenor Atterbury's career lasted from 1894 to 1931. The more than two hundred houses he designed and built were only a part of a much larger, diverse practice. He worked throughout his life both politically and architecturally to develop housing that was affordable and healthy, an activity that did not prevent him from being one of the Rockefeller's favorite architects. But his first commission, that came when he was twenty-five, was to design an Adirondack camp for the personal use of William Durant. Over the next thirteen years he did three more log buildings. He never did another. His career in rustic architecture was small, brief, and anonymous. During his lifetime his rustic work was attributed to Durant and many do so today.[1]

Trained as a classicist, in practice he was stylistically eclectic—shingle style in Maine, classical in Manhattan, and colonial revival in the suburbs. His personal preference seems to have been French Norman, but he was committed to going below the surface, regardless of style, into construction. He is remembered today as a pioneer in precast concrete housing. He held fifteen patents but he was no less interested in archaic construction. It is clear he brought a different sensibility to rustic architecture than Durant. He was not interested in bark-covered sawmill frames or faux-Swiss details. If he was going to use logs, he was going to use logs.

Opposite: Camp Uncas Lodge

Camp Uncas Lodge, Built-in furniture at bedroom

Camp Uncas Lodge
Lake Mohegan, New York,
1893-95

It sits atop a hill on a peninsula in Lake Mohegan, a singular, long rectilinear gabled-roof volume. The main lodge represents a return to the authentic, as opposed to veneered, log construction. There are few veneers or layers in the lodge. It is far more structurally complex and structurally expressive than anything at Pine Knot.[2]

The plan is long, thin, and except for porches, one-room thick. Three major living areas, each focused on a fireplace, are arrayed on the ground floor in a line separated by casework and stairs.

The three bedrooms above are defined by the same cross walls, also with stairs, fireplaces, and service areas between.

Structurally, it is a log-walled building with a log-frame building within. The ground-floor framing is a series of solid log joists running across the short dimension of the building, spaced at about three feet, supported by the exterior longitudinal walls. The two long walls have horizontal bands of windows that weaken their bearing capacity so a series of additional log girders are needed running parallel to them. These take the form of a pair of frames in each of the three rooms—two log columns supporting log girders spanning between the cross walls, something like a series of Japanese toriis. These transverse log beams create a layer of intermediate space between inside and outside, which on the ground floor, some contain long benches.[3]

The second-floor bedrooms sit within the roof loft volume but they also have long horizontal windows provided by dormers. The upper floor is thus two interlocking gable roofs, one steeply pitched to form the walls, one flatter to create the dormers, and there are thus two sets of rafters to support them. The roof rafters are logs as well, more widely spaced and less regularly located to make possible the variations of roof geometry.

Section looking west

East elevation

Camp Uncas, Lodge, fireplaces and furniture built-ins

The roof rafters are supported primarily by the exterior log walls, although there are occasional columns here as well. The dormer rafters are supported by a complex series of beams and logs connecting to the roof rafters below. Smaller elements are made of smaller logs, such as the built-in furniture in the spirit of H. H. Richardson and Richard Norman Shaw, but built of peeled logs that grow out of and into the log structure.

It has a frame and skin quality that is at moments almost Corbusian. It is not a chalet. Other than the log brackets supporting the end gables, there are few Swiss features, no scroll work or volutes.

Even within the confines of Camp Uncas the lodge was unique. The 20 or so buildings that make up Camp Uncas are not so haphazardly arranged as Pine Knot and have something like a master plan. The buildings at Uncas fall into three loosely defined types in three different construction systems.

The romantic parts of Uncas, the guest areas, like all Adirondack camps, consist of a series of pavilions—guest cabins, a boat house, service cabins, and eventually a large dining hall. But the main lodge is larger and more complex than anything at Pine Knot, combining a number of rooms. The lodge is built of solid logs. Most of the other guest buildings were mill-framed inside and rustic outside.

Uncas, like all camps, was to a degree self-sufficient in terms of food production and the service/support buildings, the working farm part of the camp that produced necessary food staples for what could be a large occupancy, are located in a separate cluster. They are built of sawmill lumber and clapboard siding with few romantic overtones. Atterbury is known to have designed two buildings there: one of the first, the main Lodge, and later the one of the last, the Dining Hall.

Durant's financial woes caused him to lose Uncas by default to J. P. Morgan after two years. Durant's solution to his continuing problems was to build much larger lodge and camp nearby.

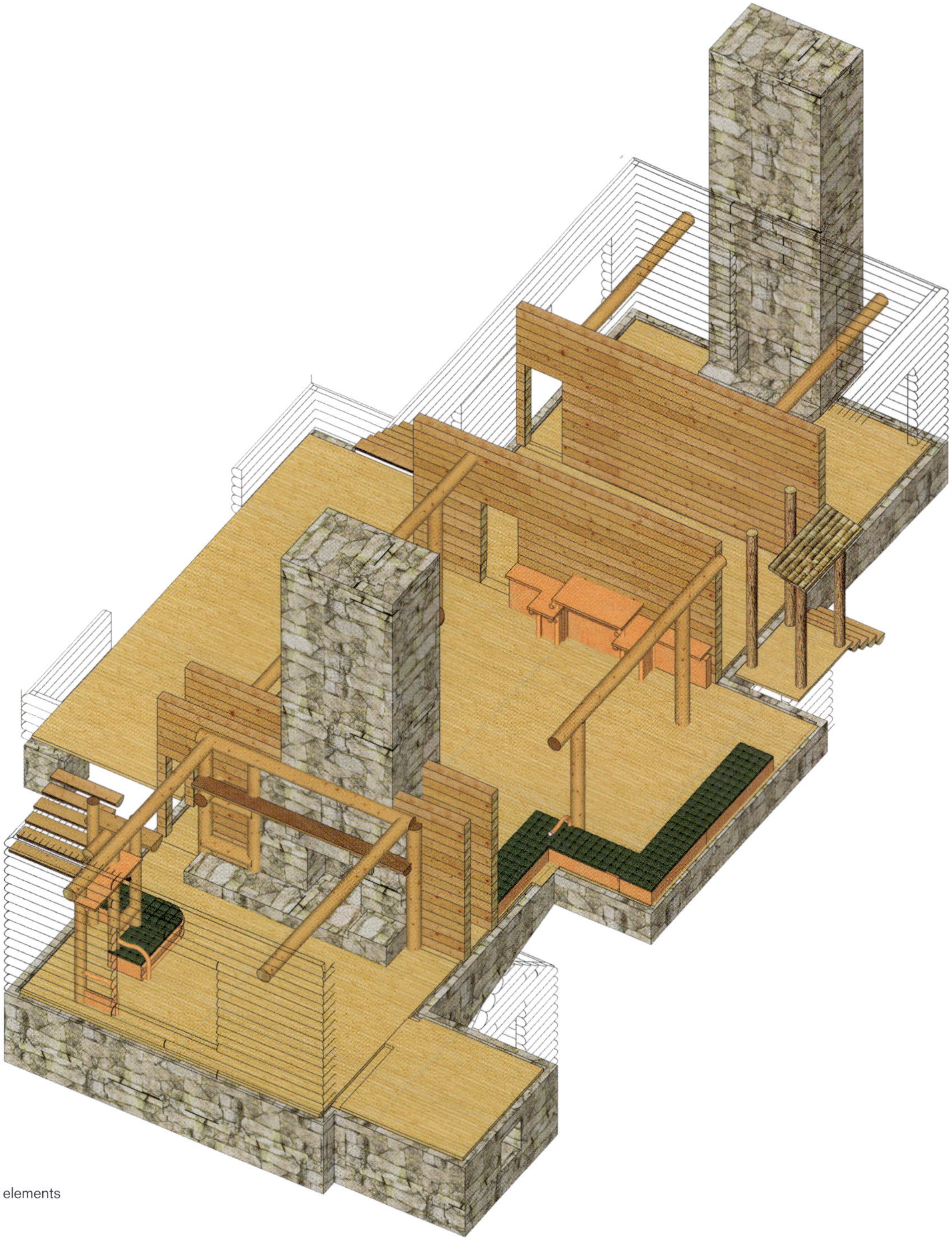

The furniture/structure elements

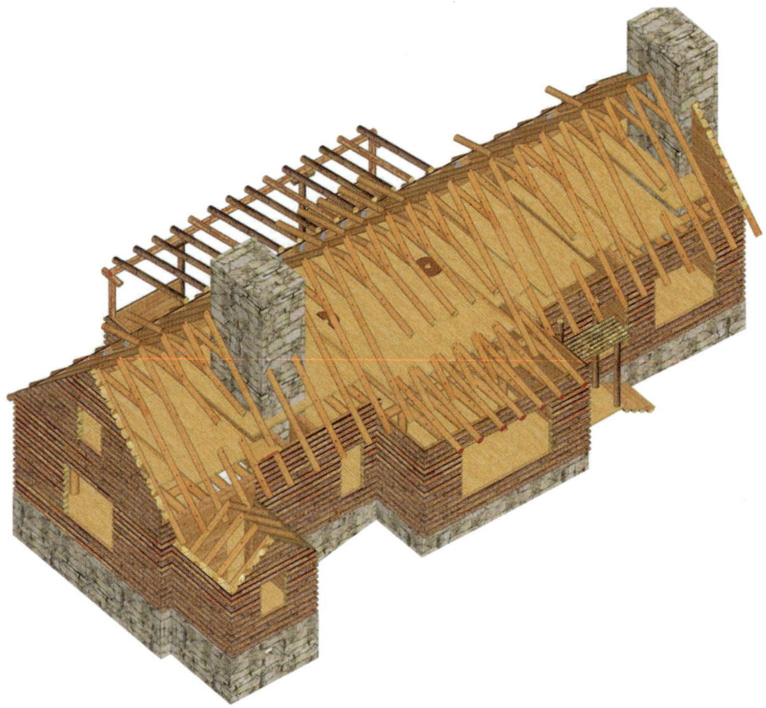

Camp Uncas Lodge, roof framing

Structurally it is a log walled building with a log frame building within. The roof framing is 9-inch log rafters, spaced at 2 feet 6 inches. with 9-inch horizontal ties.

Camp Uncas Lodge, floor framing

The second floor framing is a series of solid log joists running across the short dimension of the building supported by the exterior longitudinal walls.≠

Camp Uncas Lodge
Wall Section

In contrast to the many buildings in this text that use half-log siding on milled framed lumber, the Uncas Lodge is an authentic log cabin with solid 9-inch log walls squared off on their inside face. The roof beams, roof trusses and floor beams are peeled 9-inch logs.

The exterior walls are solid. They sit on a stone foundation wall. The floor and roof structure are largely exposed. Only the floor, roof decking, and some interior paneling are built of sawmill lumber.

The roof of shingles and boards is supported 9-inch log rafters, spaced at 2 feet 6 inches. With 9-inch horizontal ties.

The second floor is 9-inch log beams, spaced at 2 feet 6 inches.

Some rooms, particularly on the second floor, have walls with wood paneling.

Sagamore Lodge
Sagamore Lake NY, 1897

The compositional differences between Uncas and Sagamore may owe something to the more elaborate and controlled site plan that involves a sequence reminiscent of an English garden.

The lodge, the principal building, sits at the lake edge at the end of north-facing promontory. It is approached from that direction where it appears dramatically from a distance emerging from the forest, but it then disappears and the final approach to the lodge is from the opposite, south side along a long axis. Unlike Uncas it is a building viewed from a distance from both sides and it is far more of a singular volume, far more dramatic in its profile, far more symmetrical in its disposition, and far more rigorous in its spatial divisions than Uncas.

From a distance the lodge is a literal interpretation of a chalet with a profile similar to the Pine Knot Chalet. As one approaches it becomes clear that it is a heavily rusticated one. The log-built Swiss features of the type used at Pine Knot reappear here such as the two types of log brackets. What is typically the most conspicuous element of the chalet facade, the long balcony rail of flat boards with elaborate profiles cut out of them, is here reinterpreted with log slabs.

The architect of the main building, the lodge, is again almost certainly Atterbury but a different Atterbury.[4] The complex roof, the meandering wall structure, and the long low roof of Uncas are gone. The straightforward solid-log structure is also gone, and the result, if not a complete return to the rustic veneer, is a complex hybrid of solid and veneer. The chalet is back. Some of the structural purity is gone. It is a second type of Atterbury rustic building—the hybrid of whole logs and half logs. The reason for the change from Uncas is not clear. Perhaps a desire for a more refined interior, perhaps a desire for a more environmentally effective wall.

The lodge is half or perhaps a quarter of a log cabin. The exterior walls are milled wood studs covered on both sides to give the appearance of a solid-log wall. The ground floor and roof joists are solid logs and are structural. The lower floors are real structure; the walls are not; the upper floors are framed with milled joists hidden by a ceiling. There are many hybrid conditions. Since some logs must project beyond the corner at their ends to form corners and brackets, those ends walls must be solid. Veneered nostalgia was briefly replaced by constructional realism, but it was a short-lived phenomenon.[5]

Section looking north

South elevation

Wall is cut away to show that, except for the logs supporting the second floor, the framing behind the rustic skin are milled lumber.

The lodge at Sagamore has a real log roof and floors, but the walls are a rather thick half log veneer. After the completion of the railroad, the steamships, and local sawmills, Adirondack siding is often half logs on conventional framing rather than solid logs. In terms of structural expression this is problematic but in terms of practical concerns it is a much better wall. Solid-log construction is dependent on chinking of the many horizontal joints between logs. In a bark layered wall or a half log faced frame wall these joints do not exist.

Much of the building material had ceased to be indigenous and much of the labor as well. Carpenters and masons were literally hired off the boat at Ellis Island to work at Sagamore.

At the time many felt this was a better solution, a more "practical" option. Nearby is Kirtland Cutter's design for the Carnegie Camp, "North Point," built in 1903 on Raquette lake just north of Pine Knot. North Point is constructed of a sawmill frame of square posts and joists that is clad with an incrustation that makes it appear a building in the Swiss tradition of square-hewn logs. Before building began, Mary Clark Stott, who owned a camp nearby, wrote a letter to her cousin Lucy Carnegie advising how to go about building in the Adirondacks recommending the exterior be built of, "rough unplanned wood covered with slabs which gives the appearance of logs," which will "wear much better. The inside could then be plaster or whatever."[6]

Unlike Pine Knot there is a clear master plan at Sagamore, one in which constructional types play a key role. The first move was to divide servants and service areas from guest buildings, the latter on the lakeshore, and the former shielded by trees farther back. Constructional types are divided in the same way. The guest buildings are log-faced rustic buildings. Service buildings are utilitarian industrialized constructions of sawmill studs and clapboards.

Sagamore Lodge

Wall Section

It uses two different building systems. In contrast to the Uncas lodge, it is a composite of a real, exposed log construction and a concealed, milled construction hidden behind a veneer of half logs. The exposed structure is logs. The concealed structure is milled lumber.

The ceiling of the ground floor is truly rustic, with 10-inch logs 2 feet 2 inches on center and wood deck spanning between the walls.

But those walls are only a veneer-10-inch spruce half-logs with sheathing and studs with interior paneling.

On the other floors milled lumber floor joists spaced at16 inches are used instead of logs where the structure is not visible.

The roof construction is shingles and boards supported by 9-inch logs where they are visible. The concealed rafters are probably milled.

In the porch construction spruce brackets and beams support the balcony.

Sagamore Lodge: Center room, ground floor

Sagamore Dining Complex, 1898-1927

Immediately adjacent to the lodge is a second building type, the much-enlarged and altered dining complex. It is dramatically different in form and material from the lodge, a rambling structure with a bark and small log veneer. It is the Pine Knot construction type. This suggests another architect, perhaps Durant himself. Durant's rustic architecture built independent of Atterbury is more often than not only skin deep. Even in its original form it was far more varied and irregular than the lodge. If there is a Durant-designed building at Sagamore this is probably the one. It has few log walls. Like the later buildings at Pine Knot, it is a series of mill-framed buildings given a rustic incrustation of bark with log trim.

The original building at Uncas is solid log construction. The Sagamore lodge was half real. Each of Atterbury's log buildings is fundamentally different including his last at Uncas.

Sagamore Lodge on the left and Dining Hall on the right

Sagamore Playhouse, 1901

Durant sold Sagamore in 1901. Alfred Vanderbilt, the new owner, added a recreation room, the Playhouse, at the south end of the dining complex. It is a return to the solid-log construction type used at Uncas but, due to a long span, considerably more adventurous.

It is the work of a Lake Placid architect, William Coulter, a leading Adirondack-based designer of the rustic style. It has many of the structural qualities of an arts and crafts building, something conspicuously absent from most of the buildings associated with Durant. The complex structure of the Playhouse is somewhat in the spirit of the wood roof of an English church. If it had been framed with conventional trusses with a single horizontal bottom chord the large hall would be crossed by numerous wood members, effectively dividing it into an upper and lower space. If the horizontal chord is eliminated, the roof beams push the two sides of the structure apart, which are otherwise held together by the chord. The long horizontal beam holds them together.

The hammerbeam roof used in countless wood churches is a popular alternative to the truss but not always a structurally successful one as evidenced by the large number of these buildings to which horizontal metal tie rods have been added to provide the horizontal connectors. The steel tie rods in the playhouse today show clearly the problem that is common in this condition.

Primary frames

Girders

Wall and porch framing

Camp Sagamore Playhouse, William Coulter, 1901, sectional perspective

Camp Uncas Dining Hall, 1905

Uncas Dining Hall
Lake Mohegan, New York, 1905

In 1905 J. P. Morgan, after acquiring Camp Uncas, added a Dining Hall. It is the work of Atterbury, but it was for a different client and perhaps for that reason, or perhaps because Atterbury had an experience with the lodge that convinced him solid logs were problematic, it uses half log siding. It is a third type of Atterbury rustic building, two small buildings inside a larger, all three faced with half logs.

The exterior is far more a single volume. The exterior is a half-log veneer. The interior rooms are surfaced with half logs, real logs, and flat boards imitating square logs. In the volume between the two, which is considerable, is the real structure of the building—2x4 studs and 2x10 joists. The exact structure of the farm buildings but clad with a rustic fantasy. Log brackets support the roof overhangs like those at Pine Knot, adding a Swiss flavor as well.

But despite surface similarities with the lodge, it is a very different kind of architecture. It is in terms of comfort far more practical. In terms of appearance far more picturesque. In terms of authenticity, it bears no comparison with the main lodge. It returns to the Pine Knot stage set-rustic veneer on industrial-approach to design.

In the end Atterbury did only one real log building for Durant, his first, the lodge.

East elevation

Camp Uncas Dining Hall, longitudinal section, 1905

Camp Uncas Dining Hall
Wall Section

The Uncas Dining Hall appears similar to the main lodge of ten years earlier but the actual construction is radically different. The typology of a pure, all solid log structure Atterbury used at the Uncas Lodge is replaced here by Its opposite—a log-veneered, milled frame building. Logs are exposed; studs are concealed

In contrast to the solid log walls of the lodge the exterior wall here is 8-inch spruce half-log slabs on wood sheathing supported by 2x4 studs and wood-paneling interior finish.

The interstitial spaces and their finish wood paneling and stud and joist structure are relatively independent of the exterior, forming independent volumes within the whole.

Conclusion

Atterbury's engagement with real log construction was brief. He did one more building in the Adirondacks in 1907, a "camp" for Anna Lusk on Upper St. Regis Lake. His interest in logs was short-lived and evidently minimal, but he was interested in a broader vision of the rustic. He designed a large working farm, Surprise Valley Farm, built of crude stonework that sat on the Newport shoreline two miles from the neoclassical marble palaces of the Vanderbilts and the Astors. Atterbury did much to define the rustic in the twentieth century but he had little interest in it.

In 1930, John D. Rockefeller hired Atterbury to design two gate houses for the carriage roads of his estate on Mount Desert Island. It was understood that since Rockefeller was going to give his estate to the Park Service to expand Acadia National Park, the gatehouses would become park buildings. Rockefeller sent Atterbury on a tour of the park buildings in the West to seek inspiration. He compiled an extensive report but was generally unimpressed and his answer on return was French medieval—half-timber frame infilled with brick. No logs were needed.

While much of what Atterbury had achieved has been erroneously attributed to Durant, the latter may account for this odd bit of history. If Durant was nothing like a designer, he was something of a tastemaker, and he probably set out the palette of materials Atterbury was to use.

But the exploration of constructional rigor that avoided rustic veneers while combining sawmill lumber and logs continued, particularly at the Adirondack League Club, focusing less on the romance of logs and more on the reality of building with them and a rarity in Adirondack architecture—old fashioned nineteenth-century structural rationalism.

Gate houses, Rockefeller estate, Mt. Desert Island, 1932

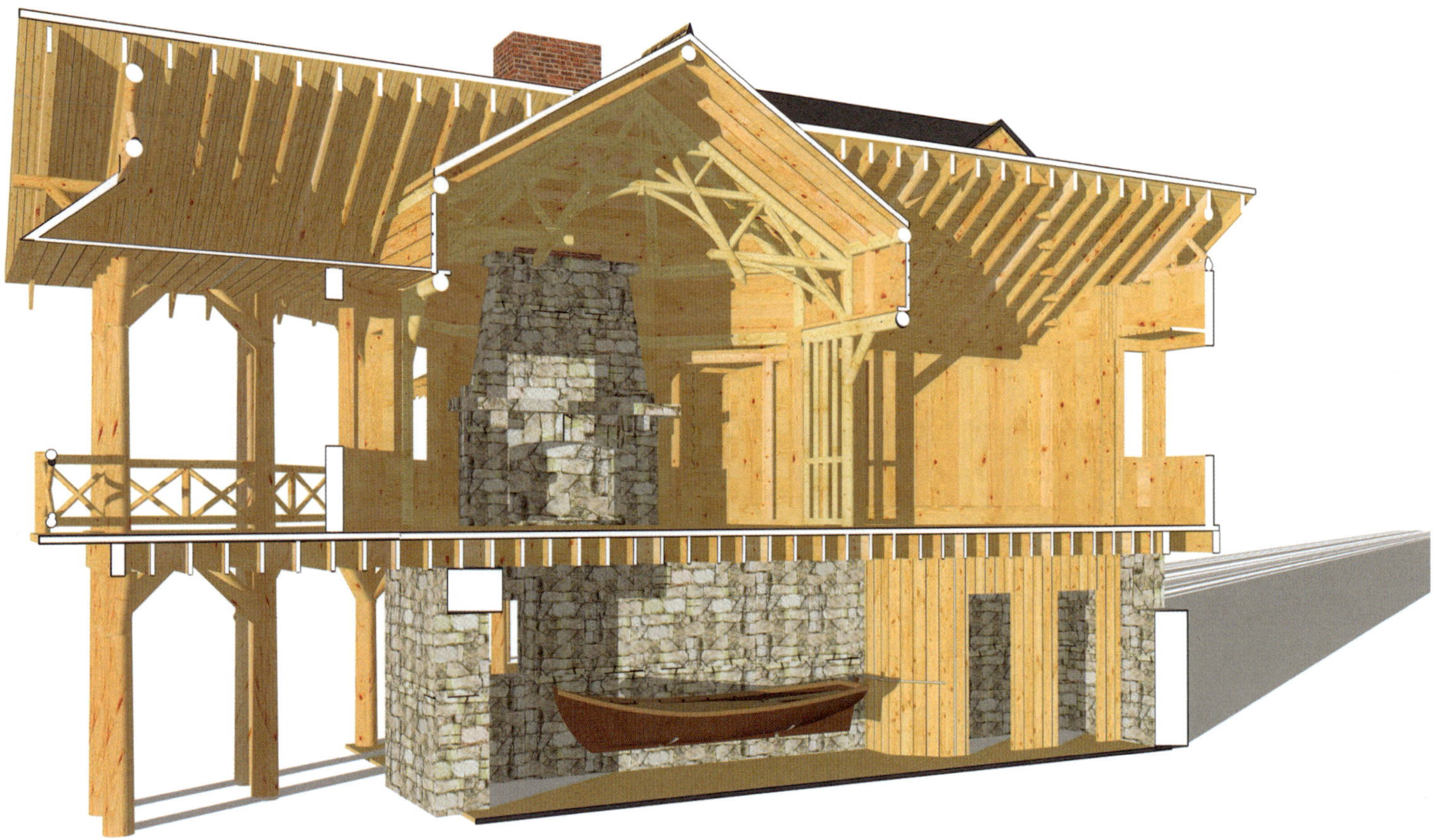

Camp for Charles Huttig

WILLIAM WICKS AND AUGUSTUS SHEPARD

The year 1890 was a watershed in Adirondack history. The State Forest Preserve had been created simultaneously with the timber industry's shift to far more destructive methods of harvesting to obtain pulp instead of timber. Simultaneously, large areas of wilderness that had previously been accessible became closed private preserves and 1890 saw the creation of largest of these, the 91,000 acres of the Adirondack League Club (ALC) and in 1892 the means to access the ALC was completed, the second Adirondack railroad, the Mohawk and Malone. Its builder was W. Seward Webb who, like Durant, was a large landowner and enabler of both the timber industry and the tourist industry.

Curiously, the arrival of the railroad triggered two larger efforts that were, at least in intention, far more altruistic. Both the ALC and Webb sought to develop systems of forest management that were sustainable and renewable. The second was the emergence of a culture of architecture and construction that went beyond the stage-set back drop of Durant's Pine Knot and its pseudo-rustic veneers covering a hidden industrial sawmill frame. A small group of architects sought a culture of building that utilized indigenous craft in combination with the newly established sawmill industry, that dealt with reality, not just appearance, where both types of craft were simultaneously visible, where both the mark of the axe and the sawmill could be seen.

The epicenter of both events was the small town of Old Forge on the Fulton Chain of Lakes, about 25 miles west of Raquette Lake. The ALC lands were to the south of Old Forge. In time it contained about a hundred individual camps spaced out along the shorelines of Little Moose and Honnedaga Lakes with a central lodge. This huge track of land was not just a summer camp but an investment. The surrounding forest was to be selectively and sustainably harvested. One of the founding members was Bernhard Fernow, the head of the USDA Forestry Division, who developed a system of forest management for the ALC. It was essentially selective clear cutting and replanting. What stands out about the ALC is how much we know about its designers. Much architecture of interest was built in the Adirondacks in these years. In many cases the architects are unknown, let alone their intentions. A majority of the ALC camps were designed by two members who were architects—William Wicks in the beginning and later Augustus Shepard. Both were original designers and both wrote highly detailed books describing their work, its motivations, and methodologies.

But again, this would not have happened without the arrival of the railroad at Old Forge two years after the club's founding. The railroad ran southwest from Plattsburgh, a terminal on the New York Montreal line, and provided access to Webb's estate, Camp Santanoni, and the camps around Old Forge, but it also served the expanding timber industry. Webb, unlike Durant, was financially successful and interested in forest management.

In 1896 Webb hired Gifford Pinchot, the future head of the US Forest Service, to study his forest lands. This was published in book form in1898 as *The Adirondack Spruce*.[1] His methodology differs significantly from Fernow's. His recommendation to sustain long-term production was the continued forest production of spruce and the key to this was to not cut spruce with a diameter under 12 inches.

The arrival of the railroad did not just provide access to ALC and other camps. As it had done before it created its own building culture. The year it arrived George Deis built a large sawmill on the river at Old Forge that supplied milled lumber to most of the camps built at the nearby ALC. The dramatic increase in construction created a new class of builder. Three of these were locals who had worked as hunting and fishing guides, building log cabins and shelters in the offseason. With the arrival of the railroad and the creation of the sawmill they became full-time contractors and craftsmen. One of these former guides, George Goodsell, was to build many of the ALC camps, working with craft and precision, working comfortably with both logs and sawmill boards.[2]

But whatever their debt to indigenous craft, the nature of these camps would have been very different without Wicks and Shepard and their particular take on log and sawmill construction. It was not the rustic veneer atop an industrial frame of Pine Knot or North Point. It was not just about rustic appearance but rustic reality, in art and life.

William Wicks

Wicks, a Cornell/MIT trained classicist, had established a successful practice in Buffalo with Edward Green. Their most conspicuous work is the Albright Gallery, but Wicks had a passion for the rustic, particularly the Adirondack cabin, and made a detailed study of the log cabins and shelters in the West Canada Creek area near Old Forge. The result was a small book, *Log Cabins and Cottages* (1889), not only still in print but still in use as a do-it-yourself log cabin building manual. Wicks advocated not just rustic architecture but the rustic life. Like Kephart and Burroughs, he felt he was connecting to a primal, archetypal self:

Some recent anthropologists regard the amusements of the chase, as cultivated by civilized men—hunting, fishing, and the like—as 'traces in modern civilization of original barbarism.' If there is any truth in this theory, then the writer must confess that he is in a large measure a barbarian… As man has brought with him from barbarism to civilization traces of his original condition, so he must take back to 'the forest primeval" some traces of civilization.' [3]

Wicks' book is a schizophrenic text in several ways. The first half is a step by step, axe blow by axe blow, set of instructions on how to build a simple log cabin. It describes preindustrial methodologies. There are no instructions on rustic veneers, half-log siding on sheathing masquerading as solid walls, no clapboard siding on studs masquerading as hewn square logs.

FIG. 54.

FIG. 55.

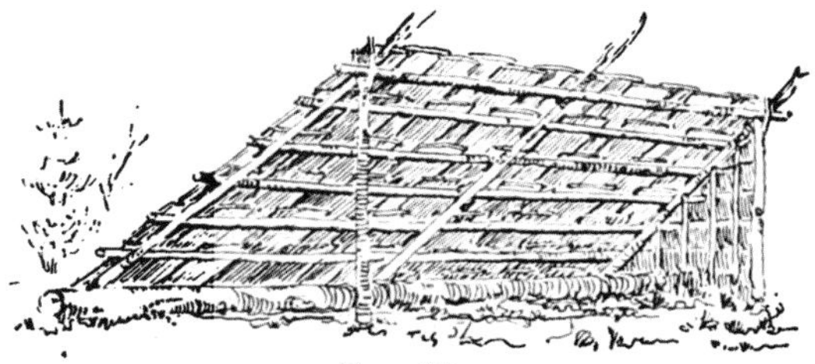

FIG. 56.

FIG. 57.

William Wicks
Types of Lean-to

They are simple generic cabins, built in the woods with nothing more than an axe, crosscut saw and trees. There is an embodied acceptance in the text that materials from the sawmill—floor boards and window sash—were always necessary and at times sawmill sheathing and shingles. Wicks wrote that, "as far as possible they should be made on the spot and with the material at hand."[4]

The second half of Wicks' book is decidedly an odd fit. It shows small plans and perspectives of 30–40 of Wicks' own rustic buildings. All are much larger, and structurally and spatially more complex than the simple log cabins that are shown in the first half. Nowhere can one discover how to build a truss, a covered porch, a balcony, or anything larger than a single room or two, assemblies that appear in abundance in Wicks' illustrated designs. Unfortunately, few of Wicks' buildings are well documented, so how he dealt with these larger problems in practice is nebulous.

Wicks was part of a larger phenomenon, perhaps one he provoked, the revival of authentic log construction. Just as the industrialized Adirondacks, with its massive timber harvests and sawmill-driven building industry was nearing realization, there was in some quarters a revival of the old ways while attempting to reconcile the two technologies in a way that would avoid the stage set of Pine Knot. It is not an accident that return of the authentic log cabin coincided with creation of the railroad and the timber industry.

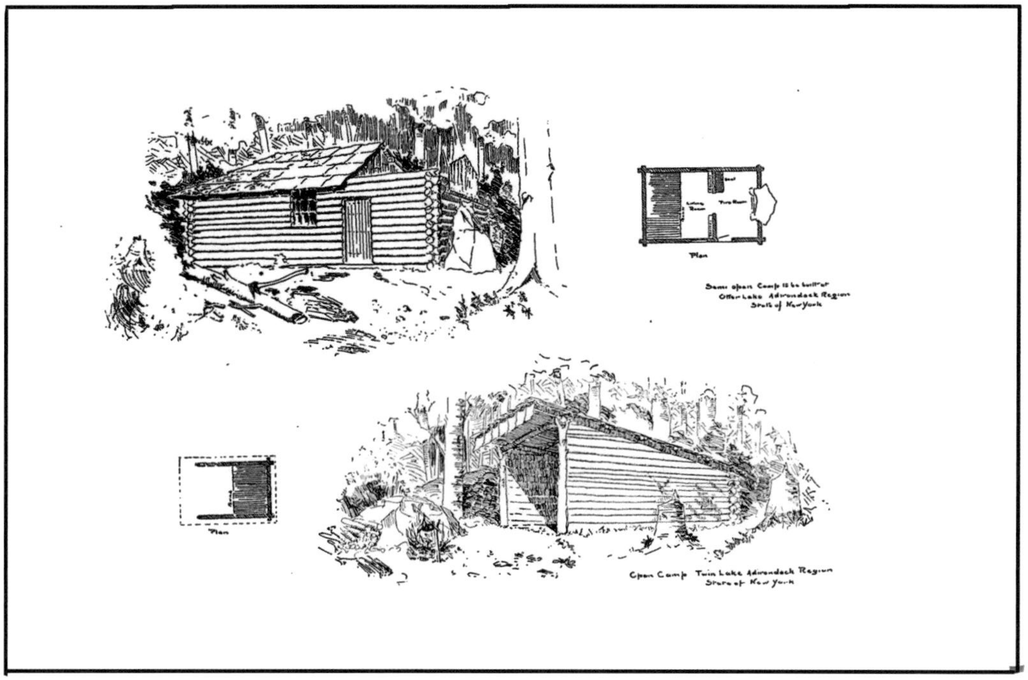

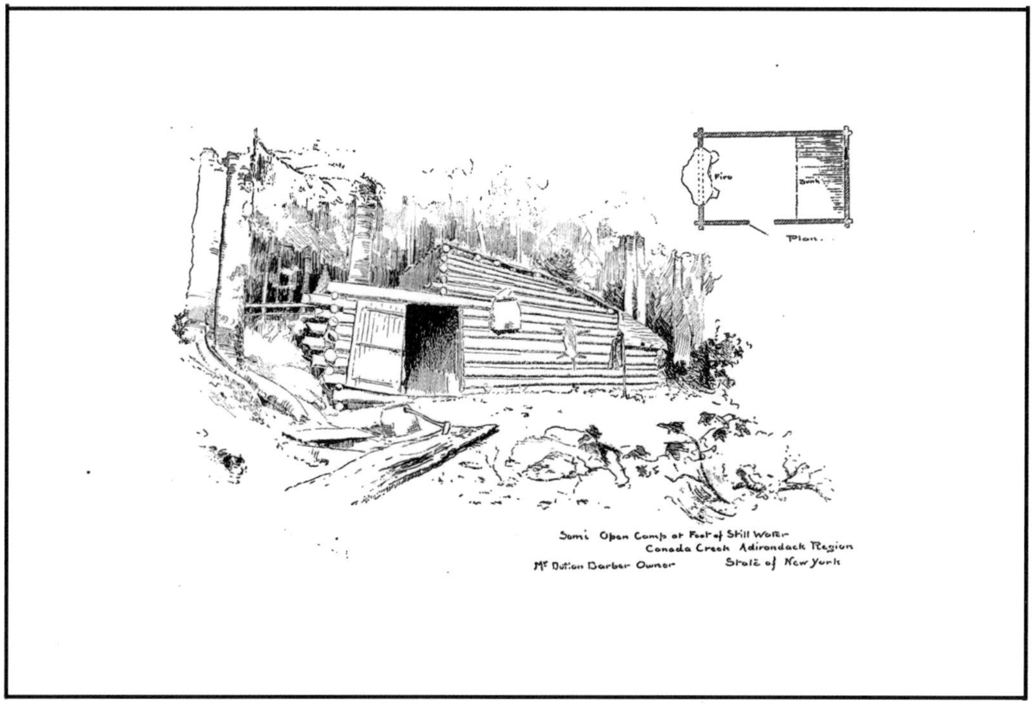

Pages from Wicks' *Log Cabins and Cottages* (1889)

William Wicks, Camp Rabbit Wild, Honnedaga Lake NY

Augustus Shepard

Augustus Shepard was 15 years younger than Wicks and his career lasted well into the 1930s, which may explain his eccentric take on the rustic. Shepard exhibited little interest in the primal urges that fascinated Kephart and Wicks. Comfort was his goal and he insisted that his buildings were not log cabins but summer houses. Of all the rustic architects Shepard may be the least rustic. But there was absolute clarity as to his architectural intentions, the expression of nature through the expression of structure. He wrote:

Visible construction may be said to stand as an architectural symbol of nature's growth, and these camps make their strongest appeal in the fact that their designs are so definitely based on structure. This is evident in the roof trusses, the peeled log and pole beams and split pole studs, so frequently used ... Little has been added merely to lend decorative interest ... Simplicity is the keynote of the design as it is of nature.[5]

But his work was not just about structural honesty, it was about structural expression. Shepard wrote: "The style of these buildings, if we must use that word, is a style inspired by the woods. And thus it is in the design of these camps in the woods we see the structural element logically emphasized."[6] Shepard felt that the boundary between inside and out should be unnoticed and that the structure of the building should be that of the trees. A newspaper reporter said of his work: "Paint or plaster have no place in these camps deluxe. Only natural wood is used for walls and ceilings, hempen rope for molding, peeled poles for decorations as well as useful purposes. And he twists them into unbelievable beauty."[7]

One of the rare pictures we have of Shepard shows him relaxing in a boat, and an interest in boating would explain much about his architecture. Adirondack boathouses received as much design and attention as the main lodge. Uncas and Sagamore have large, well-crafted rustic ones but they are typically on the lake shore, somewhat detached from the main lodge.

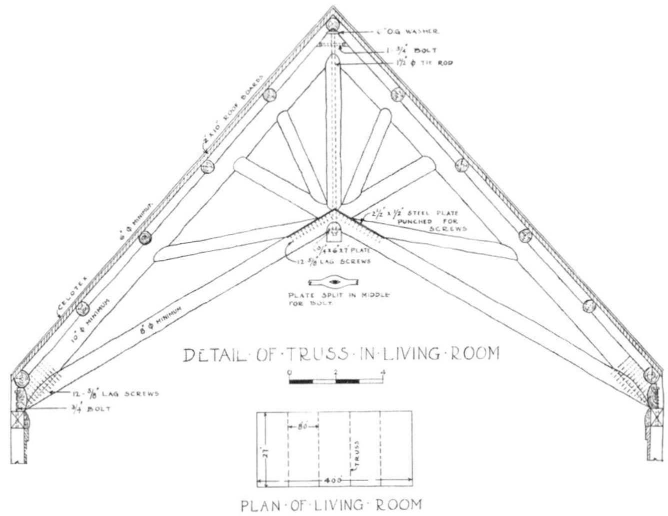

Aten Camp, Lakefalls, New Hampshire.

Camp for Charles Huttig
Honnedaga Lake, NY, 1909

In many Shepard camps the lodge is moved to the lakeside, with boathouse below and living area above, surrounded by a deep porch, The boathouse becomes the central pavilion of the camp. Shepard's 1909 camp for Charles Huttig on Honnedaga Lake is laid out symmetrically on the water's edge, anchored by a central pavilion with living and dining above and boathouse below. Two rows of bedrooms and service rooms extend from either side along the shore. Circulation is largely exterior, along a continuous porch facing the water. The plan resembles a Palladian villa more than an Adirondack camp. There is far more of the symmetrical in Shepard's work than the picturesque. The roof has an oriental sensibility; the trusses suggest English Gothic; there are some Swiss brackets but no gingerbread balconies. Historical or stylistic references are atypical.

The braced column and beam framework is largely exposed. The large spaces—dining, living and recreation rooms—used trusses. Trusses are often the key element in a Shepard camp. In the Huttig House living room it is a two-way system with two pairs of hammerbeam trusses perpendicular to one another that form an interlocking rectangle set within a flat eight-sided space overlooking the lake. He rarely used trusses of the king post type, which have continuous horizontal chords across the bottom of the triangle. The Huttig truss is a variation of the English hammerbeam with curved brackets that avoid the bottom chord as at the Sagamore Playhouse. This can be structurally problematic but it avoids the perception of a spatial division between the space above the truss and the room below. Shepard experimented with several truss types in his many houses. He did many variations on the scissor truss which does not have a horizontal bottom chord. The trusses are often set in a simple parallel arrangement such as the living room in the Aten Camp, Lakefalls, in New Hampshire. It is a short step from structural expression to structural exaggeration and one Shepard occasionally took. Many of his trusses appear unnecessarily complex from an engineering viewpoint. Much of his furniture has an oversized truss-like character. In the Riker Camp a series of mini-trusses form a kind of overweight freeze in each room. Shepard was willing to conceal structure but never construct false structure.

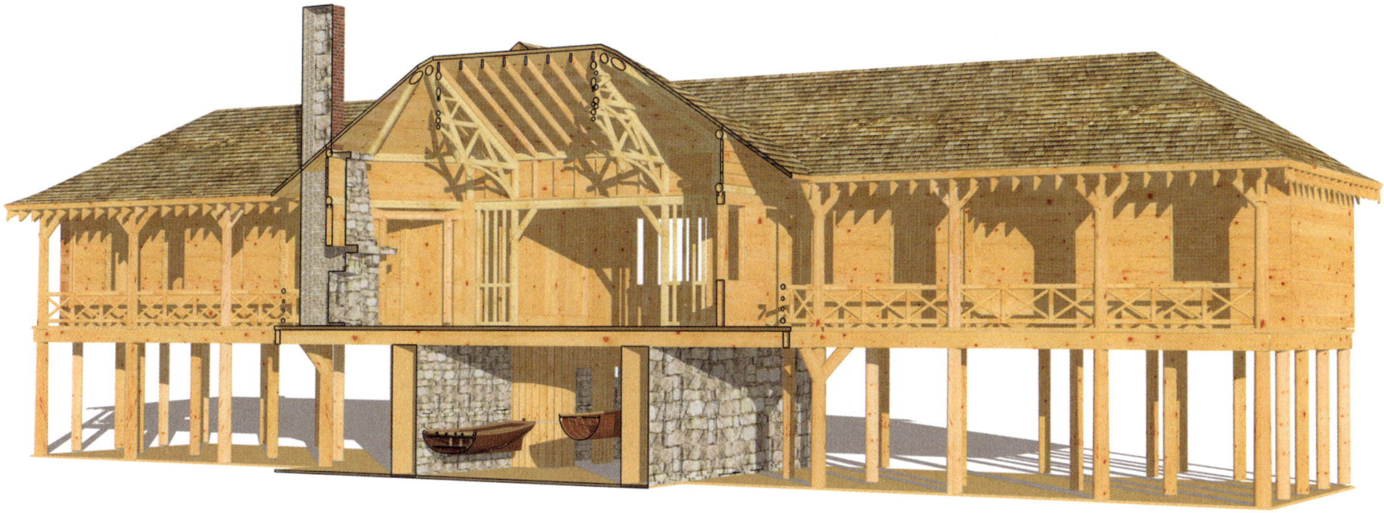

Section looking inland

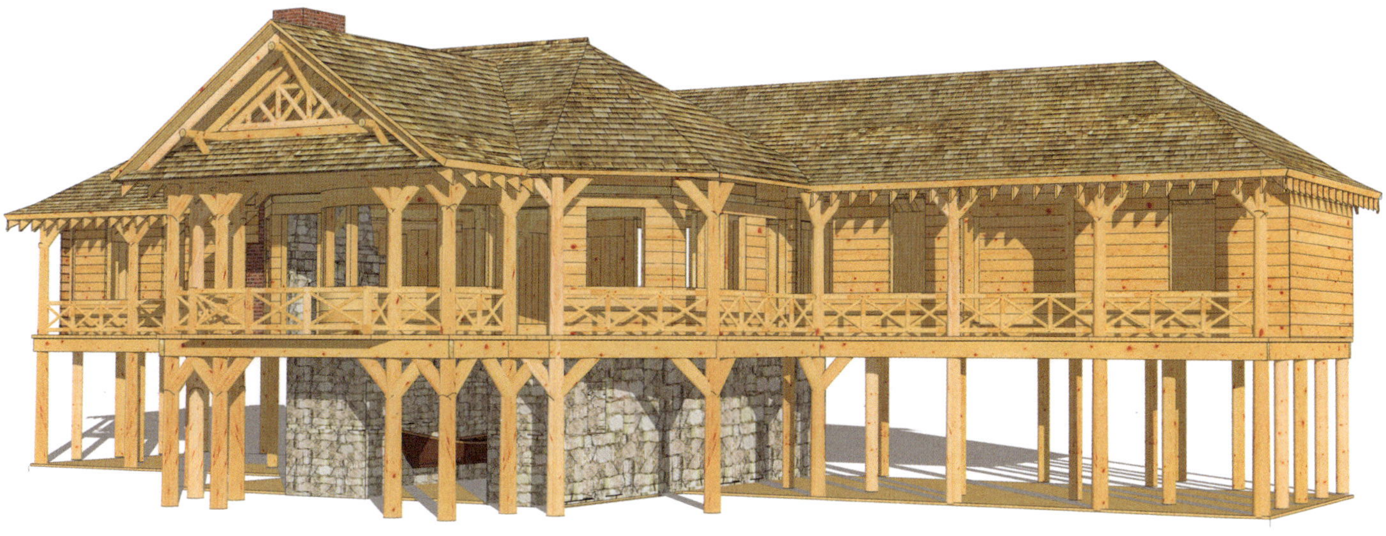

Elevation on lakeside

Camp for Charles Huttig
Wall Section

Shepard wanted to do more than reveal the log structure, he wanted to express it. The peeled-log wood trusses are all exposed and perhaps a bit overdesigned. The floor and roof structure are largely exposed.

The less dramatic roof construction of shingles and boards on milled joists spaced at 16-inches is largely concealed.

The wall constriction is shiplap siding on log studs, set within a log frame.

Shepard developed a series of wall and floor systems that, while they used logs, did not use them in the traditional log cabin manner. Both wall system and floor/roof system used closely spaced log verticals or horizontals supporting mill-sawn sheathing or decking. None of his published or documented work uses conventional log cabin wall construction. A typical wall would be logs flattened on one side spaced at two to three feet faced on the exterior with horizontal sheathing and siding or simply various types of wide clapboard or tongue and groove boards. At the same time there are no chinking problems; there is less timber in contrast to the traditional log wall. A typical floor would be peeled logs, also spaced at two to three feet, supporting 2x10 ceiling boards. The similarity of the two systems creates a visual unity of wall and roof or floor. He made frequent use of half logs but never disguised them as a solid log wall. On occasion he would use milled studs or joists instead of logs but in his rustic work he typically exposed them. These buildings have few cavities. Everything, especially structure, is exposed. Shepard's constructional language is decidedly polished and refined. Some of it is not rustic at all. There is no bark inside or out. Logs are peeled, polished, and relatively knot free. Joints between logs are precisely made. There are no twisted brackets or twigs. He wrote: "Every detail possesses some structural significance. ... If a certain element is not found to be sufficiently decorative or interesting in its bare structure, other structural materials which possess a greater natural interest have been substituted."[8] If one believes what Viollet-le-Duc believed about rustic structures, that it was logical building, Shepard's best work is the logical outcome.

Perceval McIntosh Camp

Conclusion

As for the larger plans for forest management, both Fernow's clear cutting/replanting and Pinchot's selective harvesting were imperfectly implemented and failed, but both were scientifically flawed. Acid rain has been the cause of the loss of about half of the red spruce forests in the Adirondacks at high altitudes. Much of the Adirondack forest has grown back but it is a different forest.

The architectural legacy of the Adirondacks is two very different types of building. One was a pseudo-rustic architecture to accommodate a pseudo-rustic life in Isiah Berlin's terms, playing at being woodsmen. This was a stage set architecture, one of bark and half log veneers that concealed an industrial sawmill frame below. On the other side there is the deeper and far more authentic buildings that actually were logs—Atterbury's Uncas, Robertson's Santanoni, Coulter's Sagamore rec hall, and Shepard's houses. They are for the most part what they appear to be—frames and walls made of logs faced with exposed siding from the sawmill. The lives clients led in these buildings are unlikely to have been genuinely any more rustic than those that lived in the log veneered cabins nearby but they did so with fewer architectural pretensions.

It would be in error to see one as playing at rustic and one as genuinely rustic. Neither could have existed without the railroad. The railroad not only brought the clients, it brought most of the technology, most of the materials, and most of the craftsmen. All were the end product of the process of creating a railroad. It also brought the nostalgia for what it eliminated.

Augustus Shepard.
Typical Wall Section.

Shepard rarely used the traditional log cabin construction of stacked rows of horizontal logs.
The typical Shepard wall is rather a series of vertical 6-inch peeled logs 2 to 3 feet apart covered with a siding of one layer of shiplap boards or two layers- 1-inch clapboards on sheathing.

The roof is similarly constructed of shingles and boards on peeled 6-inch logs 2 to 3 feet apart resting on a wood plate.

It is a system that uses considerably less lumber than conventional log construction while expressing the frame.

THE CHALET

THE CHALET: KIRTLAND CUTTER IN CHICAGO

The mention of the 1893 World's Columbian Exposition in Chicago evokes certain images—the massive white neoclassical buildings around the lagoon signaling the rise of the American Renaissance, Louis Sullivan's Transportation building marking the beginning of the fall of the Chicago School. The fair does not evoke images of log cabins but there were two significant ones there, and in their own way they too influenced the architecture that was to come. The smallest of these was not really a log cabin and not really in the fair. Buffalo Bill had set up his Wild West show just outside the fairgrounds. The last episode in every show was "The Attack on the Settler's Cabin," in which a log cabin housing a settler and his family were attacked by Native Americans, then rescued by Buffalo Bill. The cabin had to be quickly demounted and moved and appears to have been painted boards. It is one of many examples of increasing interest in the log cabin as an object of legend.[1]

The Idaho Pavilion was a real log cabin at the fair but it was far more. It was a chalet with the Alpine romance of a chalet, but one made of logs. The image of the chalet had little to do with the building's primary purpose. The Idaho building may have evoked nostalgia for the pioneers, as Buffalo Bill's settler's cabin did, but it was just as much a timber showroom. It was an advertisement. It was not the container for the exhibits; it was the exhibit, showing Idaho's most substantial products, timber and ore. So both the romance of the log cabin and the demonstration of the unlimited endless resources of America were on display at the fair, particularly in the state pavilion of Idaho.

Each room was finished in a different type of wood and there were twenty-two types of lumber. Equally represented was mining, hence the stone-walled ground floor that contained white magnesia, lava, marble, mica, and granite from individual mines in the state. In the history of the West, mining is perceived in a romantic way; it is here as well, represented by picks and shovels mounted on the walls. The exhibits gave an equally romantic view of the timber industry.

The pavilion was the work of Kirtland Cutter of Spokane. It was clearly inspired by the Swiss chalet, and Cutter had previously built at least one chalet-inspired building, and he was to build at least ten more.

Cutter said later in life that he had studied Swiss architecture firsthand when he traveled through Europe as a young man, but he was not specific about his sources. Most of his chalets conform to type described by Ernest Gladbach's *Der Schweizer Holzstil* based on examples around Lake Brienz. He may have learned of them from Gladbach's text or from architect-designed copies of traditional models.

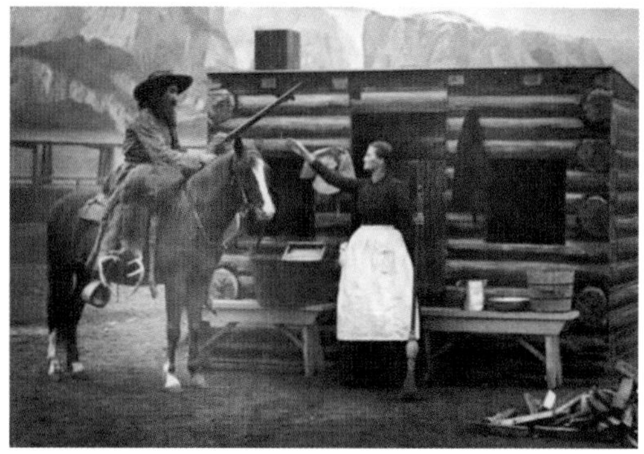

Attack on the Settler's Cabin
Scene from Buffalo Bill's Wild West Show

Opposite: The Idaho Pavilion, World's Columbian Exposition
Chicago, 1893

Ladies' Reception Room

The Idaho Pavilion was a familiar generic chalet type by 1893, a wide multi-story box topped with low slope gable-fronted roof with long balconies, both supported with brackets. It is much like William Durant's Pine Knot and its possible model, Victoria and Albert's "Swiss Cottage" on the Isle of Wight.

The general form of the Idaho building is the familiar wide, flat, symmetrical, low-sloped projecting roof we have come to associate with the type, symmetrical with a central axis on which sits a fireplace. It has its requisite Swiss features—a long low-pitched roof with large eaves. Stones on the roof, and brackets formed by extending the top logs at each log plane completes the connection to the Swiss prototypes.

But while it follows the details of the traditional model the material is decidedly transformed. All the traditional squared timbers of the chalet became round bark-on logs. The ground floor is stone walls. Atop this is a wood volume formed by five log planes running parallel to the central axis and six running perpendicular to it, creating a series of boxes that define the spatial divisions of the building. These walls do not always form room divisions as the log planes are hollowed out to form connecting spaces. As in the Swiss model the end of the log wall planes extend beyond the corners and though the exterior walls so they create vertical fins that are visible at the corners and on the face. Brackets are formed by extending the top logs at each log plane in a stepped profile.

The exterior wall of the building is all logs excepting its stone base and stucco-covered chimney. Nine-inch diameter logs make up the entire wood structure save for the floor, roof deck and sheathing. It is a solid load-bearing wall structure with few cavities.

Section looking northwest

Southeast elevation

View from southeast

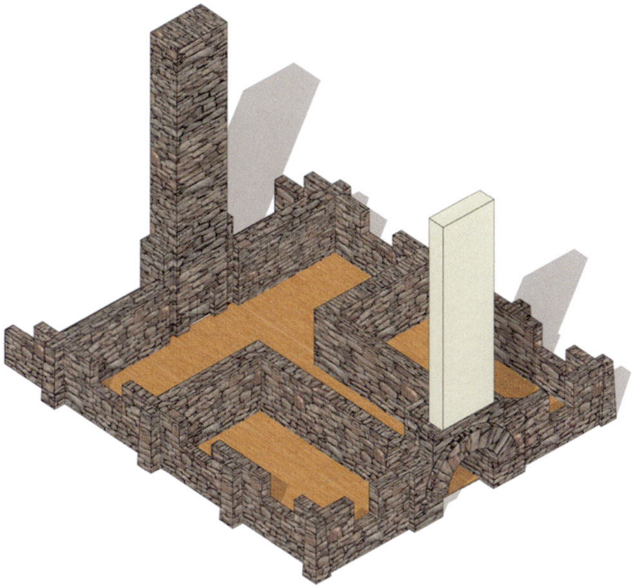

Stone ground floor walls and chimneys

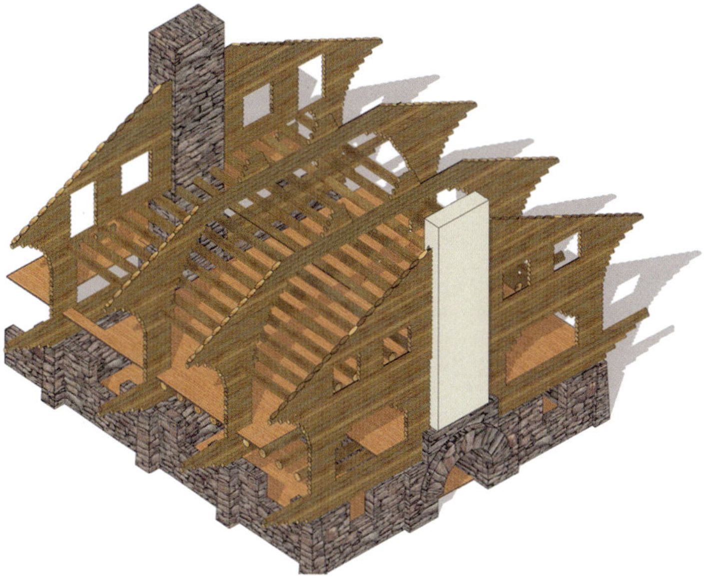

Log beams spanning between walls supporting floor

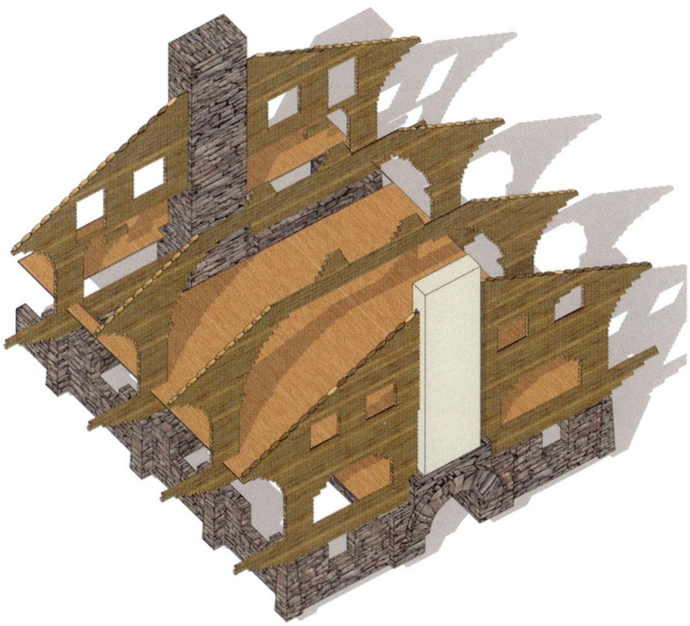

Parallel log walls perpendicular to circulation axis

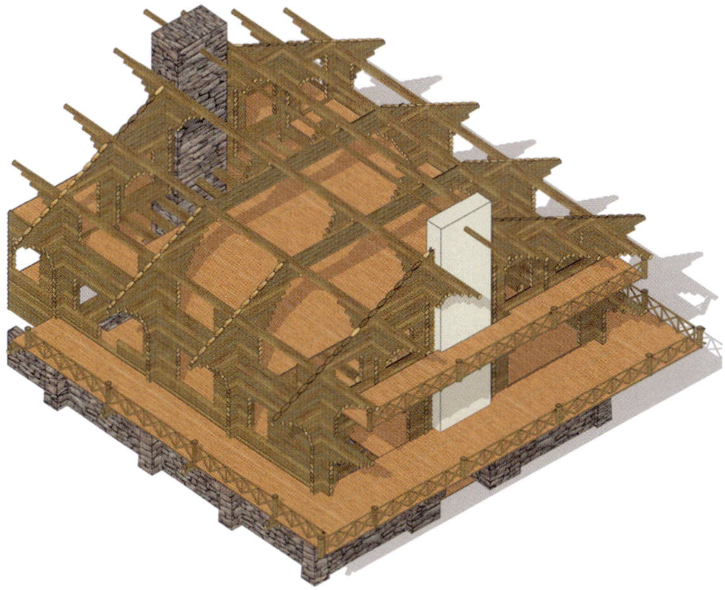

Six log walls parallel to circulation axis supporting roof

There are no log trusses. There are no log columns. Long spans are accomplished by stacks of horizontal logs working together as a deep beam. Vertical supports are accomplished the same way. There is no concealed milled balloon frame. There is no structural skeleton. Cutter had rusticated the chalet as Adam and Chambers had done with the Greek temple. Cutter had also returned it to it constructional origins.

There are two types of brackets in traditional chalets. One is a series of parallel squared logs, each of which projects beyond the one below, or a single square timber at an angle of about 45 degrees, braced against the wall. Durant uses both of these but he makes them of logs, not squared timbers. A series of projecting parallel logs support the second floor. A series of 45-degree brackets support the projecting roof. This was a practice followed by many who came after. But whatever past the chalet evoked here it had found a new purpose—a mass marketing device.

The Idaho building was widely praised. It was transported to a new site and re-erected. An exact copy of it was built in Hampshire by an English banker, but despite the success of the Idaho building and the obvious potential of Cutter applying it to his work, between 1893 and 1907 he built only one log structure, a church in Chelan, Washington in 1898. He built three chalets in the years immediately after but not of logs. His early practice ranged from houses for wealthy executives to large hotels. Stylistically they span the spectrum from Queen Anne to Palladian. As was the case with many rustic architects, rustic work was a small a part of much larger eclectic and diverse practice, He was to return to the log chalet, but not for some time.

The rustic architecture of the West is inextricably linked to the industrialization of the West and with the destruction it caused. Rustic architecture could be, as it was here, an imaginative hybrid of the industrial and the primitive, or it could be a romantic patina overlaying the hidden grim reality. This was as true in architecture as it was in life. The Idaho pavilion had little structural deception in the form of veneers, but this cannot be said of its intentions in representing the realities of the mining and timber industries.

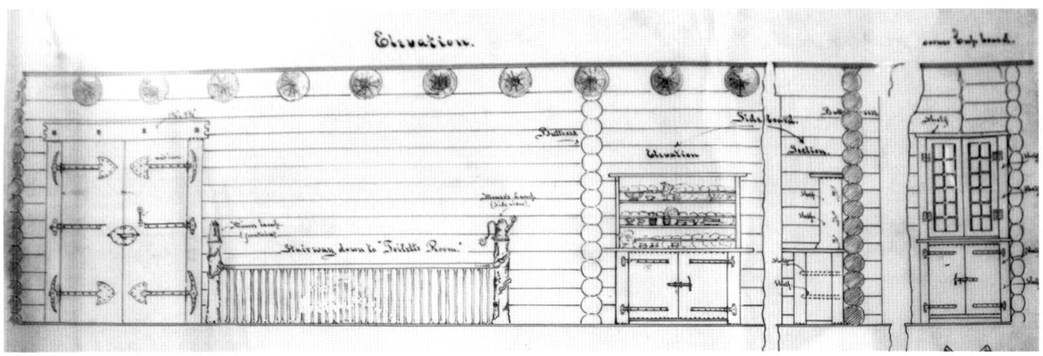

Ground floor interior elevation
Showing mining-themed hardware and lights

Idaho Pavilion
Wall Section

It has no frame, no columns, no trusses.
All vertical supports are planes of logs.

The exterior walls are solid. The floor and roof structure are largely exposed.

The entire assembly is a combination of 8-inch and 16-inch logs. The floor and roof are constructed of boards on 16-inch logs 3 feet on center. The roof has no rafters but is supported by the 8-Inch log walls that spatially define the building.

The stone base, made of various ores from Idaho, is essentially part of the mining exhibit.

Little of Cutter's subsequent work is equally authentic in using complete log construction.

South elevation

Section looking north

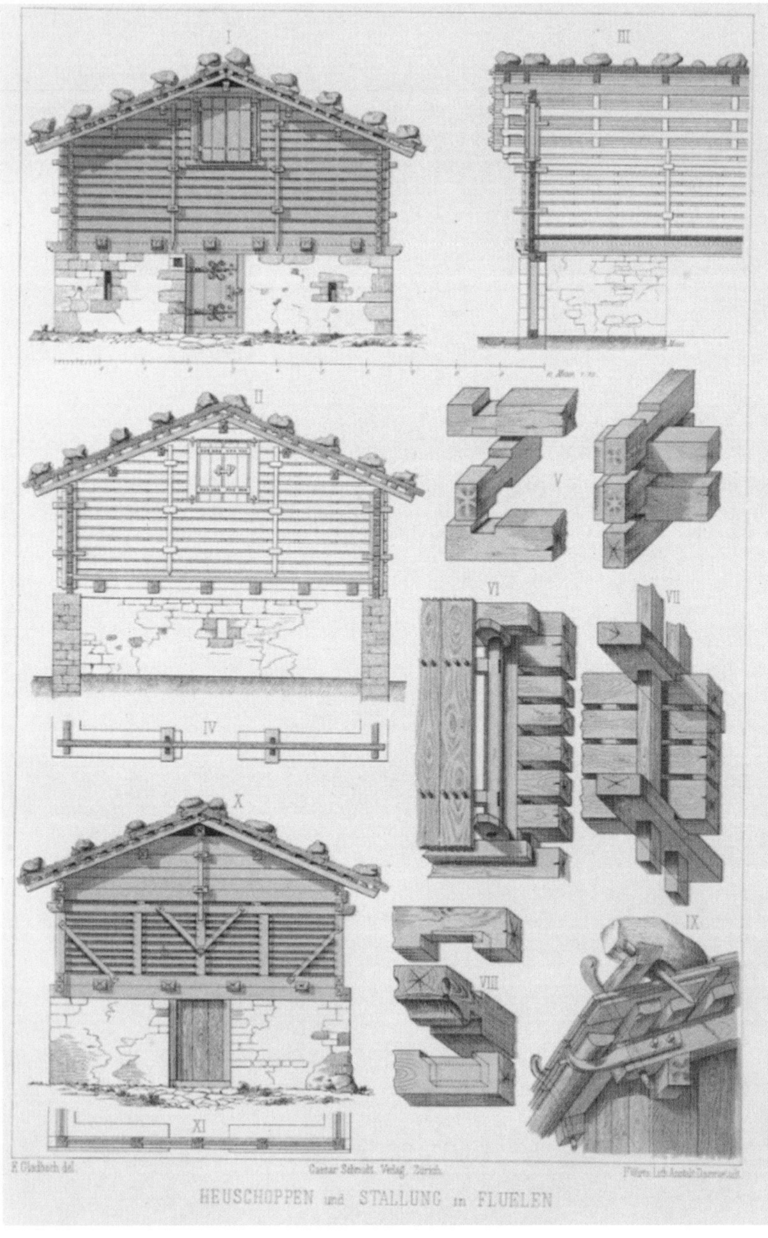
E. Gladbach del.
Caesar Schmidt, Verlag, Zürich
F. Wirtz Lith. Anstalt Darmstadt
HEUSCHOPPEN und STALLUNG in FLUELEN

E. Gladbach del.
Caesar Schmidt, Verlag, Zürich
F. Wirtz Lith. Anstalt Darmstadt
KAES-SPEICHER IN BOENIGEN

THE LOG CHALET

While it is not clear what particular building was the inspiration for William Durant's Swiss chalet at Pine Knot, imitating the chalet was by then a well-established formal tradition, demonstrated by the history of the building that probably did inspire it.

In 1853-54 Queen Victoria and Prince Albert built a summer retreat for themselves, a "Swiss Cottage" in the garden of Osborne House on the Isle of Wight. It was a stage for Victoria and Albert to play at being rustic and a place for their children to play at being middle class. Both educational program and architectural design are thought to be drawn from Albert's childhood as his boyhood home at Schloss Rosenau has a similar Swiss cottage.[1]

The practice of retreating from the life of the everyday to something like the Swiss chalet was something of a trope by 1854. The chalet was more of an idea that came from literature and less of a form that came from architecture, but what ties its many manifestations together was a return to origins. Albert's program—to return to personal origins in tandem with a return to cultural origins—was also something of a trope. It might be personal origins. It might be historical. It might be archetypal origins.

For many non-architects the chalet might represent a return to political origins, to what was for some the source of democracy, the Alps, as it was for Jean-Jacques Rousseau. It might be a return to origins that were fictional. The influence of any of one building in popularizing the chalet pales beside that of Johanna Spyri's immensely successful children's book *Heidi* of 1881, the story of a young girl who is forced to leave her Alpine home for an unhappy, unhealthy life in the city, but who eventually returns to her origins and her grandfather in the mountains. As Irene Cieraad writes: "Heidi echoed the later nineteenth-century passion for honest, rustic simplicity and the appreciation of the noble handicraft of woodwork in contrast to industrial production."[2]

In some cases the chalet meant a return to the origins of building as well, to logs, bark, and thatch. Despite common themes there were critical differences between the Osbourne chalet and the older ones—Prince Albert's Chalet in appearance has little in common with the Swiss cottages of 50 years earlier—the Duchess of Bedford's Swiss cottage at Endsleigh or Lord Cahir's Swiss cottage in Ireland. Prince Albert's Swiss chalet was all precision and polish, smooth planed lumber with precise fittings. Cahir and Endsleigh were rustic. Roofs were thatch, timbers were logs, with the bark on in the case of the later.

John Ruskin saw the chalet this way, a return to the origins of architecture itself, not by means of archeology but by understanding the process that created it. He wrote:

One feels that the peasants whose hands carved the planks so neatly, and adorned their cottage so industriously, and still preserve it so perfectly, and so neatly, can be no dull, drunken, lazy boors; one feels, also, that it requires both firm resolution, and determined industry, to maintain so successful a struggle against 'the crush of thunder, and the warring winds.' Sweet ideas float over the imagination of such passages of peasant life.[3]

To Ruskin the chalet was the work of the indigenous craftsmen—clever but unsophisticated, knowledgeable in craft but not in architectural history, working with limited resources and tools, using materials that were readily available—the innocent designer in the Alpine landscape.

John Ruskin, *Chalet in the Luetschine Valley*

E. E. Viollet-le-Duc, A Himalayan Chalet

Opposite: Pages from Ernest Gladbach's 1886 *Der Schweizer Holzstil*

For many nineteenth-century thinkers the vernacular was seen as the functional, the origins of building that were free of style and whim, straightforward solutions using the tools at hand. E. E. Viollet-le-Duc, the nineteenth century's leading structural rationalist, saw the chalet from this perspective, but in a decidedly ugly way. The chalet for him represented a return to genetic origins. He saw an inherent connection between landscape, climate, and race—in this case the mountain people-the Aryans:

Now whether it was the result of natural predisposition or of the environment by which the various races of mankind were surrounded at the outset. ... It happened that these races adopted certain methods of construction,—methods whose original elements are handed down from age to age, and make their appearance at the present day.[4]

Viollet-le-Duc's conjectural drawing of the original chalet, in his case located in the Himalayas, is also a rough log building—the prototype for many chalets to come. Irene Cieraad argues that the chalet was yet another version of the primitive hut:

Nineteenth-century tourism to the Alpine regions thus represented a journey into Europe's past. ... The mix of neo-gothic details combined with references to other regions distant in time or place that was characteristic of the late nineteenth-century international chalet style was an appreciation of both rustic simplicity and exoticized primitivism. ... to visit even these places was to travel into Europe's pre-industrial past.

It is significant that all of these precedents are "primitive." The chalet designs of the1810 period such as Cahir and the conjectural prototypes of writers on the chalet—Rousseau, Ruskin, and Viollet-le-Duc—were all rustic. They were built completely or partially with logs. They were returns to the origins of building, and those origins were logs. This was something that was not true of the vast majority of chalets being built by 1850 or even existing chalets dating back many years. Timbers were square. Boards were smooth.

In the early nineteenth century there was considerable difference of opinion as to what exactly a chalet looked like. Julie's (Rousseau's) chalet was thatched, requiring a steep roof. John Nash's Swiss cottage in Ireland is not much different than his faux-rustic vernacular English cottages at Blaise Hamlet.

Ruskin came closest to describing the characteristics that came to be identified as the chalet: 1. symmetry 2. a low-slope roof often supported with widely spaced logs, 3. wide overhanging eaves to prevent the windows from being clogged with snow, 4. a long central second-floor balcony with a railing of slats usually with cut out profiles, 5. large wood brackets to support them, 6. logs and rocks placed on the roof to hold it down in storms.

Fig. 41.

Rustic log cabin chalet from *Der Schweizer Holzstil*

Refined log cabin chalet from *Der Schweizer Holzstil*

Above Left: The Swiss Cottage at Osborne House, Isle of Wight
Right: Refined log chalet from Gladbach's *Der Schweizer Holzstil*

The Refined Chalet

The 1860s saw the first examples of rigorous, detailed documentation of traditional chalets, publications containing examples that were to be widely copied in America. Amédée and Eugène Varin's 1861 *L'architecture pittoresque en Suisse*, contains a great deal of constructional description, seeing structural expression as essential to the chalet. They show us a very different chalet. While they illustrate a conjectural primitive log prototype. The buildings they document use squared timbers. They are the refined, not the primitive.

It was Ernest Gladbach's 1886 *Der Schweizer Holzstil* that cataloged in meticulous detail the chalets of Switzerland. Gladbach's emphasis is also heavily structural and he identifies several basic chalet types, but the most important of these was the box type—a building built up like a log cabin—but with squared timbers. It is a type common in Western Switzerland and Gladbach documented a number of vernacular examples around Lake Brienz. Gladbach did much to codify, some say partially invented, what is still the prevalent image of what a chalet looks like. The basic form is a symmetrical wide low slope roof. If this type is a rustic building, it is it is a precisely crafted one. Boards were planned and frequently ornamented. Joints were made like cabinetry. While the type probably originated as a log cabin, and while some chalets Gladbach illustrated were made of round logs, the type had evolved into something more sophisticated.

The volume is formed of an eggcrate of parallel and perpendicular walls built of squared log timbers forming the rooms of the building. The solid horizontal wall timbers overlap when they meet, as in any log structure, and are notched at the corners in the same way as a log cabin, but with far more precise craftsmanship. This causes the log planes extend beyond the corners and the internal walls to extend though the exterior walls creating thin vertical piers that are visible at the corners and on the face of the wall. There are solid square beams to support the floor, solid rafters to support the roof and brackets to support the eaves, balconies, and roof rafters that extend well beyond the wall. These brackets are also built of stepped horizontal rows of square timbers, usually aligned with the projecting walls. The result is a solid structure with few cavities. While there are numerous projections to support eaves and balconies, there is no frame. This building type required sophisticated craft and a great deal of labor. Gladbach refers to some of their precise complex jointed assemblies as jewelry. They were decidedly not primitive. The box type was to dominate subsequent chalet design in Switzerland and, in appearance at least, in America. By mid-century the image of the chalet had undergone a transformation. Whatever it was culturally or politically, it was no longer a return to constructional origins. The bark, thatch, and tree trunks of Endsleigh and Cahir are gone, replaced by sawn and planed square lumber.

Prefabrication

Prince Albert's Chalet was prefabricated and shipped to the site—constructed of wood panels joined with metal fasteners. It is not clear where the parts were fabricated but it was certainly not Switzerland and possibly America. But it plays its role of being Swiss, complete with the requisite rocks on the roof. The chalet had become a prefabricated industrialized commodity.

Prefabrication was very much in evidence at the 1896 Exposition in Geneva for which a number of chalets were constructed. All or almost all were of the box/wall type. Equally significant was the process that created them. Like Prince Albert's chalet they were made from factory produced prefab parts and shipped to mountainside sites for assembly. This is hardly surprising given the complexity of parts the system required. Timber was typically unavailable on site and was imported to the factories.

William Dana, who wrote the comprehensive history of the chalet, described the Swiss type: "These *châlettes* are portable ... being constructed at the [factory} and then dismounted and shipped . ... Châlets of all sizes are designed at the [factory] and constructed bodily in the yards, then knocked down for shipment to any point"[5] These were not rustic chalets. The logs, bark, and thatch were gone and the logs and stone were gone from the roof. Having gone back to its origins it had become civilized again. In America the process was to be reversed.

The American Chalet

The chalet was to become no less popular in America. At first glance it seems this was the result of simple nationalism, or more correctly, simple capitalism. The Rockies were the Switzerland of America and the chalet was an excellent marketing ploy to drive tourists to the Rockies and away from the Alps. But the ideology was still there. American publications on the chalet in the period 1900 to 1915 tell a similar story, echoing precisely the ideological foundations described by their European counterparts.

Louis Steelman wrote in *House and Garden* in 1911:

There is about the Swiss chalet a rugged, honest picturesqueness, a simple, candid strength that I find in no other type of habitation ... It seems to typify—as plain as a house can ever hope to represent a man—the hardy, fearless, simple mountaineer—whose life is spent among the heights and broad vistas and who lives a simple frugal, happy, sincere life.[6]

Wendell Corthell writing in Gustav Stickley's *Craftsman* magazine in 1903 echoes Rousseau and Ruskin on the virtues of Swiss character:

Here is the only true republic in Europe, a republic of far more freedom, dignity and real democracy than that of France, or even that of our own. A land is here without a 'Boss,' where every member is free to cast his ballot and have his full share in the general corporation ...

Switzerland has no castles, no walled towns. She has been governed for five hundred years by her own people and without the help of kings. ... The Swiss are the freest people in the world, the Athenians of modern times.

And again, seeing a fit between building form and landscape:

In the plains, where there is much rain, the roofs are steep, to throw off the water, while in the mountains, where there is much snow, they are made flat and dotted with stones to hold the snow, which aids to keep the house warm. The wide, overhanging eaves, from three to nine feet, which are universal, are to protect the occupants from the summer sun and winter snows.[7]

And something like structural rationalism:

A true chalet does not cover its exterior with paint, or hide its interior wood by paper and hangings, which can never be beautiful as the natural grain of the wood ... Instead of hiding the materials employed and the methods of their employment, every effort is made to show the joints and their fittings, the boards and timber, so that what is there by necessity becomes an object of decoration and harmony.[8]

Andrew Jackson Downing was more skeptical about the chalet as prototype. He wrote in 1841:

From the Italian style it is an easy transition to the Swiss mode, a bold and spirited one, highly picturesque and interesting in certain situations. To build a Swiss cottage in a smooth cultivated country, would, both as regards association and intrinsic want of fitness, be the height of folly. But in a wild and mountainous region, such as the borders of certain deep valleys and rocky glens in the Hudson Highlands, or rich bits of the Alleghenies, positions may be found where the Swiss cottage, with its low and broad roof, shedding off the heavy snows, its ornamented exterior gallery, its strong and deep brackets, and its rough and rustic exterior, would be in the highest degree appropriate.[9]

But as we have seen there were two models of the chalet that could be followed. One was based on Gladbach's box with walls of squared horizontal timbers, interlocking corners and finely crafted and precisely joined brackets balconies of planned lumber. The other model was to return the chalet to its origins, to return Gladbach's box to its rustic log original, just as Robert Adam had done with the classical temple. American architects pursued both these strategies, but both presented considerable constructional problems.

Above: Sagamore, stepped bracket in logs
Below: Gladbach, stepped bracket in finished wood

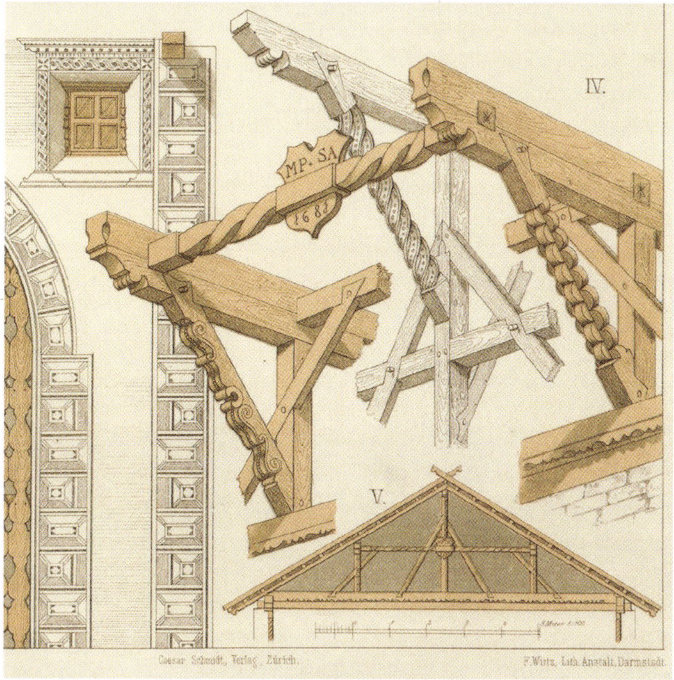

Above: Sagamore Lodge, slopped bracket in logs
Below: Gladbach, slopped bracket in finished wood

American Construction and Swiss Construction

Those American architects wishing to adopt not just the imagery but the construction methodology of the chalet faced some basic contradictions. American wood construction was based on the balloon or platform frame system that required far less lumber and less precise craftsmanship, e.g., hammers and nails, than Gladbach's massive, meticulously fitted piece of cabinetry. The result was often the illusion of a Swiss-type construction veneered on top of a balloon frame. William Dana wrote: "Whereas in Switzerland the age-old custom of tiers of beams laid horizontally persists in the transplanted chalet vertical boards and cleats and shingles or shakes as a covering to a wooden skeleton prevail."

An 1897 *Architectural Record* article described in detail the constructional superiority of the Swiss system over the American:

Another cause of the inferiority of wood architecture in America is the manner of placing the boards on the walls, the upper ones usually overlapping the lower. ... the joists are not visible and give no idea of the internal structure of the house.

In Switzerland, too, and the other countries where the woodworking art has flourished and created a style, instead of masking and hiding the material employed, every effort has been exerted to make the most of its decorative properties; hence the joists are exposed, the projections of the upper floors emphasized, and the joist left uncovered; the roofs are developed and the eaves extended, protecting the house and producing the finest decorative effect imaginable with their supporting brackets. Inside, wood forms are the basis of the ornamentation.

The Swiss chalet has an imagery that is easy enough to mimic but it has a construction system antithetical to American building. It was prefabricated and joined with the type of precision prefabrication made possible. The American chalet was built on site, often with local materials, limited tools and at times limited skills.

The connection to the log cabin was, to many Americans, a large part of the chalet's appeal. Returning to the rustic log prototype chalet eliminated some of the craft problems but created others. It eliminated Gladbach's complex elements and their ornaments that required sophisticated milling equipment and a great deal of labor. The basic character of the traditional American log cabin was that it was a system that one used when there was plentiful natural material and no sophisticated or heavy equipment—that is, built with an axe. The structural members of Gladbach's chalet interlock with the precision of furniture. The round members of the traditional American log cabin have a space between and are heavily dependent on being properly sealed or "chinked" to provide the interior with any degree of thermal comfort.

It was in many ways a poor choice of model—ill-suited to American conditions yet having an imagery dependent on that methodology. If the chalet was to be used in an authentic way it would have to overcome numerous problems.

Two Chalets

Nevertheless, by the end of the century the image of the chalet was ubiquitous, perhaps because the thoughts of a Rousseau or a Ruskin had found their way into popular culture, perhaps simply because of the romance of the Rockies as the Switzerland of America.

Thus two different versions of the chalet were to emerge in America, constructed in very different ways. The first type was refined, but veneered, one that appeared to follow closely Swiss examples but was in reality clapboard faced balloon frames masquerading as solid square-logged Swiss chalet. American architecture was to build countless chalets of this type, but it was also to invent a new chalet, or more correctly return to an old one—one that was rustic. There were American architects, the Greene brothers, Maybeck, and others who worked within this system, taking the Swiss sources as models building with the balloon frame and avoiding the literalism, but the faux-chalet was far more common.

The second type was less common but far more interesting. It was rusticated and solid, the chalet built with solid logs in which image and reality largely corresponded. It was built with solid timbers and floors in the Swiss fashion, but it was built of rough logs, not refined squared timbers. It did with the chalet what Adam and Chambers had done in rusticating the classic temple by returning to the log construction where, in popular myth, it began. This was the rustic chalet, one that made its way into countless forest retreats for the wealthy and into the national parks at some critical locations. It was inspired by a return to rustic origins in spirit, in architecture, and construction. It was a return not just to nature but to constructional, primitive origins.

It often resembled Prince Albert's chalet but it is transformed. It was rusticated. Square milled timbers must be logs with the bark on. Railings and brackets of planed wood and jig-sawed profiles must be twigs, often with the bark on.

The main lodge at Sagamore and the Chalet at Pine Knot follow this model aesthetically but not constructionally. Both are veneers of half logs or bark and poles.

THE RAILROAD

RAILROADS, NATIONAL PARKS, AND THE NORTHERN PACIFIC

Opposite: The Three Sisters Wilderness.

If you travel east from Eugene, Oregon up the McKenzie River Valley into the Cascade Mountains about 80 miles you will arrive at the top of McKenzie Pass. Here the tall, dense Douglas-fir forest is divided by a lava bed of jagged boulders. It extends to the south to the three pyramidal peaks of the Three Sisters, barren of trees but often covered with snow. Whenever one of my colleagues speaks of the fluidity and continuity of organic form I think of this place. There is nothing fluid about it. You can visualize the glaciers tearing away the rock. The lava bed, mostly devoid of vegetation, seems to have just finished cooling. It is a landscape of torn edges and jagged boundaries, a kind of cubist collage of timber and geology. To me and to thousands of other visitors this is one of the most powerful landscapes in the West.

There is a small observation building there, a simple elevated stone cylinder with openings framing distant views. From the observatory platform one can see in the distance the numerous isolated peaks that characterize the Cascades. Mount Rainier, 300 miles away, is too far to be visible, but the thought of it, if you are an environmentalist, raises a question. Why is Mount Rainier a national park while the Three Sisters Wilderness is not? There is a one-word answer-the railroad, specifically as we will see, the Northern Pacific Railroad.

Rainier is not an isolated case. If you look at the nine national parks that exist today and that existed in 1910 you will find some exist because they contain natural eccentricities—the trees of Sequoia for instance—but in the creation of four of the first nine parks—Yellowstone, Yosemite, Rainier, and Glacier, and three of the oldest national monuments that became national parks, the railroads were a primary if not the primary agent in determining their preservation. To be sure there were idealists, organizations, and altruistic politicians who played their part, but it was the railroad who had the money, the power, and the legislative influence. In 1906, John Muir was a vocal advocate for the expansion of the Yosemite Reserve into the national park we know today, but it was E. H. Harriman, president of the Southern Pacific Railroad, who lobbied congress to make it happen. To understand how the parks were created, what they became, and what architecture was placed there, you must begin with the transcontinental railroads.[1]

In popular history the construction of the first transcendental railroad in 1869 has been portrayed as heroic, admirable, and inevitable, allowing for some political shenanigans along the way. The publication of *Railroaded* by Richard White in 2011 telling the story of the transcontinental railroads constructed in the last half of the nineteenth century was one of a series of reevaluations. It is a tale of scoundrels, wrecking the country environmentally and financially in the service of an infrastructure much of which was unneeded and unwanted.

There was little need for a railroad that traversed the entire western half of the country in 1862 when it all began. There was a need for regional lines in California. There was a need for lines connecting Chicago, St. Louis, and Kansas City to the farms to their east, but there was no need for lines between the vast territory west the 98th meridian (about the middle of Kansas) and east of the Cascades/Sierra Nevada Ranges—the high plains and the mountains.

The typical market for the railroad, farming, often failed to materialize in this dead zone in sufficient quantities. As settlement moved west of the 98th meridian to more arid areas, the dream of the yeoman farmer and his 160 acres literally evaporated. Cattle seemed more suitable, and large-scale experiments with cattle ranching were plentiful, but had largely collapsed by 1887 due to bad weather and poor management. Raising cattle in the East and California was less dangerous and more profitable. White writes:

Regional lines in California and the Midwest could have handled most of the productive traffic. ... The development of the rest of the region would have been delayed without multiple transcontinentals, but what would have been lost? Mines that glutted the market for silver? The Catastrophes that befell both cattle and buffalo on the Great Plains? The suffering of those who settled lands that could not sustain them all over the West? The calamities that afflicted Indians who lost their land, their way of life, and often their lives? [2]

The lack of income was exacerbated by the enormous amount of capital and the enormous amount of debt required to build the railroads. Congress provided bonds but what they gave in abundance was land, massive quantities of it, as a subsidy for building a transcontinental line. The Northern Pacific received 42 million acres (the size of New England), the largest land grant in US history. Since the railroads did not take title to a particular part of the grant until the track that served it was complete, there was pressure to finish the track as quickly as possible. So they had to create markets and they had to do it quickly. All of these problems were exacerbated by often incompetent management, poor design, and competition from the duplication of routes by other railroads.

When the railroads did succeed in the dead zone between its profit centers it was through an odd trinity of mining, timber, and tourism, all of which were inextricably connected, particularly the last two. Unfortunately, the first two of these were the most environmentally destructive.

So the railroads pursed aggressive strategies to create customers. The railroads worked to create the parks not out of altruism but out of economic necessity and in the process they built hotels, also out of economic necessity, but they did a great deal more. They determined where certain parks were to be, the nature of their landscape, and the nature of the architecture the railroads built there. In order to understand the architecture, one must understand the larger process it was a part of. Beginning with Yellowstone, a large group of writers and artists produced, by commission of the railroads—paintings, photographs, pamphlets, articles, and ads to recruit visitors. In such a system a lodge or hotel, whatever its architectural qualities, was a marketing device to be used in an advertising campaign.

Thus the railroad played a role in defining the nature of both the built landscape and the buildings of the parks. The railroad and its agents were ultimately responsible for the rustic architectural legacy established by the Old Faithful Inn at Yellowstone, the Many Glacier Hotel at Glacier, and the buildings at the south rim of the Grand Canyon. The railroads also determined the character of building industry that produced it, since building the lodges was only a small part of the larger project of building the railroad.

But if the railroads deserve the credit for the creation of many of the parks and the character and quality of the architecture that was built there, these two positive items were relatively small components on a long list of negative consequences that add up to a process that was destructive on a monstrous scale.

The construction of the railroads accelerated certain processes that were probably inevitable—the annihilation of the buffalo and the massive quantities of land taken from Native Americans and their confinement to reservations. But there are many other acts of destruction for which the railroad was the primary culprit.[3] There was the environmental damage of failed farms and ranches, but the most troubling in some respects is that the same process that served to preserve small fragments of wilderness as parks also destroyed a far greater area of wilderness in the process. In nineteenth-century thinking it was all inevitable and beneficial. To the modern sensibility these are odd contradictions—the simultaneous destruction and preservation of the West.

Our contemporary ethical templates are often hard to locate in nineteenth-century minds, but the ledger is this: the creation of the national parks and their architecture was inextricably linked with larger acts of physical and social destruction.

The Northern Pacific and Yellowstone National Park

All great institutions have a creation myth and so it is with Yellowstone National Park.

On the evening of September 19, 1870, we are told, the members of the Washburn-Doane expedition, after exploring the Yellowstone area, were sitting around a campfire at the junction where the Firehole and Gibbon rivers join to form the Madison. They were discussing the future and inevitable development of the area and the fortunes to be made. Then, according to Nathaniel Langford, Cornelius Hedges, "then said that he did not approve of any of these plans—that there ought to be no private ownership of any portion of that region, but that the whole of it ought to be set apart as a great national park, and that each one of us ought to make an effort to have this accomplished."[4] The result, according to the same legend, was the creation of the first national park in 1872. The Park Service reenacted this event in something like a pageant for many years, but there is a great deal of evidence that this particular conversation never happened at all. These individuals were at that place at that time and some were to play a role in the creation of the park, but in a far less altruistic way.

But if the men at this campfire seemed to, at least at this moment, wish to preserve the West as it was, two of them were to play major roles in the destruction of large parts of it. Gustavus Doane, leader of the military escort, had eight months earlier participated in the Marias Massacre in which the US army slaughtered 200 smallpox-infected Piegan women, children, and old men. Nathaniel Langford, the narrator of the campfire story, was a vocal advocate for the park and in time become the park's first superintendent, but he was no preservationist and he was an employee of the Northern Pacific Railroad.

The critical conversation in the creation of Yellowstone is highly likely to have taken place in a room in Philadelphia on June 4 or 5 when Langford visited Jay Cooke, president of the Northern Pacific Railroad. The Northern Pacific was involved with Yellowstone National Park from the start. The building of the Old Faithful Inn and in fact the creation of the Park was a small part of a much larger phenomenon—the highly expensive construction of the decidedly unprofitable Northern Pacific Railroad. Cooke, like his counterparts in transcontinental railroading, needed to create a market for his unneeded railroad. The creation of Yellowstone owes a great deal to populist altruism but it owes just as much to capitalist greed.

Cooke had argued for the creation of the park, realizing the potential market it would provide and had hired Langford as his chief publicist, arranging for him to write articles in *Scribners* on his return. Langford immediately went on the road making speeches in major cities of the East Coast in support of the park idea, an endeavor organized and paid for by Cooke, and each of Langford's presentations sang the praises of the Northern Pacific as well as the park. Ferdinand Hayden, of the US Geological and Geographical Survey, was in the audience at the lecture in Washington, DC and as a result organized the Hayden expedition to Yellowstone, which ultimately resulted in the founding of the park. While nominally financed by the government, Cooke's fingers and his money were all over the Hayden Expedition. Cooke paid for the transportation. He also paid for Thomas Moran, then an unknown painter, to join the expedition, hoping he would produce a work of art to reinforce the promotion of Yellowstone. On their return, Hayden, along with Langford and others lobbied successfully for the creation of the park.

Cooke was successful in creating the Park, but it was, at least for him, of little consequence. On March 1, 1872, Congress established Yellowstone National Park. Eighteen months later, Cooke declared bankruptcy causing the Panic of 1873 and the Depression of 1873-79. The Northern Pacific escaped bankruptcy until 1875,

The route of the Northern Pacific in relation to Yellowstone National Park in red

1 Mount Rainier National Park
2 Yellowstone National Park

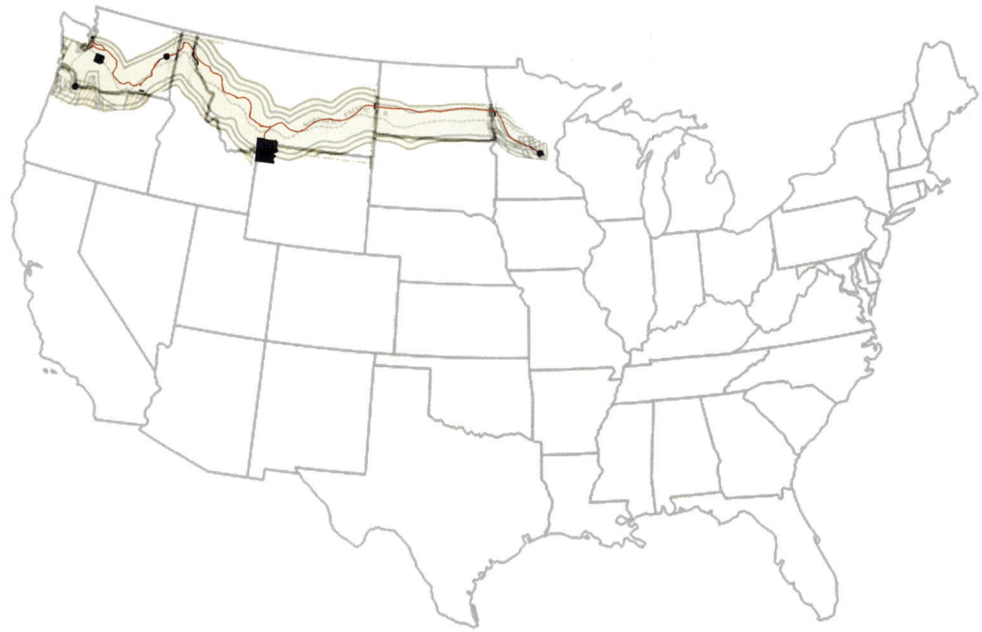

Key portions of the land grant to the Northern Pacific

but it was a transcontinental railroad that ended in Bismarck, North Dakota. There was a national park but it was largely inaccessible and would be until the railroad arrived.

The Northern Pacific was not completed until 1883. The completion of the branch line that would bring passengers to a point nine miles from Yellowstone was timed to coincide with the this and visitation the Park increased from 1,000 in 1882 to 5,000 in 1885.[5] But again, a small success lead to a large failure. The Northern Pacific's completion coincided with its second financial collapse. The Northern Pacific like most of the transcontinentals produced little revenue and was financed by a mountain of debt, but it seems to have been particularly cursed over its long life. It underwent another bankruptcy in 1893.

The Environmental Cost

At the time the Northern Pacific declared bankruptcy in 1875, there were no railroads in the state of Montana. It was to be twenty-seven years until the railroad came anywhere near a park entrance, at and it was one year after that arrival that construction started on the Old Faithful Inn, arguably the first rustic national park building, a project that was planned and financed by the Northern Pacific Railroad acting through an intermediary.

In the course of those twenty-seven years the state of Montana was radically transformed in every way—socially, physically, economically—and from an environmental view not for the better. The railroads were responsible for the ruined lives of many farm and ranch failures. As well as accelerating the annihilation of buffalo and dispossession of the Native Americans.

In the case of deforestation, however, the Northern Pacific's actions were direct. The forested area of Montana prior to white settlement was 23,320,100 acres. By 1909 this area had been reduced to 18,000,000. In the course of a quarter century Montana had lost a quarter of its forests.[6] A great deal of this was consumed by the railroad for ties and infrastructure.

The impact of the railroads on the forests of the West was not just a question of the way they facilitated the harvesting and transport of timber but in the massive quantity of timber the railroads consumed themselves.

The destruction was not necessarily in the way one would expect. After 1870 the railroads primarily burned coal rather than timber. The critical need was railroad ties. An 1878 report estimated that a typical railway used between 2,200 and 3,500 ties per mile, and the need continued indefinitely after construction was completed as 15 to 20 percent of the ties had to be replaced every year. Building the Union Pacific Railroad required 2,300 wood ties per mile. Most of these ties were unsuitable for permanent use and were replaced following the railroad's completion. If one assumes that an acre provides 200 ties, each mile of track required twelve acres of forest for ties alone.[7]

Equal in its visual impact was the demands made by the geometry of building a railroad and the quantity of timber required to do so. The ideal railroad is a level straight line with little deviation. The key problem is the rising slope as one moves west across the US. In the late 1800s the standard maximum slope was set at 4.5%. but the American Standard Grade was set much lower at 2.2%.[8] In short, railroads do not do well in mountains. One need not look far in the American landscape to see the effects of this. A massive amount of wood that was required for bridges, viaducts, snow sheds, sidings, and other infrastructure. The Marent Gulch Trestle, 226 feet high and 750 feet long, the highest bridge in the United States at the time, required 800,000 board feet of lumber all cut near the site, and all thrown away two years later when a steel bridge was installed. In 1884, a snow shed built in the Sierra Nevada by the Central Pacific required 65 million board feet of lumber. Charles Sargent published a series of maps showing that the construction of any railroad resulted in the of clearing of a swath of trees at least five miles on either side of the railroad.[9]

Michael Williams writes:

In 1887 ... the annual drain was nearly 300,000 acres: 249,214 acres for the maintenance of tracks and poles, and 47,673 acres for the construction of new track ... By 1876 the railroads were deemed to be making greater inroads than agriculture into the forests, 'which were being removed entirely too rapidly.'"[10]

The railroad helped finance many of the lumber companies that supplied them with ties and sometimes continued as major shareholders. The Northern Pacific contracted with a single company to provide its lumber controlled by the Montana Improvement Company. It was arguably the Northern Pacific's own creation as they provided 50% of the capital.[11]

The railroad's consumption of timber continued after its completion as lumber replacement was also massive. The railroads had created another monster of timber consumption—the copper mines at Butte. The Montana Improvement Company supplied this as well. In 1888, the Butte mines were using 4,000 board feet of timber a day.[12]

One might assume that Nathanial Langford who was so instrumental in creating Yellowstone Park was disturbed by this. He was an enthusiastic participant. For him and for many, no contradiction was seen between development and preservation. Langford became the first park superintendent, but during his five-year term he visited the park only two to three times. Insofar as he had a vision it was not about preserving wilderness. His first priority was sawmills:

Leases have been sought for the construction of saw-mills in parts of the property where timber could be spared. The manufacture of lumber will prove a lucrative employment whenever the erection of public houses shall be commenced. In fact, with roads such as I have recommended, the business might be extended to reach the settlements of Montana, in most of which lumber commands a high price. A large portion of the park is covered with a heavy growth of pine timber, fit only for manufacture into lumber.[13]

The bare fact is this. Yellowstone Park is 2,221,700 acres, mostly in Wyoming. In creating the national park, the Northern Pacific (with the help of the Union Pacific after 1881 and the Great Northern after 1887) destroyed a wilderness forest 2.5 times that size in Montana.[14]

It might seem we are off topic if we are discussing rustic architecture, but we are at its center for these are the men that not only made that architecture possible but those who created and defined it. What is problematic is that certain parks and certain rustic structures were the benevolent byproducts of the expansion of the railroads westward. This would be true if the railroads were indeed necessary and inevitable. They were neither.

The larger picture missing from the popular history of Yellowstone is the railroad and the role it played in the creation of the park and its rustic buildings. The construction of the Old Faithful Inn and all of the other hotels at Yellowstone was a part of a of a much larger enterprise—the long, difficult, expensive, and unprofitable construction of the Northern Pacific Railroad. The railroad did not just support the establishment of the park, it politically caused it to happen. It did not just transport the visitors to the park, it created the market that convinced them to come. It did not just finance the construction of the inn; it shipped the material at no cost and probably provided many of the workers.

However we understand what to us are the contradictory motives of those who built the railroads, created the parks and their architecture, we cannot deny the relationship. The railroads determined the character of parks and the character of the architecture within them. The technology of building the architecture was determined by the technology of building the railroad. The imagery of the architecture was part and parcel of the railroads advertising campaigns. The forms of the architecture were in some ways inspired by the structures of the railroad.

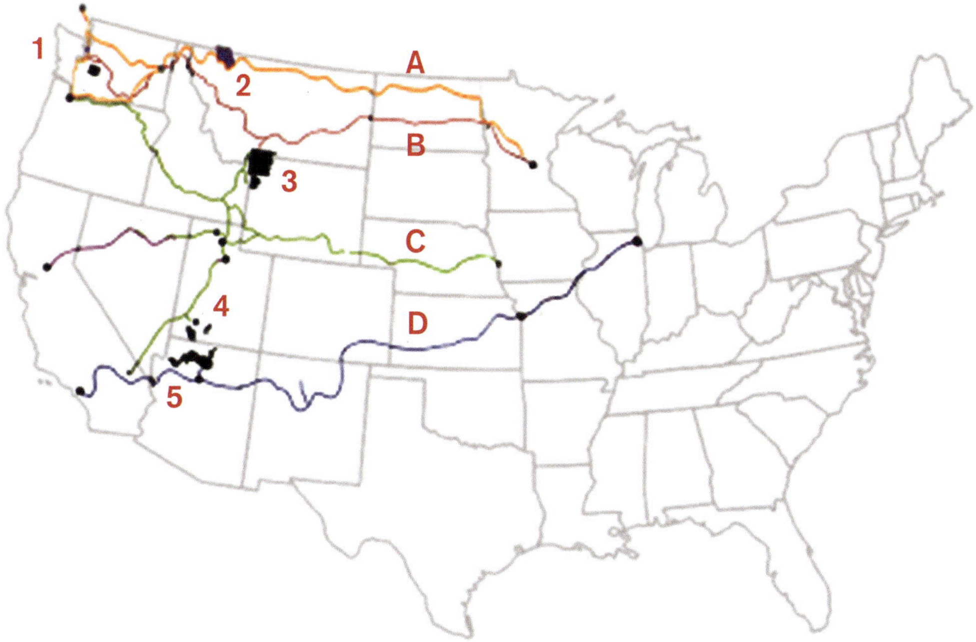

Transcontinental railroads in this text

A Great Northern
B Northern Pacific
C Union Pacific
D Atchison, Topeka, and Santa Fe

National Parks linked to railroads
1 Mt. Rainier
2 Glacier
3 Yellowstone
4 Bryce and Zion
5 Grand Canyon

SUBLIME IMPERIALISM

"You can't create a railroad from nowhere to nowhere."

—Cornelius Vanderbilt on the Northern Pacific[1]

In 1853 Isaac Stevens, standing at the eastern boundary of the Columbia River basin, contemplated the task he had just completed. He had been charged by Congress to survey a potential route for the Northern Pacific Railway beginning at St. Paul and extending to what is now Washington State. And on that day in that place, he had determined to his own satisfaction that it was possible. The area of land separating the Missouri and Columbia watersheds was level and pleasant, unlike the treacherous mountain gorge he had anticipated. He remarked of the valley that: "Nature seemed to have intended it for the great highway across the continent."[2]

The remainder of Steven's report is dry and technical, but on this occasion, he remarks on the role of the divinity in his task. He certainly believed in manifest destiny, that God wanted them to build a railroad that would completely transform the land he was traversing, and he seems to believe that the divinity, or at least nature, has sculpted the mountains in a way to expedite the process. Stevens was in awe of the landscape before him even as he was in the act of changing it.

This is one of many instances of the sublime, religious vision in the history of western exploration. Often characterized by an awe and humility in the presence of the forces of nature that covers an inner arrogance. We have already met two of its conspicuous practitioners in the Yellowstone campfire story. Even more humble than Isaac Stevens in the face of nature was Nathaniel Langford whose expedition to Yellowstone eventually led to the creation of the park. His actions as an agent of the railroad and as superintendent of the park suggest a man who was avaricious, arrogant and environmentally indifferent but in his description of his first visit to Yellowstone he is transfixed—in awe of its grandeur and humble in the face of it. He wrote on his first view of Yellowstone Falls.

As I took in this scene, I realized my own littleness, my helplessness, my dread exposure to destruction, my inability to cope with or even comprehend the mighty architecture of nature. More than all this I felt as never before my entire dependence upon that Almighty Power who had wrought these wonders. A sense of danger, lest the rock should crumble away, almost overpowered me.[3]

His companion, Gus Doane, had similar reactions:

No sound reaches the ear from the bottom of the abyss; the sun's rays are reflected on the further wall, and then lost in the darkness below. The mind struggles and then falls back upon itself despairing in the effort to grasp by a single thought the idea of its immensity.[4]

As we have seen Langford was no John Muir and Doane was a war criminal. Neither was humble. Langford's motives may have been complex, but Yellowstone was to him as much an economic opportunity as anything else. The examples of Stevens, an engineer planning transcontinental railroads, and Langford, scheming in the service of the Northern Pacific, provide a key to under-

Thomas Moran, *The Grand Canyon of the Yellowstone,* 1872

W. H. Jackson, "The Grand Canyon of the Yellowstone from the East Bank," 1872

standing the vast contradiction of the creation of any transcontinental railroad, including the Northern Pacific, and its architecture. These incidents are examples of what Barbara Novak describes as a particularly American sublime, one that was at once religious, nationalistic, and commercial. The American sublime of the nineteenth century was not the English sublime of the eighteenth:

Thus the sublime was being absorbed into a religious, moral, and frequently nationalist concept of nature, contributing to the rhetorical screen under which the aggressive conquest of the country could be accomplished. The older sublime was a gentleman's preserve, an aristocratic reflex of romantic thought. The Christianized sublime, more accessible to everyone, was more democratic, even bourgeois.[5]

This view of the sublime is of some assistance in answering a difficult question. How is it that those who were engaged in the destruction of so much wilderness could be simultaneously dedicated to the preservation of another part?

Ascribing it all to hypocrisy and cynicism does not quite dispense with all the facts. There are a number of answers, none completely satisfying. If the various presidents of the Northern Pacific had been scoundrels on the order of Thomas Durant understanding would be easier. Jay Cooke, who began it, started his career as an abolitionist working to finance the Union cause. Henry Villard, who finally completed the railroad, was a Civil War hero, one of the first modern war correspondents. Frederick Billings, his predecessor, had fought to preserve Yosemite and dedicated much of his time and his fortune to propagate the ideas of George Perkins Marsh, the founder of modern environmentalism. Perhaps the explanation is that they, like everyone else, were at the mercy of forces they could not control.

To many who love the rustic buildings of the parks this is of no great relevance, but this indifference is not so easily borne, for what was going on at a massive scale in Montana was going on in Yellowstone at the small. The economics and technology of the railroad were inextricably linked with the economics and technology of the great hotels that it created and to the architecture that came out of it.

This was the new American sublime, one in which a sense of the power of nature could become a sense of divine authorization, even predestination; a sense of not of helplessness but empowerment in that one was doing God's will, connecting to the sense that it was the American landscape that possessed these divine revelations in quantity. In the end it added to the sense of smallness a degree of arrogance. Robert Doran writes:

on the one hand, being overwhelmed/ dominated by the encounter with the transcendent in art or nature induces a feeling of inferiority *or* submission*; on the other, it is precisely by being overpowered that a high-minded feeling of* superiority *or* nobility of soul *... is attained. The tension between these two poles of a single experience—of being at once below and above, inferior and superior, humbled and exalted—produces the special dynamism of the sublime.*[6]

There was something else that was different about the new American sublime. To Burke and Price, the sublime was the provenance of nature. It should not be attempted in architecture. But American architects felt otherwise. There was no reason a building could not be as sublime as a landscape.

YELLOWSTONE: BUILDING A RAILROAD, BUILDING A PARK

The railroads must have ties.
—Theodore Roosevelt[1]

In 1877, the US army, anxious to assert their control over the Lakota Nation following their humiliating defeat at the Little Bighorn and death of George Custer the previous year, set out to build two forts along the Yellowstone and the Bighorn rivers. One, Fort Custer, was located upriver and only15 miles from the battlefield. The second, Fort Keough, was at the junction of the Tongue and the Yellowstone. Four companies of soldiers and 200 civilian workmen were dispatched by riverboat to the two sites. If this story were a movie, men with axes would have felled trees and placed them, with the bark on in vertical rows to form a stockade, sharpening the ends for additional protection. But this was not the case. These forts, like many of the day, were a series of individual buildings. Nor were the buildings all logs. They brought with them a portable sawmill. The buildings were built not out of logs but of milled lumber. Portable sawmills were usually steam powered, requiring wood for fuel, although some used water turbines. They were made in modules that were combined into a complete mill and required about four days to assemble.[2]

The buildings of the forts were not conventional balloon frame buildings but rather solid walls of stacked pieces of lumber six inches wide by two inches thick. The slabs were cut from local cottonwood timber and some lodge poles from the Lakota encampment of 1876 served as fuel for the sawmill.

Further downstream work had started on the second post, Fort Keough. Rough-cut lumber was secured at the government sawmill near the Yellowstone River and all the fine finished lumber was shipped in on steamboat. Since the majority of buildings were frame structures, a number of items still had to be brought by steamboat—138 kegs of nails, 21 bundles of window sash, and 18 boxes of glass. Here, something like log cabins had been built as temporary shelters—upright logs buried in the earth with a similar log roof. Chinked with mud, they leaked badly and were vermin infested, and their inhabitants quickly and happily moved into the milled-timber structures.[3]

It is not really surprising that a power sawmill was in use in so remote an area at so early a date. The pioneers of American myth may have journeyed west with an axe, but the portable sawmill was not far behind them, in fact if they came west by steamboat or rail, it probably came with them. Log technology, the log cabin, and the axe dominate the myth and popular history of the West but the portable sawmill and its allied architecture was no less ubiquitous.

This technology was not indigenous to Montana and neither was the architecture it created. The architecture that emerged in these forts is not rustic. It features gambrel roofs, double-hung windows with shutters, and porches. If these buildings speak of any place it is of the world the soldiers and their families had left to come there. If a log cabin was suggestive of anything to them it was probably discomfort and squalor.

Log crib trellis on the Columbia and Nehalem Valley Railroad, Columbia County, Oregon, 1906

Officers' quarters at Fort Custer after1877

Buckeye portable sawmill

This anecdote illustrates the great misunderstanding about how the rustic architecture of the West came about. Although these events took place five years after the creation of Yellowstone National Park 300 miles away, they illustrate two aspects of the Western building industry—the enormous quantity of materials, tools, and expertise that needed to be imported and that log construction was often avoided and temporary.

The Railroad/Timber Industry

To understand how Old Faithful Inn and other hotels at Yellowstone were built one must understand the specifics of how the Northern Pacific was built. The railroad created hotels because it badly needed customers, but it needed lumber more. It needed to create a timber industry, of which the hotel building industry was to become a small part, a part that embodied the basic characteristics of the larger system. The Montana Improvement Company, financed by the Northern Pacific, set up a series of portable/temporary sawmills along the route. The railroad financed the creation of timber mills, temporary and permanent. There were five in 1882 and seven by 1886, at which point a massive permanent mill was created at Bonner near Missoula. Here the confluence of the Blackfoot and the Clark Fork allowed for logs to be floated down both rivers.[4]

Critical to this system was the use of portable sawmills, which were set up along the route so that logs from nearby forests could be sawn into milled timber. There was much use of the axe to be sure but in the narrative of the conquest of the wilderness it is the portable sawmill that mattered and as soon as the railroad arrived so did the sawmill.

The S Bridge at Coeur d'alene, 1891

Marent Gulch Trestle

The Structures

The legacy of the railroad and its timber industry went far beyond technical methodology. It was this technology that produced the Old Faithful Inn but more critically it was the infrastructure of the railroad and the road system, of the trestle bridge and the crib, even the tie, that contained so much of the formal language for much of the Old Faithful Inn. An equally important legacy of the railroad was one of forms—the trestles and viaducts of the railroad—that proved to be just as important as the log cabin.

The simplest and perhaps the most important of these elements was the log tie. To save time only the top and bottom of a log was sawed off to give parallel horizontal surfaces top and bottom, one to sit on the ground, one to support the rails. This was the same methodology and the same form that over time became the preferred method for building a log wall, providing two wide flat surfaces to form the horizontal joints achieving an air and watertight connection since the horizontal surfaces were easier to seal than the horizontal joint of two round logs. It capitalized on the virtues of sawmill construction while keeping them hidden.

The second of these elements was the trestle, which were numerous and substantial—such as the 750-foot-long Marent Gulch Trestle. The typical Northern Pacific trestle was not a product of carefully calculated, materially efficient engineering. It relied on plentiful material and labor to achieve a structure in a minimum of time. The design of the structure owed something to necessity and vernacular tradition, but it owed as much to Herman Haupt. Haupt, general manager Northern Pacific from 1881 to 1885, had spent the Civil War heading a unit charged with constructing similar trestles for military railroads in the eastern states, a job that used very similar designs answering to the same criteria, speed of construction, use of local material, and unsophisticated joinery.[5]

The Northern Pacific trestles were typically built of a three-way grid of closely spaced verticals and horizontals. Over-designed, relying on experience rather than calculation, they were built in haste with the understanding that the immediate completion of the railroad was paramount. The railroad was built with materials at hand, e.g., logs.

The third element was the most rustic form of trestle or bridge, the crib or corn crib, in which logs were simply piled on one other in alternating 90-degree directions. This required the least skill, the least heavy equipment, and the most material. More popular with logging railroads than transcontinental routes, they were found throughout the Northwest.

While the trestles, cribs, and bridges built by the logging companies often used raw logs with the bark on, the railroads generally preferred sawn lumber since it greatly extended the life of the structure.

Building at Yellowstone

The building culture of Yellowstone National Park was a small part of the building culture of the Northern Pacific railroad. The nature of that culture—its sophistication, its materials, its access to tools, and the knowledge to use them—was directly related to the railroad.

Yellowstone needed buildings, but in the beginning it needed roads more, and those roads needed a great deal of infrastructure. The technology of building a railroad infrastructure became the methodology of building a transportation infrastructure within the park, and by extension, a way of building hotels.

On March 1, 1872, Yellowstone National Park came into being. It was largely inaccessible. There was no railroad to get you there. There were no good roads in the park, only some poorly maintained trails. The only hotel was a one-room log cabin with no beds, just a floor. According to official records the park had 300 visitors in its first year.[6]

But the unromantic fact was that the building culture at Yellowstone was directly dependent on the distance between any building site and the railroad. Before the railroad's arrival in 1882 most of the buildings in the park were log cabins built with axes, most with sod roofs.

Before the railroad first reached the vicinity of the park in the 1880s, log construction was prevalent but to many, particularly park administrators and the Army, it was something to be avoided. This all changed in 1882 when the railroad reached a point near the northern edge of the park. Once the railroad provided an alternative via portable sawmills and building components shipped in from farther away, logs were quickly abandoned when possible. By 1900, larger buildings at Yellowstone were built of milled lumber or stone. There were still plenty of log cabins, primarily for small utilitarian buildings, particularly if they were at remote locations.

This arrival made many things possible, not all of them good. It meant an increase in the number of visitors. It meant the need to house, feed, and transport them, but also meant the need for technology to do this—the machinery, the manpower, the skills. It meant materials unavailable on site were more accessible but it also meant the ability to clear whole forests in a short time. The same system was put in place that was used elsewhere to build infrastructure—portable sawmills.

The first hotels were inseparable from the timber industry. The first of these was built by a dubious group called the Yellowstone Park Improvement Company. It was formed by a local banker, the division superintendent for the Northern Pacific and Rufus Hatch, a New York investor known for his, "unusual and unsavory activities."[7] Their individual interests were those of the railroad—mining, lumber, and tourism. The Yellowstone Park Improvement Company had a bad reputation in 1883 and has a worse one today. In terms of tourism, they wanted a monopoly on all businesses in the park. They wanted long-term leases on seven sites of 640 acres each, greatly in excess of what a hotel would require and obviously intended to become a major investment of its own with the right to cut timber and quarry stone in unlimited quantities.

The plan was to bring in twenty sawmills and get to work cutting logs and producing lumber.[8] They also wanted to build a railroad through the park to Cooke City to enable the mines there to connect to the main route. All these propositions, and the sheer fact of the monopoly, generated howls of protest, from the superintendent, from Congress, and even the Army. The monopoly remained, but the train idea was soon abandoned and the parcels rented were reduced to ten acres total.

The hotel under construction showing stud and joist frame

National Hotel
Yellowstone National Park, 1882-1884

The first manifestation of the newly available technology appeared quickly and conspicuously–the National Hotel in Mammoth, just inside the park and about ten miles from the end of the line. It was designed by L. F. Buffington of Minneapolis, began in the fall of 1882, and timed to coincide with the completion of the railroad. The hotel that the Yellowstone Park Improvement Company constructed was different in every way from the small ones that were existing. It was much larger in size; it was a wood framed box planned to hold 250 rooms, eight times as long as it was deep, with a long, rambling shingle-style facade with seven gables and a tower. It was different in every way in building construction. While the lumber was from the park, most of the technology, particularly the labor, was not and all material other than milled structural lumber and occasionally shingles came from outside—windows, hardware, lighting, finish wood, other constructional materials, and a large number of carpenters had to be brought by train and wagon.

But it was not a log building. The railroad brought in two sawmills and a shingle mill. The construction lumber was cut on site and sawn into studs and joists. A contemporary architect might admire the use of indigenous materials, but quantitatively this was an issue. An estimated 1,686,000 board feet of lumber were cut in the park. Assuming the number of board feet in a lodgepole pine forest on average is 23,000 board feet per acre, 73 acres of forest had been lost. This left a large scar on the landscape, which caused a public outcry.[9]

But this was only a tiny part of a much larger enterprise being conducted at a much larger scale by the Northern Pacific and the Montana Improvement Company: the technology the railroad brought with it, the technology of modern industrial wood building, and with it the inevitable environmental destruction.

But as is common in the history of the Northern Pacific, a small success proceeded a larger failure. The Northern Pacific financially collapsed immediately after its completion. The failure of the Yellowstone Park Improvement Company was not far behind.

The area that felt the full technological impact of what the railroad could bring was at Mammoth—the end of the railroad at the northern edge of the park and in 1884 the only real entry. Many of the park's main attractions were to the south.

Golden Gate Trestle, 1885

Baronett Bridge with log-crib support, 1871, rebuilt 1877

Building infrastructure

Even when finished the Northern Pacific ended five miles from the park boundary, and most of the planned hotels were at sites at least 50 miles farther into the park on poor roads. Equally important to hotel construction in Yellowstone was the road infrastructure inside the park. Given its rugged topography it required a large quantity of bridges, viaducts, and retaining walls. This was done by the Army. In August, Lieutenant Dan Kingman was sent to the park to take charge of turning its primitive trail system into roads. The first government sawmill arrived in Yellowstone in 1883 courtesy of the Army, a 30-horsepower portable steam sawmill with a 58-inch saw. The army preferred sawn lumber but logs remained necessary in many cases. The army faced the same problems and built the same structures as the railroad—bridges and trestles. Two of these devices were to be of considerable significance for future rustic architecture.

The first was the log crib. The early bridges at Yellowstone were built with log cribs supporting log trusses. If crib trestles and bridges were not common on the Northern Pacific route, they were commonplace in the Yellowstone Park infrastructure. The park's oldest bridge, the Baronett Bridge, was a crib bridge, built in 1871 (rebuilt 1877). The type continued in use well into the twentieth century. A common type is exemplified are the 10 bridges built on tributaries of the Yellowstone in 1892 of hewn logs supported by four cribs built much like a log cabin but smaller and taller at 6 by 20 feet by 25 feet high. Two crib abutments anchored either end and two cribs formed interior piers.

The arrival of the railroad allowed for steel bridges but log cribs continued to be used. Crib bridges were still being built ten years later. Again, as anywhere else, the location of the railroad in relation to the building site was a factor. In July of 1902 the components for 30 steel bridges to be located in the park were delivered to the new railroad terminus at Gardiner at the north end of the park.[10] The Crawfish Creek Bridge and Kelley Bridge were log crib bridges built the same year perhaps because they were well south of the park and the railroad. But things were changing and in terms of infrastructure, logs were on the way out. In the early 1900s elements like trestles were replaced with concrete. At the moment the log trellis and crib began to disappear from the infrastructure it began to appear in the architecture.

The second railroad element to migrate into architecture was the log trestle. The most conspicuous of these constructions was the 1885 Golden Gate Trestle, a gridded and trussed road support through a steep walled canyon built of wood. It was very much of the gridded cage type invented by Haupt for the Army and used by the Northern Pacific, except that it was built of logs, not milled lumber.

The Hotel System

As the roads began to take shape hotel construction began in the park proper to the south of Mammoth. Following the failure of the Yellowstone Park Improvement Company a replacement was organized—the Yellowstone Park Association. Three of its four owners were Northern Pacific executives, and after 1898 they owned all of it. It got off to a slow start in part because of the state or nonexistence of the road system, but Lieutenant Kingman and the Army were at work on that and in 1890 things began to take shape. The program was for three large hotels to be built in the interior of the park. Nicholas T. Haller of Washington, DC, who never visited the sites, was the architect.

By 1891 they had built hotels at Lake Yellowstone, the Canyon, and the Lower Geyser Basin (the Fountain). All were constructed, as was the National Hotel, with sawn lumber, although they were much farther from the railroad. Despite the protest over the amount of forest destroyed to create the National Hotel, the policy of cutting timber in the park became the methodology of the hotels that followed. Sawmills were brought to the building site. Trees were cut from nearby forests and the typical studs and joists of the balloon frame emerged. After 1882 and before 1904 all the large hotels built in the park were built of milled lumber. And the majority of the buildings

Nicholas T. Haller, Canyon Hotel, 1891

Nicholas T. Haller, Lake Hotel, 1891

built by the government between 1886 and 1908 were of sawn wood. Log buildings continued to be constructed, primarily at remote sites with difficult access.

But much of the material and all of the labor for the hotels had to be brought from the outside. The remoteness of the hotel locations hampered delivery of building materials that had to be brought by train and hauled to the site, and made recruiting and retaining reliable construction workers difficult.

The first of these, the Lake Hotel with 80 rooms, the smallest, was built in the same way the National Hotel. The lumber was cut nearby but it was not used as logs. A great deal of material had to brought in, first by train then by wagon, which caused considerable delays. This included windows, plumbing, finish wood for the doors and stairs, and lime for the plaster and plasterers to apply it.

Craftsmanship was not indigenous pioneers wielding axes. Workers also came from far away by rail. Superintendent F. A. Boutelle expressed his concern that: "the breaking of a single piece of the sawmill ... or the sickness or incapacity of a workman brought out from St. Paul, will stop the work until they can be replaced."[11] The Fountain Hotel was built in the same way. The scarcity of qualified available workman is illustrated by construction of the old hotel at the canyon. It was a prefabricated system described as a, "ready-made house...screwed together."

The second Canyon Hotel was also wood studs and clapboards. It is possible that all the materials for the Canyon Hotel were brought in by train, some from as far as Minneapolis. A report to the Department of the Interior stated: "All the lumber, roofing, lime, etc., have been purchased mostly here and in Minneapolis, and is ready at Mammoth Hot Springs."[12]

In comparison with the old log hotels the new hotels were larger, housed in more habitable buildings, and built with more industrial technology, but in all other ways were minimal. All were boxes with minimal surface area. Public spaces were small. There were few porches and no large lobbies. Their external character was equally minimal—clapboard siding with double-hung windows. There were a few projections such as dormers or bay windows.

There was one last log hotel built at Mammoth following the arrival of the railroad, the Cottage, built by the Henderson family in 1885. Lieutenant Kingman requested that Henderson and others be allowed access to his sawmill and use milled lumber rather than logs. Kingman wrote to his superiors that the result of denying this request would be a, "building of rough logs and mud, and it will be an eyesore, and will disfigure the Park."[13] So, the Cottage was built of logs. Henderson wrote to the government protesting that the YPIC had cut him off, forcing him to use logs, crushing the life out of, "primitive log cabin builders" like himself and, "constructing partial hotels nearby that would render their property worthless."[14]

The previous discussion deals almost entirely with the building of hotels, but in the early years except for tent camps, that was what was being built. The park was administered by the Department of the Interior with a minimal budget, a minimal staff, and a minimal need for buildings.

Park Buildings and Logs at Yellowstone

The second superintendent, Langford's successor, Philetus Norris, had a more romantic view of the role of superintendent as evidenced by a curious artifact left behind—a photograph of himself "on the job." He stands in buckskin shirt leaning on a rifle in front of a painted landscape background. Other nineteenth-century park superintendents exist only in portraits with suits, ties, and watch chains. It suggests Norris was someone who would see the act of building a blockhouse log cabin with an axe in the forest a romantic if not mythical light. He was the first superintendent to love the log cabin and the last for some time to come.

He constructed the first official park building—the Blockhouse. It consisted of two sheds on either side of a larger office with an octagonal turret—the gun-room—above. It was of better construction than the other cabins but not by much. It was, "built of well-hewn logs notched and spiked or pinned together log by log as is laid up."[15] The timber was local, although certain items probably windows, hardware, and perhaps shingles were brought in from Bozeman with considerable difficulty.

Norris' successors at Yellowstone who went on the record saw log construction as emblematic of all that was wrong with the place. The third superintendent, Patrick Conger, hated the blockhouse. He wrote: "The house now occupied is nothing but a log cabin at the best, sadly out of repair, roof leaky and the force of the winds shakes the plaster out of the cracks between the logs constantly, rendering the house hardly habitable, especially during the cold season."[16] He began his first year, 1882 with a small building program—a small park headquarters and two service buildings at the Firehole Geyser Basin. They were built of hewn logs similar to what Norris had used in the Blockhouse, but Conger detested the log cabin/sod-roof building system and began work to eliminate it. Conger's attitude was fairly typical—log construction was a necessary but inferior system of building.

At the end of Conger's first year the railroad arrived and at least three sawmills arrived soon after—two for the hotel builders, one for Kingman's road builders. And a primary element of Conger's program for his second year was building facilities but of milled lumber, not logs. Conger's building program for his second year was to first build a series of shops and service building at the Park Headquarters at Mammoth, and he wanted sawn lumber and frame buildings.

Conger had no direct access to this new sawmill technology. His solution was to buy milled lumber from the hotel owned by the YPIC who had imported sawmills for the hotel construction. Conger wrote in his report to the Secretary of the Interior:

You will observe by consulting the enclosed drawings that I propose to build of sawed lumber. I have chosen this style for the double reason that it will be cheaper, besides far more valuable. A house built of logs has to be checked and pointed, and usually this has to be done every year as long as they last; while a house constructed of sawed scuttling and nailed well will always keep its form, is neat and tasty besides being warm and durable.[17]

But again, distance from the railroad mattered. Conger proposed that five assistant superintendent's cabins be distributed throughout the Park. This presented additional difficulties as there were few roads which were good enough to bring workmen and material to these locations. Getting equipment and material to Mammoth was one level of problem; getting it to a place like Lake Yellowstone was another. Nevertheless, he wanted sawn lumber, frame building, board siding and shingle roofs.

There is little evidence of a sophisticated log cabin craft building at Yellowstone but rather a crude architecture of necessity. So, it is clear in 1885 that while a tourist at Yellowstone might find the log cabin evocative, those who built them, those who worked in the private or public side, saw log construction as an inferior, inadequate, and antiquated means of building that should be disposed of as soon as possible.

The Blockhouse

Philetus Norris

Corps of Engineers Building, 1903

Fort Yellowstone
Yellowstone National Park

In 1886, the administration of the park was taken away from the Department of the Interior and turned over to the Department of War, e.g., the Army. It meant a substantial increase in park personnel, which meant a substantial increase in housing and other accommodations. The initial building program, like that of the hotels, used a great deal of portable sawmill lumber. Camp Sheridan consisted of about 15 milled-wood frame buildings. Like the hotel builders, the army cut their lumber in the park. If anyone saw anything romantic about log buildings it is unrecorded.

This is not to say the Army had no aesthetic ambitions. In 1894 a Commissioner's House was constructed of stone from nearby quarries, the first in Mammoth. This was the site for trials of those accused of poaching or other destructive acts. The clear desire was to evoke the character of a government building, and a seat of authority and gravitas, in the form of masonry, was required. The Army wanted more like it. The inspector general wrote: "The buildings at this post are all frame, convenient and fairly comfortable. [but] It is respectfully submitted that at this station, the one which is probably seen by more foreigners than any other, save, perhaps, West Point, a more dignified shelter for the troops of the country would be in better keeping." Starting in 1891 Camp Sheridan was replaced by Fort Yellowstone, built of stone. Captain Castner, head of construction, wrote a long letter giving his reasons for stone construction rather than brick or frame, including: "Stone was relatively cheap," and, "Stone possessed architectural values."[18] All of the early wood hotels are gone. Fort Yellowstone is still there.

The arrival of the railroad did not mean the immediate demise of log cabin construction, but when it was used in subsequent years it was because the builder had no access to milled lumber, carpenters, and frame building, either because the site was too far from the railroad over bad roads. In the same years four log houses were built for soldier outpost stations at Lower Geyser Basin, Upper Geyser Basin, Lake Outlet and Grand Canyon. Nineteen log cabins were built for the use of patrol parties during the winter and five cabins previously built were repaired.

Conclusion

So, in the years 1895 to 1900 neither the Army nor the concessionaires constructed any log buildings of consequence at Mammoth. If anyone admired log buildings in these years it was tourists in search of adventure including "roughing it" that required a certain amount of mandatory discomfort. It is not that there were not examples of log construction rustic architecture before 1900. Atterbury's work in the Adirondacks, Cutler's Idaho Pavilion of 1893, but in 1990–1905 log rustic began to appear in a number of small buildings, some very near Yellowstone.

In 1902-3 the Northern Pacific finally reached Gardiner just outside the northern entry of the park and access to building materials and building technology took another leap. Once the railroad was in place, however, it was much easier to transport timber from sawmill to building site, provided the site was near the railroad. There is a particular economic geography to the nineteenth-century railroad in that the cost of a material or service is less in relation to the distance between two points than it is related to the distance of any point from the railroad. Two prominent examples are the El Tovar Hotel (1905) at the rim of the Grand Canyon immediately adjacent to the Santa Fe Tracks and the Glacier Park Lodge (1913) at Glacier National Park immediately adjacent to the Great Northern.

This happened at Yellowstone as well. All of this was a major determinant in the way buildings were built, particularly the ability to deliver materials and skilled labor to a building site that might be miles from the track. In 1902 the Northern Pacific finally extended the line serving Yellowstone the last three miles to the northern park boundary and celebrated by building a station serving the park at Gardiner. The Gardiner train station was designed by Robert Reamer and was indigenous largely in appearance. Large timbers shipped in from Bitterroot County, Montana three hundred miles away, supported the porte-cochere. Subsequent rustic buildings used mostly indigenous logs and this exception presumably was due to the site's immediate adjacency to the railroad making the transport possible. It is perhaps Reamer's most authentic rustic building. The log construction is not an incrustation on a frame of industrialized milled lumber unlike many rustic structures to follow. The station was quickly followed in 1904 by Reamer's second rustic building, the Old Faithful Inn, also paid for with Northern Pacific funds.

So, this was the state of architecture and building in the park in 1900. There were no logs in the large hotel buildings. There was nothing rustic about them. This was about to change dramatically. From external appearance it would appear a giant step backwards. The stud was replaced by the log; the sawmill was replaced by the axe. But the reality is that the sawmill system remained more dominant than ever. What was about to change was the appearance. It was simply given a rustic coating.

THE RUSTIC

R. Farrington Elwell, *Pahaska Tepee Hunting Lodge*,

RUSTIC BEGINS: TWO LOG CABINS

Many, if not most of those who worked in Yellowstone before 1895, whether railroad men, civil servants, or soldiers, had little use for the indigenous log cabins they found there—walls full of cracks, uninhabitable in winter, often missing a floor. Conger, Kingman, the Army and many others all found them squalid. But while there was prejudice against log cabins at Yellowstone, they continued to be constructed. Between 1886 and 1908 16 soldier stations, small buildings in remote locations with difficult access were built throughout the park. Eleven of them were log cabins.[1]

There is no reason, nothing inevitable, that determined the rustic style selected for the Old Faithful Inn. It was not unprecedented, but for hotel architecture of the turn of the century it was not typical. Buffington's 1883 National Hotel at Yellowstone was typical of the period. The popular East coast resorts, Bar Harbor and Long Branch, were dominated by the shingle style. Major western resorts of the day were anything but rustic. The Antlers Hotel in Colorado Springs (1901) was Italian Renaissance. The del Monte in Monterey (1897), built by the Southern Pacific, was a stick-style palace. The Hotel Colorado in Glenwood Springs (1893) was modeled on the Villa Medici. What did not exist in 1895, at least at a large scale, was a log cabin hotel.

So what was it that changed at Yellowstone? How did the log construction to which the administrators of Yellowstone were aesthetically indifferent and functionally hostile become the mandatory language of park architecture? As an aesthetic choice it was an innovation that, like the portable sawmill, was not indigenous. However common the log cabin in the West and however common the log cabin transformed into a hotel was to become, the romantic image of the log cabin came from the East.

The log cabin certainly had a place in the American consciousness. Since the 1840 election it had never lost its mythical aura. From Currier and Ives prints to Thomas Cole paintings, its history is well documented, usually as a kind of Edenic first house and first step in the civilizing of America, something that would eventually lead to clapboard house or perhaps a stone one.

In the years after 1895 there is a change; the romanticized log cabin moves to the West, and over the next 10 years a different type of log cabin begins to appear in Montana, in fact in the Yellowstone area. Strange as it may seem the log cabin, the one with aesthetic intentions, was something of an import to Yellowstone. It had a multitude of sources but conspicuous examples were brought in by two artists—Joseph Henry Sharp and William F. Cody.

Absarokee Hut
Crow Agency, WY, 1899

Let us return to our 1876 starting point, Fort Custer on the Little Bighorn River where the Army brought their sawmill in 1877. The Army abandoned the fort in 1898. In 1900 the only community nearby was about 15 miles south of the fort, the Crow Agency, also the site of the Battle of the little Bighorn. Despite the Army's love of the sawmill and disdain for the log cabin, there were log cabins being built—by the Native Americans—the Absaroka or Crows.

Several years later in the same location a very different log cabin was under construction for Joseph Henry Sharp. Sharp was a painter, had studied in Europe and taught in Cincinnati, but since childhood had wanted to paint Native Americans. Beginning in 1899, he spent winters in Montana, painting portraits of 200 Native American warriors who had participated the Battle of the Little Bighorn. As he began to spend time in Montana he went to work on his own home. Samuel Reynolds, the agent of the Absaroka Nation, gained permission for Sharp to build a log cabin on the reservation and in 1905 Sharp completed a small log cabin called Absarokee Hut.

Sharp saw the West with different eyes than Army officers or hotel architects and wished to find an aesthetic he felt was there rather than bring his own, and he chose logs. He said of it:

I have been painting Indians in the various reservations for fifteen years, and have built my 'hut' in just this spot because I wanted to paint the winter landscape here as well as the Indians—to paint them day after day and month after month. At first I just had a studio out in the fields and then we decided that we ought to build a house so that where we were working best we should also live best, and here are the pictures of what the house has grown to be indoors and out: plain outside, comfortable within, near the work of our life, almost the essence of it.[2]

Since Sharp's focus was Native Americans, it might seem odd that he defined living in a log cabin as the "essence of his life," but many Absaroka were living in log cabins during Sharp's time there.

Sharp's cabin had one large room and one small. Walls and rafters were pine logs with the bark off, cut on the reservation. Bricks for the fireplace were salvaged from the ruins of Fort Custer. The walls were decorated with buffalo skulls, shields, skins, Navajo rugs, a buffalo robe decorat-

Absarokee Hut

ed with porcupine quills. There is a candelabra made by suspending elk antlers from chains. But there were European items–something like a stained glass window, and at least one piece of oak Craftsman furniture mixed in with the local version of the same.

Sharp was a reader of Gustav Stickley's *The Craftsman,* and in 1906 Stickley published the house along with Sharp's description. *The Craftsman* said that the house demonstrated, "what can be accomplished in the most remote territory, in the most primitive conditions, with the simplest ideals, and only local materials at hand to work with—a home constructed without asking a favor of civilization, grown, as it were, out of the very soil, an answer to a need." Sharp wrote that the house was built by, "Indian boys with a carpenter to superintend them. Naturally the design was along the simplest structural lines, for the workboys were untrained, acquiring skill as they built the house." The information Sharp supplied to Stickley omitted some facts. The Crow Agency owned the cabin. In fact, the construction "workboys" were local convicts from the agency jail.

Perhaps partially as a result of his correspondence with Sharp, Stickley developed an interest in log construction. In a 1907 issue *The Craftsman* published "Three Craftsman Log Houses:"

But the impression given by all is the same—that of a simplicity and directness that is purely primitive, allied with a justness of proportion, a decorative use of structural features, and a fineness of finish that suggests a cultivation which has gone far beyond conventional elaboration.

But of course, the logs had the value of evoking history:

Of all forms of building that remain to us as records of the ingenuity of man in devising places of shelter, none makes such an intimate appeal to the imagination as the house of logs. Especially is this true in this country of comparatively recent civilization, where it is only a few generations since hardy pioneers were forced to make clearings in the virgin forests, and where the natural thing for them to do was to build shelters of the trees they had cut down.[3]

Pahaska Tepee

Pahaska Tepee for William F. Cody, Wyoming, 1902-3

William F. Cody's seems to have had a memory of a log cabin that never existed. Log cabins had not played any role of substance in Cody's previous life. He probably didn't own one until he was 50. The house he grew up in is a white clapboarded frame box. The house on his ranch in North Platte was a white clapboard balloon frame, a somewhat over-ornamented Queen Anne affair that he built for himself. But he was at heart a showman, and the showman in him needed a log cabin.

Every performance of the Wild West show ended with the attack on the prefab fake settler's cabin, by Native American's of course, playing themselves, followed a by a rescue. Cody built a small log cabin in his back yard in North Platte, a kind of replica/shrine of the log cabin where (he said) he went to school.

Beginning in 1895 Cody began on a somewhat smaller scale to build an empire like Durant's or the Northern Pacific. He bought land southeast of Yellowstone and convinced the Chicago, Burlington, and Quincy Railroad to build a branch there. He founded the town of Cody at the end of tracks and built a hotel with the intention of building more lodges to the east near what would become the southern entry to Yellowstone. He bought at ranch nearby, the TE, and moved into the existing headquarters, a small log cabin, providing him with what might have been his first domestic experience of one, and he soon added on. But the log cabin was to be another piece of his marketing plan.

In November 1901 Cody had selected a site for a hunting lodge. About 50 miles west of Cody and just outside the Park. Pahaska Tepee was constructed sometime during 1902 or 1903. His architect was no unschooled rustic genius. Abraham Archibald Anderson was born in New Jersey, studied art in Paris in the 1870s with Auguste Rodin among others, and had a successful career as a painter. But like many in this story, Anderson had two lives. He owned a ranch in northwestern Wyoming, where he designed his own log home. Construction was completed on Cody's lodge

Pahaska Tepee

in 1905, and was opened to guests. It is cabin-sized but monumentally scaled—a two-story log structure enclosed by porches on three sides with a double-height hall with a stone fireplace at the opposite end.[4]

So, if the utilitarian log cabins of Wyoming and Montana were being replaced by something more industrial and less uncomfortable a new set of log cabins was appearing with better chinking in between logs and with the romantic aura of the life that was disappearing.

All of these cabins incorporated a nostalgia of a fictive imaginary cabin—one that captured the spirit of the West that was about to disappear. Stickley to evoke memory of "hardy pioneers." Cody's nostalgia for a non-existent boyhood, backed by a strong capitalist desire for self-promotion was perhaps a deeply felt affection in the form of a marketing device. The settler's cabin becomes a hotel. Two of these cabins are immediately adjacent to Yellowstone and were built just before or concurrently with the Old Faithful Inn.

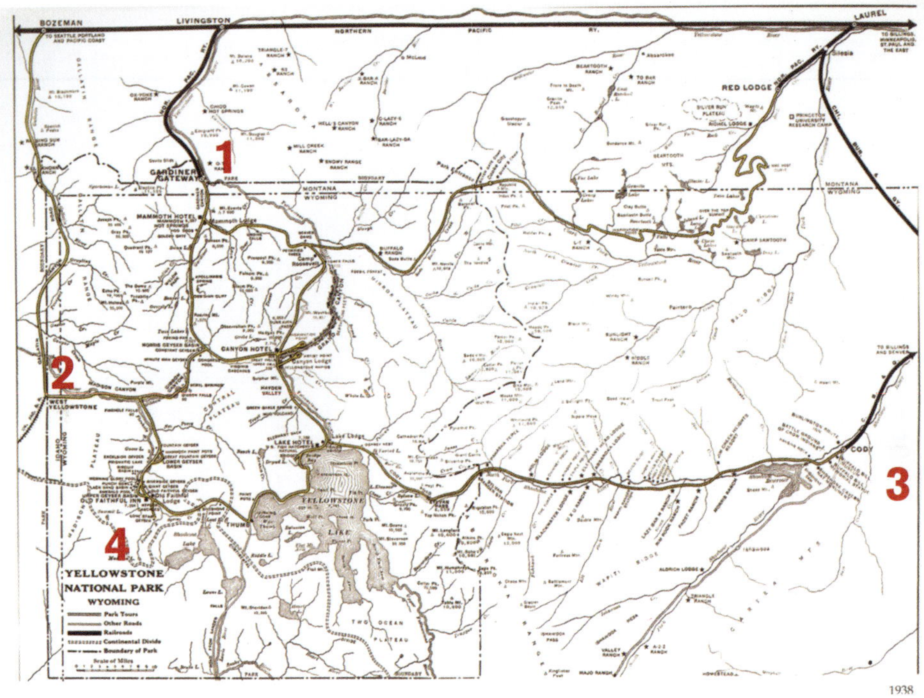

Railroads and roads in Yellowstone Park c.1905

1 Northern Pacific Depot
2 Union Pacific Depot
3 Road connection to Burlington Depot in Cody
4 Old Faithful Inn

Three Railroads

In 1903 the Northern Pacific, having finally extended the line serving Yellowstone to the northern park boundary, celebrated by building a station serving the park at Gardiner, and 1905 was a watershed year in Yellowstone park history. It was the year an adequate, albeit unpaved road system was finished through the park. In 1907 the Northern Pacific lost its monopoly of transport to the park. The Union Pacific Railroad had reached West Yellowstone, 40 miles closer to Old Faithful than the Northern Pacific depot at Gardiner. In 1901 the Chicago, Burlington, and Quincy reached the town of Cody near the park's southeastern edge. All three railroads were interested in building hotels and the Union Pacific and the Northern Pacific were interested in doing so at Old Faithful.

Something else was different in 1904—something that railroad brought from the East—the romance of the log cabin. The new railroads wanted to build hotels of logs. All proposed log hotels were designed by architects from the East. The first of these, as we have seen, was Cody's, working with the Burlington, who built Pahaska Tepee just east of the park in 1905. What was probably the most critical log cabin precedent, however, was built immediately adjacent to the Old Faithful Inn site, a photographic studio for F. Jay Haynes in 1897. Haynes began as a photographer for the Northern Pacific, then became the park photographer, then a concessionaire in the park, but in 1904 he was a partner in a park stage line connecting to new the Union Pacific station in West Yellowstone.

In 1897 Haynes built a log studio at the Upper Geyser Basin designed by Edward Donohue, a St. Paul architect. Superintendent Anderson said of it: "This cabin is the most beautiful and most appropriate in the park." [5] But it was part of a larger plan. Haynes wanted to expand into the hotel business and he was going to do so not with the Northern Pacific but with the Union Pacific.

In 1905, E. H. Harriman, president of the Union Pacific Railroad, came to Yellowstone to meet with Haynes. They likely discussed the increasing need for more hotel facilities to serve the growing numbers of Yellowstone visitors. Following his visit to the park, Harriman immediately ordered construction of railroad tracks from Ashton, Idaho to the park's western border in Montana, what is now West Yellowstone.

Haynes commissioned Donohue to design a hotel for the Upper Geyser Basin and the design used log siding. Other than the logs there is little about it that is rustic. It was never built but the seed of the idea was planted. The convergence of these three railroads on the Upper Geyser Basin were a serious challenge to the park's existing hotel monopolies, but they were no match for Harry Child, already the main park concessionaire and manager of the other hotels in the park. While the other railroads may have provoked interest in a log hotel at the Upper Geyser Basin, ultimately the inn at Old Faithful was built by Child, who was closely linked to the Northern Pacific and the inn was financed by the Northern Pacific who gave Child a large loan.

Harry Child had secured the concession for the new hotel at the Upper Geyser Basin but he wanted something more. He controlled the large hotels in the Park, but they were neither luxurious nor particularly marketable. All were efficiently designed clapboard or shingled boxes with minimal one-story lobbies. A far more exciting if less comfortable way to see the park was a tour through the tent camps that featured cookouts, evening campfire celebrations, and just enough rustication to be exciting. The evening campfire was a key attraction of the many tent camps in the park. An example:

Grace Hurley applauded 'the nightly campfires' that were 'one of the most pleasing features of [our] trip.' She elaborated on the close-knit atmosphere and warm fellowship that inevitably sprang up. ... entertainers are always ready[;] gathered around the blazing pines, travelers from all sections of the world meet on a common basis, cares are forgotten, humanity's natural kinship manifests itself and all are friends before the 2nd day's trip is completed.[6]

This was something the existing hotels with their box massing and small one-story lobbies could not easily accommodate. Child decided to pursue hotel designs that did the same. There would be campfire events but they would be indoors, in rooms with a flavor to the outdoors—the rusticity of the campsite minus the discomfort.

He commissioned a design by William Bement, one of his employees, for a group of nine smaller buildings in lieu of one large hotel. It owed much to the long-established tent camps and those ideas remained in the final design. The individual cabins were to have something similar, "A large reception hall with a large fireplace at one end over the hall will be a rotunda so that people on the second floor can obtain a view of the hall," the *Livingston Enterprise* reported. The campfire atrium idea also seems to have been decided on before the arrival of his architect, Robert Reamer. The *Butte Miner* reported: "Opposite the entrance of the office will be a large fireplace before which the guests can assemble in the evening and which will afford a fine place for telling stories and other amusements."[7]

A sensibility had emerged that was not found in the Canyon, Lake, or Fountain hotels, one that was decidedly primitive, at least in appearance. Ruth Quinn, among others, has detailed the early stages of the design, particularly the fact that the decision to do a rustic building was made well before Robert Reamer, the architect of record, was hired. While Child selected Reamer, he may, just as much as Reamer, have selected the style and there were many others, particularly with the Northern Pacific, who were suddenly interested in logs. Quinn catalogs numerous alternative sources of the log idea. In 1897 when a proposal was made to move part of the Fountain Hotel to the Upper Geyser Basin. J. W. Kendrick, chief engineer for the Northern Pacific, suggested that the inn be sided with logs, "to get the effect of a log house" and that the roof should be altered to give it a less barn-like appearance, which result could be secured by the introduction of dormers as well as a broad veranda toward the front.

Northern Pacific Depot,
Gardiner, Montana, 1903

Reau Campbell, who published *Campbell's Complete Guide to Yellowstone* in 1909, claimed the rustic details were his idea and that he had given sketches to Child and others before Reamer was involved in the project.[8]

It could be argued that I am giving rustic architecture more analysis than it deserves, but just as the transcontinental railroads were not inevitable, in 1870 neither was the log architecture they built. The use of rustic architecture, whether it originated in England the Adirondacks or Central Park was not inevitable.

The history of the Canadian Pacific Railroad is similar to that of the Northern Pacific and the Great Northern. The architecture that it built is not. Between 1881 and 1885 a transcontinental railroad from Ontario to Vancouver was built with a series of hotels along the way. Bruce Price, a leading American shingle-style architect, designed the first Banff Springs Hotel. Over the years a different style, or perhaps we should say brand, emerged—Chateaux, French culture having an obvious Canadian appeal. Thus the Chateau Frontenac, the Chateau Montebello. There is no rustic log palace, no Old Faithful Inn, on the Canadian Pacific. Regardless of sources, the romantic narrative of the log cabin was not so much based on the vernacular culture of the West as a romantic aesthetic imported from the East. It may have been an indigenous form, but it had to travel to the East and back to become romanticized and by 1904 that idea had arrived at Yellowstone.

The uncomfortable fact is that the source of national park rustic, the style which is thought so deeply American, was neither vernacular nor indigenous to the West or in many respects to America. However much it owed to indigenous forms and craft it owed more to the forms and technology of the East and to designers like Calvert Vaux and A. J. Downing and individuals like Gustav Stickley and Buffalo Bill.

In 1903 the Northern Pacific, having finally extended the line serving Yellowstone to the northern park boundary, celebrated by building a station serving the park at Gardiner. The Gardiner train station was designed by Robert Reamer and was indigenous largely in appearance. Large timbers shipped in from Bitterroot County, Montana 300 miles away, supported the porte-cochere. Subsequent rustic buildings used mostly indigenous logs and this exception presumably was due to the site's immediate adjacency to the railroad, making the transport possible. It is perhaps Reamer's most authentic rustic building. The log construction is not an incrustation on a frame of industrialized milled lumber unlike many rustic structures to follow.

But in any case the log-built Gardiner station was quickly followed in 1904 by Reamer's second rustic building, the Old Faithful Inn, also paid for with Northern Pacific funds.

Northern Pacific Depot, platform

CLEARANCE
AND
BUSSES
CARS

THE OLD FAITHFUL INN

Opposite: Old Faithful Inn

The Old Faithful Inn's place in the modernist canon has fluctuated widely since it opened in 1904 but its populist appeal has never wavered, and that appeal is not some whim of aesthetics. The inn represented something that was great about American character. It was an invention growing not just out of the character of the place, but its very materials. It is as if the stone and timber of the site had magically taken on something very close to their natural form in the guise of a hotel. In 1913 Charles Francis Adams wrote that it: "looks as though it grew there, and the fact is, every timber and twig in it did."[1]

No less important to its populist appeal was the way it was made or rather, who made it. It was not just the materials that were indigenous, so too was the craft that formed them. *The Western Architect* wrote in 1904: "[It is] A product of the Forest made with ax, saw and hammer."[2]

This legend of the anonymous enigmatic craftsmen who built it became a key part of the inn's aura, that it was not just built of indigenous materials but also by indigenous craft—has grown in importance over the years and has been repeated countless times since 1904, sometimes word for word. This is from the Historic Structures Report of 1973:

The type of men who built it, the journey-man forest-craftsman—proud in their skills, hardened to and disdainful of weather extremes—were a product of frontier conditions. Men of their stamp, possessing mastery of the ax, adz and drawknife, independent and accustomed by their lifestyle to free use of their own initiative, can still be found today—but almost certainly not in sufficient numbers to so quickly build a structure of such dimensions.[3]

And reached a hyperbolic level in a *Chicago Tribune* article of 1986:

Each log had been hewn by hand, chopped by burly Swedish 'tie hacks' swinging double-bitted axes. Once cut and stripped of branches, the logs were loaded aboard wooden sledges and dragged across the snow by teams of Clydesdale horses.[4]

This view of the origins of the inn dovetails neatly with an idea growing in popularity in the same years it was built, what has come to be called the Turner thesis. In an 1893 paper Frederick Jackson Turner argued that the condition of Western settlement—the constant repetitive reinvention required as civilization moved west-gave rise to a culture that was uniquely American. Turner wrote:

The wilderness disappears, the 'West' proper passes on to a new frontier, and in the former area ... a new society has emerged from its contact with the backwoods. Gradually this society loses its primitive conditions, and assimilates itself to the type of the older social conditions of the East; but it bears within it enduring and distinguishing survivals of its frontier experience.[5]

It is easy to see the inn as the perfect illustration of Turner's premise, as one of these, "enduring and distinguishing survivals," a creation without precedent, growing out of the limitations of the place in combination with the enterprise of those who inhabited it.

If the popularity of the Old Faithful Inn has endured, the popularity of Turner's thesis has not. It still gets plenty of attention, from historians at least, but those assessments are overwhelmingly negative. This perhaps makes one wonder how the inn's reputation might stand up if submitted to the same scrutiny through the same lens. The scholarship on the inn conducted over the last 25 years, an immense amount of analysis applied to a small body of evidence, has deprived the notion of the inn as the work of local pioneer craftsman and of much of its poetry.

Karen Reinhart notes that the use of power equipment, if not documented, was certainly necessary for its construction. Harvey Kaiser wrote of, "Allusions to pioneer building techniques" while Ethan Carr is more blunt stating the inn was built with "pseudo pioneer construction techniques."[6] An analysis of the inn's actual construction suggests that these assessments are if anything, too kind, given the immense gap between the handicraft appearance of the inn and the industrialized reality it conceals. Nevertheless, these same analyses reveal there is some truth to the populist visions of the inn, but it is only a partial truth and it may not be the truth we wish to hear.

The story of how the inn at Old Faithful was built has been told many times. How Harry Child, the main park concessionaire, acquired a large loan from the Northern Pacific Railroad, how Child selected Robert Reamer, an unknown architect, to design the hotel. The larger picture missing from all of this is the railroad and the world that it made and designed. The railroad was not indigenous; it was not handcrafted, and in 1870 it was not yet romantic. The construction of the Old Faithful Inn was a small part of a of a much larger enterprise—the long, difficult, expensive, and unprofitable construction of the Northern Pacific Railroad. The inn is in part a product of a building culture shaped by necessity and indigenous craft in the unique conditions of the West, but it is just as much the product of an imported industrial technology and imported material.

The Indigenous and the Industrial

That the inn is a hybrid of the indigenous local craft and the generic imported industrial is clear in the palate of materials. It is frequently said of the building that it was constructed out of the very materials of the site, as Adams did in the quote that begins this chapter. A great deal of it is, but the truth is more complex. Most of the primary materials of the hotel naturally occur on the site—lodgepole pine and rhyolite stone. The stone for the foundation and fireplaces came from Black Sand Basin two miles away, but it was in the end only a facing on concrete, at least at the foundations. The pine logs came from the Upper Geyser Basin, near the Firehole Cascades, 15 miles north of the inn, and were hauled by horse-drawn sledge to the site, but while the lodgepole pine is from the park most of it was not used as logs. As with the earlier hotels, logs were cut into lumber on site. It is possible that much of the milled lumber was brought by train and then wagon as well.[7]

The completion of the railroad and the road system in the park one year before construction began on the inn had an effect. As always, a change in the transport system meant a change in the building culture. Eighty percent of the exterior is cedar shingles shipped to the site from the Pacific coast, a mill in Aloha, Washington.[8] This seems like a long way to go for cedar but this is another case of railroad geography. Aloha is one of the western termini of the Northern Pacific Railroad who shipped the shingles and other materials at no cost. Windows, plumbing, heating systems, hardware, and furniture were also shipped to Gardiner by train and to the Upper Geyser Basin by wagon, many times over snow as much of the construction took place in the winter.[9]

The materials that were local required highly industrialized labor and equipment to take their organic form and the inn is constructed in part with locally available methods but those methods are far more industrial ones than the craft of the axe and the drawknife. The labor was indigenous as tradition holds but not in the way many would like. In regard to the legendary craftsmen who built the inn, those indigenous, rustic masters of the axe and adze, there is little definitive information. There is large quantity of anecdotal evidence that they had been or were railroad construction workers, probably, "railroad trestle builders," probably on loan from the Northern Pacific who had a financial interest in the inn's quick completion.[10]

This seems credible given the circumstances of its construction but the strongest argument for the inclusion of railroad workers and railroad trestle technology is the forms, details, and techniques of the interior of the inn. The language here is not that of the log cabin but unmistakably that of the railroad and road infrastructure, particularly log ones. The evidence is apparent before one enters the door. The six log cribs supporting the porch are the same as those used to support the Baronett Bridge, built in 1871, one of the park's oldest. Cribs were being used to support the road bridges being built in the northeast corner of the park at the same time.[11]

Log crib at entry to inn

Log crib at Baronett Bridge, 1871

The inn before 1913

The obvious question is why, given the unpopularity of the log cabin in the early years of Yellowstone, did Child and Reamer return to log construction? The answer is that they did not.

The inn was built as were its predecessors. A portable sawmill was brought to the site and logs were cut into studs and joists. What was different was that some of the logs remained logs.

It was certainly ironic and arguably absurd. Just as a vast network of transport and infrastructure was nearing completion that would enable all the power and sophistication of the American building industry to be brought to bear on the building of a hotel at Yellowstone, the corporate giant responsible elected to pursue a marketing strategy that featured a rustic life in a log cabin with campfire. All of that power was put to work to construct a rustic shelter. The inn would be a building whose construction reflected this contradiction. The inn employs systems of construction that spanned the distance between two worlds—from the primitive to the industrial. They included a normative milled-lumber frame, a real frame of solid logs from the site, and a system of log-clad walls and ceilings that allowed the former to masquerade as the latter. Let us begin with the most interesting and original of these—the large log frame of the central pavilion, the lobby.

The Old Faithful Inn is not, as often claimed, the "world's largest log cabin."[12] It is not any kind of log cabin. Log cabins do not have spans of one hundred feet. Child's idea of four small lodges with atria centered around campfires had been combined into a single large one that would require a very large cabin. Within the enclosure, which is primarily shingles, some type of structural frame was necessary. The principal component of this system is the tightly spaced gridded log trellis that supports the balconies and lobby roof. All of the exposed columns, struts, and beams of the lobby, the balcony, the columns that support the roof truss system, the dining room trusses, the exposed exterior supports, and the ground-floor walls of the bedroom wings are all real, solid lodgepole pine logs cut from the forest nearby. It is genuinely rustic if we discount the power cranes used to erect it. The construction of that scaffolding no doubt required the use of the axe, adze, and drawknife a great deal of the time but it is not log cabin technology. It too is a product of the railroad.

The story of the design process of the inn is a fragmentary history. The only drawings that survive of the original design are an incomplete set approved by the Department of the Interior in May 1903. Given that construction was to begin in a month, this set should have been a final and definitive description, but some issues are clearly not resolved. There is a complete if not detailed plan. There is a meticulously drawn and detailed elevation of the main facade and both drawings are very similar to the finished building. The interior by contrast is incompletely documented and dramatically different from the constructed inn. What is missing is a convincing description of the structure of the main hall, that is, how the huge roof of the lobby was to be supported. Although a section survives, it is incomplete, inconsistent with the plan drawing and not entirely plausible. It shows two largely independent structures—a gable roof spanning 100 feet supported by a series of king-post trusses four stories high. This roof structure covers a second independent structure of two floors of mezzanines overlooking the atrium holding the fireplace. The mezzanine floors are supported by a tightly spaced grid of log columns. The trusses supporting the gable roof are composed of rather small diameter logs with a bottom chord over 90 feet long and truss diagonals that are over 60 feet in length. These lengths are not impossible to find in lodgepole pine but it would not be easy. In any case, the structure that is drawn appears to be a rather anemic one for such a major structural role. But whatever its possible shortcomings it was not implemented.

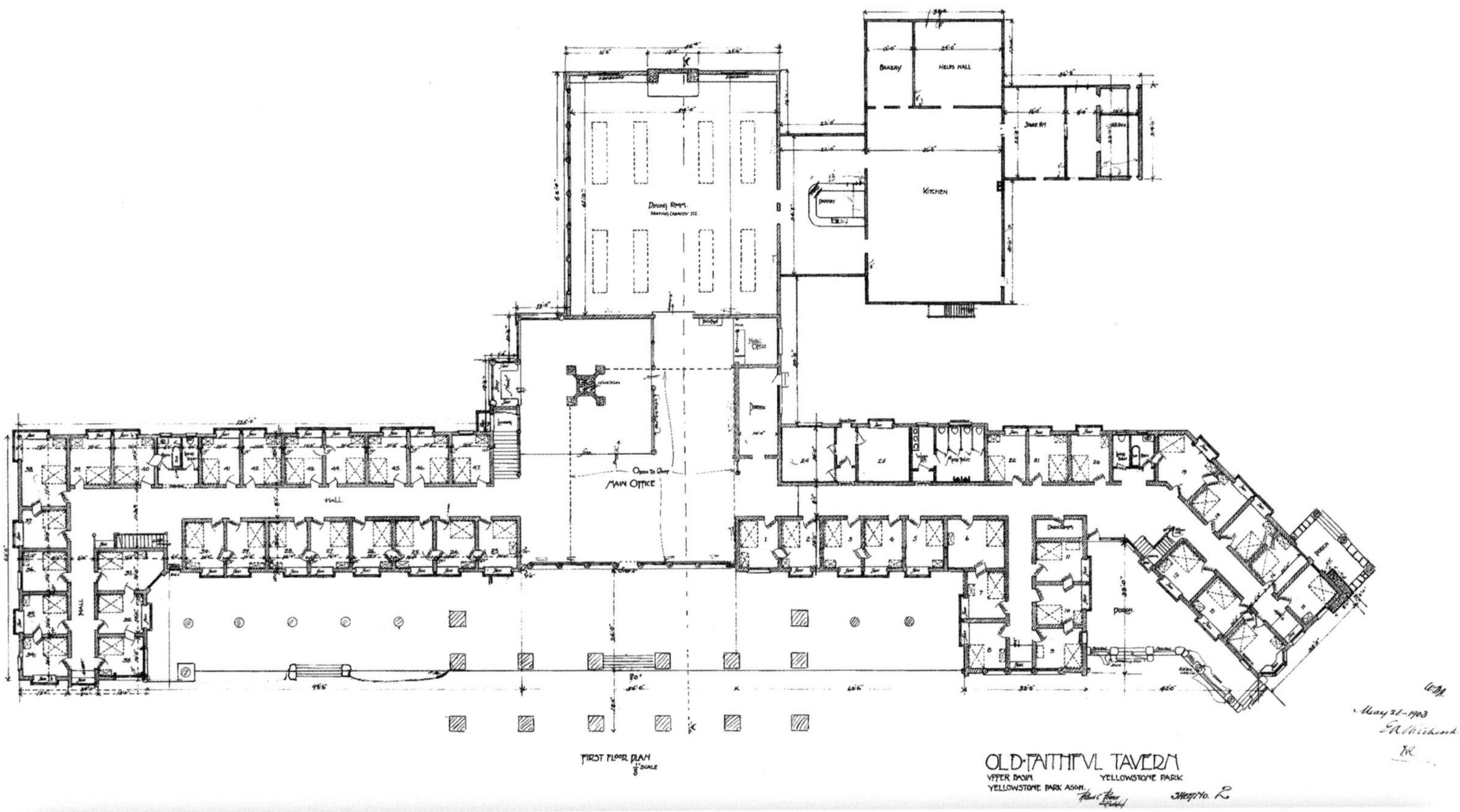

Drawings presented to the Department of the Interior in May. 1903

What happened next and exactly why is a mystery, undocumented by drawings or memos, apparent only in the finished product. The kingpost trusses were eliminated and the small grid of log columns supporting the mezzanines below was extended outward and upward to support the roof, transforming itself into something like a gridded cage of logs in the process. It has inspired a variety of metaphors, the inside of a whale, a cave, but those who see a railroad trestle are close to the mark.

We know little of Reamer's aesthetic thinking. What little he said often contradicts reality, and there are no clues as to why he chose this trestle-like structure to support the roof. It is not an illogical solution for this particular structural problem, but neither is it the obvious one. It may have been constructional necessity. Perhaps the large trusses proved difficult or impossible to build. It may be he wanted to avoid the "engineered" look of trusses. Perhaps it was a flash of creative genius, perhaps he had created a problem that he had to design his way out of and this readily available construction system, the familiar log trellis used on the Northern Pacific line and the Golden Gate Trestle within the park may have provided it.

Many look at the lobby of the inn and see not a trellis but a forest, and Reamer may have been one of them. The S-shaped brackets clearly imply tree branches. Perhaps Reamer wished to create the clearing in the forest complete with campfire and the trellis, in some ways very close of a literal forest, was a readily available way to do so. So, is it a forest or a trellis? It is both.

The ambiguity of the very real train trellis and the entirely representative log forest finds its way into the engineering. Structurally the frame is part trestle and part truss—a cubic cage of tightly spaced logs on the north side of the lobby and a series of log trusses on the south side over the fireplace area. The southern system is a triangulated engineered truss, the northern a gridded cage. The entire system is built of lodgepole pine logs of the same diameter. There is no clear point where the gridded cage stops and the trusses begin.

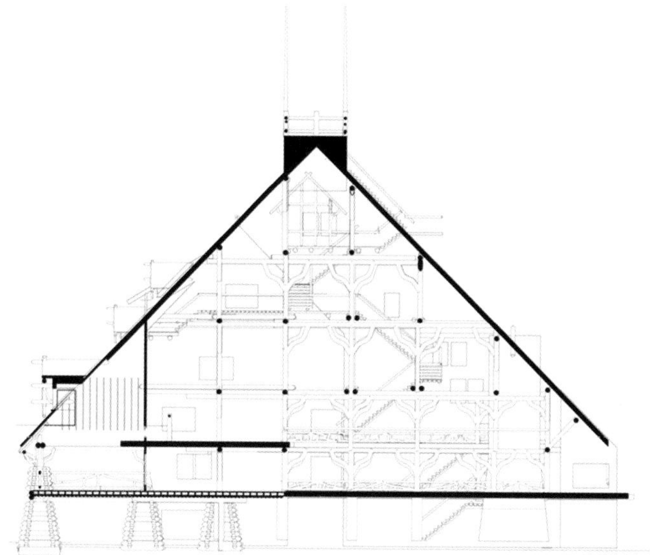

The structure as built

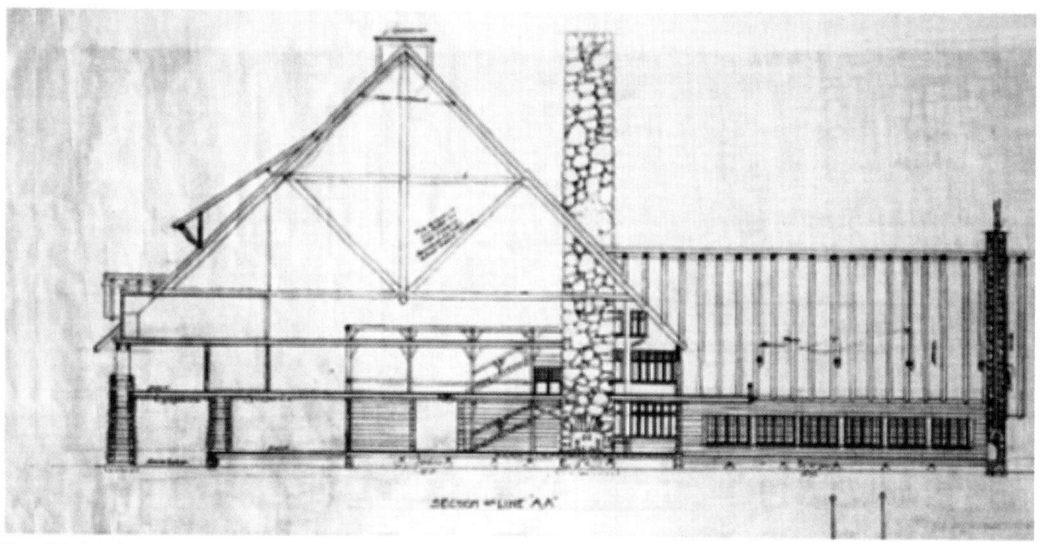

The original design
The structure as shown in 'preliminary drawings, May, 1903

Trellis and truss structure as built

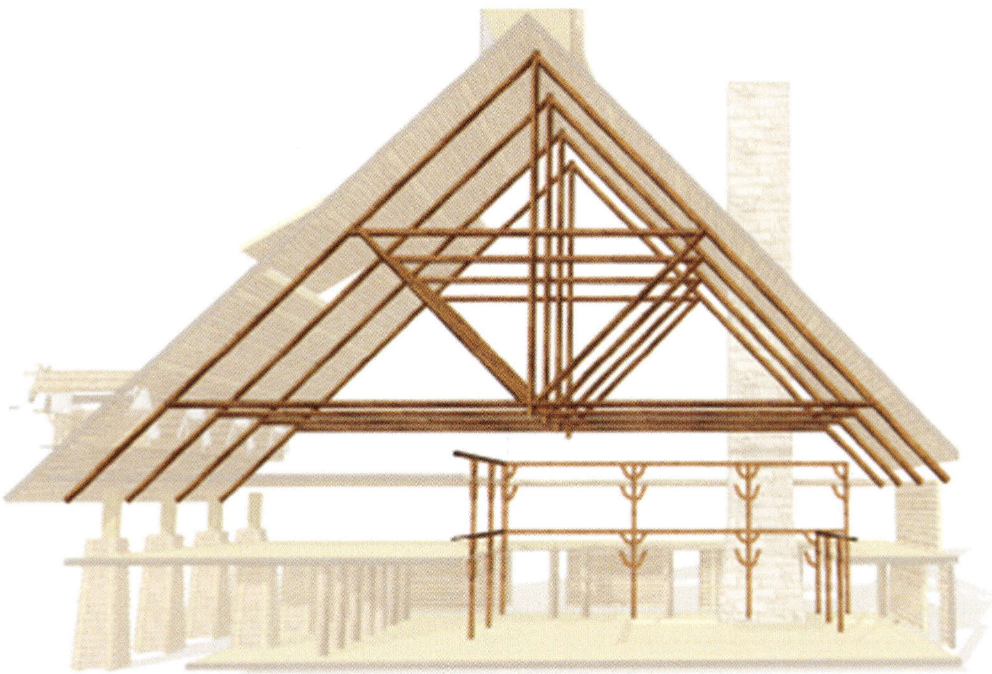

Kingpost truss structure
As shown in preliminary drawings

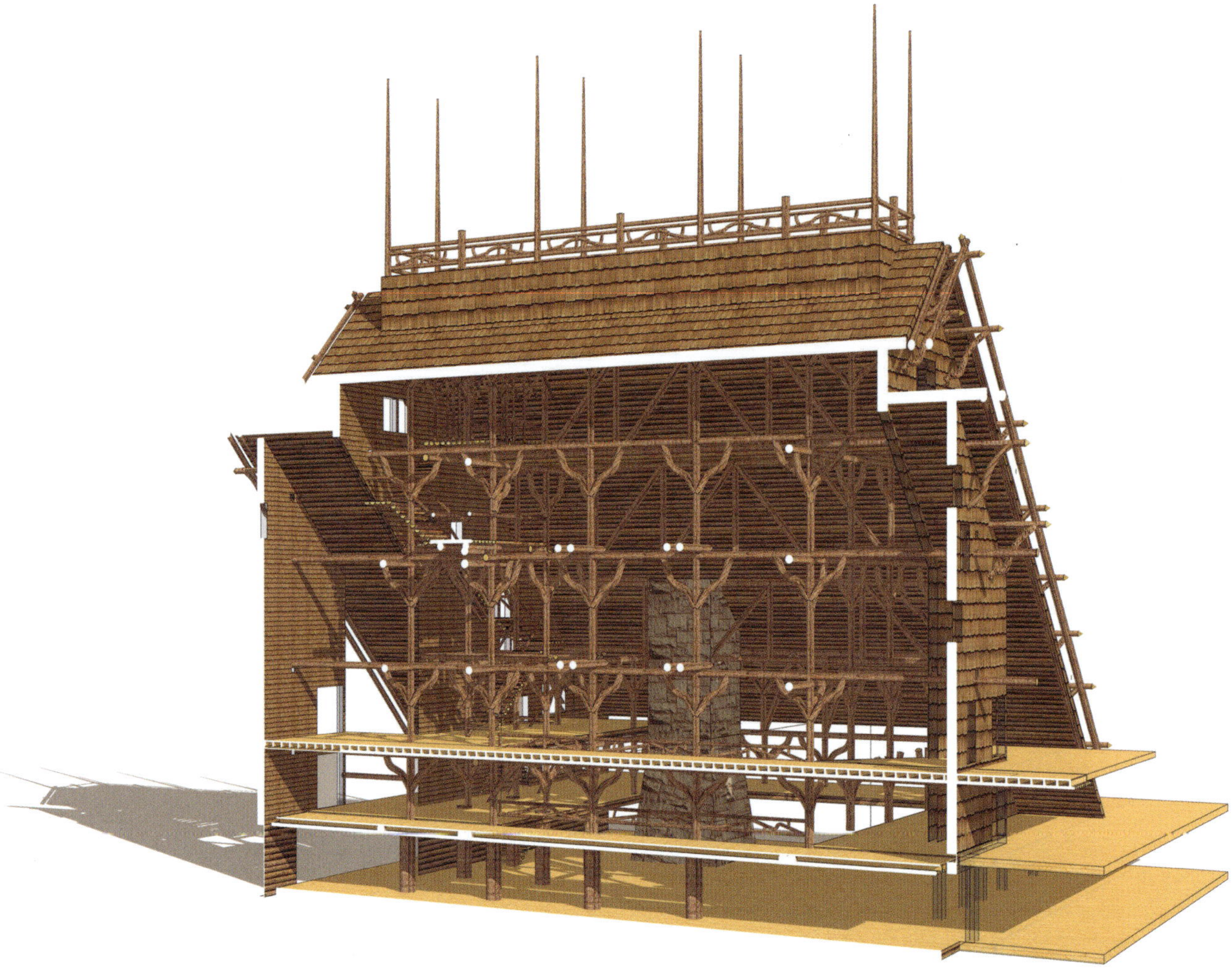

Section looking south

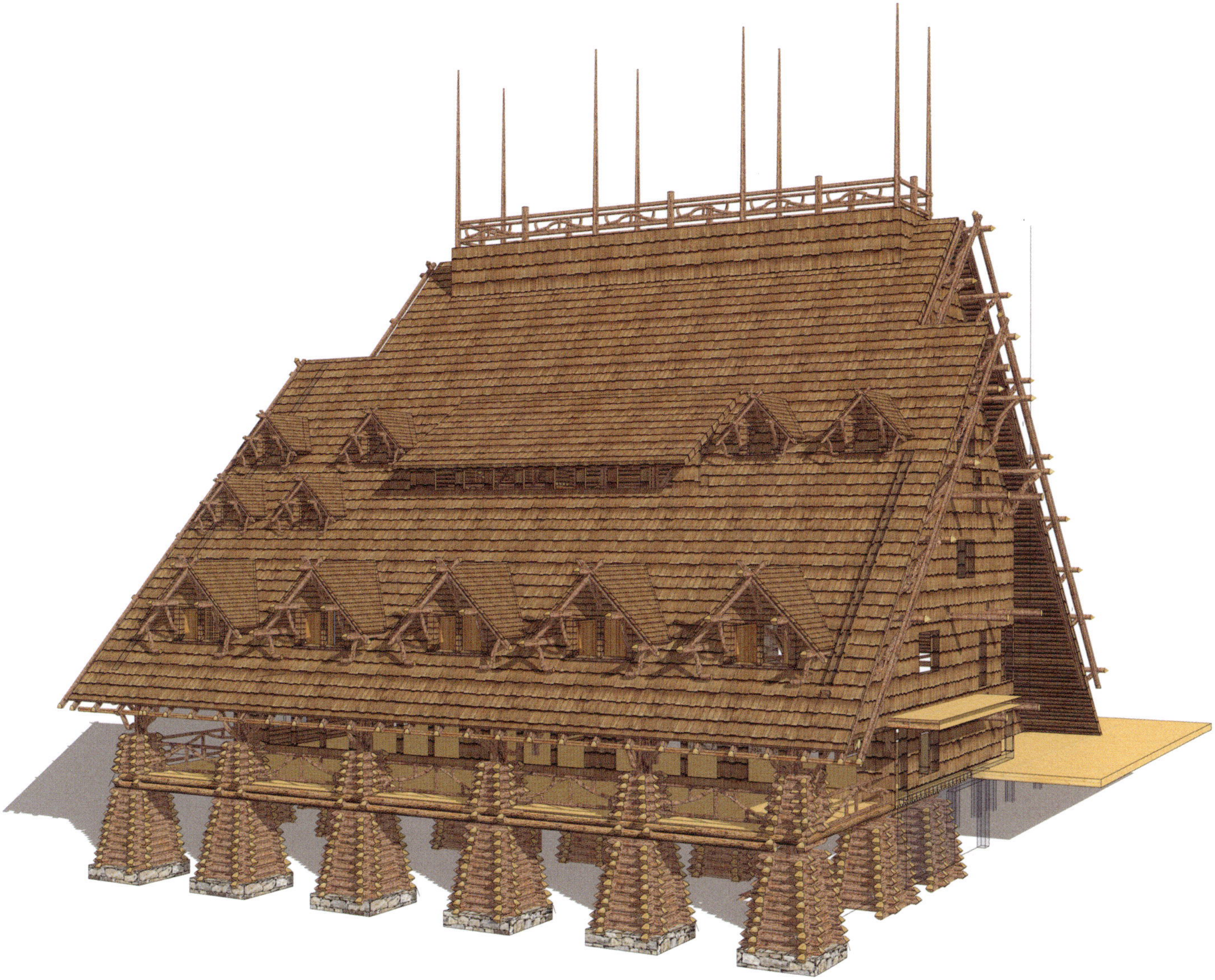

North elevation

Section at fireplace atrium

The inn is a simple post and beam structure of 8-inch log columns and beams, excepting the larger columns at the lower level, that are equally spaced forming a gridded cage of cubes. A primary reason for the dual system is that covering the large open atrium containing the fireplace with the cage of logs could not be done without filling the space with columns, so over the atrium the log trellis is transformed. Starting at the fourth of the six levels the brackets drop out and diagonals are added to transform the grid into three trusses spanning the length of the lobby parallel to the ridge. The structure changes from a bracketed post and beam system into a long span truss system as it ascends.

The ambiguity of the merging of the real trellis with the representative forest finds its way into the joinery as well. Different parts of this log structure have their own character and aesthetic with multiple types of joints, some constructive, some sculptural. In the joints of the truss the logs flow into each other like welded steel pipes so that they are seamless and continuous. The logs of the cubic cage by contrast appear not to be joined at all. The connections are side to side so that the logs extend past and around each other much like a log trestle joint but it allows the logs to appear as individual objects, not just a cage.

The system of joinery follows a different set of values—that of the metaphorical forest, the surreal one-the curved and double curved diagonal bracing at each corner of the cage. It resembles one of the most common wood building systems, found in wood barns all over the world, a post and beam system with 45-degree brackets at the corners to brace the structure.

The brackets at the inn are S-shaped logs that are almost the inn's trademark. These occur at most of the corners of the cage but rarely in the joints in the truss. Perhaps these were intended to be structural, but restoration architects say they are not so their role seems to be sculptural.

Reas Pass trellis
near West Yellowstone on the UP Shortline, 1909

The log cage at the inn

The log cage trellis structure

The log truss structure

The log cage joint

The log truss joint

Although lodgepole pine, this is the tree in its twisted form. The *Gardiner Wonderland* wrote:

Hundreds of miles of forest was searched for gnarled and twisted branches and trunks of trees. Nature's forest cripples were collected by the thousand and the odd freaks of tree growth were seized upon and made part of the big hotel. ... Logs everywhere, and the oddest and most fantastic have entered most prominently into the architect's intricate scheme of interior decoration.[13]

According to the *Washington Evening Star* "five woodsmen were brought here Wisconsin to look up freaks of timber for this purpose."[14]

This is the craft of the surreal-the revelation of inner forces within the log. The twisted struts bring with them the memory of what they are and where they came from. The forces that over time that made it the shape and the forces acting on it today, so it is not just a glib observation that the inn is the architecture of nature is present.

The marks of the saw are hidden. The marks of the axe are exposed. The narrative is that of the rustic westerner and hand-tooled craft, not the railroad and its industrial sawmill. The dream of the temple growing out of the trees of a forest—the dream of Alexander Pope—was being realized across the West in 1905-1910 as we will see, but the inn is different. It is simultaneously a literal railway trellis and a metaphorical forest. Not something a lover of the rustic would like but something far closer to the reality of the forces that created the inn—the massive power of nineteenth-century industry working in tandem with an indigenous craft sensibility. William Empson and Robert Venturi have written on the difference between confusion and ambiguity, a single work of art that generates multiple readings and which is not a problem but a virtue.[15]

Stair platform at window

Stair to tree house

The Journey

The Old Faithful Inn does not face Old Faithful. About half of the rooms look out on the Geyser Basin to the west of Old Faithful. The other half look away from it. The entry drive parallels the main facade and is on axis with Old Faithful so one sees it as they approach the building but once inside viewing a geyser eruption, in the original design, required a journey. On entering the view is focused on the fireplace/atrium. To see the geyser one must turn to the left, ascend the meandering, complex series of connecting stairs that wind through the trellis/forest that ultimately led to a long narrow observation deck on the ridge of the roof. This stair was the primary mechanism linking the building interior to the site and the primary route for the tourists to follow. Halfway up is a long balcony and window looking out to the Geyser Basin with Old Faithful to the right. The stair continues upward first to a small, twisted log tree house-like cabin looking down on the lobby, then exits through the roof to an exterior stair leading to a viewing platform where Old Faithful can be seen without obstruction. Originally there was a searchlight on the terrace illuminating eruptions at night. Understandably, many wanted a more accessible view of the geyser from the hotel that required less work, and in 1927 a large porte-cochere was added to the front topped with a large viewing platform connecting to the more easily accessed second floor lobby. The stair is usually closed but can be seen by appointment.

Stair to roof terrace

A Ground floor stair
B Platform at window over looking Geyser Basin
C Tree house
D Exterior stair
E Exterior viewing platform

The Campfire/Fireplace
It is composed of a stone mass with eight different hearths, four large at the center of each side, four small ones at the corners.

Old Faithful Inn
Lobby
Wall Section

The lobby is a crafted, solid log frame enclosed by a building envelope built of milled studs, joists, sheathing, shingles and log brackets. It is a real log megastructure wrapped with a faux-rustic enclosure.

The roof consists of shingles on sheathing and joists of milled lumber with a half-log veneered ceiling below hiding the roof joists. Likewise, the underside of the wood floor of 2x8 milled joists and decking is faced with half-logs, hiding the milled lumber behind.

Only the ground floor exterior walls are true log construction. The upper wall is shingles and sheathing on milled studs. Interior walls are 2x4 stud with wood paneling on two sides.

The interior lodgepole pine trellis, by contrast, is quite real.

The Guest Room Wings

Of course what has just been described above is not even half the hotel. There remains the exterior enclosure of the lobby and the rooms themselves, housed in two wings. Both are also combinations of the rustic and the industrial but in a far less interesting way.

Reamer said in a newspaper interview that: "It was my ambition ... to construct a building without a piece of planed wood in it. In all the big structure there is not a foot of smooth finished board or molding ... sawn board enter(s) so little into its construction that they can hardly be said to form a part."[16] If this indeed was his ambition, "to construct a building without a piece of planed wood in it," it was one in which he failed. In fact, there is plenty of exposed milled lumber in the wood paneling of the rooms, and the concealed parts of the structure, which make up more than 50% if one counts the additions, is all "planed wood." The log enclosure of the world's largest log cabin was not logs either. The typical exterior wall of the lobby is solid logs, but most of the lobby enclosure is the underside of the roof. What appears to be log construction in the underside of the roof is mostly half logs hiding a joist frame. Many interior walls are half-logs hiding a stud frame. These parts of the building are rustic when visible and industrial when hidden—logs with the bark on covering the milled construction that supported them.

The two wings of rooms are of similar construction. The inner frame of studs and joists was truly industrial, built of the familiar, wood balloon or platform frame of 2x4s, 2x6s, and 2x8s from the on-site sawmill—stud and joist milled lumber framing, used wherever the wood construction is concealed, which is the vast majority wood structure is. The construction photograph that survives show this clearly. Concealing the milled lumber is not strictly necessary and in rustic buildings built in Yellowstone in the 1930s it was often exposed. But at the inn this would not serve. An exposed log trellis might be acceptable but not a 2x4 with the marks of a circular saw. It had to be concealed here to maintain the rustic fiction of the lodge of logs and to conceal the evidence of the machine technology necessary to build it.

Old Faithful Inn
Guest Room Wing
Wall Section

There are actually very few real log walls in the parts of the inn beyond the lobby, almost all on the ground floor.

Structural Elements

In contrast to the main lobby there is little log structure in the wings that hold the guest rooms.

The majority of the structure here is the familiar product of the sawmill—the platform frame of milled 2-inch wide rafters and16 milled 2-inch wide floor joists.

Only the ground-floor walls are solid lodgepole pine log construction.

Structure and Finish Elements

The vast majority of exterior walls above are cedar shingles on sheathing and milled studs and there is almost no log structure save for the dormer brackets and a few ornamental elements.

The interior walls of the upper floors are studs with finish wood paneling.

Surreal elements at the inn

There is much here in the spirit of the Stourhead Root House—the S-shaped supports of the interior brackets and exterior window supports, the distorted elements of the stairs, surreal intrusions into a rigid rectilinear order.

But the inn remains an aesthetic hybrid of the industrial and rustic. Some of it is not very different than the Pine Knot Chalet—a frame of sawmill lumber is covered with shingles and half log siding—the rustic over the industrial. The lobby log cage that supports the roof and balconies is a different architecture and a different narrative of history. What one sees is the real structure. It is both trellis and abstract forest, both surreal and engineered. If there is an applicable lesson here it is that rustic architecture is at its best when it draws on the real technology that created it or on nature directly and not on nostalgia.

This is the great enigma that is the Old Faithful Inn. All of the contradictions in this narrative are there—all the false histories, all the true histories. It abounds in structural expressionism and structural deception. It exhibits both craft and industry, the veneered and the authentic. It uses material from the site and material from the coast. It exhibits the romantic imagery of the West. It exhibits the industrial reality that created it. It hides its debt to the railroad while it celebrates it.

The inn influenced all subsequent national park architecture, but that influence was more generic than specific. Its legacy is a palette of materials and details, of bark and logs, and not of forms. Subsequent rustic park buildings used other structural methodologies. The nearby 1928 Geyser Hall has a central spaces as large as the Old Faithful Inn lobby, but is spanned by deep log-built trusses, essentially a steel truss of logs. The lodges built at Glacier National Park of 1913-1915 are Roman in scale. All of these structures are monumentally oversized in relation to the inn. The inn has an anthropomorphic quality of scale that is missing from other rustic era lodges of the era. Strangely, Reamer's system was never used again in quite the same way, and more strangely, the language of the inn was rarely if ever used again by Reamer.

The Canyon Hotel
Yellowstone National Park, 1910

Child did not need more hotels so much as he needed to improve the rather bland but serviceable hotels in place at Canyon, Lake, and Mammoth Hot Springs. Reamer's approach to altering each of these is puzzling and wildly inconsistent. Having established so conspicuous an example of a new direction for architecture with the inn, after becoming the "father of Parkitecture," he seems to have lost all interest in it. Even while working on the inn he was simultaneously added four-story-high classical portico to the Lake Hotel.

In 1910 Reamer began work on an addition to the Yellowstone Canyon Hotel, more than doubling its size, including an enormous portico and lobby. It was an obvious opportunity to continue the language he had developed for Old Faithful, but excepting the portico this did not happen. It was a different building in every way from the inn built only six years earlier. It was far more refined than its predecessor and deliberately in the spirit of the European spa than the Swiss chalet. It was a different model of the tourist visit to Yellowstone, one that was the product of a European experience of nature, one in which what was rustic was outside the hotel. Reamer took the European model only so far. There were none of the clipped shrubberies of Marienbad or the rose gardens of Baden Baden, but it was a change, a pivot point between cowboy-style campfire cookouts and dances with dinner jackets and ballroom dancing that were to come. If the life inside was more refined so was the detailing—far fewer twigs and less bark, more polish and more veneers.

It was also about this time that Reamer became familiar with the work of Frank Lloyd Wright. He came to embrace Wright's idea about how one learns from nature. Wright described his work as organic, never as rustic. Literalism, e.g., the tree trunk used as a column, a wood branch beam with the bark on, are absent from his work. Tree trunk literalism is the essential strategy of the Old Faithful Inn, but Reamer rather dramatically took up Wright's methodology. There is a very different attitude toward the relation of natural form to building form in the Canyon Hotel than at Old Faithful. Wright's process required that nature be abstracted. It had to be conventionalized. Reamer or at least his publicist agreed. J. H. Rafferty describes the decoration of the dining room:

The pillar, transom, chair and linen motif of decoration is the branch of the pine tree conventionalized.

This motif, severe but characteristic, is carried out simply and with quiet consistency wherever the need of conservative and yet decorative relief is apparent. It is apparent in the chair backs, in the shadowy transom-lattice, in the pillar capitals, and even in the margins of the thousands of rugs which are being made exclusively for the new Canyon Hotel.[17]

This is very close to Wright's process of conventionalizing nature. He wrote in 1908 of the Susan Lawrence Dana house (Springfield, IL, 1902):

From one basic idea all the formal elements of design are in each case derived and held together in scale and character ... its grammar may be deduced from some simple plant form that has appealed to me, as certain properties in line and form of the sumac ... the motif is adhered to throughout.[18]

This is not the rustic architecture of the Old Faithful Inn. While there is plenty of timber, the bark-on logs are gone. Gone also are the surreal, twisted lodgepole pine brackets, the most dramatic of the Old Faithful Inn's rustic elements. Fragments of the rustic language remained but were confined to the exterior. It seems Reamer may have contemplated an incrustation of surreal log images similar to the inn, but they are subdued in the final design, and they are completely missing from the major exterior log structure. Many, including later park superintendent Horace Albright, endorsed the change of aesthetic. There is an often-cited quote from Reamer about the relation of his work to nature: "To be at discord with the landscape would be almost a crime. To try to improve upon it would be an impertinence."[19] It is often cited in relation to the Old Faithful Inn as an explanation of his work there, but the comment was made as part of a description of the Canyon Hotel and in the context he was being self-critical, admitting that he had erred at the inn in literally imitating nature.

Culture of building

The change in hotel culture and architectural language brought with it another—abstraction of form, probably not by accident occurred simultaneously with the birth of a new building culture at Yellowstone, perhaps caused by the change in style, perhaps the cause of it. Perhaps the inevitable results of the never-ending expansion and improvement of railway and road system. All the previous methods for obtaining, transporting and crafting material underwent a drastic shift.

The completion of an adequate road system in 1905, one year after the Old Faithful Inn was finished, and the arrival of the Union Pacific in the same year may have affected this. What had been a local economy of construction in 1890 had become by 1910 a national one. The site-based materials and technology were gone. Gone are the portable sawmills, the trees harvested from the park. Unlike its predecessors the Canyon Hotel was built from lumber milled off site. The *Anaconda Standard* reported at the hotels opening that, "every pound of material within this great structure, which stretches along the mountainside for 700 feet and is full five stories in height, was brought in by freight wagon and sleds from Gardiner, forty miles away, and for several months, through snowdrifts 10 to 12 feet in depth."[20]

The labor was imported as well as it had been often in the past, but that had been the constant complaint of those constructing in the park, the difficulty in acquiring skilled labor and craft. It was now more accessible and with it came refinement in craft and technology. Gone also is the indigenous craft of axe and adze, real or mythical. There are no logs in the interior, not so much as a twig. A few vestigial log elements remain on the exterior as a kind of rustic transition to the forest beyond.

The trestle is gone, the truss is back, constructed of sawn lumber and iron cables, both covered with a thin wood veneer. Beams and columns are typically veneered. The interior is clad—painted and laminated—with precision. There are many yards of plaster.

Dining Room Canyon Hotel

Sumac window, Dana House, F. L. Wright

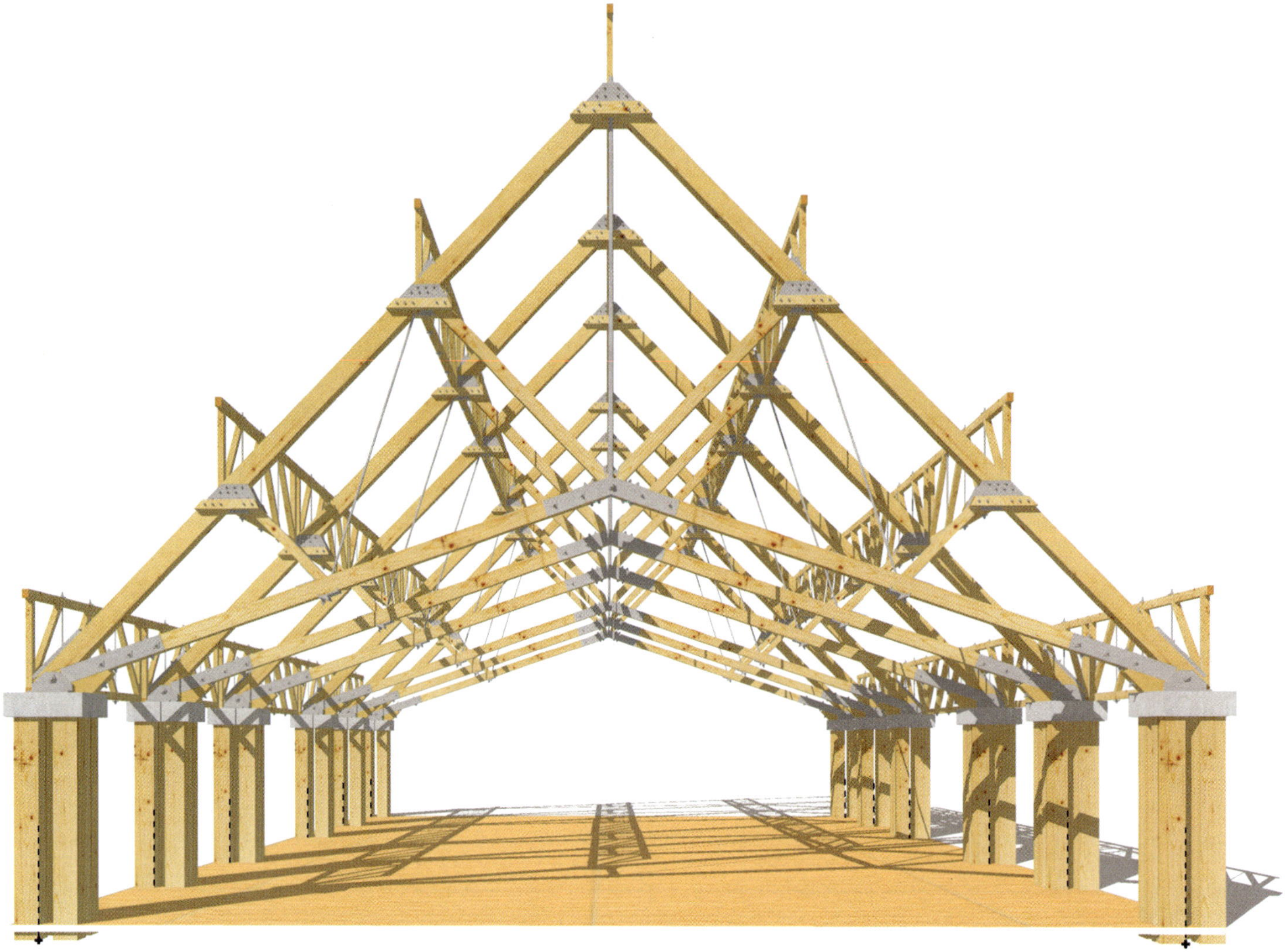

Canyon Hotel: Truss Construction

The top chord 12x12 Douglas-fir

Connecting them are 2 1/2" wrought iron rods
1/2" cast iron plates connectors

The bottom chord 10x10 Douglass fir

All members and connectors have finished wood casings

Lounge, Canyon Hotel

Conclusion

Reamer designed many more buildings at Yellowstone, but few of them are rustic, and he never again used the surreal trestle and log crib vocabulary of the inn.

The success of the Old Faithful Inn led to expansion—large extensions to the east in 1913-14 and to the west of the original building in 1927. If the additions had not been by Reamer, they could understandably be criticized for insensitivity. They are little more than plain long boxes—simple three-story double-loaded unbroken corridor buildings, a regular block of rooms on either side of a corridor. They have far more regular roof lines, far taller and far broader facades, and are far more massive in appearance. Gone as well is the rustic structure. In its place is an ordinary four-story milled wood frame. There is a rustic incrustation tacked on to this block and elements such as log wrapped window mullions. A straight block with a mansard roof, it has little of the character of the original. It was a design that no one except Reamer liked, particularly Horace Albright, the park superintendent at the time, and the criticism was deserved. He and Harry Child, the client, objected to the flat roof. Reamer felt that a gable roof would overwhelm the original, and won the argument. But the addition remains an insensitive extension of the original.[21]

The most dramatic addition came in 1927 when the porte-cochere was extended and partially enclosed. The major structural members here are steel, although concealed. The inn has survived 110 years of snow, earthquakes, fires that came incredibly close, and heavy use but not without considerable reinforcement and renovation.

Of the many other buildings Reamer did at Yellowstone few could be called rustic and his lack of interest in his earlier work seems evident. In 1913 he remodeled the old National Hotel at Mammoth. He added nothing that was rustic and he took away a great deal that was picturesque. Reamer is credited with the design of the exteriors of 1925 Lake Lodge (by the HSR), a

West addition to the inn, 1913-1914

Porte-cochere and observation deck, 1927

log building as rustic as exists at Yellowstone but Reamer's biographer credits it to Fred Willson.[22]

A sad final act in Reamer's career at Yellowstone was built near Old Faithful in 1929. Reamer was hired to build a store and dormitory for Hamilton Stores. His first design was Spanish Colonial built out of concrete. The Park Service rejected the design and told him that if he was going to use concrete, he should imitate wood construction and the executed building is concrete imitating log walls. Reamer seems to have strategically avoided a repetition of the building that gave him his place in architectural history. But if Reamer was anxious to leave behind the rustic style he had done so much to establish others were just as quick to pick it up.

If you search the web you will have no difficulty finding an image of Abe Lincoln leaning on an axe. You will not find an image of Lincoln or any other president leaning on a portable sawmill, but it would be a more accurate portrait of the West. The axe and the drawknife were the essential tools of the mythology of Western building, but the portable sawmill and milled lumber were the reality. Nevertheless, the Turner thesis, despite its unpopularity, has a certain validity when applied to the inn. It was born out or the circumstances, the possibilities and limitations of the West, but it is a hybrid—a building just as industrial and global as it was rustic and indigenous, and the indigenous technology was more that of the railroad and less that of Swedes with axes. It is understandable that we wish it were otherwise, that we wish the craftsman of the inn was some vestigial mountain man and not a railroad worker, and that its forms came from the forest and not some viaduct. But the reality remains, and returning to the larger view, it is a less pleasant reality. The construction of the transcontinental railroads in the late nineteenth century was, as Richard White has shown, a process that was environmentally destructive, economically devastating, and at the time they were built, largely unnecessary, and however much we value the inn and the park we must accept that they were in Turner's words "enduring survivals" of that process.

Morgan J. Rhees, *The Youth of Lincoln*, 1892

1861 Portable sawmill Ad

THE LONGS PEAK INN

In 1885 Enos Mills made his first climb of Longs Peak. Over the next 37 years 303 more were to follow.

Mills had moved to the Longs Peak area near Estes Park at the age of 14 and found work in his uncle's hotel, nine miles from the Longs Peak summit. He bought the hotel in 1902 and his guiding trips began in earnest.

Longs Peak is 14,259 feet high and the trip requires a change in elevation of about 4,800 feet, in the course of which one crosses a boundary, the elevation above which trees do not grow, somewhere above 11,000 feet. This zone, the timberline, became Mill's favorite haunt and the source of his own particular view of rustic aesthetics. It was in this place, above the forest and below the treeless peaks where he learned not just about the structure of nature but the structure of architecture. In 1903 he began working for the federal government as a Colorado Snow Observer for the US Department of Agriculture, a job largely of his own creation that he held for three years. It involved extensive hiking in the tree line zone, a job that allowed him to spend more time there but over a greater expanse of landscape.

Simultaneously, Mills was pursuing the things that made him famous. A chance meeting with John Muir in 1889 inspired Mills to pursue a similar career and in his day he was almost as well-known, lecturing and writing on the Rockies. One of his texts *Trees That Twist*, describes in detail the forms trees take in the timberline zone. Mills looked beyond the contorted surface of a tree to find its internal structural order, his own take on what came to be called vitalism. He describes a "Douglas spruce," a lumber type used for ship masts and airplane frames:

In places the bark was torn off, and as I examined it I discovered that the fibers of the wood were twisted round and round like the turns of a screw. I chopped deep into the tree and found that it was twisted nearly to the center. ... In questioning numbers of people about twisted trees I was told that the wind was the chief cause of this deviation from the normally straight grain.[1]

He believed that the "distorted" nature of these trees was not the product of wind but of internal forces and that these logs had considerable structural advantages:

It is almost an impossibility to split these larger twisted trees. Limbs or knots run through the coiled spirals like so many iron bolts or reinforcing rods of steel. ... Trees of this twisted type are more durable for outside timbers; and when sawed they often are more attractive for veneer or for polish than the woods of more straight grained trees.[2]

Lobby

Opposite:
Longs Peak Inn, Estes Park, Colorado

What was perceived as the highly erratic and irregular forms of these trees were not distortions of a "normal" type but the logical result of structural necessity.

In 1906 the Longs Peak House burned to the ground. In a remarkably short period of time Mills rebuilt it in very different form. Thus, in 1906, two years after the Old Faithful Inn was completed another, considerably smaller, hotel was finished in Estes Park Colorado. It was not so well known as the inn at Yellowstone, but it used the same style at its least classical and most naturalistic, if not surreal, manifestation. It began with a solitary mountain epiphany:

I was on a mountain side one day leaning against a tall dead spruce when a woodpecker began hammering near the top seventy feet up. The vibrations of his tapping came thrilling to me as through a sounding board and also gave a bell like ring to the air. I struck this tree trunk with my ax and it resounded like a steel column. It was sound from surface to center and it was attractive too. It was a time stained monolith. It then occurred to me that these fire killed timbers which covered the mountains by the million would make an appropriate building. ... I had determined build a house of these timbers.[3]

Most of the inn is normative log construction but it contained a variety of timbers, many that are structural, that were fire-scared, gnarled, twisted tree trunks, some of which extended a full story height above the roof line. These surreal elements, huge, almost freestanding sculptures, dominate the simplicity of the rest of the building. Mills may have seen Native American houses in his 1892 trip to Alaska, which could account for what Mills called the "totem pole" like qualities of the new inn.

Mills went through a series of unsuccessful experiences with master carpenters who sought to regularize the structure, until he found one that had worked on shoring mine shafts. Mills wrote:

"We avoided conspicuous craftsmanship. Joints were neither concealed nor emphasized. We mortised, inset and spiked, pinned, bolted, and clamped. There were no frills nor freaks, no

Longs Peak Inn, lobby

Longs Peak Inn, lobby and stair

Longs Peak Inn, main lodge

Longs Peak Inn, guest cabin

striving for effect, and the simple lines produced substantial and pleasing results."[4]

Mills' description of his work is exactly that of Claude Levi-Strauss' *bricoleur*: "We did not follow a carefully thought-out plan, but constantly re-adjusted an experimented. The finished structure was a good combination of the rustic and the artistic."

Mills did not see himself as making aesthetic decisions but following his natural impulses. His stories about building often have a parallel story about an animal shelter, in one case a beaver who Mills watched build a dam during his break. One of Mills' faults as a naturalist was a tendency to ascribe human traits to animals. He adopted two orphaned grizzly cubs that lived with him until they died. He wrote extensively on the habits of beavers, particularly their "architectural" habits, and no doubt he saw himself working a similar manner at the inn. Mills seems to have seen himself as just another animal following its natural instincts constructing its habitat.

Mills' attitudes to what we think of as "wilderness" or "preservation" are enigmatic. He did not see the industrialization of the Western landscape in a negative way. In 1893 Mills traveled to the Columbian Exposition in Chicago, but he stopped first at the high altitude mining town of Ward. His wife/biographer records that: "The mountaintop mines of Colorado though often lonely spots through the long winter, were scenes of contentment," and Mills stayed six months in Ward. Like Muir and Olmsted, he spent a large part of his life in environmentally destructive industries and saw no conflict between them and his passion for conservation. As a young man he established a pattern of working the winter in mines and spending the summer in Estes Park guiding tourists. He lived and worked intermittently in Butte, Victor, and Cripple Creek from 1896 until 1902. Mills' mining work was more than a pastime or source of secondary income. He rose to the position of "stationary" engineer in Butte and it seems that if his life had been slightly different he might have spent his life as a mining engineer. It was not a counterpoint in his view of nature but a part of it. It is odd that a preservationist should work at so destructive operation as the Butte copper mines, but he seems to have been strangely content there. Mills never saw any contradiction in his love of mining and his passion for preservation. Muir after all had worked at a sawmill at Yosemite.

If Mills was probing his subconscious as a kind of proto-surrealist he did not see himself that way, in fact in his own mind he was a structural rationalist. He did share with the surrealists a belief that he was reaching beyond external shape and appearance to the inner life within, not surprising for a man who wrote an autobiography of a pine tree. Mills died in1922 and the inn, alas, burned in 1949.

Mills is remembered today as a vocal advocate for the creation of Rocky Mountain National Park. He had no help from a railroad in this but he had something better, help from the fledgling automobile industry in the form of the Stanley Brothers who owned the nearby neoclassical Stanley Hotel, and together they were successful. Mills was for his time a militant. Like Muir he favored forest preservation, not forest management as advocated by Gifford Pinchot, his former employer in the Forest Service. Also like Muir he began thinking Pinchot was an ally and ended thinking him an enemy.

Since the days of Robert Adam, William Chambers and the eighteenth-century rustic garden pavilions there had always been two schools of rustic design. That of Chambers, the classical rewind, the primitive hut, following most of the rules of classicism but with an incrustation of bark. But there was also the rustic of the Root House, the collage of found objects, each of which was unique, forms that were not a segment of a platonic solid, that did not follow the conventions of architectural composition, where structural members did not take their most efficient and most direct form, where forces did not take the shortest path to the ground, where external order was not imposed from without but grew from within.

So did Mills create a new aesthetic of the natural that found its way into rustic architecture, or were designers such as Mills simply adopting the traditions of the Adirondacks placing themselves in the tradition of Italian grotesque, the English hermitage and Olmsted and Vaux's shelters? Familiarity with these traditions seems unlikely but words like grotesque would for Mills simply have been wrong. It is not the forms that were different. It is that they were perceived as, if not the norm, then the natural and not the freakish or distorted.

THE SURREAL

Yosemite National Park is one of the most photographed places in America and, given that it is also home to some of the largest trees in the world, the Sequoias at the Mariposa grove, it could be assumed that they received a great deal of photographic attention. But what was probably for many years the most photographed tree in Yosemite was less than 20 feet tall. It was a Jeffrey pine located atop Sentinel Dome on the south side of the canyon rim near Glacier Point. The tree died during a drought in 1977 and now even the dead trunk is gone, but it had a long life—400+ years—and the last one hundred of these achieved considerable fame. It began when Carlton Watkins photographed it in 1867, but its reputation took off after Ansel Adams made his classic photograph in 1940. For the next 37 years countless tourists stopped their car, took the short hike up to Sentinel Dome and did the same.

The appeal of this view is self-evident. The tree is isolated, seems to grow from the rock on which it sits and in Adams' photograph, even frames the mountain range beyond. This altitude is the natural habitat of the Jeffrey pine but this tree was distorted from the norm beyond recognition. This is the upper altitudes of the forest near the timberline. Its isolated position exposed it to the frequent massive winds at the high canyon rim.

There are moments in the Old Faithful Inn that look backward to the traditional log architecture of Switzerland and America. There are constructivist elements in the inn—joints that seem to look forward to modernist works such as Gerrit Reitveld's furniture. And there are elements that can only be called surreal. These are the twisted lodgepole pine logs, usually S-shaped, that occur throughout the building as brackets—supporting balconies, dormers, and eaves, and as diagonal braces at the tops of small columns. For those who see the lobby as a kind of metaphorical forest, these are probably the reason. It is a short step from the appreciation of the Jeffrey pine to the enjoyment of the twisted brackets of the inn. In the classic duality of European aesthetics—the beautiful and the picturesque—this is clearly the latter. Uvedale Price in his *Essay on the Picturesque* says that this type of distortion is acceptable:

There is often a sort of spirit and animation in the manner in which old neglected pollards stretch out their immense limbs. ... and in every wild and irregular direction. On some, the large knots and protuberances add to the ruggedness of their twisted trunks. ... such as the finest timber in health and vigour, cannot exhibit.[1]

In this tradition there is the concept of the ideal form of the tree, something like the representation of a tree in a tree identification book—symmetrical with no missing branches and defined by an ideal shape: conical, spherical, etc. Trees like the Yosemite Jeffrey pine are distortions of this ideal type caused by wind, snow, exposure, and circumstance. This is the Platonic view of the world in which a sphere is an ideal form and a grapefruit a distortion of that ideal. In the lexicon of English landscape theory this is the grotesque—distorted and disproportional.

Ansel Adams, Glacier Point

Like most of the tenets of the English landscape tradition, the picturesque found its way to America. Thomas Cole despised it. He wrote in 1842:

All nature is not true. The stunted pine, the withered fig tree, the flower whose petals are imperfect are not true ... the imitation of art should be the imitation of the perfect as far as can be in Nature.[2]

But other Americans saw something else. These trees were not the distortions of some ideal. They were simply autonomous forms. There was no deviance. Yellowstone offers a particularly rich environment for this. Olin D. Wheeler, a writer for the Northern Pacific, saw the Old Faithful Inn in this way. The tree trunks might be distorted but distortion was characteristic of Yellowstone:

The forests of the park abound in freaky, abnormal tree growths. All sorts of irregularly formed limbs and bulging, warty boles are to be seen and of these, in large degree, wherever possible to use them, is Old Faithful Inn, and to them does it owe its quaint originality. These abnormal growths are in perfect keeping with the unusual character of this Wonderland, and Old Faithful Inn, a unique hotel home in a unique land, harmonizes completely with its strange surroundings. ... Most of us have got beyond the point where we are surprised at any of the manifold forms in which Nature reveals herself to us. We may never before have seen some particular phase of her work and may understand but vaguely, if at all, how the result was accomplished, but we are now, usually, prepared for any new manifestation of her processes and handiwork upon which we may stumble, expectedly or unexpectedly.[3]

The bristlecone pine is another tree that grows at the timberline, and it also is typically perceived as "distorted." John Muir called the bristlecone pine, "irrepressibly and extravagantly picturesque, ... offering a richer and more varied series of forms to the artist than any other species I have yet seen." He wrote: "there is an infinite variety of arching forms, standing free or in groups, leaning away from or toward each other in curious architectural structures. ... the outside glowing in the light, masses of deep shade beneath, giving rise to effects marvelously beautiful."[4]

It was a short step of course to apply this thinking to the eccentricities of the Old Faithful Inn. The logs like all the others in the building are lodgepole pine. The name of the lodgepole pine explains a great deal about its form. According to tradition they were popular with the Lakotas and other Native Americans for tepee poles because they were long, thin, and straight. But they are sometimes called twisted pine and their Latin name is *Pinus contorta*, tangled pine.

It can be argued that there is no ideal form of a tree. Each form was the product of circumstances. In 1915 *The Craftsman*, in an article on rustic furniture, touched on this:

Each rustic chair has its own personality of detail, its own originality in logs and branches, its own quaint irregularity of lines, which, though they may be copied in a general way, can never be exactly repeated by either Nature or man. Perhaps this is the reason that we are so fond of rustic furniture—because it is a product partly of the beauty of the woodlands and partly of the skill of man—a pleasant hyphen, as it were, between the primitiveness of the one and the civilization of the other to mingling of natural and cultured loveliness. ... For every log, branch and twig has its own partic-

ular form, its own little idiosyncrasies, its own personality—whether sturdy and formal, severe and massive, light and whimsical, or fancifully distorted into unexpected and amusing forms.[5]

For those who believe the form of the Old Faithful Inn and its construction are unique and original American inventions growing out of pioneer culture and the Wyoming environment, these brackets are an illustration of this, growing out of the mind of Robert Reamer and most writings on the inn iterate this idea. A few brave souls have pointed out possible links to the Adirondacks. But this thinking is not substantially different than what Uvedale Price said in 1794, that the shapes are not "distorted" but the manifestation of an inner life.

In rustic design at least, the line between picturesque and surreal is hard to locate. Four years after the inn was completed Henri Bergson published *Creative Evolution,* presenting the idea of the *elan vital*, an event naturalists like Muir were almost certainly unaware of, but they are ideologically connected. Herbert Read wrote extensively on the subject of vitalism, particularly in the work of artists of the 1930s such as Henry Moore and Jean Arp, about how inner forces determined external form. Read wrote:

Modern civilized man regards that faculty which attributes spiritual or vital qualities to inanimate objects as the mark of a primitive stage in human development; and it would be a mistake to identify modern art with any revival of such 'animism.' But modern man at his most 'civilized' (the modern scientist) has restored a degree of animation to matter, which a short time ago was regarded as merely inert.[6]

"Perfect" Jeffrey pine

Bristlecone pine

J. R. Pope, Camp Kill Kare,
Bed by Charles Hiscoe

The surreal rustic in fact lasted into the age of European surrealism as in the work of Charles C. Hiscoe at Kamp Kill Kare.

As to the validity of the concept of the ideal form distorted by circumstance it is a concept our brain constructed. A contemporary cognitive scientist might argue the opposite. The sphere comes after our brain constructs a concept based on reality but that is not real in itself. Muir thinks of the tree in this way. It takes the form that nature gives it and nature gives each tree a different form. There is no distortion.

THE FOREST RUIN

Thomas Moran, *God's First Temples*, 1867

SACRED GROVES

God used to rage at the Israelites for frequenting sacred groves. I wish I could find one.
—Annie Dillard[1]

To the ancient Christian mind, the sacred grove was suspect. The Old Testament injunction against them Dillard refers to was a result of the association of groves with the ancient Canaanite cults, and the association of tree worship with pre-Christian religion gave the sacred grove a bad name among some Christians.

But for eighteenth-century British writers such as Warburton who linked churches and forests, this was not true. The theory that the origin of Gothic architecture is in tree branches was a belief held by Goethe, Hegel, and Coleridge. One might also argue that the forest/basilica metaphor is so glib and obvious as not to merit a critical investigation. But the connection is not so obvious and in the eyes of many historians of Gothic architecture, completely wrong. Paul Crossley called the idea "nonsense." Paul Frankl, dean of Gothic historians, gave it little attention. Joseph Rykwert writes that in medieval texts the symbolism of the forest simply does not exist.[2] In any case the popularity of the idea that nature, including the forest, is a manifestation of God's existence and order is largely a product of the Enlightenment. For much of Christianity's existence nature was the manifestation of the evilness of this world in contrast to the perfection of the world to come.

By the early nineteenth century European romanticism and American transcendentalism had made the equivalence of forest and temple all but doctrine. Take for example the small group of writers, including James Fenimore Cooper, William Cullen Bryant, and Washington Irving that formed the Bread and Cheese club in the 1820s.

Bryant wrote in "A Forest Hymn," "*THE GROVES were God's first temples.*" Cooper, in a passage in *The Deerslayer,* speculates that the origins of the church are to be found in the forest:

The arches of the woods, even at high noon, cast their somber shadows on the spot, which the brilliant rays of the sun that struggled through the leaves contributed to mellow, and, if such an expression can be used, to illuminate. It was probably from a similar scene that the mind of man first got its idea of the effects of gothic tracery and churchly hues, this temple of nature.[3]

For Irving it is not that the forest makes us think of the church but rather the church that make us think of the forest. In 1828, after visiting Seville Cathedral, Irving wrote: "The light of the painted windows more dim and vague has the effect upon me of a walk in one of our great American forests."[4]

But the metaphor worked both ways. Four years later in a cottonwood grove on the Arkansas River he wrote:

I was reminded of the effect of sunshine among the stained windows and clustering columns of a Gothic cathedral. Indeed, there is a grandeur and solemnity in our spacious forests of the West that awaken in me the same feeling.[5]

The forest as cathedral idea had a life in painting as well, particularly in Asher Durand's 1855 depiction of a divine grove *In the Woods.*

All these epiphanies describe a moment of serenity, a sense of being comfortably situated in a wilderness. But the forest did not always evoke such responses. It might evoke a sense of serene unity between an individual and the natural, but it could evoke many others. Not surprisingly the grove of giant sequoias or redwoods of the West evoked a different response.

The Redwood Grove

The groves of trees that moved Irving and Bryant—cottonwoods on the Arkansas and hardwoods of the Hudson Valley—are by North American standards of size not that impressive, and one would thus expect like-minded observers to have more "sublime" reactions in the presence of exponentially larger sequoias or redwoods, sublime in the sense of the typical Western experience—humbling, awe inspiring, even frightening—the forest as sublime cathedral.

Sublime experiences described by Burke, Kant, and others have a common set of characteristics: a sense of one's own smallness and insecurity, a sense of being at the mercy of a much greater power, a sense of humility in the presence of greater forces. The sublime landscape might be great size, great age, great power, and as Kant described it, could simultaneously evoke a sense of one's own power to control it. Any number of natural features may provoke these reactions: great heights—mountains; great depths—waterfalls; ragged geology or fractured ice. Sublimity is about immensity. There is a sublimity of size, of endless space, but also or in the case of the redwoods, of time. J. D. Grant, chairman of the Save the Redwoods League, wrote: "The Redwood has been witnesser of great events. ... It has seen the rise of civilization. It has looked upon the growth and fall of empires."[6] In 1891 Laura White, a leading redwoods preservationist, took a hike with six friends in the redwood grove at Muir Woods. One by one each mentions an historical event—the birth of California, the battle of Bunker Hill, the crusades, and reflects that the redwoods were alive at that time.[7]

As we have seen, Barbara Novak and Robert Doran see the particularly American, particularly Western sublime as an enabling device for what was being done to the West. Its landscape might evoke a sense of our insignificance, but at the same time a sense that we were part of an inevitable, divinely determined course of events.

The forest might evoke spiritual serenity as it did for Bryant, it might evoke the anxiety and pleasure of the sublime, but it also might evoke a sense of something lost or about to be lost. It might be a ruin. Ruins that manifest both size and age can have the same humbling effect as landscapes so almost inevitably there is the comparison the forest to ruins. Stanton Kirkham, a journalist, saw, "the fluted columns of some noble order of architecture, surviving its builders like the marble temples of Greece."[8]

In the work of the "great" painters of the American West, Thomas Moran and Albert Bierstadt in particular, it is rare to see a depiction of a simple forest grove like Durand's. It seems that trees alone are never enough. There must be distant vistas and detailed foregrounds. There must be dramatic focus—the falls of the Yellowstone, the Grand Canyon, but the forest as ruin had its place. In 1867 Thomas Moran painted a forest scene to which he gave a quote from Bryant, *God's First Temples*, as a title. Bierstadt exhibited a simple forest painting, *Giant Redwood Trees of California,* in 1874. Including human figures in paintings of redwoods was more or less mandatory in order to portray the size of the trees, but Bierstadt chose to paint a family of Native Americans, who were long gone from the redwood forest by this point, living in a hollow at the base of a tree. Simon Schama calls the painting "Sylvan Domestic" and perhaps it could be seen this way in 1874 but in subsequent years it would have been difficult, as it is today, to see it other than a depiction of disappearing culture inhabiting a disappearing environment—the ruins of a culture within the ruins of nature.[9]

But the forest/cathedral could also be reassuringly majestic. It might evoke a sense of pride of place, and to those who had implemented that destiny. As William Dudley, a botanist from Stanford put it: "The nation that could so effectively preserve the inoffensive plants ... was indeed a nation worth living for." They were not just ruins, they were monuments to America's destiny.[10]

The groves were not just America's Switzerland; they were America's Chartres. And in an era when the national inevitability, economic gain, and patriotism were housed comfortably together, the redwoods were emblematic of patriotism. Richard White sees the need for monuments, as central to the creation of the national parks:

The United States was a young nation lacking both an ancient history and a cultural tradition rich in art, architecture, or literature. Americans looked to scenery as compensation for the cultural riches they lacked. They hoped nature at its most monumental would provide the inspiration, the sublimity, and the glimpse of timelessness that American culture had not yet achieved. It became a matter of national pride that the new country set apart areas such as the Yosemite Valley of California or the Yellowstone country of Wyoming as symbols of national greatness. These 'earth monuments,' proponents claimed, rivaled in grandeur the monuments of Europe's antiquity.[11]

But the idea of ruins suggests more than historic nostalgia. It suggests George Simmel's idea of the metamorphosis of architecture into nature. And if the landscape of the West could evoke this quality, then so could the architecture. It could take on the quality of the forest. Architectural equivalents of all of these types of the forest/temple were to be built-the grove of serenity, the intimidating and inspiring giant forest, the monument and even the forest in ruins.

Equating the redwood or sequoia groves not just with European cathedrals but European ruins was an idea popular not just in aesthetics but in marketing. It was a key tenet of the "See America First movement." But a sense of the power of nature could become a sense of divine authorization, even predestination, a sense not of helplessness but empowerment in that one was doing God's will. Connecting to the phenomenon of scenic nationalism was the sense that it was the American landscape that possessed divine revelations in quantity. In the end it added to the sense of helplessness a sense of empowerment. It is a way of understanding how an individual could simultaneously cut down a forest in one place while preserving another and displace an indigenous population while reflecting on the melancholic greatness of a ruined pueblo.

Asher Durand, *In the Wood*, 1855

Albert Bierstadt, *Giant Redwood trees of California*,1874

The Church the New Jerusalem San Francisco, 1895

To hold a church service in a cathedral-like grove is easy enough and was commonplace in 1900. To build a church that literally resembled a grove of trees is more problematic and less commonplace, but 1895 saw the completion of a masterpiece of the type—the Church of the New Jerusalem—in the Pacific Heights area of San Francisco. In many ways it was the work of its pastor, Joseph Worcester, a Harvard educated intellectual and Swedenborgian minister.

He undoubtedly was familiar with the writings of Cooper, Bryant, and Irving, and after he moved to California in 1864, he knew John Muir personally. That said it is probably not particularly important if Worcester had read Bryant's *Forest Hymn* as he had certainly read the work of Emanuel Swedenborg, the founder of his denomination.

Swedenborg is not much read today. His work to the modern mind seems an odd combination of theology and science fiction, but his influence was extensive. Ralph Waldo Emerson thought enough of him to write a long analytical essay on his work and the lines between Swedenborg's writings and Worcester's ideas about architecture, and his church, are unmistakable.

The outside of the church and some of the inside shows an Italian and Mission influence—brick bearing walls on the outside, redwood paneling and plaster on the interior. The roof is milled redwood decking on redwood milled wood joists, sawn and planed (although the joists are worked with an adze to give a fictive hand-worked character), but the major transverse beams are given additional support by a series of segmented arches made of unpeeled logs of madrone. Madrone is a small tree native to the West with brightly colored red bark and berries.

Mabel Clare Craft, the *House Beautiful* correspondent, tells the story:

Worcester was in the Santa Cruz Mountains and he selected the lusty young madrones for the pillars of the temple. He told the young mountaineer on whose wood lot they grew the purpose for which they were destined. The mountaineer was a practical young fellow to whom the tree meant nothing more than its market price. But as he cut the trees he grew thoughtful. Doors hitherto unsuspected opened to him. ... One day he said to the clergyman, 'No hands but mine have touched those trees and I can't bear to think of them being handled as freight. If you will let me carry them to the city in my wagon it shall not cost you any more than by train.' [12]

These are ideas we have seen before, the idea of architecture literally made from trees, in Stukeley, Wrighte, and others. What we know of Worcester's architectural thinking is from secondhand sources, but it is clear that the thought of Swedenborg was the generative factor in several ways. To Worcester and Swedenborg all objects in the world are signifiers of concepts. Swedenborg believed that different kinds of trees signify different truths.

Swedenborg's writings are highly mystical visions and contain elaborate descriptions of other worlds on other planets, but certain passages describe precisely parts of Worcester's church. The church is signified by a forest. Swedenborg wrote:

They are constructed of trees, not cut down, but growing in their native soil. ... by cutting and pruning the branches when they are tender, they fit and prepare them so that while they are growing they may intertwine and unite to make the base and floor of the sanctuary, and rise on the sides for the walls, and bend above into arches for the roof. [13]

The Church of the New Jerusalem is not a massive European-style cathedral. It is built of wood to avoid the monumentality of stone. Swedenborg wrote of his imaginary church: "the inhabitants do not dwell in high places, but upon the ground in low cottages, because high places are for the Lord who is in heaven, and low ones are for men who are on earth."[14] It has a small-scale domesticity of the sanctuary and the fireplace, to avoid the monumentality of size.

Church of the New Jerusalem today

Original sanctuary

Madrone log structure

A. C. Schweinfurth, First Unitarian Church, Berkeley, 1896

The church is thus entered informally, through a side garden rather than on the axis of the sanctuary. The interior had a decidedly domestic character, with a fireplace where an altar would have been located. William Keith, the noted California landscape painter, painted four murals on one wall, and vintage photographs show the interior as a forest with multiple cuttings from various trees, branches of pine and fir.

To Mabel Craft, however, Worcester's church was something of this world. Like the eighteenth-century English temples of Stuckely, Wrighte, and Warburton this was Gothic architecture returning to its origins, "this temple of the trees," as they called it.

The first thing that impresses you is the Gothic effect which the little room expresses so forcibly. Who was it that said that the first Gothic idea was conceived in forest aisles where the interlacing branches formed the groined roof. ... Not by pillars or columns is the roof upborne but by great tree stems still covered with native bark. The trees are madrones and there are six pairs of them. You seem to be in a forest.[15]

If Worcester had multiple influences, he had multiple architects that he influenced. While the architect of record for the church was A. Page Brown, Bernard Maybeck and A. C. Schweinfurth were working in Brown's office at the time. There is much speculation as to their contribution, but the work of each of them differs in significant ways from the church. Maybeck, at least for the next 10 years, showed little interest in bark-on, unmilled log rustic. His coworker, Schweinfurth showed more. Two years after the church was finished Schweinfurth completed the First Unitarian Church in Berkeley. Its basic form is an established shingle style type—a wide gabled box with a low slope. No vault, just wood trusses, although it does have shingle buttresses. At the two entries, however, one at each corner, is a thick oversized column from the trunk of a redwood. It has most of the elements of a primitive classic column. This is a specific architectural reference very unlike Worcester's church. It is primitive Doric as described by Vitruvius and Laugier, not primitive Gothic as described by Pope and Warburton. Unfortunately, Schweinfurth died at 36 in 1900 and what role rustic architecture might have played in his future is unknown. Maybeck built a number of houses over the next five years. Most of these were wood, many had a rustic character. None of them used logs but the idea of metaphor of the grove was to return in his work.

The idea of equating a church with a grove of trees is prevalent in Swedenborg's doctrine. But there is a critical difference with other forest/temples to follow. Swedenborg and Worcester saw the grove/sanctuary as a means to destroy the monumentality of stone. The idea of the log temple or log church was to have a long life in rustic architecture and in California but as a means of achieving monumentality, not avoiding it. Whatever spiritual reactions these buildings evoked they were monuments to capitalist enterprise.

To the biblically-minded the life of the world to come, the one described in the book of Revelation, was a shining city, the new Jerusalem. To Worcester and to Swedenborg the paradise to come was the new Eden—the return to the natural order that had been lost, and it was a decidedly domestic small-scale Eden. Its intrinsic virtue was that it was not monumental, whether that of St. Johns heavenly city or New York. The architectural model he described, the temple that was a forest, had a long life in the rustic architecture to come, but it was anything but domestic and not at all anthropomorphic. To serve the purpose of the American future, monumentality was exactly what was needed, the overwhelming sublime of the redwood grove.

THE PORTLAND FORESTRY BUILDING: THE TEMPLE OF CAPITALISM

Opposite: Portland Forestry Building, interior

The world's fairs and international exhibitions of the turn of the twentieth century had the primary mission, if not the sole mission, of economic promotion, and it was the mission of the pavilions built by the timber industry to promote its products. The Chicago Fair in 1893 featured conspicuous example of a log building representing the forest industry, the first of many to follow.

At the Louisiana Purchase Exposition in St. Louis in 1904, Oregon, for the first time in the history of such fairs, provided a state pavilion representing the Oregon timber industry. It was the mission of the pavilion to make it clear to the world that Oregon's leading export was timber and that they had the largest supply in the country. A publication prepared for the fair stated: "The State of Oregon has approximately three hundred billion feet, B. M., of standing timber ... a much greater amount than is possessed by any State in the Union." Oregon had not only the largest supply of timber; it had the largest timbers: "Oregon ships the longest squared timbers in the world; sticks 125 to 150 feet long are often cut in the mills at Portland."[1]

The St. Louis Fair celebrated the one hundredth anniversary of Lewis and Clark's journey at the location of its departure. A fair in Portland the next year would celebrate the one hundredth anniversary of Lewis and Clark's arrival at the Pacific.

Thus, one year after the Old Faithful Inn was constructed, another rustic building was rising in a more urban setting, Portland, Oregon, at the Lewis and Clark Centennial Exhibition of 1905. Most of the exhibition's architecture was Spanish Renaissance but the Forestry Building was not. It had a specific message and methodology. It was built to demonstrate that Oregon possessed an unlimited supply of the largest trees in America. It would not be constructed of pine twigs like the Old Faithful Inn, but it would use the largest Douglas firs in the world and it would use them en masse.

Like many rustic buildings, it has been called the "World's largest Log Cabin" and for once it probably was, but the pavilion's architects had an entirely different precedent in mind—they were classicists.[2] Ion Lewis of Whidden and Lewis was educated at MIT and had worked for Carrère and Hastings. His assistant A. E. Doyle had studied at Columbia and worked for Henry Bacon. The bulk of their subsequent work was classical. It is not impossible that they had seen the rustic drawings of Adam and Chambers, but this hardly mattered. This was log classicism of another order.

And thus the building's interior was simply built of huge tree trunks in the role of classical columns. It consisted of three halls forming an H, each framed by 48-foot-high log columns five feet in diameter, roughly the proportions of an Ionic column. Two small logs were placed at the side of each column top to simulate Ionic capitals. The 46 exterior Doric columns of the Parthenon are 6.2 feet in diameter and are 34.1 feet high. The log columns of the Forestry building were 30% larger.

The exterior tells a different story, a non-classical one. It had a traditional albeit oversized Swiss flavor. Ten years had passed since the Chicago fair and Cutler's Idaho pavilion/chalet but the concept was obviously remembered.

Forestry Building
Portland, Oregon, 1905

The Forestry Building resembled, particularly at its ends, the type of chalet illustrated in Gladbach's *Der Schweizer. Holzstil* but many features reminiscent of the chalet are missing. There were no flat board railings, no stones on the roof, no profiled rafters. In their place was something considerably more monumental. Obviously, there was a proportional problem in using the chalet form at a greatly enlarged scale. It was solved by using massive overscaled components. The first-floor exterior was constructed of horizontal logs three feet in diameter with a shingled story above. The Swiss features were confined to the short ends. The shingles were three times normal size with an 18-inch weather instead of the typical 6 inches. The result was a surprisingly successful merger of a Swiss chalet and giant Greek temple. However conceptually uncomfortable the marriage of chalet and temple, the message was clear—the power of the Oregon timber industry, and it did this quite literally. Worcester built a church of logs to avoid monumentality. The Portland Pavilion's architects used logs to achieve it.

There was an obvious misfit between the industrial reality of the building and the nostalgic image of craftsmanship. Fair promoters wished to make a link to the pioneer craftsman, proclaiming that: "primitive methods were adhered to as far as possible" including old fashioned tree nails, rough-hewn doors, and wrought iron hardware.[3] Its members were, "bound together as the pioneers of the state bound their first rude cabins."[4] Fair literature says that it was built without milled lumber or fasteners other than spikes, but the milled lumber is simply hidden. How and when pioneers had moved logs 48 feet long and 5 feet in diameter more than 70 miles and then erected them as uprights was not explained.

West elevation

Section looking east

The "architect" of the building in a metaphorical sense was Simon Benson. A Norwegian immigrant, he began work in the lumber business in Wisconsin but seeing that lumber's future was in the Northwest he moved to the area around the mouth of the Colombia River and began to assemble land to harvest timber. But his success, which as considerable, owes less to his land acquisition and more to his innovations in transporting logs from forest to mill. He developed what he called an all-steam system. He began by making widespread use of the donkey engine, a steam driven device invented in California in 1883 for hauling large logs. He built small railroads to avoid the use of oxen and developed a method for building "Benson" rafts, rafts of logs to float them down the Columbia to his mill at Oak Point, Washington or beyond, enabling him to ship large quantizes of logs to his sawmill in San Diego for the California market.

It is hard to imagine the Portland Building would have happened without what he had to offer. He had the money to build it, but he also had access to the logs, which were gigantic, far too large to move on roads, and he knew how to get the logs from the forest to Portland. The 300 logs required came from the lower Columbia River. They were floated up the Willamette to Guild's Lake. A 1,500-foot-long tramline was constructed to move them to the site powered with a donkey engine that was four times the power of the standard model. So the building was a monument to something beyond quantity and size. It was about the power to move, assemble, and create it.[5]

Columns being erected

A Benson raft

Major and minor rafters resting on trusses

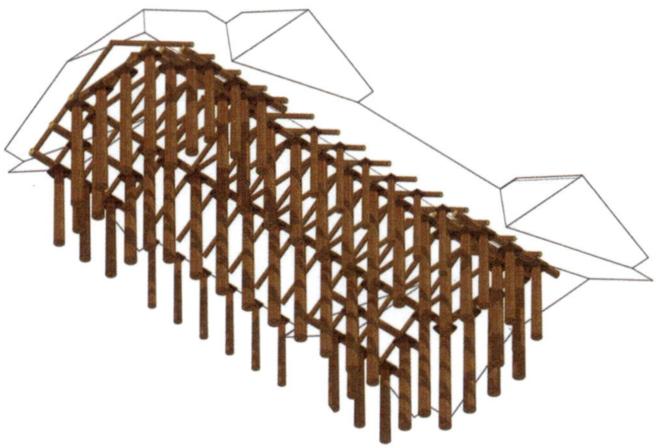

Log trusses between columns

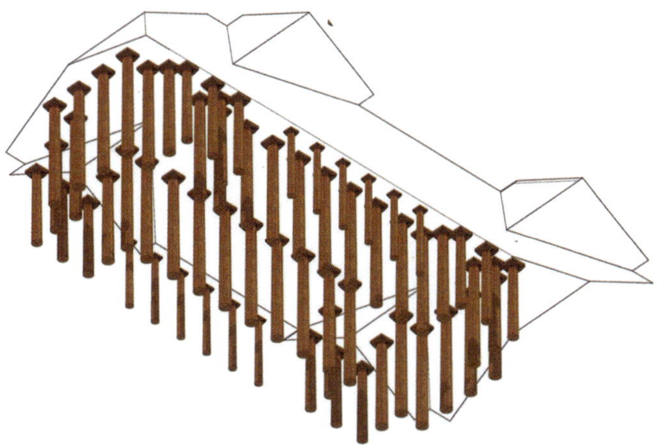

Columns

The desire to inspire awe at the immensity of the building's elements—a kind of economic sublime—succeeded. The building surpassed expectations, attracting the most visits and the longest ones. The *Oregonian* wrote:

Visitors from the east and even the plains of the West catch sight of the Forestry building, they are so taken by surprise that they make no efforts to hide their astonishment and amazement. The enormous logs used in construction of the building are one of the mediums by which visitors, are enabled to form an idea of the tremendous growth obtained by Oregon trees. ... Visitors to the Exposition have been known to spend an entire day at the Forestry building, so fascinated by the quaintness of the house of logs and bark, that the other buildings held no attractions for them.[6]

The building served a commercial purpose, showing the endless natural resources of the North American Continent. Its enormous elements were not freaks to be gazed at, alongside the two-headed cow at the fair. They demonstrated the (apparent) limitless power of the timber industry and its ability to cut any tree, however large, and move it, however great a distance, over however difficult a terrain.

But the building did more. For a strategy whose motives were overtly capitalist it evoked a plethora of spiritual reactions. A common metaphor was expressed by the *Oregonian*: "the immense structure [is] representative of the Oregon forest as nature herself." And in that capacity, it could appeal to desires beyond turning lumber into a commodity. The *Builder* saw it as an original creation saying: "Nothing more original in design can be conceived," not as architecture, but, "almost entirely a work of nature."[7]

However original, many felt it was decidedly classical. The *Oregon Daily Journal* called it a temple. The novelist Hallie Erminie Rives was near the mark when she called it, "a dream of some primeval, Druidical Pericles." The *Oregonian* as well as Kirtland Cutter called it Oregon's Parthenon.[8] To the contemporary architect or scholar, the evocation of Laugier's or Chambers' primitive hut—the log ancestor of classicism—is inescapable. The building was not classicism transformed; it was classicism before it was transformed.

But the most popular analogy was the least architecturally accurate, that it was a cathedral. To many the forest was God's cathedral, as it was to Pope and Bryant, so the comparison to a church was inevitable. The director of exhibits said: "Its 52 columns of shaggy giants, the innumerable alcoves and galleries, in short, the whole construction of the building reminds one of nothing so much as of the Gothic edifices of the Old World, unless it be Nature's shrines on the mountain sides, whence these giants come."[9]

The idea that the building has a spiritual if not religious dimension was given a decisive boost when an organ was installed. The *Oregonian* wrote: "The tones of the organ will rumble and roar until the visitor will wonder if he is in a Gothic cathedral set down in a Druidic forest."[10] It added:

No one ever failed to be impressed with the somberness of the Oregon fir forest, with its immense trunks and high waving branches and about the base of the trees a stillness of night at noon. Something of the majesty of the majesty of the Oregon forest will be conveyed to the Fair visitors when the Organ moans in the Forestry building.[11]

Some thought the metaphor should become a reality, that when the fair was over it should be preserved as a church. J. M. Edwards wrote:

Should not an Inscription, 'Dedicated to the great Creator who planted these trees,' be placed over the massive door ... Should not the Forestry building be fitted and furnished as the city's cathedral of the forests, wherein to hold devout service of worship each sabbath afternoon. ... Should not a nation great and mighty be proud of a Rome City Beautiful wherein a forestry cathedral of ancient trees?[12]

Section at central court

Section at central court

Section at end transept

Section at end transept

Clearly there is an element of the sublime in this thinking, and its most typical characteristic of the sublime, sheer size. The *Builder* wrote: "Standing in one of the spacious corridors of the Forestry Building and awed by the great fir and cedar columns—children of a virgin forest ... the visitor must needs fall susceptible to its fascinating grandeur."[13]

Certainty the photographs of individuals dwarfed by the columns speak of a kind of timber Karnak, an expression of the power including the power of the American industrial tidal wave (including the American timber industry) encountering the forests of the West.

Reactions to the Forestry Building recall two familiar themes but two that are often oddly juxtaposed. On the one hand there is awe, the true experience of the sublime, the sense of one's smallness in the immensity of the universe in general—standing in the artificial forest of 50-foot-high trees. One could feel what Langford and Doane had felt in their solitary epiphanies at Yellowstone Falls. It is what Muir had felt standing atop Glacier Point in Yosemite. There is also a glow of nationalistic pride, that they live in a place that could produce such forests, real or artificial, in abundance, and that they possess the power to harvest, move, and erect the gigantic objects to and at this place. And probably a sense of manifest destiny as well, the belief that all of this was divinely inevitable. No doubt the organ helped with this.

Barbara Novak writes that in nineteenth-century America the sublime, the sacred, the patriotic, and the inevitable had become one and the same. All those sentiments can be found in visitor's reactions to the Forestry Building. What we saw aesthetically in the landscape and what we saw in the art that depicted it was what we saw in the architecture that came to inhabit it.

But like many sublime structures it is a memorial to something that is lost or disappearing. There is a third theme at the Forestry Building not that of a church or forest, but the museum/memorial/ruin. Most of the exhibits paid tribute to the power and competence of the Oregon forest industry, something hardly necessary given the nature of the building that housed them.

View from balcony

Column erection

To J. M. Edwards, who wished to see it converted into a church, it was not the evidence of the endless supply of giant timber that was Oregon, but the opposite, the last time a construction like this would be possible. It was a ruin, a monument to what was being destroyed. He wrote:

Should not the public spirit of the city of Portland dedicate the site and the building for a perpetual memorial of the grand old forests? ...Man has and is subduing all growths In nature and never again In this present era will restless man wait for great trees to grow wild and untrameled to their perfect fullness and beauty, Therefore it is necessary to preserve that which is.[14]

William Curtis photograph at the Exhibition

The forest was not the only thing being memorialized as it disappeared. Also included in the building's exhibits was an exhibition of the photographs of Edward Curtis. It was a point early in Curtis' career. In two years he would receive the funding that was to make his massive documentation of Native Americans possible. The show resulted in one of the first articles on his work published in the journal of the exhibition. But it was perceived almost as a memorial.

The author Gertrude Metcalfe saw Curtis hurrying to document the Native American before they disappeared, which was inevitable and imminent: "It is a dying race, and in a few years there will no longer be an opportunity to study the rich symbolism of tribal life [they are] hastening with fatal rapidity toward total extinction."[15]

Marion Macrae, writing for the *Sunday Oregonian* saw the building as a forest, as did Bierstadt in his painting, where it was not hard to see the already vanished Native Americans:

One looks down through the columns of colossal timbers which support the building and wonders and dreams. Perhaps some of the pictured redmen on the wall rode through the primeval forest from which these monster trees were taken by the white invader perhaps a tepee stood under that tree or a brave stood behind this one waiting for wild game or the hated paleface. Another glance at the pictures and it is hard to believe that It was not the whisk of a war bonnet down through the

Stair

Portland Forestry Building
Wall Section

Structural elements here are greatly oversized and excessive in number given the far more modest actual structural requirements, but the building had to serve both monumental and commercial purposes.

The upper wall construction is shingles on boards on studs, with the studs exposed on the interior Shingles are oversized, 18 inches to weather, to keep them in scale with the massive logs below.

The lower exterior wall is constructed of horizontally stacked logs 3 feet in diameter with tops and bottoms sawn off to create a flat surface at the horizontal joints between logs.

The vastly oversized interior framing begins with log columns 48 feet-high and 5 feet in diameter. Spanning between each pair is a simple triangular truss Of 36-inch logs.

Above this is a roof structure of boards on tightly spaced log rafters sitting on log purlins

shady trees a hundred feet below. ... climb another stairway to the quaint attic away up under the huge rafters. Here is the forest primeval again. Here is where these pictures should always be hung to make them realistic, and here they are at home. The Indian ... seems to belong to the forest and the forest to him.[16]

This then is another familiar theme of the sublime, the mourning for what is lost or about to be lost. It is for obvious reasons often found in combination with acknowledgment of the inevitability of the expansion of European/Eastern American culture. It is another case of someone monumentalizing and memorializing something they have destroyed. The building is after all a monument to the timber industry and all its destructiveness.

Well before the end of the fair, efforts were underway to preserve what had been intended as a temporary building, but it was expensive and would require that the temporary wood foundation be replaced with a concrete one. A major donor came forward to pay for the foundation. He was one of the building's biggest fans, James J. Hill, president of the Great Northern Railway.

While true classicism may evoke permanence, few things are less permanent than any wood building, unless it is any building for a World's Fair. Perhaps in the depths of our consciousness we know that this is the reality. Materials are not endless, power has its limits, and buildings do not endure. It was saved after the fair and used by the city until it burned in 1964. But it left a legacy in an unexpected place, the hotels of the West.

The Old Faithful Inn opened in 1904, and the Forestry Building in 1905, but they have far more differences than similarities—one classical, the other surreal. The inn was anthropomorphic scale In the Forestry Building the individual dwarfed by the architecture.

View at balcony level

Lumbermen's Building and House of Hoo-Hoo.
Panama-Pacific International Exposition-San Francisco-1915

BERNARD MAYBECK: THE GROVE OF REDWOODS

What is the tallest tree in the world? What is the oldest? If you answered that either one is a sequoia, as found in Sequoia National Park, you would be wrong. The giant sequoia (*Sequoiadendron giganteum*) is neither. The oldest trees are bristlecone pines (*Pinus longaeva*) located to the east in Great Basin National Park. The tallest is the giant sequoia's close relative, the *Sequoia sempervirens*—the coastal redwood. The giant sequoia's habitat is scattered. The area of the coastal redwood is far more specifically bounded. It grows in a dense, originally continuous forest in a 450-mile-long strip of land along the California coast starting at Monterey and ending near the Oregon border. The strip's western boundary is the Pacific and at its widest point it is only 35 miles deep.[1]

Bristlecone pines and giant sequoias make poor building lumber. Redwood, however, has always been a popular building wood. It is softer than many building woods, but it's clear grain, its natural resins that impair decay and its color make it desirable. In part for these reasons, it has always been the least protected. The redwood groves passed into private ownership well before the rise of national parks and paid the price.

Redwoods had been logged since the 1850s, but sophisticated technologies increased the quantity of lumber harvesting by a factor of four in the 1880s and its effects were soon apparent. The idea that redwoods were rapidly disappearing and ought to be preserved begins to be heard about 1898, no doubt a result of the increase in logging and the scars left as a result of the new logging technologies, but in 1900 85–90% of the old growth forest was still intact. Despite herculean efforts, today only about 5% of the old growth remains. So quantitatively the fight to save the old growth redwoods cannot be called a great success. A central problem was land ownership. Yosemite was preserved as early as 1864. Sequoias were never popular for commercial lumber, and the park was set aside in 1890. But in 1900 virtually all the redwood forest was in private hands, which needed to be purchased to become a park, no easy thing politically or economically. But if the results of this movement are not numerically impressive the fragments that remain are, and if the individuals that fought to create them are not all that we hope they might be, in the process they produced some significant architecture.

Opposite: House of Hoo Hoo

Bernard Maybeck

Just before Bernard Maybeck's death in 1957, a city-wide discussion was taking place in San Francisco about the fate of his most conspicuous building, the Palace of Fine Arts. Built as a temporary building for the Panama Pacific Exhibition of 1915 of plaster casts on hidden wood framing, it was, after 40 years, badly deteriorated. When asked what should be done Maybeck replied:

I think the main building should be torn down and redwoods planted around—completely around—the rotunda. ... As they grow, the columns would slowly crumble at the same speed. Then I would like to design an altar, with the figure of a maiden praying, to install in that grove of redwoods. ... I should like my palace to die behind those great trees of its own accord, and become its own cemetery.[2]

This was no off-the-cuff remark as it closely parallels what Maybeck had felt about the building when it was built. The Palace of Fine Arts was to be a portrait of a ruin. He wrote in 1915 that it should be:

An old Roman ruin, away from civilization, which two thousand years before was the center of action and full of life, and now is partly overgrown with bushes and trees—such ruins give the mind a sense of sadness. ... Great examples of melancholy in architecture and gardening may be seen in the engravings of Piranesi, who lived a century ago, and whose remarkable work conveys the sad, minor note of old Roman ruins.[3]

In a 1915 book on the palace Frank Todd wrote: "He has gone back to the classic age for his elementary forms, standing where a young Greek would have stood; and he has come forward again to the present, putting his building on the edge of a tarn and giving it the melancholy of old ruins by a landscape treatment intended to throw it into the background."[4]

Maybeck wrote of the melancholy evoked by the art on display there, which included Arnold Böcklin's *Isle of the Dead,* portraying a burial on an island ruin, and said: "we must use those forms in architecture and gardening that will affect the emotions in such a way as to produce on the individual the same modified sadness as the galleries do."[5]

This is a type of melancholy we have met before—the melancholy of the English romantics—of William Shenstone, of picturesque ruins. The melancholic contemplation of ruins was a well-established aesthetic pastime by 1915. For Maybeck it had been a far more personal and painful experience. He had seen the ruins of San Francisco after the earthquake and fire of 1906 in which his office and many of his drawings were lost. In 1923 he had contemplated the ruins of Berkeley following the fire that destroyed 584 homes. Nineteen of those houses he had designed and one of them was his own. The large scar contained the ruins of the landscape that he and his colleagues in the Hillside Club had worked to create. But the melancholic aspects of Maybeck's vision may have been something else as well. Whenever it is mentioned, it is concerned with redwoods and to one who loved redwoods there was much to be melancholic about.

Despite his fascination with redwood groves, Maybeck the preservationist is not easy to locate. While the members of the Hillside Club, to which he belonged, wrote in "What the Club Advocates:" "The few native trees that have survived centuries of fire and flood lived because they had chosen the best places. They should be jealously preserved. Bend the road, divide the lots, place the houses to accommodate them!"[6] And while Annie Maybeck was forever famous for forcing the city of Berkeley, on the spot, to divert a street around an oak tree,

The Palace of Fine Arts before restoration

Arnold Böcklin's *Isle of the Dead*

Wyntoon, on the McCloud River, 1903

Maybeck's tract "Hillside Building" speaks far more of preserving topography and how to plant new trees rather than saving existing ones. Many of his clients were preservationists, including members of organizations such as the Sierra Club, the Outdoor Art Club, and individuals such as Laura White, a vocal redwood preservationist. At the same time his clients and colleagues in organizations like the Bohemian Club included lumbermen and in time he did buildings for them, from exhibition buildings to lumber mill towns.

The vision of a of redwood grove as a point of departure might not seem the obvious point to explain the Palace of Fine Arts but it is even less so for another work he describes in the same way, Wyntoon. This was a large castle for Phoebe Hearst located in a forest on the McCloud river in Northern California built in 1903. Steeply pitched tile roofs were supported by thick stone walls to form a pyramidal composition. The roof and floors were wood framed and the inner face of the roof deck was faced with bark. It had no columns to speak of, but in describing the work, Maybeck began with the description of a forest:

The idea of composing this construction in the primeval forest on the McCloud River resulted from several causes. First, the six trees in a semicircle. Second, the immense size of these trees. Third, the distance from railroad and expense of transportation. Fourth, climate. Fifth, forest fires. Similar conditions existed in the Middle Ages, and, consequently, without effort, the Gothic composition resulted.[7]

Wyntoon's massive stone walls did not save it from what must have seemed something of a curse to Maybeck. It burned in 1929.

Wood had a special significance for Maybeck. Speaking at the dedication of a building he designed for lumbermen at the Panama Pacific Exhibition he said that: "genuineness can best be carried out in wood finish. ... rather than to use the sham of plaster, the monotony of which becomes so tiresome, while in the natural wood finish, figuration and beauty of grain gives rest to the eye in its endless variety."[8] But redwood had an importance went beyond color, texture, and grain.

The Bohemian Club Lodge, 1904

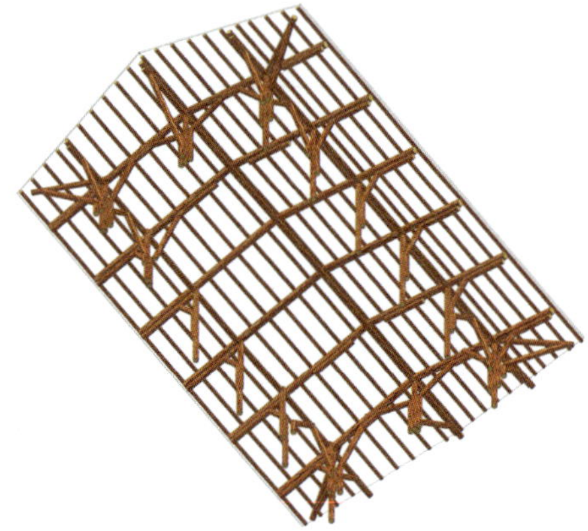

View from below showing log framing

View from below showing finished wood paneling covering logs at the interior

View from below showing walls

Maybeck built his first commissioned work in Berkeley in 1895, a house for Charles Keeler. Over the next four years he built three houses adjacent to it. All have exposed interior structure. All are unpainted and all were built completely of redwood—redwood studs, redwood joists, redwood sheathing, and redwood shakes. Of course, Maybeck used a variety of materials in his long career and he was not alone in his use of redwood, particularly in Berkeley. His daughter-in- law wrote that: "There was an abundance of everything of land—of space—of redwood"[9]

The concept of the grove of trees, particularly redwoods, could not be more appropriate to a building built in 1904. It was built of redwood and built in one of Maybeck's favorite redwood groves, the 160-acre stand of old growth trees on the Russian River where the Bohemian Club held their summer retreats.

The Bohemian Club was started in 1872 by a group of artists, journalists, and other self-described bohemians, all men, who sought to escape from San Francisco for short periods into the woods to enjoy the rustic life, camping out and putting on theatrical productions. Today it is famous or infamous as a powerful conservative organization, but, although never a liberal organization, its members included the writers Frank Norris, Mark Twain, and Jack London. From the beginning the group realized they would need members with higher incomes in order to do be sustainable, so prominent businessmen were included. It contained some of the most passionate defenders of the redwoods such as David Starr Jordan and some of those most responsible for the destruction of the redwood forest—Andrew Hammond for example. It also contained architects, John Galen Howard, Willis Polk, and Maybeck.

From the beginning they sought out groves of giant redwoods for their meetings. Finally settling at their current location, Meeker Grove, about 75 miles north of San Francisco along the Russian River in a large stand of redwoods, eventually growing to 2,700 acres. There were no buildings at the Bohemian Club for the first 30 years of its existence. They camped in tents or in the open and when a lodge was built in 1903-4, Maybeck, who had joined the club that year, was the architect.

The design began as a grove of redwood trunks, 14 of them in a rectangle supporting a large overhanging roof with a single floor below and sited on a steep hillside. Given the hillside the projecting face of the main space is a full two floors above grade. Rather than showing the forest of redwood supports below, the underside of the room is enclosed with a wall of smaller redwood trunks supporting bark strips. *The San Francisco Call* wrote that: "the architect did not disturb the younger of the redwoods, around which the structure was constructed, thus furnishing additional support for the building," implying, poetically but incorrectly, that the live trees were supporting the structure.[10] The exterior is pure rustic. No logs are squared. No bark is removed. The logs come from the site and are cut only to length. The exterior was faced with wide strips of redwood bark or redwood shakes. Its boundaries are porous. The surrounding platform balcony is faced with an open grating of tightly spaced redwood sticks. Rafter ends project beyond the roof edge, giving a porosity and irregularity of the building edges that adds considerably to the ruin aspect of the building's imagery.

The interior tells a different story. It is a precise type of craft, the craft of the machine. Logs are covered with finished wood. Interior walls are sawn and planned redwood. All is tight and precise. The Bohemian Club is not just about rustic nostalgia. It contains wood used at every level of finish from bark-on logs to planks planed smooth. It is a historic recapitulation, repeating the entire history of wood construction from its origins in tree trunks to milled lumber. It is done in layers—machined and finished on the interior, rustic and imperfect on the outside. The completely rustic Maybeck building is almost unknown. More common is this kind of progressive replication of architectural history from a primitive exterior to a finished interior.

This brings us to a Maybeck building of 1903, the LeConte Lodge at Yosemite for the Sierra Club. The Sierra Club was founded in 1892 by John Muir in concert with a group of faculty from UC Berkeley and Stanford. Its goals, then and now, were both recreation and preservation. Muir was the only president during his lifetime, but another key member was Joseph LeConte, professor at Berkeley. LeConte died while hiking in Yosemite Valley in 1901 at the base of Glacier Point. The Sierra Club built a lodge there in his honor. (It has been moved.) Its authorship is problematic. It may be a Maybeck building and if so, it is his first building in a national park. The Sierra Club Bulletin of 1903 credits John White, an architect who shared offices with Maybeck and was his partner briefly in 1906, with the design. There are similarities with Maybeck's early and later work and a Maybeck influence has always been assumed. More recent scholarship credits Maybeck with the design. If so, it is not one of his masterpieces and bears little resemblance to our image of a national park building. The plan is an eight-sided polygon with two projecting wings to form a V. The stone walls are smooth and dressed. The steeply pitched roof is supported by redwood scissor trusses with something like a hammerbeam roof in the polygon.

LeConte Memorial, Yosemite NP, 1903

There is not much rustic about it. This is a memorial and the stone is treated accordingly. Rustic architecture existed in 1903 but it did not exist in the national parks. The Old Faithful Inn was built the same year.

Maybeck built a number of buildings between 1904 and 1915, some of his most significant, but they fall outside the discussion of his rustic architecture. In 1911 he built his only completely rustic design. While working on a house in a forested area near Ukiah in northern California he bought land there and began building a log cabin. His daughter-in-law describes the construction:

The Maybecks ... vacationed there for many years. They hiked in the rain under a tarpaulin, singing. They camped on a ridge and built half a log cabin. They cut small firs and Maybeck put a nail and loop of rope on the small logs and drew them along. We rolled stones for a fireplace, and often were reduced to eating fried oatmeal, but drank the fresh, sweet spring water.[11]

Parsons Memorial Lodge
Yosemite National Park, 1915

Twelve years after the LeConte Lodge, Maybeck did another building for the Sierra Club, also of stone, also in Yosemite, but this time high above the valley in Tuolumne Meadows at an elevation over 8,000 feet. It was closed in the winter and subject to heavy snow. It uses the same material as LeConte but in a very different way and is much more of a ruin.

The building is wider than LeConte with a low-pitched roof closer to the classic chalet profile. In "Hillside Architecture" Maybeck had written that in their climate roofs should shed rain but not snow, which might explain the low pitch in relation to the Berkeley houses. Supporting the heavy snow loads was an obvious issue and Maybeck and his partner/engineer Mark White had explored a number of truss and rafter types finally settling on small diagonal braces at the ends but requiring that temporary supports be placed at midspan while it stood unused in the winter. Maybeck developed a clever but deceptive masonry wall type, using heavy mortar at the center of the wall but eliminating it at the face so that the wall appeared a simple unmortared wall of rough stones. Along with the peeled log roof it gives a rough quality completely missing from LeConte. This might seem an obvious opportunity to build a large log cabin but Maybeck chose, as he often did in the forest, stone.

Two years before Maybeck had built the Parsons Lodge, his last national park building, he began his first for the timber industry. The Brookings family of Washington, DC planned to enter the lumber industry by building a mill and housing at the mouth of the Chetco River on the Oregon Coast. After Maybeck was hired he convinced them to expand the project into a town plan. The venture failed 10 years later and only a hotel and a few houses were built. The buildings were meant to be temporary and were simple milled wood frame structures built with lumber as it emerged from the mill. There is not much rustic about these buildings and not much of architectural interest. There is little in Maybeck's plans to indicate that he saw this in any way rustic, as a return to the forest. Understandably so, but five years later a similar town was built down the coast at Scotia for the Pacific Lumber Company. Several rustic gems were produced: the Winema Theater (1920) and the Scotia Saving Bank (1921).

Section looking southwest

View from northeast

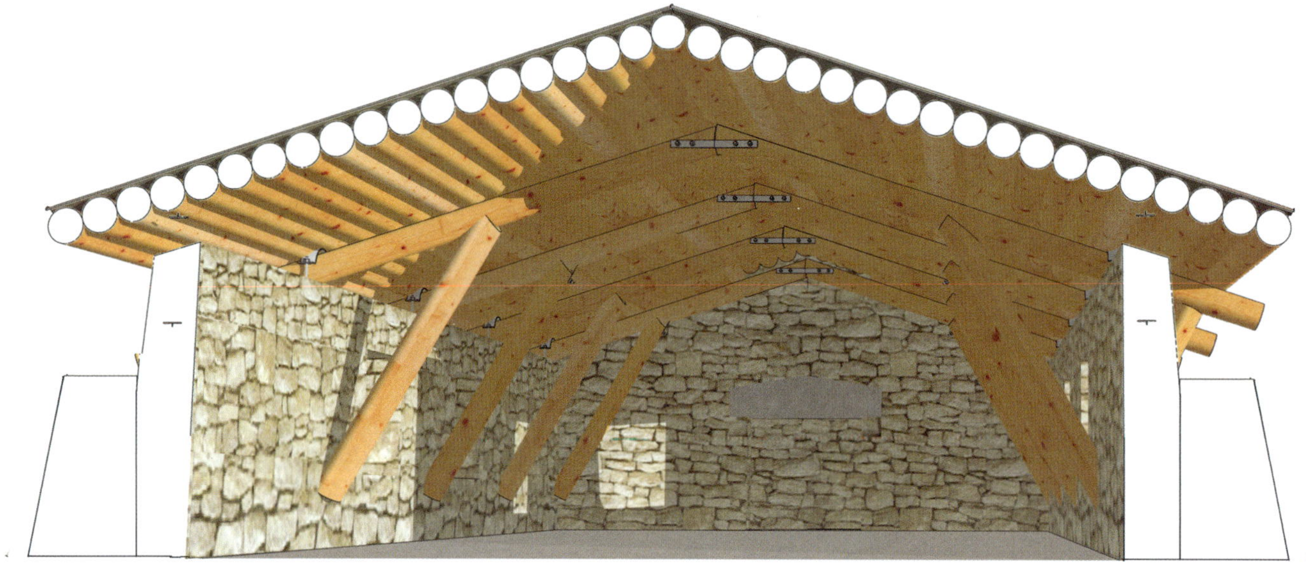

Section looking south

Interior view looking southwest

Parsons Memorial Lodge
Wall Section

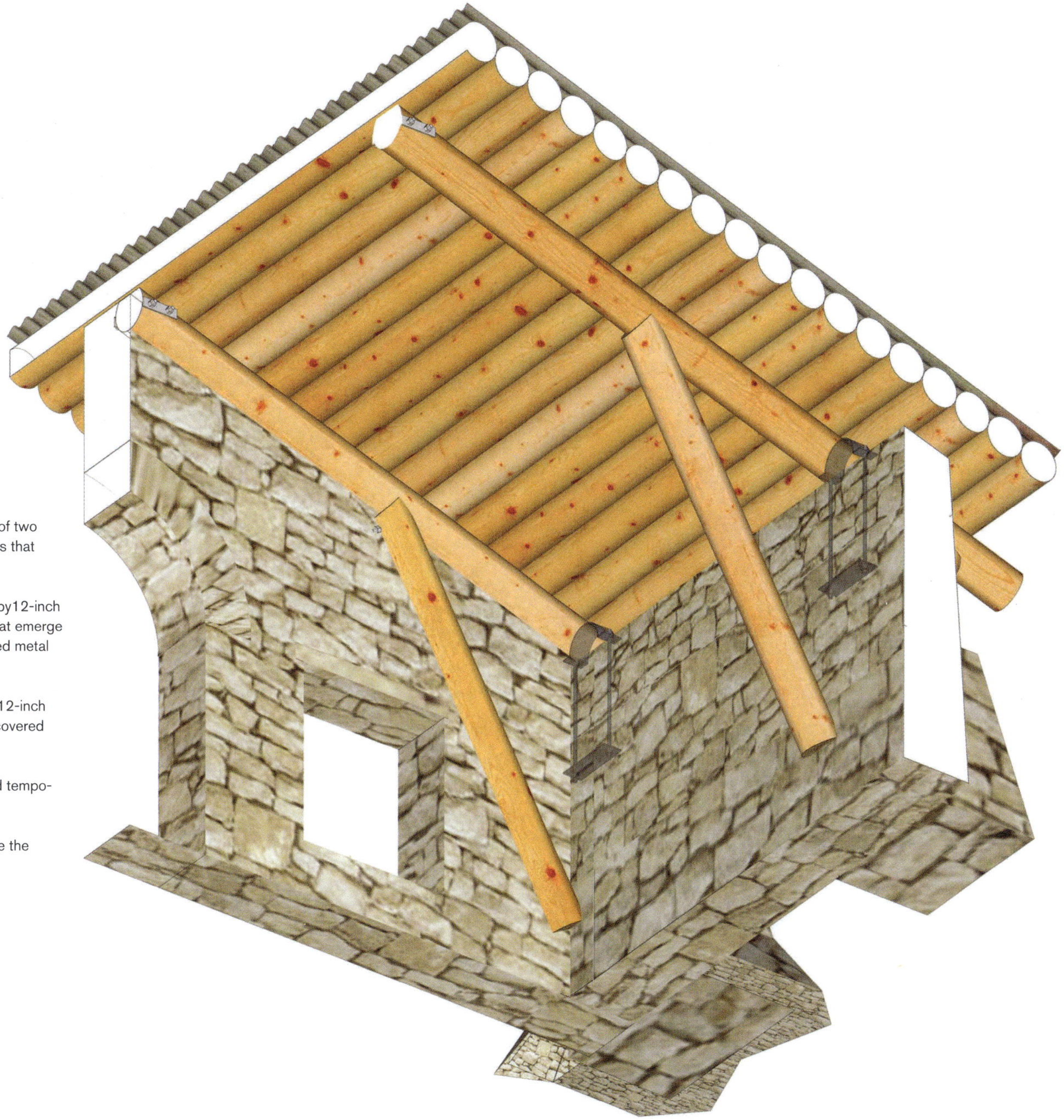

Five rigid frames at a low pitch, composed of two linked Y-shaped 12-inch round log elements that support the roof.

The rafters are supported at their midspan by12-inch log braces connecting to the stone piers that emerge from the wall. Each Y shape has a concealed metal tie-down within the stone wall.

Atop these frames is a continuous deck of 12-inch logs with no spaces between, that is then covered with corrugated galvanized metal sheeting.

The roof is subject to major snow loads and temporary supports we put in during the winter.

The stone piers have recessed joints to hide the connecting mortar.

The Chicago Fair of 1893 established the tradition of constructing oversized rustic log buildings at international exhibitions to promote the lumber industry, built either by timber producing states or forestry associations. Subsequent fair pavilions grew in size and thematic scope over the next 25 years, evoking the romance of American history (St. Louis, 1904), simulating the transcendental experience of nature (Portland, 1905), always proclaiming the greatness of America, while simultaneously demonstrating the massively destructive national timber harvest that was underway. The rustic bark-on classical style begun with the Lumberman's Building in Portland was continued in the Forestry Building at the Seattle Exhibition in 1909, but it reached its ultimate and predictable conclusion at the Panama Pacific Exhibition of 1915 in San Francisco. Foulkes and Hogue's Oregon Pavilion was a log replica of the Parthenon, complete with bark-covered capitals, columns, triglyphs, and metopes, built with logs shipped the 600 miles by water from the forest to San Francisco. There was nothing subtle about it. It was larger than the original. Two columns were added to the 46 of the Greek prototype so that one column could represent each of the 48 states.

The Panama Pacific Exhibition was the event that took Bernard Maybeck from obscurity to fame and produced his most conspicuous building, the Palace of Fine Arts, but this was only one of three buildings he designed at the fair. A more intriguing building in this history is his oversized rustic timber pavilion, the House of Hoo Hoo, an exhibition building for a society of lumbermen.

The House of Hoo Hoo
Panama Pacific Exhibition, 1915

Section looking south

North elevation

View from west

The Hoo Hoo are a fraternal society of lumberman. They perform service and engage in humorous tongue in cheek rituals, but their ultimate goal is advancing their industry. It was made clear to Maybeck that his task was to display to the public all the wood products of the West Coast with or without humor. From the contemporary view Maybeck was essentially switching sides. His clients of 1903 were the most radical of forest preservationists. The clients of 1914-1920 were those in the process of destroying it.

The concept of representing a redwood grove was again the point of departure but it was a grove in a very different state. The House of Hoo Hoo was a large building entered through a forecourt of equal size. There is no symbolism here. The forecourt was a fairly literal representation of what a redwood grove looks like after it is clear-cut. Trellises sit on huge stumps. Buildings even grow out of them. Redwoods were typically not cut at ground level but at a point at least ten feet above grade. The wood in the trunk below this point was given little value. It made sense to start higher up the trunk where the trunk was thinner and the grain straight. Thinner is a relative concept as trunk diameters of old growth trees were commonly 4–10 feet in diameter but can reach 25. The remains of a forest following logging was a series of these gigantic redwood stumps, which over time would be occupied by other plants.

Section through entry court, pylon and meeting room

The image of the ruins of an old growth redwood forest were where Maybeck began.

The redwood structures of the large forecourt may have been logs but they were arranged in Beaux Arts fashion. The long forecourt was entered between two large freestanding cylinders in the form of redwood stumps. Semicircular exedra of tree trunks supporting trellises of milled redwood terminate each end of the long axis, The two large free-standing cylinders, 16 feet in diameter and 40 feet high, mark the center axis with the building entry. In reality, these were hollow constructions of wood studs and joists faced with redwood bark. Maybeck had intended the two trunks to be linked at the top with a flower box reminiscent of an entablature that would have given the whole something of the feel of a rusticated and overgrown triumphal arch, but this was vetoed by the client.

The columns of the semicircular exedra of tree trunks at the short ends of the court were smaller versions of the hollow pseudo-tree stumps; the trellis beams that spanned between are log faced dimensional lumber, supported by redwood tree trunks. Again none of these are actual tree trunks but are constructed of a cylindrical milled stud frame supporting the outer curved section of peeled bark or slabs. As it appears in photographs the building may not be as primitive as Maybeck intended. He wanted trees planted

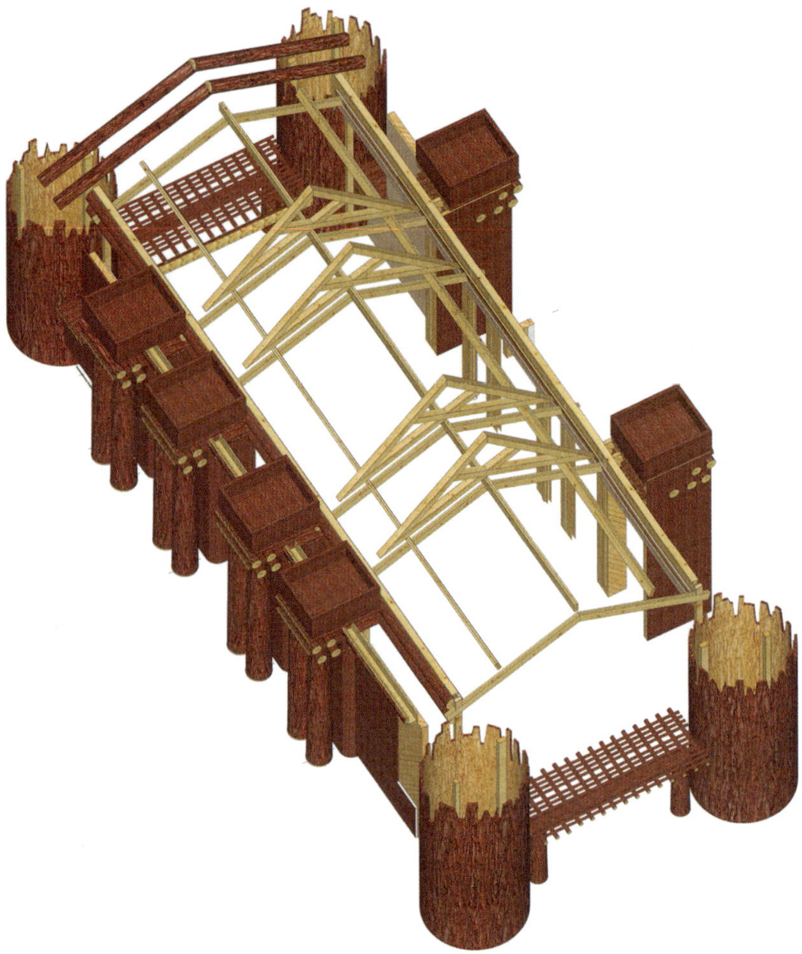

Rustic enclosure

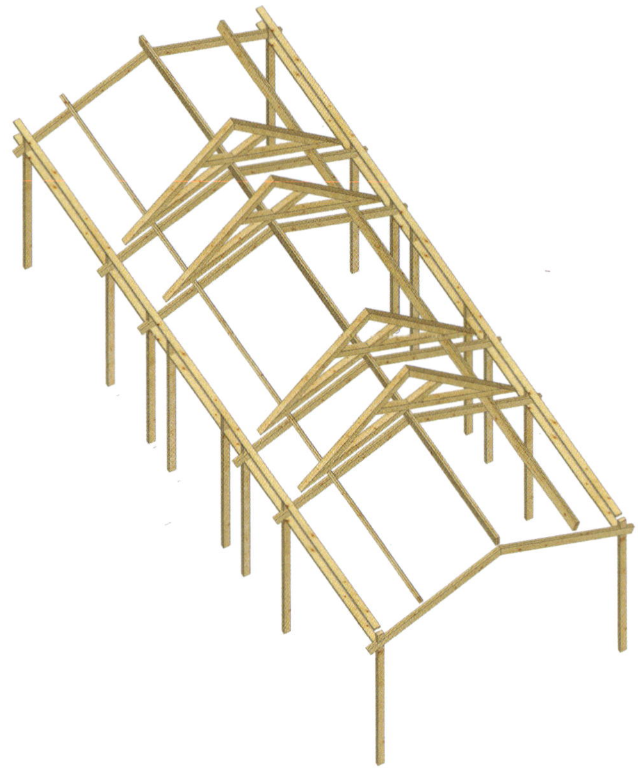

Concealed timber frame

inside the stumps and on the roofs, in addition to the triumphal arch, but the client declined. Maybeck's notes on the landscape plan are telling: "These spaces to have flowers or shrubs about four or five feet high. The idea being to so cover the redwood bark on the house and imitation tress so a close view cannot be obtained of the fake."[12] He directs that the planting to be located to keep the viewer at a distance from the building, less they notice the bark was only a veneer. This was Maybeck the set designer.

The main pavilion was faced on both sides with four paired clusters of solid tree-trunk columns 2.5 to 3 feet in diameter. Each was planed to be one of the eight commercial trees of the West—the coastal redwood, sugar pine, white pine, Douglas fir, Oregon pine, western hemlock, western spruce, red cedar, and Port Orford cedar. It is not clear from photographs that this was done as all appear to have been redwood. Atop these columns were a series of large flower boxes and the columns were topped with shorter horizontal logs giving them the look of Ionic columns. These four column piers of the exterior themselves were unmistakable replications in logs of the similar piers of the nearby Palace of Fine Arts. These columns framed only the central space of the building and the side wings were in part supported by four more hollow redwood columns, this time with rather clumsily detailed wood studs and joists emerging to support the roof beams above. The space inside these columns was sufficient to provide room for the men and women's toilets.

The interior was one of Maybeck's theatrical spaces. There is a large assembly hall at the center, another with a large hearth on the short side, and a stage space at the center of the long side. The stage/theater form here takes on a deeper significance given the theatrical nature of other parts of the building and the open balconies overlooking the "performance" space.

The central hall had three large bays divided by four small ones in an ABABABA pattern. The roof was supported by four pairs of scissor trusses that align with the spatial divisions.

Interior

Entry elevation

House of Hoo Hoo
Wall Section from Interior

The building was a rustic log exterior enclosing a finished wood interior, forming a progression from the rugged and raw to the polished and refined. The exterior was bark-on redwood; the interior was precisely finished pine and fir. There were no bark or log surfaces in the interior.

The actual framing was rarely exposed although often expressed. Trusses and girders were not visible, only the cladding. The bottom chord of the truss extended below ceiling and was encased with fir, as were the structural roof members and the girders. The infill panels are white pine.

The thick, hollow exterior walls were formed by milled-stud walls covered with redwood bark on boards on the exterior and interior wood paneling. Most of the interior wall paneling was white pine with fir trim covering the milled studs of the wall.

There were a variety of finish wood species since the building was essentially a product showroom, but they provided a key to the structures they were cladding.

House of Hoo Hoo
Wall Section from Exterior

The outside appearance was deceiving, as one might assume that the building was rustic throughout, but like the Bohemian Club it was two buildings—one rustic on the exterior, one polished and finished on the inside. The stepped roof planes alternated between the top and bottom chord of the trusses so that the latter were effectively hidden. The ceiling was pine with fir strips cladding the structural elements.

The roof was framed with wood trusses between alternating roof profiles. Spanning between the trusses were girders of and milled joists with fir casings.

The entry portico was solid redwood columns with capitals and entablature in imitation of the Ionic order. The original plan was that each column would be a different species. It appears they were all redwood in the finished building.

They were topped with flower boxes similar to those at the nearby Palace of Fine Arts. They were flanked by redwood bark-faced piers The soffit and fascia had a half-log facing.

The building itself probably caused some environmental damage as it required 32,000 square feet of redwood bark, peeled from living trees. This entire structure might as easily serve the cause of preservation since it illustrated so well the destructiveness of the lumber industry.

The roof has alternating high and low sections with the low section fixed to the bottom chord of the truss and the high section of the roof fixed to the top, something a visitor would have no way of knowing as the trusses are completely hidden. Columns of built-up milled timber support the trusses but they also are concealed. One saw the effects of the structure but not the structure. This may be a consequence of the space's real function. Columns are recessed and hidden. Wood paneling in a variety of species steps forward. Since it was meant to be a demonstration of the possibilities of the materials and the timber industry, the interior was something close to a wood products showroom detailed with conventional finish trim and paneling, not rough finished bark. Like many Maybeck buildings that might be thought of as rustic it was more a series of transformative exercises from primitive to the refined.

Each rustic Maybeck building retells us the larger history from creation to ruin repeating the history of the development of wood construction. It is a rare rustic Maybeck building in which there are not contrasting levels of craft and finish.

While at first glance it appears completely a different animal from the Palace of Fine Arts, the two buildings have remarkable similarities with the House of Hoo Hoo playing the role of primitive hut, the ancestor of the Palace of Fine Arts. Thus the "order" of the House of Hoo Hoo was a replica of the order of the Palace of Fine Arts, built of bark and logs complete with the flower boxes. Was it a return to origins, or a new creation or was it just advertising for the lumber industry? Perhaps to Maybeck each required the presence of the other. This is yet another fictive history. It proceeds backwards from the Palace, not forward from the Lumberman's Pavilion. The latter is rather a vernacular Paestum concocted out of a real Parthenon. The House of Hoo Hoo was a statement of first principles but informed with the knowledge of hindsight, a cleaned up and clarified mythical ancestor omitting the embarrassing and elaborating the admirable. To Maybeck, however, it was an evocation of the glory of a lost world, the ruin, the forest as drawn by Piranesi.

House of Hoo Hoo order

Palace of Fine Arts order

Glen Alpine Springs Resort
Dining Hall
Lake Tahoe, California, 1921

Another rustic Maybeck design, and yet another retreat for Maybeck, was the Glen Alpine Springs Resort near Lake Tahoe where he vacationed regularly with his family. In 1920 he designed a dining hall there but that same year the entire complex burned. Maybeck then designed a totally new resort. Understandably he began to explore non-flammable materials and wood buildings and this is evident at the Dining Hall at Glen Alpine.

The original plan is the same diagram as the LeConte Lodge—an eight-sided polygon with two projecting wings at an acute angle perched on a small level area in the hilly terrain. The central pavilion was the kitchen; the two wings held dining and assembly. The two wings are a variant on the archetypal Maybeck space we have seen so often: one bay by three defined by eight stone piers. The center bay is slightly wider so that the piers project.

The corrugated metal roof is steeply pitched and rather than having a sharp peak, given a rounded transition to join the two faces. This dramatically changes the profile but it probably a response to the problem of joining the two corrugated sheets at a sharp angle to make a waterproof joint. Making a separate curved roof section for the peak meant there would be two lapped joints on the face of the roof rather than one butt joint at the peak.

The stone surfaces are more evenly faced and the stones more evenly coursed into roughly rectilinear shapes than at Parsons but he used the same stone wall methodology with open joints on the exterior and mortar on the interior.

The massive stone piers, the absence of lintels, and the thin sheet metal roof evokes a different type of ruin than a log building. After the San Francisco fire and earthquake and the Berkeley fire of 1923 he pursued yet another type of ruin, a fireproof one, one that is externally stone and steel.

Wood framing at Assembly Hall interior

Dining Hall

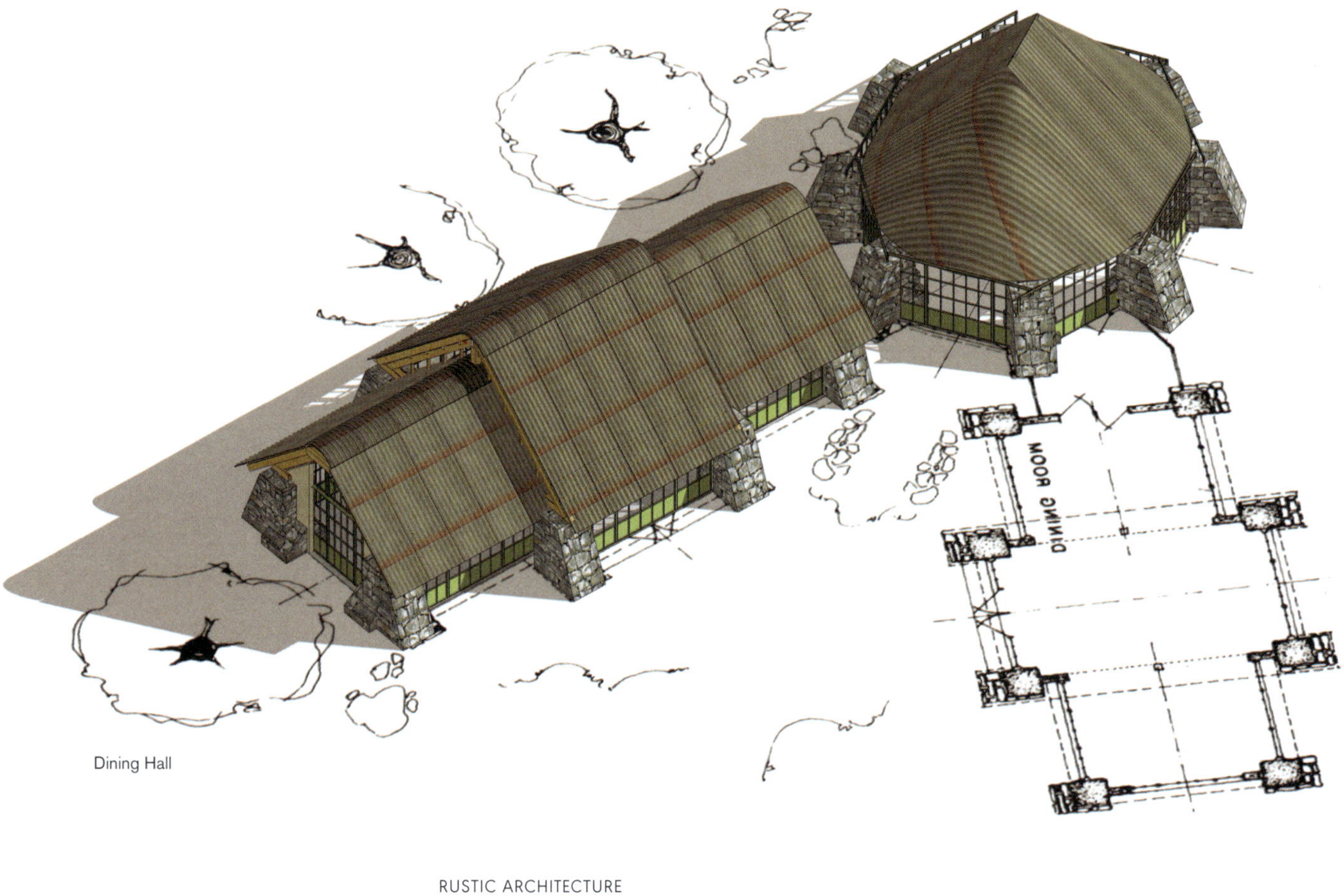

Dining Hall

Section looking east

West elevation

Dining Hall
Wall Section

The roof and exterior walls are composed of non-combustible materials. The roof is corrugated iron sheets on 3x12 purlins. Wood is confined to the interior.

The purlins are connected to the structural frames resting on the concrete piers. The frame is composed of two 3x12 boards with blocking between. It is supported at midspan by an 8x8 wood column and two 2x8 braces sandwiched between the two 3x12s at the joint.

The walls have internal concrete piers and external stone piers. The voids between are filled by Fenestra window an extremely thin but not particularly rustic steel window system.

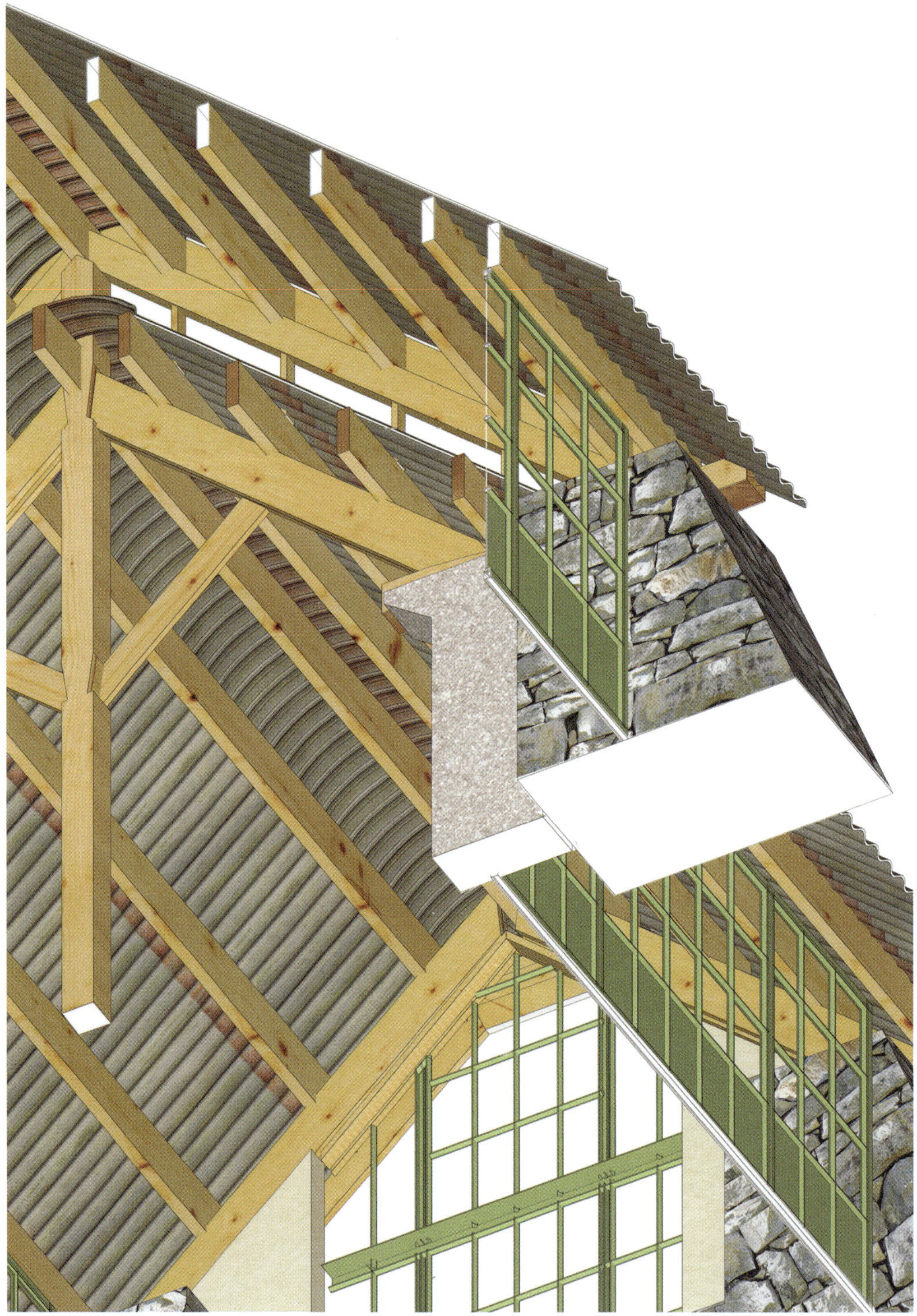

Assembly hall

House of Hoo Hoo

Conclusion

This has been an eclectic ramble through Maybeck's work, ignoring significant moments and focusing on his rustic work. This group of rustic buildings, while characterized by consistent formal strategies and ideological unity, were created to accommodate programs and serve clients working at cross purposes.

Maybeck's clients included the most dedicated forest preservationists of the day and at the same time many of those working hard to harvest the Western forest in its entirety. While he fought to preserve the landscape of Berkeley, he then went on to help plan the destruction of a forest in Oregon. It is disappointing that while he did buildings for both the Sierra Club, a group of idealists dedicated to preservation, and for the Bohemian Club, a group of largely conservative businessmen vacationing in the woods, he never joined the former or showed much interest in its activities, while he attended the summer retreats of the Bohemian Club every year until his death in 1957, by which time it was well on its way to becoming what it is today, a bastion of conservative politics and in many aspects an anti-environmental organization. During the discussion of the creation of Redwood National Park in the 1960s, Ronald Reagan, Bohemian Club member, gave us his memorable quote: "A tree is a tree. How many more do you have to look at?"[13] Many in the Bohemian Club agreed and in 2011 the club sought a special logging permit that would allow it to cut more than 1 million board feet each year in the grove where they held their meetings. The request was denied.[14]

But the truth is we should probably be glad Maybeck was not active with the Sierra Club. In these years it had problems of its own that are more offensive than those of the Bohemians. Joseph LeConte, for whom Maybeck's memorial at Yosemite was named, embraced the "science" of Eugenics, the idea of selective breeding to improve the human race based on the idea that some races were inferior to others. Other founding members of the Sierra club held similar views. One wishes the fact that these opinions were held by so many who argued for the preservation of the redwoods was simply coincidence but it is a coincidence that is all too common and there is a clear line connecting the fear for vanishing redwoods with fear for the vanishing Nordic race, as conspicuously represented the work of Madison Grant.[15]

Maybeck seems to have been more interested in building evocative memorials to redwood groves that had been lost than in preserving those that remained. Maybeck's attitude toward the destruction the old growth redwood forest is more evocative than systematic and owes more to artistic vision than scientific analysis.

We have seen the evocative qualities of the ruin in several manifestations—the redwood grove, the Forestry Building in Portland, Worcester's forest/church in San Francisco, and Maybeck's buildings have many of these same qualities and intentions. They may evoke nostalgia for a place and time that is gone—the remnant of past glories as in the ruins of Europe. They may, like the type of ruins Simmel describes, speak of the constant war between the human-made and the natural. They may evoke a sublime reaction, an awe in the face of extreme age and massive size the sublime monumentality of the Western landscape or the Forestry Building.

But while Maybeck's ruins have these qualities, they are ultimately a different type. What is different is what he saw in Bodkin's *Isle of the Dead* the strange but quite real phenomenon of "pleasurable melancholy." The objects of Maybeck's landscapes, whether buildings or fragments of preserved nature, were to evoke the same sensibility as it occurs in Piranesi's views of the Forum and Caspar David Friedrich's *Abbey in the Oak Forest*, Maybeck's works contain within them the images of very real ruins that were very personal—a clear-cut redwood forest, the ruins of San Francisco after the earthquake, the ruins of Berkeley after the fire and the charred carcass of Wyntoon and his own house in Berkeley. While famous for his bottomless optimism and enthusiasm for going forward after massive setbacks, Maybeck had within him something of William Shenstone, someone who enjoyed, "that pleasing melancholy which proceeds from a reflection on decayed magnificence."

THE MONUMENT AND THE CHALET

901. Glacier Park Hotel
© Marble

THE GREAT NORTHERN RAILROAD

If he'd of lived he'd of been a great man. A man like James J. Hill. He'd of helped build up the country.[1]
—*The Great Gatsby*, F. Scott Fitzgerald

By 1886 James J. Hill had determined that he was going to own a transcontinental railroad. There were two ways that he could do this. First, he could build one. He could extend his existing lines which ended in North Dakota across Montana and Idaho to Tacoma. Or he could buy one, namely the perpetually financially troubled Northern Pacific. By the end of the century, he had done both. In 1893 the Great Northern Line was complete from St. Paul to Seattle and by 1901 he had acquired financial control of the Northern Pacific.

Hill is sometimes portrayed as an "admirable" member of the builders of transcontinentals in contrast to men like Thomas Durant. Hill was certainly more financially successful. A character in Fitzgerald's *The Great Gatsby* tells us that James J. Hill was a great man. Cornelius Van Horne, owner of the Canadian Pacific Railroad, called Hill a "Master of Humbug."[2] But regardless of character Hill had to deal with the same problem as his peers. The Great Northern was well managed, well designed, and financially stable, but he was building a large expensive piece of infrastructure much of which was largely unneeded over much of its length and might not be for some time. He had to create his own customers. He had three potential markets in the far West—farming, timber, and mining—and pursued them all. Richard White wrote, "Western North Dakota, eastern Montana and much of eastern Washington were too arid, too infertile, too distant from markets to sustain the density of settlement and agricultural development that Hill's Great Northern promised."[3] Hill enjoyed more success with timber, but all produced long term massive damage, environmental and social.

James Hill had no interest in tourists and not much in passengers for that matter. He preferred to ship timber, ore, and grain. He had an agrarian vision of the world he was creating, a nation of small farmers connected by a railroad, but as the railroad moved west the profitable markets were to be found elsewhere, particularly timber and mining. Whatever virtues "wilderness" possessed were not part of the equation.

Ultimately the Great Northern was to transform both the landscape and the architecture of the West but this was inseparable from the creation of its principal market—timber—and its principal obstacle, Native Americans.

Opposite: Tepees in front of the Glacier Park Lodge

Piegan tepees at the Glacier Park Lodge

Timber and the Creation of Rainier

An area where Hill succeeded was timber. He had demonstrated an ability to run a far more efficient operation that his competitors, but he still needed ties and infrastructure. Like all railroads Hill needed to create his own timber industry and did so conspicuously by setting up a large mill in Somers, Montana. Hill invented a triangular tie that required less timber but he still used massive amounts. In the drive to build the line to Montana he used 100 million board feet of timber and ties to build 733 miles of track, obliterating 7,500 acres of forest in the process.[4]

But timber became a major source of income. He declared in 1905 that, "one acre of timberland possessed more intrinsic value to a railway corporation than forty acres of agricultural land."[5] Hill's actions caused a profound transformation of the Western American landscape well beyond what was typical of railroad construction. The Great Northern was finished at the moment at which American timber industry underwent a monumental shift. The forests of the central US were disappearing. The forests of the Northwest held a seemingly limitless supply. The shift would have happened without Hill, but Hill not only had the railroad, he owned a great deal of forest. In 1864 Congress had granted 62,000 square miles, an area a little less than the size of the state of Washington, to the Northern Pacific Railroad to facilitate the construction of a transcontinental railroad. Despite its many failures and troubled history, it retained that grant and when Hill acquired the Northern Pacific, he acquired what remained of that land, much of it timberland in the Northwest.

In 1890 Frederick Weyerhauser, a friend and neighbor of Hill, owned the largest timber company in the United States, but at the same time faced a serious problem. His fortune had been made in the forests of the Great Lakes area and that timber was rapidly diminishing. He needed to look elsewhere and the obvious place was the Pacific Northwest. Hill had the opposite problem. He owned vast area of timberland but had insufficient resources to make use of it himself. In January 1900, Weyerhaeuser, in the largest private land transaction in American history to that date, bought 900,000 acres of timber in Washington from the Northern Pacific Railway. Glacier National Park at one million acres is only a little larger.[6] While Hill and Weyerhauser received a great deal of criticism for this, one result was the creation of the fifth national park. The terrain around Mt. Rainier was in Hill or Weyerhaeuser's view, not very useful. It was not good timberland. It certainly could not be effectively farmed. Thus, just before the sale to Weyerhaeuser, Hill traded 450,000 acres of the area that is now Mount Rainier National Park to the government for more suitable timberlands elsewhere, and in 1899 Mount Rainier National Park was established. President Harrison had created a Pacific Preserve in 1893, but this deal produced a full-fledged national park.

Stephen Puter, who went to jail for his role in various land fraud schemes, accused Hill of exchanging the "worthless bleak territory" surrounding Mt. Rainier for valuable tracts in every state penetrated by its lines. Puter wrote:

The entire idea of making a National Park out of the unprepossessing country surrounding Mt. Rainier, was clever in the extreme. ... In short, Mt. Rainier owes its distinction in this respect to the fact that the Northern Pacific Railroad Company owns a lot of land in the neighborhood. Had the Jim Hill corporation possessed the odd-numbered sections adjacent to Mt. Shasta, in California, Mt. Hood, in Oregon, or Mt. Anything, in Anywhere, there is no question but what Congress would have wisely recognized the utmost importance of making National Parks out of them also.[7]

The legacy of the Northern Pacific grant lives on. Derrick Jensen wrote in 1995:

In 1864 the Pacific Northwest's forests had not yet been logged and extended from the Continental Divide across parts of the Columbia River Watershed to the Pacific Ocean. Across this

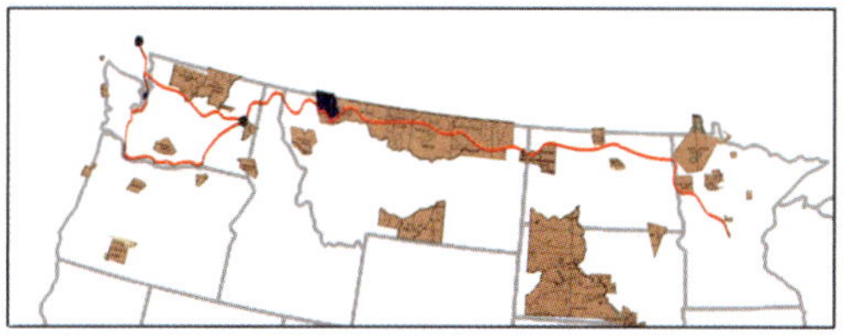

Above: Native American reservations in Montana in 1883. Great Northern route in red.

Below: Route of Great Northern Railroad in relation to Glacier National Park

same region today, watersheds are unraveling and the spotted owl, the marbled murrelet, the grizzly bear, many runs of salmon, and other species of flora and fauna have become threatened, endangered, or extinct through ... excessive logging.[8]

Jensen also argues, with many others, that it was all illegal. The Northern Pacific had forfeited the land under the unfulfilled terms of the grant long before Hill purchased the Northern Pacific.

Late in his life Hill spoke of the need for preservation of timber, soil, and water, but he vigorously opposed the US Forest Service, arguing that private owners should handle this or perhaps the states, but not the Federal Government. So, regardless of his motives, James J. Hill can be credited with making possible a national park and in time was to create another, but both were part of a larger enterprise that was far less altruistic.

James J. Hill and the Piegans

All of the transcontinental railroads adversely affected Native Americans, but Hill is exceptional here as well and not in a good way. Even more than other railroads, he had to build across their lands. In 1890 Hill and the Great Northern Railroad began in earnest their efforts to build a railroad that would connect their Minnesota lines with Puget Sound. To avoid duplication the route of the Northern Pacific he had to build north of the Missouri and the state of Montana north of the Missouri belonged to Native Americans—the Blackfoot or Piegan lands to the west and the, Gros Ventre, Arikira, Hidatsa, and Mandans to the east. Obviously, he needed the right of way but in truth he wanted the surrounding land to be open for development. Both would require an act of congress and the President's signature and after some lobbying and the help of Senator Henry Dawes, both were obtained as it required minimal consultation with any of the Native Americans.

The original Piegan lands were about 28 million acres. Today they are 1.5 million. Major reductions in Piegan land took place throughout the nineteenth century. The last of these in 1895 made up much of what is now Glacier National Park. The Piegans were in need of money. Hill and others wanted the reservation opened for miners and farmers. George Bird Grinnell, who acted as the Piegan's advisor, wanted to pave the way for a national park. The tribe sold the parcel in 1895 to the US government with the understanding that the Piegans would maintain rights to hunt, cut timber, and have general access. When Glacier National Park was established in 1910 with the strong support of Hill, these rights vanished. The boundaries of Glacier National Park thus contain a large strip of land, 800,000 acres, that once belonged to the Piegans.[9]

The Hill family and the Great Northern Railroad in some cases enabled, in others directly caused, and in all cases directly benefited from what was essentially the cumulative theft of about 90% of the land traditionally inhabited by the Piegans. This was not the end of the Hill family's long and complex relationship with the Piegans, for the Hills were to come back for many other things before they were through.

In 1901 James J. Hill controlled both the Great Northern and the Northern Pacific and in order to avoid possible anti-trust action, turned the management of the Great Northern over to his son Louis.

Roderick Nash identifies two visions in the American psyche of what the landscape of the West might be—the pastoral landscape or the uncontrolled wilderness.[10] If one were to look for real manifestations of these two visions, one need look no further then James J. Hill and his son and successor Louis. James was the pastoralist. He saw the West as Jefferson saw it, a vision of yeoman farmers. Louis by contrast, looked at the West, or at least the mountains, and saw wilderness. He loved the outdoors, he loved Montana, and in his own way he loved the Piegans. Louis was to build not a railroad but a national park.

LOUIS HILL: MONUMENTS AND CHALETS

Horseback riders on the trail along the north slope of the Ptarmigan Wall at Glacier NP, circa 1932.

In 1911 Louis Hill, one of the wealthiest men in America and the president one of the country's largest railroads, announced he was going to give it all up, resign from his job, leave his mansion in St. Paul and move to Montana. He told a reporter: "I have a home now in the Glacier Park." He told another reporter that his chief desire was to avoid railroad business and his greatest pleasure was hunting and fishing miles away from railroads or telegraph wires in the wilds of Montana or Oregon. In 1912 he said that he had given up the presidency of the Great Northern to devote his time to painting.[1]

This seems to be one more example of the retreat to the wilderness in search of the alternative life, but Hill was no Horace Kephart. Hill's motives were more complex and more contradictory. Three things drew him to the West:

One was his genuine love of the outdoors.

Hill truly enjoyed roughing it in the backcountry on occasion. His affection for the landscape of the West is best illustrated not by anything he wrote but by the hours he spent painting it. But while he was different than his father, he was not so different as first appears. Despite his determination to leave his job and home for the Montana wilderness he was bringing his business interests with him.

The second motive was timber.

As much as he wanted to enjoy the West, he wanted to exploit it. In 1910 Louis Hill became a primary investor in the Oregon and Western Colonization Company who owned 868,969 acres of timber in Oregon. Their intention was over time to harvest and sell the timber, then sell the cleared land to farmers. The company was never the success he had hoped but it is significant that seven months after congress had, at Hill's urging, created Glacier National Park. He was involved in a scheme to eliminate a forest 4/5 the size of the park. His plan was to destroy as much forest as he was preserving.[2]

The third was his vision for Glacier National Park.

The Park was created in 1910 and the Hill family's power and influence played no small part in that event, as their railroad constituted the park's southern boundary. Congress had neither the means nor the desire to develop it, but Louis Hill was happy to take on the job, including the financing. Glacier National Park was to be the great project of Louis Hill's life. He was not a figurehead in that role but closer to a micromanager. Over the coming years he gave much of his time and a great deal of his money and his personal vision to making a very particular type of park.

In the end Louis did not retire to Montana. While he spent a great deal of time in the West, he maintained his primary residence in St. Paul and while he stepped down as director of the Great Northern, he remained chairman of the board until 1929. His declaration of 1911, while not insincere, was directed at the press and their readers.

See America First ad for the Great Northern

A reporter once said of Hill that it was too bad a man with such a gift for public relations was wasted as the president of one of the country's largest railroads: "He believes in publicity. ... The detail of running a railroad bored him. Being boss of or eight thousand miles of rails didn't seem worthwhile." Hill's statements to the press were always self-serving and often exaggerated. It is significant that while Hill took backcountry trips, he once took 25 reporters with him. But at least one reporter thought him sincere: "He believes in the Northwest ... and will now spend his time developing whole territory."[3]

There was at the core of Louis Hill a man very much like his father, a ruthless competitor, and he bears equal responsibility with his father and his peers for the damage done by the railroads, particularly to the forests and Native Americans. On the surface he appeared to be sensitive to these issues and in some ways he was. At times he appears to advocate preservation. James J. Hill fought the idea of the national forests, and Louis had been a longstanding vocal critic. On June 10, 1910, Louis "dropped a bomb" at public meeting when he announced that in the future, he would support the forest management polices of Gifford Pinchot and the US Forest Service.[4]

His attitude toward Native Americans was equally complex. The Great Northern had already taken a great deal from the Piegans indirectly, but in 1912 Louis needed one more thing from them, land for his hotel. He wished to buy 160 acres of Piegan land just outside the park adjacent to the Great Northern station in East Glacier. The Piegan's were badly in need of money and asked for $41/acre. Hill manipulated the price down to $25.

But having performed one more outrage on the Piegans he then became (in his view) their greatest friend and at a time when their culture was systematically suppressed. Louis Hill celebrated and popularized that culture, collecting, exhibiting, and commissioning their traditional art, providing them with jobs, many of which involved teaching their culture and history to visitors. In the past this was seen as patronage. In the present it is often described as exploitation, but Louis' desire to help the Piegans, however self-serving and misguided seems to have been genuine.

A glib reading of the park that emerged from this that it was an artifact, a reminder, evoking nostalgia for something the railroad had destroyed—the forests of the West and the culture of Native Americans who inhabited it. The story of Hill's Great Northern Railway leaves us with the same paradox as that of the Northern Pacific, that the preservation of two national parks and the creation of the architecture that they contained was part of an enterprise that was on the whole environmentally destructive to the American landscape, particularly its forests, and socially destructive of its inhabitants, particularly the Native Americans.

But in so doing the Hills established a very different type of rustic architecture than the one Durant or the Northern Pacific had created, one that spoke as much of the transformative power of American industry as it did of rustic escapism, one that duplicated the simultaneous arrogance and humility that many experienced in the face of the landscape of the West and one that exemplified their nostalgia for its past.

When Hill began work on the Glacier Park Lodge, his first and largest building at the park, he began by borrowing the drawings of the Portland Forestry Building to use as a guide. Like that building it would house gargantuan tree trunks and remnants of Native American culture, and with the same intention. It would be a monument to what the Great Northern had accomplished and a demonstration of its the magnitude of its constructional ability. It would at the same time be a museum of what had been lost in the process. It would be a constructed ruin, evoking lost cultures and forests. It would be as much a memorial as a museum, in the eyes of today, a reliquary holding of the trophies of colonialism.

The Return to Origins: Switzerland

This was one side of Louis Hill, the head of the Great Northern, the timber baron, the monument builder. There was another—the one wanted a life in the backcountry, housed in a different architecture, one much less monumental and far more domestic.

Louis Hill lived from 1903 to 1948 in a neo-Palladian house with a columned portico in St. Paul. But he exhibited little passion for classical architecture. His other life—the fisherman and the painter—was lived in chalets. He built them everywhere. He built one in on a farm near St Paul. He built the Belton Chalet on the east side of Glacier National Park. He built one at Swiftcurrent lake on the west side of the park. He built one 25 miles north of the park at Watterton Lakes National Park in Canada that he never lived in, and when he bought a lot at Pebble Beach California in 1910 at the heart of the climate and culture of Southern California, he built a chalet as well.[5]

He saw an aesthetic appeal of the Swiss landscape, but also saw its capitalist potential, as evidenced by his associations with the "See America First" movement. Despite its name, the See America First movement was obsessed with Switzerland. A large part of the fixation on Switzerland was about cash. In the eyes of its members money was being spent there that should be spent in the United States. The *Anaconda Standard* gave a precise figure reporting that in 1911 400,000 Americans visited Europe and, assuming each spent $1000, $400,000,000 in revenue was being lost annually.[6] Louis Hill was only a bit more subtle saying that: "millions of dollars are being spent every year in the continental Switzerland by people who go there for the scenery which does not compare with Montana scenery."

His attitude had patriotic if not jingoistic origins as well: "Uncle Sam has Alps of his own right up in Glacier Park. He also has more than a composite of all landscape beauties to the found anywhere upon the face of the earth"[7]

The cynic might argue that Louis Hill's interest in the chalet was shallow, that he had no interest in the sentiments of Rousseau or Viollet-le-Duc or cared that Switzerland was the home of the uncorrupted natural man, but it is just as likely he thought of it as a European vacation at a lower price including a stay at a chalet, that the chalet was an effective marketing device. But Hill's love for the chalet transcended his economic motivations. Despite his passion for the chalet, Hill left us few explanations for his great obsession with it. He had visited Switzerland, honeymooned there, but in his frequent comments on Switzerland his only point is that the landscape and fishing was inferior to that of Montana.

The travel writer Mary Roberts Rinehart, who worked for Hill, urged her readers to, "heed the call of the mountains," that a trip to Glacier was the way to find one's true self, to peel away the layers of civilization, to return to origins:

The veneer, after all, is so thin. Throw off the impedimenta of civilization, the telephones, the silly conventions, the lies that pass for truth. Go out to the West. ... Let the summer rains fall on your upturned face and wash away the memory of all that is false and petty and cruel. Then the mountains will get you.[8]

Hill genuinely enjoyed the rustic life of the mountains, but, as for many, the search for this authentic life was usually temporary and easily reconciled with lives that were not authentic, which dovetailed quite neatly with a one-or two-week vacation, something that was certainly true of Hill.

The obsession with Switzerland went beyond the financial potential of diverting Americans from visiting it and it had an appeal beyond sublime epiphanies and scenic monumentality. Of equal value, especially to Louis Hill, was a different image of Switzerland, less grand and more nostalgic, of Alpine meadows and hand-crafted huts, a pastoral one, less intimidating and more comforting than the monumental hotels he was to build. There was the appeal of Swiss culture itself, celebrated by writers from Wordsworth to Johanna Spyri, author of *Heidi*. This was not about the simultaneous pleasure and horror of the Alpine peak or chasm. It was about the serene Alpine landscape, the gently rolling Alpine meadow, but it was just as much, if not more, about the chalet that sat in the meadow.

We have seen in previous chapters a multitude of reasons for the chalet's popularity. Its significance in this context was as the location of the "other" alternative life.

Kirtland Cutter's original design for Hill's chalet at Belton

For some it was a recreation of a non-existent idyllic childhood as it was for Prince Albert. For others it was an opportunity for the wealthy to experience the joys of the humble life as it was for Duchess of Bedford or Lord Cahir, or it was the refuge from the urban malaise as it was for the fictional Heidi.

There is a nostalgia for a time that was better, for a place that had been lost or was about to be lost although it is an experience that is rather generic, and usually mythical, the natural life we had lost after we became overcivilized. The chalet represented a counter life, what Jackson Lears describes as the search for authentic experience that characterized this era and the chalet was the home of the authentic life. As Irene Cieraad wrote, a journey to Switzerland was a return to origins. The life in the Alpine chalet was a mechanism for finding one's true natural self, to achieve a life that is natural and uncomplicated by stripping away the veneer of civilization.[9]

The authenticity of the architecture of the chalet was seen as the result of its designer's lack of self-awareness, the absence of aesthetic intent, resulting in a perfect marriage of site, necessity and place. The Swiss were not alone in possessing this virtue. Similar cultures could produce similar results—not just the Swiss chalet built by the Alpine farmer, but the log cabin built by the pioneer, and the Native American tepee. All of these were popular vacation cabins for those seeking the authentic.

For William "Adirondack" Murray log cabins and lean-tos were not just the essence of the Adirondack experience, they were the essence of those who made them. And the guides who built them were "wise" with a wisdom nowhere written in books.

Many saw the West in the same way as the Swiss landscape. George Bird Grinnell, writes of an experience there. After asking the mountains to tell him their history queries its long-vanished inhabitants, the Piegans, in the same way:

Tell us of the people, whence they came and how the tribes were divided; what was their life in the ancient days, how did they hunt, with whom warred they? Ye have seen it all. Ye know, and if ye would reply, could solve these mysteries, but ye are silent. ... But we would know more than your history. We would know what ye have seen, what has gone on before ye. We ask in vain.[10]

The Piegans were playing the role of the Swiss for Grinnell and others—the source of indigenous wisdom. All of this architecturally represented a return to origins. In 1900 tribal cultures were seen by many as the equivalent of our own primitive ancestors. Their architecture was ours at its point of origin.

The Piegans had an obviously limited architectural vocabulary to draw on, but it got good use. There were times in the early years of the Glacier hotels when the tepees seemed to outnumber the chalets. There are more unique and less iconic examples of Piegan architecture, such as the medicine lodge structures that they were forbidden to build on the reservation, and in several instances the Piegans were brought into the park to build these. Hill's interest in Native American art was genuine, although it could be glib and stereotypical when marketing was involved. In any case something more was needed programmatically. The chalet would have to do.

Conclusion

In 1910 Louis Hill, although still chairman of the Great Northern Railroad, was spending a great deal of his time on the creation of Glacier National Park undertaking a program that would ultimately result in the building of two large lodges and at least nine small ones. He envisioned two very different experiences, so he built two very different types of hotel.

It would begin with a stay in a comfortable hotel, with fine dining and a view of the mountains. It would be followed by a second, a journey by horseback through the mountains, across the roof of America, one that would be decidedly less comfortable where the food would not be so fine, where one would be physically and emotionally challenged, where one would see as much height as one wanted and more, an escape into another life in another part of the American wilderness that remained.

The first step was a large hotel adjacent to the Great Northern tracks that would serve as the base camp for the real Glacier experience. In time another large hotel was added for the same purpose. The second phase was modeled on the Swiss hut-to-hut hiking concept, a one-to two-week backcountry trek. The prescribed route of experience at Glacier is a giant loop, a series of them, starting at the large hotels closer to the railroad then travel by horseback to a chain of smaller lodges or tent camps traversing the Continental Divide in the process. Glacier's huts were to be a one-day ride apart—some at high elevations, some closer to the lodges.

Hill's two visions of the West were not easily compatible and manifested themselves in two very different ways of experiencing it. These were thus manifested in two very different types of architecture—the monumental log temple and the domesticated log chalet. The log temple was to be a structure that would do what the Portland Forestry Building had done, an idealized space that could produce a sense of awe equal to that of a grove of fully grown Douglas-firs, filled with Native America art, even Native Americans. Beneath it all was the certainty that the landscape, the railroad, and the building were the products of inevitable forces of which Hill was only the agent.

But he also wanted the chalet in the mountains with all its association of an alternative natural life, a return to primal origins, much like his own homes.

This was a reflection of the two sides of his personality—the monument to American industry and its inevitability, and the escape from that world to a hut high in the mountains.

Piegans tepees at Logan Pass

THE AMERICAN SUBLIME

I wished for the pencil of Salvator Rosa or the pen of Thompson, that I might be enabled to give to the enlightened world some just idea of this truly magnificent and sublimely grand object, which has from the commencement of time been concealed from the view of civilized man.[1]

—Meriwether Lewis on viewing the Great Falls of the Missouri

The history of the Great Northern leaves us with the same question as the history of the Northern Pacific. How is it Louis Hill could be simultaneously engaged in the destruction of so much wilderness and the preservation of another part? How could he have been so sympathetic and supportive of Native American culture in the wake of taking so much of it away? As with Nathaniel Langford at Yellowstone, the feelings of the sublime as described above by Barbara Novak and Robert Doran offer a key.[2] It is easy to see how a sense of one's insignificance in the face of the inevitable order of nature could lead to an arrogance if one thought they were acting in its service, something particularly true of those who built railroads. It is easy to understand how a sense of awe at the magnitude of natural objects could be turned into a marketing strategy or how a sense of the unique character of the American landscape could evolve into American nationalism. Issues that are for us polar extremes—preservation versus development, the commercial versus the spiritual—were for many in the nineteenth century issues with far more fluid boundaries.

There are a number of concepts that are particular manifestations of the humility and arrogance of this version of the American sublime found in both the landscape and the architecture. The most common is magnitude. The nineteenth century-American struggling to explain the aesthetic significance of a natural phenomenon invariably resorted to dimensions. Many of the early descriptions of Yellowstone are mathematical. The Washburn expedition's first impulse on seeing Tower Fall was to measure its height. Every pinnacle and canyon, it seems, must be measured and have its immensity recorded with awe. John Muir cannot describe a sequoia without giving us not just the height and diameter but the thickness of the bark and the number of the cones (240 on one branch).[3]

A key element of what has been called scenic nationalism was to argue the equivalence of American monuments to those in Europe and thus the celebration of the mountains and canyons, the "ruins" of the West, and a key component of American superiority was magnitude. Thus the landscape of the West became not just sublime but monumental.

A second characteristic of this version of the sublime, as we have seen, was age. The redwoods were larger than any tree in Europe but they were also, many believed, older. They had witnessed history. They were American ruins, even if not human-made. It is a characteristic of the topography of Yosemite and Glacier National Parks, that the marks of their geologic history are so prominently on display. There is nothing uniquely American about landscapes of magnitude or age. We are just as likely to associate them with Switzerland, but that in fact was a reason for their appeal to Hill and others.

America in the late nineteenth century faced a problem in the area of tourism; it could not compete with Europe. It lacked the cathedral, the ruin, the romance provided by historical background at a time when only white Eurocentric history had significance. For both national pride and the economics of tourism it needed an equivalent. It needed its own monuments. The American landscape provided one, not just the American landscape but the sublime American landscape that had no European equivalent, Yellowstone and the Grand Canyon in particular. Richard White describes this as monumentalism:

The United States was a young nation lacking both an ancient history and a cultural tradition rich in art, architecture, or literature. Americans looked to scenery as compensation for the cultural riches they lacked. They hoped nature at its most monumental would provide the inspiration, the sublimity, and the glimpse of timelessness that American culture had not yet achieved. It became a matter of national pride that the new country set apart areas such as the Yosemite Valley of California or the Yellowstone country of Wyoming as symbols of national greatness.[4]

Again, the second key component of sublime monumentality was age. George Bird Grinnell described the mountains there as if they were the ruined, overgrown landscape of the Roman Forum.

Not for the first time in the aesthetics of the West, geology plays the role of ruins. The mountains, like the forest, supplied a needed history.

Besides size and age there was another significant quality of the sublime of the West. Dugald Stewart, in his 1855 essay on the sublime spoke of "primitive" sublimity that dealt with the most basic force of the universe, gravity, or more correctly, the defiance of gravity. He described the, "Feelings excited by *literal* sublimity," created by "assimilating the poetical effects of the two opposite dimensions of Depth and of Height."[5]

This version of the sublime has no better illustration than John Muir. In 1869 he stood at the edge of a cliff near the top of Yosemite Falls. While finding the view transcendent, he wrote: "I could not hope fearing a little that the rock might split off and let me down, and what a down--more than three thousand feet." The night was a different story and Muir, alternating between sleep

Thomas Moran, *Above Tower Fall*

Glacier Point, Yosemite

and dream, wrote, "again and again I dreamed that I was rushing through the air above a glorious avalanche of water and rocks ... I said this time it is real—all must die and where could mountaineer find a more glorious death."[6]

All of these aspects of the sublime produced a certain type of architecture, an architecture that also had to serve as part of a marketing strategy. It is easy to see why both Hills were taken with the Portland Forestry Building. By intention it exemplified all of these qualities. Magnitude was present in every gigantic log column. It was a literal representation of the immensity of the forest of the Northwest. It gave to many visitors a sense of the natural and divine forces that had created it, a sense of awe and our smallness in the face of it. At the same time, it gave a sense of the power of American industry that was capable of harvesting, transporting, and erecting it and a sense that it was all the inevitable result of progress.

It might have also provided an assurance that certain things were not true which in fact were, that the American forest was not unlimited, that it was perhaps not the will of God that we cut it all down with no heed for the results, and that those that did so, those that built the railroads were in many cases motivated primarily by greed and fear of their own economic collapse.

The selling of the West and the national parks required monumentalizing the landscape, but it also needed something imbued with, romantic history, to rival that of Europe. Something that would evoke nostalgia, perhaps melancholy, but not dread. Something that was not sublime but pastoral, a landscape experience that did not make one feel small. The American landscape did not just have to be monumentalized. It also had to be domesticated.

GLACIER NATIONAL PARK: THE HOTELS

Opposite: Central atrium, Glacier Park Lodge.

In February 1912 an article the *Timberman*, a journal of the Western logging industry, announced that the Great Northern Railway was going to build a replica of the Forestry Building at the Portland Exposition in Midvale, Montana.[1] Almost as an aside it mentioned that building would be used as a hotel. The building, the Glacier Park Lodge, was in fact under construction. The emphasis on the fact that it was a museum and the offhand mention that it was to be a hotel was almost certainly intentional. Louis Hill wanted to build such a replica and while he wanted to build a hotel, he also wanted to build a museum. This was Louis Hill, the master of public relations, at work

The Glacier Park Lodge was the first of several hotels to be built by the Great Northern in Glacier National Park. Adjacent to the railroad station, it was the point of departure for experiencing the park, preferably by traveling to other Great Northern hotels, but it was also a conspicuous reminder of the Great Northern's role not just in the park's creation but in the development of the West. If the American Landscape was to perform the role of the ancient monument had played in Europe, so could the architecture.

The Portland Forestry Building was a demonstration that whatever emotions could be evoked by the landscapes of the West could be evoked by its architecture. It was an architectural condensation of the great forests of the Northwest and it inspired the same kind of humility and awe in the face of the forces of nature that Novak describes—the American sublime. But if it made the visitor feel small it also presented them with the fact that the power existed to do the almost impossible—to harvest gigantic logs, move them hundreds of miles, and erect them into a gargantuan building. It was the perfect combination of spiritual epiphany and product placement, simultaneously cathedral and billboard.

Alfred Runte and Richard White argue that the monumentalization of the landscape was essential to the creation of the national parks. Hill sought to do the same with the architecture, to monumentalize it as the landscape had been monumentalized. Hill was certainly not averse to advertising the products his railroad hauled, e.g., timber, but his ultimate desire was to build a monument to the world of the Great Northern. A monument to what it had created and a memorial to what it had destroyed.

One of Hill's publicists, Mary Roberts Rinehart, wrote, "if you are willing to learn how little you count in the eternal scheme of things. ... go ride in the Rocky Mountains and save your soul."[2] A phrase no travel agent could love, but precisely the perception of the sublime Novak describes. Rinehart was writing about the landscape but she could have been talking about the lodge. It might not make you feel insignificant, but it could certainly make you feel small.

This is the rustic architecture of the monumental, and that required magnitude. There are too many columns and they are too close together but this is all necessary. Everything is excessive in the way of monumental classicism—oversized, over-designed, and superfluous in number.

Glacier Park Lodge
East Glacier, Montana, 1913

In April 1912 construction began and it was construction that defied classification. The new hotel was to be built of solid logs five feet in diameter and 40 feet tall. It is less a cathedral and more a temple with the bark on. It was not an architecture of layers and nailed on motifs. It was solid.

The oversized logs greatly complicated the process. There was an assumption in the beginning that logs of adequate size could be found locally. After much searching and discussion, it was decided to purchase them from the Pacific Fir Company and to haul them the 500 miles from Aberdeen Washington—a western terminus of the Hill-controlled Northern Pacific Railroad and a major port for shipping timber.[3] It may be that trees were unavailable in adequate size locally, or that they were dispersed and inaccessible and could not be easily transported to the site. It was not just that there were plenty of large logs in the coast, but there was an infrastructure there to harvest and move them to the railroad.

The plan is a long, extended hip-roofed H shape. Inside is a long hall the height of the building holding 60 gargantuan log columns suggesting a Roman basilica built of logs. They are Corinthian in a proportion with a ratio of 1:10, but Ionic, rather rustic Ionic, in detail. Here as elsewhere everything is oversized. The 60 40-feet high columns are old growth Douglas-fir trunks. They had the authority of age as well—estimated at 300 to 800 years old when they were cut.

Like a classical temple its effect is the result of freestanding columns. When you look at a temple you do not see walls but columns in front of walls. The log columns at Glacier, both interior and exterior, had to stand free of the building envelope. The edge of the third floor is pulled back from the columns inside and out, and walls rarely touch them.

Section looking west

East elevation

The characteristics of the monumental rustic find their way into the details. The balcony railings are classical forms—two squares with X's connected by horizontals but made of small logs. But on the whole there are few small elements. There is no small classical order as might be found in a Renaissance building. Everything is large.

Later national park architects would understandably try to minimize the size, mass, and particularly the height of their buildings for fear of competing with the landscape, and they would certainly avoid the excessive quantity of material used at the lodge, which not only had gigantic columns but far more than structurally necessary. Louis Hill directed his architect to the contrary. He was building a monument and gravitas required great size, weight, and number. Hill proclaimed that the building had the greatest frontage of any hotel and that it was only 125 feet shorter than the US Capitol. It is actually only about three quarters of the capitol length but it was important to Hill to believe otherwise.[4]

The Forestry Building was largely classical on the interior and largely Swiss on the exterior. At the lodge the classical dominates on the exterior as well. The exterior of the Forestry Building had been giant logs, laid up in the traditional fashion. That was the original intent for the Glacier Park Lodge, but at the same time it was decided to bring in logs from the Northwest it was decided the exterior would be shingles on studs. It became less of a chalet and more of a temple. Samuel Bartlett, the architect, classicized the exterior into a vernacularized baroque arcade. Again, as in a Greek temple, the columns stand free of the walls. The wall is recessed to make it appear an open arcade. The exterior columns are peeled cedar, smaller than the interior Douglas-fir columns, but still large at 35 feet. The steeply sloped roof has a long dormer to lower the eave to hide the hotel rooms on the exterior and emphasize the columns in front.

The Swiss elements where they exist are subdued. There are pediments at each end and at the projections on each side of the long elevations. Swiss gables are used only at the short ends. There is none of the Swiss gingerbread found in later hotels at Glacier.

The exterior order

The interior order

Lodge seen from train station

Columns on flat car in foreground. Central columns of lodge at rear.

The structure is of three types of timber that corresponded roughly to three types of construction. There were three sources of timber as well. First there were the logs. Much of the lumber was transported by railroad to Glacier—the large logs from the forest of Oregon and Washington through Aberdeen, some of the largest trees on the North American continent. Getting them to the site was one problem. Getting them erected was another. But the railroad was nearby and cranes on flatcars were brought in to lift the columns.

There was a second system, still monumental, of large timbers but sawn into large rectilinear lumber as big as 12x20 inches, exposed as well, used in the lobby spaces with low ceilings. And there was a third, studs and joints, that frame the large blocks of hotel rooms that were largely hidden. The lumber for the second and third systems was milled at local mills or from the Great Northern's own mill at Somers 100 miles to the west, but like the site, directly connected to the track. Ironically, the industrial frame is local: the rustic log frame is imported.

The Glacier Park Lodge has a constructional straightforwardness and integrity not all that common in the rustic architecture of the time. There are no half-log wall facings, no sawmill lumber faced with log veneer, no deceptive structural elements.

There is not much that is indigenous in methodology or materials in the lodge. It is no less a product of the machine age as Albert Kahn's Packard plant in Detroit, under construction at the same time. And there is a whole other building inside the Glacier Park Lodge that is not logs but lumber. Like the Old Faithful Inn this was a new American architecture, a "enduring and distinguishing survival," as Frederick Turner would say. Whatever vernacular elements and techniques it embodies, Its great size and the size of its components proclaim the technology and the power of the railroad at its most conspicuous.

It is telling that rather late in the process Hill made an attempt to involve Robert Reamer in the design. In February of 1912 Hill invited Reamer to visit him in St. Paul. Probably because the design was too far advanced, or perhaps because Hill preferred working with Samuel Bartlett, the architect of record and his "house" architect, Hill decided against the idea. But the larger issue is that what Reamer had done at the Old Faithful Inn was foreign to Hill's vision of the Glacier Park Hotel.[5] The Old Faithful Inn is built of small logs that are not much larger than a person. There is an anthropomorphic scale, a humanism in the Old Faithful Inn not found in the Forestry Building or the Glacier Park Lodge. The essence of Glacier Park was elements much larger than the human body. The language of the Old Faithful Inn has the anthropomorphic qualities of a high renaissance building. The language of the Glacier Park Lodge is monumental baroque classicism. It aimed for the power the massive oversized baroque era embodied, what Heinrich Wölfflin described as "a search for the intimidating."[6]

The building was finished but Hill was only halfway there. The museum remained. Gravitas required not just magnitude; it required history, here provided by the Native Americans and their campfire. A 1912 newspaper article written prior to completion described Hill's vision for the hall:

An open campfire, built in the center or the lobby upon a huge stone, 16x16 feet. A large hood which hangs down over the lobby campfire will carry the smoke up a mammoth chimney. The glow from the burning logs will light the lobby nights. Indian tepees pitched in corners of the spacious lobby will be used as card and tea rooms. ... Two canoes are to be suspended from the high timbered lobby ceiling. Indian boys wearing buckskin clothing and moccasins will glide noiselessly through the building as "bell hops" and Indian maidens will be the chamber maids.[7]

Like the Old Faithful Inn, it was to have an indoor campfire, but in this case a Native American one. In an odd way Albert Bierstadt's painting *Giant Redwood Trees of California* showing a group of Native Americans dwarfed by a gigantic grove of trees which they inhabit, was realized.

An open fire pit was placed at one end of the hall. Suspended above it was hood connected to a 50-foot-tall metal chimney. A small log hut housing a movie projector hung beside it. A hundred-year-old Buffalo skin "council" tepee, with the fur still on, was placed nearby. The vision was only partially realized.

So Hill, whose father had played a role in the great Piegan land grabs of 1887 and 1895 and who had himself overseen the smaller swindle of 1912 that gave him the site for the hotel, wanted to build something between a museum and a ruin that evoked not just nature but the past—a vision of a lost America. During his lifetime Louis Hill was praised for his very real support, employment, and artistic patronage of the Piegans. Today he is criticized for his exploitation of them and his appropriation of their culture. Hovering above it all is his probable belief in the historical inevitability of the Great Northern and its consequences.

Over time the fire-pit and tepee disappeared but Hill's vision for the museum had already begun to extend far beyond the Piegans.

In 1913, as the building neared completion, Hill contacted Frederick C. Frobese, a Seattle-based "scholar and artist" to both collect and make copies of Native American art particularly totem poles. Obviously Hill was thinking of housing Native American artifacts beyond what the Piegans might provide and Frobese fueled this idea. He wrote to Hill in January 1913:

I would like to make part of this lobby into a veritable museum [with]. ... 4 very large totems, a couple of ancient Haida War canoes decorated with many totem ... and carved bears ... some warriors with their curious and fantastic armor of ancient Haida Pattern, a specimen of an Orca whale[8]

The war canoe never materialized but the lobby concept was expanded into a museum to link to the larger world of the Great Northern, including the Pacific coast. Frobese made six totem poles copied from Haida originals. This was cultural appropriation, but Frobese argued that he was authorized to make them since they were the family totems of his father-in-law. Hill was unconcerned with cultural appropriation in any case and ordered seven more poles from the Hudson Bay store in Seattle. His vision extended well beyond the West Coast. He added 36 Chinese lanterns plus Chinese hats he had bought in San Francisco. They are the finishing touches in this monument to the unstoppable force that was America and the Great Northern Railroad.

This melange was essentially the world of the Great Northern, representing their markets from America to Asia. Providence had provided the means for the Great Northern to connect to the Pacific and expand economically in the process, but the Hills saw no reason they should stop there. The markets of Asia waited. This is what Roderick Nash calls the dream of the "Passage to India."[9] Roughly put, it meant that the economic future of the US was not just to grow to the coast, but to keep going, to Japan and China, to complete the vision of Columbus.

The Glacier Park Lodge opened in July 1913. If there was any doubt as to the impulses that created it they were clarified two months later when James J. Hill's 75th birthday was celebrated there, and they were celebrating far more than a birthday. Two hundred veterans of the Great Northern's construction were brought by train to dine in the great hall where they were served by waiters and waitresses dressed in Native American clothes. What better symbol, or manifestation for that matter, could be found of what Hill had done for the railroad and to America.[10]

Glacier Park Lodge was the product of the Louis Hill that was the always dedicated and sometimes ruthless president of the Great Northern, an agent of larger forces of progress and their consequences. This Hill suggests an attitude toward the West resembling the phenomenon that Novak and Doran describe—humble in the face of the Western landscape while arrogant in one's awareness that it was their destiny to change it.

A group of tourists and Piegans gathered around the fire pit—a posed photograph

View of the opposite end of the hall showing the Buffalo Council Tepee.

Glacier Park Lodge
Wall Section

The interior Douglas-fir columns support the roof framing of 10-inch and 12-inch log rafters spaced at 4 feet 6 inches.

The framing of the hotel rooms themselves is almost completely concealed and built entirely of milled lumber.

Floors are 2x12 joists and interior walls are 2x6 studs, all spaced at 16 inches. Ceilings and wall finish are Sackett (gypsum) board.

There are large exposed milled beams at first floor ceiling. The hotel room wing above is supported by exposed 12x16 squared sawmill timbers.

The balcony railing here, like other details in the hotel, is rustic 6-inch round bark-on logs in the form of a classical railing rather than Swiss gingerbread used in later hotels.

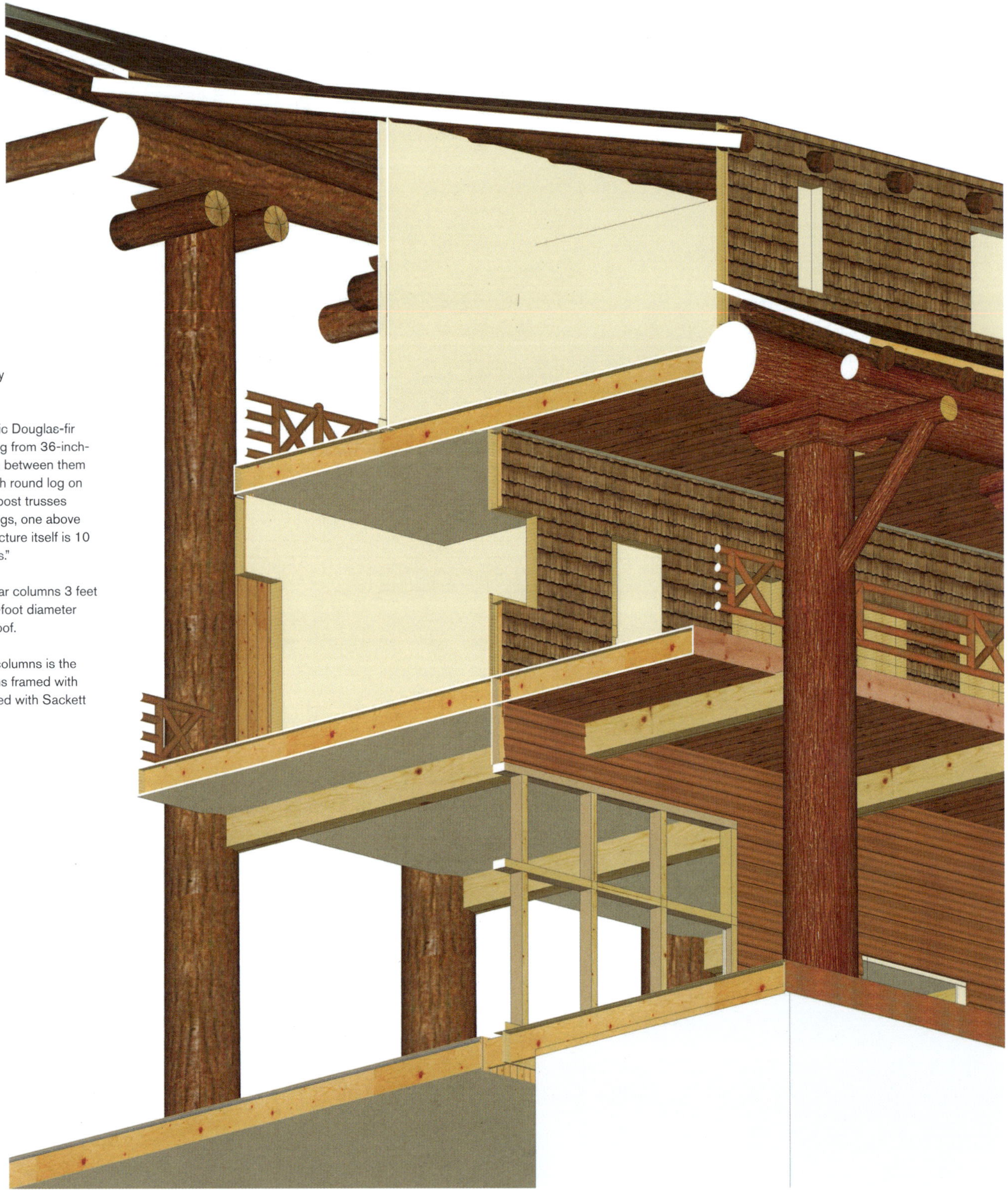

Glacier Park Lodge
Wall Section

The main frame is massively over-structured.

Interior columns are gigantic Douglas-fir trunks 38 feet high, tapering from 36-inches to 22.-inches. Spanning between them is the entablature, a 36-inch round log on which sits a series of kimgpost trusses made of 18" and10-inch logs, one above each column. The roof structure itself is 10 inch and 12-inch log rafters."

At the exterior 22-foot cedar columns 3 feet in diameter, topped by a 3-foot diameter beam, support the porch roof.

Between the two rows of columns is the 4-story block of hotel rooms framed with studs and joists and covered with Sackett (gypsum) board.

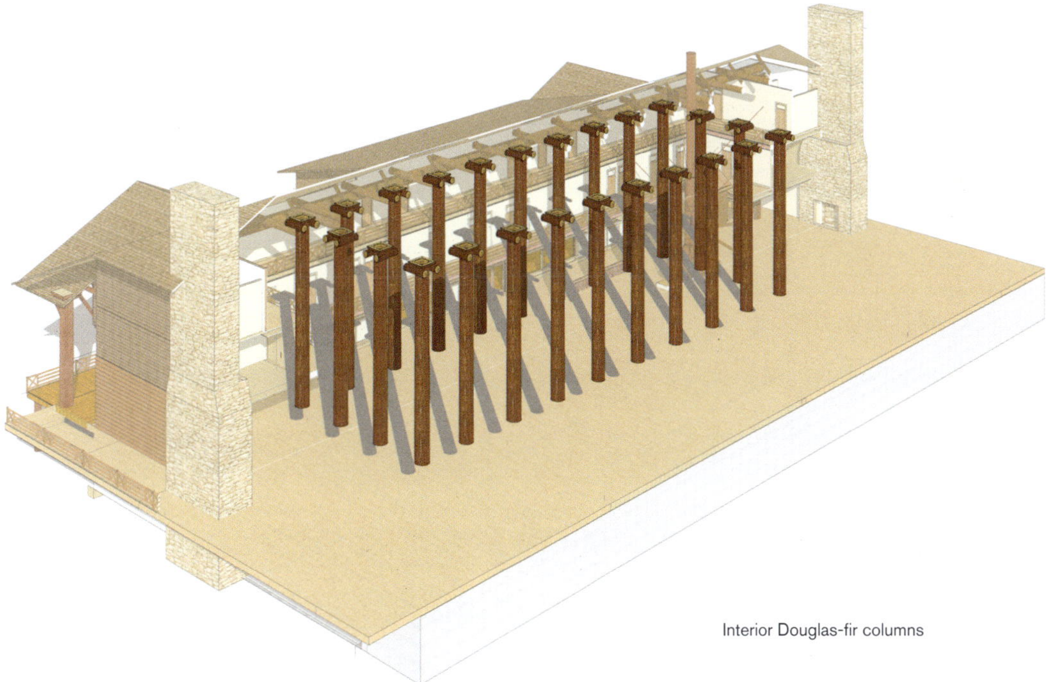

Interior Douglas-fir columns

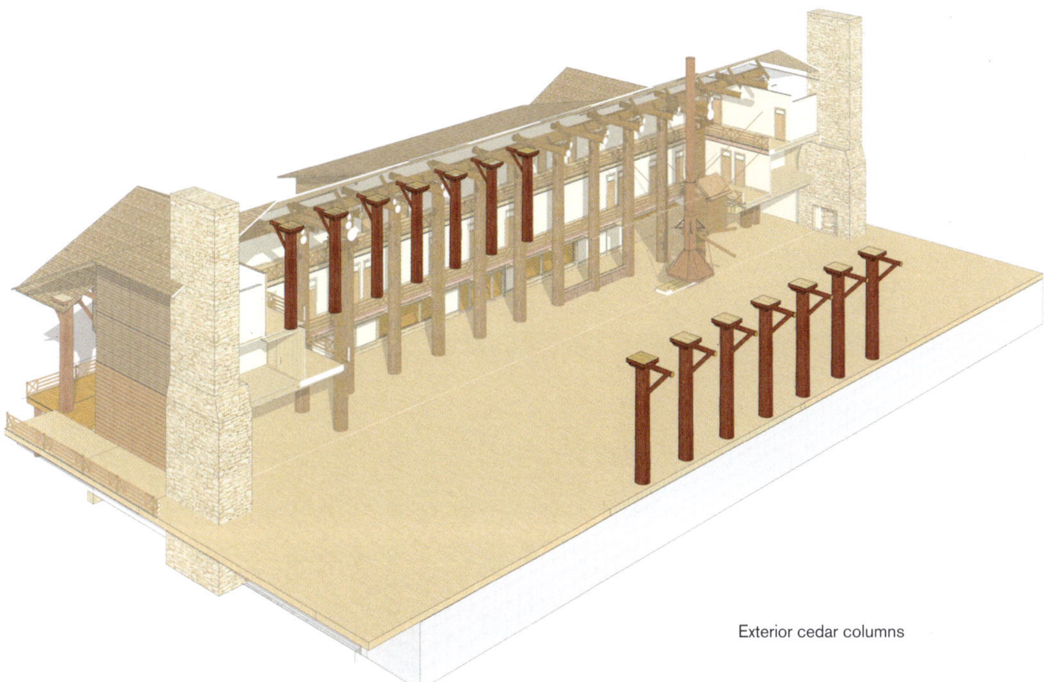

Exterior cedar columns

The Belton Chalet
East Glacier MT, 1911

Work began immediately on an extension to the Glacier Park Lodge, far less classical and far more Swiss than the original. It was a harbinger of what was to come, another side of Louis Hill was simultaneously at work on the other side of the park.

Two years before work began on the Glacier Park Lodge, 50 miles to the west, in Belton on the western edge of Glacier National Park, Louis Hill completed a house for his family, a chalet. This was about the time he announced he was moving to Montana. In a way Hill did move to Montana, though not as dramatically as he implied, spending his summers there. But in any case he did not stay long at the Belton Chalet and it became one of his many hotels. Hill was clearly more engaged with his chalets than the typical Adirondack millionaire. There was the Louis Hill who had become president of the Great Northern in 1907 that had pursued his role with enthusiasm and purpose, and when the occasion demanded could be no less ruthless than his father, the one who built the Glacier Park Lodge. This was the other side of Louis Hill—the avid fisherman, the passionate hunter, the dedicated landscape painter, the lover of the wilderness trek, the one who wanted to escape from an overcivilized world, who wanted to move to Montana and live in a chalet, who wished to escape from his real life to a place of nostalgic imaginary origins. Perhaps these were fragments of a larger "other," the other life he might have led, the other person he might have become.

Hill looked at chalet architecture in depth. He wrote to a St. Paul bookshop asking for the best volumes on the subject and obtained Gladbach's and Varin's encyclopedic and highly technical works.[11] But his interpretation of what he saw could be quite shallow, and often so was the architecture, consisting of a thin layer of motifs rather than integral form. It was a language of association in which ornaments overlaid a construction, in which a correspondence of structural representation and structural reality was often absent. The chalet did not manifest the values associated with it; it simply represented them.

The two Louis Hills produced two architectures, on the eastern side of the park, the monumental gravitas of the giant forest of the Glacier Park Lodge. On the west the nostalgic, melancholic domesticity, the return to origins, of the Belton Chalet. The two were soon to appear simultaneously in the buildings that followed at Glacier.

Left: Corner detail at roof bracket

Right: Detail at false-log corner

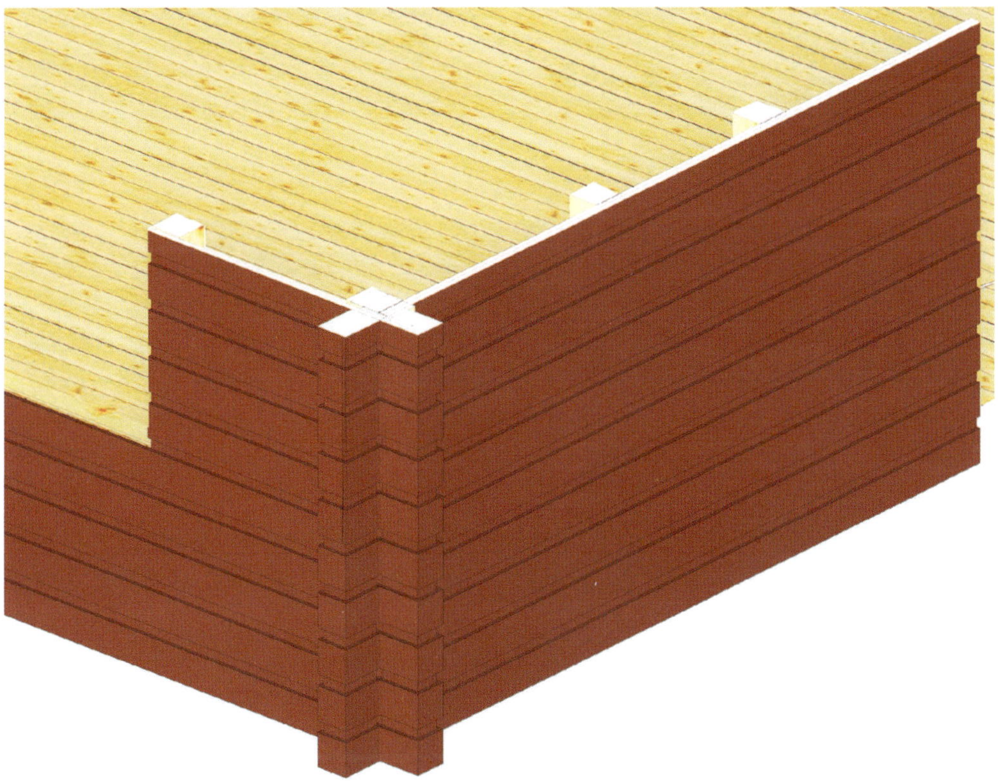

Cutter's false-log corner detail
North Point Camp
Raquette Lake, NY

An example of Cutter's false-log corner detail, also used at the Belton Chalet.

It is a severe misfit between image and reality, Making a wood stud wall with siding appear to be a Swiss type squared-log cabin. What appears to be overlapping and interlocking log ends is a single piece of timber.

Entry to the Hotel before the addition of the canopy

Many Glacier Hotel
Glacier National Park, 1914-1917

Meanwhile at the eastern park boundary, the Park Service wanted a larger hotel deeper into the park, to the north of the Glacier Park Lodge at Swiftcurrent Lake. George Bird Grinnell, editor of *Forest and Stream*, had popularized the Swiftcurrent Pass Valley on the east side of the park as a tourist destination and Swiftcurrent Valley at its lower end was an obvious location for a hotel, in the mountains but accessible from the plains. Hill had planned a hotel there as early as 1909, and in 1914-1915 he built the central portion and an annex was added in 1917. This was the most remote of the large hotels. The railroad was 40 miles to the south. What was critically different constructionally was the location. It was equally dependent on the railroad for construction, but in comparison with the Glacier Park Lodge it was difficult to access. It was not at a high elevation but it was much deeper into the park and much farther from the railroad and without adequate roads. The architect of record was Thomas McMahon but Hill was in many ways his own architect. He was a micromanager in his relationships with his architects, and he wanted them close at hand. He admired the Portland Forestry Building and he borrowed the plans during the design of Glacier Park, but he did not hire its architects. Hill interviewed Robert Reamer for the Glacier Park Lodge but decided not to use him. Kirtland Cutter was master of the rustic chalet and Hill hired him at least twice and fired him at least once, but Hill preferred to work with architects in St. Paul who were regularly used by the Great Northern—Samuel Bartlett and Thomas McMahon. McMahon designed the first version of the Many Glacier Hotel and the last, but in between Hill brought in Cutter to modify the designs. Cutter left the project before its completion but he left his mark as is evident in the similarities to the Lake McDonald Lodge, which Cutter did design.

Ray Djuff said that one reason Hill dispensed with Cutter's services is that he thought Cutter was not using enough Swiss details.[12] Given the quantity of Swiss details in his other work this seem odd, but as we have seen for Cutter there were two types of Swiss detail—the literal details, those made with jigsaw cut profiled boards and there were rustic details based on literal details but made of logs. There is very little of the first type at Many Glacier Hotel; there is a multitude of the second.

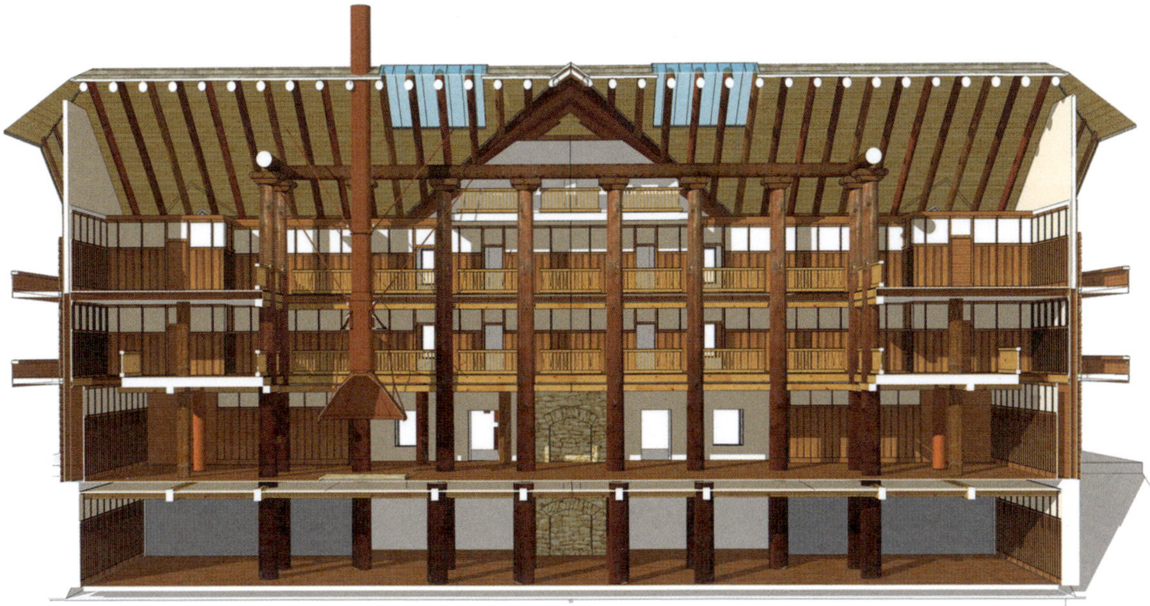

Section looking east

Lake elevation

Many Glacier Lodge Wall Section

It is far more refined and finished and far less rustic with far fewer logs that the Glacier Park Lodge.

The courtyard frame is smaller than the Glacier Park Lodge and framed with peeled logs,

It is built of log 48-foot columns tapering from 36-inch to 18-inch-22-inch logs.

There is a 22-inch log beam entablature on top of the columns running along the long side of the atrium supporting 12-inch horizontal logs, one at each column, that connects to every third 12-inch log roof rafter to form trusses.

The roof is 2-inch tongue and groove boards on 12-inch log rafters 4 feet on center.

The interior walls are 2x6 studs covered with Sackett (gypsum) board and wood paneling.

The floor construction is 2x12 floor joists with a Sackett board ceiling with an exposed 10x10 milled beam at the edge.

Unlike the Glacier Park Lodge, the balcony railing is boards in Swiss profiles, not logs.

There are two interlocking systems of form, language of symbols and means of construction, but the Many Glacier Hotel is far more the chalet and far less the log temple. There is a degree of monumentalism—a central log hall in the spirit of the Forestry Building. But there are also elements of the chalet, typically manifested in exterior ornament. The hotel was to establish the sublime, gravitas, and size of the rustic classical on the one hand and the smaller scale domestic/nostalgic Swiss features on the other. There is a large, monumental log hall but smaller than the Glacier Park Lodge. The Many Glacier Hotel is not just less rustic, it is more refined. The plan consists of four separate pavilions in a chain along the lake—some of the pavilions are rigidly symmetrical, others awkwardly composed and haphazardly joined. The first and third of the four wings from the west are simply blocks of rooms. The key components are the main lobby, the second in the chain, and the dining wing, the last.

The second, the entry/lobby pavilion, is a concentric plan in which a central hall of log columns following the Roman temple model of the Glacier Park Lodge, is surrounded by a wood stud-framed block. It is crossed by a central axis of circulation entered from the land side and marked on the front facade by a central fireplace and the broad symmetrical front gable. The procession begins at the entry on either side of the fireplace on the entry side, extends through the log hall and ends at a terrace overlooking the lake.

The hall is smaller than that of the Glacier Park Lodge. The columns are not quite so big—four stories tall, 36 inches at base, and 18 inches at top. The width of the space is the same but the length is only seven bays in contrast to the Glacier Park Lodge's 12. The columns resemble the Ionic of the Glacier Park Lodge. They are peeled, however, perhaps because they could not be harvested in the winter, a requirement for keeping the bark, perhaps because the bark was damaged in transit. There were other factors. The Many Glacier Hotel is the most literally Swiss, the most refined of the hotels at Glacier, and it was to be the most elegant with little or no bark. The railing infill panels are not small logs but Swiss thin flat boards with cut out profiles.

The log hall is surrounded by the platform framed block of the larger building. That platform frame is largely concealed but there is a heavy timber frame in the corridor around the hall to transition between the two and the round log beams in the surrounding corridor transition to square profiles. But this is the extent of the rustic. Of the three hotels it uses the fewest unmilled logs—only in the central hall and two vestibules.

Internally the theme is again Native Americans in the ruins of the forest, but with more authenticity. The open pit fireplace with hood is repeated at the end of the log axis of the hall—a rather high-tech one. A proto-modernist stair is located at the opposite end. The hall contained a smaller but probably better museum. Hill's understanding and use of Native American culture and art could be glib and his use of it exploitive, but here he demonstrated a deeper engagement. A pictographic tradition had been started among the Piegans. Medicine Owl and 11 other Piegans were asked to create a kind of individual graphic autobiography. The result was a mural canvas of Blackfoot history 180 feet long. A second mural was placed in the Dining Hall. The "museum" is not as broad in its subject matter but various types of Japanese paraphernalia are located throughout the lobby, more reminders that the Great Northern literally had its eye on the horizon.

View of roof from main lobby

Many Glacier Hotel
Wall Section

If the Glacier Park Lodge is about classic rusticity, the Many Glacier Hotel is about Swiss refinement.

Interior walls are 2x6 studs and 2x12 joists with 10x10-inch milled beams at the balcony edge Sackett board (gypsum board) form the ceilings and wall finish with wood paneling in the corridors.

The exterior walls are 2x6 studs with 1x12 siding 9-1/2-inch to weather on studs.

There is a multitude of Swiss paraphernalia in the exterior- the profiled balcony railings and brackets, the elaborate profiles in the boards around the windows and the trim at the string course.

Opposite:
Details of facade facing lake

Many Glacier Hotel Dining Room

The most complex and intriguing of the four pavilions of the Many Glacier Hotel, and a highly eccentric one, is the last, the Dining Hall. The industrial technology made accessible by the railroad is implicit in the gigantic logs of the Glacier Park Lodge. They could not have been moved, let alone erected without it. In the Dining Hall of the Many Glacier Hotel the industrial technology is on display. The truss in the Dining Hall has the quality of a tensegrity structure composed of logs in compression and exposed steel cables in tension. There is a similarity in detail to the steel trusses used by the Great Northern at stations, sheds, and other building throughout the West, and since A. H. Hogeland, the chief engineer for Great Northern, was also in charge of park construction it was a connection easily made. In the dining room the technological of railroad engineering is quite explicitly demonstrated down to the cables and bolts.

In1910 Robert Reamer had used a similar timber and cable truss for the lobby of the Yellowstone Canyon Hotel. The trusses are visible; they are the principal feature of the room but what one sees is the wood casing that encases the real truss, hiding the cables and presenting the appearance of a traditional wood truss. Rustic architects had been using cables for years, usually hidden. Cutter was to do so at Lake McDonald. At the Many Glacier Hotel, they were finally exposed.

It is a building that is both highly original and terribly confused, in terms of form. An open trellis runs along the wall below the truss next to the windows as if to domesticate the high-tech truss above. It suggests an ambivalence about the radical technological departure. The Dining Room roof structure was covered with a suspended ceiling in 1937, supposedly for acoustic reasons but one suspects it was far too dissonant a technological intrusion for a Swiss hotel. It has been removed.

Details of wood and steel cable truss

Lake facade

While the log frame is solid, the facade of the outer building holding the rooms is Swiss veneer on a structural frame of milled studs and joists. This is the most refined of Hill's buildings at Glacier. Here the monumental and even the rustic are suppressed to highlight the Swiss connection. Everything that was rustic before is now Swiss. The Many Glacier Hotel was not a return to origins, it was a return to Switzerland.

All gables that were pediments at Glacier Park Lodge are now the Swiss jerkinhead type. Elements that were round logs with the bark on in previous buildings are here made from rectilinear boards with elaborate jigsaw profiled Swiss-style cut outs on barge boards and rafter ends, window trim and door jambs. Swiss-style balcony rails inside and out and Swiss-style balcony brackets that support them. At the same time there is a precision in craft here that is missing in Glacier Park Lodge.

In these parts of the building the dominance of the chalet is complete. The Swiss paraphernalia is multiplying. There are Swiss waiter and waitress costumes and a red cross and shield of Switzerland on every door. The monumental hall with its giant logs is getting smaller. The bark is gone altogether and the craft is becoming more precise.

The timber came from two very different sources. Again, the most rustic elements, the logs, were shipped by rail from Washington and Oregon, then hauled the 40-mile, five-day wagon trip from the tracks to the site. Many other building components made the same journey. The most industrial, the studs and joists, came from the park. The industrialization of the Swiftcurrent Valley was underway by 1911. Timber for milled lumber was cut in the park at Grinnell Lake further west into the mountains. The logs were floated down Lake Josephine to a new sawmill next to the hotel. In this case Hill built the sawmill. There were thus at least two sawmills in the park by 1914 and the railway was cutting about one million board feet of timber annually for construction purposes in the park.[13]

But if Hill had lost interest in the monumental, he had not abandoned the rustic, as was clear from other construction going on in the park.

The Many Glacier Hotel and the Glacier Park Lodge were points of departure for something far more truly rustic in every sense—a horseback trip to the wilderness, to the American Alps, and Hill was in the process of completing a series of backcountry chalets. Two of them, St. Mary's and Going to the Sun Lodge, were on St. Mary Lake, 10 miles to the south of the Many Glacier Hotel. The sites are not dissimilar to the Many Glacier Hotel but the experience was and so was the architecture. Neither was a large full-service lodge and the stay there would be less comfortable and more challenging. Both are built entirely of logs and abound in rustic details. They are all logs probably because they were part of the back-country experience of the park. Construction returned to origins.

The Many Glacier Hotel by contrast was the luxury hotel where the vacation would not be arduous and the architecture would be polished. The image of the chalet was a marketing strategy—it was an indication of comfort. In simple terms it was the luxury hotel and the architecture was more refined. It is also the most glib. Industrial construction covered with Swiss paraphernalia and symbolism.

Did this preference for the Swiss in architecture reflect a change in Louis Hill's view of the West? Perhaps because the Many Glacier Hotel is farther from the railroad and closer to the mountains, perhaps because time had passed since James J. Hill's death, Louis felt, having memorialized his father and the Great Northern, he could move on.

Louis Hill built one last hotel, just across the Canadian border from Glacier National Park. It is copied from a book in Hill's library of chalets, High House at Wolfenschiessen, published in Gladbach's *Der Schweizer Holzstil*. The chalet image has become dominant and the log monumentality of the Forestry building is gone. There are no logs, only sawn squared up timbers. It is the pure chalet. Nothing is rustic.

Prince of Wales Hotel, Waterton National Park, Alberta, 1927

THE GLACIER PARK CHALETS: INTO THE WILDERNESS

In 1884 the parts of Theodore Roosevelt's private life seemed to be falling into place. He was living in New York with his wife Alice, who was pregnant with their first child, and his mother. Two days after the baby was born, both his wife and his mother died within hours of each other. The popular version of Roosevelt's life is that, grief stricken, he left his home, his fledgling political career, and his only daughter for the Badlands of North Dakota where he began a cattle ranch and where he stayed for almost two years, and that he returned a new man, remarried, resumed his political career with a vengeance, and reentered history. He came to consider it as the defining moment of his life without which he would not have been president.[1]

Reality is a bit more complex. His retreat to the desert was at least in part a political exile. His longest stay in the Badlands was only four months and he made frequent trips to New York between in pursuit of his political ambitions. His memoir, written even before his wilderness sojourn was over, is filled with misleading descriptions and falsehoods.

Roosevelt if not a day-to-day stockman, made a point of rolling up his sleeves and doing his part or at least putting on a show of doing his part when there was manual labor to be done, and this included building a new cabin "Elkhorn." Hewn (squared) cottonwood logs formed the walls, and Roosevelt did his part, cutting logs but producing less than half of the number each of his companions did. After two days he left them to finish the job, it seems to the satisfaction of all concerned. Like most rustic cabins of the West "built from local materials" it was no less an industrialized product. Elkhorn required 16,000 board feet of milled lumber, mostly for the roof deck, rafters, floor, floor joists, interior partitions, and windows, all of which had to be shipped the 500 miles by rail from Minneapolis to Medora, then brought by wagon, one assumes, the 35 miles to Elkhorn. Roosevelt described the 60-foot-long covered porch at Elkhorn:

From the low, long veranda, shaded by leafy cotton-woods, one looks across sand-bars and shallows to a strip of meadowland, behind which rises a line of sheer cliffs and grassy plateaus. ... The story-high house of hewn logs is clean and neat, with many rooms so that one can be alone if one wishes to.[2]

The accuracy of his observations here are remarkable given that the time it was written the cabin was not finished, let alone the porch. Roosevelt simply made it up. But we should not be too hard on Roosevelt. He was not so much living a lie as acting out an ancient ritual—the wilderness as a test, a trial to be endured and overcome. Like Moses, Elijah, and Christ, he went into the wilderness to face his demons and was reborn.

This is the primitivism of self-discovery, the trial that must be endured. Roosevelt was constructing a narrative of his life which required a certain degree of editing, if not factual invention.

Opposite: Granite Park Chalet, Glacier National Park

Elkhorn Cabin

Horseback party with Grinnell Glacier and the Garden Wall beyond, 1932

Philip Terrie writes that the "trial" was an essential part of the Adirondack experience. It might have begun as a spiritual sublime meditation but it became a test, physical and mental, even a trial.

[It was a] part of a growing cult of recreation, exercise, and health. The Adirondacks—and similar wilderness retreats throughout the United States—moved from being the home of God to being the place where, the dominant culture declared, men from the elite and middle classes developed the muscles, self-reliance, and independence needed for success.[3]

For many the visit to Yellowstone was an adventure, and in the early days it was. For David Clary it was "the romantic era of the park who reveled in the luxury of 'new' things, who really felt as they wandered through this fascinating region that they were treading virgin soil." A visitor to Yellowstone wrote in 1882, "How great has been our privilege to follow so closely the trail of the Indian and the pioneer."[4] So in the early days a trip west was an adventure, a chance to escape the ordinary for the challenging, allowing for some imagination, to reenact the great adventure of the West. Given the widespread desire for authentic experience, given the railroads' need to use that demand as a marketing strategy, how was the solitary trial in the wilderness to be accomplished? A large part of the answer was to be provided by another resident of Medora, ND, Roosevelt's friend and neighbor, Howard Eaton, who had already begun to market Roosevelt's wilderness trial as a commodity.

In 1879, four years before Roosevelt's arrival in Medora, Howard Eaton came there from Pittsburgh and established the Custer Trail Ranch. One year later the Northern Pacific railroad arrived in Medora, and with it an alternative business. He captured deer, elk, and buffalo and shipped them to zoos and private menageries in the East. In 1882 he started taking guests on hunting trips, but also offering the simulated cowboy life—range riding, roping, and roundups. Eaton did not invent the concept of the dude ranch, but he did invent the term for the advertisements he placed in eastern newspapers. The simple fact is that Eaton was taking the Roosevelt experience—the Western trial, the tempering of character—and mass marketing it to the middle class.

In 1883, the year Roosevelt bought his ranch, Howard started taking pack trips to Yellowstone National Park and introduced longer tours to the Grand Canyon as well. But the completion of the Great Northern Railroad farther north opened another market.

Dudes: West Glacier Montana, 1915

Five years after Glacier National Park opened, Eaton arranged a 300-mile horseback trip through the eastern side of the park, and set up something like a celebrity cruise with the well-known mystery writer Mary Roberts Rinehart, Three Bears, a Piegan chief, and the artist Charley Russell. A party of 42 tourists supported by two wagons and 33 horses left West Glacier and headed east toward the continental divide. Eaton's party stayed only in the tents that they brought with them. No promotional opportunity went unexplored. In addition to movies and publicity photographs Rinehart published *Through Glacier Park: Seeing America First with Howard Eaton.*

Converting the Roosevelt experience—the test of the wilderness—into a marketable commodity required some discretion of course. How it can be acted out, if it can be acted out, in a context of mass tourism seems a dumb question of course. It can't. It was Eaton's job to determine how many tests and how much trial a tourist could undergo in four weeks. And it was Rinehart's job to convince the tourist that this was a good idea.

The trip was to be transformative, a kind of ordeal to mold character, a trial to establish one's worth. Rinehart's memoir details how each day involved some challenging task to be accomplished, some obstacle to be overcome involving horses, mountainous trails, scarcity of resources, and lack of physical stamina, but each obstacle is overcome with resulting sense of accomplishment. She wrote:

That 's what it is, partly. A sense of achievement; of conquering the unconquerable; of pitting human wits against giants and winning—a sporting chance. ... But you are doing this thing yourself. Every mile is an achievement.[5]

Travelers are assured, however, that it is all perfectly safe: "And, after all, it is miraculously easy. ... It is a triumph of endurance rather than of courage. If you have got it his far, you are one of us, and you will go on." After several weeks they emerged as new men and new women, as Roosevelt had emerged from his:

As the days went on there was a subtle change in the party. Women, who had to be helped into their saddles sat the beginning of the trip, swung into them easily. Waistbands were looser, eyes were clearer; we were tanned; we were calm with the large calmness of the great outdoors, and with each succeeding day the feeling of achievement grew.[6]

This was a variation in this wilderness test, one that was about altitude. It was about the sublime and intimidating but at the same time empowering experience of mountaintops. Their pack-trip had a destination, the Triple Divide, where the watersheds of the Atlantic, Pacific, and Hudson's Bay meet: "I shall never forget my joy at reaching the summit and the horror that followed when I found I was on a rocky wall about twenty feet wide which dropped a half-mile straight down on the other side to a perfectly good blue lake."[7] This involved another test of will—heights: "A pass is not an opening but a barrier which you climb with chills and descend with prayer. A pass is a thing which you try to forget at the time and which you boast about when you get back home."[8]

The rise of eighteenth-century ideas of aesthetics coincided with the rise of an idea that before the Enlightenment had been all but unthinkable, that the Alps were beautiful, but in a sublime way, which meant pleasure but with strong elements of awe, humility, fear, and empowerment. Robert MacFarlane in his study of the aesthetics of mountains speaks of the phenomenon of elevation,

What really elevated the cultivated mind in the second half of the century was elevation. ...As a concept it coincided perfectly with the Romantic glorification of the individual. A summit was somewhere one could stand out—could be outstanding. The mountain-top also provided an icon for the Romantic ideal of liberty: what could more obviously embody freedom and openness?[9]

The phenomenon of experiencing elevation contained not just the idea of a challenge but real danger, and that is what many early Alpine tourists were after. In the case of Switzerland, it gave rise to the passion for mountaineering, which was truly dangerous. MacFarlane writes: "More and more people began to expose themselves to the pleasures—and the dangers—of height, and the notion of a summit as a goal in itself began to emerge." So elevation was yet another test, but one not limited to mountain climbers:

The difference between those who died on the mountains, those who took a Thomas Cook tour to the Alps and those who merely read about mountains or gazed at their representations was one of degree and not one of kind. ... There was a near-perfect marriage between the attention-seeking mountaineers and the ascension-seeking public.[10]

The Glacier Experience

Louis Hill clearly saw the experience of the American West, particularly the mountains, like the experience of the Alps, as a test, a trial that led to strength. He wrote to a Boy Scout Leader in 1923 who had just led a group through the Park, "they learned to care for themselves and their horses like real old timers, and to live in the open without trimmings. The development of those youngsters in hardihood, self-reliance, and physique was delightful to see."[11] The test included elevation. In 1926 the Great Northern Railway brought to Glacier the well-known British mountaineer Dorothy Pilley where she climbed 25 peaks in 19 days.

Dorothy Pilley on the Ptarmigan Wall

Porch at Two Medicine Chalet

Louis Hill wanted to prove he was up to the test as well and elevation was part of it, and he did so in characteristic fashion. In 1912 Hill invited 25 newspapermen from all over the US to come to Glacier, not to relax at the lodge, but to prove themselves, taking them on a week-long horseback pack trip through Glacier Park "traveling along he brink of eternity." One reporter noted, "Mr. Hill invited newspapermen from all over the country to have the times of their lives in Glacier National Park. That they did, riding a staggering number of miles over the most precipitous trails, meeting formally scores of undeniably real Indians and some first-class Montana snow storms."[12] Hill presumably received 25 newspaper stories in return.

The Chalets

The ritual for visiting Glacier was carefully choreographed. There were a number of possible itineraries, usually beginning at the Glacier Park or Many Glacier Hotels, usually on horseback, but almost all involved a trek to a high point on the continental divide and a return to the point of departure. The focus of the trip was often literally an Alpine-style elevating experience. A Great Northern ad from 1912 offers a package vacation that includes a two-week horseback trip stopping at seven chalets starting at Glacier Park Lodge crossing the Continental divide, visiting Sperry Chalet and Sperry Glacier, going up 2,500 feet in the process and returning to the Glacier Park Lodge. A visit to a high-country chalet typically featured a walk up a mountain summit or along a glacier. The destination of the trek was usually a view, if not from a peak, then over a precarious precipice "the roof of the Continent."

A series of backcountry chalets or tent camps, all about a one-day horseback ride apart, punctuated its length. They were something like Adirondack camps with separate buildings for dining and sleeping. Thus, simultaneously with the construction of the large Glacier Park hotels work began on smaller backcountry chalets. Originally there were 12 tent camps. Within a year or two by the addition of more permanent buildings were added to nine of them to create chalet camps.

The programmatic model of this experience was Swiss. Given the popularity of mountain climbing in Switzerland there was an obvious need for high altitude housing since a climb lasted several days and in 1863 the Swiss Alpine club built their first overnight hut at Grünhorn on the Tödi, the highest mountain in central Switzerland. By 1890 they had built 37 more. The early huts are architecturally minimal, sometimes stone, but usually stucco with few brackets, projections, or ornaments. They are typically called huts rather than chalets and they bear little resemblance to those illustrated by Gladbach or to the elaborately encrusted Many Glacier Hotel.

Hill's plan for the Glacier backcountry was clearly inspired by the Swiss hut system. Many sources cite the fact that Louis Hill made a careful on-site study of Swiss tourism. None specifies any detail as to what was being studied, but something he was clearly looking at was the Alpine huts. But these form what was a conceptual rather than an architectural model for the backcountry experience of Glacier.

Typical ads for the lodges of the day such as Old Faithful emphasize the high level of comfort and amenity in lodging, food, and everything else. It was Adirondack style playing at rustic. The Glacier chalets, however, were something else. This was a form of test so it was about denial but not too difficult a test. One gave up comfortable means of travel for horses. One gave up privacy in housing. One gave up a certain quality in food but it was served on a tablecloth. One experiences the awe evoking sublime view, but safely from a balcony.

In truth there is not much of the chalet in these buildings. The roofs of the chalet buildings of the camps are often topped with the logs and boulders used to hold down the roofs, as in Switzerland, and are log bracketed, but on the whole Swiss quotations are rare. It is an architecture of raw logs. It was more a return to hypothetical origins and less of a visit to Switzerland

In a May 1914 article, the *Spokane Chronicle* announced that Cutter and Malmgrem had been hired to design the chalets in Glacier National Park.[13] In fact, by that date many were finished and under construction. It seems certain that Cutter was involved in the design of some of the chalets but which ones and how much is uncertain.

There were three types of chalet camp in three types of location. The first type was not really any more in the backcountry than Lake McDonald or Many Glacier Hotels. Others were deeper into the park, at least a day's ride away up one of the deep valleys that led up to the continental divide. Many of the first two types are located at the base or the side of a lake and were built largely of logs. The third type, most remote and the most elevated, were the high-altitude, long view, precariously located destination chalets where the pack trip ended before heading back down the mountain. These used a great deal more stone. All were very much part of the narrative of the retreat from the overcivilized world, the arduous trek up the mountain by horse, and the ascent to the elevated sublime view. In construction, they were real logs. In style they were not Swiss but primitive.

In the life one lived there, however short the time, was, to a degree, primitive as well. For the most part they were like the journey itself, a trial by withdrawal from "overcivilized" life.

The backcountry chalets were a return to origins both in their operation and their architecture construction systems and architectural forms. The backcountry chalets bore only a vague resemblance to the large hotels. None of the large hotels used log walls. All of the backcountry chalets did except those at high elevations that were stone. Out of necessity, construction and craft of those in remote locations used local materials and handcraft to a degree. This was not always possible. Packing in milled lumber is difficult; packing in a sawmill is impossible. But despite their aura of backcountry axe-craft they are in some ways no less industrial than the large hotels below. Windows and doors meant milled lumber was needed, which meant sawmills close at hand. Altitude mattered in architecture as well. Their rustic qualities owed much to radical differences in building technology but they were also the product and expression of a very different experience. Primitive (in the sense of primal) living meant primitive architecture.

If the construction methodologies were handcrafted, the designs were industrial in organization, standardized to a degree Walter Gropius would have admired. Each camp was composed of anywhere from three to 15 separate buildings, but in most cases each building followed a set of standardized plans.

Two sizes of dining room and kitchen units: 18'x76' and 42'x85'.

Two types of log cabin housing units—28'x28 or 18'x18'.

Two types of larger dormitories, the larger ones are 28'x84', such as the log ones at Two Medicine. The dorm at Sperry has the same plan but with stone walls is 31'x89'.

There were unique buildings at key locations such as Granite Park, the highest of the chalets.

Despite the dependence on the industrialized world all of the chalet buildings are genuinely rustic. Most were built of solid unlayered log walls and log beams. As a rule logs came from within two miles of the site. But milled lumber was still necessary for floors, roof decking, and interior partitions between bedrooms. Sawmills or access to milled lumber was necessary.

Even before construction began there were sawmills available, two in the Swiftcurrent Valley that could serve those easily accessible by road. Milled lumber had to be hauled by horse or boat to the backcountry, and the high-altitude destination chalets, much farther away and much higher up in areas with poor timber, horses were the only option. The degree of industrialization was inversely proportional to the distance from the railroad or even the highway.

Gunsight Chalet

Two Medicine Chalet

St. Mary's Chalet

Dining Hall

Dormitory

Two Medicine Chalet
Glacier National Park, 1912-1913

Two Medicine was the first type of chalet, at a lower altitude and closer to the train station and the Glacier Park Lodge than the Many Glacier. It was accessible by bus or wagon from the Glacier Park Lodge and many visitors came for one night. But it was a very different experience from the lodge in a very different kind of architecture. Many Glacier was all refinement; Two Medicine was all rustic. Two Medicine was not much more remote than the Many Glacier but the experience was different in every way, as was the architecture.

Thematically, Two Medicine had a clearly Native American focus. The first iteration was a 1911 tent camp of tall tepee-like pyramid tents. Piegans performed the Sundance ceremony there during which, through complex rituals, they constructed a medicine lodge—a roughly circular open log structure with a center pole. They had been forbidden to do this on the nearby reservation except on the Fourth of July, and Hill gave them an opportunity to relive the life they had lost.

Within a year buildings were added, first three standardized cabin units, then in 1912 two log chalets, a dining hall, and in 1913 a dorm. In 1915 the larger dining building was built, one of the few log structures of any of the chalet groups that survives. The roof of the Dining Hall projecting end is supported by columns, but the dorms are simple boxes with dormers and use a simple vocabulary of logs. The walls are solid, cut from within one mile of the camp on the south side of the lake. Like other chalets the construction was authentic out of necessity.

Chalet is a strange term for these buildings given the paucity of any traditional Swiss elements or details. There are logs and stones on the roof, some log roof and balcony brackets, one chalet-like wall screen, and the occasional jerkinhead gable, but there are no jigsaw cutouts, no tacked-on pseudo-constructive ornaments and very little that was not logs. There were 11 more chalet camps of the Two Medicine type, clusters of standardized log buildings, more remote but not so high as the destination chalets.

Section looking west

East elevation

Two Medicine Chalet
Wall Section

This is far more authentic log construction than many rustic buildings and more truly rustic in its accommodation.

The exterior walls are solid logs.
The floor and roof structure are largely exposed.
All logs are of the same diameter.

The wall is constricted 6-inch logs.

The floor construction is 1x6 tongue and groove boards on 6-inch log beams on 6-inch log floor joists.

The roof is shingles and boards on 6-inch log rafters resting on 6-inch log girders spanning between log cross walls.

Stones and logs on the roof are there in imitation of Swiss chalets rather than serving a functional purpose.

The High Elevation Chalets

Granite Park Chalet, started in 1914, was a high altitude, remote destination chalet, sited on a cliff edge with a balcony and porch on each side. It also used local stone from nearby, although it was later expanded with log extensions. It is a unique type, not one of the standard modules.

Of all the rustic architecture in the national parks the Glacier chalets come the closest to the rustic intention—not just the kind of architecture but the experience Kephart and Burroughs had sought, an authentic alternative experience, a life closer to nature, not just in location but sleeping, eating, and living-somewhere closer to our origins. Their work was a product of the industrial America. The site could provide no suitable lumber, and it was all packed in by horse up the Swiftcurrent Valley. The contractor was no local axe man but the Evensta Company of St. Paul, a large contractor that regularly worked for the Great Northern Railroad.

Clearly the difference in architecture and the difference in craft between the backcountry chalets was a reflection of the nature of the experience. It certainly involved different levels of comfort but there was something more. If they did not contain the ornamental paraphernalia of the chalet as the Many Glacier did, they exemplified the rustic spirit of the chalet—the primitive origins of building—and it was, even for a short time as authentic experiences go, closer to the reality than many.

Richard White sees this need for a "trial" to be yet another manifestation of a late nineteenth-century malaise:

In a world where more and more Americans did not know nature through their work, Western nature had a new role to play. Nature would keep native-born Americans 'true' and 'hardy.' ... the fear of softness and weakness among middle-class men provoked a movement to restore manliness, vigor and strength—in a word, character. Not work but leisure would lead men back into nature, particularly Western nature.[14]

Granite Park Chalet

Sperry Chalet

Sperry Chalet
Glacier National Park, 1914

Those chalets at higher elevations, the destination chalets, were built of stone walls with timber floors and roofs because of the scarcity of good timber at that elevation and the difficulty of transporting it up the mountain. Sperry Chalet is at 6,500 feet; Glacier Park is at 6,670. Both are more than 2,500 feet higher than the Glacier Park Lodge. Each is sited at the edge of a precipice.

Sperry Chalet was one of the highest and more remote chalets, 50 miles from the Glacier Park Lodge. It was the place one turned around to go back. Both of the main buildings sit on the cliff edge with long balconies facing the view down the valley to Lake McDonald. It began in 1911 as a tent camp. A dining room and a large dorm were added in 1914. At this altitude, close to the upper limit of the tree line, trees are smaller and fewer. Alpine timber, even when available, was often unsuitable. Hill suggested that they whip saw the logs, a laborious hand powered process, cutting them in half to save lumber, but in the end, it was built with stone walls.

The Sperry dormitory uses the same plan and the same roof form as the log ones at Two Medicine and St. Mary's but is built with much thicker and heavier stone walls. The Sperry dorm is a documented Cutter design, which probably explains the difference. The dormitory also has the same alternating gables as the wood dorm at Two Medicine. The beams and rafters are logs. The roof and floor decks are milled lumber. There are minimal details, rusticated log brackets supporting balconies, gables, and the cantilevered roof ends.

The local stones in the dormitory are three times the size of those used in the dining hall buildings and used like logs. Stones were drug on a sledge from a quarry nearby. Douglas fir timber was brought from below. If the materials were indigenous the craft was not. Italian stonemasons made the trek to the timberline, as did much of the lumber. The *Timberman* reported in October 1913:

A pile of lumber, said to contain 75,000 feet, is being landed at Glacier hotel, on Lake McDonald, and will be taken to Glacier camp on the trial across the mountains, to complete the buildings that are being put up there. There is nothing notable about that, but when it is remembered that the distance is seven or eight miles, all up hill, with a grade approaching 25 per cent a good

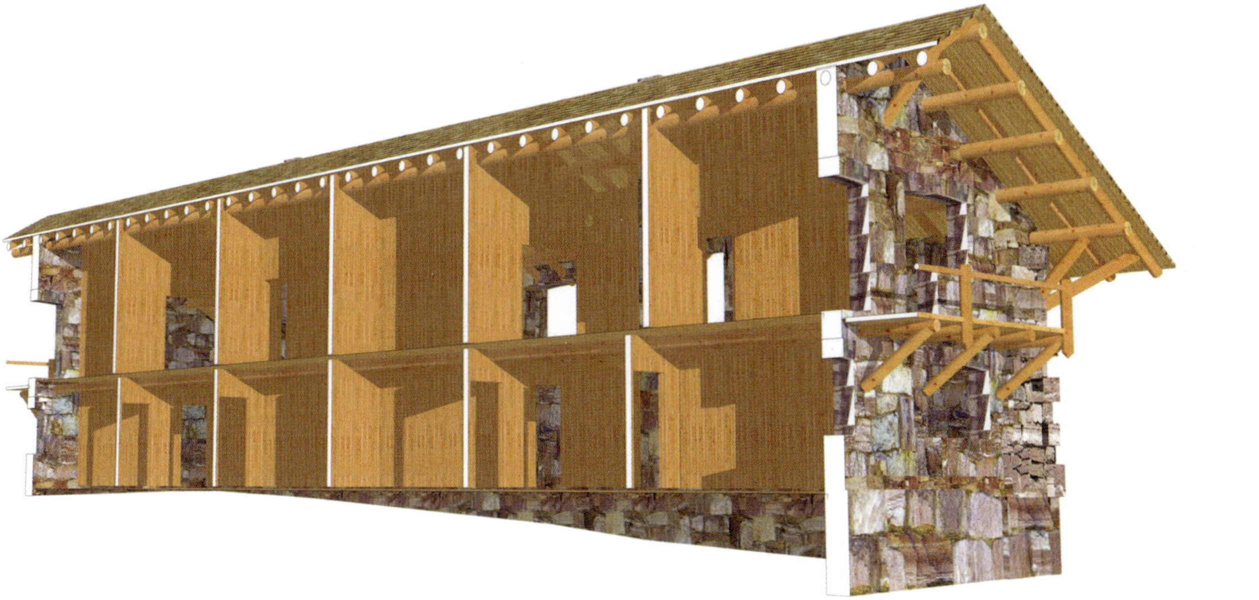

Section looking west

East elevation

Sperry Chalet Dormitory
Wall Section

The plan is the same as the Two Medicine dormitory but the walls are solid stone, a material more readily available than usable logs at the higher elevations.

The floor and roof structure are largely exposed.

The roof is constructed of shingles and boards on 6-inch log rafters.

The floor is constructed of 1x6 floorboards on 6-inch logs 3-feet on center.

There are two types of bearing wall: exterior stone walls and 2x4 stud walls on the interior, both resting on stone foundations. There are Interior columns at unknown locations.

share of the way, that there is a good trail, but no wagon road, and that the lumber will all have to be dragged up by horses, it will be conceded that it is a good-sized job.[15]

Conclusion

Louis Hill brought his vision for Glacier to realization, but it was relatively short lived and never very profitable. The completion of Hill's large hotels and chalets about 1916 coincided with the creation of the Park Service. The symbolic end of the story came in 1925. All of the hotels in the park had made extensive use of timber cut in the park. The sawmill Hill had built during the construction of Many Glacier was still operating in 1925. Perhaps Stephen Mather, the Park Service's first director, was self-reflective enough to realize the absurdity of a permanent sawmill owned by a private enterprise in a national park. After years of letters demanding its removal, the sawmill was dynamited in 1925 on his orders.

Mather was a populist with ambitious expectations of park visitors and far less interested, if at all, in providing wilderness trials. He wanted to maximize visitation and he understood early on that automobile travel was the answer. The result in the case of Glacier, as it was in many parks, was the construction of a highway across the Park and over the mountains, in this case, the Going to the Sun highway, begun in 1921 and completed in 1932. It is often cited as a masterpiece of national park landscape design but Glacier lost something when it was constructed, something less populist, more elitist, but certainly more profound. It now requires very little effort and not much time to ascend the mountain and return. The chalet system as a business was gone by 1945. Today the journey that Rinehart, Eaton, and their companions traversed by horseback over two weeks is duplicated by 4,700 automobiles in a two-hour journey every summer day. Only parts of two chalets remain in operation, Sperry and Granite Park. If you sit on the porch of Granite Park today you will see a long line of cars making their way down the highway to Lake McDonald.

Kirtland Cutter, Kootenai Lodge, Swan Lake, Montana

KIRTLAND CUTTER IN MONTANA

At this point it is no surprise that Kirtland Cutter, America's foremost chalet designer, reenters the story. I have already described Louis Hill's on-again off-again employment of Cutter and the latter's fragmented contribution to Hill's buildings at Glacier, but Cutter's most critical and personal contributions to the Glacier Park region came through his work with other clients, at the Lake McDonald Lodge at the western entry to the park, and the Kootenai Lodge, 60 miles to the south.

Cutter, as we have seen, had developed two very different versions of the chalet. It could be literal. It could be precise, planed wood, jigsaw profiled elements. The exterior of the Many Glacier Hotel, although only partially by Cutter, is a conspicuous example. Or the chalet could be the rusticated version of traditional Swiss forms and details in which these literal elements are approximated in logs. Details such as brackets or bargeboards that were typically flat surfaces with ornate complex profiles are translated into rough logs. The Idaho Pavilion is an example. The Glacier Park Lodge, although not by Cutter, uses this type of log chalet detail.

These two strategies were to become two very different languages of architecture—one of refined and finished wood trim, bristling with the precise paraphernalia of the modern crafted chalet, and a second type, rougher and more ancient, of axes and logs. It was a difference that was more than skin deep. Buildings in the refined mode tended to be standard wood-frame construction with encrustations of glib, Swiss-style elements. It was a system that invited structural deception. The log chalet tended to be more integral and solid, less layered and less glib, as it was a system that demanded, out of necessity, a marriage of structural reality and structural expression.

Cutter does not appear to have been a man of deep thought or to have possessed any theoretical underpinnings that determined his design, and his rustic work has little to do with the bulk of his design, which is eclectic, but he could not avoid the obvious. The log chalets are the perfect illustration of a return to European origins, a primitive hut. They are not archaeological reconstruction, but a repetition of the process Robert Adam followed in his rustic work, a primitivizing of the contemporary. The chalet is taken backward, returning it to its log origins.[1]

Cutter was to use both versions of the chalet in his last two rustic buildings, but in very different ways. We have already seen these two characteristics of Cutter's work, but the work at Glacier saw a dramatic change in his log architecture.

He had an expertise in the rustic vocabulary of the log cabin and the rusticated chalet, but he was taking on projects exponentially larger in scale and complexity. These were products of the industrial age using an industrial technology, but with a vocabulary of logs. Specifically, he was shifting from a language of log walls to one of log frames.

Like Reamer before him, Cutter faced the problem of using a log cabin building vocabulary for large, long-span spaces to construct a large multi-story building. His log houses and the Idaho Pavilion were constructed primarily of log planes. Connections between rooms were made by interrupting the continuous plane of horizontal logs to make an opening, leaving sufficient logs above to form a beam, as at Idaho. There was no log truss, no log columns, no structural log frame to speak of. To build a hotel this way was not impossible, but it was clearly a cumbersome system for the larger spaces such as the hotel lobby. But it was hardly a new problem for Cutter. Most of Cutter's work was not rustic. He had built hotels but he had never built a rustic building at that scale. He had done a number of steel-frame buildings and it was no great leap to build one that only appeared to be rustic or was only partially rustic, and he was about to face the question in multiple commissions.

In 1909 John Lewis owned a small hotel on Lake McDonald the west side of what is now Glacier National Park. The creation of the Park in 1910 meant more business but it also meant the arrival of a powerful competitor, the Great Northern Railroad. Lewis decided to meet them head on with his own new large hotel and the Lewis Glacier Hotel (now the Lake McDonald Lodge) was built from 1911 to 1913.

Lake McDonald Lodge
Glacier National Park, 1913

The Lake McDonald Lodge, begun the same year as the Glacier Park Lodge, is a hybrid of rustic monument and quaint chalet but it is far more chalet and far less log monument. John Lewis and Louis Hill were bitter enemies but they agreed on one thing, the architectural virtues of the chalet, so it is no surprise that Lewis hired Cutter. There remained the question of what exactly the chalet style was.

So between 1913 and 1917 three large hotels were built in the park quickly in succession. Despite differences in architects and owners, the three have much in common. All faced the same issues of dependence on the railroad for construction but difficulties in accessing it. All had many of the same aspirations. Like Hill's large hotels Lake McDonald sought rustic monumentality, but like the Many Glacier Hotel this was encased in the smaller scale domestic/nostalgic language of the chalet. The site presented challenges far beyond the Glacier Park Hotel that sat adjacent to the track. Access to the Lake McDonald Lodge site in 1910 was only by horse or a 10-mile boat ride.

The lodge that followed is the work of a new Cutter. The Lake McDonald Lodge proper is a symmetrical object, three volumes forming a long rectangle extending along the lake edge.

At the center is the monumental element, a cube containing the full height lobby and primarily supported by an almost freestanding log frame. It is flanked on either side by two slightly narrower volumes containing the hotel rooms that are platform-framed, clapboard-faced boxes with Swiss jerkinhead gables on each side. All sit atop a stone ground floor (now covered with stucco).

The hotel entrance faces the lake, since visitors arrived by boat before 1922. The cube between the gabled volumes is traversed by an axis of circulation. The procession along this axis passes through a series of log rustic structures from the lake-side entry through a log-framed hall to the fireplace on the opposite wall. In the process one passes through three sets of log "orders" in the classical sense.

Section looking southeast

Lake elevation

The first order in this series of log structures are the balcony support columns at the entry coincident with the wall facing the lake. This is Cutter's inverted trapezoid order. It is an order supporting the openings in the log walls. This was to become Cutter's trademark order in the classical sense of an order—the inverted trapezoid—and was used in the lobby, balconies, dining room, and in numerous buildings to follow. Cutter's orders are less literally classically based than others, but they have the same characteristic articulation of parts and carefully defined transitions.

The second in the series of orders is a row of doubled columns with brackets in the entry just behind the first order in the one-story lobby leading to the large hall. It is a preview of what is to come—a smaller version of the hall structure. Each of the three columns is doubled and has a 45-degree bracket connecting it to the beam it supports. The double log order of the lobby extends upward into a central second-floor terrace.

The third order, the most complex, are the elements that make up the frame of the log hall. It is a pyramid on a cube. Each corner of the cube is defined by three 28-foot-high bark-on log columns.

Columns and beams are connected by log brackets at 45 degrees, a common device to provide lateral bracing in a heavy timber frame, but used here as part of another order. This cubical log frame is topped by a pyramid formed of log trusses rotated at 45 degrees to support the X-shaped trussed assembly above.

There are two systems of joining the logs here in stark opposition. The logs of the frame itself are co-planer and inserted into one another. The log beams supporting the floors around the lobby are joined in an over and under constructivist way so that visually they remain separate entities. There are steel fasteners and reinforcing in the log frame.

Order 3: Monumental Doric

Order 2: Upright with brackets

Order 1: Inverted trapezoid order
The front row of columns is a later addition.

Lake McDonald Lodge

The larger log halls at the Great Northern hotels are transformations of classical buildings. The almost freestanding frame that defines the hall is not particularly classical and not so monumental. Cutter's hall space has some of the character of the central halls of the other two hotels but with smaller and fewer logs and some decidedly un-classical elements—diagonal bracing and the pyramidal roof of engineered log trusses. It is structurally logical. It has no specific recognizable precedent. It is certainly not Swiss. It suggests some preindustrial barn frames and the tall unenclosed hay sheds of the West but it can also be seen as a steel form translated into wood.

The fourth of the log orders in this sequence is that surrounding the fireplace. The fireplace here is an Inglenook rather than open campfire of Hill's lodges. It is covered with an open log trellis that is an extension of the main bracketed frame. The stone of the fireplace is covered with Native American graffiti, actually the work of the painter Charles Russell.

Both of Cutter's approaches to the chalet, the literal and the rustic, are present in Lake McDonald Lodge. The gables of the Glacier Park Lodge are the classical pedimented type, that emphasizes the height of the wall and thinness of the roof. The gables at Lake McDonald Lodge are the Swiss form, the truncated jerkinhead gable, that creates a broken horizontal roof dropping the line of the eave. The result is a lower profile, a broader roof surface that hovers over the building, subduing the monumentality and connecting it with the ground. Logs and stones on the roof complete the Swiss connection.

In the two blocks flanking the hall below the Swiss elements are all on the surface. This rusticated type of detail occurs at Lake McDonald Lodge in the elements that separate themselves from the building mass. Here, elements are logs rather than gingerbread. The balcony brackets are the best part of this in the Cutter tradition of Swiss features recreated in logs. Originally the balconies were only on the lakeside and there was none on what is now the front. The lakeside balconies were supported by rows of projecting bark-on logs and the balconies with bark-on log rails. The balconies have changed considerably. Many are now smooth peeled logs. Columns and beams were added to support what were originally cantilevers. Over time milled lumber has replaced the original rustic log railings.

Far less successful are the two building volumes the balconies cover, a variation on the system used at North Point. The surfaces of the two Swiss-like boxes flanking the log hall are essentially the skin of a chalet tacked on top of the skeleton of a milled lumber frame. Many of these elements suggest structure where there is none. What appears to be a traditional Swiss squared log construction is only a veneer on wood studs. Notched vertical wood strips represent the ends of non-existent cross walls. Fake interlocking square log corners represent the intersection of two non-existent log walls. There are other literal Swiss elements—white bands of Swiss trim with protruding logs, jigsaw profiles cut into double rafter extensions. There is in places a fake rusticity as well—door frames of milled lumber clad with thin log slabs, protruding ornamental log beams where there is no real beam. For the most part the facade is a handcrafted costume on a rough sawmill frame. The building is an odd contrast of systems, one of structural substance and one of pseudo-constructive veneers. The platform-framed boxes are neither authentic nor organic. The main lobby is a highly original industrial form executed in bark-on cedar logs. In the four-year period in which the three hotels were built the monumental Swiss hybrid evolved. At Lake McDonald Lodge the monumental log hall remained, although smaller in size, but the oversized rustic details began to disappear, replaced by Swiss gingerbread.

The timber industry arrived at Glacier National Park almost as soon as it was created. As with Yellowstone, cutting timber in the park was common practice. The 1911 Park Superintendent's report states that he planned to build a sawmill at Fish Creek at the western edge of the lake. And notes that there was a great deal of "unsightly," downed lumber in the park that could be sawn and sold for profit.[2] Like many of his day, he tended to see a forest not as an ecosystem but as a timber factory where a rotting log is a wasted resource. His intent was to produce lumber (but not finish wood) for the administration buildings and for sale, and he intended that it turn a profit.

Lake McDonald is 10 miles long. The railroad station is at the west end. The lodge was at the east end at the base of the mountains. Access to the lodge site in 1909 was only by water. With the hotel at one end of the lake and the train station at Belton and eventually the sawmill at the other, building materials had to be brought in by boat, barge, or pack horse during the summer by or sled across the ice during the winter. Some came from the park. Some came from miles away.

The cedar logs that framed the main lobby were cut near the site. The largest of these is about 14 inches in diameter, less than half the size of the Glacier Park Lodge log columns, and these timbers were more readily available. There was a sawmill on site. But much of the lumber and a great many building components had to be shipped up the lake, some from the mill at Fish Creek, some delivered by rail to Belton. Some timber came by rail to from Kalispell, but they had to be delivered in the same way.

Hill was through building lodges. Cutter was not. Cutter's last log building was private and outside the park, about 60 miles to the southwest, but is the real end of this architectural sequence. So one of Cutter's best log palaces came at the end of his career for a client all too similar to his predecessors.

Log columns and trusses of main lobby

Exterior wall of clapboards on sheathing on milled studs

Log balcony and trellis supports

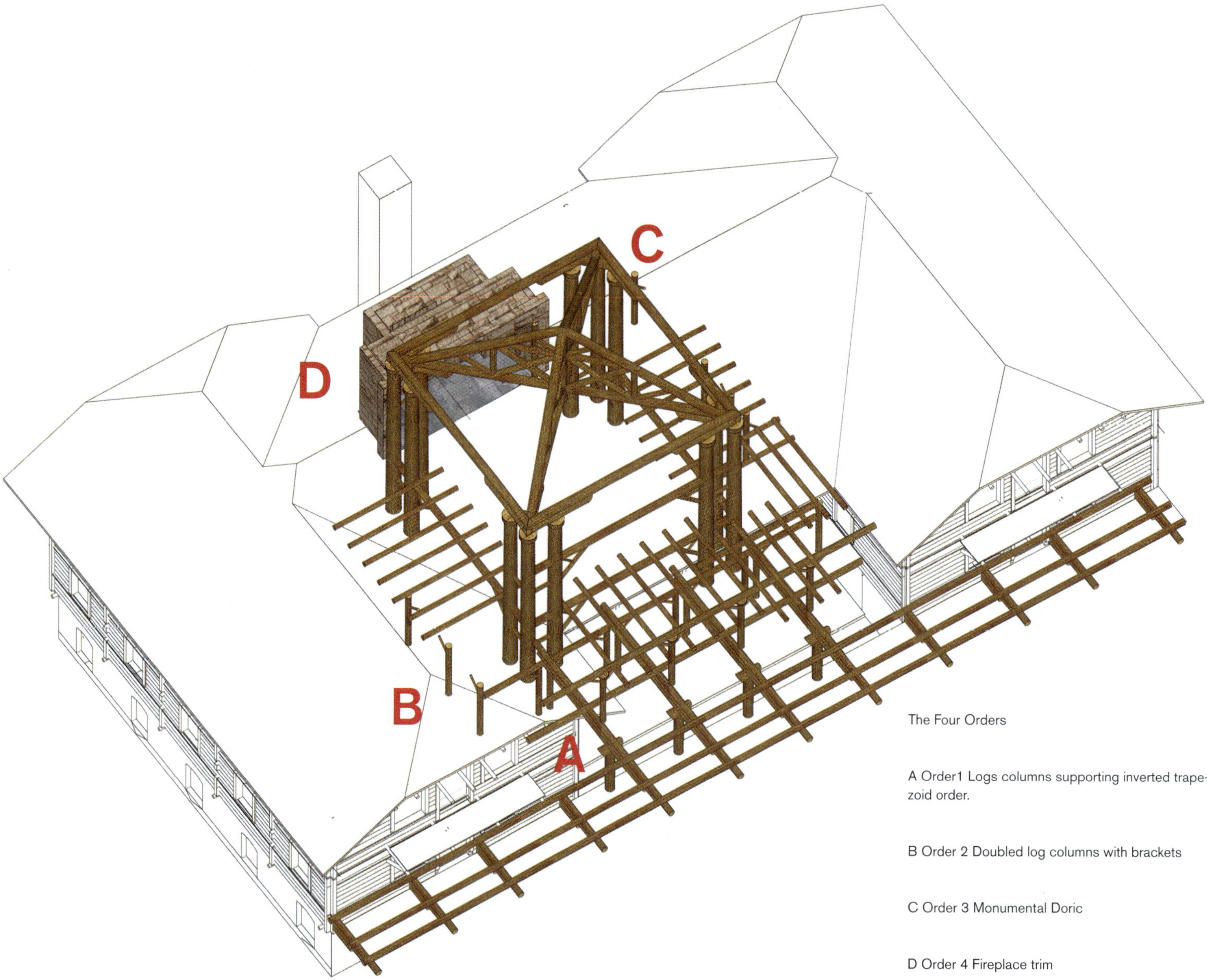

The Four Orders

A Order1 Logs columns supporting inverted trapezoid order.

B Order 2 Doubled log columns with brackets

C Order 3 Monumental Doric

D Order 4 Fireplace trim

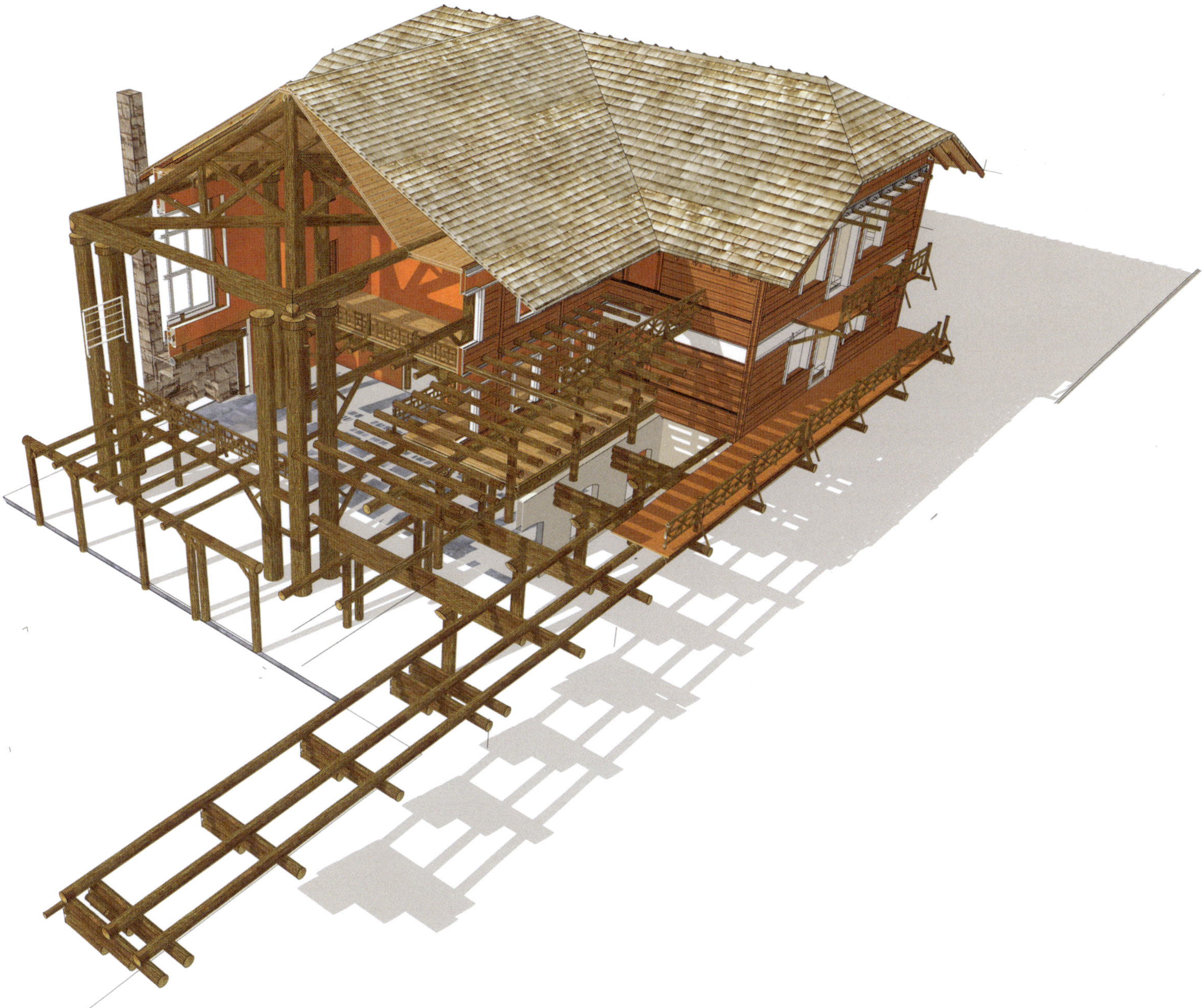

In 1906 John Ryan A. Cornelius Kelley, a key administrator of the Anaconda Company along with Orvis Evans, another Anaconda "copper king" bought a series of log cabins in the Flathead Valley near Swan Lake, Montana, which they developed into a rustic complex called Kootenai, and hired Cutter to design the main lodge. Like Hill, Kelley preserved a fragment of forest in the process of a larger act of destruction.

Kootenai is one of Cutter's last log buildings and in some ways his best in that here the log skeleton and log skin introduced at Lake McDonald are fully realized. It can be misleading to look at Cutter's rustic work in a developmental way given his multi-stylistic simultaneous explorations. At the time Cutter was working on the Many Glacier Hotel he was finishing the Davenport Hotel in Spokane, in which Hill had a financial interest, which began as Spanish Colonial and ended as neoclassical. But at the same time, in addition to the Swiss influences Cutter's rustic work is informed by classicism while looking toward modernism—toward a frame architecture.

In the large hotels built by Hill the Swiss paraphernalia multiplied. Here Cutter dispensed with it altogether. The chalet veneer is gone. There is no tacked-on Swiss trim. Like Reamer at Old Faithful and McMahon at the Many Glacier Dining Hall before him, Cutter transcended log cabin clichés into something else that was both rustic and industrial. Cutter's previous design work shows at best only a decorative interest in structure and little interest in real structural integration, as in most of the work he did after. This was the moment when he did. It is his least Swiss rustic building.

The plan is a courtyard formed by a U-shaped form—one-story wings connecting to a two-story block containing a large room with a central fireplace facing the lake. The plan follows the typical Cutter plan of a central axis traversing the short dimension of a hall with a fireplace/inglenook with balcony above at one end and a porch with a lake view at the other.

The Kootenai Lodge
Swan Lake, Montana, 1919-1920

Section looking northeast

Lake elevation

Roof Structure

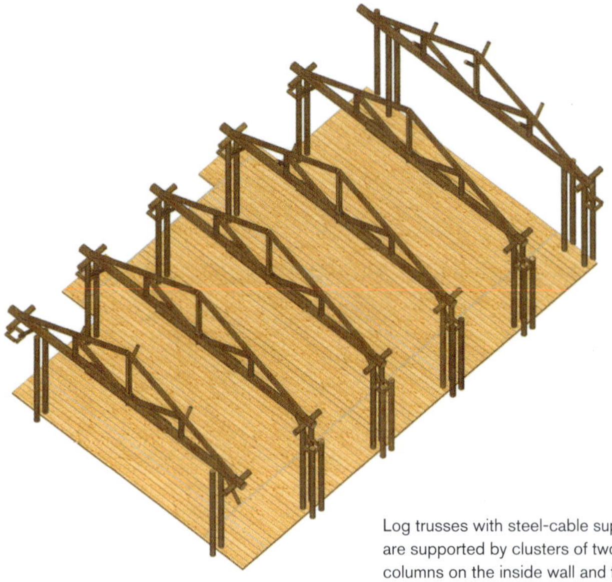

Log trusses with steel-cable supports are supported by clusters of two columns on the inside wall and four on the exterior.

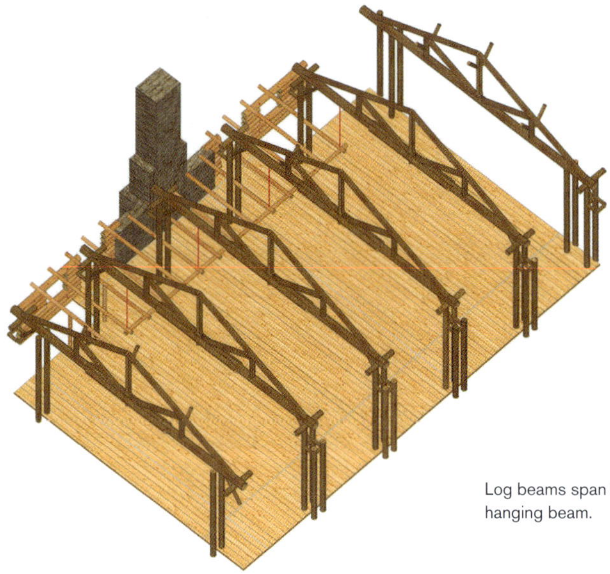

Log beams span between wall and hanging beam.

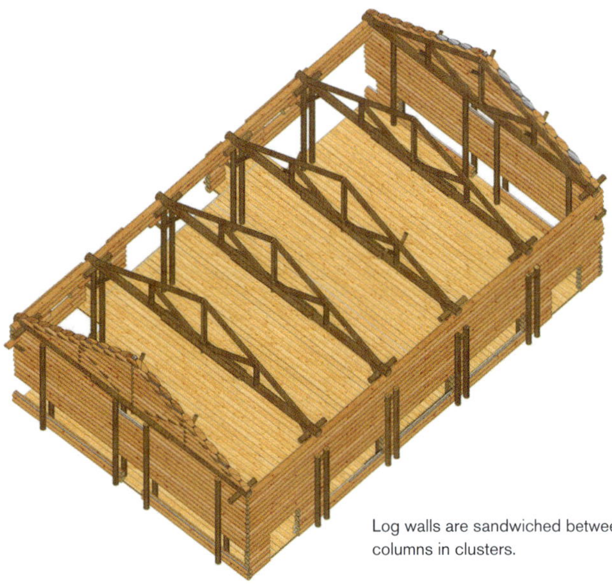

Log walls are sandwiched between log columns in clusters.

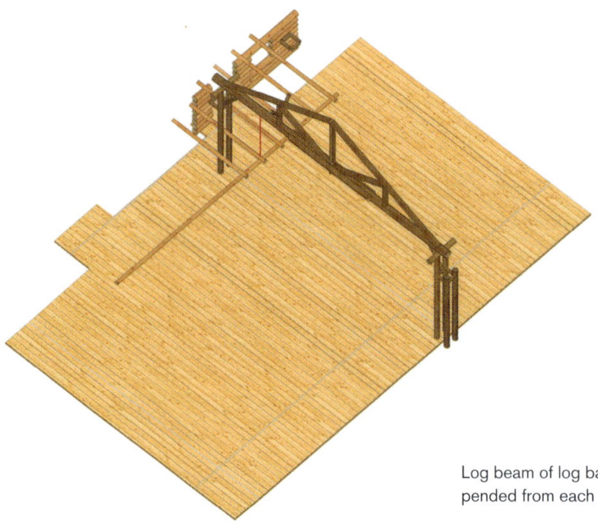

Log beam of log balcony frame is suspended from each truss.

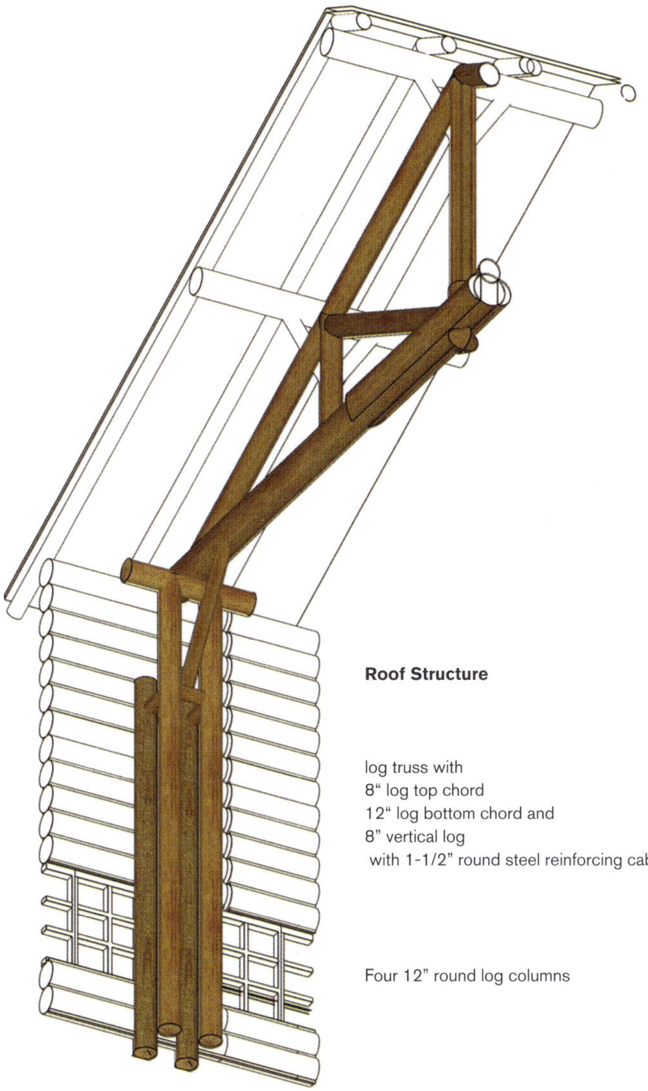

Roof Structure

log truss with
8“ log top chord
12“ log bottom chord and
8” vertical log
with 1-1/2” round steel reinforcing cable

Four 12” round log columns

The Central Hall

However rustic in detail, Kootenai exhibits an almost Corbusian modernism. The building employs something like a log curtain wall. The frame and skin become separate elements and there is no ambiguity as to which is which. Bark is used to identify the structural elements—the truss piers and porch columns. The log walls, the "curtain" walls, are peeled. They are just that—logs—not half logs on wood studs but they do not, at least in appearance, hold up the roof. This is done by the columns and trusses. But if it is proto-modern one could say this has classical influences as well, as in the freestanding columns recalling the classical temple.

The log order here is a variation of that used at the Lake McDonald Lodge. Each column is a cluster—four logs on the lake side and two logs on the court side—connected like ladders. They have a variation on the inverted trapezoid capital. The "order" of the hall structure has an affinity with original design of the atrium of the Davenport Hotel in Spokane, which featured clustered columns and brackets of similar shape and proportion to Kootenai. In a subtle way Cutter is, like Bartlett at the Glacier Park Lodge, returning classicism to nature.

The log walls may be non-bearing, although there is a long log lintel above the ground floor windows, but they are not thin. This is the only building in this chapter that uses log walls of any kind, and these are real logs, not half-log siding. The four-column log cluster served as both truss and wall support sandwiching the truss support perpendicular to the wall and sandwiching the wall itself parallel to it. Spanning between the column clusters is the roof structure, a series of log Howe trusses. The horizontal truss members have the identical section to the column with half logs added where needed as in the bottom truss chord. There are 45-degree log brackets at each truss/pier junction.

The Central Hall
Log sandwiched between columns in clusters

The porch

The Central Hall

Exposed connectors and steel of any kind are rare in rustic buildings before 1915, Reamer covered his cables at the Canyon Hotel with wood and Cutter had concealed them in logs at the Lake McDonald Lodge. But Cutter began to experiment.

An earlier version of the Hall, what might be called the "rope" design, was a combination of details from British High tech and the sort of rope lashings found in *The Boy Scout Handbook*. It uses a great deal of rope but in two ways. Many of the log-to-log joints are lashed with these temporary joints that might be used in camping. But the rope is also used like steel cables, as tension cables to support the balcony over the fireplace, which is hung from the log truss above. In this version the trusses also use exposed steel connectors at points. There are real steel cables in the structure in the king-post of the log trusses. In the original detail these were placed in a hole drilled thought the center of the log. In the final version the single log is changed to a cluster of four smaller ones and the cable is placed at the center of the cluster, not really exposing it but not hiding it either. Here Cutter stopped short of what McMahon did at the Many Glacier Hotel but he reveals the rope. In the end the wood frame joints are made in the usual way for the time, and there are no visible connectors in the structure.

Beyond the rope knots there are other instances of visible handcraft—the hand scraped peeled logs and the chopped log ends later made popular by the Park Service add to the handcrafted theme. But the lodge at Kootenai was industrial in spite of itself. The industrial revolution in building is not just implied here but evident, mixed in with the rustic.

This was the end of the exploration of the independent log frame for Cutter. He ended his career in Southern California designing primarily in the style of Spanish Colonial.

Suspended balcony structure
with column behind

Basic double column

Kootenai Lodge
Wall Section at Suspended Balcony

The two sides of the hall are almost identical except for the suspended balcony over the fireplace.

The balcony is supported by1-1/2-inch rope or steel cables at each truss connecting to a 7-inch log beam log along the balcony edge supporting transverse beams. The tension rods shown as ropes on the original drawings, today the suspension rods are logs.

The decision to uses cables rather than columns to support the balcony seems more aesthetic than functional.

Kootenai Lodge
Wall Section at Lake Facade

The shingles and boards of the roof are supported by 10-inch logs spaced at 3 feet resting on wood trusses.

The wall construction is solid12 -inch logs wall with cement chinking that run between the cluster of four columns.

The log structural frame here breaks free of the enclosing log walls to be almost freestanding. Since the bark is left on the logs of the frame and the logs of the wall are peeled the two are easily distinguished.

The roof structure is boards on 3-inch pole rafters supported by the log truss with 8-inch log top chord, 12-inch log bottom chord and 8-inch vertical with 1-1/2-inch round steel reinforcing cable inside.

Each end of the trusses is supported by a pier composed of a cluster of four 12-inch round log columns.

The 12-inch peeled log wall runs between the 4 logs of the column.

The Ethical Ledger

Throughout this narrative we have dealt with the problem that works of architecture we find admirable are a smaller part of a process we deplore. The career and architecture of Kirtland Cutter takes us into a whole new level of such destructiveness the world of mining in the West.

Cutter designed buildings for the Great Northern. Spokane was a major hub of the Northern Pacific and it fueled the growth of the major industries, gold mining, timber, and electric power.

So Cutter's client list is a true rogues gallery of disreputable industrialists, but none more so than the client for Kootenai Lodge—John Ryan A. Cornelius "Con" Kelley, a key administrator of the Anaconda Copper Mining Company, one of the copper kings of Montana. Kelley spent much of his career keeping organized labor out of the mines. Anaconda holds a great deal of the responsibility for the present state of Butte Montana. The Clark Fork River Basin in the vicinity of Butte contains more than 10 EPA superfund megasites, all the result of copper mining. The years of Cutter's career saw the Coeur d'Alene mining strikes of 1892 and 1899, provoked by horrific working conditions, reduced wages, resulting in violent and destructive strikes, brutal military suppression, producing death and destruction on both sides. Many of the executive heads of these organizations were Cutter's clients.

His lodge for Kelley was actually part of the development of major destructive industrial enterprises. The Great Northern needed ties and infrastructure and the Swan Valley south of the park was a well-located source.

An even larger consumer of Swan Valley timber was one of the Great Northern's best customers, Anaconda. Its smelters in Butte required 300,000 cords of wood a year and 4,000 board feet of lumber a day for mine infrastructure. In 1907 Anaconda bought a million acres of the Northern Pacific Montana timberlands and became a major landowner there. The site for the Kootenai Lodge was part of this grant. The timber had already been harvested from the site before construction began.

Should we blame Cutter for any of this? Carrère and Hastings designed a house for Henry Clay Frick but that does not make them responsible for the people that died in the Homestead strike that Frick is infamous for suppressing. Can we say the same of Cutter? At least one project is conspicuous in this regard. On a much smaller scale, but far more problematic, are the picks and shovels mounted on the wall of the Idaho pavilion. In the popular history of the West mining is perceived in a romantic way and the exhibits gave a romantic view of the timber and mining industries—the pioneer with the axe, the prospector with the pick—but the reality of both was anything but romantic. The Idaho Pavilion was a rustic vessel to house, perhaps hide, the evidence of the technological upheaval going on in Idaho, an event with massive environmental and social consequences.

GEOLOGY

GEOLOGY AND RUINS

In the summer of 1833, a boat owned by the American Fur Company moved up the Missouri river in Western Montana toward its source. On board were two passengers: a German nobleman, Maximilian of Wied-Neuwied, and an artist in his employ, Karl Bodmer. When they entered the area known as the Badlands where the river is flanked by stone cliffs on two sides. Maximilian remarked on how architectural the cliffs appeared, "the strange clay hills close to shore had incredible domes, some just like mountain castles on the Rhine." They not only resembled castles but at times very specific ones, "a mountain castle at Bornhofen."[1]

He made the same observation eight more times, describing gates, windows, and wall-like formations. Numerous other structures were present as well, "an old tower," "an old Gothic chapel with a chimney ... a barracks. Even the details were architectural, "Beside us were the most regular walls, which looked as though they had been constructed from thick cubical stones, the joints as regular as though [the stones had been] hewn to size."[2]

Bodmer's drawings perfectly describe this perception. It is not surprising that these rectilinear outcrops not just look like buildings to Maximilian and Bodmer, they look like the romantic buildings of their home—the Rhine and its landscape.

The members of the Langford expedition to Yellowstone saw the geologic landscape in the same way. The primary tool Nathaniel Langford used to come to terms with Yellowstone's frightening immensity was to architecturalize it, to imagine the natural landscape as a building. He describes the Canyon of the Yellowstone: "a dozen distorted channels which have zig-zagged their passage through the cement formation, working it into spires, pinnacles, towers and many other capricious objects. Many of these are of faultless symmetry, resembling the minaret of a mosque."[3] Other formations, particularly geysers, are described as chimneys, interspersed among turrets, castles, spires, and towers. Cheney Doane describes Castle Crater, "a castellated turret. ...From a distance it strongly resembles an old feudal tower partially in ruins."[4]

The frequency of architectural descriptions of geology in nineteenth-century writings on of the American West is epidemic. There are several explanations. The first is simple—homesickness. Two Germans on viewing the mountains flanking the upper Missouri saw the castles of their homeland. But the tendency to look at rocks and see buildings is more than a product of nostalgia. A psychologist might make the same observation about geologic description that the art critic might make about Western landscape painting. The Western landscape must be conceptualized or at least broken down into perceptible parts and seeing a city in a mountain is a solution. The third explanation is a bit more scientific. Geology looks like building because it must answer to nature in the same way. Not surprisingly many who saw it this way were geologists.

Opposite: Ruins at Mesa Verde

Scenes on the Upper Missouri, Karl Bodmer, 1833.
From Maximilian of Wied *Travels in North America*

Clarence King spent 1853-1866 with the California Geological Survey. He was contemptuous of observations like Langford's, but his own were not so different, "To goad one's imagination up to the point of perpetually seeing resemblances of everything else in the forms of rocks, is the most vulgar vice of travelers. To refuse to see the architectural suggestions upon the Snake canon, however, is to administer a flat snub to one's fancy."[5]

He thought the peaks of Mount Tyndall had "shaped themselves like the ruins of cathedrals. ... buttresses more spired and ornamented than Milan's. ... The form of the mountain at the head of our ravine was purely Gothic."[6]

King explored the metaphor in depth. Why do these shapes occur? What makes them take the shape of buildings? He favored the Gothic connection as opposed to the castle or minaret given the structure/form dependence of Gothic architecture.

Next to this, and more pleasing to notice, is the interest and richness of the granite forms; for the whole region, from plain to plain, is built of this dense, solid rock, and is sculptured under chisel of cold in shapes of great variety, yet all having a common spirit, which is purely Gothic. In the much-discussed origin of this order of building, I never remember to have seen, though it can hardly have escaped mention, any suggestion of the possibility of the Gothic having been inspired by granite forms.[7]

As Maximilian had Bodmer to aesthetically document his work, King had the photographer Timothy O'Sullivan whose pictures of Canyon de Chelly, of architecture resembling geology and geology resembling architecture, were a harbinger of what was to come. The architecture that King saw in geology was decidedly vertical—the piers and buttresses of Gothic. King's observations were made in the mostly igneous and metamorphic mountains of Montana and California with their residue of volcanic and glacial history. It might be expected that the geology of the Southwest with its very different record of ancient oceans would evoke different reactions, and for many it did. It was not King's vertical piers but horizontal layers.

It was for John Wesley Powell. Powell famously explored the Colorado River from Wyoming to Nevada, including the Grand Canyon. He was a professor of geology so it is not surprising that rocks were a major topic. He looked at the Canyon and saw not just its history. He saw a library:

The thought grew into my mind that the canyons of this region would be a Book of Revelations in the rock-leaved Bible of geology. The thought fructified, and I determined to read the book. ... I talked with Indians and hunters, I went among the Mormons to learn what they knew of this country adjacent to the "Kingdom of God."[8]

This is not surprising given that the stone of the Grand Canyon consists of multiple layers of sedimentary rock formed by ancient oceans—limestone, sandstone, shale, unlike the granite mountains to the north.

This brings us to John Muir, who saw in geology both the vertical and the horizontal—the cathedral and the book. Geology to Muir was also a book "like any other writing, faint and blurred according to the length of time." Like Powell, Muir saw the geology of the Grand Canyon as a great library. "The whole cañon is a mine of fossils, in which five thousand feet of horizontal strata are exposed ... forming a grand geological library—a collection of stone books covering thousands of miles of shelving tier on tier conveniently arranged for the student."[9]

But Muir also saw buildings in the rocks. Muir's descriptions of geology are among the most informed while at the same time he is the writer who most frequently saw architecture when he was looking at geology, and the architecture he saw was Gothic. An example from his description of the Grand Canyon:

Yonder stands a spiry cathedral nearly five thousand feet in height, nobly symmetrical, with sheer buttressed walls and arched doors and windows, as richly finished and decorated with sculptures as the great rock temples of India or Egypt. Beside it rises a huge castle with arched gateway, turrets, watch-towers, ramparts, etc., and to right and left palaces, obelisks, and pyramids fairly fill the gulf.[10]

So for Muir, Southwestern geology was both vertical and horizontal, the result of the horizontal strata being vertically eroded:

Walking quietly about in the alleys and byways of the Grand Cañon City, we learn something of the way it was made; and all must admire effects so great from means apparently so simple: rain striking light hammer-blows or heavier in streams, with many rest Sundays; soft air and light, gentle sappers and miners, toiling forever; the big river sawing the plateau asunder, carrying away the eroded and ground waste, and exposing the edges of the strata to the weather; rain torrents sawing cross-streets and alleys.[11]

Timothy O'Sullivan, Canyon de Chelly, Monument Rock and White House Ruins.

Thomas Moran, Tower Fall, 1872

Thomas Moran, *Castle Geyser*, 1872

But this was "The Grand Canyon of the Colorado." When describing the structure of the Yosemite Valley a different Muir emerges because the geology is different. He wrote of the Sierra: "The architect may build his structures out of any kind of stone, without their forms betraying the physical characters of the stone employed; but in Sierra architecture, the style always proclaims the nature of the rock." But these forms as we will see are not the result of sedimentation but magma. Its stone is, "built up of brick-like blocks, whose forms and dimensions are determined chiefly by the degree of development of elected planes of cleavage."[12]

This of course suggests a second point of departure of for architecture—that the lessons of the structure of rock become the key to the building that is made from it. As to what architecture this geology might imply the answer for many is already there in the Ancestral Puebloan structures of the region.

If there was an epidemic of interpretations of Western geology as architecture, there is also an epidemic of interpretations of the indigenous architecture of the West as geology. Particularly the Ancestral Puebloans of Mesa Verde and Chaco Canyon, but just as much in the living pueblos of Acoma and the Hopi Mesas. Ethel Rose wrote in *The Craftsman:*

Hopi houses were built of the earth into such perfect imitations of the strange square forms of the surrounding buttes that it was almost impossible for even the keen eye of an Indian to tell houses from turreted hills. The Hopis, through the same instinct of protective security that mottles the breast of the thrush, that streaks the tawny tiger with stripes like the shadows of jungle reeds, have achieved one of the most perfect examples of architectural fitness known to the world.[13]

Frederick Monson, also a writer for *The Craftsman*, began his career as a photographer for the railroad and then the Geologic Survey and was recognized as an expert in the geology of the West, but his great love, and the photographic work for which he is best remembered, is of Native Americans. He describes the Hopi Pueblos, which were hard to distinguish from the rocks on which they sat:

You strain your eyes to see the towns on the crest of these great cliffs, but so like are they in color and outline to the living rock, that it is impossible to distinguish them until you come within a couple of miles, when you suddenly realize that the mesas are crowned with human habitations. ... As you climb one of the precipitous trails leading to the villages, you wonder what overpowering motive could have forced these people to build their homes in such inaccessible places, but a closer look at their architecture reveals the fact that it was fear of man that must originally have caused them to build their fortress-like cities at the top of the cliffs.[14]

Monson saw the Hopi as Ruskin and Viollet-le-Duc saw the Swiss, architects who did not know they were architects, creating greatness out of limitation and necessity.

Is this relentless domination of an austere environment that forms the keynote of the whole religious and social life of the Hopi, for the Indian is much more helpless in the presence of Nature than the civilized man. Where we may frequently offer successful resistance to natural forces, the primitive man has no recourse but to yield to circumstances that are due to his surroundings. The sincerity of their faith and their absolute belief in the Nature God is most interesting and wonderful to see.[15]

But the perception of geology is different than the perception of the forest. It raises questions of theology more than aesthetics. Unlike the forest we see the mountains, if not fixed, then complete, and it is the historical record of millenniums. The nineteenth-century mind, even the educated one, might see this in a different way. Many would say these canyons are the product of a grand plan, perhaps not so literally as Stevens who thought providence had laid out the route of a railroad through the mountains but nevertheless the result of a divine order. For Langford the forms of this topography were not an accident. It was a supernatural design. He wrote, "It is a new phase in the natural world; a fresh exhibition of the handiwork of the Great Architect."[16]

King and Muir certainly gave the biblical description of creation little credence, but like many of their contemporaries they could not accept the arbitrariness of Darwin's idea of natural selection; it implied there was no design, only accidents, and they thought all of nature, especially geology had been designed. Muir followed Darwin carefully, but he too looked at nature and saw a grand plan. He wrote, "In the development of these, the Master Builder chose for a tool, not the earthquake nor lightning to rend and split asunder, not the stormy torrent nor eroding rain, but the tender snow-flowers, noiselessly falling through unnumbered seasons, the offspring of the sun and sea."[17]

In his essay of 1911, "The Ruin," the German sociologist Georg Simmel identified the precise relationship that was manifested in the ruins of Rome. "In the ruin, nature begins to have the upper hand: 'the brute, downward-dragging, corroding, crumbling power produces a new form, entirely meaningful, comprehensible, differentiated'. ... The ruin is not the triumph of nature, but an intermediate moment, a fragile equilibrium between persistence and decay."[18]

Americans looked at the geology of the West with European eyes, and like their English counterparts saw ruins in two ways—the ruin of memory and the ruin as nature.

Maximilian and Langford saw geology as the ruin of memory. King and Muir saw it as the ruins of nature. The rustic architects that soon followed them were similarly divided between literal nostalgia and abstraction of nature, as well as being divided between geology as vertical and geology as horizontal.

Our connection to a building is the mirror image of our connection to the land. It is the same as the Old Faithful Inn or the Glacier Park Lodge. If we can see the basilica in the forest, we can see the forest in the basilica. If we can see architecture as geology, we can see the geology in architecture.

THE SANTA FE RAILROAD

It is a strange journey through history to drive the 70 miles from Santa Fe, New Mexico to Las Vegas, New Mexico. Santa Fe is just what one expects, a dense collection of battered adobe walls, arcades, and log beams of Spanish Colonial architecture looking little changed from the early 1800s. Las Vegas by contrast seems all wrong. There is little Hispanic about it. The main town square is surrounded by three-story corniced brick buildings, some with porches, all looking like typical Anglo nineteenth-century railroad town. The surrounding area is dominated by Burnham and Root's Montezuma Hotel, a Queen Anne structure built by the Santa Fe Railroad when their tracks reached the city. One might assume that this is the type of architecture the railroad brought with it, that replaced the traditional Hispanic architecture of Santa Fe, but it is Santa Fe that is the new town. Las Vegas came first.

What we see today in Santa Fe is the result of rigid design guidelines that began in earnest with the city plan of 1912. There were buildings in Santa Fe that resembled those in Las Vegas but they have mostly been destroyed, covered with adobe, or painted with adobe-colored paint. The Santa Fe played their part in this as well, most conspicuously at the La Fonda Hotel. In fact, the Harvey Company, the hospitality partner of the Santa Fe, was one of the major if not the major agent in the creation of Hispanic and Native-American-inspired buildings. The architecture was only a part of a broad tourist marketing strategy of art, architecture, and performance that extended from silver jewelry to whole Disneyesque pueblos at world's fairs. The architecture of Las Vegas is authentic. It was built by the Santa Fe and their associated hotel/restaurant/tourism organization, the Harvey Company, but it was built in 1882 in the same style that they built in Kansas and Colorado. The change to Hispanic/Native American came after and in dramatic fashion.

So why did this happen? What caused this shift in taste from Anglo Queen Anne in1882 to Southwestern Hispanic/Native American in 1912? Obviously, there was a cultural shift in which the perception of the latter became romanticized, but by whom?

Historians assign a great deal of credit to Helen Hunt Jackson's 1884 novel *Ramona*. It contains short, appealing descriptions of a California Hispanic courtyard farmhouse and no doubt did a great deal to popularize that style. George James wrote in *The Craftsman* in an article titled "The Indigenous Architecture of Ramona's Country," "For any one section of the United States to claim a new and true style of architecture as its own is to make a large and rather startling claim. Yet I unhesitatingly make that claim for Ramona's country. There is no purely original and indigenous American architecture of the domestic type save that which has been developed here."[1]

In this same period there was a growing interest in Native American Culture and the Southwestern Native Americans had a special appeal. In 1879, John Wesley Powell, head of the newly formed US Department of Ethnology, sent three of his staff, including a young Frank Cushing, into the American Southwest with the charge to study the cultures of the Native Americans there. Frederick Chapin began excavating at Mesa Verde in 1889. *The Craftsman* magazine published several articles on the Hopi between 1901 and 1916.

The oldest parts of the La Fonda Hotel, on the main plaza in Santa Fe, date from 1920.

The oldest parts of the Plaza Hotel, on the main plaza in Las Vegas NM, date from 1882.

Opposite: Thomas Moran, *Grand Canyon of Arizona from Hermit Rim Road*, 1912

But the single largest factor in the romanticization of Puebloan culture is arguably the Santa Fe Railroad and the Harvey Company themselves. They may have been marketing and public relations, but it employed some of the great writers and artists of the day and its motives went far beyond filling train seats and hotel rooms. It became a major collector of distributor and ultimately creator of Native American art. The Atchison, Topeka & Santa Fe Railway was founded in 1859 with the intention of connecting Atchison and Topeka, Kansas with Santa Fe, New Mexico. Its progress was slow, but in 1883 reached Needles, California, where it connected with the Southern Pacific to become transcontinental. So, the railroad that was to become the "Santa Fe" began its progress across Arizona in pursuit of the by now familiar economic trilogy—timber, mining, and tourism. Tourism was strangely the least promising of the three at this point. We do not think of the Arizona desert as a source of timber but what is thought to be the largest unbroken strand of ponderosa pines extends from the White Mountains of eastern Arizona to the Grand Canyon.

Of course, initially the railroad was the primary consumer of timber—the perennial problem of ties-2,000-3,000 per mile—and the infrastructure required to build a nearly level roadway across the irregular geology of the West.

In 1882 a Chicago lumberman Everett Ayer built a mill in Flagstaff that could produce 100,000 board feet per day, contracted with the Santa Fe and other railroads to supply all their timber and he opened a series of lumber yards along the Santa Fe from Albuquerque to Los Angeles. He was to become one of the strongest supporters of the promotion of the Grand Canyon. Like many in his profession he strongly advocated the preservation of fragments of what he was in the process of destroying.[2]

But the Santa Fe faced the same problems as the other transcontinentals and the Panic of 1893 put the Santa Fe and many other railroads into bankruptcy. It reorganized under a new president, J. Edward Ripley, who led them into prosperity. But Ripley was, like Louis Hill, a man with a larger cultural vision and gave the company a new direction—an emphasis on tourism. Soon after Ripley's appointment his good friend Ayer, of the Ayer Lumber Company, took Ripley on his first visit to the Grand Canyon. In time the Santa Fe built a spur line between Winslow and the south rim.

The year 1893 saw a campaign to expand the tourism market. C. A. Higgins of the Santa Fe was asked to prepare a series of booklets for the railroad highlighting the tourist destinations along the route, which at that time did not extend past Albuquerque. But he soon turned to the subject that appealed to him most—the landscape and indigenous architecture of New Mexico and Arizona. His second book, *The Grand Canon of the Colorado River*, describes the sublime qualities of the canyon, despite the fact that the railroad would not reach there until three years later. His third book, *To California and Back*, is a mix of public relations and inspired cultural commentary. It describes each Harvey Company hotel and the route in glowing detail, but it also wanders off the route to discuss Native American architecture. Higgins was not working alone. He hired W. H. Jackson, photographer, to produce illustrations and he hired Thomas Moran to paint a Grand Canyon view to mass produce and distribute.

If Montana and Wyoming lacked human-made monuments to rival Europe, the Southwest had no such problems. Pueblo Bonita was built in 1150, the year the Royal portal at Chartres Cathedral was finished. To many the Acoma Pueblo is the most striking of the inhabited pueblos. Acoma dates from the thirteenth century. Sitting atop a stone mesa, Acoma's resemblance the Acropolis is inescapable.

Higgins also hired the writers Charles Lummis and George James. Lummis was an editor of his own magazine, *Land of Sunshine*, and the author of popular works about the Southwest, and another advocate of the "See America First" movement. Lummis was and is better known than James, but James was the more architecturally observant and descriptive.

To James the architecture grew directly from the nature of the stone. He wrote:

All throughout the Verde Valley are scattered scores of cave, cliff and village ruins. At many points a soft calcareous sandstone covers

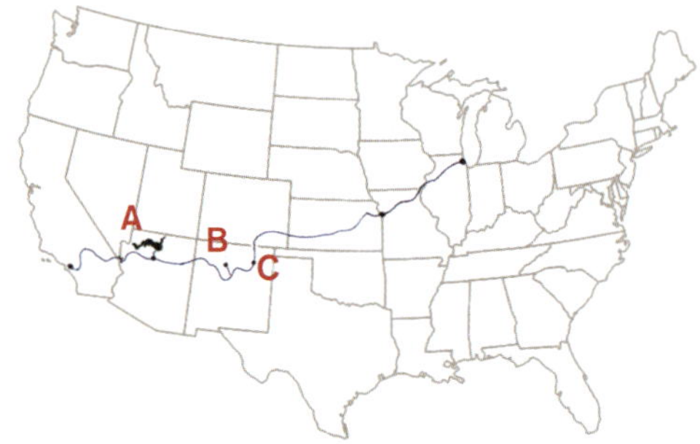

The primary route of the Atchison Topeka and Santa Fe
A Grand Canyon National Park
B Santa Fe
C Las Vegas, NM

Pueblo Bonita, Chaco Canyon, New Mexico, CE 850 to CE 1150

The Acoma Pueblo, New Mexico, since CE1150

Louis Akin, *El Tovar, Grand Canyon*, 1906

the underlying rock. This sandstone is strongly laminated, and, being of so yielding a nature, was easily excavated. In the canyons of the water courses and wherever nature had formed a cliff, the cave dweller found everything ready for his stone axe and flint hammer. Continued peckings, with an occasional heavy blow, excavated quite a cave, and thus his rude shelter was formed. ... and when he learned from the birds and the insects the lesson of mortar, mud or cement, he made a solid wall which shut in his cave.[3]

Architecture and geology had a spatial/formal connection as well. One could not say where one ended and the other began. The cliff regions of New Mexico:

are honeycombed with cave, cliff and pueblo ruins. These terms are all more popular than scientific. ... If one were to demand scientific accuracy in definition he would speak of natural caves below the surface, caves on a level with the point of entrance, caves in cliffs above the base, caves with front closed up with rudely laid unmortared blocks of rock, and caves closed up with mortared walls. Then there would be the excavated caves of the same varieties. The fact is that one kind so insensibly shades into another kind that it is practically impossible to be exact.[4]

In 1901 the Fred Harvey Company entered a new marketing area, Southwestern tourism, with a vengeance. Fred's son Ford Harvey took over the company, but it was his brother-in-law J. F. Huckel and his sister Minne that were to set the artistic and architectural policy. That year they founded the Harvey Company "Indian Department." Its purpose was to acquire Native American art both for collecting and marketing, and it rather quickly became a primary goal to produce it as well.[5]

As visitors from the East like Sharp and Cody were responsible for romanticizing the log cabin so did visitors from the East romanticize the pueblo. Stephen Fried argues that the critical date in this narrative is October of 1901. A group of 20 executives and consultants made an extensive tour of the Southwest including one of the first trips to the south rim by train. The party included Ripley, other executives of the Santa Fe, and the new management of the Fred Harvey Company.

Their guide was Charles Lummis. Although Lummis was sometimes paid by Harvey or the Santa Fe, his boosterism for the Southwest was genuine. He was also a vocal advocate for Native American causes. But if Lummis' objective was to convince the Santa Fe and the Harvey Company management that their new architecture should draw on the indigenous he ultimately succeeded. Lummis planned the trip carefully. They visited the most impressive Ancestral Puebloan structure, Pueblo Bonita at Chaco Canyon. They also visited Acoma, the city on the mesa and the most picturesque of the inhabited pueblos. Their last stop was the south rim. Their primary purpose was to select a location for El Tovar hotel. All agreed on the canyon rim except Lummis. He wrote:

The natural call of the wayfaring Philistine had been for a hotel smack on the brink: and an artist had painted a 'plan' with the caravansary dominating the canon. But he was too soon. It was recognized by the party that in the first place this would be an impudence—'You can't slap God Almighty in the face like that,' ... the element of surprise, so potent in literature and art, should not be forgotten here.[6]

El Tovar was built off the rim, but not by much, two years later. Like Hill, the Harvey Company had their own architects, and understood that whatever style they built in, it was part of a marketing strategy.

MARY COLTER: LOOKOUT STUDIO AND HERMIT'S REST

In 1905, four years after the visit of Lummis and his group to inspect the site at the south rim, work was completed on the Harvey House Hotel, now called El Tovar. The architect was Charles Whittlesey who had just completed the Alvarado Hotel in Albuquerque for the Harvey Company. The Harvey publication describing El Tovar tells us, "The architect has combined in admirable proportions the Swiss chalet and the Norway villa. ... where the traveler seeking high class accommodations also find freedom from ultra-fashionable restrictions."[1] Why Swiss or Norwegian buildings might be appropriate models for a hotel in the Arizona desert was not explained, but the reason is obvious, the Harvey Company hotels and the Santa Fe were in direct competition with the Northern Pacific who were taking that approach at the Old Faithful Inn. If rustic architecture is based on the idea that both form and material are indigenous this is neither. It is hard to imagine a building less at home in this place than a faux chalet.

Its construction was in keeping with its alien presence. No building exemplifies the great technological contradiction of national park rustic and of the rustic park lodges than El Tovar, probably the least truly rustic. It uses very few local materials except for the stone. The logs were Douglas-fir, shipped by rail from Oregon. Why the local ponderosa pine was not used, as it was in many subsequent buildings in the park is not clear, but this fact tells us a great deal about the culture and economics of railroads building buildings, that shipping material was cheaper than shipping skilled labor and equipment, as in the Yellowstone train station.

The primary structure is mostly wood stud walls of milled lumber (Douglas-fir as well) nailed together in perfect rectilinear shapes except for the marks of the circular saw along their surfaces. Little if any of this can be seen inside or out. Most of the logs of the exterior wall were half log siding on the wood stud walls. The only real rustic structures are the log beams and trusses.

The Grand Canyon was not at that point a national park, although efforts had been underway since 1882, and although it had been made a forest reserve and then a national monument, it did not become a park until 1919. One of the reasons was the presence of a number of concessionaires who wanted to maintain their market. The Santa Fe and the Harvey Company, latecomers, were not among these, and a key architectural objective in style and location was to upstage the existing commercial residents.

Opposite: Lookout Studio

Hopi House

The Harvey Company's brief affair with the rustic chalet in the desert came to a quick end, abandoned before the El Tovar was finished, when they began the construction of Hopi House not a quarter of a mile away.

Hopi House was based on indigenous regional architecture, but it was not specific to the canyon and it too is a bit foreign to its particular site. It draws on images of indigenous architecture, not geology or the qualities of local stone. Later Harvey buildings were built of Kaibab Limestone, the top layer of the canyon, the rock upon which the buildings sat. In fact, what one sees is not the local stone. The whitish local Kaibab Limestone from the site is used in the inner structural wall, but what one sees is the exterior facing, a redder Moenkopi Coconino sandstone brought from Winslow, 150 miles away, undoubtedly by rail. The facing was imported to make it look like another building, an actual Hopi Pueblo.

Hopi House is a fairly precise copy of the Hopi buildings at Oraibi 100 miles to the east. Hopi House is not a real pueblo of course. Compromises and additions were made. Hopi dwellings rarely have ground-floor entrances and are traditionally entered through the roof by ladder. Hopi House had these but it had doors as well. The ladders remain; the openings they served were closed long ago. Plaster stood in for adobe walls, concrete for earth floors. Where traditional log vigas did not accommodate the structural loads, iron rails were used as beams. Hopi house was not meant to be a ruin. It was a replication of a living Hopi village filled with Hopis. It is in odd contrast to later Harvey buildings that were built of Kaibab Limestone.

Charles F. Whittlesey was the architect of record of Hopi house. At some point Mary Colter was brought in, who is often credited, incorrectly, with the design.

Hopi House

Interior sales room at Hopi House, possibly designed by Colter

Mary Colter

There has been some controversy about the extent of Colter's involvement in the many buildings attributed to her at the canyon and elsewhere for which she took credit. Her role may have been exaggerated in the past, such as the attribution of El Tovar to her. More recently her whole career has been called a hoax.[2] On the surface it would appear that she may have been given too much credit in the past but one suspects she is not being given enough in the present. Several facts are clear. Colter rarely made orthogonal scale drawings of her designs. She provided models and evocative but imprecise perspective sketches that were translated into conventional architectural drawings by others. Throughout her career she clearly relied on others to draw the plans, sections, and details that would have been necessary for construction. This process clearly required more than just interpretation on the part of her coworkers. There were other designers involved in all these projects and it has always been clear that they were more than just draftsmen, but this is true of many modern architects such as Craig Ellwood. At the very least she worked as a designer on the Harvey projects at the canyon and one with a great deal of power and influence.

What is revealing in recent research is that it appears that the first phase of building at the canyon—Lookout Studio and Hermit's Rest—Louis Curtiss was heavily involved. Those buildings done in the 1930s—Desert Watchtower and the Bright Angel Lodge—involved Robert Raney. This could explain the substantive architectural differences between the two phases of building—one geological and one ethnographic. But these two aspects of her work have a more obvious explanation. The Harvey Company architecture was part of a marketing strategy, and each building had a role to play in this regardless of the designer.

The first two Colter buildings at the canyon, built in 1914, take their inspiration from the geology of the canyon, although they make use of indigenous building tradition in a generic way. Colter's 1930s buildings are far more in the spirit of Hopi House with literal references to Native American building and iconography.

There are two distinct Colter styles on display at the Grand Canyon. Both have historical references. The buildings that draw on Native American culture, Hopi House and the Watchtower of the 1930s, are conspicuous in their commercialization of the things that are to Native Americans spiritual and private used as marketing devices for the Harvey Company. More original, more appealing, and less offensive to the Native Americans were the buildings done without strong formal precedents such as the two that followed Hopi House.

The topmost strata of the Grand Canyon, the Kiabab limestone, is harder than the sandstone below and its sides are more vertical. This is the location of the best architecture of the canyon, certainly Colter's. While many of Colter's later buildings are fairly literal interpretations of existing Native American models and appropriate Native American iconography for the financial benefit of the Fred Harvey Company, Lookout Studio and Hermit's Rest draw more directly on the geology of the canyon. They are not without references to Hispanic or Native American forms, but they are far more abstract than literal and far more fused with the geology. The buildings have varying relations with the rock. The Lookout Studio seems to grow up out of it. Hermit's Rest is far more excavated.

Lookout Studio
Grand Canyon National Park, 1914

Both the Lookout Studio and Hermit's Rest were built to create competition with existing businesses. The first, Lookout (1914), an observation station and photographic studio to compete with the existing and highly successful Kolb Brothers' Studio, is beautifully and prominently sited at the canyon edge, literally growing out of the canyon walls. The cynic would see this as yet another marketing device to intercept the tourists on their way to the Kolb Studio just off the rim, but the building is hard to equal as a happy marriage of building and site.

Lookout Studio is one-story building roughly square in plan on a point projecting into the canyon so that the east and north sides align roughly with the rim. At the northeast corner where they meet is a square two-story tower. A fireplace inglenook is located at the center of the wall opposite the canyon. Two routes through the small building are choreographed to allow the canyon and building to unfold. One can enter at the southeast corner, walk thought the building to the tower and ascend to the raised balcony above to the canyon overlook, then turn to descend the tower and either enter the main floor facing the fireplace inglenook at the opposite end or exit to the steps into the canyon. Or one can walk past the building to the tower at the canyon edge and take the same route in reverse.

The construction system follows generic Hispanic and Native American traditions—stone bearing walls, a roof of log beams, "vigas," supporting a wood roof. All logs are the same size—columns and beams of about 10 inches. The primary roof support is a single log beam that spans the space at center just below the roof ridge that is supported by two log columns that divide the space in half. This beam supports the log roof rafters that gently slope toward the perimeter, spaced about seven feet apart. Between the log beams is a celling of flat boards, given additional support by hidden two-inch-wide joists above.[3] For the most part the structure is what it appears to be. Joints are made with steel rods that are largely invisible. Some of the columns are arranged more for scenographic effect than structural necessity. There are fake wood columns on the inside of the stone bearing walls while at least one additional real column had to be added at some point after the initial construction. As a construction it is "honest." There is no concealed steel, and little ornamental structure.

East elevation

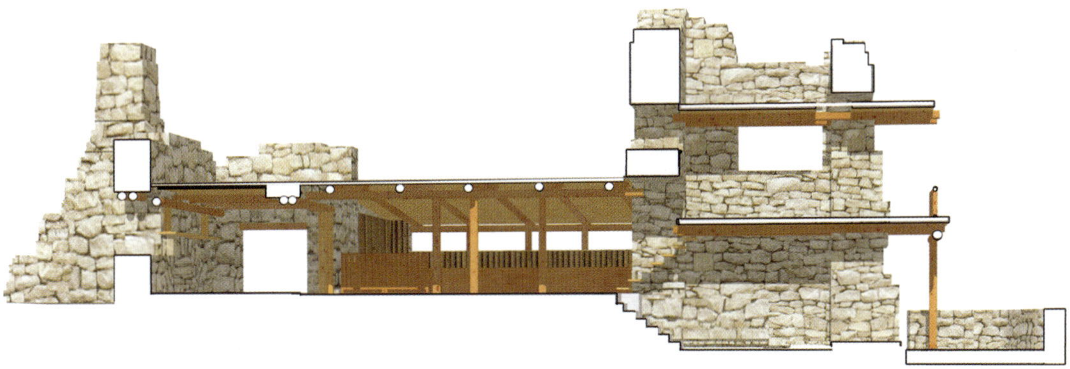

Section looking west

Lookout Studio,
Grand Canyon, 1914, aerial view

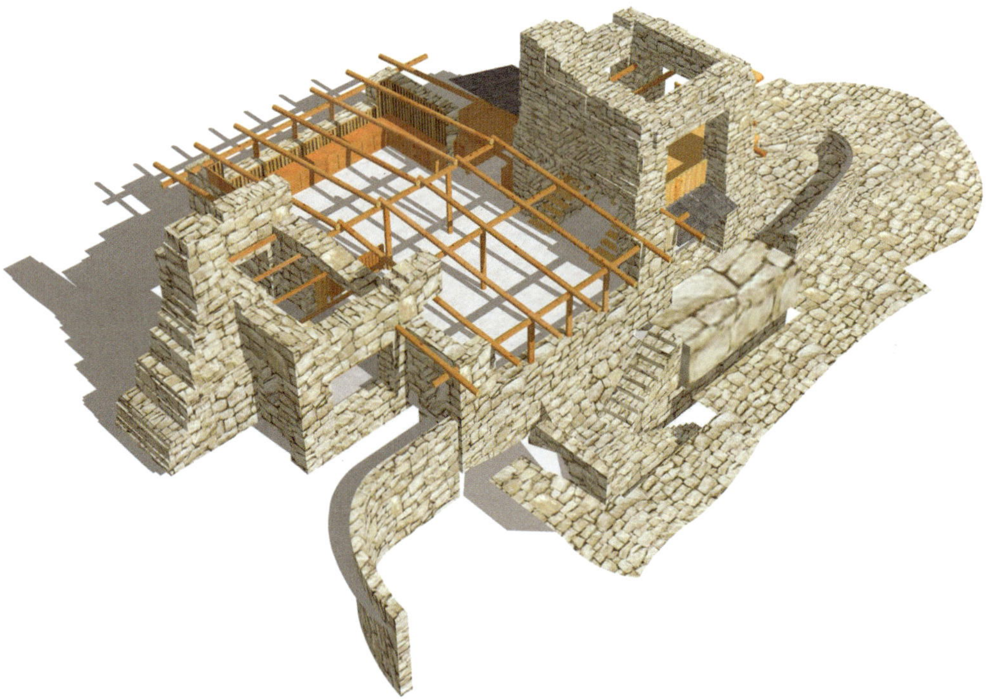

Lookout Studio,
Grand Canyon, 1914, roof framing

There are few if any literal references to history. The Swiss-like balcony rail of the tower today is an unfortunate rebuilding of a far more abstract log original. Lookout suggests a puebloan building but in other ways is very unlike them. A characteristic of most Southwestern Native American architecture is the absence of visual connections between interior and exterior. Windows are rare and small, and doors are not common. Their idea of a "view" was very different. Lookout Studio has for obvious reasons a great deal of glass. The side wall facing the canyon has a very unpueblo-like strip window—a glazed opening far larger than what could be found in any pueblo, and its log mullions are actually columns supporting the roof. The result is a structure far more original than a faux-pueblo ruin.

It is the structure of a ruin. Vertical edges are irregular. Horizontal lines are broken. Parts seem to be missing. Walls are generally battered but with frequent protrusions. Parapets are broken in a variety of profiles. Some parapets are high at their ends and low at the center or the reverse. On examination it is a systematic, composed, picturesque composition. One parapet corner is always raised, the opposite corner is always lowered and the wall between is stepped as in the top of the tower. Rough faced Kaibab Limestone often has rectilinear or polygonal edges. Straight lines—vertical, horizontal, or sloped are the exception not the rule. All blurred the boundary between building and site. Originally the junction between landscape and architecture was even more obscured by a roof garden, but this was later removed, along with one of the stone parapets, to reduce the load on the roof structure.

One can see the building as Muir saw the canyon, buildings emerging naturally from the stone geologic base, or one can see the building as the reverse, as ruins, the way Georg Simmel would see them—buildings breaking down and returning to a state of nature. This type of log structure resembles Ancestral Puebloan construction and closely resembles classic Hispanic construction with its use of vigas, log beams, and latillas—small sticks laid diagonally—but is highly abstract and archetypal in comparison with the specificity of Hopi House.

Inglenook

Interior

Hermit's Rest
Grand Canyon National Park, 1914

The second Colter building in this series at the canyon rim is Hermit's Rest, built immediately after Lookout (1914). The Bright Angel trail was a privately owned popular route to the canyon floor owned by another concessionaire. The beginning of the Harvey Company's trail to the canyon floor was located seven miles west, and Hermit's Rest was built there as refreshment area to draw tourists to the Harvey Company's trail route. It was another commercial building designed to compete with an existing concession. The architecture played a part in this by trying to look older. Like many Colter buildings it has a narrative, a story largely of her creation explaining its origin and perhaps its architecture, although in this case it seems invented or exaggerated—a hermit who lived on the site, a prospector. But this narrative of the hidden recluse probably influenced Colter's design, and again there are historical cultural references—latillas and vigas—but the building's virtues, like the Lookout Studio, are the result of a more abstract strategy.

Hermit's Rest is another of Colter's "geologic" buildings as opposed to those done in imitation of Native American buildings. Rather than growing out of the rock it is rather excavated out of it. Hermit's Rest is relatively hidden in contrast to Colter's other buildings at the canyon. It is to be discovered and unfolds as one approaches. It sits on a sloped site set back slightly from the canyon rim within the Kaibab Limestone layer, which is also its primary material. An oblong stone box running parallel to the slope is half buried in the hillside and its roof covered with several feet of earth and rock. On the uphill side is a large, cavernous inglenook, a one-quarter spherical stone vault with a fireplace inside. Projecting on the canyon side is a log beam and column porch, asymmetrical in contrast to the largely symmetrical stone backdrop. The wall above the porch has a long clerestory to light the room beyond and again the large quantity of glass makes the building decidedly un-pueblo like and in doing so makes something far more original. The stone walls are given a ruinous profile and irregular copings at least on the short sides. Thus the walls are rubble with no mortar exposed on the surface.

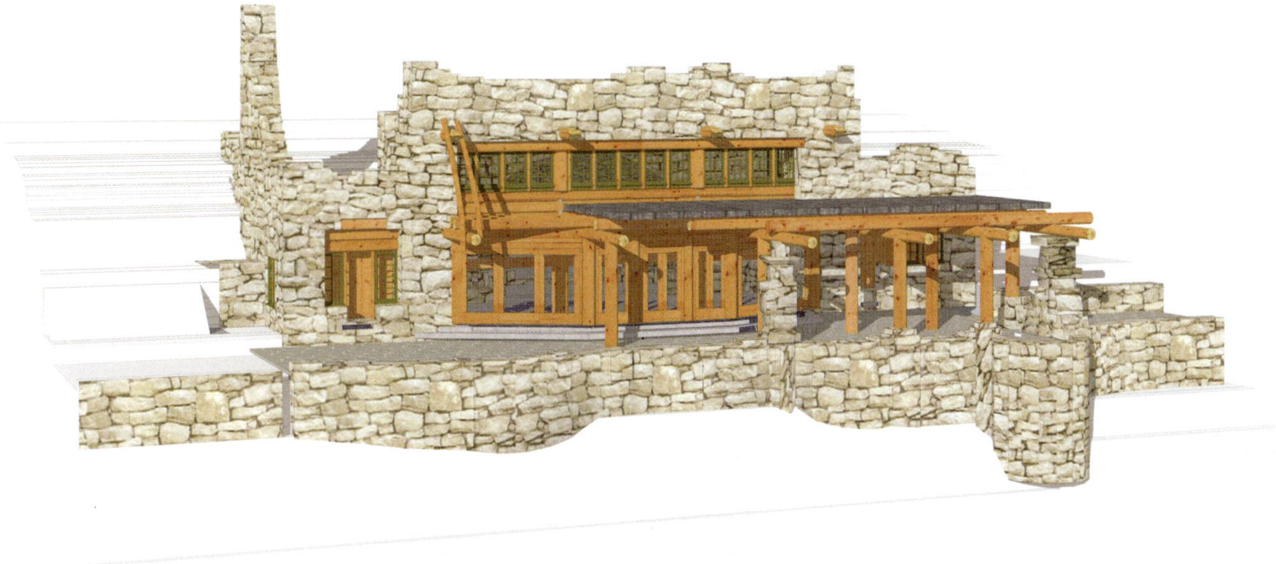

Canyon elevation

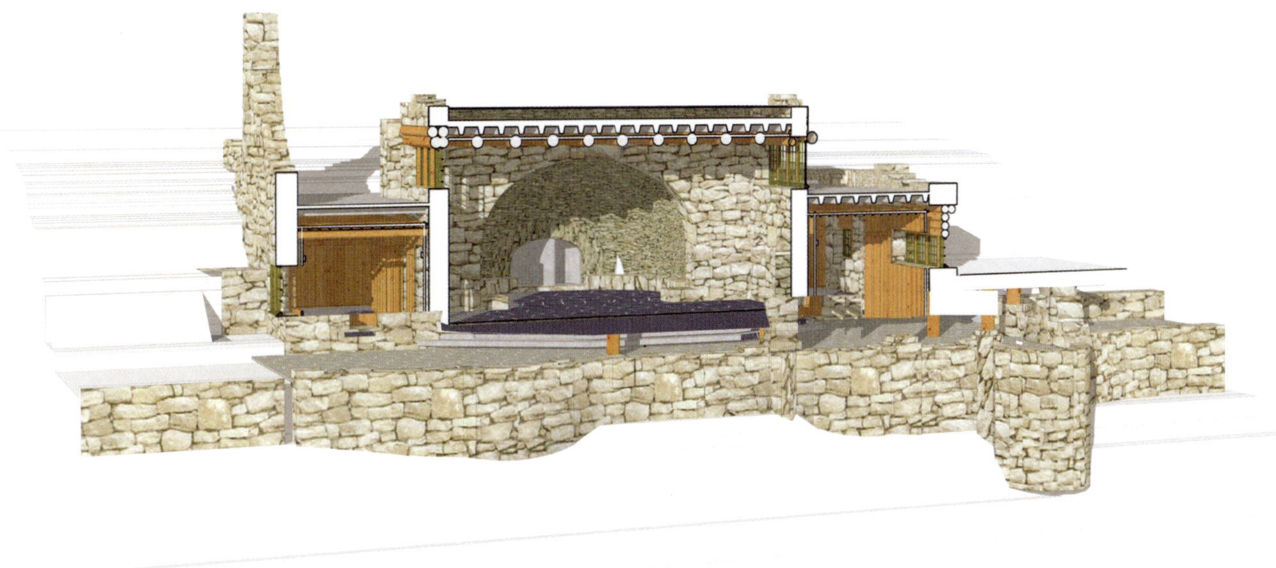

Section looking west

The truth is that Lookout Studio and Hermit's Rest are two very different buildings. Lookout Studio is an indigenous stone and wood building. Hermit's Rest is a concrete and steel building wrapped in an indigenous layer of stone and wood. Both of these, however, are architecture of a very different order than the glib replication of Native American architecture that is Hopi House. Hopi House sits on a lawn that is essentially flat. It is not a foreign object but it is a detached one. Hermit's Rest and Lookout Studio emerge from the stone and ruble that support them.

There is much about Hermit's Rest that is not anything like a pueblo—clerestories, banks of glazed doors, long timber spans, and an oversized arch, but it is the fragmented irregular tops of both buildings in combination with the increased thickness and size of the stone as the walls descend that links landscape and building so effectively.

Hermit's Rest appears to be a fairly regular building that has been abraded and eroded at its edges. The logs in the building proper are square with chamfered edges. Those of the external trellis are round logs. The stone walls are stepped with irregular edges as at Lookout. George James wrote of it:

It is a striking cave-home in the cliffs, but of majestic proportions. The rough and unhewn rocks have been cunningly put into place so that from the exterior one can scarce tell where cliff ends and building begins. But when you enter the doorway a surprise awaits you. ... you enter a room, forty-five feet wide and eighteen feet high which is one vast cave, hollowed out of the wall, shaped like a dome cut in half, the further base of which is a fireplace, the like of which must have warmed the toes of the giant Vikings when they reached Walhalla.[4]

This is a second type of ruin, the one described by Georg Simmel. It is not about memory. It is partially about geology, but it is really about nature reclaiming architecture.

View toward canyon

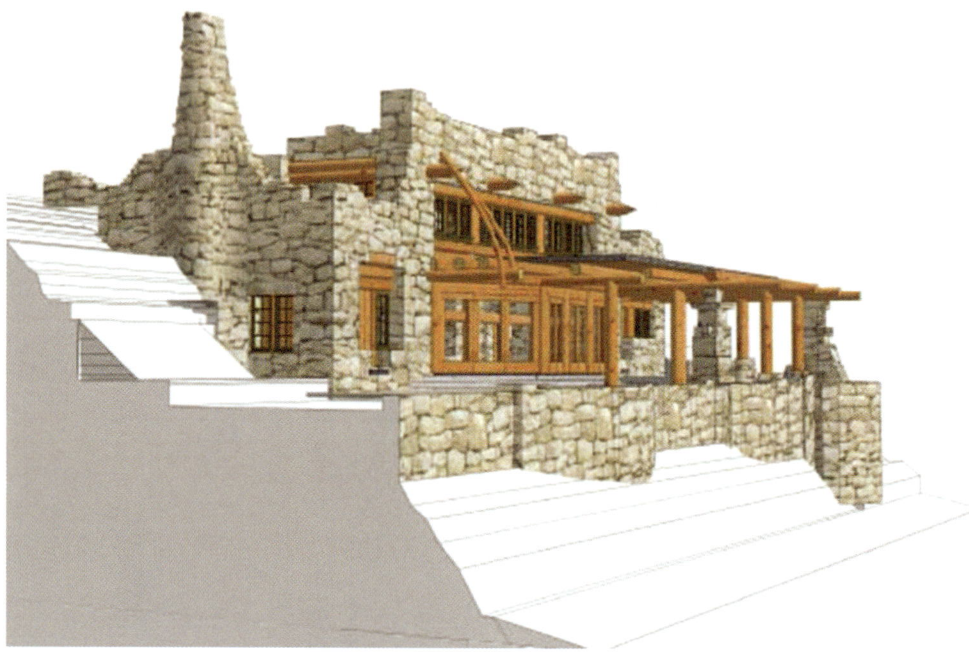

View from canyon

Inglenook

Section through canyon edge

Lookout Studio and Hermit's are, as James said they are—extensions of the landscape. If they are suggestive of Native American architecture, it is because they followed the same constraints, not because they appropriated its forms.[5]

The stone and log type of structure used at the Lookout Studio was not quite up to the structural task here, primarily because of the heavy stone and earth load on the roof, the rear retaining wall, and the long clerestory window that undermines the wall supporting the roof above. Beneath the earth covering on the roof there is a second structure—a thirteen-inch-thick concrete-ribbed slab hidden by the logs and stone below. The concrete is in turn supported by a 12x34-inch edge beam and two six-inch diameter concrete-filled steel pipe columns, encased with hollowed out logs. None of the steel or concrete is visible. The stone vault had a concrete shell behind and above the stone facing to support the substantial load of the almost 20 feet of earth above. Once again local wood and timber is supported in part by a structure of steel and concrete. It is essentially a stone-walled, steel-roofed building.[6]

After completing Hermit's Rest, Colter's work with the Harvey Company took her elsewhere and her next executed project was a sham imitation of the Taos Pueblo in San Diego for the Panama California Exposition, a return to cultural appropriation. She did not return to the canyon until 1922. By then the Grand Canyon was a national park and the Park Service would not approve building it on the rim. And by then Colter and the Harvey Company had already abandoned the geologic abstraction of Lookout and Hermit's for the literalism of Native American imitations or the romanticism of Western pioneers. But however dramatic the architectural change the logic of design was consistent. It was the purpose of Lookout Studio to sell photographs. It was the purpose of Hermit's Fest to sell refreshments and attract tourists. When it became the purpose of the architecture to sell Native American art and design it required a different package.

Inglenook

Hermit's Rest
Construction

It is two buildings, a steel and concrete one encased in a stone and log encrustation. The latter was necessary for marketing; the former needed for the structural difficulties.

It is an industrialized steel and concrete frame hidden inside a rustic wood and stone one.

The concealed concrete and steel frame is a 13-inch ribbed concrete slab supported by a retaining wall on the uphill side and12x34 inch concrete beam on the canyon side, supported by 6-inch round steel columns is filled with cement.

A 12-inch concrete vault supports the earth over the inglenook.

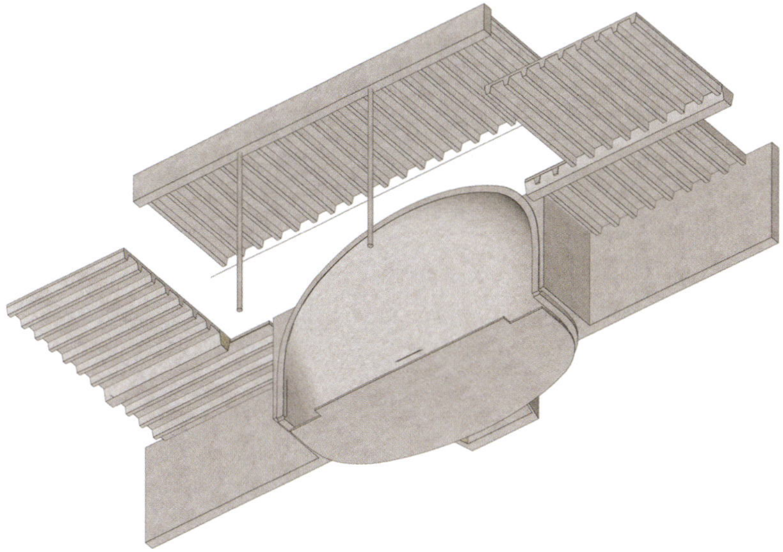

Concrete and steel structure seen from below

Portions of the stone and log structure are exposed. The concrete and steel is completely hidden.

There is a stone facing on concrete vault, log enclosures on the steel columns, and a stone encasement of the face of the concrete slab.

Portions of the stone and log frames are structural at the low roof and the porch.

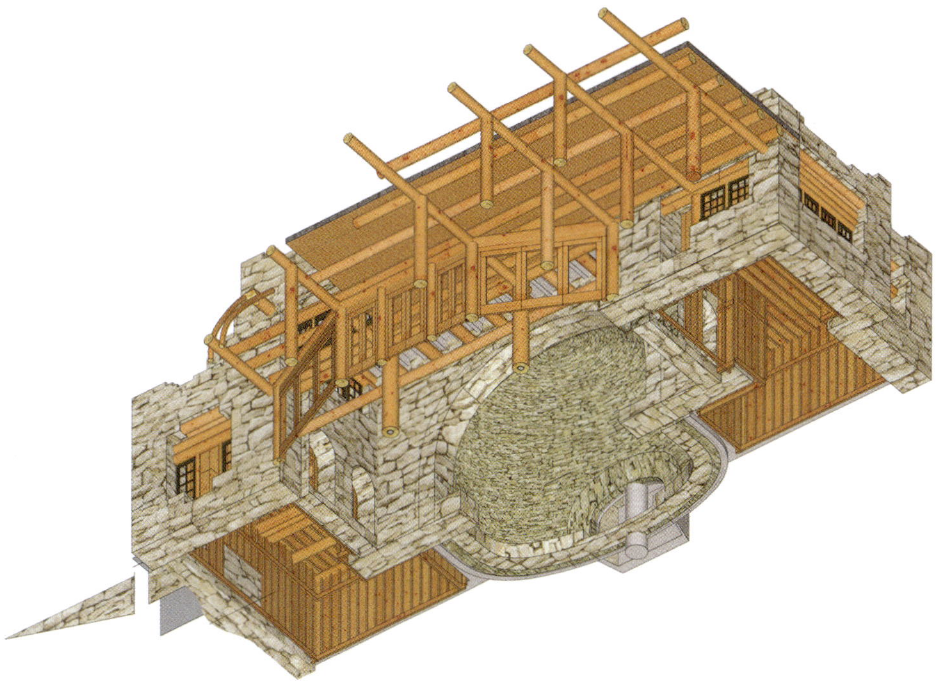

Stone and wood encrustation seen from below

Hermit's Rest
Wall Details Showing Structure Only

3-inch ribbed concrete slab is supported by the concrete retaining wall (not shown) and a 12-inch x 34-inch concrete beam supported by 6-inch round steel column filled with cement.

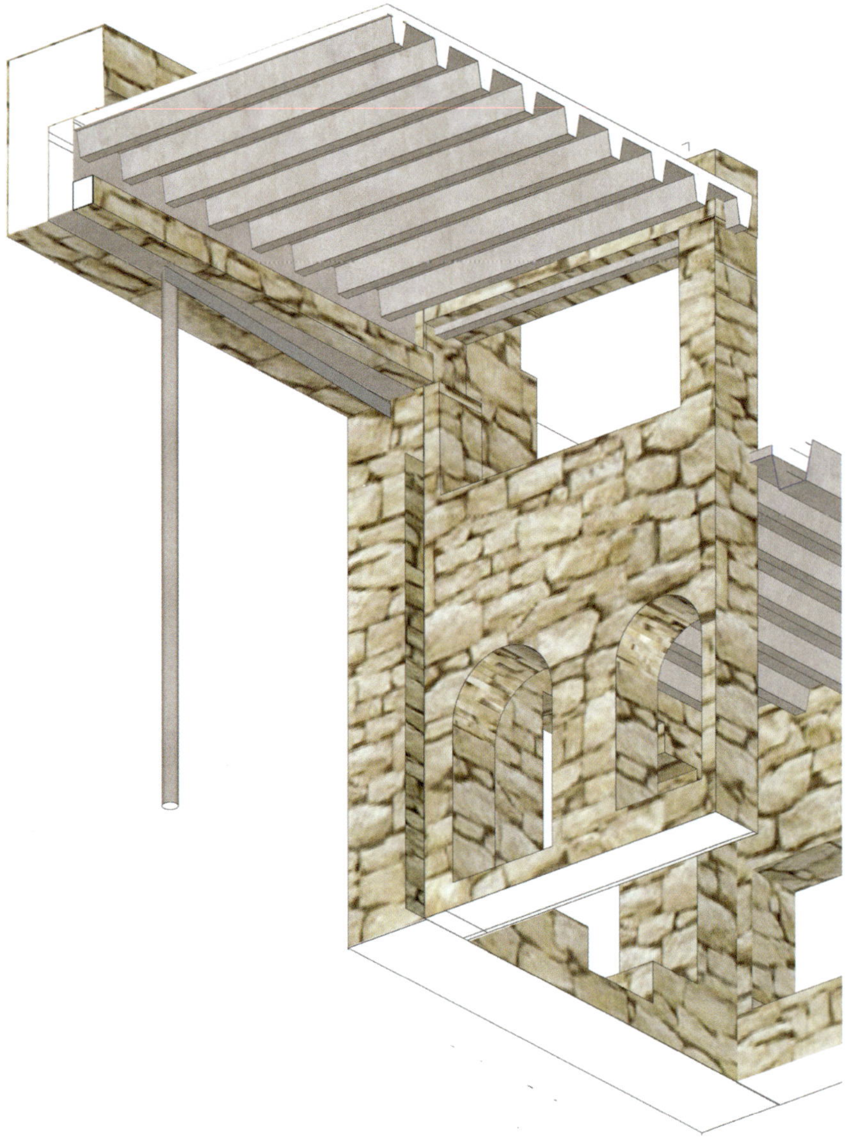

Hermit's Rest
Wall Details Showing Structure and Finishes

The high roof construction, a ribbed concrete slab is covered with dirt and rock.

The 12-inch x 34-inch concrete beam the slab rests on is hidden inside stone wall.

The ceiling construction below the slab is non-structural. Log beams are hung from 2x4 ceiling supports in turn hung from the slab. The space between beams is filled with latillas, saplings, and covered with clay.

The low roof frame is a real structure of boards on logs 3 feet on center and 3x6 joists at 30 inches on center.

There are 12-inch logs encasing the round steel column. The log frame below is non-structural.

GEOLOGY: HERBERT MAIER AND GILBERT UNDERWOOD

Granite Formation, Tuolumne Meadows, Yosemite

If John Muir saw architecture growing out of the limestone at the Grand Canyon, he saw something else at Yosemite, architecture that was already there, hidden in the granite, waiting to be exposed:

Therefore, when we say that the glacial ice-sheet and separate glaciers molded *the mountains, we must remember that their molding power upon* hard granite possessing a strong physical structure *is comparatively slight. In such hard, strongly built granite regions,* glaciers do not so much mold and shape, as disinter forms already conceived and ripe. *... it has only developed the predestined forms of mountain beauty which were ready and waiting to receive the baptism of light.*[1]

The layers of the Grand Canyon might have formed a book, but few of those layers are as hard as the various types of granite of Yosemite. There are plenty of fissures in Yosemite Canyon; there are fewer layers. The granite of the central canyon is monolithic. It is igneous rock formed by cooled lava, and as the lava cools, it fractures. It is subjected to upheaval and to glacial action that rips it apart, but it breaks along the structural fractures created by cooling, regardless of the strength of the force, the form is predetermined. Muir continued:

The whole mass of the Sierra. ... is built up of brick-like blocks, whose forms and dimensions are determined chiefly by the degree of development of elected planes of cleavage*, which individualize them, and make them separable from one another while yet forming undisturbed parts of the mountain.*[2]

The West offered two very different types of geology—one horizontal at the Grand Canyon and one either gridded or vertical, depending on one's perception, at Yosemite. Two architectures were to emerge from these two landscapes, differing in form but united by geology. The two different visions were abetted or inspired by the geology of the West, but the different forms of building were in large part the result of two different program types, two different views of the nature of building, and two different architects.

For Muir the best place to see the natural architecture of Yosemite was not on the valley floor but high up at Glacier Point where one could see that most architectural piece of geology, Half Dome, head on. When he was trying to convince Theodore Roosevelt to expand Yosemite National Park, that is where Muir took him. Muir was ultimately successful, but no less important to Yosemite's future was the creation of the Park Service itself in 1916.

Stephen Mather, the first director of the Park Service, was a Californian. Yosemite was popular and conspicuous, so it became a focus of what Mather wanted to accomplish, including what he wanted to architecturally accomplish.

Thus, as the plans for the new buildings in Yosemite Village and Glacier Point began two young architects appeared on the scene, beginning their careers there—Gilbert Underwood and Herbert Maier. They worked in the parks but usually not for the Park Service. Maier was an employee of the American Association of Museums, the instrument that funded museums in the parks. Underwood did much of his work for concessionaires. Both saw architecture in geology and geology in architecture but in very different ways.

They had different ideas about stone and about masonry. One could ask whether they found those ideas in the stone of Yosemite or brought those ideas with them, the answer seems to be both.

In the early years of the Park Service, buildings in the parks were constructed in three different ways. The Park Service itself built new building types—administration offices, ranger stations, entrance gates. Concessionaires continued to build hotels and dining facilities, and hired their own architects, although the designs had to be approved by the Park Service. There was a third, smaller, at times autonomous, but architecturally notable group—those that built the educational buildings—the museums.

If the need for museum and education buildings in national parks is obvious today, it was not in 1920. The idea that appreciating the natural landscape involved science as much as art, that it is not just a question of picturesque forms but understanding causal relationships, is older than Goethe. It is the basis of American transcendentalism, and Emerson and Thoreau's entire lives and work were structured around it. It was fundamental to Enos Mills and John Muir—two of the national parks' strongest advocates. Nevertheless, the educational mission of the parks was never a given before the late 1920s. The Park Service wanted to attract more visitors and to many a golf course seemed a better investment than a classroom. The funding for many early museums came from private donors who hired their own architect, although these buildings were subject to Mather's review as well. It began when Mather placed Ansel Hall, the chief naturalist at Yosemite, in charge of the national parks education program.[3] He sought the help of the American Association of Museums, in particular Hermon Bumpas, a former director of the New York Museum of Natural History.

Hall and Bumpas' objective was to build small "trailside" museums. Rather than the large centralized comprehensive museum, they favored a series of small decentralized and focused museums. Hall wrote of the trailside museum that, "It is an insulation remover and provides a back up between an object or spectacle, charged with dynamic information and a mind that is receptive to international impulses." Bumpas said, "To lead these people away from direct contact with nature, to beguile them into a building where they are surrounded by artifacts, and to subject them to the spell of the professional lecturer, is contrary to the spirit of this enterprise."[4]

Mather's ideas for the Yosemite Village included a large museum, but Bumpas had little enthusiasm for the village as a site. Like Muir he saw Glacier Point as the place where the geology was revealed, and immediately proposed a tiny trailside museum at Glacier Point that would focus on geology. Bumpas said: "The real museum is outside the walls of the building and the purpose of the museum work is to render the out-of-doors intelligible."[5] Hall hired a young Berkeley architect, Herbert Maier, to design it.

Herbert Maier is perhaps the best-known architect of the National Park Service era due to the popularity of his small museums at Yellowstone, but he occupies a strange position in relation to the others, in part because his buildings are almost entirely educational, in part because the Park Service was not really his client, and he did not become a Park Service employee until 1933 when the bulk of his design work was behind him. He is the only architect in this book who designed only rustic architecture, excepting his exhibition work.

The first of Maier's buildings was the trailside museum atop Glacier Point. The shelter is a small but massive granite building with battered walls, a single arched opening at the center, and a low pitch log roof. What would have been a symmetrical form has been truncated with a jagged edge on one side as if part of the building had been removed. On one end the wall has a clean edge, on the other a fragmented one, making it look like a ruin. But also following the block-like fissures of the rock upon which it sits. Maier imitated at a smaller scale, the stone around the building. The joints are tight and rectilinear, but so are the typical fissures in the Yosemite granite. At the same time the face of the stone wall is smooth as is the natural granite around it. Maier later wrote that the walls should have been thicker and the stones should have been larger to, "give the appearance of growing out of the rock." The stonework is quite different than the LeConte Memorial below where Maybeck employed the smooth granite wall. It is more fragmented than Parsons, and Maier's subsequent work is more fragmented still.

In the beginning the ruinous quality of Maier's work was literal—the fictitious residue of a non-existent history. As his work developed it retained its ruinous quality, but it became more abstract and systematic, more a strategy of fragmentation and less one of nostalgia.

With the trailside museum in place, Maier went to work on the main park museum located on the valley floor in the newly emerging Yosemite village. The program was only one-half museum, the other half administration, and the museum half had to be fireproof. Maier's building is thus a long, horizontal gabled-roof wood-framed office atop a stone-faced concrete-structured museum. The wood portions are shingled. The only visible structure are the projecting beams of the second floor. The only stone openings is the arched entry. Maier wrote, "To attempt a latitudinal impressiveness here in a building would have meant entering into competition with the cliffs; and for such competition the architect has no stomach. The horizontal key, on the other hand, makes the museum blend easily into the flat ground."[6]

Yosemite Museum

Glacier Point Museum

Gilbert Underwood

Gilbert Underwood received his education in both the traditional way—as an apprentice—and in the modern, taking architectural degrees from Yale and Harvard. It is doubtful that he learned anything of rustic architecture at either Yale or Harvard, but he did make an important contact, at the latter, Daniel Hull, who after 1921 was the chief landscape architect of the Park Service.

A large number of the commissions Hull awarded went to Underwood and Hull directed organizations like the Union Pacific toward Underwood as well, despite the fact that Underwood's office was less than a year old at the time. Given that Hull was on Underwood's payroll for some of these jobs while still employed by the Park Service, there was a complex series of conflicts of interest.[7]

Underwood had a very different background than Maier, a very different client base, and a very different vision of stone and geology. There is clearly an Underwood style of rustic building. In fact there are two styles, not just of form but of material. One is what we will call his geologic style, one certainly influenced by Colter, but perhaps equally influenced by the geologic context in which Underwood worked. The other language, of wood, the "logs out" style, a rationalist form that perhaps owes something to the Paradise Inn—was predominately wood. There is an overlap but we will examine these in separate chapters to place them in context. The wood language is discussed on pages 397–425.

Underwood's first design for the Park Service, the Yosemite Post Office and Administration Building, was rejected. Mather found it too complicated, and it was criticized for not using enough stone, a material more plentiful at Yosemite than suitable lumber. If insufficient stone is a fault, it is one Underwood did not repeat.

Despite this setback Underwood was deluged with park work in 1924-26, largely because of Hull, but the bulk of it was for concessionaire buildings—lodges and cabins, and the bulk of those were for the Union Pacific Railroad.

The Loop

Despite being the oldest of the transcontinental railroads, the Union Pacific came to the national park business rather late, perhaps because the original line did not run through any areas thought to be worthy of the designation at the time. This changed in 1923 when the Union Pacific lines reached Cedar City, Utah. The Utah Parks Company, owned by the Union Pacific, set up bus loop tours to include the canyons at Bryce, Zion, and the north rim of the Grand Canyon, returning to Cedar Breaks itself. The Park Service repaid the favor by creating destinations. Zion became a National Park in 1919, Bryce Canyon in 1928, and a new National Monument, Cedar Breaks, was created in 1924.

The land extending from Cedar Breaks to the Grand Canyon is called the Grand Staircase. The loop traversed the Grand Staircase and Underwood's architecture traversed it as well.

Stone is used in very different ways in the lodges on the loop. The lodge at Cedar Breaks was completely wood. The lodges at Bryce and Zion were largely wood with stone used as highlights. Stone dominated the North Rim Lodge, despite the extensive log walls.

Underwood probably did not think of these systems as different languages since he rarely used them in isolation. The use of stone was sensitive to an economics of location. Underwood was forced to use it in place of concrete at Bryce and the north rim at of the Grand Canyon since no usable sand was available for concrete. Fort Yellowstone, built by the army at the north end of the park in 1909 is almost completely stone, but in 1924 Yellowstone superintendent Horace Albright told his architects that stone was prohibited because of the excessive cost.[8] While the architectural geology of English grottoes and Vaux's rustic bridges of boulders may have been inspirational to Underwood, one senses somewhere in the background was the work of H. H. Richardson. Its rough glacial boulders and massive constructions that seem to be geological events, would have been hard to ignore, such as the Gate Lodge for the Ames estate.

Union Pacific lines serving national parks
1 Yellowstone
2 Cedar Breaks Bryce and Zion
3 Grand Canyon

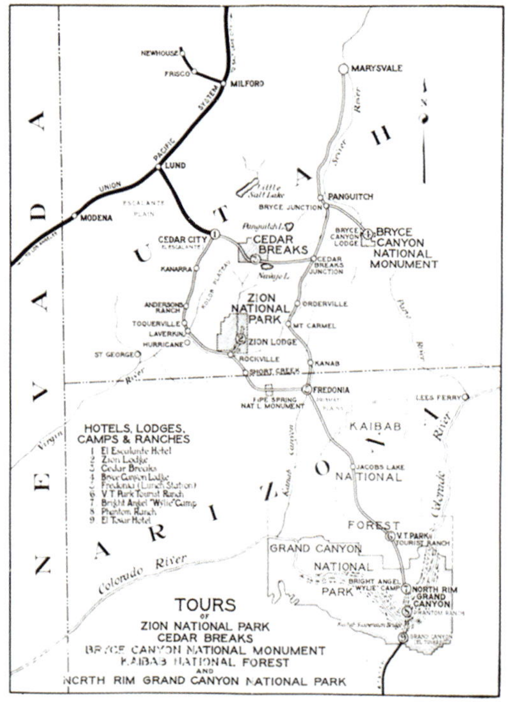

The Union Pacific bus loop map

Deluxe Cabins at Bryce Lodge
Bryce National Park, 1925

Bryce lodge was built in stages and the first stage had no stone other than fireplaces. It had few logs for that matter, built almost entirely of exposed milled lumber. Structurally the stone at Bryce Lodge is irrelevant, a latter addition to a structurally self-sufficient wood building. Far more important to Underwood's stone rustic language were the Deluxe Cabins of the second phase. However small in relation to what was to come, it is historically the foundation for all of Underwood's subsequent geologic buildings.

Concrete was difficult, but while stone was plentiful stone masons were rare and expensive. So the quantity of stone at Bryce is limited to fireplaces and some corner piers. The stone is from the park but not the canyon. The wood from the Kaibab national forest, about a hundred miles away. Nevertheless, this is where Underwood's stone language began to take shape.

That language consisted primarily of vertical stone piers. The resemblance to the geology of Bryce Canyon was obvious. But it is highly abstracted. The stone formations at Bryce are hoodoos, vertical surreal piers caused by the erosion of alternating layers of hard and soft stone. Underwood's piers have little real resemblance to them and are built of a different stone. If the language was inspired by Bryce Canyon it had for Underwood a universal applicability and he used it at Yosemite, Grand Canyon, and many other places in between, whether in granite or in sandstone.

The Deluxe Cabins are solid, chinked log walls framed by masonry piers. The duplex unit was a simple rectangle with two porches, one on the side and one on the end, giving an asymmetrical appearance to a symmetrical plan. The cabins are arranged back-to-back, and each duplex had massive stone piers at each corner, holding a fireplace and chimney at the two opposite corners. The tops of the piers rise above the roof-line, forming a fragmented composition with a large variety of vertical surfaces and jagged roof lines. The stone forms are complex but the surfaces are flat, formed of stepped rectangular shapes with square corners. There are few lintels; openings in the wall itself are small and rare.

Deluxe Cabin
Section looking south

Deluxe Cabin
North elevation

The hoodoos at Bryce Canyon

Union Pacific Dining Hall, West Yellowstone

Glazing, when it occurs, is in the wood walls between piers. Underwood's stone is far more rectilinear and far less natural than Maier's or Maybeck's at Parsons.

Here the log wall was something like the traditional type but with the inner face of the logs covered. The walls were solid logs and the horizontal joints were heavily chinked with cement to create a weatherproof envelope, in the process giving the exterior very pronounced white stripes. The log walls are actually three-quarter logs, chamfered to form a flat, smooth surface that is on the inside faced with insulite, a thin wood fiberboard, that forms the interior finish. The logs are vertical at the gable ends. All the hidden lumber is milled.

The stone piers are an obvious reference to the hoodoos of Bryce Canyon, but Underwood used the same system repeatedly at locations whose geology had little resemblance to Bryce. The same piers were used at the main lodge at Zion and the Union Pacific Dining Hall in West Yellowstone. In fact, his geologic architecture is not particularly contextual even at Bryce. It may use local stone but its forms are based on rectilinear shapes highly geometric and highly abstracted and if the types of stone varied the forms did not.

This in a nutshell was the strategy—stones in their natural state, minimal mortar joints, minimal openings with minimal lintels, and slightly irregular edges at walls and parapet. It was regularity of line that made geology look like buildings. It was irregularity of line that made architecture look like geology. While Maier preferred the horizontal at Yellowstone or Yosemite or the south rim, Underwood favored tightly spaced vertical stone piers at Bryce and the north rim of the Canyon.

Deluxe Cabin at Bryce Lodge
Wall Section

The exterior walls are solid.
The floor and roof structure are largely exposed.

The exterior log walls are solid and structural but faced with paneling on the interior so they are not seen.

The wall constriction is 14-inch logs with 1/4-inch metal dowels, building paper and 1-inch Insulite.

The floor and roof structure are largely exposed.

The roof construction is 1x6 tongue and groove sheathing supported by 8-inch log rafters spaced at 2'6," supported by 12-inch log girders.

The 12-inch stone foundation wall extends upward to form the chimneys and the corner piers.

The Ahwahnee Hotel, Yosemite National Park, 1927

Concrete beams masquerading as wood

Underwood returned to Yosemite in 1927, the site of his initial failure, fully prepared to use plenty of stone. The Ahwahnee was a new departure for the Park Service. Mather's priority was park attendance. He wanted to create facilities to make it possible and to his credit, he wanted to do so at both ends of the economic scale. He wanted tent camps and he wanted luxury hotels. In the latter category was the Ahwahnee.

There were many prototypes for the lodge at Yosemite being built in the national parks by this time, and many of these were in the familiar rustic style of stone and logs, but the use of this construction system at Yosemite presented problems. With 132,000 square feet of space in an eight-story building, a combustible wood-framed structure would have been dangerous if not illegal. Time was short; concrete and/or steel were more obvious solutions than logs and that is what it became. So the Ahwahnee today is a kind of concrete replication of its wood rustic predecessors. How Underwood felt about this is unknown. It is radically different from his other work in the disparity between imagery and construction, but Underwood was more than flexible in matters of ideology.

Despite the change of material the stone pier language is very much on display at the Ahwahnee, what Underwood called the "megalithic elements."[9] His language of stone is literally at 90 degrees to Maier's, who said that "wherever possible verticality should be avoided." Underwood's stone language does not really interface with the geology of Yosemite canyon in any case.

It is a rare visitor to the Ahwahnee that is troubled by the fact that it is a concrete building pretending to be a wood one. It is no more a rustic building than the Hotel Colorado in Glenwood Springs is the Villa Medici, which it closely resembles. In the Ahwahnee's defense there is little deception that it is rustic. It was and is a luxury hotel and the interior design, not by Underwood, makes this clear. Except for the wood, no deception is involved.

The Grand Canyon Lodge at the North Rim, 1928

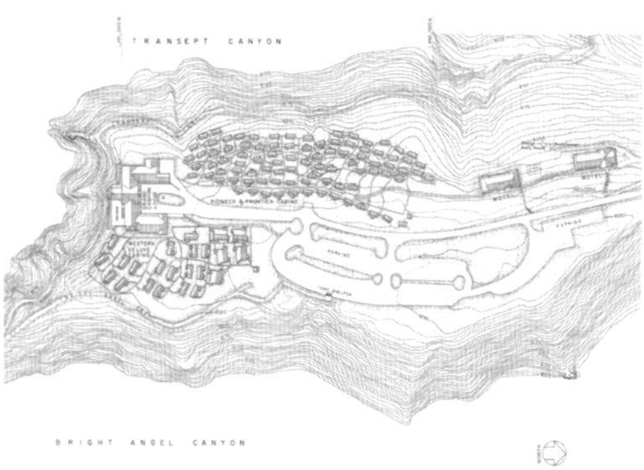

Plan: North Rim Lodge with cabins

Underwood's geologic series ends very near to where it began, at the Grand Canyon, but at the north rim. The lodge was the ultimate destination of the Union Pacific bus loop and is sited accordingly, at the end of a long, thin mesa extending into the canyon. The housing is in cabins on either side of the approach road that ends in a courtyard formed by the lodge.

It sat on the edge of the canyon in the Kaibab limestone. The building rested on a series of stepped terraces but was dramatically modulated with a series of thin, stone verticals of irregular shape and height emerging from the rock below, located at each corner and at each important intersection, rising half a floor above the roof parapet, breaking and hiding its vertical lines, projecting well forward of the wall face and well above the roof line. Much of the power of the composition comes from the multitude of vertical piers sitting atop the limestone layers, in large part because they are a bit foreign to the geology of the canyon. Kaibab limestone's natural formation at the canyon is predominately horizontal. Underwood's vertical piers have little to do with the actual structure of the Kaibab limestone, but it is both ruin and geologic formation.

From several viewpoints it appears to be made mostly of stone. The building is actually mostly wood, but a number of details act to suppress, not just the horizontals but the wood walls as well. The result gives the impression of a structure that was part of the rock or perhaps a ruin growing out of the rock. In fact, none of Underwood's stonework is really contextual. The piers at the north rim are an abstract version of the piers developed at Bryce Canyon with a slightly wider spacing. The same piers are used again in the dining hall at West Yellowstone where there is little natural rock in sight.

Section looking northwest

Southeast elevation

Porch at front entry

Canyon view from lounge

Lounge under construction

Here, geology is the key to understanding the plan of the lodge. The building was a simple U-shape forming the entry courtyard. The two legs of the U housed bedrooms, service, and kitchen. The base of the U faced the canyon and had projections along three axes. One traversed the lodge by following the geology along each of them—one parallel to the rim, one perpendicular to the rim, and one vertically from a grotto in the hollows of the rock below.

AXIS 1

The principle horizontal axis, perpendicular to the edge, continued the route of the long approach road across the courtyard, through the door, across the lobby, to a stairway into a large room extending into the canyon, a kind of giant bay window with three oversized glazed openings undivided by mullions.

The marriage of structural appearance and structural reality typical of the building was missing from the main lounge that overlooks the canyon. Probably because the span is longer and the load of the flat-roofed observation deck above heavier, it was supported by two built-up steel girders 34 inches deep, cased in wood to preserve the rustic ambiance.

Section through entry and lounge

View from west

Dining Room

Recreation Room

AXIS 2

The second axis ran parallel to the rim, extending horizontally along the canyon edge from a central vertical stone mass holding the lobby with the Dining Room on one side and the Recreation Room on the other. The long dining/recreation wing opened out to long, wide stone terraces supported by a massive retaining wall aligning with the canyon edge that was also buttressed.

The lodge was at its best in the two large spaces along this axis on either side of the entry—the dining and recreation rooms. The wall structure can be characterized as having a frame and infill system, the frame being logs and the infill being glass or rows of logs, often vertically. The Dining Room had four bays defined by log roof trusses of a type called "vaulted parallel leg truss, being two Howe trusses meeting at an oblique angle to form a ridge. It was a system Underwood used frequently. Above the trusses was an exposed structure of log rafters and purlins. The trusses were supported at the four corners of the room by stone piers. The intermediate trusses had a 26-inch round log column at each truss end. The wall spaces between the columns and stone piers were mostly glazed but there were horizontal log curtain walls, some solid, others only half logs on either side of a wood stud wall.

Much of the service area of the building, by contrast, lacked the constructive character of the major public spaces. Here there was something of a misfit of the industrial reality of the construction and the rustic appearance of the architecture. The framing, standard milled 2x4 wood studs, 2x12 joists and trusses made from 2x6 stud rafters, was all covered behind a tongue and groove ceiling or wall finish. At the eaves where rafters are exposed the truss ends were fitted with log extensions to give the appearance of log rafters throughout, an unfortunate detail that was to become commonplace in national park building.

Section parallel to canyon rim

Elevation facing canyon

Observation deck to the left, observation tower to the right, and access stair

Grotto to the left and access stair to observation deck to the right

AXIS 3

The most dramatic axis traversed the vertical elements. At the center of the base of the U was a tall, vertical, stone element with a thin tower at the top and a massive stone vault at the base. One moves through this mass vertically starting at the base—a thick-walled grotto-like space whose portals gave a view of the canyon. Its buttress-like stepped stone piers extended upward to form a half octagon that housed the giant bay window facing the canyon with a stone pier at each corner. The three main windows were dramatic, undivided sheets of glass. The buttresses extended a bit farther to support the rails of the roof terrace of the lounge. A dramatic but narrow stair led to an uncovered terrace and then to a smaller covered one. The visitor begins within the canyon wall and rises through the rim to a tower with an observation platform overlooking the south rim beyond.

Section along vertical axis

View from southwest

Grand Canyon Lodge at the North Rim
Wall Section Recreation Room

Since the second floor was divided into a number small guest and service rooms with ceilings, log construction was neither practical nor economical. As a result, second floor of this wing uses mostly milled lumber—2x4 stud walls and roof joists—and the second-floor exterior was a veneer of half logs on sheathing on 2x4 milled studs and the roof construction is milled wood trusses with false log rafter extensions.

The framing of the floor below, a single space occupied by the Recreation Room is a genuine log structure. Log joists 3 feet on center are supported by 24-inch log girders on 24-foot log column at each end. They support 12log floor joist spaced at 4-feet.

The second-floor wall was veneered logs on studs. At the lower floor the logs were solid.

Grand Canyon Lodge at the North Rim
Wall Section Dining Room

The dining room wing was a single, large, tall one-story space with an authentic and highly engineered structure almost entirely of logs. It was far more genuinely rustic than the Recreation Room opposite.

It consisted of five vaulted parallel chord trusses of 12-inch logs supported by a 24-inch column at each end frame the space. Ten-inch girders spanning between them supported the roof rafters. Many of the spaces between columns were glazed but the exterior walls here are solid 12-inch logs at least on the canyon side. With some vertical panels of 12-inch half logs.

The wall adjacent to the service wing was built of half log slabs on sheathing and studs an interior wood paneling.

The floor construction, completely hidden, was standard milled floor joists.

Dining Room
Structural Elements

Trusses

Rafters and girders

Windows and roof

Log walls

The Lodge at the North Rim was Underwood's most truly rustic building in large part because of the restrictions under which he worked. Like most of the lodges built by the railroads, this was a hybrid of industrial/railroad technology and local/craft technology. But the north rim lodge had a particular problem—it was nowhere near a railroad. The nearest was at Cedar Breaks, 150 miles to the north.

Local materials—wood and stone—were available but skilled labor, tools, and some essential materials, were not. Steel and concrete were considered, as at the Ahwahnee, but were deemed too expensive due to the cost of transport. Concrete was the logical material for the numerous retaining walls but there was no suitable sand available anywhere near the canyon. So the walls were stone. In combination with Underwood's geologic aesthetic the result was a massive amount. This came from the park, a local quarry two miles away. Concrete was confined mostly to floors and toppings. Stone masons were another issue, but some were available in Southern Utah.

The wood was not from the park but from the Kaibab National Forest 45 miles away. It was ponderosa pine but in two very different forms—logs for beams, columns, and siding—and milled dimensional lumber for studs, joists, and rafters. As had been done at Yellowstone a sawmill from Kanab, 80 miles away, was brought to the site. The foreman recalled: "The mill handles ponderosa saw-logs brought in from the surrounding national forest by truck. We handle them extremely fast. Trees are cut in the morning, brought to the mill, sawed into lumber and the boards are in their final resting place before sundown." It was powered by electricity supplied by a water-powered generator in the canyon below.

Despite its appearance from certain locations the lodge, its floors, its roofs, and many of its walls are wood. Again, the site restrictions worked to Underwood's advantage. His contract with the Park Service specified that he was to use "log construction," not veneers.[10]

Most of the wood frame walls were placed between vertical stone piers. There were two wood structures, one made of logs and one made of studs. Exposed log columns, beams, and trusses formed the main spaces. Concealed studs and joists formed the smaller service or guest rooms. The logs that enclosed these areas were really half logs or logs squared on one side, but they typically played a structural role. There were few stone lintels in the building adding to its ruined geologic quality.

If the particular conditions of Yosemite Valley mandated the construction of a faux-rustic buildings of concrete and steel, the particular conditions at the north rim were almost mandating that the lodge be of genuinely rustic construction. Limestone and ponderosa pine were readily available in large quantities. Steel, concrete, and the technology to use them were far away. Site access was difficult, and the Park Service wanted a log building.

It is no surprise that many in the railroad and its concessionaires were unhappy with this direction. A memo from the Union Pacific prepared as plans neared completion recommended that all wood trusses be changed to steel, that all stone walls be reinforced with steel columns and lintels, that certain log walls become veneered, and that the roof be made of asbestos shingles. It appears that most of these suggestions were not followed. But the all-log requirement was a condition not completely adhered to. Most of the walls of the main rooms that are exposed on both sides were solid logs. Bedroom and service areas used half logs on studs with an inner facing of fiberboard. The finished structure was by no means pure in what could be called its structural integrity.

Like all national park rustic buildings, the lodge was a technological hybrid—the generic industrial technology of the railroad—of milled lumber, concrete, and steel framing combined with a second palate of indigenous materials, local technology, and a largely fictive local craft tradition. Most of Underwood's predecessors and most of his contemporaries simply clad the former with the latter—log siding on studs or stone on concrete or steel. The rustic and local was always exposed, and the generic and industrial always hidden. Underwood in his work at Bryce, Zion, and elsewhere had found ways to fuse the two systems into something more integral and rigorous. It cannot be said that he completely succeeded at the north rim. There are spaces where structural imagery and structural reality are very close but it also contains in places steel hidden behind wood or stone. But the lodge was not only Underwood's most authentic stone building; it was his most truly rustic log building as well.

The lodge at the north rim was one of the best of the national park buildings for what it was and for what it was not. It was a marriage of site and building that equaled the natural without imitating it. It led the visitor through dramatic and profound choreographed journeys through landscape and architecture. At the same time it was free of pseudo-ruins or borrowed Native American motifs. It was by no means flawless in this regard, but it did not clad an industrial wood frame with a veneer of pseudo-pioneer craft, and it is highly superior to other better-known park buildings that do, such as the 1929 Park Administration building at the south rim.

The lodge at the north rim existed for only a moment in canyon history. A fire in 1932, four years after its completion, left it a stone ruin. It was quickly rebuilt and the Union Pacific almost systematically destroyed its best qualities in the name of good practice. The tower and grotto were eliminated because they were "noisy." They had never liked the slightly pitched roof, the tower, or the stone piers that projected above the eaves, so it was rebuilt with an overhanging roof, no parapet, few stone piers, and no tower. Eliminating the piers eliminated its sympathetic relationship to the geology below. Rebuilding the log exterior walls in stone strangely made the disconnection worse. The resulting totality, although similar in plan to the original, is a rather clumsy hip-roofed stone monolith. Underwood's rendering and a few photographs are all that connect us to the short-lived monument in park building.[11]

Stone walls

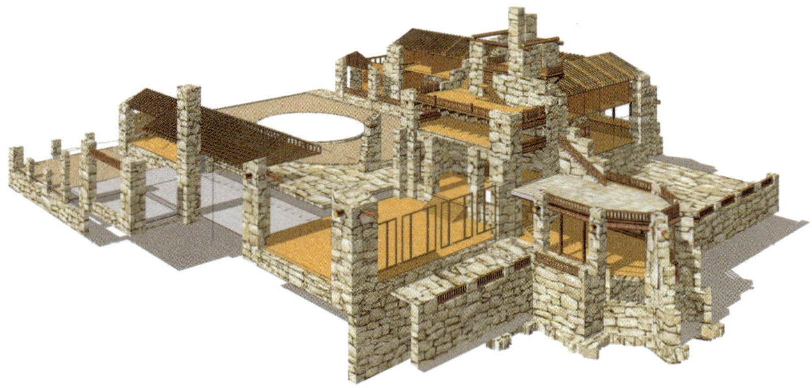

Sawn wood stud joist elements

Solid Log Elements

Yavapai Museum
Grand Canyon National Park, 1928

The three great architects who worked at the Grand Canyon—Colter, Underwood, and Herbert Maier—all adapted Powell's book of geology into a mode of building in stone, but they did it in very different ways. Maier's work contains a strong element of the geologic rustic style, established by Underwood and Colter, and that sensibility was very much on display in his next building, a trail-side museum, again focused on geology, at the Grand Canyon and something of a geological event in itself. Yavapai Point is on the south rim about two miles east of El Tovar and Hopi House. The building is composed of two interlocking stone forms—an irregular covered platform on the edge of the canyon and a low one-story stone box on the side away from the canyon. Both are built of the local Kaibab limestone.

The projecting covered platform is almost but not quite part of the rock. The building's debt to Mary Colter's Hermit's Rest and Lookout Studio is obvious, but while Lookout Studio is perched on the edge of the canyon, growing out of the rock, Maier's seems excavated. The roof is supported by four log columns. Two large wood beams running parallel to the rim support a series of log beams 36 inches apart, perpendicular to the canyon edge. Originally the terrace was completely open except for the stone railing. It was fitted with a series of telescopes to allow detailed observation of Powell's book of stone—the multiple layers of stone types that make up the canyon walls. Maier had a ceiling-high model of the canyon wall built using samples of the actual stone types brought up from the canyon below. A large relief model and real plant and rock specimens completed the simple but effective exhibit.

The stone box behind sat on a stone terrace that extended beyond the roof toward the canyon. The simple window openings have simple single-stone lintels. The outside wall is fitted with a set of projecting vigas apparently ornamental, a nod toward Puebloan and Spanish architecture, but the building has few such cultural references. It is an event in geologic, not cultural history.

Yavapai Geology Museum, Log roof framing

Yavapai Geology Museum, Roof framing with deck

In keeping with the tradition in which he was working, each of the two building segments has its own balance of nature, geology, traditional masonry, and evocative ruin. The rectilinear box facing away from the canyon has square windows with stone lintels supported by brackets and a level stone parapet. The series of projecting false vigas completes the idea of a traditional regional building not specifically Spanish or Native American, but in the irregular shape facing the canyon pure geologic form seems to take over from the image of a ruined traditional building returning to nature. There are no windows, no stone lintels, but rather a series of openings defined by vertical piers that taper dramatically upward, giving the stone openings highly irregular shapes covered by the log roof.

Two years after the building opened the wing facing way from the canyon was modified to appear far more ruinous by extending the horizontal line of the parapet into a broken profile as Colter had done at Hermit's Rest and elsewhere. It is not clear whether Maier was involved in this modification but he later said he felt the stones of the wall were far too regular—that the individual stone should have varied more in size.

As a museum it was a success and despite its eccentricity, immediately began generating imitations. Ansel Hall, head of Park Service education, proposed that five more such museums be built along the canyon rim. The 1931 Sinnott Observation Station and Museum at Crater Lake followed a similar submerged strategy and the concept appears again in the Coronado Lodge at Palo Duro Canyon in 1937.[12]

Maier and Colter both worked in the narrow territory between the abstractly suggestive and literal imitation in the relation to indigenous architecture and to geologic forms. In other words, how much should a building look like a ruin or how much should it look like a natural formation. Maier moved toward the abstract to his advantage. He at least in theory saw little difference between imitating Native America ruins and imitating Southwestern geology. Both were the result of material and environmental conditions.

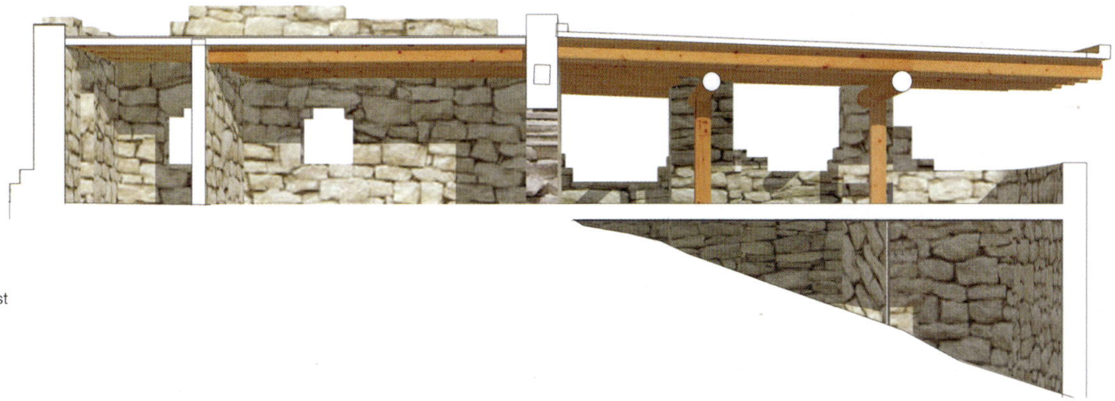

Section looking west

East elevation

Conclusion

So how are we to see Maier's building—as a pueblo ruin or a piece of geology? Arguably to Maier there was no real difference. To Maier, Native American architecture was the work of rationalism's primitive man and was similar in form to the natural because it was the result of the same forces creating the same forms.

Maier began at Yavapai what was to become his trademark—vastly oversized materials. He said, "In rockwork it is better, due to the scale of the nearest natural features, to oversize rather than undersize."[13] It was a philosophy he was to continue to pursue in stone and wood. Learning from regional architecture was important to Maier, but Yavapai is something more—a structurally rigorous building answering to the site, the program, and the nature of the materials and has no need of historical allusion. It has none of the concealed concrete or steel of Colter buildings and none of the culturally appropriated symbols. Unfortunately, the Park Service found it necessary to enclose the porch and much of the buildings character was lost in the process.

Colter, Underwood, and Maier all felt it necessary to occupy the underground. It is doubtful any of them knew of Pope's Grotto, but like many commonalities in this narrative Colter's cave with fireplace, the bottom of Underwood's tower, and Maier's excavated museum seemed to speak to a common impulse. Karsten Harries is critical of "artificial ruins" saying that they "speak of a desire to return to nature not to master it," which is perhaps why all three of these architects were drawn to them.[14] All responded to Simmel and James, geology of architecture but with different levels of literalism, with Underwood at it most abstract and Colter at its most literal.

But as always we should remember what Maier was, an exhibit designer. Columns were not structural, they were educational: "the best museum structure is that one which functions most efficiently as an interpretive agent." But all of this is only half, in fact less than half, of the rustic architecture of Maier and Underwood, who were no less engaged with wood.

Rendering of Lodge at the Grand Canyon North Rim

Right opposite: Maier had a ceiling-high model of the canyon wall built using samples of the actual stone types brought up from he canyon below. A large relief model and real plant and rock specimens completed the simple but effective exhibit.

Left opposite:'Colter was to repay Maier's complement by imitation. In 1936 she built a large stone fireplace in the Bright Angel Lodge in imitation of Maier's geologic history column.

THE DESSERT WATCHTOWER: THE HOPI, THE DINÉ, AND MARY COLTER

Let us return to a story we have passed over, Hopi House. Central to the creation of the village at the south rim of the Grand Canyon in the early years was the Fred Harvey Company. They built hotels and provided services like other railroad concessionaires but unlike other concessionaires they sold Native American art in quantity, and their role was not confined to marketing. They sold it, they commissioned it, they arranged special tours for tourists to purchase it. They arranged Native American performances as well, particularly dances, to publicize it. Architecture, obviously, was a key component of this enterprise.

The Harvey Company's Native American program had begun with exhibits of Hopi crafts and craftsmen at world's fairs, such as Chicago (1893). But as the Santa Fe moved west the market grew exponentially. Its first two large museum/gift shops were the Albuquerque Indian Building-part museum, part curio shop, and, directly connected to the Albuquerque Santa Fe station and Hopi House at the Grand Canyon, that followed soon after. Both had the same intent and the same architectural concept, marketing Native American art from multiple nations, Hopi pottery, Navajo (Diné) rugs and jewelry. Even art from the Pacific Northwest was thrown in.

Charles F. Whittlesey was the architect of record of Hopi House. It owes a great deal to Henry Voth, a missionary who had lived with the Hopi for 10 years. Voth consulted on the design of Hopi House, which is modeled on the Hopi village at Oraibi.

Voth had done much that angered the Hopi. He published precise descriptions of their religious ceremonies and folklore, often obtained by forced entry to private ceremonies where he was forbidden. Voth crossed a boundary by appropriating these ceremonies as marketing devices for the Harvey Company. Voth is responsible for the most controversial part of Hopi House, two altars built in a room on the second floor, including a four-foot-high door with leather hinges brought from Oraibi. To the Hopi then, and to many today, he was a thief, less of objects than of their essence.

Hopi House draws on images of indigenous architecture, not geology or the qualities of local stone. Later Harvey buildings were built of the local Kaibab limestone. In fact, what one sees is not the local stone. The whitish limestone from the site is used in the inner structural wall, but what one sees is the exterior facing, a redder Moenkopi Coconino Sandstone brought from Winslow, 150 miles away, undoubtedly by rail.

Room designed by Colter at Indian House

Pueblo at the Panama California Exposition in San Diego 1915
Built by the Harvey Company

Nampeyo, Jar 1890-1910

Hopi House is not a real pueblo of course. Plaster stood in for adobe walls and concrete for mud floors. Where traditional log vigas did not accommodate the structural loads, iron rails were used as beams. Hopi house was not meant to be a ruin. It was a replication of a living Hopi village filled with Hopis. Hopi House is a far less happy approach to an architecture appropriate to the canyon than Lookout Studio. But if the architecture was culturally problematic so was its contents.

The Harvey Company did just as much commissioning as collecting. They were fairly specific about what they wished the Native Americans to produce.[1] Nampeyo is an example. She is recognized as a great American artist but she was far more original and less traditional than is often assumed. She is sometimes defined as the inventor of modern Hopi pottery. She always had been a potter but her early work was for the most part simple, utilitarian, and minimally decorated. In 1895, when J. W. Fewkes began to excavate the ancient village of Sikyátki near First Mesa, Nampeyo's husband worked in the excavation and showed fragments of ancient of pottery to Nampeyo who began to imitate them. Fewkes encouraged this and bought many for himself, effectively creating a market for what was arguably Hopi revival pottery. Like other Harvey employees, she altered the design of her work to meet demand, primarily by making smaller, simpler pieces. She was a resident artist at Hopi House for two extended periods, living in a rooftop apartment with her family. They were also performers, paid to dance twice a day in the adjacent plaza. Deborah Tibbel offers a more contemporary view:

The story of Nampeyo was manipulated according to a colonial discourse which simultaneously idealized and marginalized the artistic motivations and production of colonized Others. In the case of Nampeyo, this involved a notion of Pueblo society and art as conservative, static, and incapable of independent change…the story of Nampeyo, and her relationships with numerous Euro-American patrons is the product of conflicting dominant interests, with little or no regard for Native agency. Rather, as a member of a subordinate group, Nampeyo created a niche for the concept of 'Native art' acceptable in both Pueblo and Euro-American terms, while working from within the constrained boundaries of colonial domination.[2]

The art and architecture of the Harvey Company occupies a nebulous zone. Much of it should be seen as original work of artists, not tribal tradition, but a great deal of it was not just appropriation but exploitation of artists and cultures.

Mary Colter

To artfully arrange the mélanges of art at both the Indian Building at Albuquerque and Hopi House, Mary Colter was brought in for the first of her many jobs for the Harvey Company. Early in her career Colter worked as a department store display designer, and it could be said she continued to design showrooms, this time to house Hopi products, all fitted with brand new archaic wood beams and carefully arranged dust, designing something like the kind of faux-bedrooms and living rooms one finds in a furniture showroom.

Hopi House was followed by Lookout Studio and Hermit's Rest. As we have seen, these buildings were in many ways her best, in large part because any relations they have to Native American or Hispanic structures is highly generic and involve no cultural theft. In the next Harvey Company project she was involved from inception. It was another reconstruction and there was nothing subtle about it. It was a Disney theme park of a pueblo, built for the 1915 Panama California Exposition in San Diego. It was a fairly literal model of the pueblo at Taos, as well as Hopi kivas and Diné hogans, and of course a large gift shop. Three hundred Native Americans from various tribes were hired to occupy it.

Desert View Watchtower
Grand Canyon National Park, 1933

After working with Louis Curtiss on Hermit's Rest and Lookout Studio in 1914, she worked on Harvey projects elsewhere and did not return to the south rim until 1922 to do three more projects with Robert Raney—the 1922 Phantom Ranch, the 1933 Desert View Watchtower, and the 1935 Bright Angel Lodge. A change in personnel may explain the change in architecture, but it probably is the result of differences in program and how architecture enabled the Harvey Company's marketing objectives. All three projects drew on romantic images rather than geologic form in contrast to Lookout and Hermit's Rest, but they drew on different sources in different ways. The ranch and the lodge are hotels, and are built in a wood Western vernacular and have fewer literal references to Native American building. The Watchtower, although it provided an elevated view from the canyon rim, was there to sell Native American art and when the Harvey Company wanted to sell Native American art they used a facsimile of Native American architecture. Its design and decoration are focused on that mission, one that used very specific quotations from Native American buildings at every scale from the decorative motif to the overriding form.

The Desert Watchtower was completed in 1933. A tall, tapering, stone cylinder perched on the canyon rim, it is strongly suggestive of other Ancestral Puebloan structures that Colter had studied, at times from airplanes, but at 70 feet in height and over 30 feet in diameter it dwarfs them in size.

Round Tower House, Mesa Verde

The tallest tower at Mesa Verde is only 26 feet tall and Round Tower, which is the probable model for Watchtower, is even smaller. In any case, no Ancestral Puebloan tower would be built in such an isolated and conspicuous location.

The first element one sees at Watchtower is a fake ruin, a curved stone wall. This led to a kiva at the tower base, but with doors and picture windows of course, keeping the form but fundamentally altering the nature of what is traditionally an underground windowless space. This is all an introduction to the tower and its stair ascending five levels to give view of the canyon. This is, in a way, even more incongruous than size differences as Ancestral Puebloan buildings do not have picture windows in the sense of views to the exterior. The tapered cylinder is Kaibab limestone but a number of large chert boulders were added at the base to increase the apparent mass. The stone and stonework size and pattern are drawn from the Hovenweep ruins in Colorado, built of stone closer in character to what was available at the Grand Canyon.

Many Colter buildings had a narrative, a story, often fictive, that formed the basis for the design. Hopi House was simply a fragment of Oraibi. In later buildings the narrative became more complex, as in the Hermit at Hermit's Rest. This time Colter wrote it out for the sake of the tour guides. She made it clear that this was not a copy, replica, reproduction, or a restoration but a "recreation." At times she comes very close to primitive functionalism:

The primitive architect never intentionally copied anything but made every building suit its own conditions, and each one differed from every other according to the character of the site, *the* materials *that could be procured and the* purpose *for which the building was intended. ... So, though he was guided by tradition when he built, he did not 'copy,' but in every case "CREATED" a new thing.*[3]

That Colter wrote what was for her a lengthy text on the Watchtower is understandable given that she was placing herself into a more than dubious tradition—the creation of faux-Ancestral Puebloan ruins focusing solely on their appearance and ignoring their essence.

But this is all a thin pseudo-indigenous crust covering a modern industrial product. The stonework is all for effect as it is all held up by a steel frame, a necessary lateral reinforcement given the building's height and location. The steel was prefabricated in Kansas City, shipped to the canyon by the Santa Fe Railroad and erected there by the Hichborn Company who regularly built bridges for the Santa Fe.

There is no question that Colter was a gifted composer of masses and materials but here it was in the service of a marketing device for the Harvey Company's Native American art empire. Appearance was all that mattered. Previously, in the decoration of the El Navajo Hotel in Gallup in 1923 Colter used images lifted directly from Diné sand paintings as wall decorations. Many Dinés considered this sacrilegious and put Colter on "trial" in their terms. The murals survived but she avoided this issue at Watchtower by working with Fred Kabotie who did the interior murals of the tower. He was born at Oraibi, and attended the Santa Fe Indian school where an enlightened superintendent and his wife encouraged Kabotie not only to paint but to paint what he knew, the kachinas and ceremonies of the Hopi Pueblos. He became a teacher and practitioner of painting. Strangely, although Kabotie had been drawing kachinas for sale since childhood and had provided the collector George Heye with an extensive set of drawings of Hopi rituals, he never received the kind of criticism that other Hopi artists faced for violating ceremonial secrets. Jessica Walton argues that this is a result of very selective editing and transforming on Kabotie's part so that he carefully avoided stepping over the line that others had crossed.[4] The Harvey Company was not so particular and hired other nonnative painters and gave them images of traditional Diné sacred imagery to be painted on the walls. It worked, at least temporarily, and prior to its opening there was a Hopi dedication.

Steel framing of the Tower and Kiva

Steel Frame
H Columns
Edge channel ribs
Specially formed fabricated pla

Stone Enclosure

Desert Watchtower has always been popular with the public and the Park Service management long yearned to buy it before they finally did so. The educational part of the Park Service has always hated it. It was one thing that a fake ruin was situated at so unlikely a location contrary to any plausible history, but it was something else that it was a gift shop posing as a museum. Robert Farrel, a Park Service official, wrote:

I gag. I retch. I writhe on the floor in agony. The Desert Watchtower is totally unsuited to function as an interpretive facility ... In fact, it is totally unsuited to exist at all in my opinion. ... the damn thing was built to look like an Indian ruin, thereby attempting to foster a totally false impression of Indian architecture and use of that part of the South Rim. It should be dynamited, and as soon as possible.[5]

Yavapai was completed in 1928, and Watchtower four years later. The buildings are quite different but the architects had much in common. Both sought to learn from the indigenous architecture of the Southwest; both, on paper, forbade literal copying of precedent. Maier was 24 years younger than Colter and was clearly in her debt. What is best about Yavapai draws on Colter's work at Lookout and Hermit's Rest. What dramatically separates them is that in 1930 they were moving in opposite directions. Both Yavapai and Watchtower use literal historical quotations but Watchtower had far more of them and they are far more literal. The quotations would soon disappear from Maier's work while in Colter's work they were multiplying. The abstract refinement of Lookout had become the pseudo-kiva and Puebloan tower of Watchtower. Maier was moving toward abstraction. Colter and the Harvey Company had already moved into literalism.

The Kiva

Murals at the lower levels of the Watchtower

Buildings on the Edge
Profiles of structures on the edge of the Grand Canyon

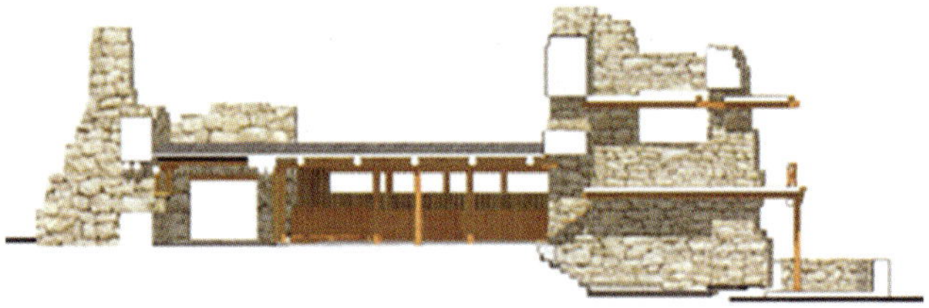

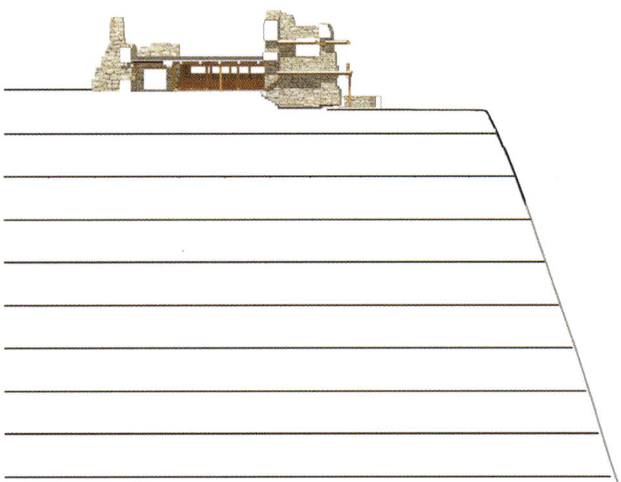

Lookout Studio

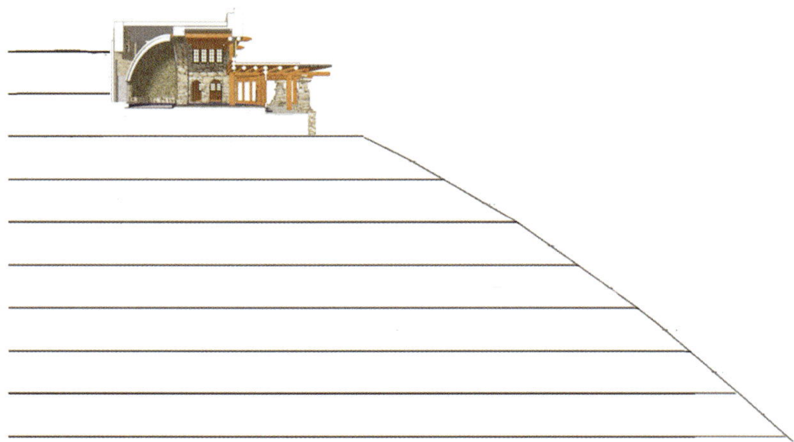

Hermit's Rest

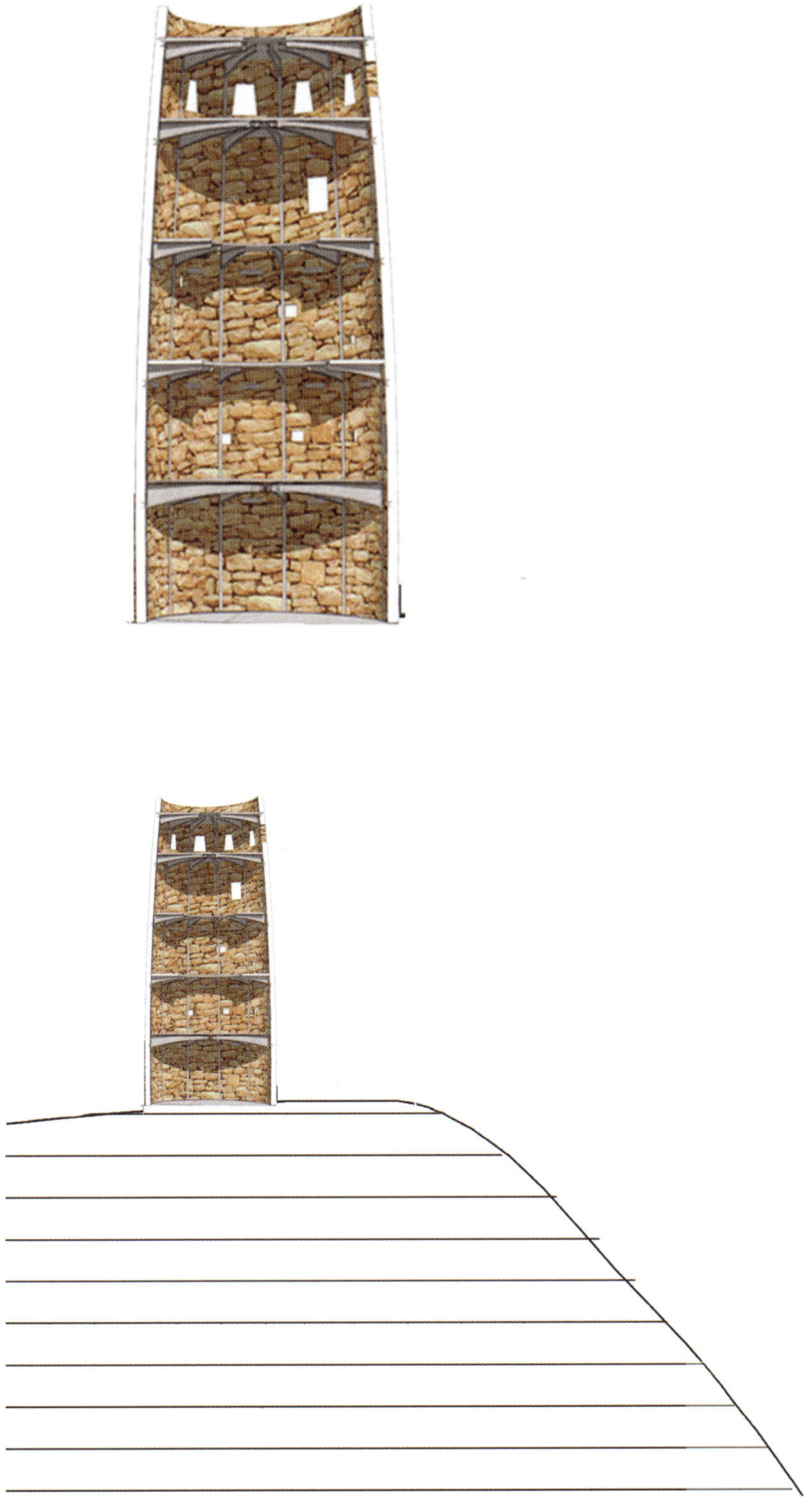

Desert Watchtower

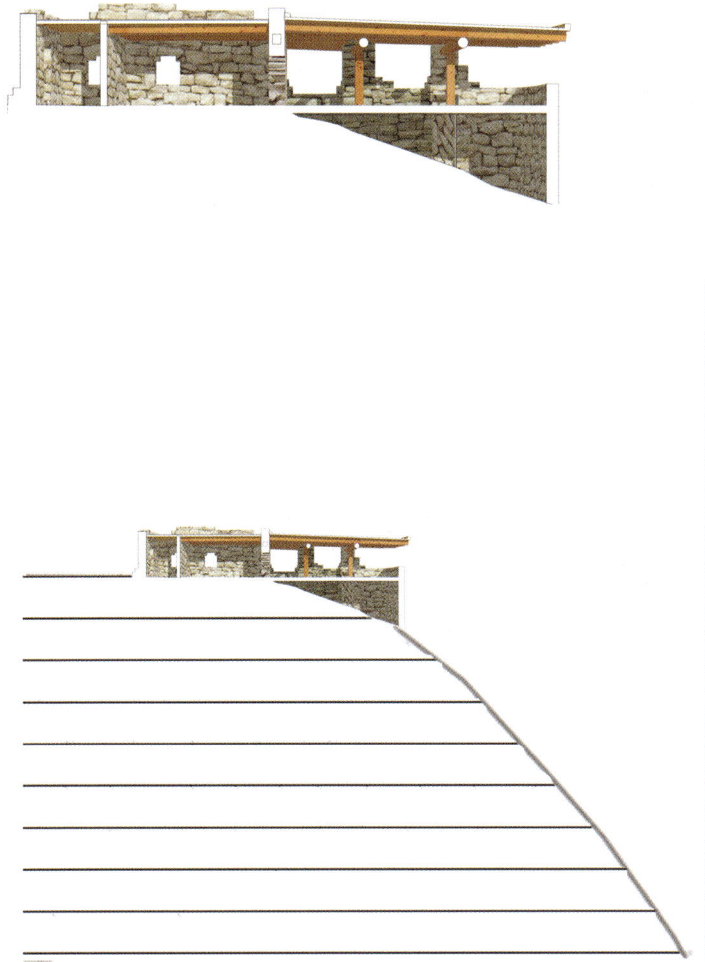

Yavapai Museum

CULTURAL APPROPRIATION

The Wheelwright Museum. Santa Fe, NM, 1937

Seton design for a tent using elements of Native American structures of the plains and the northwest

Seton Castle

Colter's work and the work of many others like her practicing in the Southwest at the time raises questions not just of aesthetics, but of ethics. Colter is only a conspicuous member of a large group of artists who practiced what today is considered cultural appropriation. In the1930s and 1940s perspectives were quite different. In the eyes of many artists, particularly the surrealists, who copied Native American iconography, they were employing universal archetypes. In the eyes of Native Americans these forms were private property.

The Museum of Modern Art's groundbreaking show "Indian Art of the United States" in 1941 included a number of Native American reconstructions, including reconstructions of three kivas painted by Fred Kabotie. Rene d'Harnoncourt, the organizer, said that "we must concede the existence of human concepts that find expression in specific art forms."[1] Many artists of the day and many who saw the exhibition believed in archetypes, Jungian archetypes. In this world, primitive art was the raw manifestation of universal subconscious forms.

Similar appropriations were going on in New York and elsewhere. Adolph Gottlieb and Richard Pousette-Dart were working on parallel lines, and the immigrant surrealists Max Ernst and Andre Breton had major collections of Native American art. There were many artists appropriating Native American art, much of it of a religious nature and no Anglos saw anything wrong with this. They were doing what Picasso and Matisse had done with African Art in the 1910s. A lesser-known practitioner of cultural appropriation was the young, unknown Jackson Pollack. Between 1938 and 1950 Pollack executed a series of paintings in which motifs of Native American art are copied in recognizable images, from Zuni pottery, to Inuit Shamanic masks, to Hopi kachinas. W. Jackson Rushing, who identified these references, goes on to say that Native American influence on Pollack went beyond imagery, that Diné sand paintings, part of a healing ritual, were the lead into his drip paintings executed after 1947.

Forty years after "Indian Art of the United States," the intellectual mood was very different. In 1984, MoMA tried to recreate the success of the 1941 show when "Primitivism in 20th Century Art: Affinity of the Tribal and the Modern" opened. To the numerous critics of "Primitivism," the problem is simple. This is cultural colonialism. Susan Hiller writes:

Cultural Colonialism ... is an ideology that extends the idea that spoils of war might include art objects along with other valuable goods as proof of conquest and territorial sovereignty, to the appropriation and incorporation into the body of European culture of 'the diverse cultures of the whole world and of all history.'[2]

A reflection of the changing attitudes is the fate of the Wheelwright Museum in Santa Fe. In 1937 an eight-sided hogan-shaped building was constructed outside of Santa Fe. Frances Newcomb, an Anglo who lived on the Diné reservation, created versions of sand paintings, traditionally executed temporarily in sand as parts of healing rituals, which were placed on the walls. A non-indigenous artist executed a sand painting on the floor. Today the "hogan" is there but the paintings are not. By the 1970s, attitudes toward the building had changed. The Diné Nation objected to the teaching of Diné culture by those who were not Dinés. In 1977 the museum returned several Diné sacred artifacts. The museum also gave 80 oil versions of sand paintings, based on Franc Newcomb's paintings, to the Diné.

These attitudes had very direct architectural consequences, as exemplified by the work of Ernest Thompson Seton. Seton achieved both wealth and fame pursuing his great loves, first as an artist and illustrator of wildlife, then as an author, then as a scholar of Native American Culture. *Two Little Savages* or *Wild Animals I Have Known* are not read very often today but at the turn of the century they were bestsellers. In 1930 he bought 2,500 acres three miles from Santa Fe with the plan for founding an institute for the study and teaching of Native American Culture, "The College of Indian Wisdom."

He described Santa Fe as the "primitive spiritual capital of nature in America,"[3] but by 1930 this was a well-worn path, certainly for the artist wishing to connect to the primal and the spiritual. The Southwest offered this in abundance. Aby Warburg came in 1895, D. H. Lawrence in 1922, Georgia O'Keeffe in 1929.

Serving as his own architect, Seton began with a ring of adobe and timber buildings facing a plaza housing an office, a print shop, and a crafts shop/museum of indigenous artifacts. Several guesthouses faced the plaza, two of which were built of old Santa Fe Railroad cars encrusted with adobe. All the other structures were built of stone, timber, and adobe bricks. They contained traditional Hispanic elements, but all were adorned with Native American symbols, totems, and other paraphernalia from across North America. Seton's passion for "honest construction" was very much linked to his understanding of Native Americans as we will see.

Seton built a school building, and here the Native American debt was more literal. The buildings were what might be called improvised versions of Native American archetypal buildings—kivas, hogans, and tepees. North of the plaza was the "Indian Village," in reality the student housing. It contained temporary and permanent structures tepees, wickiups, a few log cabins, a dining hall, a pueblo/kiva constructed by a resident of the San Ildefonso Pueblo, and a Navajo hogan that doubled as the auditorium. Seton Village was a strange amalgam in which kivas and hogans rest side by side with stuccoed railway cars.

After the college opened in 1932, work began on a house for himself, "Seton Castle," a 6,900-square-foot mansion on a hill overlooking the rest of the camp. It contained a large gathering space, a studio, a museum, a 70,000-volume combination library/living room, a portico, numerous bedrooms, and eventually grew to 45 rooms. It may have been primitive in a way. It was no tepee, rather a cluster of adobe and timber buildings facing a plaza. They contained traditional Hispanic elements and materials, but all were adorned with Native American symbols, totems, and other paraphernalia from across North America.

Seton was a vocal advocate for Native American rights, defending land from encroachment and campaigning for the abolition of indigenous boarding schools. However sympathetic Seton may have seemed in the 1930s, the activities of the college—reenactments, and recreation of Native American rituals, structures, and artifacts would call down a firestorm of criticism if performed today. Seton was an ambivalent reenactor in any case, never willing to abandon his own culture completely or permanently. The college closed in 1941. Seton died in 1946 and the castle burned down while being restored in 2005.

His attitudes toward learning from tribal culture were commonplace in the 1930s. His creative processes are distinguished from many of his contemporaries who were inspired by Native American work only by their literalism. Seton was criticized even in his lifetime for these recreations of Native American structures. Most of his recreations that have not disappeared have been destroyed. Many other reproductions of traditional Native American structures have suffered similar fates, even when the work was executed by Native Americans themselves. Seton's activities, however, were of a different order. In his recreations of Native American art from a wide spectrum of tribes, he felt no queasiness about adapting and transforming the prototypes and later even combining and inventing. Some of the results have lost almost all resemblance to the object of origin.

Seton Castle

All of these constructions, whether buildings, shanties, or tepees were for Seton not cultural appropriation but reenactments of archetypes. Seton thought his response to the wilderness, to the natural world, was based on a deep-seated genetic inheritance, a reconnection with something we all possessed.

It is doubtful he knew Jung's work but he certainly understood archetypes, and archetypes are not proprietary. This kind of thinking was reinforced by what was still a prevalent attitude about all tribal societies, including Native Americans in Seton's lifetime. That they were societies like his own simply in the formative primal stages and he was in that sense their descendant.

His life and his architecture were a return to origins. Seton built many of structures for himself in his life, from shanties to tepees to mansions. All were a reenactment for Seton, a reconnection with something like a collective memory, one that was very different from his intellectual legacy from his actual parents, from whom he was estranged.

Seton was a great believer in both genealogy and genetics. His version of primitive man was present in his deepest thoughts but he had multiple origins. In his early designs he was his Anglo ancestor. In his later work it was the archetypes of Native American art. "from Emerson came the thought, 'if ye be of good ancestry cast aside your judgment, and trust yourself indomitably to your instincts. ... So what are out instincts? The accumulated wisdom of our ancestors—our best inheritance; the power that builds us up out of the lower orders of men."[4]

But the larger criticism was directed at the idea of "primitivism." It is true that the concept of the primitive in architecture is very much dependent on the concept of primitive man, and if one reads what is written about the Swiss or Native Americans—geniuses who created the models being followed—they are all dependent on a stereotype of what primitive man was. What was admirable about Seton was that he was innocent. He dealt only with necessity, that he was unschooled in tradition or history—allowing him to be seen as inferior while being admired.

These structures are something like the type of ruin exemplified by Shenstone's druidic hermitage, something that evoked the simultaneous pleasure and pain in contemplating something that has been lost except for its fragments. In the case the Piegan tepees, relocated to the monumental forest hall of the Glacier Park Lodge, one might take pleasure in what had been accomplished and regret at what had been destroyed. In the case of buildings that incorporated Native America elements, genuine or artificial, they play a role similar to the spolia of ancient Roman buildings that incorporate fragments of cultures they had subdued into new construction. These were the ruins of literalism.

This is, as we have seen, the second type of ruin—that of reclaimed nature. William Gilpin called a ruin, "a work of nature rather than of art." Georg Simmel had described the ruin as a manifestation of "the great struggle between the will of the spirit and the necessity of nature." [5] This was what Bodmer saw in the cliffs on the upper Missouri in 1833 and George James saw at the Hopi mesas in 1911. The line between the building and the landscape, between the natural and the human made, was gone. The Watchtower was a ruin of memory. Yavapai was a ruin of nature.

This multiplied possibilities. Boundaries were fluid; overall form was indeterminate; completeness was impossible because the formal goal was indeterminate.

RATIONALISTS AND ROMANTICS

LITERARY RATIONALISM

John Burroughs, Slabsides

I do not believe that beauty can be created overnight. It must start with the archaic.
—Louis Kahn[1]

A familiar character to readers of architectural theory is primitive man. He appears in Laugier's *Essay on Architecture* in 1753, in *Towards a New Architecture* in 1923, and plays supporting roles in the work of other writers from William Chambers to Adolf Loos. Primitive man has remarkably consistent attitudes. Like the modern architect, he designs and builds buildings but he has many advantages over his descendant—primarily that he does not know that he is an architect and he knows nothing of architecture. He is unencumbered by knowledge of precedent. He is unconcerned with critical reception. He is concerned with aesthetic effect, but only in a direct, intuitive way. This gives him a distinct advantage. He can solve the problem of building in a straightforward, commonsense way using only the materials and methods at his disposal, considering only the conditions of the site and climate and the problem at hand. The results, all these writers agree, are superior to the work of the academically trained, historically knowledgeable, and aesthetically self-aware, professionally trained designer. The works of primitive man are not necessarily beautiful and certainly not refined. They are filled, however, with an intense vitality.

Put another way, you can say that the appreciation of the vernacular is the idea that someone can create something beautiful with no intention of doing so. If one designs something that is direct, functional, unpretentious, and free of frivolous aesthetic intentions, aesthetic quality will follow.

The appreciation of the vernacular is perhaps one of the many things we owe to the Enlightenment and its creation, the English garden culture of the eighteenth century, the idea that an everyday object—a tool, a bowl, a shed—can have an incredible beauty. Uvedale Price, writing in *On the Picturesque*, sees the simple country cottage as this type of vernacular, "there is a peculiar relish which arises from many rude and even mean, but strongly marked picturesque circumstances; and that peculiar relish, as it does arise from those circumstances."[2]

We have already met primitive man in several locations, particularly Ruskin's Swiss village. He said of the chalet that "was nothing in itself" but that it possessed "beauty, that of fitness and humility."[3] Along with the veneration of the vernacular came the veneration of its creator, the anonymous craftsman. The Swiss builder has no aesthetic intent or aesthetic knowledge, is unaware of precedent. He is not an architect, simply a clever person solving a problem in a direct, logical, and functional way.

It is with the structural rationalists of the last half of the nineteenth century that we arrive at the idea that the vernacular designer is not just the architect's equal but the architect's superior, particularly in the writings of Viollet-le-Duc.

Jack London at Wolf House

In his introduction to the *Discourses on Architecture*, he begins with a lament for the modern architect: "We suffer a wrong today which we cannot remedy; we have come too late into the world. The ancients, in preceding us, have robbed us of the simple and beautiful ideas which we otherwise perhaps would have had. ... the duty of the artist has become very difficult. We labor under an infinity of old prejudices and habits belonging to dead civilizations." And later, "civilized man ... is an extremely complicated animal, as he is transformed by an education which obliges him to contend forever against his instincts." Far better was the condition of the designer in a primitive civilization where, "The task of the artist was then comparatively easy." He writes of the primitive designer: "Among them, a false gesture, a movement which does not clearly and directly indicate a definite intention, a desire, or a fear is impossible: they are never affected, mannered, or vulgar; whether beautiful or ugly, they all are stylistic, because their instincts are simple, and the means by which they accomplish their purposes direct and natural."[4]

A large part of the appeal of the vernacular was its directness and "honesty." It was critical, at least for Ruskin or Viollet-le-Duc, that the form of these objects and buildings not become stylistic motifs, but ways of building that were free of fakery and sham. For Ruskin this meant the absence of deceptions, particularly covering one thing with another in a deceptive way, e.g., a gold watch that is merely plated, or it might be what appears to be a log cabin that is merely log siding.[5] Viollet-le-Duc went further demanding not just structural honesty but structural expression.

The cult of the designer as natural man found its way to America but took some time to be accepted. A. J. Downing admired the work of the unschooled craftsman but he thought true art required artistic intent. Downing says of the typical American log cabin that: "these are only manifestations of the grosser wants of life; and the mind of the civilized and cultivated man as naturally manifests itself in fitting, appropriate, and beautiful forms of habitation." Accidental aesthetic appeal is not enough to make architecture, that requires a, "civilized and cultivated man." But idea of the veneration of the architect who does not know that they are an architect was widely accepted by 1906. Three of its best-known apologists were of an unlikely type: three popular writers none of whom was thought of even in a minor way as a writer on architecture.

Jack London

While one might expect the author of *White Fang* to focus on the log cabin, London's primitive man was not all that primitive, more like an engineer designing a house as if it were a sailboat, minimizing space and material. He is not self-conscious about aesthetics, but he seems more likely to be a nautical engineer than a pioneer with an axe.

In 1906, *House Beautiful* asked several authors, including London, to describe their ideal home. London's article reads a bit like a German modernist manifesto of the 1920s. Space should be functionally allocated, bedrooms should be minimized, large hallways should be eliminated. Rooms should be sized according to need. The pretentious spatial excess of the conventional mansion must go. One should lay out a house the way one would lay out the deck of a ship. London was in fact building a sailboat, a 45-foot one, at the time he wrote the essay. Lightness was important as well:

A sky-scraper is beautiful that is intrinsically and structurally light and that has a false massiveness of pillars plastered on outside. ... The true sky-scraper is beautiful, and it is beautiful in so far as it is true. In its construction it is light and airy, therefore in its appearance it must be light and airy.[6]

The central focus of London's essay shows the influence of Ruskin and deals with honesty. He described a neoclassical house he owned in Oakland:

I am hurt every time I look at it. No drunken rowdy or political enemy can insult me so deeply as that house does. ... After it was built, the criminal that constructed it nailed on, at the corners, perpendicularly, some two-inch fluted planks. These planks rise the height of the house, and to a drunken man have the appearance of fluted columns. ... the planks are topped with wooden Ionic capitals, nailed on. ... They have no use, no work to perform. They are plastered gawds that tell lies that nobody believes.[7]

The implication is that such conventions of architecture are a pretentious wrapper on the true building, and if the building is to be true, they must be removed. But his dislike of conventional architecture went deeper. London was not just an author; he was a socialist author and architecture, it is said, is the art of the establishment. London had written that as a young man he had seen that "Above me towered the colossal edifice of society, and to my mind the only way out was up. Into this edifice I early resolved to climb." But in time he saw that he did not want to occupy this edifice but to destroy it, "setting the whole edifice rocking." He wrote: "Some day, when we get a few more hands and crowbars to work, we'll topple it over, along with all its rotten life and unburied dead, its monstrous selfishness and sodden materialism." And above all stripping away of all shams and symbols of wealth and prestige.[8]

In 1911, London, who five years earlier had passionately argued for frugality of space in houses, began construction on a 15,000-square-foot home for himself, "Wolf House," in Sonoma. In general, it is rather disconnected from his essay and in some ways contradicts it. It was no sailboat, neither polished nor lightweight. The building might be called monumental rustic, an oxymoron that describes the ambivalence of its creator. London's desire was for something like a classical villa constructed of bark-on redwood logs atop a massive stone and concrete base. It was literally two buildings.

Economy of material, essential in nautical design, was of no importance. London's clear intent was to achieve solidity and mass, and with both comes monumentality. He wrote: "I am really going to throw out an anchor so big and so heavy that all hell could never get it up again. In fact, it's going to be a prodigious, ponderous sort of anchor."[9] It's monumentality may in part be attributed to London's experience watching and later writing on the 1906 San Francisco earthquake and the fires that followed. He sought monumentality in the sense of permanence through mass and solidity writing: "My house will be standing, act of God permitting, for a thousand years."[10]

At the same time Wolf House was decidedly rustic, something that can in part be attributed to the site. The ground floor, built of massive sections of volcanic stone taken from the site, contains a stone vault to house manuscripts. The upper floor is built of bark-on redwoods, also from the site. London's farm was within the narrow strip along the California coastline that is the natural habitat of coastal redwoods.[11] Its rustic classicism was perhaps a way to avoid the obvious alternative of a neoclassical mansion. The prohibition against functionless cladding remains. Structure was largely exposed, although, as is common in rustic building, a large amount of milled lumber was hidden.

Both rustic and monumental elements owe something to the architect Albert Farr, whose drawings included twig extensions to the columns. But the monumentality seems to answer a need beyond a refuge from earthquake and fire. The young man who wanted to topple the colossal edifice of society had decided to join it. The socialist author came to agree with one of America's most conspicuous capitalists. London was widely criticized for building the house. To many of London's admirers it was hypocritical.

Wolf House was a compilation of all the contradictory aspects of London's life, a mansion for a hero of the working class, a classical palace of rustic logs. Just before London was to move in, the building burned to its stone base, creating the impressive ruin that remains today. The result was a stone foundation that would last for centuries supporting an upper floor of wood that was gone before it could be inhabited.

Wolf House

Albert Farr's rendering of Wolf House

The same view today

Burroughs at Slabsides

John Burroughs

John Burroughs in his day was as famous as Muir, the confidant of presidents and millionaires. Burrough's model of primitive man is probably himself, longing for the simplicity of the old rustic life. He wielded his own axe and built his own cabin (at least in part)—in fact several.

Burroughs had no desire to leave his birthplace in the Catskills and while his work forced him to move elsewhere as a young man, at the age of 37 he returned home. While he wrote of the virtues of forest solitude he was rarely alone. He received and encouraged frequent visitors from near and far, functioning something like a Delphic oracle of the Catskills. In 1895 he built a single-room log cabin, Slabsides. It is a simple two-story cabin with porch, apparently constructed of a combination of sawn lumber and logs. The porch columns are clusters of two to three small tree trunks. The second-floor beams are logs. The sides are not logs but half logs on a milled frame with horizontal boards with battens on the interior. The cabin contains a great deal of Adirondack-style log furniture and bookcases and shelves supported by small logs. His dream seems to have been to recreate an idealized childhood where life was simple, unpretentious, and connected to nature.

When asked why he did not paint his cabin he said that he built it "to get away from paint and polish," to escape the "rules and regulations of well-ordered domestic machinery." Like London, he equated the layers of modern construction with the pretensions of society. The layers of historical or geographic allusion—sophisticated trim and refined craftsmanship—must be stripped away to get to the rustic core of the house, just as the complex sophisticated trapping of the city must be stripped away by returning to nature or at least to the farm. A good building required repose and repose demanded a manifestation of structure:

I think that, on examination, it will be found that the main secret of the picturesqueness of more simple structures, like fences, bridges, sheds, and log-huts, is that the motive, *the principle of construction, is so open and obvious. ... Hence the lively pleasure we feel in what are called 'timber-houses,' and in every architectural device by which the anatomy, the real framework, of the structure, inside or out, is allowed to show, or made to serve as ornament.*[12]

But for Burroughs, "honesty," the absence of structural deception, is insufficient; there must be the presence of structural expression.

The eye craves lines of strength, evidence of weight and stability. But in the wooden house, as usually treated, these lines are nearly all concealed, the ties and supports are carefully suppressed, and the eye must feed on the small, fine lines of the finish. When the mere outlines of the frame are indicated, so that the larger spaces appear as panels, it is a great help; or let any part of the internal economy show through, and the eye is interested.[13]

Thus in theory all that is unnecessary must be eliminated, leaving only the essential skeleton. In reality, like London, Burroughs' own architectural work is filled with the types of deceptive layers he condemned, particularly the half log siding of Slabsides. But regardless, if London was rustic architecture's Ruskin, Burroughs, an unlikely candidate, was rustic architecture's Viollet-le-Duc.

Ernest Thompson Seton

Born in Northern England, Ernest Thompson Seton immigrated with this family to Canada in 1866, first to rural Ontario, then to the outskirts of Toronto, and it was there he discovered his great loves: the world of nature, the culture of Native Americans, and the "primitive life." But he saw them the key to something else, his love of good building.

Seton built his first primitive cabin in 1874 at the age of 14. It was a log cabin half submerged into a bank built of six-inch diameter cedar posts with a roof of willow brush and grass. He had no axe and the building's size was thus determined by the length of the logs he could find. In fact, he was equipped with only a chisel, handsaw, hammer, and the blade from a broken plane he used to make a shovel. His great regret however was the use of nails: "These nails hurt my conscience. They were not Indian." While Robinson Crusoe and Swiss Family Robinson were on his mind, Seton's super-rational primitive man is not the English or Swiss peasant but the Native American. Seton saw Native Americans as designers who had achieved the rational out of necessity.

In 1900 Seton began work on a house in Cos Cob, Connecticut, this time with an architect and at a considerably larger scale. Seton and his architect were soon at an impasse due to what Seton describes as "fakery." He wrote, "We ripped off the architect's imitation timbers, his bogus rafters, his pretended beam ends, his dummy bolts, and his tinware hammered iron. We simplified the exterior. We put on real timbers where real timber seemed [to belong]." As a result of the experience, he wrote a series of articles in 1923 on the construction of the house, laying out the basic principles for building a primitive house which included: "Honesty," "Sound construction," and that "The Purpose must dictate the plan." In 1915 he built a second house not far away, and in this instance, he was far more his own architect.[14] Seton worked out the framing of the ground floor, sizing and locating each "real" beam in the process.

Seton described himself as, "A lover of good building, an amateur architect with lifelong experience and a traveler who has seen and studied

Ernest Thompson Seton's boyhood shanty

Ernest Thompson Seton
Seton Castle, Santa Fe, 1933

most famous buildings of the world." His views on architecture are those of rationalist modernism but his source was the Native American. The good building should appear to be what it structurally is. Structure may be exposed but under no circumstances can it be clad with something that appears to be structure but is not.

His move to Santa Fe in 1930 brought a change of focus, bringing him closer to the Native Americans of the Southwest, the ideal candidates for the American primitive man.

The structures he built there were stone, timber, and adobe bricks. They contained traditional Hispanic elements and materials, but all were adorned with Indigenous symbols, totems, and other paraphernalia. Seton's passion for "honest construction" was very much linked to his understanding of Native Americans. For Seton and many others, Native American constructions had a legitimacy that those of more sophisticated cultures lacked.

Of course London, Burroughs, and Seton were, in Isiah Berlin's terms, playing at being rustic and at other roles as well, Seton in part played the English Gentleman in his manor house. London, the laird in his mansion, and Burroughs clearly enjoyed his celebrity status. They also saw something others did not in rustic architecture, that it was the product of the authenticity of those who built it—the engineer, the Native American, the backwoodsman, the "primitive man" of architecture.

All three argued less for a rustic architecture than for a genuine architecture, one free of stylistic conventional motifs. This architecture might be raw and uncouth. But it must be genuine, straightforward, without allusions to Greece, Rome, or anywhere else. Their reasoning contains very little nostalgia. Rustic architecture did not evoke the memory of a past life in the wilderness, it embodied that world not just through its imagery but its methodology of building. This was not Durant, Morgan, or Vanderbilt playing at being primitive, this was authentic. It required not just the image of pioneer craft but the reality.

In general, there is racist thinking behind much of the writing about primitive man. Viollet-le-Duc was a racist. London, a well-known eugenicist, wrote about Native Americans but had no interest in their physical culture, nor did Burroughs. But for Seton and many others, Native American constructions had a legitimacy that those of more sophisticated cultures lacked. Most of those who admired Native Americans found it useful to think of them as "children" who, if given the chance, would grow up to behave like white men. In defense of this attitude is that rationalists thought innocence a creative virtue.

The Great Paradox

Primitive man was always present in rustic and national park architecture but he becomes more important in the twentieth century, as witnessed by the probably imaginary Swedish axmen who built the Old Faithful Inn. But those who agreed faced a great structural paradox. To London, Burroughs, and Seton the pretentious unnecessary layers of overcivilization must be stripped away to reveal the rustic, primitive, primal architecture below. But the reality was precisely the reverse. It had always been national park architecture's ugly secret that much of its rusticity was only skin deep. In the majority of the large rustic buildings, it was the rustic elements that were the cladding—pretentious or not—at the Old Faithful Inn, El Tovar, and large parts of the Adirondack lodges. If their outer rustic layer were stripped away it would reveal the industrialized sawmill frame below. It was the rustic architecture that was often "the architect's bogus trimmings" and "gawds that tell lies that nobody believes."

The rationalist thinking of these three does not reflect the attitudes of many within the Park Service or the architectural profession in the first half of the twentieth century and certainly not the railroads and the concessionaires they supported. But, within the boundaries of the Park Service, these issues were fiercely debated. There were two schools of thought, a division between the mere appearance of craft and real construction, one evoking imaginary history the other revealing constructional reality.

In the vast majority of writing on rustic and national park architecture in recent years his paradox had little consequence. The years that followed the creation of the Park Service in 1916 saw many new buildings, and some of the most prominent were rustic and primitive only in appearance—veneers tacked on to industrial frames. The inconsistency between industrial reality and rustic appearance in park building was largely unknown, and many who knew argued that it was of no consequence. Architecture, the argument goes, is about what you see, not what you know but can't see. But it is significant that three of America's most influential writers saw it otherwise, and the same period also saw architects working in the parks who applied the rigor of London, Burroughs, and Seton.

Herbert Maier had nothing at all to say about Gothic cathedrals, structural rationalism or Viollet-le-Duc, but he did have his own vision of primitive man—the American pioneer:

> *Whether he set up his abode on the forest, sod, or adobe covered plains or in a rock-strewn country, he was forced to adopt the natural material immediately at hand, and when the structure was completed it consequently echoed the identical materials and color from its surroundings.*[15]

It was not just the forms that were naturally located, so too was the craft:

> *The adaptation of indigenous and frontier construction included the use of primitive tools that led to a 'freehand architecture with an absence of rigidly straight lines and a softening of right angles.' ... And so we find that construction which is primitive in character blends most readily with primitive surroundings and is thereby less outstanding and has intriguing craftsmanlike appearance.*[16]

For Maier the appearance of the primitive and the marks of primitive tools were insufficient—the construction must be authentic. Buildings were not billboards. They were not playing at being primitive.

THE PARADISE INN: RATIONALIST PROLOGUE

By the time the National Park Service was founded in 1916, what we now call rustic architecture was well established. There was a common sensibility and something like a style, allowing for variations. But underneath it all, from the perspective of today, there was ideological confusion. There was the striking contrast of technology and craft in buildings built of saw-milled lumber encrusted with logs cut with axes. The industrial parts, the frame, were mostly hidden and as far as many architects were concerned, weren't there anyway. There was the contradiction in building lodges using "indigenous" materials brought from hundreds of miles away and assembled by craftsmen who came as far. There was ideological contradiction and in many places it was visible.

Railway executives and most tourists were not much concerned with structural honesty or structural rationalism or even consistency, but it was a concern for many who advocated of this type of architecture, the structural rigor that Gladbach and Varin saw in the chalet and the virtues Seton, London, and Burroughs saw in the log cabin. The basic rustic system we have seen, a rustic veneer overlaying the sawmill frame was to continue and become even more divergent in its construction, but constructional rigor, even structural rationalism, were to have their moment in post-1916 park architecture. It began with the Paradise Inn, finished in 1917.

Mount Rainier became a national park in 1899 but it was not a particularly accessible one. The solution came through the Tacoma Eastern Railroad. It owned a mill in Tacoma, and 90% of the freight hauled by the Tacoma Eastern was lumber from the Mt. Rainier area and in 1904 it extended its lines the 60 miles to Ashford, just outside the Park. Like its predecessors who built such railroads to access parks, transporting tourists was a task secondary to transporting timber. One hotel existed, the Longmire Springs Hotel. Another was built nearby, the National Park Inn, a wood platform-framed building, in 1906. Nothing was rustic. Ten years later the National Park Service was created. Stephen Mather, its director, encouraged a group of Tacoma businessmen to form the Rainier National Park Company and gave them an exclusive 20-year monopoly on a concession service. The result was the Paradise Inn.

The Paradise Inn is one of the most structurally expressive buildings in a national park. At the same time, it is one of the most structurally problematic. The inn was designed by Frederick Heath of Heath, Gove and Bell whose rustic work, like many in this narrative, was only a small fragment of a much larger practice. He had designed one rustic building previously, a large chalet-styled structure to house baths. He never designed another, and the many buildings he designed subsequently show structural competence but little interest in structural expression. As to his possible interest in the latter, we have only the inn as evidence.

Opposite: The Paradise Inn

**The Paradise Inn,
Mt. Rainier National Park, 1917**

It was planned to be built at Longmire, but when the original client left the project, it was decided instead to build a new cluster of buildings at Paradise, 12 miles farther from the park entrance but with views of Mt. Rainier and the surrounding ranges. It was 2,600 feet higher at 5,400 feet, and the new site had consequences for both tourists and buildings, most severely in the form of snow.

The inn is a conceptually odd but formally effective hybrid of traditional craftsmanship and structural science. There was a desire that the inn not just look archaic but be constructed in an archaic way. According to one source, the structure was originally constructed without nails, simply tightly fitted wood joints." The interior building ... is all beautiful log work put together without a nail. The logs were just fitted together."[1] The railroad was far away. Supplies had to be packed in by horse. The wood and the stone were local. The frame was erected without the use of power equipment. Since it was linked to civilization by a muddy, unpaved, one-lane road there was certainly a primitivism of necessity. This resulted in some poor decisions, albeit made with admirable intentions, that contributed to the inn's problems. The Paradise Inn, by accident or intent, is in the tradition of structural rationalism. It stands apart from its many predecessors in the Adirondacks, Yellowstone, or Glacier. The structural frame is largely visible on the outside. It is completely visible on the inside. There is a clear distinction between the structural skeleton and the skin infill. The frame is, conceptually at least, in an optimal configuration, a series of parallel triangular trusses forming a long triangular prism. It has none of the quality of a rustic encrustation cladding an industrial frame of the work of Cutler or Reamer. As a piece of honest structural expression, it was a breath of fresh air. At the same time, it has a sad history of structural problems—a poor decision in siting and a poor understanding of the structural loads it would be exposed to on that site led to innumerable structural problems and have required constant major interventions over its 100-year history.

The heaviest recorded snowfall at the Paradise Inn was 1,122 inches (93.5 ft) in 1971-1972. The lightest was still 22.2 feet in 2014-2015. The largest recorded accumulation was 30 feet in 1955. According to the Park Service, Paradise is "the snowiest place on earth where snowfall is measured regularly."[2] We do not know if the architects had access to weather data for the Paradise area but the physical evidence alone—30-foot-deep snow accumulations—would have been hard to ignore. The site was selected somewhat hastily. It was a place with views toward Mount Rainier on the uphill side and the Tatoosh Range on the opposite, but was not optimal in that regard and it sat on a slope that required a more substantial foundation than was provided. It was a site that demanded a structural response, which of course does not automatically follow from structural expression.

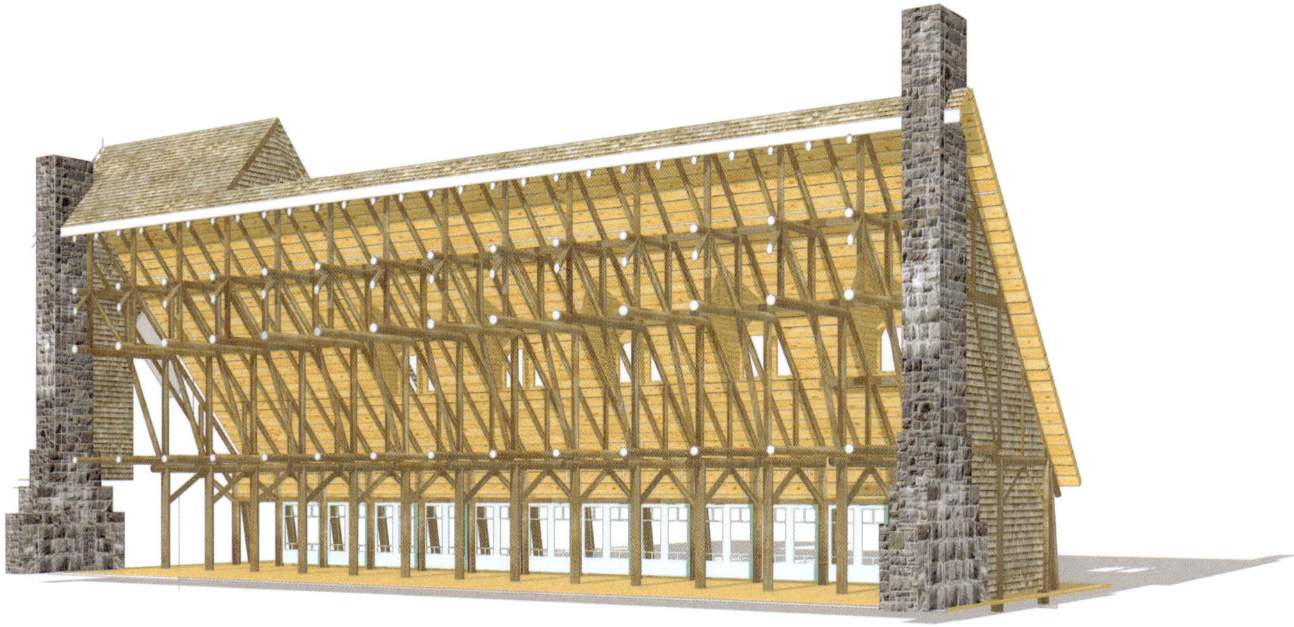

Lobby Wing
Section looking southeast

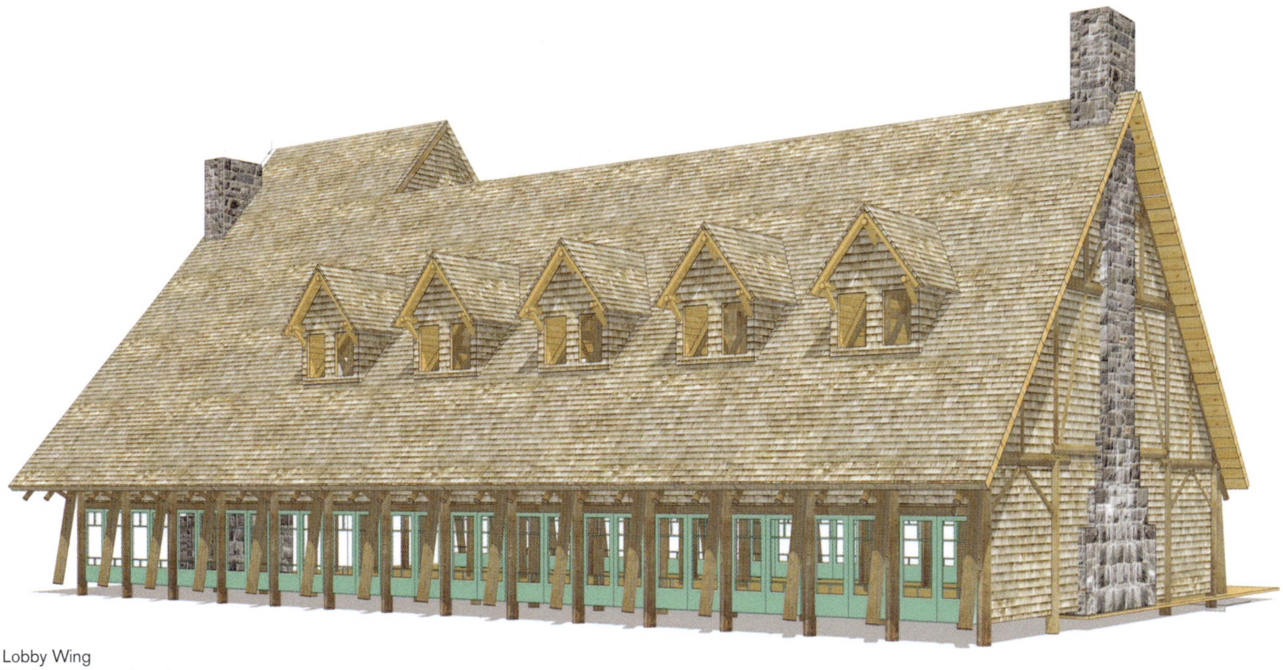

Lobby Wing
Northwest entry elevation

The program was critical to the form as well since the Paradise Inn, at least originally, was not an inn at all. The plan was for a tent camp and the original building was primarily a dining and social space surrounded by 125 tents. The building is a long triangular prism parallel to the slope holding three large rooms—a lobby, dining room, and a kitchen. A short wing of bedrooms at right angles to the prism formed a stubby tee shape. The interior is for the most part large undivided rooms with an odd distribution of space. Originally, it had only 37 rooms, served by a 5,000-square foot dining hall. Those bedrooms located above the dining hall were eight feet square in order to fit between the tightly spaced trusses. There were no adjacent bathrooms.

The reason for this is the use of a construction type we have not seen, one that exhibits a different attitude toward the frame and skin of the building. The rustic lodges examined thus far have an interior frame, the bones, that is covered by the skin. There are other buildings that have parts of the frame on the exterior, such as the Glacier Park Lodge. At Paradise, the building envelope fills the voids between the frame and is co-planer with it, forming a series of triangular and rectilinear shapes between the members of the log frame. This makes the frame highly visible. At the same time, it creates a large number of technically difficult joints where the frame and skin meet—places where thermal expansion, cracks, water, snow, and wind can work together in destructive ways. The exterior frame is felt most dramatically on the diagonal struts of the ground floor that give it a resemblance to Danish Viking longhouses.

Since the inn is triangular in section as opposed to the four-story boxes with a row of bedrooms on each side of each floor that characterizes the typical hotels at Yellowstone or Glacier, it is essentially all roof. The Old Faithful Inn, is mostly roof, and while widely admired was rarely imitated, probably because it is an inefficient shape to fit hotel rooms into. The Paradise Inn, having few rooms to accommodate, brings back the over-scaled sloping roof. It returned to a design strategy that had enjoyed great success at the Old Faithful Inn but one that had rarely been used subsequently—the gable roof with dormers.

The inn in winter

The Paradise Inn
View in late summer

At first glance the structure of the Paradise Inn appears a perfectly triangulated solution- a kind of space frame of logs. The triangular shape facilitates what could have been a structurally optimal form—a series of frames/trusses composed of triangles. This would have transferred loads more directly to the ground and added lateral stability since triangles are inherently more stable than rectangles. Certain of the triangular struts are dislocated or eliminated for spatial effects as in the lobby.

Some struts were eliminated so that the large hall would not be crossed by numerous horizontal wood members. The roof beams push against the two sides of the structure prying them apart. The long horizontal beam holds them together. The long horizontal piece is critical. At the same time, it divides the space into two horizontal layers despite the absence of a floor or ceiling above the horizontal beam. It is a common problem. It is precisely the issue and the problem of Coulter's playhouse at Sagamore Camp. The section at Paradise Inn was an unsuccessful compromise. The drawings on page 383 show what has essentially been added over the years. So, the history of the Paradise Inn has been one of constant structural additions and modifications. Horizontal timbers were added to hold the ends of the triangular trusses together. One half of these may have been there already. It is not clear.

The building's character owes a great deal to the Alaska cedar timbers of the frame. These came from the park, from the Silver Forest, several miles down the road to Seattle just below Narada Falls. It was a stand Alaska cedars that had been burned in 1885 and remained standing. Most of the logs that make up the structure are roughly the same diameter, no easy thing to do given the extreme differences in loading in the building. The inn has none of the surreal twisted logs of the Old Faithful. There is little built-in woodwork, different in character from the frame. Railings are as big as the columns they span. Table legs and newel posts are only an inch or so smaller. The ballyhooed furniture made later for the inn is much out of character.

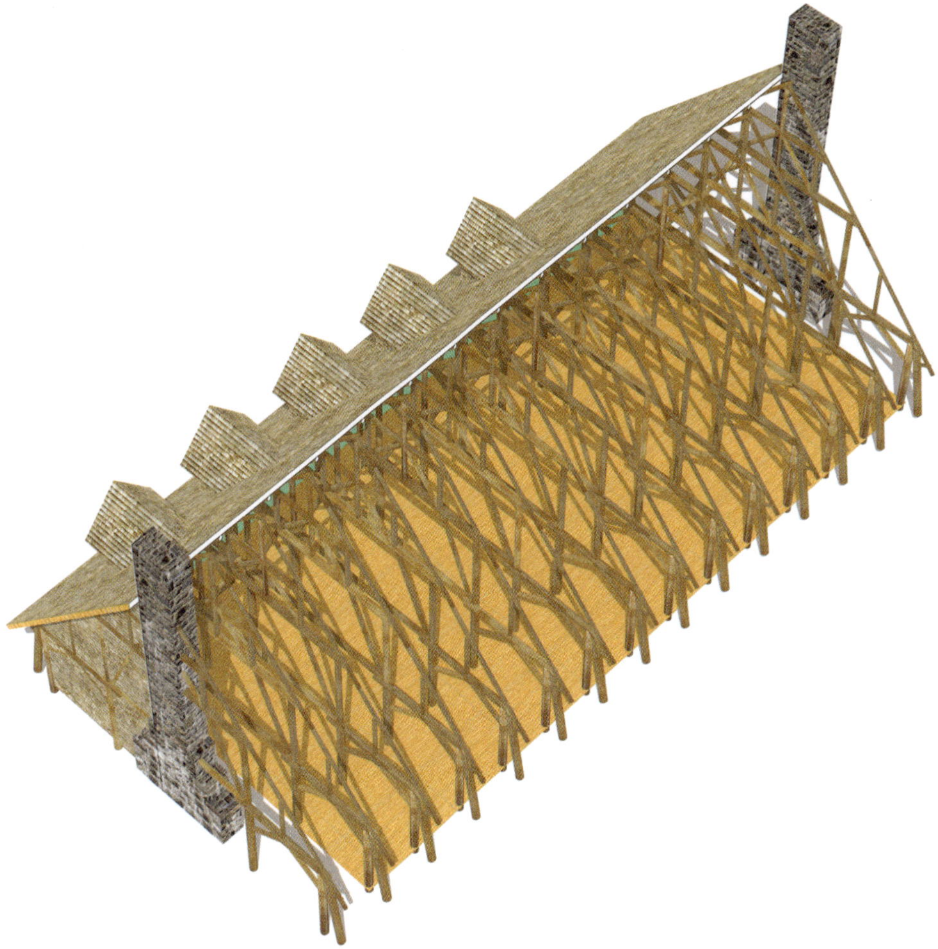

Trusses in the Main Lobby

The logs were hauled by horse and wagon to the construction site and raised into position without the use of motorized cranes. The stone was local as well, but there were large quantities of material that had to be brought up the mountain, and there is obviously a large quantity of wood required for studs and joists whose source is unknown.

The parallel triangular trusses are made of 7-15" round Alaska cedar logs. Subsequent repairs revealed a ¾" round steel bar at each joint that may or may not have been part of the original structure. In either case the joint was structurally inadequate for the forces the joint had to sustain. A wide variety of steel connectors have been added to the wood truss joints at various times to make them perform their structural task.

In addition to the structural problems of inadequate foundations, the insufficient horizontal ties, and inadequately designed joints there were other issues, particularly loading. Even if the triangular trusses had worked adequately there was the problem of resisting lateral loads at 90 degrees to the trusses. Often the diaphragm action of roofs and floors is adequate to resist this, but not in this case. Lateral bracing along the long axis of the building was achieved with the addition of steel x bracing, a balcony floor at the second level of the lounge, and cross walls such as the fireplace have been made into structural diaphragms and a great deal of construction has gone on below grade to strengthen the foundations.

Surprisingly, the inn has retained its character through all these changes. Its most serious threat, other than the periodic suggestions that it be demolished, was the wing added in 1921 to provide enough rooms for it to function as a hotel. The new wing is a conventionally framed building of little interest but was originally planned to be three times its present size with a stone tower—all of which would have dwarfed the original inn. Other alterations, such as the mezzanine floors added at the perimeter or the rebuilding of the dormers as sheds rather than gables to prevent snow accumulation, changed the original effect somewhat.

Heath's work there was done. He did not design the addition to the inn. He did no subsequent work for the Park Service. What followed architecturally at Rainier was architecture of another order altogether. There was still a great deal of architecture to come at Mount Rainier, all designed by architects of the Park Service and owe little in architectural form or constructional order to the Paradise Inn, and is in fact its opposite, Rustic architecture at its most scenographic. The Paradise Inn has a legacy but not at Mount Rainier. The rationalist tradition, or at least the tradition of not doing rustic architecture by covering an industrial wood frame with logs was to continue in the work of Gilbert Underwood, Herbert Maier, and others.

Timber joints

The Lobby
Before additional horizontal bracing and balconies were added

The lobby today

Sequence of Structural Additions

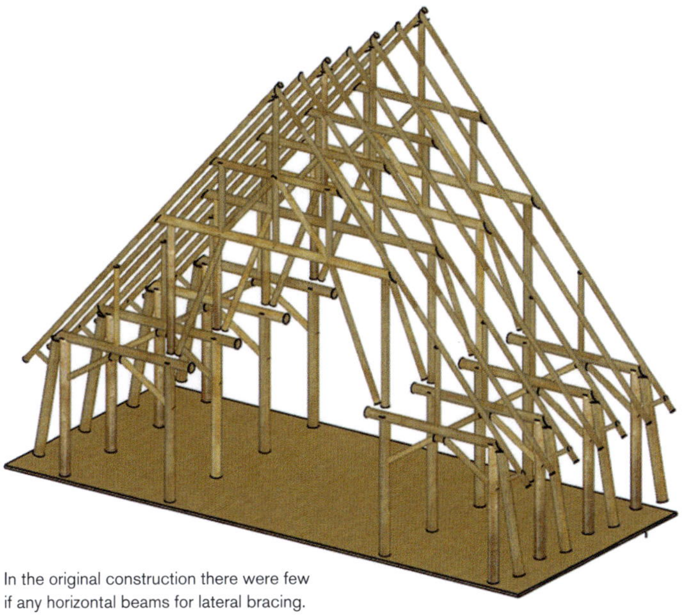

In the original construction there were few if any horizontal beams for lateral bracing.

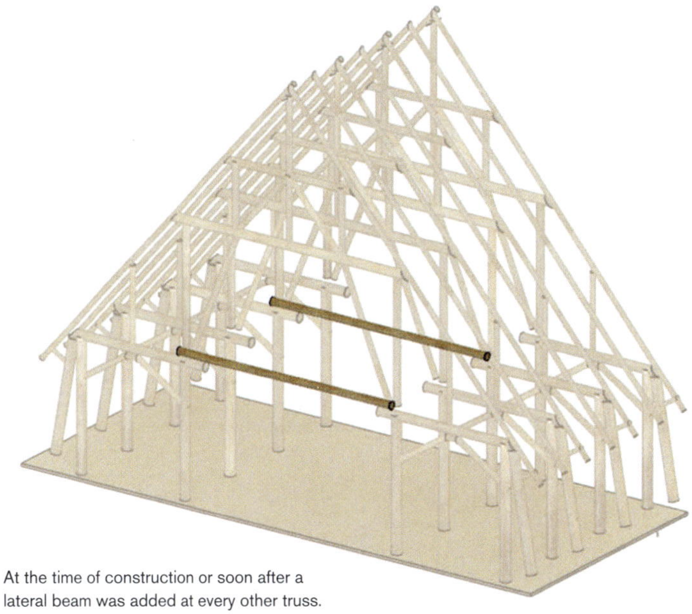

At the time of construction or soon after a lateral beam was added at every other truss.

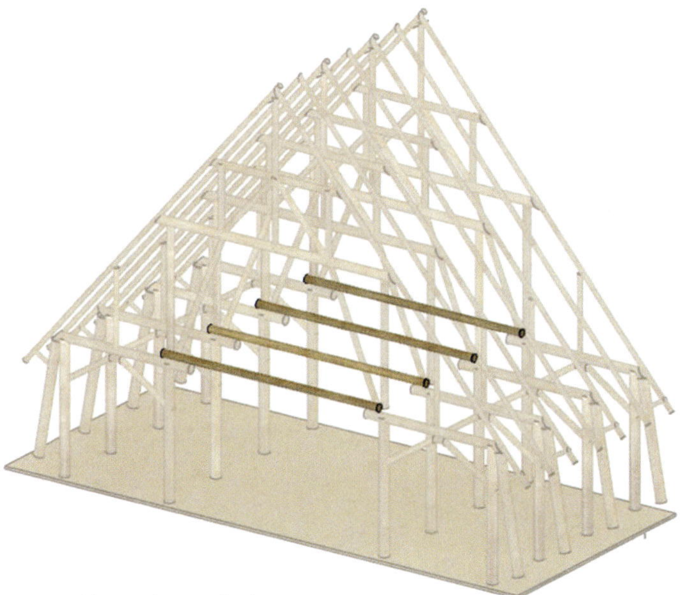

Problems with excessive snow loads continued and horizontal beams were added at every truss.

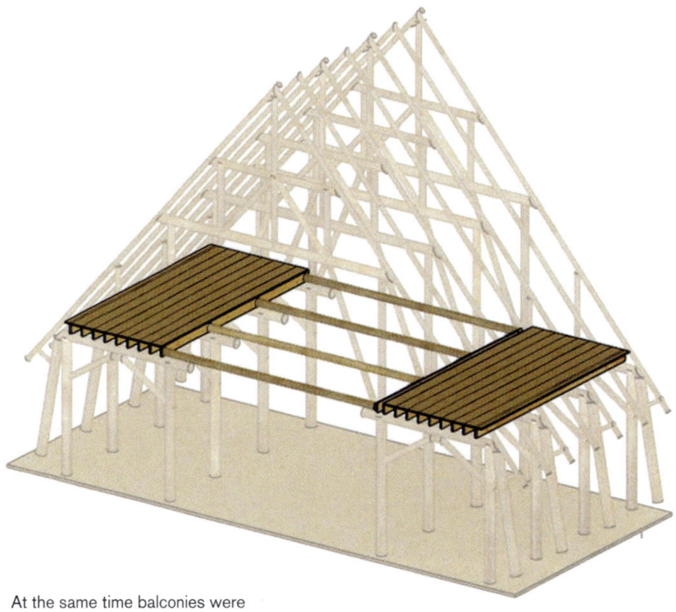

At the same time balconies were added a the perimeter.

Structural Additions

Paradise Inn
Wall Section

Approximate end wall condition after 1981 and 2008 restorations

The balcony added in 1925 is not shown.

It is a rare construction system in rustic architecture in that the walls are infill panels between the log frame as opposed to being inside the skin. It creates a myriad of joint conditions for water and wind might enter the building but it exposes the structural frame both inside and out. The floor and roof structure are largely exposed.

This wall has had considerable structural problems over the years. Concrete and steel reinforcing has been added to the chimney. The walls between the logs have been rebuilt with reinforced infill panels of 2x4 studs and plywood sheathing, covered with shingles to act as diaphragms to laterally brace the building and with improved bolted connections to the frame.

The stone foundation wall has been rebuilt with concrete.

ALBERT GOOD'S BIBLE

Over the course of 1935, a committee of six men and one woman held a series of meetings in Washington, DC to discuss proposed standards of design and prototypes for facilities in state and national parks. Their specific goal was a pattern book of existing designs that would establish and illustrate their criteria. The group included Thomas Vint, head of design at the National Park Service, and Herbert Maier, arguably the best designer of such structures. The woman was Dorothy Waugh who collected much of the material. Also on the committee was Albert Good, a designer who is best remembered today as an author. In the guidelines that followed there is a remarkable consensus from overall building form down to the smallest details—paint colors, knotholes, and log ends. But there was one question, a very large one, on which there was acrimonious disagreement. They reported, "The question, long debated, centered around honesty in the use of materials." The report was remarkably straightforward:

Only threats to turn the key on the jury until a verdict would be reached moved the proponents of the several schools of thought. Beyond all doubt every member of the committee was coerced through sheer horror at the prospect of enduring longer the enforced company of six others of heretical belief. At any rate, the perfect settlement was suavely reached by unanimous agreement to leave the matter unsettled. The committee remains stubbornly off the record on this controversial point.[1]

One group, what might be called "rationalists," thought, "that park buildings should not appropriate the semblance of primitive structures without appropriating as well all the primitive elements and methods of the prototypes. ... there is no allowable compromise with true log construction; it must be rigidly adhered to in every detail if employed at all."

There was another group we will call, for the sake of clarity, "romantics," who "argued that there are not at hand today the seemingly inexhaustible resources of pioneer days, that to insist on the use of logs in today's park structures in the spendthrift fashion of our forefathers, might be logic in the aesthetic abstract, but in practice wastes those resources the conservation of which is at the very roots of the impetus toward park expansion."

A compromise was suggested:

A straddling pacifist proposed that only the more important park structures should faithfully reproduce pioneer log construction, with the objective of preserving for observation and study the fast-disappearing frontier construction methods[2]

In summation, the park headquarters might be logs, the tourist cabin something more practical and probably industrial.

Economy was at the heart of the issue not just economy of capital—economy of labor, economy of material and the preservation of natural resources. It was asked:

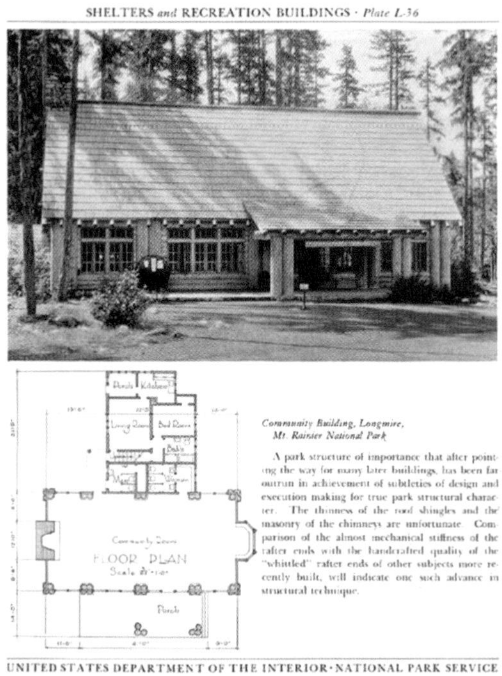
SHELTERS *and* RECREATION BUILDINGS · *Plate L-36*

Community Building, Longmire, Mt. Rainier National Park

A park structure of importance that after pointing the way for many later buildings, has been far outrun in achievement of subtleties of design and execution making for true park structural character. The thinness of the roof shingles and the masonry of the chimneys are unfortunate. Comparison of the almost mechanical stiffness of the rafter ends with the handcrafted quality of the "whittled" rafter ends of other subjects more recently built, will indicate one such advance in structural technique.

UNITED STATES DEPARTMENT OF THE INTERIOR · NATIONAL PARK SERVICE

A page from *Park and Recreation Structures* showing Ernest Davidson's Longmire Community Building

Is there justification in the fact that the amount of timber stock required for one true log structure will provide material for three or four more or less adequate and pleasing structures to bloom or blight ... in its place?[3]

But this issue was not quite the burning question it appeared to be. Their report, which evolved into Albert Good's *Park and Recreation Structures* (1938), has been called the Bible of rustic architecture. It was not really a plan for the future so much as it was a description of the past.[4] It did not describe a policy for what was to come. Rustic architecture would disappear in a few years with the outbreak of war. It was a description of the status quo, of a set of practices that had emerged after 1916 and continued until 1940. The three conditions described—(1) buildings truly handcrafted by traditional methods; (2) buildings in which the handcraft was a rustic veneer on an industrialized frame, and (3) a hybrid or technical compromise in which the handcraft and industrialized lumber sat side by side—were all in existence and had been for some time. These were created by evolution and practical necessity, not by committee, and each had its own history and its own practitioners.

The Park Service

The creation of the National Park Service in 1916, 44 years after the creation of the first national park, brought many changes. There was a centralized administration, a centralized landscape office, a chief landscape architect to approve and supervise design, staff architects to design buildings, master plans for large parks, and there was funding for the administrators and the administration buildings to house them. There were new educational programs and buildings to house them as well. Some of these were funded by private donors but designs were approved by the Park Service.

At the same time many things stayed the same after 1916, or almost the same. Hotels and services were still created by private concessionaires and many of these were railroads or companies controlled by railroads. This did not trouble Stephen Mather, the Park Service director who favored a single concessionaire for each park.

Many of the Park Service buildings are characterized by a veneer of allusions to a romanticized handicraft, pioneer-type log cabin past often overlayed on an industrialized framework. Image was what mattered and external appearance was based on fictive histories not the reality of the present.

But there was another group one that was more accepting of industrial technology particularly that of the railroad, who sought a marriage of external form and internal structural order, who explored buildings where design and construction are integral, even a sort of rustic structural rationalism.

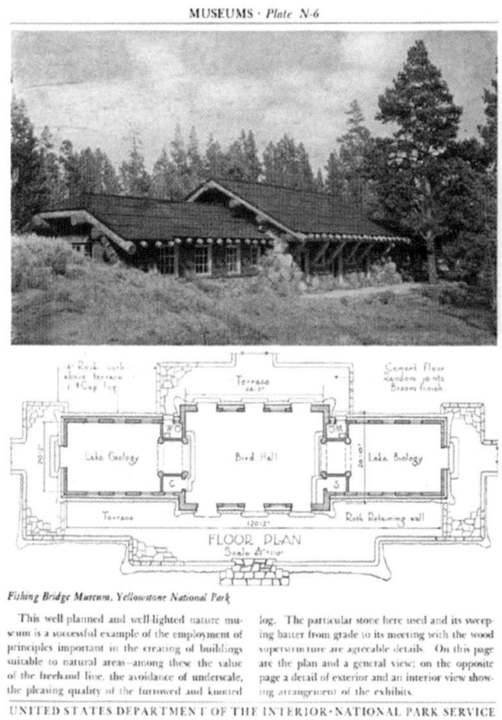
MUSEUMS · *Plate N-6*

Fishing Bridge Museum, Yellowstone National Park

This well planned and well-lighted nature museum is a successful example of the employment of principles important in the creating of buildings suitable to natural areas—among these the value of the freehand line, the avoidance of underscale, the pleasing quality of the furrowed and knotted log. The particular stone here used and its sweeping batter from grade to its meeting with the wood superstructure are agreeable details. On this page are the plan and a general view; on the opposite page a detail of exterior and an interior view showing arrangement of the exhibits.

UNITED STATES DEPARTMENT OF THE INTERIOR · NATIONAL PARK SERVICE

A page from *Park and Recreation Structures* showing Herbert Maier's Fishing Bridge Museum

The stair-step log corner. Harry Trisch at work on the West Thumb Ranger Station

STEPHEN MATHER AND THE LOG CABIN

In 1923, during the early years of the Park Service, Stephen Mather, its first director, and Gilbert Underwood, one of its primary architects, were called to a meeting in New York that was canceled at the last minute. Left with a free day, at Mather's suggestion they visited Coney Island. Mather's purpose, according to Underwood, was to show him its crass commercialism, a representation of precisely what the national parks were not about. There is no doubt that Mather was sincere and that he worked tirelessly to remove and prevent crass commercialism in the parks, but in retrospect is not so accurate a depiction of Mather. Whatever else he was, he was also a showman.[1]

Mather wanted to increase attendance in parks and he wanted to do so across the economic spectrum, from the elite to the working class. If staging a performance was required, that would happen. His star performers were wildlife but not all wildlife and not in a natural way. Predators—mountain lions, wolves, and coyotes—were hunted to extinction. Picturesque animals—elk, buffalo, and deer—were protected, fed, and directed by fences and other means to populate the roadside where they would be visible. Bears were encouraged to visit garbage dumps and bleachers were set up for tourists to watch them scavenge. Rangers on occasion were required to perform as well, but only in certain ways.[2] When a series of ranger presentations were being set up at Yellowstone campgrounds, there was an "official fear lest suggestion of lessons and study would keep people away from the Parks," and Mather directed that these talks be "not too dry or scientific" and "low-keyed and entertaining."[3]

So, inevitably, national park architecture became part of these performances: what kind of an architecture, what stage-set design, would be appropriate to Mather for these performances? In the Park Service's early years there were experiments—arts and crafts shingle-style buildings were built at Yosemite. Charles Punchard, the first chief landscape architect, explored Swiss motifs at Yosemite. But the final answer is not difficult to predict—the log cabin. During a conference in 1915 that marked the founding of the Park Service, Mather took the attendees to see a replica of the Old Faithful Inn that the Union Pacific had constructed at the Panama-Pacific International Exposition in San Francisco.[4] The inn was probably for Mather the logical extension of the log cabin language into the large building, but it perfectly illustrated the problem. Much of the inn was a rustic veneer on an industrial frame and the conditions that made that necessary were more prevalent in 1916 than in 1904. Mather and the Park Service had thus to determine how real their rustic performance was to be—painted backdrop or something genuinely archaic. The days when log construction was looked at with disdain at Yellowstone or in any other park were gone. The success of the Old Faithful Inn had completed the change in taste Haynes, Cody, Stickley, and Sharpe had begun, elevating the log cabin to its shrine status.

Old Faithful Inn replica at Panama Pacific Exposition, 1915

Abraham Lincoln Birthplace Memorial, Kentucky, 1911

The Interior: The cabin where Lincoln was not born

But these were small events in relation to the rise in national standing of the log cabin. In 1911, five years before the Park Service was established, the Abraham Lincoln Birthplace Memorial was completed in Kentucky. It was designed by John Russell Pope as a massive stone building to serve as an enclosure, a reliquary, for one of America's greatest relics, the log cabin in which Abraham Lincoln was thought to be born. (It was not.) A stone building with massive walls and minimal windows encloses a structure that, in this context, appears to be so many toothpicks. The everyday was elevated into the realm of the sacred. In 1916 John Lloyd Wright developed the immensely popular toy system known as Lincoln Logs, a set of miniature log components that came with instructions for building a tiny copy of Uncle Tom's Cabin or Lincoln's.[5]

But whatever the vicissitudes of national taste, there was one place in the national parks where construction had always been of logs and continued to be—the Yellowstone backcountry. These were the Snowshoe cabins built on site in the remote backcountry providing temporary shelters for rangers on patrol by the rangers themselves, using only the materials at the site and whatever equipment, experience, and expertise that the rangers brought with them. The Park Service's first building campaigns at Yellowstone were in two areas—rebuilding most of the Snowshoe cabins, which were in poor shape, and a second type far more conspicuous and accessible—a series of ranger stations in the park campgrounds with a meeting room attached for public events.

It was at this moment, 1921, that Charles Punchard, the first director of design at the Park Service, died and was succeeded by his assistant, Daniel Hull. This book is full of enigmas, but Hull as we will see, is hard to match. At times a romantic, at times a rationalist, he had a clear understanding and sympathy for both viewpoints. He had clear commitment to architectural integrity, e.g., no fake veneers, but tempered with pragmatism. His ideas of professional ethics were decidedly more fluid.

One of his first commissions was three ranger station/community buildings at Yellowstone. Logs were to be the material, not just logs, but logs

The Lake Ranger Station, Yellowstone National Park, 1923

assembled in the style of the pioneer. One of the first to be finished was at Old Faithful in 1921. Horace Albright, the park superintendent, also had ideas about their design. He wanted the design of the Old Faithful Ranger Station to reflect the architecture of Old Faithful Inn, with the use of "special windows, dormers and brackets under the rafters; these perhaps to be of bent limbs of Lodgepole trees."[6]

But it was the Lake Ranger Station, finished 1923 and designed by Hull, that was to become the model of what Mather wanted park architecture to be. The meeting room in plan was an eight-sided polygon with a fireplace at the center, providing an indoor replica of an outdoor campfire as at the Old Faithful Inn. Mather directed that the building be finished in what he called "trapper cabin" style, what Albright called "the stair-step method" of cutting off the ends of the logs."[7] This meant that the log ends would be at irregular length so the corners projected varying distances but increasing in length toward the ground. The flat log ends were then cut to a chisel point with an axe hiding the saw marks in the process. Reamer had done this at Old Faithful. Mather called the station "a triumph in woodland architecture ... with perfect jointing of logs."[8]

The man with the axe here was Merit Tuttle, not a trapper but a contractor from Fromberg, Montana, but he and his workman knew how to build with logs. He had built the three ranger stations, and he built many more larger log buildings such as the Lake Lodge.

The Thumb Station was finished in 1925 in a similar style. But the ranger-station log cabins represented only a small part of a larger body of structures being built in the park. In 1923, the year the lake station was finished, sixty new concessionaire cabins were built at Old Faithful Camp alone. To build them all in trapper-cabin style would be a challenge. It was already clear in 1922 that log buildings were expensive and they used far more material than frame structures. Burdened with a congressional limit of $1,500 per building the Park Service faced if not an impasse, a severe obstacle.[9]

Canyon Ranger Station, 1921

The Thumb Ranger Station under construction,1925

In 1935, 25 members of the CCC constructed a ranger station at Jewel Cave National Monument. It was a true log cabin, with no layers or veneers. The logs were cut on the site with axes and assembled in the stair-step method, pointed at the ends while the corners were double saddle-notched. The porch is half logs with log steps, log railings. The foundation is stone. The only industrial products are the concrete floor, cedar-shingles of the roof, and the double-hung windows.

Albert Good was so enthusiastic he resorted to Latin describing it as *multum in parvo* (much in little) calling it a "masterly accomplishment," and wrote:

Being almost a miniature in scale, this cabin is something of a concentrated essence of log cabin structural technique. Logs are employed for the puncheon floor and steps of the porch, both details which, in modern log cabins, usually compromise with more modern and less sturdy building methods. ... this little dwelling which marries the split millimeter pro portions of a Pullman section and the spendthrift technique of the pioneer builder.

It is a rare example of a cabin rustic in appearance that is rustic in reality, but it is arguably more a reenactment than a building. Without the industrialization of the West and the romanticization of the log cabin it would not have happened. The Park Service had found its language. It had not found the means to realize it with available resources.[10]

For Mather, and for many others, the log cabin and the axe that produced it are the symbols of what a kind of domestic technological national identity. The stud and joist platform frame is not. There was an alternative architecture, however, the lessons of the vernacular, the evocation of history, and the urge to build with natural materials are not excluded by constructional rigor and do not demand the suppression of technology as Herbert Maier and Gilbert Underwood were about to demonstrate.

Ranger station, Jewel Cave National Monument, 1935

Charles R. Peterson

PARK SERVICE PRAGMATISTS: GILBERT UNDERWOOD, DANIEL HULL AND FRED WILLSON

At the end of *My First Summer in the Sierra* John Muir wrote, "If I had a few sacks of flour, an axe, and some matches, I would build a cabin of pine logs, pile up plenty of firewood about it and stay all winter,"[1] implying that, had he access to adequate tools, he might have followed Thoreau's example and built a cabin for himself. One year later, that situation, at least in regard to tools, had changed dramatically. In the autumn of 1865 a hotel owner, James Hutchings, had packed in the equipment on mules to build a sawmill and in the fall of 1869, he hired Muir to design, build, and run it. Muir milled trees that had been blown down in a storm, and assembled the lumber into non-log buildings—the mill, two cabins, and a hotel near Yosemite Falls.

This might seem an unlikely profession for Muir, the rustic conservationist, but while he may have been the last of the transcendentalists, he was also a far more common American type—the gadget lover, the tinkerer, the *bricoleur*. His dream as a young man was to be an inventor, not a naturalist, and his first invention was a table saw to cut rough logs into square timbers. And Muir was building his own cabin, but not the conventional log cabin he imagines in his memoir. Both his sketch and his description of the cabin he did build imply that it was flat horizontal boards of milled lumber behind widely spaced log uprights. It required an axe but it also required a sawmill.

There are several lessons in this story. One is that as soon as the tourists arrived at Yosemite so did the sawmill. The other is that Muir was willing to do in 1870 what the architects of the Old Faithful Inn and El Tovar were unwilling to do in 1904, mix bark-on logs with exposed sawmill lumber in the same building. Muir's attitude toward rustic architecture was surprisingly unromantic, using whatever technology was available—axes and sawmills, logs and boards.

Fifty years later the architects and administrators of the newly formed National Park Service faced a problem filled with the same dilemma, how to build the backdrop for a life of rustic simplicity on an industrial scale with industrial methods. It was for that reason that Muir's cabin became the precursor, perhaps the ancestor, of hundreds of national park buildings built in the 1920s starting at Yellowstone.

One of these administrators, probably the key one, was Horace Albright, superintendent of Yellowstone National Park from 1919 to 1929, a period which saw one of the largest number of constructed buildings in the history of that park, but he was a good deal more. He had been instrumental in drafting the legislation that created the Park Service. In the early days he was Mather's assistant director. He served as acting director during Mather's incapacities during his battles with depression and eventually became his successor when Mather retired. During his time at Yellowstone, Albright oversaw all the western parks as well. So Albright had a great deal to say about what kind of architecture was to be built in the parks.

West Yellowstone Union Pacific Dining Hall, 1926

Albright, Underwood, Hull, and Willson

Although trained as a lawyer, Albright was neither shy nor slow to give his opinion on design. Ideologically and stylistically his architectural vision did not differ greatly from Mather's and he did his best to carry Mather's vision out, but Albright was a great deal more than this as well. His correspondence shows a pragmatic administrator, struggling to execute that rustic vision within the realities, particularly the economic realities, of the place and time.

He enthusiastically supported and applauded log buildings such as the Lake Ranger Station but at the same time he vetoed certain materials or techniques because of cost, and he faced severe congressional limits on what he could spend on any one building. There were a range of types of buildings constructed in his first years as superintendent. There were genuinely rustic, crudely hand-crafted buildings—the traditional backcountry cabins built of logs—out of necessity. There were straightforward, stud and clapboard, industrially fabricated utilitarian frame buildings—fresh from the lumber yard. Albright complained that, "The Copeland Lumber company of Bozeman came very close to being regarded for a time as the official architects for Yellowstone National Park."[2]

But the new generation of park buildings was to produce two new, very different cultures of building. There was a different type of log cabin, handcrafted showpiece buildings, commissioned by the Park Service—ranger stations, museums, and community buildings—built to send a rustic message, with an ambiance of axes, logs, and pioneers—buildings such as the Lake Ranger Station. These were central to the image and mission of the Park Service, but they were only a rather small part of a much larger building enterprise, responding to a much larger need, the hundreds of cabins, large dining rooms, and other buildings to support them commissioned by the Park Service but built and operated by concessionaires. These two types were built in two very different ways, financially and constructionally. In the end it produced two very different architectures built by two different groups of architects: small scale romantic, the craft building built for the Park Service's use, and the large-scale craft/industrial hybrids of the lodges of the concessionaires.

The primary architect who was to attack these problems for the Park Service was Gilbert Underwood, but in a rather indirect way. All of the lodge buildings and cabins were built for private corporations, the Yellowstone Park Camping Company (YPCC) and the Union Pacific, but their design required Albright and Mather's approval unless they were outside the parks. There were thus three clients and Underwood was often the architect of choice for all three.

But at the same time, Underwood was working with and for Daniel Hull, head of design at the Park Service, who was Underwood's client but also his partner. To confuse an already confused situation is the Bozeman architect Fred Willson who developed and executed many of the Hull/Underwood designs, and the specifics of his role are elusive. Willson's rustic work over the years included at least ten major buildings and over a hundred cabins. In this text I will refer to Underwood as the designer with the caveat that he may not be the sole author.

As we have seen there are two Underwood constructional languages. One is the geologic, built in stone described on pages 325-381. It is very much on display at the Bryce Cabins and North Rim Lodge. The second, the language of wood, is dominant in most of the Yellowstone cabin camps.

This was probably not Underwood's choice. Stone presented problems. It was expensive. Albright chastised Hull for using stone in some early buildings.[3] Wood was cheaper. Nevertheless, Underwood's vertical stone piers developed at Bryce show up on some of his Yellowstone buildings, but while sometimes visually prominent, they constitute simply the perimeter and are a small part of the reality, a much large wood structure.

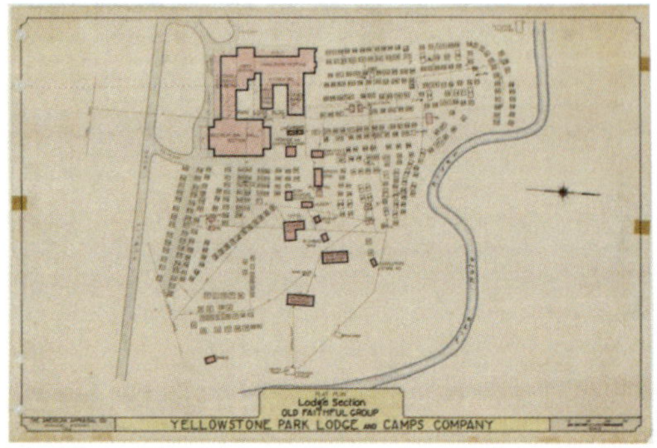

Plan: Old Faithful Cabin Camp

The New Camps

The need for cabins and their support buildings was a manifestation of a change in park policy precipitated by the rapidly increasing number of visitors. This was the system of lodges. Mather and Albright were rethinking the tradition of national park housing. Accommodations had been traditionally divided between hotels/lodges and tent camps. The almost simultaneous appearance of the Park Service and of visitors who came by automobile gave rise to numerous campgrounds in the parks. In 1919, Albright wrote that at Yellowstone there was a, "crying need for the immediate construction of several large new automobile camp grounds" over the next several years so that "as soon as possible not less that 50 major camps should be made available."[4] The Park Service sought an intermediate system—the cabin camp. These new camps would resemble the traditional elements of a tent camp—central dining, recreation, and service buildings surrounded by a number of cabins in addition to or instead of tents. The solution included two very different programs, hundreds of small cabins and large support spaces for dining and recreation.

The result was a massive building campaign. In the early 1920s, five cabin camps were created at Yellowstone by building from scratch or converting older tent camps. A new concessionaire growing out of the old tent camp franchises, the YPCC, was to build and operate them. Simultaneously, lodges of the new type were being constructed at the new national parks on the Union Pacific bus loop through Utah at Zion, Bryce and the north rim of the Grand Canyon.

The small cabins and large halls presented two very different technical problems. First, they needed a less expensive way to build rustic buildings, and they needed to build them in large quantities. In 1926 there was an addition of 159 cabins at Yellowstone. They could not afford 159 trapper cabins at a congressional cost limit of $1,500 per building. Second, they also needed a way to adopt the vocabulary of the small-span log cabin to the large, long-span lodges being contemplated. They needed a rustic way to build much larger buildings with larger spaces.

Geyser Hall at Old Faithful Camp

Logs-out cabins at Old Faithful Camp

The Economics of Log Buildings

Wood structures presented their own problems. The first was that the log wall used use excessive quantities of wood and did not always give an infiltration-proof building envelope. Reamer had reduced the quantity of logs and waterproofed the wall by using half-log veneers on a conventional wood stud wall. The log-veneered milled frame, although used at the Old Faithful Inn, is not particularly common at Yellowstone in the early 1920s, perhaps due to the efforts of Merit Tuttle, the log trapper/craftsman/contractor, but log veneers were to become quite common elsewhere. But there remained a need if not a desire for a system that used less material, less handcrafted labor, and that offered better environmental performance.

Albright might be said to have solved this first problem—the excessive wood and porous envelope of the solid-log wall, himself. A turning point in Albright's attitude and a turning point in park architecture occurred with a rather small nondescript white clapboard 1907 ranger station near Tower Fall that was being remodeled, where in 1923 Hull and Underwood were at work. Nearby was the newly renovated Haynes Picture Shop, one of a series of shops belonging to the Haynes family, one of the oldest concessions in the park. Haynes had sought to give the old mill-framed building a more rustic appearance. His solution was "[a] false log frame [that] was placed around the building to give it a paneled appearance." Based on photographs this was a series of log uprights spaced at about five feet placed on top of the existing clapboard siding. Albright thought Haynes shop was "very artistic ... one of the prettiest structures in the Park,"[5] and thought enough of it to mention it in his 1923 annual report. He undoubtedly saw something else as well, a way to make rustic building with less labor, less wood, fewer logs, and less money. Albright asked Hull to develop a design that clad the old ranger station in the same way. A false stone foundation was added, the roof was extended, and log rafter extensions were placed under them. Ordinary doors were replaced with rustic ones made of "2-inch plank with heavy iron hinges and latches."

This assembly, the "false log frame," which came to be called the logs-out system, was one that Hull had a great deal of familiarity with. In the early 1920s he had been working at Sequoia National Park where a number of rustic buildings had recently been completed that resembled Muir's cabin, such as the Giant Forest Lodge and several Park Service administrative and service buildings that used widely spaced redwood uprights with redwood bark in between. Muir's long-vanished cabin may have been an ancestor of many park buildings, whether by way of direct influence, or more likely because the Park Service architects faced the same problems using the same resources—axes and sawmills, studs and logs—and through aesthetic desire or functional necessity saw no reason to architecturally pretend the situation was otherwise. Hull—who had designed the masterpiece of all-log architecture—the Lake Ranger station, came to embrace it.

So, with the three existing building cultures at Yellowstone—real-log building, milled-lumber buildings, milled-lumber buildings with log veneers to make them look like log cabins—a fourth was added milled lumber buildings and logs worked together into a hybrid. The Park Service term for these—"frame buildings with log trim"—is inaccurate. The logs were not trim. They were usually holding up the building. Many of the subsequent Underwood/Willson buildings used solid-log walls but often they were something very much like Muir's cabin and Haynes' shop. The system that soon came to dominate Yellowstone was quite simple. There are actually two systems—logs-out and studs out. Both use a wood exoskeleton, a frame placed on the outside of the wall rather than on the interior and the inner wall using a material such as tongue and groove wood boards. It is as if the wood walls of the older hotels had been turned inside out with the verticals placed on the exterior, allowing that the verticals are two to three times the spacing they would normally have been. Diagonal studs or logs are placed at the corners for lateral bracing.

John Muir's drawing of his cabin

A cabin at the Giant Forest Lodge at Sequoia NP

Haynes' Tower Fall studio

Logs-out cabins at Lake Camp

The Logs-out System

The new system had two variations. The first type, the "logs-out" system, a hybrid of logs and milled lumber, is a series of vertical logs spaced at 3 to 4 feet to form the outer layer, supporting an inner wall built of a material such as horizontal shiplap boards. Sometimes a second interior layer was added. The second system, "studs-out," is not rustic at all. Here the vertical uprights are 4x4 or 6x6 milled posts rather than logs. Both wall systems could be load-bearing, as they were in countless cabins, or they could form the exterior non-bearing walls as they often did in the large timber-framed lodges. The obvious advantage is that both systems used far less wood than a log cabin, and required far less labor.

The logs-out system had problems. Unlike standard stud framing it provided no internal voids—places where insulation and wiring are normally accommodated. In its defense, it was used in many cases for the small cabins that were used in summer only. And if we think of it as a step up from a tent it is a bit more plausible to the contemporary sustainable architect.

Whatever its technical problems, it eliminated the fictitious craft of ersatz rustic walls of one-half split logs used at the Old Faithful Inn and El Tovar, and it presented a far more constructionally articulated wall than the flowing planes of shingles used in the Glacier inns and elsewhere.

About 1924, logs-out cabins start to appear throughout Yellowstone. The superintendent's report for 1922 states that "frame cabins with log trim' were constructed at all the camps." In 1926, 159 cabins were built in the park: 20 all frame cabins (the studs out system) at Mammoth Camp, 48 log and frame (the logs-out system) at Old Faithful Camp, 42 log and frame at Lake Camp, 45 log and frame at Canyon Camp, and four log and frame at Camp Roosevelt.[6]

Underwood and company used the logs-out and studs-out frequently but they did not abandon real log buildings. After 1927, they made frequent use of solid-log walls on the model of the Deluxe Cabin at Bryce, particularly at the north rim lodge. These cabins were, not surprisingly, more expensive to rent than the logs-out or studs-out.

The logs-out-style cabin spread throughout the western parks. They were small enough to be transported so that when the need for them disappeared in one location they reappeared in another, and many cabins of this era remain. Some have been moved more than once. Many from the Old Faithful Camp now sit beside the Lake Lodge.

The Logs Out System
Wall Section

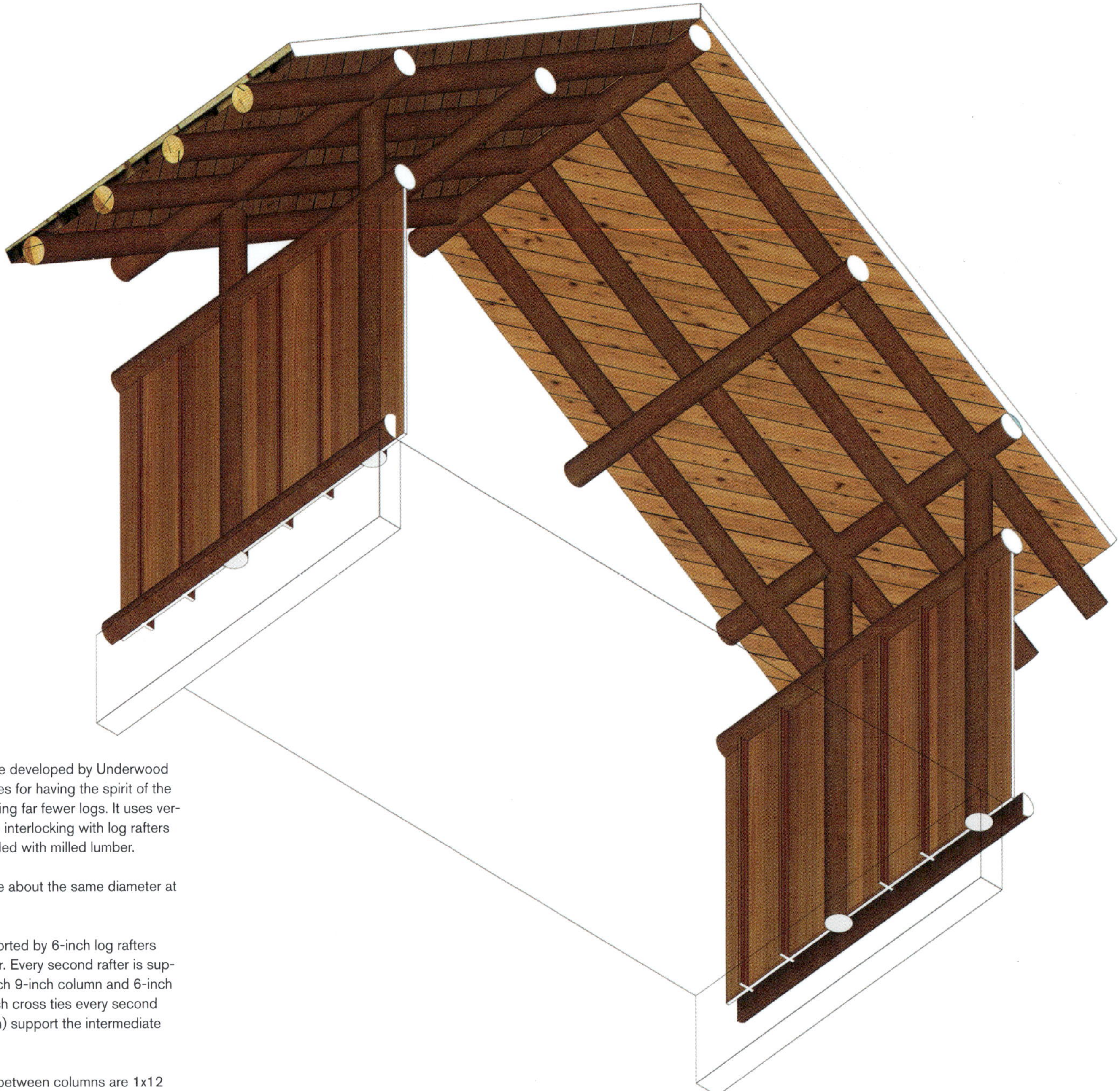

This was a device developed by Underwood and his colleagues for having the spirit of the log cabin, but using far fewer logs. It uses vertical log columns interlocking with log rafters that are then infilled with milled lumber.

All of the logs are about the same diameter at 6 inches.

The roof is supported by 6-inch log rafters 18-inchon center. Every second rafter is supported by a 6-inch 9-inch column and 6-inch purlins and 6-inch cross ties every second rafter (not shown) support the intermediate rafters.

The infill panels between columns are 1x12 boards connected with 1x4 battens.

Standardized logs-out comfort station used at Yellowstone

Engineering

The second architectural problem with the new camps was size. At the same time Underwood was immersed in the problem of defining the smallest elements of park architecture he was faced with the opposite problem, designing some of the largest buildings, containing some of the largest rooms ever built in national parks. Over the years he worked on park lodges, Underwood was asked to design increasingly larger spaces with increasingly larger spans. The 1924 Bryce dining room was small at 26-32 feet. In the 1926-27 work at Yellowstone, these spans dramatically increased to distances of 50-65 feet. If the large halls of the lodges were to be column free, something more than a row of log beams was required. Some type of truss was inevitable, exposed or concealed.

There was little, in fact nothing, in the traditional languages of the log cabin or the Swiss chalet to provide any guidance. They were domestic in scale. One could always build a giant chalet or cabin as had been done in Portland and Glacier, but the problem of how to support a 50-foot span with the elements of either language, elements that were "rustic," remained. Many rustic architects had a dislike of trusses, particularly those with an engineered look. Reamer abandoned the king-post truss at Old Faithful. Herbert Maier avoided trusses altogether.

But out of necessity the forms of modern steel construction found their way into the rustic language and there was acrimonious debate as to the virtues of the result. Out of necessity Underwood had to use the products and processes of industrialization.

Underwood's solution evolved as he came to accept the visual consequences of the hybrid nature of the enterprise-craft and industry, logs and studs. In time he came to embrace them and accepted the inevitable, that if he was to use logs it would have to be in the form of structures that were associated with steel.

Underwood's Long Span Buildings

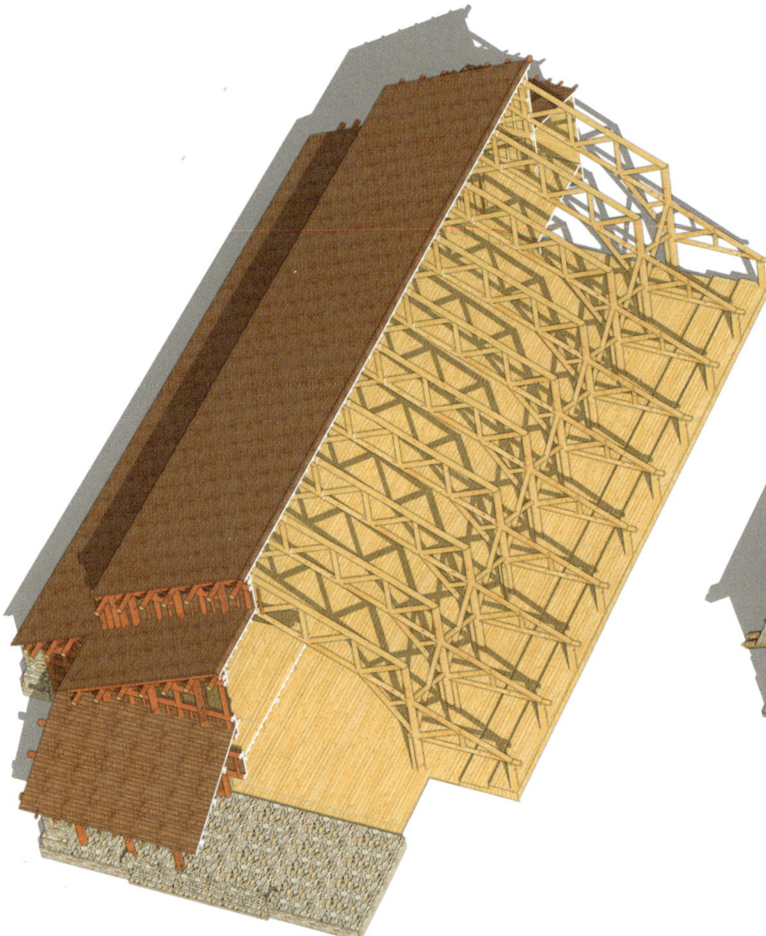

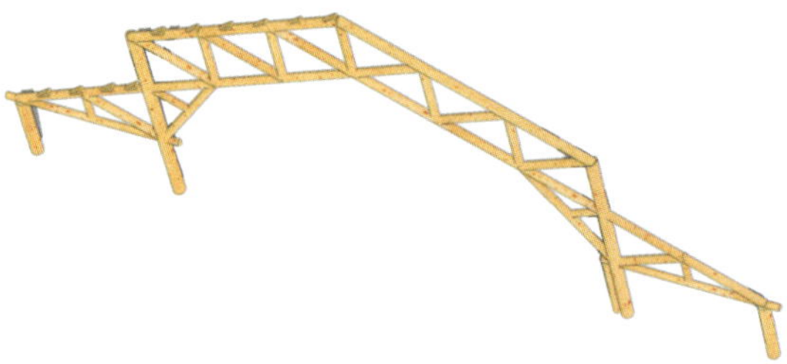

Geyser Hall, Old Faithful Lodge

Lobby, Old Faithful Lodge

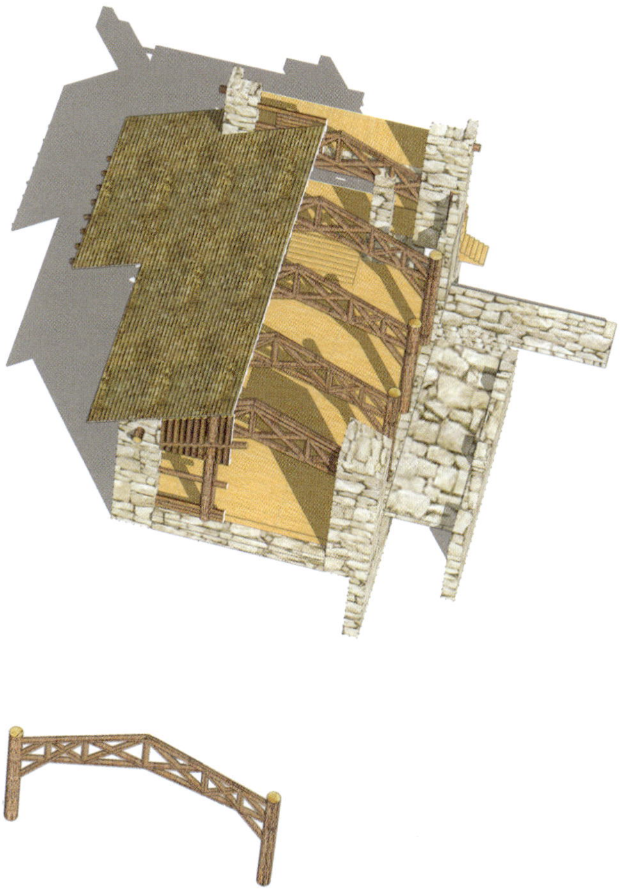

Dining Hall, Grand Canyon Lodge at the North Rim

Recreation Room, Bryce Lodge

Giftshop section looking west

Giftshop east elevation

The four lodges of the Union Pacific bus loop followed the program being simultaneously pursued at Yellowstone—freestanding cabins surrounding a central recreation and dining building. Their construction was very different. The loop began with rustic at the end of the tracks—Cedar Breaks Lodge, built entirely of logs—and ended with rustic at the Grand Canyon North Rim Lodge, built entirely of logs and stone in Underwood's geologic style. The two lodges in between, at Zion and Bryce National Parks, are very different, primarily the studs-out system—with shiplap siding the occasional stone pier. The lodge at Zion was destroyed by fire in 1966; Bryce remains.

The construction at Bryce is also different in every way from the first phase of the Old Faithful Lodge. Industrialized lumber is on full display. There is no cladding of logs. Bryce is the beginning of something new. There are very few logs at Bryce and not much stone. It is rustic architecture, but one of milled timber.

The plan is an elongated courtyard with the long side parallel to the canyon. On either side of the courtyard are the two main social spaces, the Dining and Lecture/Recreation hall. Structure is on display but it is not logs. Scissor trusses are used in the Recreation Hall as in the Old Faithful Lodge but here they are completely exposed and built with milled timbers. They interface with the roof in a way there allow the last truss to be exposed on the exterior. The flat-ceiling Dining Room is spanned with Pratt trusses. Both scissor and Pratt trusses are solid rectilinear timbers or built-up sections with exposed bolted connections. Steel rods in tension are concealed inside wood members, although their end plates are visible. There are not many logs in these spaces and not much that is traditional rustic other than the stone fireplaces.

Bryce Lodge
Bryce Canyon National Park, Utah, 1925

Roof truss structure

Lecture/Recreation structure similar to the Giftshop

Bryce Giftshop
Wall Section

A few logs are used in the lodge at locations like the entry porch, but this particular wing has none. This rustic structure uses no logs at all, only milled lumber, almost all of which is exposed.

The roof construction is shingles on boards on 3x8 rafters spaced at 26-inches resting on 6x10 purlins spanning between the trusses.

The structural frame is a series of scissor trusses supported by 8x8 columns with 8x8 top and bottom chords, a 6x6 horizontal, and two 3x6 verticals with a concealed 5/8 metal rod inside.

The truss connections are made with exposed 1/2-inch steel plate connectors and bolts.

The walls between columns are the studs-out system.

Giftshop section

Giftshop elevation

Old Faithful Lodge
Yellowstone National Park, 1927

An early and prominent example of the new cabin camps was the Old Faithful Lodge, just east of the Old Faithful Inn, a rebuilding in stages of an existing tent camp into a cluster of cabins surrounding a lodge with dining and recreation areas. It was completed in 1928.[7]

The lodge contained the first of the long-span, large-room spaces that required "engineering," the lobby. On first examination, the construction methodology appears as a continuation of the recent past, as in the housing wings of the Old Faithful Inn where an industrial sawmill frame is hidden behind a log incrustation. As in El Tovar, large pieces of structure are hidden from view. But the first phase of the Old Faithful Lodge is more complex, the beginning of a new sensibility.

The lobby has two structures—an industrial sawmill frame that is concealed and a craft frame of logs that is exposed, but the logs are not an ornamental veneer. The assembly is a hybrid of a structure of exposed logs and concealed milled timber working together.

The concealed frame is a scissor truss, a type that had always been popular with rustic architects, used by Durant, Shepard, and many others. The long chords of the scissor truss are more parallel to the roof slope eliminating the long horizontal bottom chord that vertically divided the space and it was Underwood's system of choice before 1926. The truss here, with a horizontal tie, is a milled frame of standard rectangles of sawn lumber that is largely concealed, covered with rows of 1x12 boards forming a truncated triangular ceiling. Below this is a second layer of structure, a network of logs.

The majority of the structure is hidden by the ceiling. The parallel log structure below, the rustic cladding, is all that can be seen. There is admittedly a deception here, a familiar one, of hiding factory sawn lumber while exposing the log cut with an axe at the site, but the reality is more complex. Most of the exposed logs are structural. Each log is attached to the bottom chord of the milled timber frame above in a way that makes log and frame function together as an integral structural member.

In 1924, the hybrid exposed timber/log strategy of the cabins begins to appear in the lodges, beginning with the exterior walls. The exterior wall is not log veneer but a non-bearing variation of the logs-out system turned around in this case with the 8-inch-round logs spaced at 24"—exposed on the interior—and 2x8 shiplap siding and shingles on the exterior.

But the old faux-rustic effects are still in use, An unfortunate throwback to the veneered rusticity of El Tovar is the roof eave detail—the fake projecting log rafters below the eaves that are grafted on to the real milled lumber rafters that are hidden, a detail used often by other Park Service architects. Because of this and other details the first phase of the lodge lacks the rigor of the structural expression of Underwood's later work. He was soon to leave this system of exposed log and concealed mill lumber behind and when he completed the lodge in1928 it was with a very different architecture.

Lobby facing fireplace

Lobby facing Old Faithful

Old Faithful Lodge
Lobby Construction

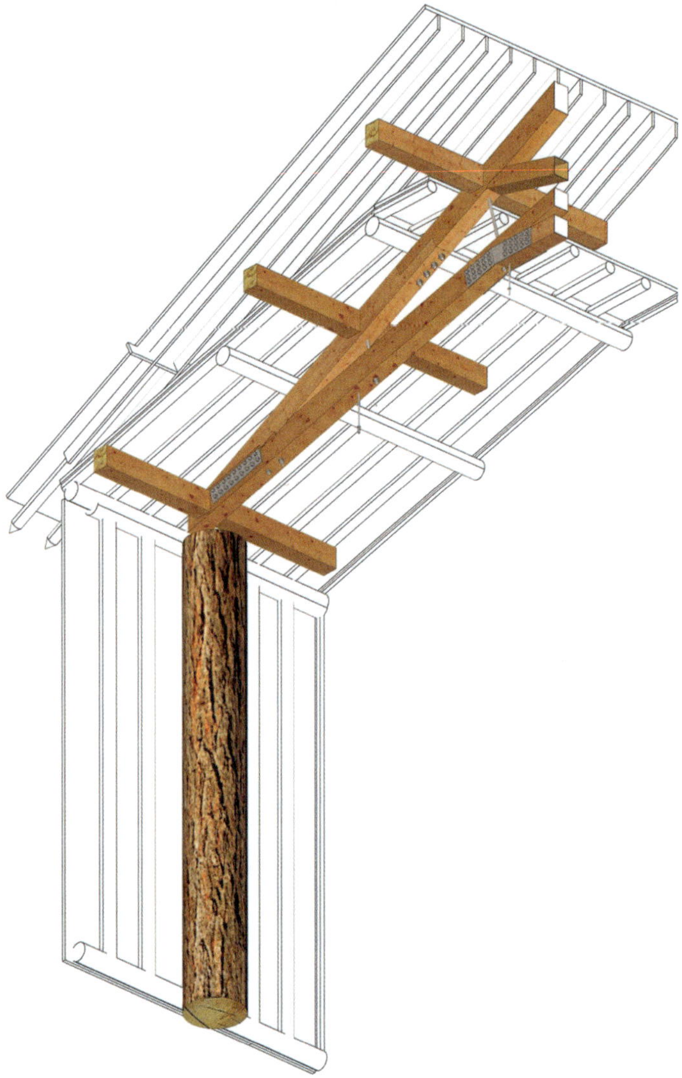

Structural frame only

Structure plus logs-out walls and ceiling

Old Faithful Lodge
Lobby Wall Section

Parts of the structure are revealed and parts are exposed. In general, the logs are exposed and the milled lumber is hidden.

The roof construction is 2x8 milled rafters16-inches on center supported by the truss. The milled lumber is all concealed and the rafters have log extensions at the eaves where they are exposed.

This structure of the trusses is 10x10 and10x14 milled lumber with steel cables and gusset plates. The bottom chord of the truss is coincident with the ceiling and would be visible but is covered by10-inch bark-on log slabs attached to bottom chord of truss. The milled lumber of the rest is concealed by the ceiling.

Each end of the truss sits on an exposed 24-inch log column.

The surrounding walls are a variant of the logs-out system, 6-inch log studs 2 feet on center with shiplap siding with the logs on the inside, The ceiling covering the structure is a similar construction.

West elevation

Section looking east

Geyser Hall
Yellowstone National Park, 1928

In 1926-27, Underwood undertook a building type that could not be more ill-suited, or challenging if you prefer, to the vocabulary of the log cabin, two gargantuan long-span halls.[8] The first was just outside the park at West Yellowstone, adjacent to the Union Pacific Train Station. West Yellowstone quickly became a main port of entry for those arriving at Yellowstone by train and a dining hall was needed at the transfer point. The result is Underwood's largest public space, a hall 65 feet wide spanned by a log structure. The second was at Old Faithful Lodge, which was still growing. In 1927, at Albright's urging, a huge recreation space, Geyser Hall, was added along with offices, shops, and services.

In both of these, Underwood abandoned the scissor truss used at Bryce and Zion for an assembly known as a vaulted parallel chord truss. It avoided the long horizontal bottom chord of the fully triangular truss but gave greater structural depth than the scissor truss. There was no avoiding the reality that it was a form drawn from engineering, a steel truss built out of logs. The truss has a very low slope in a dramatic change from Bryce, hiding the roof, but highlighting the much taller wall.

Geyser Hall has none of the exposed log hidden sawmill lumber character of the lobby of the lodge. There are no projecting fake log rafters. The projecting logs at the eaves are a continuation of the real rafters, unlike the lobby. There are no half log sidings, no milled timbers clad with slabs of bark. The exterior walls are the logs-out system, again 8-inch-round logs spaced at 2 feet, but this time with the logs on the outside with shingles covering the shiplap siding horizontals between.

Again he used the vaulted parallel chord truss for another long span of 50 feet. There is no escaping the fact that this is an industrial engineered form built of logs. This truss type became his standard, used at the Ahwahnee in 1927 and the Lodge at the North Rim in 1928.

There is a revealing sub-history in the series of long-span industrial structures—one of craft. The craft nostalgia of the Park Service created a desire for exposed fasteners, particularly wrought iron or wood dowels. Generally, in early rustic buildings, fasteners are concealed. There are no visible fasteners in the log connections at the Old Faithful Inn, nor at the Glacier Park Lodge or the Many Glacier Hotel. Hidden spikes were a common solution, as at the Paradise Inn. The sensibility that brought on the obsession with the trapper cabin with axe-cut log ends and favored a system of connections that were visibly hand made. This usually took the form of wrought iron plates and bolts. They seem to have been more commonly drawn and specified than installed. At the Ahwahnee, they were specified but not executed. Drawings for Longmire Community Building and the Ahwahnee and Kootenai lodges show them but connectors in those buildings, where they exist, are largely concealed. The structural stresses caused by the new long spans created a very real need for something larger and stronger than the old, small, hidden fasteners—something made of steel plates and bolts, which soon appeared out of necessity. Large steel bolted plates were designed for Geyser Hall that were later replaced by larger ones.

Section looking west

East elevation

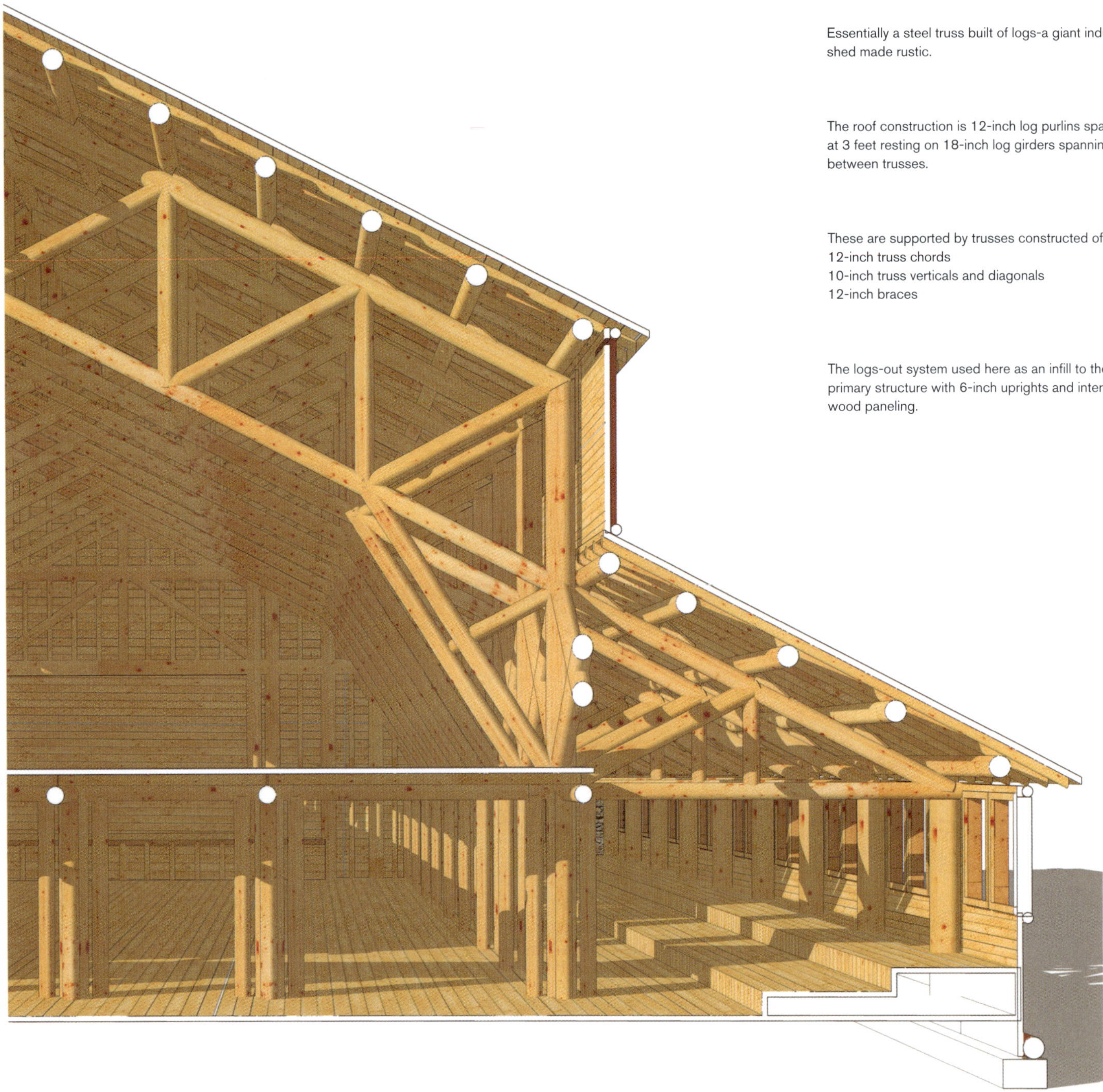

Geyser Hall
Wall Section

Essentially a steel truss built of logs-a giant industrial shed made rustic.

The roof construction is 12-inch log purlins spaced at 3 feet resting on 18-inch log girders spanning between trusses.

These are supported by trusses constructed of:
12-inch truss chords
10-inch truss verticals and diagonals
12-inch braces

The logs-out system used here as an infill to the primary structure with 6-inch uprights and interior wood paneling.

Front Elevation, Geyser Hall

Criticism

Between 1924 and 1928 Gilbert Underwood designed and built seven major lodges in the national parks along with countless smaller buildings, and if one counts all the cabins that he designed at those lodges the number of buildings he designed in the national parks extends into the hundreds. Yet, when Albert Good published *Park and Recreation Structures* in 1938, his anthology of park building designs, it contained no buildings by Underwood. Neither does *Park and Recreation Structures* contain any of the many buildings designed at Yellowstone by Fred Willson.

Perhaps one reason for their exclusion from Good's book was that in much of their work the Park Service was not really their client. Many of Underwood's rustic commissions came from yet another railroad—the Union Pacific and the YPCC. Willson's rustic work was all for the YPCC. Both had extensive urban, non-rustic practices, which others did not. But the primary reason for their exclusion is undoubtedly that Willson and Underwood's buildings were impure. They exposed far too much milled lumber and too many steel fasteners. They exhibited far too few marks of the axe and the drawknife.

Good, the spokesman in print for the romantic faction of Park Service architects, disliked the taste of engineering when found in park buildings for obvious reasons. Good liked structure, but it had to be monumental and rustic, and it did not need to be real. The appeal of rustic architecture came from its power to evoke the past, a past of axes and horse-drawn sledges, not a history suggestive of the presence of sawmills and cranes. Good's book did include projects like the Nisqually Suspension Bridge, but only as an example of the deplorable concept of executing the Brooklyn Bridge with logs and steel rods.

Albright saw their point. He was enthusiastic about the logs-out system, he was not at all enthusiastic about engineered rusticity. If Albright thought the first phase of the Yellowstone Lodge looked too much like a factory it is not hard to imagine his reaction to Geyser Hall, where the steel trusses typical of the factory and the railroad are constructed of logs. But what Albright found

Geyser Hall Wall Section

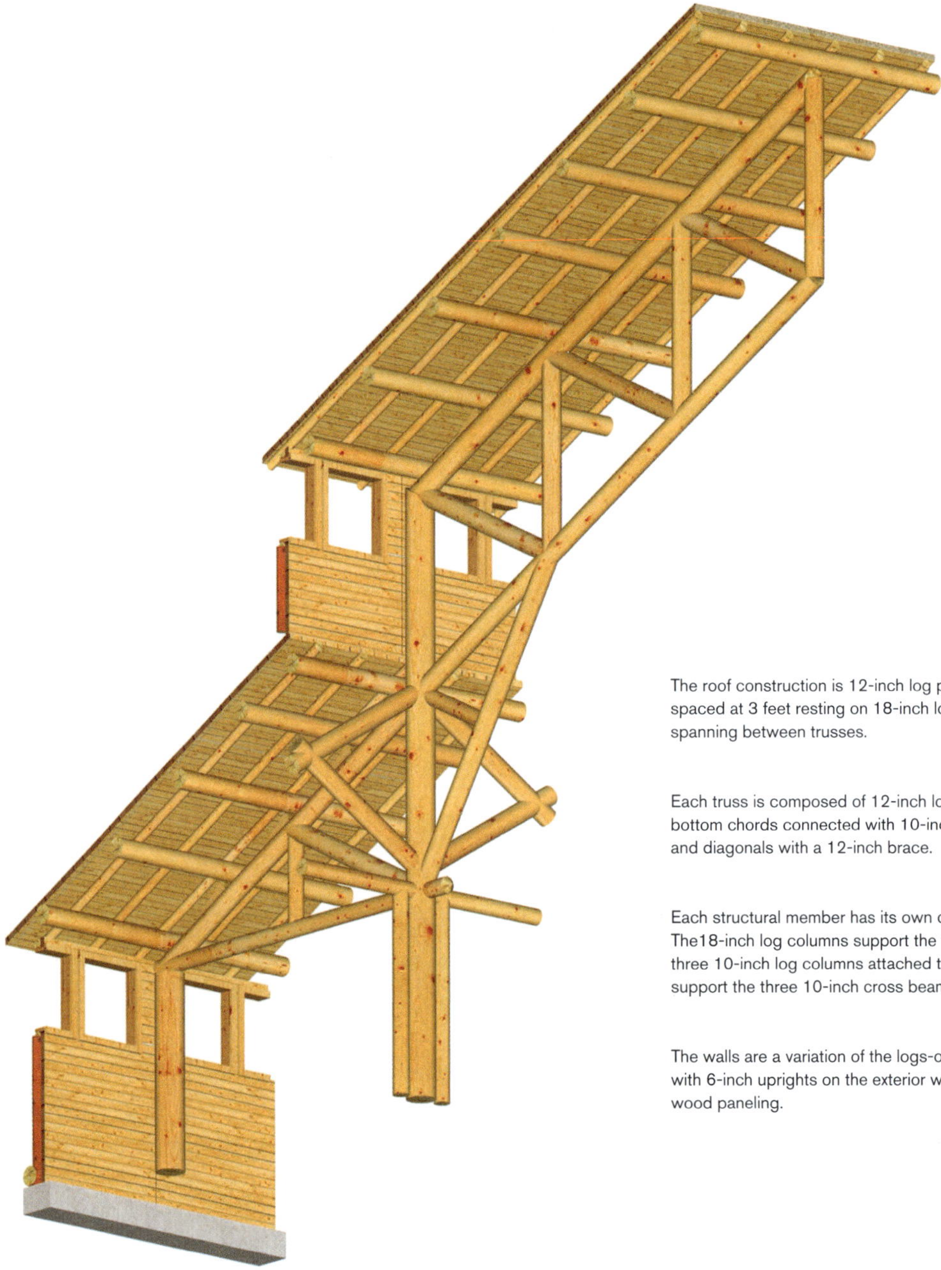

The roof construction is 12-inch log purlins spaced at 3 feet resting on 18-inch log girders spanning between trusses.

Each truss is composed of 12-inch log top and bottom chords connected with 10-inch verticals and diagonals with a 12-inch brace.

Each structural member has its own column. The18-inch log columns support the truss. The three 10-inch log columns attached to them support the three 10-inch cross beams.

The walls are a variation of the logs-out wall with 6-inch uprights on the exterior with interior wood paneling.

so distasteful is arguably what is best about Geyser Hall and the West Yellowstone hall, that they move beyond the pop historical image of the log cabin to a manifestation of the odd hybrid of craft and industry that produced them. To the judgment of history and to the observer willing to set aside nostalgic expectations, the results were not just equal but superior to the results of the pseudo-craft fantasies of some of their peers.

There are aspects of the logs-out buildings that recall the stick-style houses of Richard Morris Hunt based on French wood traditions, but the resemblance of both the studs-out and logs-out cabins to the ancient Greek or Roman temple is striking as is the resemblance to Robert Adam's rustic classicism of eighteenth-century England. The rows of these cabins that sit beside the Lake lodge today bring to mind the rows of small Greek temples at Delphi and Olympus. Underwood and Willson were not exclusively or even primarily rustic architects and they both were the products of a classical architectural education. Underwood was Ivy League and Willson had studied at Columbia and the Ecole des Beaux Arts before returning to Montana in 1910.

Underwood was not the first rustic architect to draw on the forms of engineering. Reamer avoided the king-post truss in the Old Faithful Inn but embraced the shorter spans of the railroad trellis. Louis Hill's architects used timbers so gigantic that their industrial power was explicit. McMahon had used railroad bridge technology in the log and steel cable truss at the Many Glacier Dining Room. There were others who worked for concessionaires that were far more accepting of industrial technology and far less interested in encrusted veneered narratives of pioneer craft, including Frederick Heath who designed the Paradise Inn.

The story of rustic architecture between the wars in the national parks leaves us with not just two styles of building but two histories of itself as told by the buildings—one romantic and fanciful of axes and logs and one more complex and far more truthful to the real history and a hybrid of the technology of the railroad and its sawmills, cranes and materials shipped from thousands of miles away.

Truss details

Truss details

Rationalism and Dishonesty

There are few things more painful to the structural rationalist than the Ahwahnee Hotel and its exposed concrete frame masquerading as wood. How can it be the work of the man who designed Geyser Hall?

There were deceits in Underwood's work to be sure. He and Willson were not above constructional falsehoods. At one time or another they used most of the tricks common to rustic architecture—half-log veneers, false-log rafters and there is of course the monumental deception of the Ahwahnee, a heavy timber frame made of concrete. But more often than not if they did not build something that really was a log and milled timber building, they were able to do something that used the industrial and the rustic in a credible way. The logs-out buildings have a rigor and straightforwardness that is missing from the veneered rustic narrative of other national park architects. We know little of Underwood's or Willson's thought. What were their intentions—structural rationalism, pragmatism, or simple economics?

Despite their shortcomings one might even say their occasional hypocrisy, the work of Underwood and Willson conforms far more to the ideals of Seton, Burroughs, and London of "honest" construction than the work of others to follow. It is possible that the best qualities of Underwood's work were forced on him, that the Park Service required him to use solid logs at the north rim, that the logs-out system was brought about by constructional economics.

Underwood was largely unencumbered by ideology but in his best work there is a sense of order an integrity probably born out of pragmatism.

Epilogue

Albright left the Park Service in 1933 to become president of a mining corporation. The Depression cut deeply into Underwood's prolific output and in 1932 he became an employee of the Federal Government. Fred Willson continued to work for Yellowstone concessionaires and did a number of camp buildings at Yellowstone that used logs and milled lumber together comfortably. Few of these remain. Daniel Hull left the Park Service in 1927. He joined the California State Parks system and did several buildings in the logs-out style he had done so much to promote.

In his new job, Underwood did preliminary designs for one of the last of the great rustic park lodges, the Timberline Lodge near Mt. Hood in Oregon. In reality it is not a national park lodge—it is in a national forest. While it uses the Y-shaped plan that he had used at other locations such as the Ahwahnee, many argue his involvement in the design ended after schematics were complete, if it extended that long. Many consider it to be the work of William I. Turner, an architect with the Forest Service. It is arguably one of the last of the handcrafted rustic lodges. Underwood's career extended well into the modernist era and included some fairly uninspired late national park buildings such as the Jackson Lake Lodge.

If Underwood's achievement was to merge the industrial with the rustic, one more building needs to be discussed, the Grand Canyon Powerhouse, one of the hidden gems of national park architecture. It is industrial monumentality with rustic materials. The architect is unknown. Records indicate only that he was from Los Angeles, and Underwood seems a likely suspect.

But if Underwood was largely silent on his larger architectural intentions, his companion in national park rationalism, Herbert Maier, was vocally explicit in ideological intentions and although he constructed only seven small buildings, he had no less impact.

Timberline Lodge

Timberline Lodge

Grand Canyon Powerhouse

MOUNT RAINIER NATIONAL PARK

PARK SERVICE ROMANTICS: THOMAS VINT AND ERNEST DAVIDSON

In 1927 life finally caught up with the ubiquitous, prolific, talented, and ethically challenged Daniel Hull. Mather and Albright had repeatedly expressed satisfaction with his performance and the work it produced and were untroubled by his conflict of interest and his half-time attitude to what was a full-time job, but by 1927 the Interior Department felt otherwise and Hull was forced to resign.[1] Whatever the merits of this decision it was far more than an administrative replacement but coincided with, and possibly helped cause, changes that were about to take place not just in the design but the construction of Park Service architecture. Underwood's logs-out and studs-out work would continue. The genuine log architecture of Hull's Lake Ranger Station was to continue on a small scale. In terms of the romantic/rational dichotomy, romanticism was on the rise and the rational was fading, at least in the buildings produced by the Park Service itself.

The romantic's most visible apostle was Albert Good, soon to be author of the decidedly romantic *Park and Recreation Structures*. Good in particular favored highlighting the rustic—celebrating the regional, local materials, local crafts, indigenous forms, while hiding the industrial, the character of the engineered, even if it meant a log-crafted encrustation of industrial milled lumber frames. The methodology was clear—exposing logs and hiding milled lumber—exposing axe marks and hiding power-driven saw marks, showing the mark of the tool, hiding the mark of the machine. Joints and fasteners were acceptable, even desirable, provided they conformed to the rules. The mark of the blacksmith's hammer should be visible, the trace of the welding torch must be hidden. At its best it created expressive reconnections to a past way of building. At its worst it created sham historicism.

Many of the post-1927 buildings built by the Park Service are characterized by a veneer of romanticized handicraft, a pioneer-type log cabin overlaid on an industrialized framework. Image was what mattered and external appearance was based on fictive histories, not the reality of the present.

The change almost certainly owes something to Thomas Vint, Hull's successor, who became effectively the head of design at the Park Service from 1927 to the 1960s, years during which the engineering division greatly expanded and during which he designed, supervised, or simply approved hundreds of projects, and authorship of some of these projects is multiple.

In that same year,1927, Ernest Davidson came to work for the Park Service. He was to become one of romanticism's most conspicuous advocates. His output was small but includes some of the most admired examples of this type. Vint seems to have shared Davidson's values, but since he signed almost every drawing issued by the Park Service during his tenure it is difficult to isolate his design preferences.

Vint had several assistants equal in rank to Davidson but historians have singled out two "masterpieces" of national park rustic in which Davidson was involved—the administration building at Longmire Village in Mt. Rainier, and the administration building at the Grand Canyon, both built in the late 1920s.[2]

Opposite:
Longmire Administration Building, Mount Rainier National Park

Longmire Community Building
Mount Rainier National Park, 1927

Mount Rainier was the first national park to have a master plan and the first step was to add to existing facilities. The Park Service needed a park headquarters, support spaces, and housing, and chose the old resort at Longmire, 12 miles down the mountain from the Paradise Inn, as the location. Here they built a campground, employee housing, a community building to serve the campground and a headquarters. All are the work of Davidson, working under Vint's supervision.

The first of these, the1927 Community Building, is an odd mix of real and symbolic structure. It is a large, gable-roofed rectangular meeting room with a fireplace at one end and a bay window at the other. A wing of service rooms sits to the side. The large meeting room is composed of an inner log structure, which is real, clad with a frame on the exterior that is ornamental with a veneered log wall in between. The real frame is a series of five scissor trusses made from 14-inch-round logs that support 10-inch-round log purlins and 8-inch-round rafters. The trusses are supported by pairs of 2-foot-round log columns at each end, an element almost twice the size of the truss they support, giving a monumental quality to the hall. To this is added an ornamental structure—a pair of half round logs at each column line on the exterior so that they give the impression that the interior columns are exposed on the exterior. This is the first appearance of 4-log cluster arrangements used in a number of Davidson buildings, which were never actually composed of four real columns. This log frame is enclosed by a 2x6 wood stud wall faced with slab siding inside and out, giving the impression but not the reality of a log building. The 3x8 slabs used for the false log walls are from the nearby Silver Forest, the source of the fire-polished logs in the Paradise Inn. In addition to the ornamental siding, the fictional cladding extends into the base, which is concrete clad with stone. One can argue that environmentally this wall performs better since the skin is not punctured by the frame which could create openings for water or infiltration, but the building remains a mélange of the structurally expressive and the structurally fictional.

To the rationalist it is an odd mix of the real and the symbolic, but Davidson was not a rationalist. To those who value structural rigor it is arguably the best of the Vint/Davidson buildings, but it was not so to the official chronicler of Park Service architecture—Albert Good, who felt it lacked craft and monumentality. He wrote of the Community Building, "Comparison of the almost mechanical stiffness of the rafter ends with the handcrafted quality of the 'whittled' rafter ends of other subjects more recently built will indicate one such advance in structural technique. The thinness of the roof shingles and the character of the masonry of the chimneys leave something to be desired,"[3] making an unstated but obvious comparison to the Lake Ranger Station.

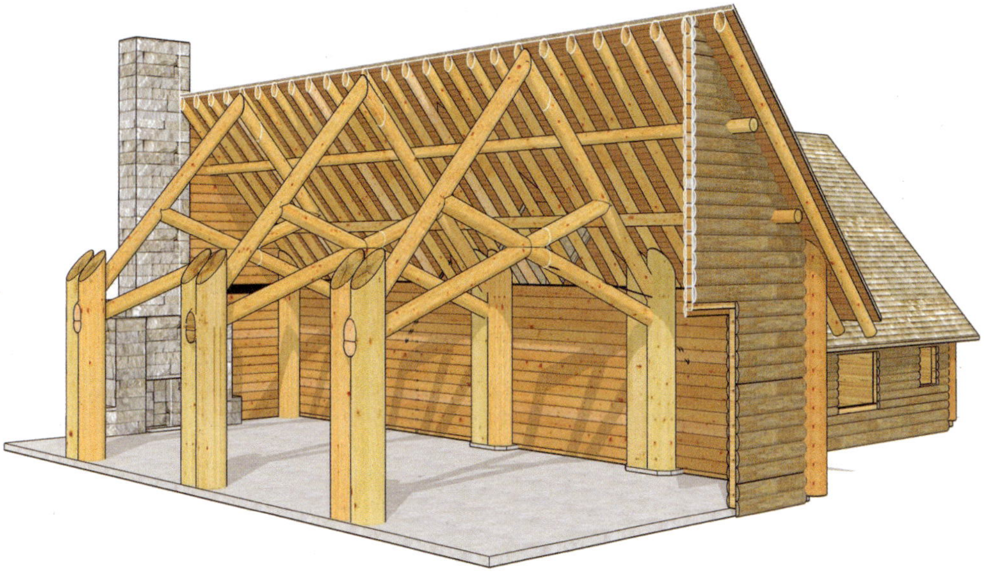

Community Building: log frame with cladding beyond

Community Building: view from north

Community Building interior

Community Building, Enclosure

The building has a log structural system on the interior that is real and a log structure on the exterior that is mostly symbolic.

The symbolic elements are the 24-inch half-round ornamental log column and half-log siding on the outside of the 2x6 stud wall.

The roof structure is quite real—shingles and sheathing on rafters and purlins.

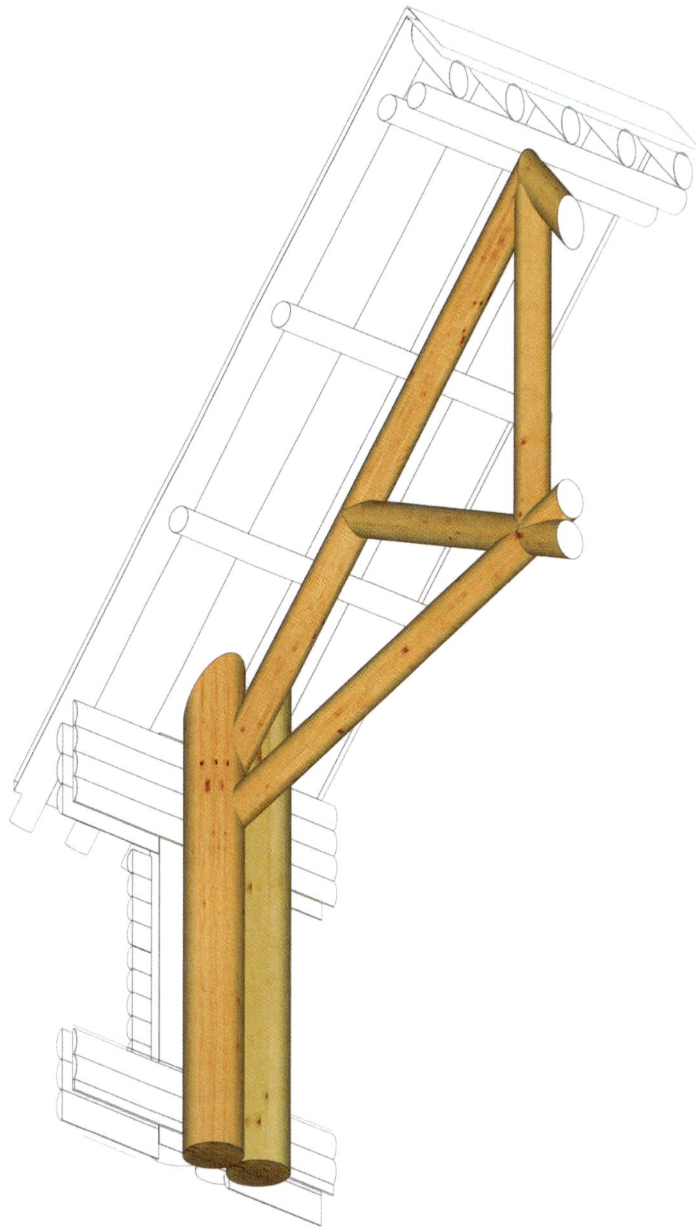

Community Building, Structure

The real structure is the internal log frames—two 24-inch-round log columns supporting 14-inch log trusses and 10-inch-log purlins.

Longmire Administration Building
Mount Rainier National Park, 1928

Good greatly preferred Davidson's Longmire Administration Building that followed one year later. It was and is frequently cited as national park rustic at its best. It is an elegantly composed facade and it has the monumental and domestic juxtaposition of this style at its best, but it is a thick veneer of local materials in fictive structural roles on top of a conventionally milled industrial frame. Being a collection of small rooms, it did not present the same architectural possibilities as the Community Building. The exterior is a massive tapering stone wall with corner buttresses that extend to the height of the second-floor window sills. It appears structural. It is not a veneer, but the interior floors it supports are standard milled 2x12 joists hidden behind a ceiling. The wall above the stone exterior, from window sill to eave, is another veneered faux-log wall and the trusses they support are milled lumber, also concealed by a ceiling. There are multiple veneers in the building. The window lintels are also two faced—a real log on the outside and a milled timber on the interior. The largest ground-floor room, the lobby, is given a veneered-log ceiling to match the veneered-log walls. The true industrial frame is hidden by the layers of pseudo-rustic craft. It is a deceptive history as well as a deceptive construction.

The 10-inch-round log rafters supporting the exterior eaves are simply rustic additions to the 2x8 milled lumber rafters that actually support the roof. Good is either unaware or untroubled by this, calling the rafters "vigorous in scale" and most agreeable."[4] The porch rafters are given the full pointed treatment. Albert Good found this infinitely superior to the "mechanical stiffness" of the Community Building:

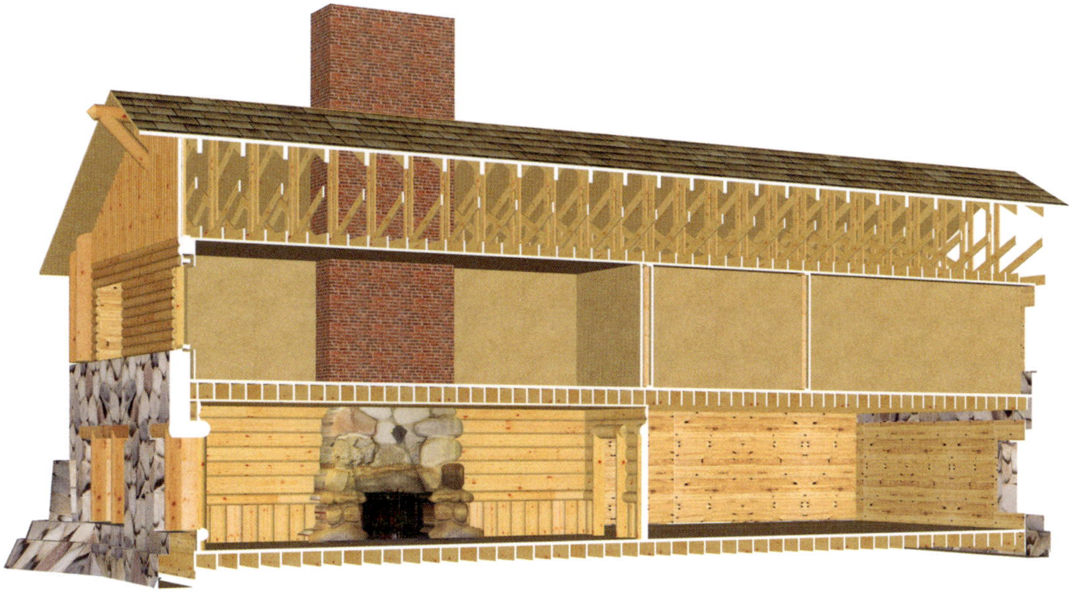

Lobby facing east

West elevation

Longmire Administration Building
Wall Section

The exterior is a veneer of false half logs on sheathing, None of what appear to be logs serve any structural purpose. The goal is to provide the illusion of handicraft in a highly industrialized construction system.

In the roof construction boards on 4x10 milled rafters are used where they are not visible. A 12' log extension is added to the rafter at the point it penetrates the wall and becomes visible to provide the illusion of a log frame behind.

At the upper wall 12-inch log slabs give the appearance of a real log wall on what is really sheathing and studs. The interior is faced with wood paneling. The interior half-log siding disguises sawmill studs and joists as rustic log structures. A log slab ceiling hides 2x12 floor joists and 1x10 board subfloor above.

At the lower wall the stone is structural but the inside of the stone wall is faced with half logs.

Good said of the Administration Building: "The rafters are appropriately vigorous in scale, and the blunted terminations of them are most agreeable" and:

Through the use of native materials in proper scale, and through the avoidance of rigid, straight lines, and over-sophistication, [it] gives the feeling of having been executed by pioneer craftsmen with limited hand tools. It thus achieved sympathy with natural surroundings and with the past.[5]

He was well aware that this was all pseudo-rustic and that it was all a great fiction, but it was necessary. Again he argued that the ideal condition in which "the character of primitive buildings was achieved by appropriating as well all the primitive elements and structural methods of the prototypes" in which "there is no allowable compromise with true log construction" was not possible. He wrote, "to insist on the use of logs in today's park structures in the spendthrift fashion of our forefathers may be logic in the aesthetic abstract, but in practice wastes those resources the conservation of which largely motivates park expansion."[6]

Axe-trimmed rafters of the Administration Building

Power-saw cut rafters and columns of the Community Building

Grand Canyon Administration Building
Grand Canyon National Park, 1928-29.

Another building by the same architects, equally admired and closely related in appearance and construction is the Grand Canyon Administration Building (now the Operations Building). Like other Vint/Davidson buildings, is a hybrid of two technologies—the imported industrial lumber and local materials crafted with local technology, perhaps by local craftsmen, but there are few rustic buildings in which one of these technologies is so clearly expressed and the other so systematically bidden. The exterior is all rustic and all local materials—the Kaibab limestone that makes up the canyon rim, the ponderosa pines of the nearby national forest. The building is square in plan with an extension forming a T. Each of the six resulting corners is marked by a stone pylon, square in plan, flaring out at the base to spread its weight, and tapering toward the top at the second-floor window sills. Atop each pylon is what appears to be a cluster of four stubby tree trunk columns supporting the overhanging roof similar to those used at Longmire.

This is what we see—local materials, the craft of hand tools and minimal processing of the material. Again, what we do not see is the industrial technology, the technology of the railroad and the non-indigenous craft and material it brought. The building is essentially an office building—a series of small rooms that do not lend themselves to any kind of structural expression, and this is a typical milled lumber stud and joist platform frame of the typical American house—stud walls support 2x12 joists and 2x8 rafters. All are covered with Celotex panels, a wood fiberboard insulation. Many of the materials are not local; most of the structure is not handcrafted. The hidden framing is Douglas fir, probably from Oregon or Northern California.

The incongruities and the rather unhappy marriage of these two systems are apparent in several awkward conditions. The square stone pylons do not extend into the building interior as they appear but are in reality L-shaped with only three half columns, not four. The roof structure is visible below the exterior projecting eave and the detail of the pseudo-log rafter grafted on to the rafter from the sawmill is used again—the same detail as the Longmire Administration Building.

Section at lobby facing east

West elevation

Composite

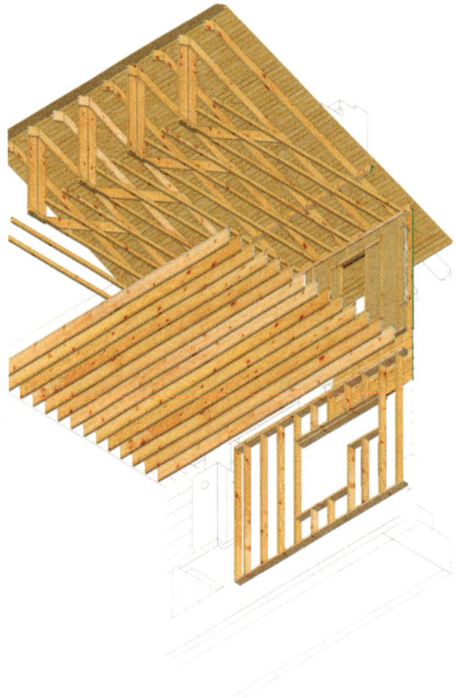

Hidden Industrial Elements:
roof truss of nilled lumber
milled wood joists, rafters and studs

Veneered Rustic Elements:
half log ceiling
half log siding
false log rafter extensions

Ethan Carr in his history of Park Service architecture notes the fact that in the administration building, "neither the rough courses of stone nor the peeled logs serve their apparent structural purposes," but he nevertheless identifies it, as do many others as, "one of the most successful of all Park Service buildings," projecting "a powerful image" of the "efficient and ethical management of the Parks.[7] In this he is undoubtedly right, but it was an image that hid the industrial reality of the building and with it the larger industrial reality of the environmental consequences of the economic processes that created parks like the Grand Canyon. It was another stage set.

Vint/Davidson buildings do have a consistency, both of compositional style and constructional strategy. They are very different from the work done by Underwood, differences that indicate conflicting ideologies not just of their respective places in the bureaucratic structure. Vint and Davidson were far more scenographic, far more concerned with external effect than internal constructional coherence, and not concerned at all with structural rigor. They were far more interested in historical association than the abstract qualities of materials, far more indifferent to the things underneath that were actually holding up the building.

Corner Details

Rarely is the misfit between exposed rustic exterior expression and concealed industrialized internal reality so great as it is here. The half-log ceiling, the half-log siding on the walls, the false-log rafter extensions are purely ornamental, veneered rustic elements. The Industrial elements are hidden, the real structural and constructional elements, the roof truss of milled lumber, the milled wood joists floor and the wood stud walls, are all hidden behind them.

A log slab ceiling hides 2x12 floor joists and 1x10 board subfloor on the interior. False half-log columns at corner on stud and joist frame Visible framing, rafters, and brackets are logs. Concealed framing is milled lumber.

Sunrise Visitors Center, one of the "Blockhouses," 1930, 1943

Vint and Davidson's work continued in its focus on evocative imagery and suppression of technology. Their last work at Mount Rainier were some of the Park Service's last rustic buildings. They were also their least successful, even by their own admission. This was the Sunrise Community in Yakima Park at Mt. Rainier. A major development at the northern part of the park, it was a part of the first park masterplan, but it was unfinished and today is a large parking lot with widely spaced buildings around its perimeter. Davidson wrote:

It is true that, purely from a landscape viewpoint, the whole development might be classed as a failure since the area is far less attractive than it was before the first idea of development took root. On the other hand, the project may be considered one of the great successes since the general appearance and result is far superior in appearance to those other development with which comparison may be made, and 'just grew,' like Topsy.[8]

Sunrise is the site of the last Vint/Davidson (with A. Paul Brown) buildings at Rainier and the one in which historical fancy overwhelms both structural rigor and programmatic sense. Davidson explains:

We wished to build into the structures as much of local or historical interest as might be secured without sacrificing other values. Yakima Park was known as a summer rendezvous of Yakima and other Indian tribes. Since their 'architecture' offered no possibility of adaption, the next step was taken to the time when white pioneers of the locality erected buildings for protection against Indians or other enemies.[8]

The result is two blockhouses, each a standard 2x4 stud and 2x10 joist box clad with a massive veneer of 12-inch-round logs. The second floor has ornamental beams and the second floor is topped with round, fake, rafters.

Started in 1930 but not completed until 1943, these were two of the last rustic buildings of the era and in its pseudo-fortification motif has a strange affinity with the first park building, Norris' Yellowstone blockhouse. This was not just a case of using pseudo-rustic elements in an industrially produced building. Setting aside the appropriateness using an imaginary fortification, particularly one to subdue Native Americans, as an administration building, it was a case of creating a fictive history and a fictive constructional veneer to illustrate it.

A number of writers on national park architecture have acknowledged the disparities between image and reality in this type of work and find it no more troubling than a Robert Stern colonial building of brick veneer. But Sunrise is a rather sad end to an original American phenomenon, the strange industrial craft hybrid that was rustic architecture, emphasizing romantic imagery over constructional substance, a recollection of a non-existent history by means of a glib veneer. It cannot be said to be historic, only pseudo-historic.

But, evoking the trapper and his axe was part of a larger intention that each park, or at least each region would have its own language growing out of its own indigenous traditions. William C. Tweed in the Park Service history wrote:

The goal was to build a structure that reinforced the historical patterns of the Rocky Mountain region. This theme of regional cultural content as a part of non-intrusive architecture would grow to include not only log cabins, but also Indian Pueblos, Spanish colonial adobes, and 'New England colonial' frame structures.[9]

'The Nisqually Bridge

There is one more rustic structure at Rainier that must be mentioned, one that although built of logs suggests another architecture. Albert Good liked the new national park buildings at Longmire. He thought the Administration Building a masterpiece. The Community Building had shortcomings but was on the right track. There is one structure did not like—the bridge crossing the Nisqually River that connected the two buildings. Writing in *Park and Recreation Structures* the normally verbose Good is speechless on the subject of the Nisqually River Suspension Bridge of 1923-24 saying, "Space here permits the showing of these bridges, but by great good fortune does not allow for comment or analysis disclosing of other than a neutral position."[10]

The Nisqually River Bridge is essentially a suspension bridge built of logs excepting the steel cables. The bridge itself is a Howe-truss suspended by steel cables from larger cables spanning between two Douglas-fir trapezoidal timber towers (originally constructed of whole logs). The whole structure has a miniature quality. The towers are only 30-feet high. The steel cables are attached to metal shoes atop the towers and anchored to the rock on the east side and a concrete dead man on the west. Steel rod suspenders, attached by metal crimps to the cables, support the timber deck beams with steel stirrups. The deck is strengthened by a Howe-type stiffening truss (minus the usual vertical metal reinforcing rods but braced by horizontal boards across the center). The bridge was unfortunately rebuilt with milled lumber in 1951-52. It was an extreme example of Western engineering finding its way into Western rustic architecture and as such was a great moment if one sees such hybrids as this architecture at its best, as in the Old Faithful Inn or the logs-out cabin. But this, to Good, is precisely the problem. The monumentality of logs and stone that Good thought mandatory is absent.

To these Americans the log cabin and the axe that produced it are the symbols of what and who we are, whatever that is. The portable sawmill and the platform frame are not, in the public imagination, up to the symbolic job. They are just as much the truth if not more of the truth than their more popular symbolic counterparts, but popular opinion has determined otherwise. There is an alternative, however, one represented by the Nisqually Bridge. But this was a choice that did not need to be made. The lessons of the vernacular, the evocation of history, and the urge to build with natural materials are not excluded by constructional rigor and do not demand the suppression of technology as Gilbert Underwood had already demonstrated and Herbert Maier was about to.

On paper, Maier and Good were of a piece. They even wrote an article together and Good was consistent in his praise of Maier's work. But Good's highest praise went to Davidson and those like him. When it came to actual building Maier and Good represented the polar extremes of rationalism and rustic scenography and it is easy to see that in the debate within the Park Service on "honesty" they almost certainly sat on different sides of the table. Maier, despite a small output of small buildings, is to many the best of the rustic architects. He was hired as an exhibition designer and designed the exhibits for all his buildings. Other than his work in museums he has no architectural work that is not rustic. Maier, like nineteenth-century rationalists, saw the rational within the vernacular. Maier's work was about much more than what he said he was about. It was not just an educational tool. It was not just a replication of vernacular traditions. It was an architecture that used the tools of nature, in appearance and reality, to build something that could sit beside nature and belong.

The Nisqually Bridge at Longmire

Norris Museum
STAFF ONLY

HERBERT MAIER AND THE ROOFLESS MUSEUM

How shall the magnificent specimens in these roofless museums of nature be adequately labeled?
—Herman Bumpas on national parks[1]

For Maier and Good the appropriate architecture of the West or of the Southwest was already there in the form of the indigenous vernacular, and the rustic architecture that they were designing grew out of that architecture. In their minds it owed nothing to Europe, eighteenth-century England, or the Adirondacks. It was an idea that emerged from their own version of primitive man, an American one. As Frederick Jackson Turner would say it was an architecture that was an "enduring and distinguishing survival."[2] Their concept of a regional vernacular, which had a strong nationalistic component, was very much of a piece with the culture of the 1930s. It was a time, as Alfred Kazin points out, of a new cultural nationalism, of which Maier's work was only a small part:

Here, in the vast granary of facts on life in America put away by the WPA writers, the documentary reporters, the folklorists preparing an American mythology, the explorers who went hunting through darkest America with notebook and camera, the new army of biographers and historians—here, stocked away like a reserve against bad times, is the raw stuff of that contemporary mass record which so many imaginative spirits tried to depict and failed to master.[3]

While Kazin warns that it is: "evidence of a nostalgia too easily content with the trappings of sentimental autobiography and romance; evidence of a need to retreat into the solid comfort of descriptive facts." It had its virtues: "Yet in that signal literature of empiricism which embodies the failure of so many to discriminate ... between the need for the past and the comforting surface of that past, is the record of what most deeply interested the contemporary imagination."[4]

The Park Service group that met in 1935 to establish design standards for new buildings, which included Herbert Maier, agreed on two things. First, that park buildings should be subordinate in size and form to the landscapes they inhabited. And secondly, in the spirit of the age, that their designs should draw from the local vernacular traditions of the region. This was Albert Good's vision, that park architecture would draw on local vernacular traditions from Michigan to Mexico.

In 1935, Conrad Wirth, the chief planner of the Park Service, authorized the creation of a comprehensive collection of American vernacular architecture to inspire park design. It never materialized but Maier himself undertook an extensive research effort to collect and document the "close to one hundred types of indigenous frontier construction" that were supposed to exist.[5]

Good's *Park and Recreation Structures* grew out of the 1935 committee's work and Maier appears to be the hero of that text, but the evidence of his design suggests he was the odd man out. He differed with his colleagues on two key points. In truth, despite his great interest in the vernacular it had little real influence on his work.

Opposite: Norris Museum

The second subject on which he was at odds with some of his colleagues was structural expression. In the Park Service debate on constructional "honesty" that took place in the preparation of Good's book, it is easy to assume that Good was on the romantic side of the argument and had little interest in structural authenticity given his text. It is easy to assume that Maier, on the basis of his work, was on the other side of this argument despite his collaborations with Good. The evidence of his work suggests a clear commitment to structural authenticity and a clear lack of interest in pseudo-craft or veneered rusticity.

In a speech given in 1935, and in an article written with Good the same year, Maier laid out his guidelines for building in a wilderness landscape. Both documents are important, but they are highly incomplete and do not really explain his designs. He saw his architecture as intrusions into contexts that could not be improved upon, and he wanted his buildings to be subordinate to the landscape. His tone is humble and modest, mostly it is a list of what he would not do. But he explains only some aspects of his work. Many of his critical design strategies are not even mentioned. His modesty in prose hides an aggressive methodology in practice. On paper, arguing for restraint while practicing exaggeration and overdesign. The key to understanding Maier is to know that he was a good deal more than what he said he was, and his design strategies have far less to do with vernacular precedent than they have to do with his perceptions of nature itself.

But he did set out his design intentions, at least in part. They are, in his own words:

- Limited height

Wherever possible, verticality in park buildings should be avoided. This usually calls for a roof low in pitch. It too frequently occurs that the roofs of park buildings unnecessarily dominate the entire design and are conspicuous from a long distance.[6]

This is a rule he followed religiously. All of his Yellowstone buildings are one story with low pitch roofs. But while there are few rustic buildings as low to the ground as Maier's, they are composed of monumentally sized components used in excessive quantities. They are oversized and overdesigned, arguably competing with nature. Architecture could never match nature with the size of its buildings. It could with the size of its components.

- Use of the irregular line

Structures could be made inconspicuous [by the] elimination of the lines of demarcation between nature and man-made structures with an absence of rigidly straight lines and a softening if not the absence of right angles.[7]

Maier maintained that the "irregular line" found in vernacular buildings was the result of what he called the freehand architecture of the pioneers. But the truth is that Maier's buildings, some of his best, are characterized by long, straight horizontal lines, roofs in particular. He used the irregular line selectively. There are many instances, the stone bases of his buildings for example, where he uses a combination of fragmentation and enlargement to erode the edge between the natural and the constructed, and if the eaves are straight, the support structure is often considerably more erratic.

- Appropriate scale

One of the principle phases of park development ... is rockwork in general. The rock selected should first of all be proper in scale. That is, the average size of the rocks should be sufficiently large to justify the use of masonry.[8]

By scale he meant the size of the components—logs or rocks. Buildings were to be in scale with their surroundings. Maier recommended buildings of a heavy rustic scale only in mountainous forested areas.

In practice not many places proved unsuitable for monumental masonry or logs. There are very few Maier buildings in which the components could be called small scale in his sense of the word. The largest log at the Old Faithful Inn is about the same size as the smallest log at the Fishing Bridge Museum. The stones at Yavapai might be described as small-scale but Maier said later that the stone was undersized. Differences between Maier buildings in varying cultural and climatic locations are typically in the proportion of wood to stone, not the size of the stone. By scale, Maier usually meant monumentality, and monumentality meant weight and large components but not a large building.

- The use of appropriate craft

[The] tools of the frontiersman consisted usually only of an ax, a pick and a shovel, and a pair of hands. ... this absence of precision tools resulted in a freehand architecture with an absence of rigidly straight lines. ... construction which is primitive in character blends most readily with primitive surroundings."[9]

This passage, from the article Maier wrote with Good, is telling. The premise is that the character of the original indigenous architecture was not just the result of indigenous materials and climate but of the "primitive" set of tools, resulting in what they called a "freehand" architecture.

Good had criticized park buildings that had rafters with flat-sawn ends, calling them stiff and mechanical. He much preferred rafters with "whittled" ends, that is, cut to a chiseled end with an axe, but this was simply giving an industrial milled wood frame a veneer of rustic nostalgia.

The importance of the hand tool that left its mark, usually the axe, is something both Maier and Good professed to believe but something Maier did not practice. All his museums have the "stiff and mechanical" industrial square ended rafters. Maier did only one building in which this idea was applied. It is his only log cabin, near the Norris Geyser basin at Yellowstone. It has stepped corner logs with axe-cut ends and joints sealed with wood strips instead of concrete. It exhibits all the handcraft traditions that Good demanded, but it highly atypical for Maier. In all of Maier's other work at Yellowstone he avoided the pseudo-craft that Good praised. There is no after-the-fact axe work to create a fake impression of pioneer craft.

The Clipped Gable • (over)

THE CLIPPED GABLE

(photo on reverse side)

Clipped gables may frequently be used to good advantage in eliminating what might otherwise be a too prominent "point"; however, there is no precedent for the use of the clipped gable in American pioneer architecture.

The selection of color for paint and stain is a very important item. Warm browns have been found to be the best medium for lessening the importance of a structure. Green roofs are difficult to handle. It is most difficult to harmonize this color with nearby tree foliage and because green pigments usually fade to unpleasant hues.

It is frequently desirable to paint window muntins a lighter color than the walls in order to take advantage of their architectural value. These cross-bars must be quite broad in order to be in scale with other oversized members.

(Yellowstone Lake Museum, Yellowstone National Park)

An Example of Poor Scale • (over)

LOOKOUT

(photo on reverse side)

Stone walls are too thin - should have at least twice the thickness shown. Stones used in building are too small especially along lower courses where building should give appearance of growing out of the solid rock. Roof is too light - shakes should be thicker or courses doubled. Floor should be of flagstones or cement rather than of wood. Stone arch over opening is poorly done.

(Glacier Point Lookout, Yosemite National Park)

• Use of Indigenous Material • (over)

USE OF INDIGENOUS MATERIAL

(photo on reverse side)

Here the use of native materials, such as rocks, logs and shakes causes the building to blend with, and become a part of, its surroundings.

Note that the windows are broken up into smaller lights. It is difficult to incorporate large sheets of glass in the design of buildings of this type, since glass is somewhat out of harmony with rough rockwork. Glass was a scarce article to the pioneer builder.

The building has been framed with 2" x 8" studs supporting log rafters. The rock base and corner pylons have merely been laid to the frame.

(Yellowstone Lake Museum, Yellowstone National Park)

• Heavy Scale in Mountainous Areas • (over)

HEAVY SCALE ONLY ADAPTABLE TO MOUNTAIN AREAS

(photo on reverse side)

It should be borne in mind that this heavy scale is suitable only to mountainous areas where forests abound. The same type should necessarily be lighter in scale in less mountainous regions. But every effort should be made to steer clear of the "twig" type of architecture which flourishes under the name of "rustic".

The photo shows an open foyer of a national park museum where material interpreting the immediate subject matter may be exhibited in the semi-outdoors. Note the satisfactory relation in scale of the log work and roofing to the rockwork. Shakes are 1" thick, doubled at each course, however, an equally heavy effect would have been obtained by doubling every fifth course only.

(Norris Geyser Basin Museum, Yellowstone National Park)

Pages from Maier's unfinished design manual

The System

He arrived at a rather complex typology to do this. All four Yellowstone buildings use a tripartite system.

- At the top, a log roof structure that is configured to spatially work in tandem with the exhibition system while eroding the boundary of the building envelope. Breaking up the top of the building to make it less of an object with constructivist joints, extended beams, and the absence of trusses.

- In the middle, a wall system of studs covered with shingles on the exterior and wood or plaster on the interior. In his later work the hidden studs of the walls become the major vertical structural element. There are no log walls and few columns.

- At the base, a structurally autonomous encrustation of stone to link building to site, always overscaled, taking on its own life and flowing across the site. The forces of nature at work are revealed, using the surreal sculpting that Mills and Reamer had developed.

Fishing Bridge Museum under construction

Again, there is far more to Maier than he explained or what his Park Service colleagues saw. Understandably, he wished to appear humble, subordinating his work to the landscape by following ancient traditions. He claimed to draw the totality of his inspiration from American vernacular precedent. In truth he learned very little from vernacular architecture. He preferred to draw his inspiration from nature itself. But he was far more inventive. He went directly to nature not through a false narrative of craft.

Structural Rationalism and Structural Narratives

Ethan Carr notes that Maier's "boulders and logs were not veneers, but usually served their apparent structural function."[10] He attributes this to the fact they are smaller and less complex than buildings like lodges or administration buildings. But there is more at work in Maier's architecture than pragmatism.

There is an absence of the usual deceits that characterize the work of Vint and Davidson. There were no square-milled rafters that changed magically into logs when they extended beyond the wall that conceals them. There were no half-log sidings on 2x4 stud walls. There are no milled 2x12 floor joists covered with half-log ceilings, no fake log columns or beams. Half-log siding was avoided by avoiding log walls.

At the same time there are deceptive elements in Maier's work, deceptions of craft in particular. Milled-wood studs are hidden while peeled logs are exposed. Little of the stone in Maier's Yellowstone buildings plays a structural role. It typically sits in front of a structurally self-supporting wood frame and supports only itself.

The key to understanding Maier, particularly his inconsistencies, is to see him as what he was. He was not a structural rationalist. He was an exhibition designer. He was not trying to demonstrate gravity at work, as a rationalist might. He wished to put structure to work as an element of the exhibit. He used real structures, but it was structure in service of a concept of exhibition, as a narrative device.

He designed not only the buildings but the exhibits, and each exhibit was indigenous as well, describing the specific character of the nearby landscape. Museum buildings were interpretive agents, and the stone and wood are part of the structural narrative. Maier wrote describing his Yavapai Museum, "the best museum structure is that one which functions most efficiently as an interpretive agent."[11] Every Maier building has a structural narrative organized around an exhibition concept.

Following his building at the Grand Canyon, Maier continued his work for the American Association of Museums. Another all-stone building by Maier, outside of the national park system and funded by a Rockefeller grant, was a trailside museum at Bear Mountain State Park, just north of New York City, where the trail literally bisects the long thin museum, an idea he was to use again when he headed west.

Madison Museum
Yellowstone National Park, 1929

In 1928, Maier and the association received a grant from the Laura Spelman Rockefeller Memorial to build four small "trailside" museums at Yellowstone. Maier worked closely with the Park Service and Bumpas, the father of the trailside museum concept, was very much involved. Trailside was meant quite literally. Each exhibit relates to features immediately adjacent to the museums. All are small one-story buildings. All are constructed with bases of stone topped with oversized log roof structures above. All use a strategy of gigantic stone, oversized logs, and over-designed structure. The first of these was at Old Faithful and survives only in photographs. The buildings at Madison Junction, Norris Geyser Basin, and at Fishing Bridge are largely intact.

The Madison Museum was less a trailside museum than a shrine and that is what it was originally called. It marks the site where, according to Nathanial Langford, the national park idea was born during an evening campfire in 1870. The main public room, the exhibit space, was a wall structure with an internal log frame. Attached was a service wing. The exhibit space is more a theater/tableau than exhibit with a large, glazed end wall designed to frame the location of the famous non-existent campfire conversation at the river junction in the distance.

The structural narrative here is a proscenium that both frames and points to the shrine. The key elements in this are two inverted U-shaped frames, log columns, and a lintel, that support the roof above, creating prosceniums to frame the campfire site in the distance. The frames in turn support five beams running parallel to the view, three inside and the two lowest beams are outside the walls. This is Maier the exhibit designer, using columns and beams less as structure and more as visual guides.

Cutaway view from southeast

View from southeast

The rafter ends are supported by the long horizontal beams outside the building, which are supported by four pairs of sloping columns sitting on the edge of the foundation. In theory this makes the structure a complete frame and the shingle wall merely an infill, but construction photographs show they were built simultaneously making either wall or beam redundant. To the rationalist, the complete frame has a conceptual purity, but Maier's subsequent work uses another system. There are heavy brackets as well. These brackets became something of a Maier trademark. Here they extend beyond the rafter ends like a high-tech outrigger. As is typical of Maier, there are brackets everywhere. Every beam with the slightest projection receives one.

The log structure employs highly indirect methods of support. There is a fragmented, disconnected quality to the log frame, in part because it is configured to frame the view.

The stone base of the building is irregular, producing, "the elimination of the lines of demarcation between nature and human-made structures…rock walls splay out near the base and especially at the corners so as to give a feeling of natural outcropping and to prevent a fixed line of demarcation at the ground."[12] This was the irregular line, the result of "freehand" architecture.

The building does not so much meet the ground as the rock literally rises up to form the building. Stone accentuates the corners but extends outward toward the site. A dramatically flared stone base expands out of the wall at the corner as do the roof supports. As large and as heavy as it is, it was to be even larger and heavier in future trailside museums.

Below the roof gable is a triangular infill of Swiss boarding with cut outs, a rare example of literal stylistic reference in Maier's work and something he did not do again. He wrote, "Our exteriors should carry no gingerbread, twig architecture, or peanut brittle" and, "every effort should be made to steer clear of the 'twig' type of architecture which flourishes under the name of rustic."[13]

Originally there was a large window in the exhibit space with an engraved glass representation of the campfire. When the campfire story was discredited, it was removed.

Window facing the campfire site

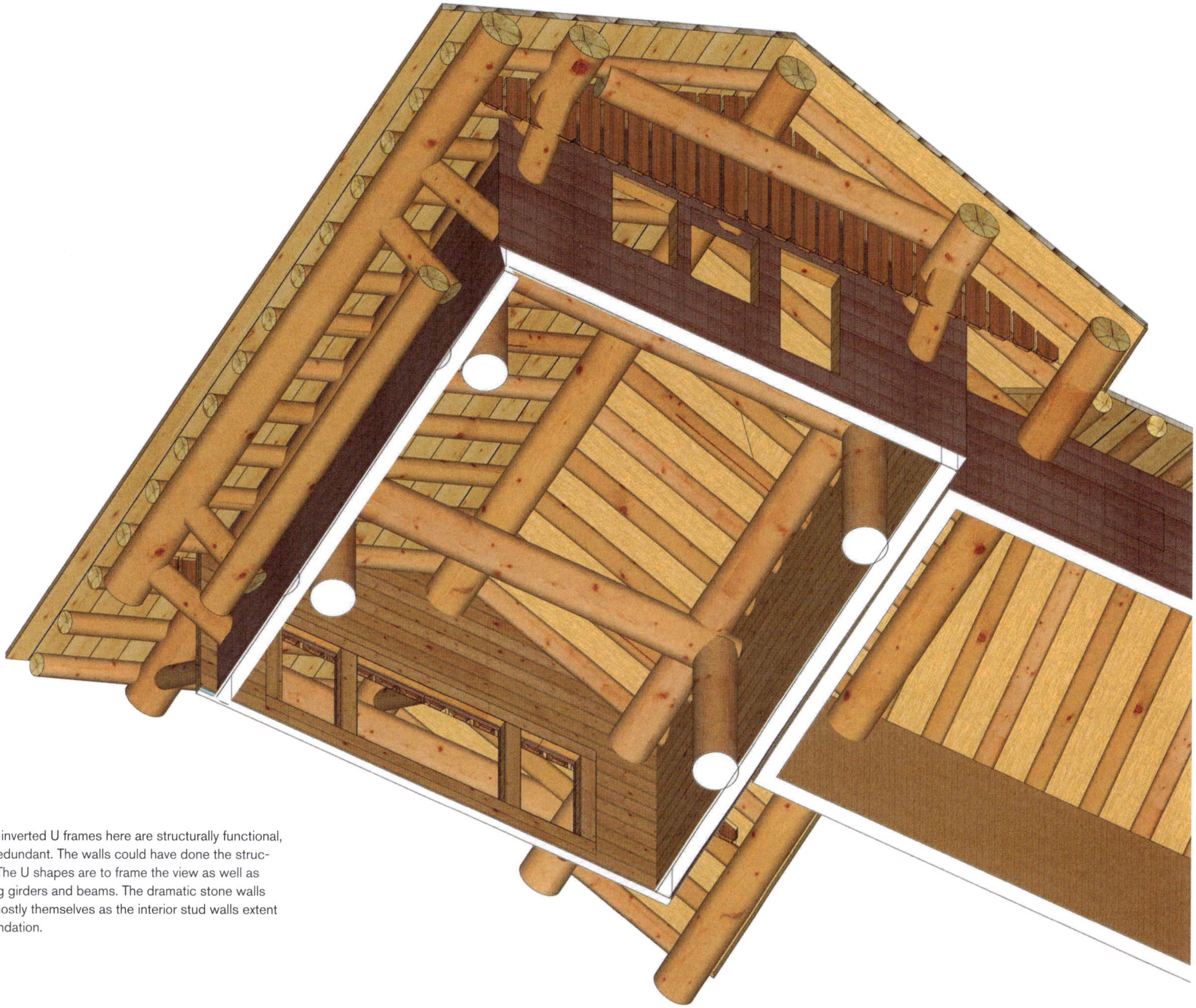

While the inverted U frames here are structurally functional, they are redundant. The walls could have done the structural job. The U shapes are to frame the view as well as supporting girders and beams. The dramatic stone walls support mostly themselves as the interior stud walls extent to the foundation.

Roof structure seen from below

Norris Geyser Basin Museum
Yellowstone National Park, 1929

Trailside museum is a misleading term here. The trail goes through the building, and, in theory, a visitor emerges wiser than they entered. The Norris Museum forms a gateway to the path that winds through the Norris Geyser basin. Flanking the gate are two exhibit rooms entered from the porch, smaller in height and size, one devoted to local geology and one to birds.

The structural narrative here is the choreography of moving through the gate. It is essentially its own room—a wood-roofed stone box with openings on two sides to allow the trail to pass through. It is two structures, a wood structure inside a stone one.

At Bear Mountain he had used a stone arch for the gateway to the trail. Here he used a truss, The two stone masses flanking the opening remain separate, connected only by the wood structure. Maier is using fragmentation again to soften the contrast between the building with the natural surroundings. In the front of the central pavilion the roof projects well beyond the stone wall and is supported by brackets.

The log structure within the stone box is largely unnecessary as the roof beams could have been supported by the stone, but the complex log structure inside is there to serve the exhibition narrative. One passes through four equally spaced gates. They support the four equally spaced log trusses above, but while these are real structural elements their primary purpose is to create a threshold as part of the exhibit narrative. The first and last gates are breaks in the enclosing stone wall marking the threshold from the entry plaza to the gate room and then the exit to the trail to the Geyser basin.

Section looking south

View from north

Maps framed by the log portals

Between them, within the stone box, are two additional log gates. They are something like the U-shaped prosceniums used at Madison but here the uprights are formed from split tree trunks, effectively creating double columns, one shaft upright, the second angled so that each column has two shafts to support the lintel. The vertical logs are twisted in a manner that recalls the Old Faithful Inn but they are much larger. They have what Maier called, "the pleasing quality of the furrowed and knotted log."[14] These logs are much closer to the real tree and highlight the "natural" gate that perfectly frames a map the same size as the door opening on the opposite wall. It is a surreal type of detail Maier used but used sparingly, usually in this context creating a metaphorical tree. The visitor is effectively traversing a very small forest.

The two interior gates frame maps on the wall beyond, but they also support the long girders of the flanking exhibition spaces and since the entry to those two exhibit rooms is between them, they also form two thresholds. Trusses are not common in Maier's work. He uses one here to form the gate, but typically, he preferred to separate the logs into individual elements to appear more natural and less mechanical, as he does in the side wings. The structure of the two flanking wings leads us through. Two major log beams run parallel to the ridge supporting log rafters at midspan while the stud wall supports them at the other. There is no ridge beam, another fragmenting device. For the most part the rafters are supported by the walls. Maier abandons the concept of the complete log frame he had used at the Old Faithful and Madison museums apparently because the stud wall was sufficient support without the external frame, but probably also to fragment the exterior framing and blur the separation of building and landscape. Again, there are brackets everywhere allowing the roof to project far beyond the walls that support it.

There is no axe craft here. Log rafter ends are square but the logs themselves are clearly chosen for their slight irregularities. Again, while Maier admired the irregular "freehand" line created by the primitive tools of the frontier craftsman, he never again indulged in the pseudo-axe work of his log cabin experiment nearby.

Maier's brackets continued to grow in size and number. The numerous brackets are very similar to those used by Cutter at Glacier. Cutter's are longer, but Maier's are three times the diameter of Cutter's. These brackets might seem excessive, even ornamental, but given the heavy winter snow loads at Yellowstone, perhaps not. The projecting eaves of Maier's museums were braced with temporary vertical supports through the winter in the 1930s.[15]

The stone base here has begun to operate almost independently of the building, growing the narrative of landscape connection. Stone climbs the walls and spills onto the paved terrace, formed steps, and retaining walls.

There was strong rationalist element in Maier's work (and a strong monumentality) and an equally strong element of the surreal, an appeal based not on nostalgia but the expression of the forces of nature, nowhere more conspicuous than in the stone base, flowing like lava into the landscape.

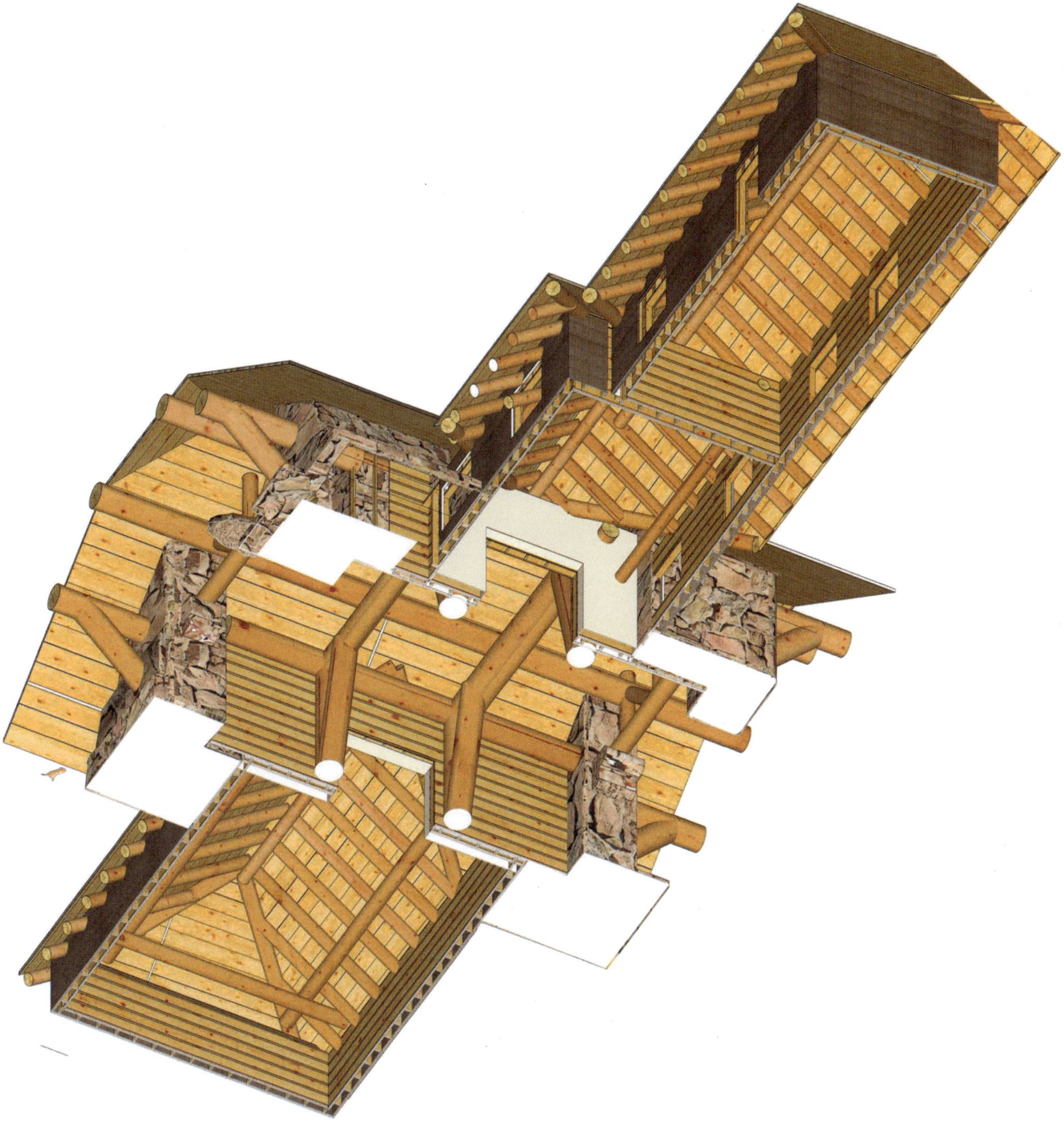

Portals and roof framing
View from below

Truss at main gate

Portal into exhibit space

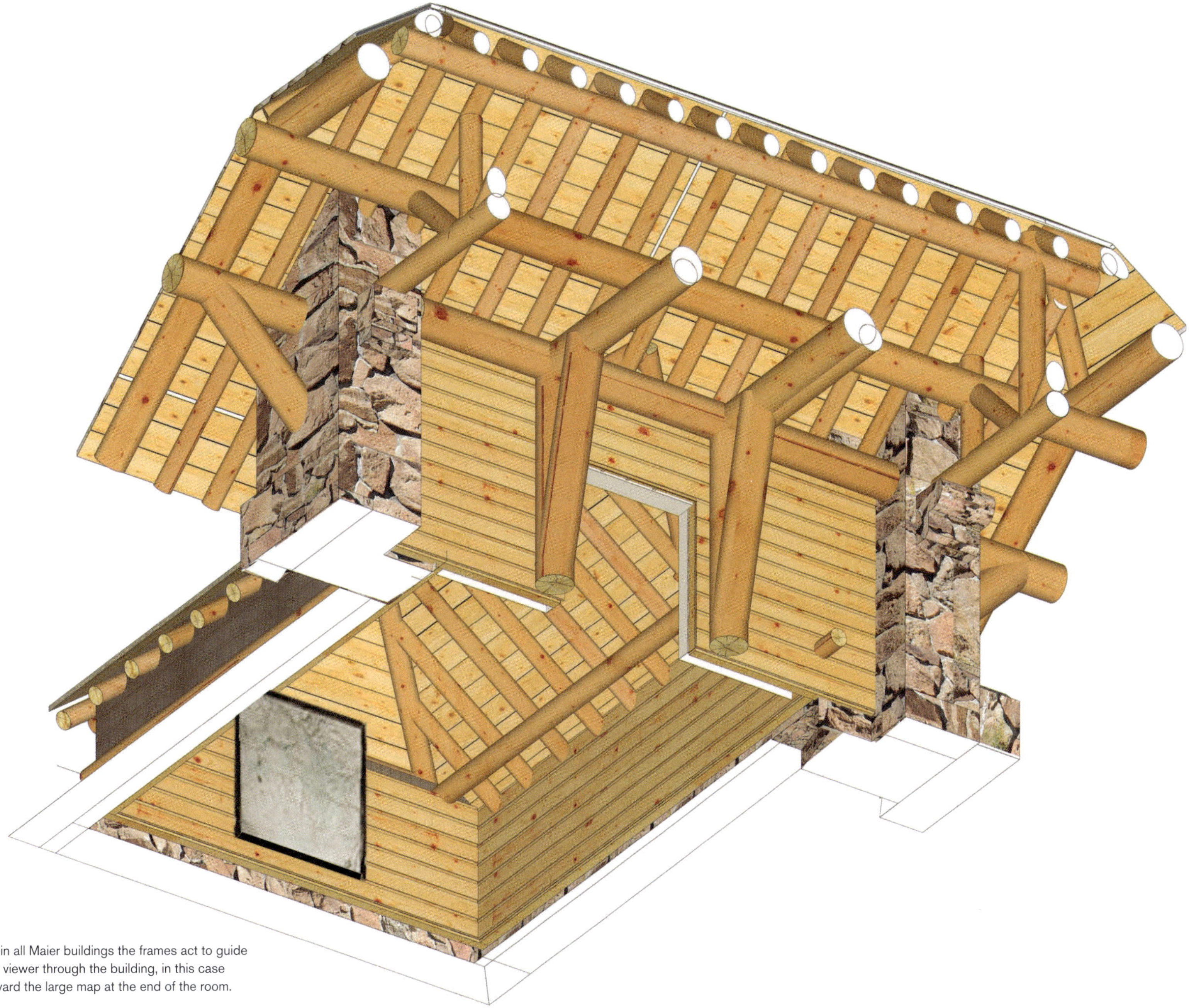

As in all Maier buildings the frames act to guide the viewer through the building, in this case toward the large map at the end of the room.

Portals and roof framing
View from below

Fishing Bridge Museum
Yellowstone National Park, 1930-1931

It sits at the end of a long approach drive on the north shore of Lake Yellowstone, placed between the visitor and the lake. It is a rather low, thin building with a long axis running parallel to the shore of the nearby lake, paralleled by long terraces of stone steps.

It is another trailside building in which the trail goes through the building, but unlike its predecessors there is no gate or proscenium. The structural narrative here is the walk along the lake through the long thin exhibit spaces and the structure is deployed along this route. There are three double doors in front and three double doors in back. This is the trailside idea at its most porous. But these doors are far less articulated than the interior portals along the long axis. There are three rooms along this axis each dealing with a natural phenomenon that is immediately adjacent—geology, birds, and Lake Yellowstone. This time, all the gables face the same direction, giving the building a long, low profile.

Along the central axis are a pair of double portals between the three rooms reminiscent of Japanese torii gates similar to those used at Norris. All the columns are forked tree trunks with one branch connected to the log lintel placed at the doorways adding a touch of the surreal. He wrote, "exposed log members should be selected knotty."[16] It is a highly metaphorical forest that one travels through. The two log-supported lintels are structural in the small room; the two in the large are not, but their primary role is not structure but as a narrative of nature. Maier preferred rough logs with twisted grain and projecting knots, but he used elements like the split columns sparingly.

As he had done at Norris the side walls with their hidden milled studs are used to help support the log rafter ends, abandoning the complete log frame for the hybrid. Between the walls, five major log beams run the length of the roof.

Section looking south

View from North

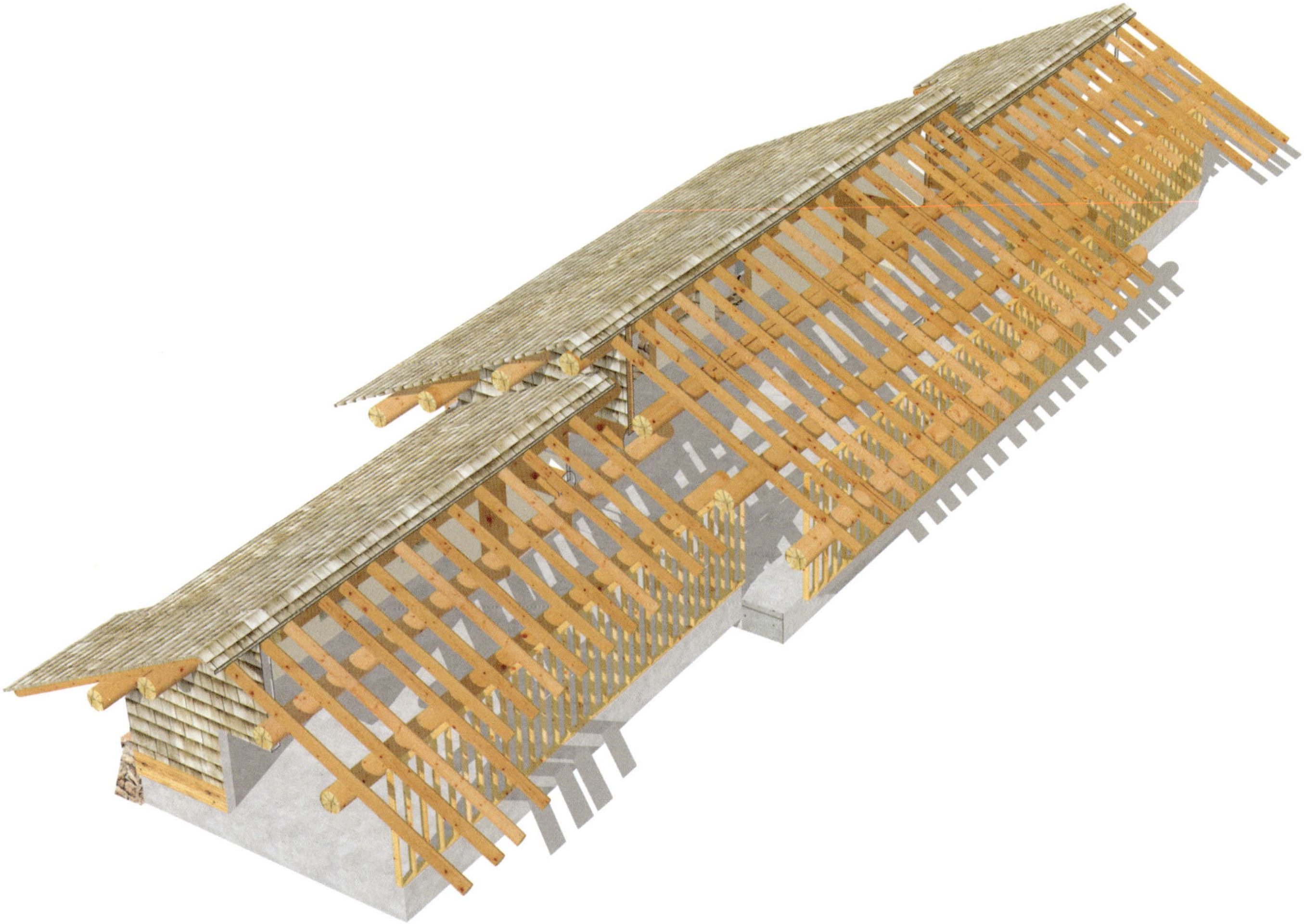

All log joists and girders are exposed and supported by stud walls encased in shingles and plaster.

Fishing Bridge Museum framing

The rafters are supported by longitudinal beams and another series of transverse beams parallel to the rafters but more widely spaced at every seventh rafter. The bottom layer of beams is not on original drawings, suggesting additional support was added. A log horizontal to form a truss might have been a more effective way of doing this but Maier rarely used trusses and used none at all here, perhaps feeling the partiality of the multiplicity of rafters would add to the partiality of the whole, putting aside the architectural for the natural.

At the two flanking wings the rafters project well beyond the roof edge. At the center section there is an exterior horizontal log beam holding the ends of the rafters, supported by heavy brackets but pulled back from the roof edge. Both details produce a more constructivist assembly, that is, a greater expression of parts since there is no beam tying them together visually as there was at Madison. This is another instance of Maier's particular methodology of fragmentation, creating an irregular edge, sitting on the boundary between the architectural and the natural.

Everything in the building is oversized, often massively. Everything except the building itself, which is small and low subordinating itself to the surroundings. All the structural elements are visually disconnected, fragmenting the volume and softening its edges.

Maier's advocacy of the broken line is not so rigidly applied in practice. The building has three strong horizontal lines—the ridge line, the eaves, and the ground. In between these what would normally be horizontal lines are broken—the edges of the shingles and the tops of the stone walls. The "freehand line" is to be found in the undulating shingle courses and the irregular stone base.

Again, the corners receive special attention. Stone walls rise upward, shingle roofs extend outward, rafters increase in diameter, roof corners flare upward in a way reminiscent of Japanese architecture. The stone moves like lava horizontally and vertically, structurally expressive while connecting to the ground in a very literal way.

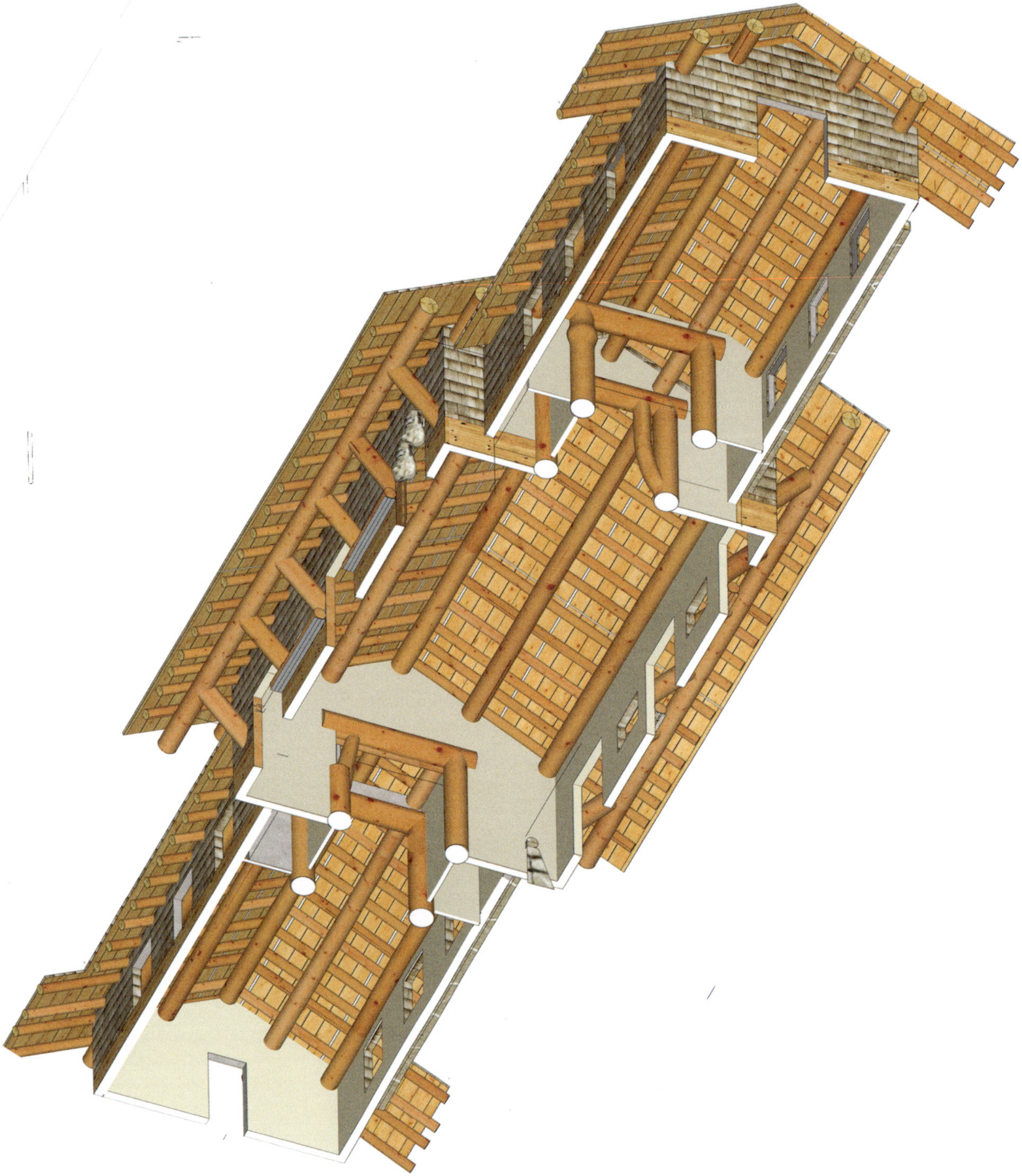

Portals and roof framing
seen from below

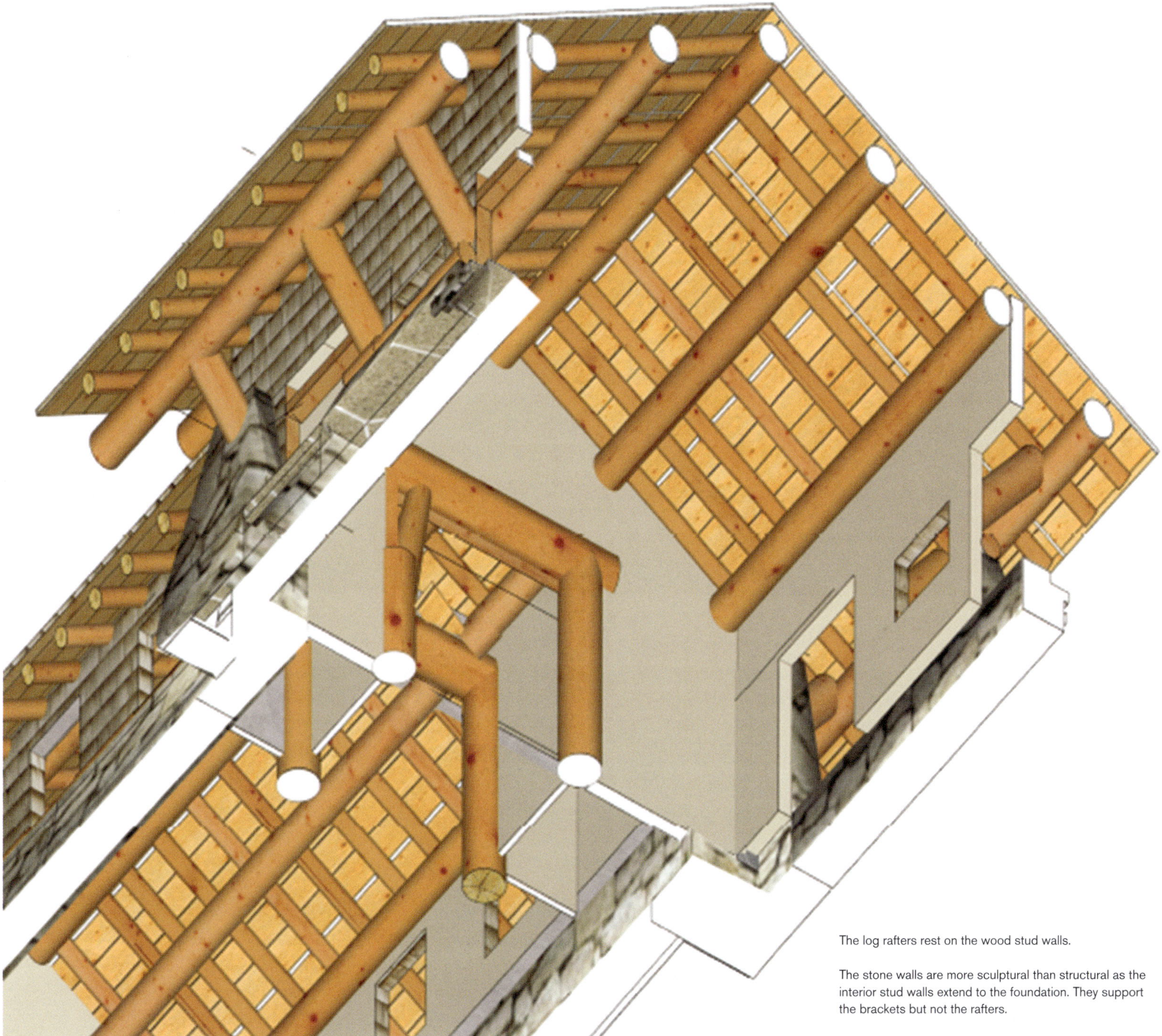

Portals and roof framing
Seen from below

The log rafters rest on the wood stud walls.

The stone walls are more sculptural than structural as the interior stud walls extend to the foundation. They support the brackets but not the rafters.

While the logs are always exposed, the milled studs are always concealed by shingles on the exterior and plaster on the interior.

Influences

Maier's explanations of his intentions are not so much inaccurate as they are selective, claiming to draw the totality of his inspiration from the American vernacular. Maier has little to say about those characteristics of the building that are not drawn from indigenous materials or regional forms. In fact, his work owes far more to distant non-vernacular precedents, to Switzerland, Japan, and Massachusetts than it does to Wyoming. Maier uses the Swiss jerkinhead "clipped" gable, which he admits had no precedent in American pioneer architecture but created the "irregular" roof line.[17] All of Maier's buildings use oversized log brackets resembling a heavyweight version of the Swiss-style bracket. There are Japanese suggestions in the roof in the upturned corners. And one cannot look at the stones in Maier's work without thinking of H. H. Richardson's Ames Gatehouse. But he could have drawn from the many who had already used these forms in American rustic buildings, perhaps by Underwood's work at Bryce Lodge, and it is hard to believe Maier did not know Cutter's buildings.

There are not many specific references to vernacular precedent but certain elements of Fishing Bridge are highly suggestive of the wooden lodges of the indigenous cultures of the Northwest coast such as the Kwakwaka'wakw (Kwakiutl), especially the log supported lintels at the doorway that also support two of the major longitudinal beams. Hermon Bumpas who worked closely with Maier was a former director of the New York Museum of Natural History, where he had set up the of Northwest coast hall of Native American art and would have been very familiar with these buildings. It is possible that Maier's work designing dioramas for Bumpas in Buffalo exposed him to this and other traditions.

But his work is not about vernacular tradition. It is about a response to the natural context. He had little interest in illustrating any kind of craft. If his forms were inspired by the vernacular they were heavily modified by other precedents, often the landscape itself. In the end his exhaustive catalog of the American vernacular seems less important than his imagination.

But Maier generally avoided literal historical quotation as carefully as he avoided the image of modern technology. While he may have shared rationalist tendencies with Underwood, he scrupulously avoided anything suggestive of modern engineering. Maier was a rationalist of a different order than Underwood. There were plenty of sawmill studs in Maier's building but few were exposed. The massive sculptural stone foundations are often not really structural. But some aspects are misleading, most are expressive and allowing for the stone, and none are shams. Each element performs the functional role it appears to perform.

Postscript

Maier's buildings have a constructional rigor that is all too rare in the national park architecture of the period. Their construction speaks to a different kind of architecture, one where external appearance is the result of a corresponding internal order. One that, as Kazin said, discriminated "between the need for the past and the comforting surface of that past."

The 1930s were an era of regionalism and nationalism, in literature, in painting, and in architecture in Europe and America. It produced the Villa Mairea, Taliesin West, Colonial Williamsburg, the early Breuer houses inspired by New England vernacular, and countless American colonial and Spanish revival buildings. It also produced the Nazi Völkisch movement in architecture. Maier's attitude toward primitive man and Indigenous Americans has much of the concept of innocent rationalism, an idea that demeans both pioneers and Indigenous Americans. Regionalism and nationalism were sensibilities Maier was comfortable with, but there were several versions of Maier: the regionalist, the exhibit designer, and the Maier who wanted his work to sit within nature—following the rules that nature had inspired but not mimicking its forms.

All but one of Maier's major Park Service buildings survive, although Yavapai has been heavily modified. The exhibits he designed, which were for him inseparable from the architecture, have not fared as well. Fishing Bridge is the only survivor. In defense of the Park Service, the exhibits required scientific updates but all the others have been replaced by the big type, short text, large color picture, touch and go exhibits of the contemporary park experience.

Fishing Bridge Museum marked the end of Maier's work for the American Association of Museums and the end of his career as a standalone designer. He joined the Park Service and Civilian Conservation Corps where he served as a regional design director in the Southeast. He was rarely the architect of record for any buildings produced during his administration, but anyone who has seen the small buildings at Turner Falls State Park in Oklahoma or Bastrop State Park and Palo Duro Canyon Park in Texas has seen the hand of Maier at work.

America's and the Park Service's love affair with rustic architecture was nearing its end. In 1940 George Nason, a landscape architect with the Park Service wrote in "Architecture and its Relationship to the Design of Parks," that, "Rude buildings are an affectation. They can only be produced by an effort so deliberate and self-conscious that they lay the designer open to the charge of sophistication. They are not a protest against over-elaboration but an elaborate protest against progress in architecture. ... The glorified pioneer structures of today are a species of tawdry circus showmanship, not examples of simple honesty. They are designed to awe rather than usefully charm. ... simplicity and restraint are cardinal virtues in parks." He thought that national park architecture should recognize contemporary architectural standards and strive toward "well-conceived, well built, modern buildings."[18] The war was a year away, and it would be many years before any national park buildings of consequence would be built, and they would not be rustic ones.

CONCLUSION

There will be many who feel this text is an unnecessary journey into subjects of peripheral importance. The value of the classic rustic American buildings is evident to the eye. Knowledge of who built them or why does not change their serene presence in the forest or desert. The Western landscape, particularly the parks, is essential to who we are, and so is the architecture it produced. Likewise, whatever unpleasant modern technical realities lie hidden below their rustic craft exteriors are not visible and not important.

This text examines in detail thirty rustic buildings. Excepting single-family houses, thirteen were hotels and hotel buildings that were built directly or indirectly by the railroads. Four were built to promote the timber industry as advertising. Four were built by the Harvey Company to sell items to tourists. Eight were built by the Park Service for ranger stations or museums. Whatever the experiences these buildings sought to provide, whatever values the sought to embody—a life closer to nature, an existence less industrialized, a non-urban life in a minimal shelter—whatever self-reliant craft was employed, whatever Indigenous traditions were used, whatever Native cultures were emulated, were all things the railroads were in the process of destroying. The railroads committed simultaneous, contradictory acts of preservation and destruction, saving fragments of wilderness as part of a process that required the obliteration of the greater part of that wilderness through timber harvesting and mining. The creation of rustic buildings was no less contradictory, importing industrial technologies to create an architectural imagery of the Indigenous architecture it was destroying.

A short evaluation would be that both the experience and the architecture were a sham. A two-week visit to one of the parks and hotels was not really a rustic experience and neither was the architecture. Both provided the illusion of a connection to nature and a disconnection from culture, and since it was all a performance, the architecture was only a stage set for playing at being rustic—an industrial fabrication with no more authenticity than a canvas backdrop at the opera. It was an all too appropriate veneered container for a veneered life—steel-framed kivas, half-log faced cabins, faux-Indigenous symbols. All were advertising, a marketing tool built by the railroads to financially support the railroad. The Indigenous architecture was commodified and mass marketed, a small part of the larger commodification of the landscape. The establishment of the Park Service in 1916 created a situation that was strangely similar. They were doing marketing in their own way, they simply measured profit in number of visitors, and if Hopi Pueblos could be commodified for the purpose, so could log cabins.

But it is not so simple. There were authentic experiences. There were authentic buildings and there was some truly great architecture that can stand alone outside the tainted history if its creation.

I will close with one more story of a wilderness experience and since I began with Horace Kephart's, I will end it with Philip Johnson's.

Opposite: Kengo Kuma, Birch Moss Chapel

In 1925, Philip Johnson, age nineteen, spent the month of August in Yellowstone National Park, joining a group from the Forest Service studying declining elk populations. This involved at least two four-day pack trips on horseback into the backcountry. According to Johnson's biographer, the trip was arranged by Johnson's mother and seen as something like a miniature version of Theodore Roosevelt's wilderness trial in the Dakotas. In terms of real hardship, Johnson's trek could not have been much of a test, but it was one he almost failed, being in fear, discomfort, and misery for its duration. But in the end, he felt it a valuable experience. He returned east and resumed the career trajectory that would end with him as the dining at the highly fashionable, very expensive Four Seasons restaurant on Park Avenue on an almost-daily basis.[1]

So, was Kephart's experience real and Johnson's experience a sham? Clearly parts of Johnson's ordeal were truly challenging, at least for him. Kephart's retreat to the woods, although genuine, allowed him to leave his marital problems behind, but not his alcoholism and depression. So the answer is no. The wilderness experiences of Kephart's counterparts, in the form of mass tourism, were mostly authentic, some more fictitious, and most somewhere in between.

The character and quality of the rustic architecture that responded to these impulses was the same. Some buildings were authentic in spirit and execution. Many were hybrids of authenticity and illusion.

How are we to evaluate the architectural results? Of course we cannot judge the buildings without judging those who built, commissioned, and designed them.

Perhaps the railroad owners, as they claimed, were powerless in the face of forces they could not control, but those forces were the forces of capitalist greed and were by no means inevitable. What they perceived as divine intention or laws of history played little part.

But for every Thomas Durant there was a Louis Hill. Whatever drove him it was not greed. Looked at in its totality over its 20-30-year life, the great Glacier Park enterprise was a poor investment. Financially he would have had a better return if he had focused on his timberlands in Oregon, something of which he was well aware. Regardless of intentions, can we enjoy the architecture he produced independent of the larger acts of destruction that made it possible? I said in the beginning that some buildings are associated with values we despise while other embody those values. There are many in this book that do, there are many that do not.

Monuments

Buildings like the Glacier Park Hotel were monuments that exhibited as much melancholy as self-congratulation—monuments to what has been accomplished, monuments to what has been lost. The Many Glacier Hotel and Maybeck's House of Hoo Hoo are also memorials to what has been lost culturally, prominently displaying the artifacts of Indigenous cultures that were "disappearing," exhibiting regret but not remorse. And it must be said that whatever the buildings' virtues it does embody values that we deplore.

But for every Glacier Park Hotel there is a Grand Canyon North Rim Lodge that drew whatever monumentality it possessed from the landscape. It has the qualities of a ruin but is silent on the subject what sins the Union Pacific committed in the process of creating it. At the same time there is much to admire in buildings like these. In a history full of veneers, the Glacier Park Lodge is also a monument to authenticity, a clear demonstration of the power of the forces, including the industrial ones, that produced them.

Appropriation

The architects benefited from the devastation of the railroads but did not abet them. Their embodied sins were caused by their desire to learn from non-Western sources, particularly Indigenous cultures, in many cases colonizing the indigenous artifacts and exploiting the inhabitants.

And while their attitudes are in many ways sympathetic, they are also patronizing. To clients and architects of 1900 Indigenous peoples were like children. However compelling their art, it was the product of innocence and naiveté. They and their culture, in time, would grow up to be like us. By learning from them we could reconnect to our origins in the natural world. It was also an attitude that established our superiority over them. Some anthropologists of the day and all of those of the present would disagree.

In the architects' defense it can be argued that what was community property in 1930, is now seen as the stolen property of the individual artist and their culture. Put another way, what artists saw in 1930 as Jungian archetypes unconsciously shared by all are now seen as highly personal possessions. But the end result was theft through appropriation.

Many see these buildings as the artistic residue of an American Imperialism, what Susan Hiller calls "cultural colonialism."[2] Just as Edwin Lutyens' work in India is the residue of a British colonialism despite the extent to which it is modeled on Indigenous architecture, so is the "colonial" architecture of the West. Renato Rosaldo takes this view. It is what he calls Imperialist nostalgia:

Imperialist nostalgia thus revolves around a paradox: a person kills somebody and then mourns his or her victim. In more attenuated form, someone deliberately alters a form of life and then regrets that things have not remained as they were prior to his or her intervention. At one more remove, people destroy their environment and then worship nature. ... Imperialist nostalgia uses a pose of 'innocent yearning' both to capture people's imaginations and to conceal its complicity with often brutal domination.[3]

But for every Desert Watchtower there is a Yavapai Museum that employs the lessons of history without mimicking its forms. And for every Mary Colter who appropriated art forms there was a Herbert Maier, who made a life study of Indigenous architecture, learned from history, but rarely copied it. There was even a different Mary Colter, the one that gave us Lookout Studio.

Authenticity

Some of these buildings were industrial-made frameworks veneered with the spolia of conquered Indigenous people with faux-rustic covering of an industrial reality with a mythic imagery of the primitive. Some were authentic, using material close to its natural state and clearly expressing their actual craft, although at their best they coexist with the visible craft of industrial necessity.

It may seem I have used the "honesty" argument as a tool to belittle architects who employed rustic veneers as part of a trite continuation of the idea of an "honest" building. Appearance is all that matters the argument goes. We are constantly reconstructing history in its own image but without its original technology, from Colonial Williamsburg to modern Berlin. But if we are doing an ethical evaluation of these buildings, it is a much larger question than "honesty" or the presence or absence of constructional expression, but in the case of rustic construction these rustic veneers are problematic in ways that go well beyond concepts of constructional deception.

Rustic architecture was not just another style. It claimed for itself a cultural significance that other styles did not. Its buildings were the mechanism to pursue an authentic, natural life, an alternative to the status quo to house a life that was an alternative to the status quo. How could the wilderness experience be genuine if the rustic architecture was a sham?

The larger question is history. Any building is telling us a story. All buildings have narratives, and the buildings examined here have historical narratives. Many of those are fictive veneers telling fictive histories. If the architecture is part of the history being revealed, should it not tell us the truth about itself?

But for every rustic veneered Grand Canyon Administration Building there is a Fishing Bridge Museum whose apparent structure is the real one.

And for every Ernest Davidson there was a Gilbert Underwood that gave us the logs-out system.

It is also clear that those rustic buildings that drew on nature have aged historically better than those that drew on fictive history, whether that of Indigenous cultures or pioneers, given that the latter have had to bear the brunt of the changes of historical judgment. The veneer of fictitious history has worn off leaving the truth of the damage to the environment and to the Indigenous culture that these buildings were enabling. We still recognize the inevitability of progress, many of us are far less certain that it is divinely ordained.

But having said that, the fact remains that despite these serious flaws in many of these buildings there is much in the Glacier Park Lodge that was demonstrating the power of American industry. One wishes the meticulous craft applied to the surfaces of the Desert Watchtower and the Grand Canyon Administration Building had been put to better use. Like the authenticity of the wilderness experience, the value we place on the architecture is subject to fluid boundaries.

But if it is the task of this kind of architecture to return us to nature, by means of material close to its natural state, used in is natural position, and modified with a minimum of craft, drawing on lessons learned from Indigenous buildings, it is a far superior tool to mimicry, trite imagery, glib nostalgia and fictive histories.

It is clear in all these cases problems were averted and value was achieved by designs drawing directly on natural form and processes rather than those that drew on literal precedent and fictive histories, particularly in the case of "ruins," and what is admirable about rustic architecture and what is most problematic are on display there.

In the course of this narrative two types of ruin have emerged and reemerged. The first type is the ruin of memory, meant to recall a specific place or moment, perhaps a fictitious one. Some of the Grand Canyon buildings, such as Hopi House, are variations of the ruin as memory.

This is the ruin of Caspar Friedrich, something that evoked the simultaneous pleasure and pain in contemplating something that has been lost except for its fragments. The Indigenous museums in the Glacier hotel lobbies prominently displaying the artifacts of Indigenous cultures are fictitious ruins, ruins of what has been lost, not just the forest, but cultures that were "disappearing." There, one might take pleasure in what had been accomplished while feeling regret at what had been destroyed. In these buildings, Indigenous elements, genuine or artificial, play a role—something like the spolia of ancient Roman buildings that incorporate fragments of cultures they had subdued into new construction. These were the ruins of literalism.

The second type of ruin was the ruin of reclaimed nature. Georg Simmel described the ruin as a manifestation of "the great struggle between the will of the spirit and the necessity of nature." This was what George James saw at the Hopi mesas in 1909 and what Bodmer saw in the cliffs on the upper Missouri in 1833.[4] The line between the building and the landscape, between the natural and the human-made, was gone. Hopi House was a ruin of memory. Lookout Studio was a ruin of nature.

The ruin of reclaimed nature is far less problematic. Underwood and Maier buildings, with a ruinous quality that is more about nature and less about culture illustrate how a great many problems can be averted by going to the natural directly and avoiding culture.

Lookout Studio and Yavapai suggest the ruins of the past, but they are arguably of the second type—the ruin of reclaimed nature. This type of design multiplied possibilities. Boundaries were fluid, overall form was indeterminate, completeness was impossible because the formal goal was uncertain. The most fundamental qualities of architecture—the boundary between inside and out, between having shelter and having none—is eroded and ambiguous.

There is no better example of the ruin blurring the boundaries of the natural and human-made than Underwood's lodge at the north rim of the Grand Canyon. And there are many other buildings in which both are present, the literal sensibility and the natural sensibility are housed in tandem, from the Old Faithful Inn to the Lake McDonald Lodge.

Whatever fictive claims have been made for these buildings, there were moments when the architecture began to separate itself from its historical fictions in the literal sense and became more ambiguous and abstract, drawing more on nature directly, and when it readily acknowledged it was using industrial technology that had produced it to do so.

Arguably there is an architecture here that is not about or not solely about drawing on nature or archaic cultures, one that is a hybrid. An architecture that employed the vast industrial capacity of the railroad, the abundance of natural resources, as well as the demand for an alternative authentic way of building to create an architecture that left history whether that of the Indigenous inhabitants or pioneer settlers behind to create something largely original.

So perhaps in this instance Frederick Jackson Turner was right. Many rustic buildings are "enduring and distinguishing survivals of its frontier experience."[5] His thesis has a validity when applied to the Old Faithful Inn, Geyser Hall, and Kootenai Lodge. They were original American inventions born out or the circumstances, the uniquely American conditions of the West.

We have seen many arguments that the architecture presented here stands apart, that it was a response to the particular malaise of the turn of the twentieth century—the desire to escape the overcivilized for the authentic. But there is much evidence that the desire remains for an experience and an architecture that engages nature in a direct way to erase the filters and barriers between ourselves and the natural world we occupy, with or without railroads and mass marketing. We are still escaping.

In 1958, Edward Abbey took a job with the Park Service as a kind of solitary wilderness caretaker in a remote section of the Utah desert. He wanted to escape not just from companionship but the entirety of culture to the wilderness. In 1999 Andrea Zittel moved from Brooklyn to the California desert near Joshua Tree National Park. In 2004 she began the construction of the Wagon Station Encampment—a collection of "sleeping pods" reflecting a "sci-fi pioneer aesthetic." She states, "I'm so drawn to the frontier mentality and that idea of having to figure everything out from scratch. ... Everybody has their desert fantasy; my particular fantasy was probably living on an alien landscape."[6]

Andrea Zittel, Wagon Station Encampment (2004-ongoing) at A-Z West in Joshua Tree, California.

Donald Judd left New York for Marfa in West Texas in the 1970s never to return for any length of time.

The rustic impulse is a sensibility that will not go away. Contemporary manifestations abound—Kengo Kuma's Birch Moss Chapel, Sou Fujimoto's Geometric Forest House, and John Pawson's Roadside Chapel in Lutzingen, Germany. It is a counterculture housed in a counter architecture, a parallel reversal to our actual life and the architecture must at least appear to do the same.

And the turn of the century malaise is arguably still with us. There remains a desire to occupy for time a life unlike the one we lead, disconnected from the world we have created but connected to that natural world that we sometimes occupy and the best of the architecture provides the stage for that to happen—an alternative architecture responding to a vision of an alternative life.

There is a persistent thought, not just in Western Art but in Western culture, that there was a time before this time, perhaps an ancient one, that was better. A time when we were closer to nature and farther from civilization, where we were not separated from the natural world by complex technologies but connected to it by primitive ones. When we did not own the natural world but belonged to it. Where we had more by having less. It is of course one of the oldest archetypes, the loss of Eden.

John Paulson, Roadside Chapel in Lutzingen Germany

Sou Fujimoto, Geometric Forest

Acknowledgements

I owe a great debt to many people I do not know— Jackson Lears, Patricia Limerick, Barbara Novack and Richard White whose work provoked this exploration. Particular insights into the issues those ideas raised came from Gordon Campbell, Irene Cieraad, William Cronon, Susan Hiller, Robert MacFarlane, Roderick Nash, Renato Rosaldo, James Schlett, and others whose thoughts informed the questions I have tried to address in this text, seeing rustic architecture through the lens they created. The conclusions, of course, are mine and not theirs.

There have been a number of histories of rustic architecture, particularly in the national parks, by Christina Barnes, Ethan Carr, Ray Djuff, Harvey Kaiser, Jeffrey Limerick, Richard Wilson, and Alfred Runte, and they are the foundational work for this text along with studies on the American forest by Michael Wiliams and Barbara McMartin. More focused insights came from authors of monographs, biographies, and studies of individual buildings, architects, parks and regions by Mark Barringer, Arnold Berke, Kenneth Cardwell, David Colley, Wesley Haynes, Ruth Kirkregions, Francis Kowsky, Leslie Freudenheim, Craig Gillborn, Henry. Mathews, Eileen McCormack, Gladys Montgomery, Caroline Welsh, Virginia Grattan, Ruth Kirk, Henry Matthews, Ruth Quinn, Mark Wilson, Sally Woodbridge, Biloine Young and Joyce Zaitlin.

The Park Service has produced its own historians—including Mary Shivers Culpin, Laura Soullière Harrison, Henry Law, Barry Mackintosh. Linda Flint McClelland, Karen Reinhart, Kiki Leigh Rydell and William Tweed, and much of this book relies on the body of comprehensive scholarship they have produced as well as the work of restoration architects, including AHBL Engineers, James R. McDonald of A&E Architects, Page and Turnbull, Inc., Crawford and Sterns Architects, and many others.

Perhaps they and some readers, perhaps many, will take issue with some of my harsher assessments of the individuals in this history and the buildings they made, feeling I have been overly critical or cynical, particularly in my comments on the history of the Park Service and the buildings built in the parks. I can only hope that my admiration for the best of this work and the best qualities of those who made it is evident, and I prefer to think that, if I have been critical of some of the buildings traditionally recognized as masterpieces, I hope I have also drawn attention to some neglected ones.

Few moments in architectural history are as accessible and thoroughly documented as the history of national park architecture. By contrast the rustic architecture of the Adirondacks involves inaccessible buildings whose histories, if they exist, are often mostly anecdotal, and this contrast is evident in the text. There are thus many institutions and hundreds of individuals who personally assisted me in researching and assembling this material. Catherine Kisluk, archives specialist at the National Park Denver Service Center, who retrieved many if the construction drawings referenced in this book. I owe as much to the National Archives at College Park, Still Picture Reference Team, Sarah Bselrani, Archivist, Gene Morris and Holly Reed; the Adirondack Experience, Jenny Ambrose Director of Archives & Special Collections and Ivy K. Gocker library director; the Ansel Adams Publishing Rights Trust, Claudia Rice General Manager; A&E Architects Missoula Montana, James McDonald Senior Preservation architect; the Ashmolean Museum of Art and Archaeology, University of Oxford; the Buffalo Bill Center of the West, Mack Frost office of digital services; Camp Pine Knot, Robert Rubendall, Director; the Central Park Conservancy; the City of New York Municipal Archives-Department of Parks Collection; the Eastern Washington State Historical Society, Northwest Museum of Arts & Culture Research Archives, Jeff Creighton Archivist; the Environmental Design Archives, University of California, Berkeley, Cyrana Dowel Research Services Archivist; the Estes Park Museum; the Gilcrease Museum, Garrett W. Gibson Director Rights & Reproductions; the Glacier National Park Museum & Archives, Jean Tabbert Museum Curator, and Anya Helsel Librarian; Keith Smith of Glacier Park Collection; Scott Tanner at the Great Northern Railway Historical Society; Glen Alpine Springs Inc., Carol Lynn Tice, administrator; the Indiana University Archives, Bradley D. Cook Curator of Photographs; the Jack London State Historic Park, California State Parks; the Kansas Historical Society, Sara J. Keckeisen Librarian; Kootenai Lodge Estates LLD; the Minnesota Historical Society Library, Jennifer Rian Reference Librarian; Minnesota Historical Society, Anne Thayer; the Montana Historical Society Library and Archives, Roberta Gebhardt library manager; the Mount Rainier National Park Archives, Brooke Childrey Park Curator; the National Archives at Seattle, Patty McNamee Archivist; the Open Parks Network at Clemson University Libraries, Nick Richbell head of special collections; the Oregon Historical Society, Scott Daniels Reference Services Coordinator; Oregon State Archives, Todd Shaffer Reference Archivist. Philmont Museums, David Werhane Director; the Sagamore Lodge, Garet D. Livermore Executive Director; the Seton Legacy Project at the Academy for the Love of Learning in Santa Fe, David L. Witt Curator; the Union Pacific Museum, Patricia LaBounty Curator; the Yellowstone Stereoview Homepage. Paul Rubinstein; the Yellowstone National Park Archives, Heritage and Research Center, Alicia Murphy Park Historian, Anne L. Foster Archivist; and Andrea Zittel and Regen Projects. I also need to thank Nancy Eklund for help with the copy editing.

I also owe a great deal to the universities where I worked in the years this book was under development, the University of Virginia, the University of Texas Austin, the University of Arkansas and Washington University, St Louis, and my colleagues at those institutions, especially Robert McCarter.

I am particularly indebted to the McDowell community, Chiwoniso Kaitano, David Macy and the fellows and staff there who provided a residency that allowed me to complete the last segments.

I owe just as much to those at ORO for their patience and support Gordon Goff, Jake Anderson, Pablo Mande, Brooke Biro and many others.

My greatest debt, however, is to the man to whom this book is dedicated. In July of 1940 Presley Ford, a twenty-five-year-old CPA from Osage county, Oklahoma, carrying only a backpack, got off a bus at the Prince of Wales Hotel, just across the Canadian border from Glacier National Park. He took a ferry to the south end of Waterton lake on the northern edge of the park and over the next twelve days hiked its length and breadth, zig-zagging from east to west, crossing the crest of the Rockies four times, moving south and ending 171 miles later at the park's southern boundary. In doing this he would have seen all of the hotels and chalets described in this text, buildings that were about to disappear, but they were something in which he seems to have had little interest. He slept in a small tent that he carried with him, that when erected, was not much larger that his sleeping bag. He cooked his meals on a fire in front of it. At the south end of the park he boarded a train at the station across the road from the Glacier Park Hotel and returned to his life as an accountant, a life to which he was no less dedicated than he was to the natural world. It was his third such hike in the mountains, his longest and his last. Service in the Navy, marriage, and children soon followed. He did not return to the mountains for seven years, and when he did it was a life of car-camps and day hikes, mostly with his family, and while he hiked hundreds of miles in the following years, never again were they so remote, so solitary, so minimal, or so primal. He said his three wilderness treks were "scattered pleasant memories across my lifetime." It was he who introduced me to the writings of Horace Kephart, but the concept of a "malaise of over-civilization" had no resonance with him. He had no quarrel with the world. He said his wilderness trips were a time to step out of his life and look back into it, but I have never quite believed that was all it was. I think that these solitary treks were the product of a different a part of him, one that I, and perhaps even he, did not completely understand.

Notes

The Malaise of the Overcivilized

1. Matthew 11: 6–8 (*Disciples' Literal New Testament*).

2. Horace Kephart, *Camping and Woodcraft* (MacMillan, 1917), 18.

3. John Burroughs, *Talks: His Reminiscences and Comments* (Houghton Mifflin, 1922), 197.

4. John Muir, *Our National Parks* (Houghton Mifflin, 1901), 1.

5. T. J. Jackson Lears, *No Place of Grace* (Pantheon, 1981), xv.

6. Lears, *No Place*, xv.

7. Michael Wallis, *Oil Man: The Story of Frank Phillips and the Birth of Phillips Petroleum* (St. Martin's Griffin, 1995).

8. Seneca the Younger, *Epistles XC* (1–100 AD), https://www.loebclassics.com/view/seneca_younger-epistles/1917/pb_LCL076.401.xml?readMode=recto p401.

9. Isiah Berlin, *The Roots of Romanticism* (Princeton University Press, 2001), 99.

10. Jan Harold Brunvand, *American Folklore: An Encyclopedia* (Garland, 1996), 9.

English Origins

1. Albert H. Good, *Park and Recreation Structures* (US Government Printing Office, 1938), 2.

2. Good, *Park and Recreation Structures*, 2.

3. Christopher Hussey, *The Picturesque* (1927: reis. Archon, 1967), 130.

4. Uvedale Price, *An Essay on the Picturesque, as Compared with the Sublime and the Beautiful* (Robson, 1794), 37.

5. William Chambers, *The Floricultural Cabinet and Florists' Magazine*, December 1, 1832, 267.

6. Arthur Thomas Bolton, *The Architecture of Robert and James Adam* (Scribner's, 1922), 55.

7. William Chambers, "The Origins of Buildings and Orders," *A Treatise on Civil Architecture* (J. Haberkorn, 1759).

8. William Wrighte, *Grotesque Architecture, or Rural Amusement* (1790: reis. I. J. Taylor, 1767).

9. Joseph Spence, *Anecdotes, Observations and Characters of Books and Men: Collected from the Conversation of Mr. Pope and Other Eminent Persons of His Time* (John Russell Smith, 1810).

10. William Warburton, *Pope's Collected Essays: The Works of Alexander Pope Esq.* (Knapton, 1752), 277.

11. William Stukeley, "The Creation, Music of the Spheres," quoted in David Boyd Haycock, *William Stukeley: Science, Religion and Archeology in Eighteenth-Century England* (Boydell, 2002), 211.

12. "An Epistolary Description of the Late Mr. Pope's House and Gardens at Twickenham," *The Newcastle General Magazine, or Monthly Intelligencer* I (January 1748): 26.

13. William Shenstone, *Men and Manners* (Bradford and Conrad, 1804), 85.

14. William Gilpin, "Observations Relative Chiefly to Picturesque Beauty, Made in the Year 1772: On Several Parts of England; Particularly the Mountains, and Lakes of Cumberland, and Westmoreland," part 2 (R. Blamire, 1786), 188.

15. Georg Simmel, "The Ruin" (1911), *Hudson Review* 11, no. 3 (Autumn 1958): 380.

16. Price, *An Essay on the Picturesque*, 61.

17. John Plaw, *Sketches for Country Houses* (J. Taylor, 1800), 3.

18. Price, *An Essay on the Picturesque*, 32.

19. Richard Payne Knight, quoted in John Macarthur, *The Picturesque: Architecture, Disgust and Other Irregularities* (Routledge, 2007), 130.

20. Joseph Addison, "Remarks on Several Parts of Italy, etc.," (1705), *The Works of Joseph Addison* (W. Durell, 1811), 24.

21. Addison, "Remarks," 374.

22. Joseph Addison, *The Tatler* 161 (April 29, 1710), *The Works of Joseph Addison* (W. Durell, 1811), 138.

23. Joseph Addison, *The Spectator* 415 (June 26, 1712), *The Spectator: Complete in One Volume* (A. Wilson, 1813), 144.

24. Edmund Burke, *A Philosophical Enquiry into the Origin of Our Ideas of the Sublime and Beautiful* (1757: reis. Harper & Brothers, 1844), 58.

25. Burke, *A Philosophical Enquiry*, 66.

26. Price, *An Essay on the Picturesque*, 123.

27. Joseph Addison, *The Spectator* 415 (June 25, 1712), *The Spectator: Complete in One Volume* (A. Wilson, 1813), 599.

28. Immanuel Kant, *Kant's Critique of Judgement, trans. and ed.* J. H. Bernard (1790: reis. Outlook, 2020), 98.

29. Robert Doran, *The Theory of the Sublime from Longinus to Kant* (Cambridge University Press, 2017), 10.

Downing, Vaux and Olmsted: The Rustic in America

1. Ronald Shafer, *Carnival Campaign: How the Rollicking 1840 Campaign of "Tippecanoe and Tyler Too" Changed Presidential Elections Forever* (Chicago Review Press, 2016).

2. Andrew Downing, *The Horticulturalist* 2, no. 8 (February 1848): 44.

3. Andrew Jackson Downing, *A Treatise on the Theory and Practice of Landscape Gardening* (1841: reis. Cambridge University Press, 2018), 379.

4. Downing, *A Treatise*, 380.

5. Francis Kowky, *Country, Park, City: The Architecture of Calvert Vaux* (Oxford University Press, 1998), 74.

6. "Greensward" Plan, April 28,1858, in *Frederick Law Olmsted, Landscape Architect, 1822–1903*, ed. Frederick Law Olmsted Jr. and Theodora Kimball (Putnam's Sons, 1928).

7. William Stillman, *The Autobiography of a Journalist*, vol. 1 (Grant Richards, 1901), 101.

8. Kowky, *Country, Park, City*, 122.

9. "Greensward" Plan, *Frederick Law Olmsted, Landscape Architect*, 48.

10. Eleventh Annual Report of the Board of Commissioners of the Central Park for the Year Ending December 31, 1867 (Wm. C. Bryant, 1868); and https://www.centralparknyc.org/articles/central-park-rustic-architecture.

11. Frederick Law Olmsted, *The Papers of Frederick Law Olmsted: The Years of Olmsted, Vaux & Company*, 1865–1874, vol. VI (John Hopkins University Press, 1977), 355.

12. Olmsted, Vaux, & Company. Report of the Landscape Architects, Sixth Annual Report of the Commissioners of Prospect Park, January 24, 1866, in Brooklyn Park Commissioners, *Annual Reports of the Brooklyn Park Commissioners, 1861–1873*.([Brooklyn] Commissioners, 1873).

13. Olmsted, Vaux, & Company. Tenth Annual Report of the Commissioners of Prospect Park. January 1870a, Brooklyn Park Commission. *Annual Reports of the Brooklyn Park Commissioners, 1861–1873* ([Brooklyn] Commissioners, 1873), 58.

14. "Structures in Rustic Work," *The American Agriculturalist* 29 (December 1870): 457.

Thomas and William Durant

1. "Adirondack," *New York Times*, August 9, 1864.

2. "Adirondack." *New York Times*.

3. "Adirondack." *New York Times*.

4. Richard White, *Railroaded* (Norton, 2011), 19–20; David Bain, *Empire Express* (Viking, 1999), 154.

5. William Murray, *Adventures in the Wilderness: or, Camp-Life in the Adirondacks* (Fields, Osgood, 1870), 38.

6. "Luxurious Camps in the Adirondacks," *New York Sun*, July 10, 1904.

7. By Most Accounts, Lake Kora was the "Grandest of Great Camps," accessed May 20, 2024, https://www.lakekora.com/about.

8. "Republican Rascality," *Buffalo Times*, October 20, 1897.

9. Craig Gilborn, *Durant: The Fortunes and Woodland Camps of a Family in the Adirondacks* (North Country Books, 1981). Gilborn describes Durant as an artistic director, rather than a designer.

10. "Camp Pine Knot," Raquette Lake, NY, National Historic Landmark Nomination, US Department of the Interior, National Park Service, 2004.

11. "Little Cottage in the Woods," accessed May 20, 2024, https://www.wwdurantstory.com/blog/little-cottage-in-the-woods.

12. "Adirondack Camps Theme Study," National Register of Historic Places, Multiple Property Documentation Form, US Department of the Interior, National Park Service, 2000 (updated, 2007), 20. https://www.nps.gov/subjects/nationalhistoriclandmarks/upload/Adirondack-Camps-Context-Final-508-Compliant.pdf

13. Barbara McMartin, *The Great Forests of the Adirondacks* (North Country Books, 1994), 30.

14. William Stillman, "Autobiography of W. J. Stillman," *Atlantic Monthly* 85 (1900): 623.

15. McMartin, *Great Forests*, 75.

16. McMartin, *Great Forests*, 70, 108.

Grosvenor Atterbury

1. Peter Pennoyer and Anne Walker, *The Architecture of Grosvenor Atterbury* (Norton, 2009). For Durant's attributions, see Craig Gilborn, *Durant: The Fortunes and Woodland Camps of a Family in the Adirondacks* (North Country Books, in association with the Adirondack Museum, 1981).

2. "Camp Uncas," Bolton Landing, New York, National Landmark Nomination, US Department of the Interior, National Park Service, 2008.

3. "Camp Uncas" Landmark Nomination.

4. https://static1.squarespace.com/static/54f382d7e4b09389aa3b9d1e/t/566096bfe4b0e83ffe7e28cd/1449170859386/2014+Sagamore+Annual+Report, accessed May 20, 2024. Atterbury's involvement with the design of Sagamore is documented but not specifically described. Based on the dramatic difference In every way between the lodge and the other buildings I attribute the design to him.

5. "Sagamore Lodge," Bolton Landing, New York, National Historic Landmark Nomination, US Department of the Interior, National Park Service, 2000.

6.Mary Clark Stott to Lucy Carnegie, January 7, 1902, held in the collection of the Adirondack Museum, Blue Mountain Lake, NY.

William Wicks and Augustus Shepard

1. Gifford Pinchot, *The Adirondack Spruce* (The Critic Co., 1898).

2. Goodsell Museum, accessed May 20, 2024, https://www.webbhistory.org/Tribute_to_George_&_Jennie_Goodsell.htm.

3. William S. Wicks, *Log Cabins and Cottages: How to Build and Furnish Them* (Forest and Stream Publishing, 1908), 7.

4. Wicks, *Log Cabins*, 8.

5. Augustus Shepard, *Camps in the Woods*, ed. R. W. Sexton (Architectural Book Publishing, 1931), 25.

6. Shepard, *Camps*, 25.

7. Lurene Butler, "Furnishing the Camp Cabin," *Brooklyn Daily Eagle*, October 11, 1931.

8. Shepard, *Camps*, 28.

The Chalet: Kirtland Cutter in Chicago

1. Richard White, "Frederick Jackson Turner and Buffalo Bill," accessed May 20, 2024, https://www.studythepast.com/his378/turnerandbuffalobill.pdf.

The Log Chalet

1. "The Swiss Cottage," accessed May 20, 2024, https://www.english-heritage.org.uk/visit/places/osborne/things-to-do/swiss-cottage/.

2. Irene Cieraad, "Bringing Nostalgia Home: Switzerland and the Swiss Chalet," *Architecture and Culture* 6, no. 2 (2018): 265.

3. John Ruskin, *The Poetry of Architecture: or, The Architecture of the Nations of Europe* (G. Allen, 1892), 43.

4. Eugène Emmanuel Viollet-le-Duc, *The Habitations of Man in All Ages*, trans. B. Bucknall (Sampson, Low, Marston, Searle & Rivington, 1876), 381.

5. William Dana, *The Swiss Chalet Book* (Comstock, 1913), 49.

6 Louis Steelman, "The Swiss Chalet Type for America," *House and Garden* 20 (1911): 289.

7. Wendell Corthell, "The Use of Wood in Switzerland," *The Craftsman* 5 (1903): 31.

8. Corthell, "The Use of Wood," 37.

9. Andrew Jackson Downing, *A Treatise on the Theory and Practice of Landscape Gardening* (1841: reis. Cambridge University Press, 2018), 338.

Railroads, National Parks, and the Northern Pacific

1. "Park Junkie," accessed May 20, 2024, https://parkjunkie.com /history-of-yosemite/.

2. Richard White, *Railroaded* (Norton, 2011), 461.

3. William T. Hornaday, *The Extermination of the American Bison*, 1886–1887 (US Government Printing Office, 1889).

4. "The Washburn-Doane Expedition of 1870," accessed May 20, 2024, https://www.nps.gov/parkhistory/online_books/yell/cramton /sec3.htm.

5. "Yellowstone National Park Visitor Statistics Page," accessed May 20, 2024, https://www.yellowstone.co/stats.htm.

6. Gifford Pinchot, Forester, and R. Kellogg, Assistant Forester, "The Timber Supply of the United States," 11 *Forest Service Circular* (published by the US Department of Agriculture) 66 (1909): 7, table 2.

7. Franklin B. Hough, *Report upon Forestry, from the Committee Appointed to Memorialize Congress and the State Legislatures, Regarding the Cultivation of Timber and the Preservation of Forests* (Salem Press, 1878), 125–27.

8. James Vance, *The North American Railroad* (John Hopkins University Press, 1995), 209.

9. Charles Sargent, *Report on the Forests of North America (exclusive of Mexico)* (US Government Printing Office, 1884).

10. Michael Williams, *Americans and Their Forests: A Historical Geography* (Cambridge University Press, 1989), 347.

11. Edward Bernie Butcher, "Analysis of Timber Depredations in Montana to 1900," Master's thesis, University of Montana, 1967, 33.

12. Kathryn L. McKay, Trails of the Past: Historical Overview of the Flathead National Forest, Montana, 1800–1960: Final Report of a Historic Overview, Flathead National Forest, Kalispell, MT, US Forest Service, 1994, http://npshistory.com/publications/usfs/region/1 /flathead /history/contents.htmhttp://npshistory.com/publications /usfs/region/1/flathead/history/chap10.htm.

13. N. P. Langford, Report of the Superintendent of the Yellowstone National Park for the Year 1872, US Department of the Interior, National Park Service, 1873, 3.

14. Pinchot and Kellogg, "Timber Supply," 7, table 2.

Sublime Imperialism

1. M. John Lubetkin, *Jay Cooke's Gamble: The Northern Pacific Railroad, the Sioux and the Panic of 1873* (University of Oklahoma Press, 2014), xv.

2. Isaac Stevens, *Final Report of Explorations for a Route for a Pacific Railroad, near the Forty Seventh and Forty Ninth Parallels of North Latitude, from St Paul to Puget Sound, by Isaac Stevens under the Direction of the Secretary of War.* vol. xii, book I (Thomas H. Ford, 1860).

3. Nathaniel Pitt Langford, *Diary of the Washburn Expedition to the Yellowstone and Firehole Rivers in the Year 1870* (Self-published, 1905), 32.

4. The Report of Lieut. Gustavus C. Doane upon the So-Called Yellowstone Expedition of 1870 to the Secretary of War, delivered to the 41st Cong. 3d sess., Executive Document no. 51 (Fort Ellis, Montana Territory, December 15, 1875 [1870]), Eighth Day, August 29th, accessed May 20, 2024, https://www.nps.gov/parkhistory /online_books/yell/cramton/appm.htm.

5. Barbara Novak, *Nature and Culture: American Landscape and Painting, 1825–1875* (Oxford University Press, 2007), 33.

6. Robert Doran, *The Theory of the Sublime from Longinus to Kant* (Cambridge University Press, 2017), 10.

Yellowstone: Building a Railroad; Building a park

1. Theodore Roosevelt, "Remarks at a Meeting of the American Forest Congress," January 5, 1905, accessed May 20, 2024, https://www.presidency.ucsb.edu/documents/remarks-meeting-the-american-forest-congress.

2. Paul L. Hedren, *After Custer: Loss and Transformation in Sioux Country* (University of Oklahoma, 2012), 50.

3. Josef Warhank, "Fort Keogh: Cutting Edge of a Culture," Master's Thesis, California State University, 1983, 9.

4. Scott Kuehn, "History of Logging and Lumber Mills in Missoula, MT," http://www.forestrydays.com/Forestry_Days /History_of _Logging.html.

5. Herman Haupt, *Military Bridges* (D. Van Nostrand, 1864), 31.

6."Yellowstone National Park Visitor Statistics Page," accessed May 20, 2024, https://www.yellowstone.co/stats.html.

7. In *Railroaded* (Norton, 2011), Richard White calls Rufus Hatch "the bad one." [472]

8. Robin Winks, *Frederick Billings* (Oxford University Press, 1991), 289.

9. Dick Blust Jr., "The President Arthur Expedition: The Fishing Trip that Helped Save Yellowstone," WyoHistory.org. April 29, 2019, https://www.wyohistory.org/encyclopedia/president-arthur -expedition-fishing-trip-helped-save-yellowstone; United States Department of Agriculture. Forest Service, Lodgepole Pine: An American Wood FS- 253, 5.

10. "Captain Chittenden," *Semiweekly Billings Gazette*, October 28, 1902.

11. Report of the Secretary of the Interior, 1890.

12. United States, Congress, House, Committee on the Public Lands (1892), 256.

13. Lt. Dan Kingman to Secretary of the Interior, March 25, 1885, on deposit at Yellowstone National Park Archives, Yellowstone, WY (National Archives affiliate).

14. Yellowstone National Park Report to Accompany H.R. 9597, United States, Congress, House, Committee on the Public Lands (1892), 270.

15. Annual Report of the Department of the Interior, 1881, 489.

16. Annual Report of the Department of the Interior, 1881, 489.

17. P. H. Conger, Superintendent, "Mammoth Hot Springs," Wyoming, US Congressional Serial Set, vol. 2162, Department of the Interior, Yellowstone National Park, Office Superintendent, November 3 1883, 20.

18. Annual Report of the Chief of Engineers, United States Army, to the Secretary of War for the Year 1892 in Four Parts and Atlas; and Mary Shivers Culpin, "A History of Concession Development in Yellowstone National Park, 1872–1966," National Park Service, Yellowstone Center for Resources, Yellowstone National Park, WY, YCR-CR-2003-01, 2003.

Rustic Begins: Two Log Cabins

1. Kiki Leigh Rydell and Mary Shivers Culpin, *Managing the "Matchless Wonders": A History of Administrative Development in Yellowstone National Park, 1872–1965* (National Park Service and Yellowstone Center for Resources, 2006), YCR-2006-03. See Appendix A, Government-Built Buildings Constructed in Yellowstone National Park, 1879–1973.

2. Joseph Henry Sharp, "Home Department: A Real Lesson in House Building," *The Craftsman* 10, no. 3 (June 1906): 408.

3. "Three Craftsman Log Houses" *The Craftsman* 11, no. 6 (March 1907): 742.

4. "Pahaska Teepee" Park County, WY, National Register of Historic Places Inventory, no. 1072, US Department of the Interior, National Park Service, 1973.

5. Report of the Acting Superintendent of the Yellowstone National Park to the Secretary of the Interior, US Department of the Interior, National Park Service, 1897, 5.

6. Grace L. Hurley, "Coast to Coast, 1915," unpublished diary, entry for August 18, 1915, [45], held in the Yellowstone National Park Archives.

7. "To Be Housed in Log Cabins," *Butte Miner*, November 28, 1902; and "A Unique Plan: Tourists Will be Housed in Log Cottage at Upper Geyser Basin," *Livingston Enterprise*, November 22, 1902.

8. Ruth Quinn, *Weaver of Dreams: The Life and Architecture of Robert C. Reamer* (Leslie and Ruth Quinn, 2004), 4.

The Old Faithful Inn

1. Charles Francis Adams, *What Jim Bridger and I Saw in Yellowstone National Park*, 1830–1913 (publisher unknown, 1913), 12.

2. Yellowstone National Park, R. C. Reamer. Architect," *The Western Architect* III (October 1904): 4–6.

3. Old Faithful Inn," Park County, WY, National Register of Places Inventory-Nomination Form, US Department of the Interior, National Park Service, 1973.

4. James Coates, "Yellowstone Inn: A Rustic Masterpiece Worth Gushing Over," *Chicago Tribune*, September 30, 1966.

5. Frederick Jackson Turner, *The Frontier in American History* (1893: reis. Henry Holt, 1921), 205.

6. Ethan Carr, *Wilderness by Design* (University of Nebraska, 1998), 62. See also Harvey H. Kaiser, *Landmarks in the Landscape: Historic Architecture in the National Parks of the West* (Chronicle Books, 1997), where Kaiser writes of "allusions to pioneer building techniques"; and Karen Reinhart, "Old Faithful Inn: Centennial of a Beloved Landmark," *Yellowstone Science* 12, no. 2 (Spring 2004), where Rinehart notes that the use of power equipment, if not documented, was certainly necessary for its construction.

7. Michael Williams, "Industrial Impacts on the Forests of the United States, 1860–1920," *Journal of Forest History* 31, no. 3 (July 1987): 118.

8. Regarding the Aloha Mill and Shake Company, see https://www.trainorders.com/discussion/read.php?11,3995337.

9. https://yellowstoneinsider.com/old-faithful-snow-lodge-cabins/;. The use of off-site lumber is suggested by an ad in the *Billings Gazette* of June 1903 seeking the services of several teams of wagons to haul "a large amount of lumber and other building material to the Upper Geyser basin and Lake Hotel for 3–4 months."

10. References to the use of railroad workers can be found in the following: Kaiser, *Landmarks in the Landscape*, where Kaiser writes, "according to legend they were trestle builders" [140]; Karen Reinhart, "Old Faithful Inn Centennial of a Beloved Landmark" *Yellowstone Science* 12, no. 2 (Spring 2004), where Rinehart writes, "some of the workers may have been 'on loan' from the railroad, that had a vested interest in the Inn's timely completion" [8]; and "Old Faithful Inn Flooring Restored in Cody," *Cody Enterprise*, February 24, 2014, where the author writes, "workers from the Northern Pacific Railroad who were familiar with constructing trestles" worked on the inn.

11. Major Hiram Chittenden was constructing log crib bridge supports at Tower and Canyon junction on the loop road. See "The History of the Construction of the Road System in Yellowstone National Park, 1872–1966," part 1, chapter VII, http://npshistory.com/publications/yell/hrs-roads/chap12.htm.

12. See, for example: "Old Faithful Inn Largest Log House in the World," *Butte Miner*, March 20, 1905.

13. "Interview with W. H. Merriman," *Gardiner Wonderland*, March 23, 1905.

14. William Curtis, "At Old Faithful Inn," *Washington Evening Star*, August 23, 1909.

15. William Empson, *The Seven Types of Ambiguity* (New Directions, 1930); and Robert Venturi, *Complexity and Contradiction in Modern Architecture* (Museum of Modern Art, New York, 1966).

16. "Interview with W. H. Merriman."

17. J. H. Rafftery, *A Miracle in Hotel Building, Being the Story of the Building of the New Canyon Hotel in Yellowstone Park* (Yellowstone Park Hotel Company, 1911), 13.

18. Frank Lloyd Wright, "In the Cause of Architecture," *Architectural Record* 23, no. 3. (March 1908): 161.

19. "Canyon Hotel Opens," *Anaconda Standard*, August 4, 1911.

20. "Canyon Hotel Opens.".

21. Ruth Quinn, *Weaver of Dreams: The Life and Architecture of Robert C. Reamer* (Leslie and Ruth Quinn, 2004), 153–54.

22. "James R. McDonald, Architect, Lake Lodge," Yellowstone National Park, Yellowstone, WY, Historic Structures Report, US Department of the Interior, National Park Service, 1997.

The Longs Peak Inn

1. Enos A. Mills, *Trees that Twist*, ed. Elizabeth M. Mills and Eryn V. Mills (Mrs. Enos A. Mills, [n.d]), Kindle, 43.

2. Mills, *Trees that Twist*, 68.

3. Enos Mills, "A Home of Forest Fire Logs" *Sunset* 47, no. 2 (May 1921): 66.

4. Enos Mills, Esther Mills and Arthur Chapman, *The Story of Longs Peak Inn* (Mrs. Enos A. Mills, [n.d]), 4.

The Surreal

1. Uvedale Price, *An Essay on the Picturesque, as Compared with the Sublime and the Beautiful* (Robson, 1794), 32.

2. Thomas Cole, *Thoughts & Occurrences: The Journal of Thomas Cole, kept from 1834 to 1848*, quoted in Barbara Novak, *Nature and Culture: American Landscape and Painting, 1825–1875* (Oxford University Press, 2007). Cole's journal is held the New York State Library. Albany, NY.

3. Olin D. Wheeler, *Wonderland* (1895: reis. Northern Pacific Railway, 1906).

4. John Muir, *Steep Trails*. ed. William Badè (Houghton Mifflin, 1918).

5. "Rustic Seats and Shelters, Formal and Fantastic," *The Craftsman* 28, no. 5 (August 28, 1915): 515.

6. Herbert Read, *The Philosophy of Modern Art* (1953: reis. Fawcett, 1967), 212.

Sacred Groves

1. Annie Dillard, *Teaching a Stone to Talk: Expeditions and Encounters* (Harper & Row, 1982), 87.

2. Paul Crossley, quoted in Mailan S. Doquang, *The Lithic Garden: Nature and the Transformation of the Medieval Church* (Oxford University Press, 2018), 13; Joseph Rykwert, *On Adam's House in Paradise* (MIT Press, 1972), 100; Paul Frankl, *Gothic Architecture* (Yale University Press, 1982), 275.

3. James Fenimore Cooper, *The Deerslayer* (1841: reis. George Routledge and Son, 1867), 185.

4. Washington Irving, *The Life and Letters of Washington Irving*, vol. 2, ed. Pierre Munroe (Putnam, 1862), 331.

5. Washington Irving, *A Tour of the Prairies* (John Murray Albemarle, 1835), 47.

6. J. D. Grant, *Saving California's Redwoods* (Save the Redwoods League, 1922), 4.

7. Laura White, "A Day in the Redwoods of Lagoon Creek," *Overland Monthly and Outwest Magazine* 18, no. 105 (September 1881): 257–60.

8. Stanton Davis Kirkham, "The Forest," *In the Open* (Paul Elder, 1908). accessed May 20, 2024, https://www.quotegarden.com/trees-redwoods.html#:~:text=Their%20immense%20trunks%20might%20be,only%20the%20forest%20cathedrals%20know.

9. Simon Schama, *Landscape and Memory* (Alfred A. Knopf, 1995), 197.

10. William Dudley, "Forest Reservations," *Sierra Club Bulletin* I (January 1896): 254–57; French Strother, "Saving the Big Trees: The Need of Further National, State, and Private Protection for the Remnants of the Groves that Are Being Cut," *The World's Work*, June 1909.

11. Richard White. *It's Your Misfortune and None of My Own* (University of Oklahoma Press, 1991), Kindle, 410.

12. Mabel Craft, "A Sermon in Church Building," *The House Beautiful* IX, no. 3 (February 1901): 132.

13. Emanuel Swedenborg, *Arcana Coelestia* (1758), tr. J. Potts (_____,1892), https://sacred-texts.com, 10504.

14. Swedenborg, *Arcana Coelestia*, 1015.

15. Craft, "A Sermon," 128.

The Portland Forestry Building

1. Edmund P. Sheldon, "The Forest Wealth of Oregon," *Lewis and Clark Journal*, March 1904.

2. "Lewis and Clark Centennial Exposition, Forestry Building, Portland, OR," Designers, accessed May 20, 2024, https://pcad.lib.washington.edu/building/13170/.

3. "A Glimpse in the Forestry Palace," *The Sunday Oregonian*, July 09, 1905, part 3.

4. "A Glimpse in the Forestry Palace."

5. "A Building that is an Exhibit," *Field and Stream* 9–10, no. 2 (June 1905): 183; and "Lewis and Clark Centennial Exposition, Forestry Building, Portland, OR," Building History, accessed May 20, 2024, https://pcad.lib.washington.edu/building/13170/.

6. "A Glimpse in the Forestry Palace."

7. "A Glimpse in the Forestry Palace"; Blaine Phillips, "Lewis and Clark Exposition: Architecturally, Originality of Design a Feature of the 1905 Worlds Fair," *The Builder* (St. Louis) 12, no. 4 (April1905).

8. "Architectural Splendors of Portland Excite Outspoken Admiration," *Oregon Daily Journal*, June 1, 1905, section 2; "Hallie Erminie Rives' Impressions of the Fair," *Sunday Oregonian*, September 3, 1905, part 4; Elizabeth McClue, "Oregon's Parthenon is 25 Years Old," *Weekly Oregonian*, June 1, 1930; Henry C. Matthews, *Kirtland Cutter: Architect in the Land of Promise* (University of Washington Press, 1998).

9. "Forestry Club Revels in Outings at the Fair," *Sunday Oregonian*, October 1, 1905, part 3; "The Oregon Cathedral," *Lewis & Clark Journal* 4, no. 1 (July 1905).

10. "Organ Will Peal Tones of Forest."

11. "Organ will Peal Tones of Forest," *Morning Oregonian*, May 19, 1905.

12. Vast Cathedral of the Forests," *Oregon Daily Journal*, July 30, 1907.

13. Phillips, "Lewis and Clark Exposition."

14. "Vast Cathedral of the Forests."

15. Gertrude Metcalfe, "The Indian as Revealed in the Curtis Pictures," *Lewis and Clark Journal* 1, no. 1 (January 1904): 13.

16. Marion Macrae, "Noted Indian Pictures on View at the Fair: Great Ethnological and Artistic Work Undertaken by E. S. Curtis," *Sunday Oregonian*, June 18, 1905.

Bernard Maybeck and the Grove of Redwoods

1. "Coast Redwood (Sequoia sempervirens)," Forest Research and Outreach, University of California Agriculture and Natural Resources, accessed May 20, 2024, https://ucanr.edu/sites/forestry/California_forests/http___ucanrorg_sites_forestry_California_forests_Tree_Identification_/Coast_Redwood_Sequoia_sempervirens_198/.

2. Herb Caen, "Ten Second Interview," *San Francisco Chronicle*, January 18, 1953.

3. The Palace of Fine Arts," *Transactions of the Commonwealth Club of California, San Francisco* 10, no. 10 (August 1915): 373.

4. Frank Morton Todd, "Introduction," in Bernard R. Maybeck, *Palace of Fine Arts and Lagoon: Panama-Pacific International Exposition*, 1915 (Paul Elder, 1915).

5. Maud Wotring Raymond et al., *The Architecture and Landscape Gardening of the Exposition* (Paul Elder, 1915), 172.

6. Bernard Maybeck, "Hillside Building," Berkeley, CA, ______, 1906, Hillside Club records, Bancroft Library, University of California, Berkeley, CA.

7. House of Mrs. Phoebe, a Hearst in Siskiyou Co., Cal., Maybeck & White, Architects," *American Country Houses* (Bates and Gill, 1904), 65.

8. House of Hoo Hoo," *The Bulletin: A Monthly Journal Devoted to Hoo Hoo* 21, no. 225 (November 9, 1914): 14.

9. Jacomena Maybeck, *Maybeck: The Family View* (1980: reis. Berkeley Architectural Heritage Association, 1991), 2.

10. "Bohemians Will Soon Open Their New Forest Retreat," *San Francisco Call*, May 9, 1904.

11. Maybeck: *The Family View*, 11.

12. Bernard Maybeck, Drawing: Ground Plan, Panama-Pacific International Exposition: Lumbermen's Building & House of Hoo Hoo, 1914–1915, Bernard Maybeck Collection, University of California, Berkeley, Environmental Design Archives, Berkeley, CA.

13. Lyn Nofziger, *Nofziger* (Regnery Publishing, 1992).

14. Susan Ives, "Elite Club Blocked from Logging Giant Redwoods," *High Country News*, April 1, 2011.

15. Jonathan Spiro has recounted the sad history of this group in his book *Defending the Master Race: Conservation, Eugenics, and the Legacy of Madison Grant* (University of Vermont Press, 2009).

The Great Northern Railroad

1. F. Scott Fitzgerald, *The Great Gatsby*, (1925: reis. Knopf Doubleday, 2021), 137.

2. Walter Vaughn, *The Life and Work of William Van Horne* (Century, 1920), 357.

3. Richard White, *Railroaded* (Norton, 2011), 503.

4. Michael Malone wrote in *James J. Hill* (University of Oklahoma, 1996, pps. 122–23) that in the drive to build the line to Montana, the Great Northern used 100 million board feet of timber and ties to build 733 miles of track. Looked at another way, assuming a railroad requires 3,000 ties per mile (Franklin Benjamin Hough, Report upon Forestry [US Government Printing Office, 1878), part 1, 125–27), and that one acre produces 100 ties (Report on the Relation of Railroads to Forest Supplies and Forestry [US Forest Service, 1887), then 21,000 acres of forest were obliterated in the process.

5. "In a speech delivered at Portland, Oregon, during the Lewis and Clark Exposition of 1905, James J. Hill, the great railway magnate—and incidentally heavily interested in Western timber lands—declared that one acre of timber land possessed more intrinsic value to a railway corporation than forty acres of agricultural land." Quoted in Stephen A. Douglas Puter and Horace Stevens, *Looters of the Public Domain* (Portland Printing House, 1908), 471.

6. Greg Lange, "Frederick Weyerhaeuser makes one of the largest land purchases in United States history on January 3, 1900," https://www.historylink.org/file/5241 HistoryLink.org Essay 5241, Posted 2/19/2003.

7. Puter and Stevens, *Looters of the Public Domain*, 368.

8. Derrick Jensen and George Draffan, *Railroads and Clearcuts* (Keokee, 1995), 4.

9. Yessenia Funes, "The Forgotten Land Grab that Gave Us Glacier National Park," *Gizmodo*, January 1, 2018, acessed May 20, 2024, https://gizmodo.com/the-forgotten-land-grab-that-gave-us-glacier-national-p-1821698.

10. Roderick Nash, *Wilderness and the American Mind* (Yale, 1965), 6.

Louis Hill

1. "Louis Hill Didn't Care for Railroad," *Fergus County Democrat* (Lewistown, MT), May 28, 1912; *Oakland Tribune*, December 25, 1911.

2. loine W. Young with Eileen R. McCormack, *The Dutiful Son: Louis W. Hill* (Ramsey County Historical Society, 2000), 169.

3. "Who's Who and Why? J. J.'s Son," *Saturday Evening Post* 185, no. 1 (1912): 19.

4. "Radical Opponent of Pinchot-Roosevelt Reclamation Project won over by Pinchot," *Star Tribune Minneapolis*, June 12, 1910.

5. Young, *The Dutiful Son*.

6. "Men of the West Gather at Lake," *Anaconda Standard*, August 29, 1912.

7. "Suggestion for Uncle Sam to Enter See America First Campaign," *Post Office Clerk: Organ of the United National Post Office Clerks of the United States, The Association* 11–12 (1911): 105.

8. Mary Roberts Rinehart, *Through Glacier Park: Seeing America First with Howard Eaton* (Houghton Mifflin, 1916), 24.

9. Irene Cieraad, "Bringing Nostalgia Home: Switzerland and the Swiss Chalet," *Architecture and Culture* 6, no. 2 (2018): 265–88.

10. George Grinnell, "The Rock Climbers," *Forest and Stream* 29, nos. 39–40 (December 29, 1887): 448.

The American Sublime

1. Journals of Meriwether Lewis, quoted in Bruce W. Smalley, *Lewis and Clark Trail Guide* (Digital Scanning, 2003), 43.

2. Barbara Novak, *Nature and Culture: American Landscape and Painting, 1825–1875* (Oxford University Press, 2007), 33; Robert Doran, *The Theory of the Sublime from Longinus to Kant* (Cambridge University Press, 2015), 11.

3. John Muir, *Our National Parks* (1901), in *The Complete Works of John Muir* (Madison& Adams Press, 2019) Kindle, 571.

4. Richard White, *It's Your Misfortune and None of My Own: A New History of the American West* (University of Oklahoma Press, 2015), 410.

5. Dugald Stewart, "On the Sublime," in *The Collected Works of Dugald Stewart*, ed. Sir William Hamilton, vol. 5 (Thomas Constable, 1855), 299.

6. John Muir, *My First Summer in the Sierra* (1911), in *The Complete Works of John Muir* (Madison & Adams Press, 2019), 687.

Glacier National Park: Hotels

1. "Forestry Building in Glacier National Park," *The Timberman*, February 1912, 51.

2. Mary Roberts Rinenhart, *Through Glacier Park: Seeing America first with Howard Eaton* (Houghton Mifflin, 1916), Kindle, 61.

3. A. H. Hogeland to H. H. Parkhouse, March 14, 1912, held in the Minnesota Historical Society, St. Paul, MN.

4. "The 1914 Season at Glacier National Park," *See America First* 5, no. 3 (1914): 109.

5. L. W. Hill to Robert Reamer, telegram, March 2, 1912, held in the Minnesota Historical Society.

6. Heinrich Wolflin, *Renaissance and Baroque* (Cornell University Press, 1966), 43.

7. "Pacific Coast Hotelmen View Indian Equipped," *Aberdeen Herald*, November 11, 1912; "Sacred Tepee Is Revered," *Pickens Sentinel* (Pickens, SC), May 7, 1914.

8. Frederic. C. Frobese to Louis Hill, January 1913, held in the Minnesota Historical Society.

9. Roderick Nash, *Wilderness and the American Mind* (Yale University Press, 1967).

10. "Northwest Honors Hill," *New York Sun*, September 17, 1912.

11. Louis Hill to St. Paul Book & Stationary Co., (undated), held in the Minnesota Historical Society.

12. Ray Djuff and Chris Morrison, *A View with a Room* (Far Country Press, 2001), 88.

13. Bill Yenne, *Glacier National Park* (Arcadia, 2006), (unpaginated).

Into the Wilderness: Glacier Park Chalets

1. Roger Di Silvestro, *Theodore Roosevelt in the Badlands: A Young Politician's Quest for Recovery in the American West* (Walker & Company, 2012).

2. Theodore Roosevelt, *Hunting Trips of a Ranchman* (1885: reis. Modern Library, 1998), 18.

3. Philip G. Terrie, *Contested Terrain: A New History of Nature and People in the Adirondacks* (Syracuse University Press, 1999), 63.

4. David Clary, *The Place Where Hell Bubbled Up: A History of the First National Park* (Homestead Press, 1972), 50.

5. Mary Roberts Rinehart, *Through Glacier Park, Seeing America First with Howard Eaton* (Houghton Mifflin, 1916). Kindle, 189.

6. Rinehart, *Through Glacier Park*, Kindle, 362.

7. Rinehart, *Through Glacier Park*, Kindle, 61.

8. Rinehart, *Through Glacier Park*, Kindle, 138.

9. Robert MacFarlane, *Mountains of the Mind* (Vintage, 2003), 152.

10. MacFarlane, *Mountains of the Mind*, 162.

11. Fred Gignilliat to Louis Hill, January 23, 1923, held in the Minnesota Historical Society.

12. "Who's Who and Why? J. J.'s Son," *Saturday Evening Post* 185, no. 1 (1912): 19.

13. *Spokane Chronicle*, May 1914.

14. Richard White, *The Republic for Which It Stands: The United States during Reconstruction* (Oxford University Press, 2017), 615.

15. "Montana," *The Timberman*, October 1913.

Kirtland Cutter in Montana

1. Irene Cieraad, "Bringing Nostalgia Home: Switzerland and the Swiss Chalet," *Architecture and Culture* 6, no. 2 (2018): 265–88.

2. *Report of the Superintendent of the Glacier National Park to the Secretary of the Interior* (US Government Printing Office, 1911).

Ruins

1. Prince Alexander Philipp Maximilian of Wied, *Travels in North America, 1832–1834: A Concise Edition of the Journals of Prince Maximilian of Wied*, ed. *Marsha V. Gallagher* (2017), Kindle, 237, 234.

2. Maximilian of Wied, *Travels*, 253, 263.

3. Nathaniel Langford, *Diary of the Washburn Expedition to the Yellowstone and Firehole Rivers* (Self-published, 1905), 19.

4. Report of Lieutenant Gustavus C. Doane upon the so called Yellowstone Expedition of 1870, United States, Senate, Third Session of the Forty First Congress, 1870–71, vol. 265, 30.

5. Clarence King, *Mountaineering in the Sierra Nevada* (1871), Project Guttenberg, Kindle, 2517.

6. King, *Mountaineering*, 1091.

7. King, *Mountaineering*, 1087.

8. John Wesley Powell, *Canyons of the Colorado* (1891: reis. Library of Alexandria, 2020), 6.

9. John Muir, "The Grand Cañon of the Colorado" (1902), in *The Complete Works of John Muir* (Madison& Adams Press, 2019).

10. Muir, "Grand Cañon," in *The Complete Works of John Muir* (Madison& Adams Press, 2019), Kindle,1595.

11. Muir, "Grand Cañon," Kindle,1607.

12. John Muir, "The Treasures of the Yosemite" (1890), in *The Complete Works of John Muir*, Kindle, 1628.

13. Ethel Rose, "New Hopi Architecture on the Old Mesa Land from Notes by Ethel Rose." *The Craftsman* 30, no. 4 (July 1916): 374.

14. Frederick Monson, "Pueblos of the Painted Desert: The Hopi Build Their Dwellings on the Cliffs," *The Craftsman* 12, no. 1 (April 1907): 6.

15. Monson, "Pueblos," 22.

16. Langford, *Diary of the Washburn Expedition.*

17. Muir, "Grand Cañon," Kindle, 1613.

18. Georg Simmel, "The Ruin," (1911), *Hudson Review* 11, no. 3 (Autumn 1958): 379; William Gilpin, "Observations, Relative Chiefly to Picturesque Beauty, Made in the Year 1772: On Several Parts of England; Particularly the Mountains, and Lakes of Cumberland, and Westmoreland," part 2 (R. Blamire, 1786), 188.

The Santa Fe Railroad

1. Reprinted in George James, *Through Ramona's Country* (Little, Brown, 1909), 305.

2. "Logging Railroad Resources of the Coconino and Kaibab National Forests, Arizona," National Register of Historic Places, Multiple Property Documentation, E2, US Department of the Interior, National Park Service, 1995.

3. James, "Aboriginal American Homes," *The Craftsman* 8, no. 5 (August 1905):463.

4. George James, "Aboriginal American Homes," 640–49.

5. Stephen Fried, *Appetite for America: How Visionary Businessman Fred Harvey Built a Railroad Hospitality Empire that Civilized the Wild West* (Banham Books, 2010).

6. Charles Lummis, "A Week of Wonders," *Out West* 16 (January 1902): 24.

Mary Colter: The Lookout Studio and Hermits Rest

1. W. H. Simpson and Fred Harvey, *El Tovar: A New Hotel Grand Canyon of Arizona* (Fred Harvey, 1905), 9.

2. Fred Shaw, *False Architect: The Mary Colter Hoax* (Fred Shaw, 2018), Kindle.

3. Page and Turnbull, Inc., "Lookout Studio, Grand Canyon National Park," AZ, Historic Structure Report, US Department of the Interior, National Park Service, 2009.

4. George Wharton James, *Arizona, the Wonderland: The History of Its Ancient Cliff and Cave Dwellings* (Page, 1917), 102.

5. University of Arizona Preservation Studies Program, "Hermit's Rest," Grand Canyon National Park, AZ, Historic Structures Report, US Department of the Interior, National Park Service, 2007.

Geology: Gilbert Underwood and Hebert Maier

1. John Muir, "Studies in the Sierra" (1874–1875), in *The Complete Works of John Muir* (Madison & Adams Press, 2019), Kindle, 1629.

2. Muir, "Studies," Kindle, 1614.

3. Linda Flint McClelland, *Presenting Nature: The Historic Landscape Design of the National Park Service, part III, A Policy and Process for Design, 1916–1927* (US Department of the Interior, National Park Service, Cultural Resources, Interagency Resources Division, National Register of Historic Places, 1993).

4. Ralph H. Lewis, Museum Curatorship in the National Park Service, 1904–1982, US Department of the Interior, National Park Service, Curatorial Services Division, 1993, 34.

5. H. C. Bumpus Jr., *Hermon Carey Bumpus, Yankee Naturalist* (University of Minnesota Press, 1947), 104.

6. Herbert Maier, "The Purpose of the Museum in National Parks," *Yosemite Nature Notes*, May 1926, 38.

7. McClelland, *Presenting Nature.*

8. Horace M. Albright to D. H. Hull, August 8, 1924, held in the Yellowstone National Park Archives, Yellowstone, WY (National Archives affiliate).

9. Joyce Zaitlin, *Gilbert Stanley Underwood, His Rustic, Art Deco, and Federal Architecture* (Simon/Pangloss Press, 1989), 70–71.

10. H. C. Mann to S. J. Mayo, May 10, 1927, held in the Minnesota Historical Society. Union Pacific Museum (Council Bluffs, Iowa). The telegram indicates that the government required solid logs. An undated memo by H. C. Mann suggests that trusses be steel covered with logs, that rafters ends be joists and not log extensions, that studs should be turned at 90 degrees to the logs. It is not clear that any of these were done.

11. Gilbert Underwood to F. E. Lewis, July 25, 1934, held in the Union Pacific Museum. Several sources speculate that Underwood had little if anything to do with the rebuilding, but the Union Pacific Archives indicate that he was very much involved.

12. Ansel F. Hall, "Studies for Museum Development in Grand Canyon National Park" (1934), Internet Archive, accessed May 20, 2024, https://archive.org/details/studiesformuseum00hall.

13. Herbert Maier, "Proceedings of National Park Service Conference of State Park Authorities, Washington, DC, February 25, 1935," mimeo (National Park Service, 1935), 91.

14. Karsten Harries, *The Ethical Function of Architecture* (MIT, 1997), 243.

The Desert Watchtower: The Diné, the Hopi and Mary Colter

1. Stephen Fried, *Appetite for America: How Visionary Businessman Fred Harvey Built a Railroad Hospitality Empire that Civilized the Wild West* (Banham Books, 2010).

2. Deborah Elizabeth Tibbel, *Nampeyo and the Sikyatki Revival: Creating a Legend with Hopi Ceramics* (University of British Columbia, 1994), ii.

3. Mary Colter, "Manual for Drivers and Guides Descriptive of the Indian Watchtower at Desert View and Its Relation Architecturally to the Prehistoric Ruins of the Southwest" (Fred Harvey, 1933), in *Architectural Regionalism: Collected Writings on Place, Identity, Modernity and Tradition*, ed. Vincent B. Canizaro (Princeton Architectural Press, 2007), 181.

4. Jessica Welton, "The Watchtower Murals," *Plateau* (Museum of Northern Arizona), Fall/Winter 2005.

5. Robert L. Farrel to Volney Wesley, November 7, 1967, held in the Grand Canyon Museum Collections, AZ.

Cultural Appropriation

1. Rene d'Harnoncourt, quoted in "Back to the Indian," *Washington Star*, February 1941.

2. Susan Hilller, *The Myth of Primitivism* (Routledge, 1991), 3.

3. H. Allen Anderson, *The Chief: Ernest Thompson Seton and the Changing West* (Texas A&M University Press, 1986), 216.

4. Ernest Thompson Seton, "Spirit of the Woods," *Century Magazine* 103 (December 1921): 216.

5. William Gilpin, "Observations, Relative Chiefly to Picturesque Beauty, Made in the Year 1772: On Several Parts of England; Particularly the Mountains, and Lakes of Cumberland, and Westmoreland," part 2 (R. Blamire, 1786), 188; and Georg Simmel, "The Ruin" (1911), *Hudson Review* 11, no. 3 (Autumn 1958): 379.

Literary Rationalism

1. Richard Wurman, *Louis Kahn: What Will Be Has Always Been* (Rizzoli, 1986), 91.

2. Uvedale Price, *On the Picturesque* (Caldwell, Lloyd, 1794, 1842), 303.

3. Ruskin said of the chalet that it "was nothing in itself" but that it possessed "beauty, that of fitness and humility." John Ruskin, *The Poetry of Architecture* (1837: reis. John Wiley & Son, 1873), 31.

4. Eugene Emmanuel Viollet-le-Duc, *Discourses on Architecture*, vol. 1 (Osgood, 1875), 21, 175–76; 23, 176.

5. John Ruskin, *The Seven Lamps of Architecture* (1849), in *The Works of John Ruskin*, ed. E. T. Cook and Alexander Wedderburn (George Allen, 1903), 60.

6. Jack London, "The House Beautiful" (1906), in *Revolution and Other Essays* (Macmillan, 1910), (unpaginated), accessed May 20, 2024, https://www.marxists.org/archive/london/revolution/ch07.htm.

7. London, "House Beautiful."

8. Jack London, "What Life Means to Me" (1906), in *Revolution and Other Essays*, accessed May 20, 2024, https://www.bartleby.com/lit-hub/upton-sinclair/jack-london-8/./.

9. Jack London to George Sterling, May 28, 1905, in Gregory Hays and Matt Atkinson, *Jack London's Wolf House* (Valley of the Moon Natural History Association, 2010).

10. Hays and Atkinson, *London's Wolf House*, 6.

11. Coast Redwood (Sequoia sempervirens)," Forest Research and Outreach, University of California Agriculture and Natural Resources, accessed May 20, 2024, https://ucanr.edu/sites/forestry/California_forests/http___ucanrorg_sites_forestry_California_forests_Tree_Identification_/Coast_Redwood_Sequoia_sempervirens_198/.

12. John Burroughs, "Roof-Tree," in *The Writings of John Burroughs: Signs and Seasons* (Houghton Mifflin, 1904), 270.

13. Burroughs, "Roof-Tree," 270.

14. Ernest Thompson Seton, "The House that is Mine," *House and Garden* 43–44 (October 1823): 52; Ernest Thompson Seton, "The Story of Wyndygoul," *Country Life in America* 16 (September 1909): 446.

15. Herbert Maier, quoted in Linda Flint McClelland, *Presenting Nature: The Historic Landscape Design of the National Park Service*, 1916–1942 (US Department of the Interior, National Park Service, Cultural Resources, Interagency Resources Division, National Register of Historic Places, 1993), 237.

16. Herbert Maier, "Proceedings of National Park Service Conference of State Park Authorities," Washington, DC, February 25, 1935," mimeo., US Department of the Interior, National Park Service, 1935, 91, 85, quoted in McClelland, *Presenting Nature.*

Paradise Inn: Rationalist Prologue

1. Paul Sceva, *Recollections by the Old Man of the Mountain* (n.p., 1972), 140.

2. https://www.nps.gov/mora/faqs.htm.

Albert Good's Bible

1. Albert H. Good, *Park Structures and Facilities* (US Department of the Interior, National Park Service and Quinn & Boden, 1935), 21.

2. Good, *Park Structures and Facilities*, 8.

3. Good, *Park Structures and Facilities*, 8.

4. Karen Kingsley, "Corps Craftsmanship," *64 Parishes*, Summer 2015, accessed May 20, 2024, https://64parishes.org/corps-craftsmanship Good's book,... became the bible of park structures."

Stephen Mather and the Log Cabin

1. Joyce Zaitlin, *Gilbert Stanley Underwood, His Rustic, Art Deco, and Federal Architecture* (Simon/Pangloss Press, 1989), 56.

2. Kiki Leigh Rydell and Mary Shivers Culpin, *Managing the "Matchless Wonders": A History of Administrative Development in Yellowstone National Park* (National Park Service, Yellowstone Center for Resources, 2006), 99; Haines, *The Yellowstone Story-A History of Our First National Park*, vol. 2, 303–304.

3. Rydell and Culpin, *Managing*, 99. The authors explain, "Educational promotion wasn't much of a success at first. No one in Washington took any interest in it except Mr. Mather, spasmodically; Congressmen smiled over it; and with a very few exceptions the concessionaires opposed it." [10]; Haines, *History*, vol. 2, 303–304.

4. "How a Conference in Berkeley in 1915 Helped Create the National Park Service," *100 Years: Panama-Pacific International Exposition*, March 23, 2015, accessed May 20, 2024, https://ppie100.org/how-a-conference-in-berkeley-in-1915-helped-create-the-national-park-service.

5. Diana Baily, ed., Abraham Lincoln: A Living Legacy, US Department of the Interior. National Park Service. 2008.

6. Rydell and Culpin, *Managing*, 86.

7. Rydell and Culpin, *Managing*, 86–87.

8. Rydell and Culpin, *Managing*, 102.

9. Annual Reports for Yellowstone National Park, 1920–1923, US Department of the Interior, National Park Service, accessed May 20, 2024, http://npshistory.com/publications/yell/annual reports_1920-1923.pdf].

10. Albert H. Good, *Park and Recreation Structures* (Washington, DC: Government Printing Office, 1938), 85.

Park Service Pragmatists: Gilbert Underwood, Daniel Hull Fred Willson

1. John Muir, *My First Summer in the Sierra* (1911), in *The Complete Works of John Muir* (Madison & Adams Press, 2019), 755.

2. Horace Albright to Director National Park Service, July 7, 1926, Yellowstone Archives.

3. Horace M. Albright to D. H. Hull, August 8, 1924, held in the Yellowstone National Park Archives.

4. Horace Albright, quoted in Kiki Leigh Rydell and Mary Shivers Culpin, *Managing the "Matchless Wonders": A History of Administrative Development in Yellowstone National Park*, National Park Service, Yellowstone Center for Resources, Yellowstone, WY, 2006.

5. Rydell and Culpin, *Managing*, 90–91.

6. Superintendent's Report for 1926, US Department of the Interior, National Park Service.

7. Horace Albright to Director, National Park Service, July 11, 1925, Yellowstone National Park Archives. [The authorship of the new camps, particularly this one, is complex. Hull and Albright are the designers, but Willson's name is on the contract drawings. Albright said, "In general I do not think the landscape engineer (Hull) should not do more than make rough sketches," and that is perhaps what happened here—that Willson executed schematic designs by Hull and Underwood.]

8. Geyser Hall is often attributed to Underwood, but the drawings identify Willson as the architect. Based on the forms alone, Geyser Hall is definitely in the vocabulary of Underwood and not that of Willson, exemplified by the Lake Lodge.

Park Service Romantics: Thomas Vint and Ernest Davidson

1. Ethan Carr, *Wilderness by Design: Landscape Architecture and the National Parks* (University of Nebraska Press, 1999), 177–79; "Presenting Nature, The Historic Landscape Design of the National Park Service," part III, "A Policy and Process For Design, 1916–1927."

2. "South Rim Ranger Operations Building, Grand Canyon National Park," Historic Structure Report, US Department of the Interior, National Park Service, 2000. Park Superintendent Tomlinson called the Administration Building. "one of the finest every constructed with national park funds." Accessed May 20, 2024, https://www.nps.gov/places/longmire-historic-tour-administration-building-exhibit panel.htm#:~:text=Park%20Superintendent%20Tomlinson%20called%20the,new%20facility%20opened%20in%20Ashford.

3. Albert H. Good, *Park and Recreation Structures* (Washington, DC: Government Printing Office, 1938), 8.

4. Carr, *Wilderness by Design*, 132–32.

5. Good, *Recreation Structures*, 80.

6. Good, *Recreation Structures*, 4.

7. Ethan Carr, *Wilderness by Design*, 132–32.

8. Erwin N. Thompson, "Mount Rainier National Park," Historic Resource Study, National Park Service, Denver Service Center, 1981, 168, quoting from Ernest Davidson, White River Inspection Trip, October 28–31, Park Development, Construction Programs, Archives, Mount Rainier National Park, Seattle, WA.

9. William Tweed, Laura Soulliere and Henry Law, "Rustic Architecture, 1916–1942, Part III, The Formative Decade, 1918–1927," National Park Service, Western Regional Office Division of Cultural Resource Management, February, 1977, unpaginated, accessed May 20, 2024, https://www.nps.gov/parkhistory/online_books/rusticarch/part3.htm.

10. Good, *Recreation Structures*, 198.

Herbert Maier and the Roofless Museum

1. Ralph H. Lewis, "Museum Curatorship in the National Park Service, 1904–1982," US Department of the Interior, National Park Service, Curatorial Services Division, 1993, 34.

2. Frederick Jackson Turner, *The Frontier in American History* (1893: reis. Henry Holt, 1921), 205.

3. Alfred Kazin, *On Native Grounds* (1942: reis. Doubleday, 1956), 381.

4. Kazin, *Native Grounds*.

5. Herbert Maier, "Proceedings of National Park Service Conference of State Park Authorities, Washington, DC, February 25, 1935," mimeo., US Department of the Interior, National Park Service, 1935, 85, quoted in Linda Flint McClelland, *Presenting Nature: The Historic Landscape Design of the National Park Service, 1916–1942* (US Department of the Interior, National Park Service, Cultural Resources, Interagency Resources Division, National Register of Historic Places, 1993), 237.

6. Herbert Maier and Albert H. Good, "Structures in State Parks, An Apologia," *Civic Annual* (journal the American Planning and Civic Association), 1935, 171–75.

7. Maier, "Proceedings of National Park Service Conference," 85, quoted in McClelland, *Presenting Nature*.

8. Maier and Good, "Structures in State Parks," 193.

9. Maier, "Proceedings of National Park Service Conference," 85.

10. Ethan Carr, *Wilderness by Design: Landscape Architecture and the National Parks* (University of Nebraska Press, 1999), 144.

11. Albert H. Good, Park Structures and Facilities (US Department of the Interior, National Park Service and Quinn & Boden, 1935), 21.

12. Maier, "Proceedings of National Park Service Conference of State Park Authorities, 83.

13. Herbert Maier, "Inspector's Photographic Handbook," n.d. [1935], Photographs of Engineering Activities, Entry 127, RG 79, National Archives, Washington, DC.

14. Maier, "Inspector's Photographic Handbook."

15. Memo to Park Naturalist C. Max Bauer, October 25, 1939, Yellowstone National Park Archive, Yellowstone, WY (National Archives affiliate).

16. Maier, "Inspector's Photographic Handbook."

17. Maier, "Inspector's Photographic Handbook."

18. George Nason, "Architecture and Its Relationship to the Design of Parks," *1940 Yearbook, Park and Recreation Progress* (Government Printing Office, 1940), 57.

Conclusion

1. Mark Lamster, *The Man in the Glass House: Philip Johnson, Architect of the Modern Century* (Little, Brown, 2018), 27.

2. Susan Hiller, *The Myth of Primitivism* (New York: Routledge, 2006), 3.

3. Renato Rosaldo, "Imperialist Nostalgia," *Representations* 26, special issue, *Memory and Counter-Memory* (Spring 1989): 107–22.

4. William Gilpin, "Observations Relative Chiefly to Picturesque Beauty, Made in the Year 1772: On Several Parts of England; Particularly the Mountains, and Lakes of Cumberland, and Westmoreland," part 2 (R. Blamire, 1786),188; and Georg Simmel, "The Ruin" (1911), *Hudson Review* 11, no. 3 (Autumn 1958): 379.

5. Frederick Jackson Turner, *The Frontier in American History* (1893: reis. Henry Holt, 1921), 205.

6. "Andrea Zittel is Drawn to the Frontier Mentality," accessed May 20, 2024, https://www.facebook.com/watch/?ref=search&v=599515655074366&external_log_id=cf6d5e8d-280c-43b1-90f5-0c87b26ad843&q=Andrea%20Zittel%20is%20drawn%20to%20the%20Frantier.

SELECTED BIBLIOGRAPHY

General

Anderson, Nancy. *Thomas Moran.* Yale, 1977.

Barnes, Christine. *Great Lodges of the National Parks.* W. W. West, 2022.

Carr, Ethan. *Wilderness by Design: Landscape Architecture and the National Park Service.* University of Nebraska Press, 1998.

Clark, Alexandra. *Colorado's Historic Hotels.* The History Press, 2011.

Gilpin, William. "Observations, relative chiefly to picturesque beauty, made in the year 1772: on several parts of England." R. Blamire, 1786.

Kaiser, Harvey. *Landmarks in the Landscape: Historic Architecture in the National Parks of the West.* Chronicle Books,1997.

Kazin, Alfred. *On Native Grounds.* Doubleday, [1942]1956.

Limerick, Patricia Nelson. *The Legacy of Conquest: The Unbroken Past of the American West.* Norton,1987.

Limerick, Jeffrey, Nancy Ferguson and Richard Oliver. *America's Grand Resort Hotels.* Pantheon Books, 1979.

Mackintosh, Barry. *Interpretation In The National Park Service: A Historical Perspective.* National Park Service, Department of the Interior, 1986.

Nash, Roderick Frazier. *Wilderness and the American Mind.* Yale University Press, 1967.

Novak, Barbara. *Nature and Culture: American Landscape and Painting*, 1825-1875. Oxford University Press, 2007.

Runte, Alfred. *National Parks: The American Experience.* University of Nebraska Press, 1987.

Runte, Alfred. *Trains of Discovery: Railroads and the Legacy of Our National Parks.* 5th ed. Roberts Rinehart Publishers, 2011.

Rushing, W. Jackson. *Native American Art and the New York Avant Garde.* University of Texas, 1995.

Simmel, Georg. "The Ruin." *The Hudson Review* 11 no. 3 (Autumn, [1911] 1958): 380.

White, Richard. *Railroaded: The Transcontinentals and the Making of Modern America.* W. W. Norton & Company, 2011.

Williams, Michael. *Americans and Their Forests.* Cambridge University Press, 1989.

Zaitlin, Joyce. *Gilbert Stanley Underwood.* Panglos, 1989.

The Malaise of the Overcivilized

Berlin, Isiah. *The Roots of Romanticism.* Princeton University Press, 2001.

Barrus, Clara. *The Life and Letters of John Burroughs.* Houghton Mifflin Company, 1925.

Burroughs, John. *Talks: His Reminiscences and Comments.* Houghton Mifflin, 1922.

Cushing, Frank. *My Adventures In Zuñi.* Legare Street Press, 2022.

Ellison, George and Janet McCue. *Back of Beyond: A Horace Kephart Biography.* Great Smoky Mountains Association, 2019.

Kephart, Horace. *Camping and Woodcraft.* MacMillan, 1917.

Lears, T. J. Jackson. *No Place of Grace.* Pantheon, 1981.

National Register of Historic Places Nomination Form, Charles M. Russell House and Studio, United States Department of the Interior: National Park Service, 1973.

Wallis, Michael. *Oil Man: The Story Of Frank Phillips & The Birth Of Phillips Petroleum.* St. Martin's Griffin,1995.

Wallis, Michael. *Beyond the Hills: The Journey of Waite Phillips.* Oklahoma Heritage Association,1995.

English Origins

Addison, Joseph. *The Tatler. in The Works of Joseph Addison Complete in Three Volumes.* W. Durell & Company, 1811.

Addison, Joseph. *The Spectator*, in *The Spectator: Complete in One Volume.* A. Wilson, 1813.

Bernard, J. H. ed., *Kant's Critique of Judgement.* Outlook, [1790} 2020.

Burke, Edmund. *A Philosophical Enquiry into the Origin of Our Ideas of the Sublime and Beautiful.* Harper & Brothers, [1757] 1844.

Campbell, Gordon. *The Hermit in the Garden: From Imperial Rome to Ornamental Gnome.* Oxford University Press, 2014.

Chambers, William. "The Origins of Buildings and Orders." in *A Treatise on Civil Architecture.* J. Haberkorn, 1759.

"An Epistolary Description of the Late Mr. Pope's House and Gardens at Twickenham." *The Newcastle General Magazine*, or *Monthly Intelligencer*, January 1, 1748.

Felus, Kate. *The Secret Life of the Georgian Garden.* I. B. Taurus, 2016.

Hall, James. *Essay on the Origin History and Principles of Gothic Architecture.* Forgotten Books, [1813] 2013.

Hussey, Christopher. *The Picturesque.* Archon, [1927]1967.

Hussey, Christopher. "Endsleigh Cottage." *Country Life.* CXXX (1961): 246-296.

Knight, Richard Payne. quoted in John Macarthur, *The Picturesque: Architecture, Disgust and other Irregularities.* Routledge, 2007.

Marschner, Joanna. *Queen Caroline: Cultural Politics at the Early Eighteenth Century Court.* Yale University Press, 2014.

Newman, Mark. *The Wonder of the North: Fountains Abbey and Studley Royal.* Boydell Press, 2015.

Price, Uvedale. *An Essay on the Picturesque, as compared with the Sublime and the Beautiful.* Robson, 1796.

Stukeley, William. "The Creation, Music of the Spheres." quoted in David Boyd Haycock, William Stukeley: Science, Religion and Archeology in Eighteenth-Century England. Boydell, 2002.

Shenstone, William. *Men and Manners.* Bradford and Conrad, 1804.

The Swiss Cottage. "Irish Heritage." Accessed May 8, 2024, https://heritageireland.ie/places-to-visit/the-swiss-cottage/

Thacker, Christopher. *The Wildness Pleases*. Croom Healm,1983.

Warburton, William. *Pope's Collected Essays: The Works of Alexander Pope esq: in Nine Volumes Complete*. Knapton, 1752.

Woodbridge, Kenneth. *The Stourhead Landscape*. National Trust, [1982] (2001).

The Rustic in America: Downing, Vaux and Olmsted

Beveridge, Charles E. and David Schuyler, eds. *The Papers of Frederick Law Olmsted: Creating Central Park*, 1857-1861 Vol III. John Hopkins, 1983.

Colley, David. *Prospect Park: Olmsted and Vaux's Brooklyn Masterpiece*. Princeton Architectural Press, 2013.

Downing, Andrew Jackson. *A Treatise on the Theory and Practice of Landscape Gardening*. Cambridge, [1841] 2018.

Eleventh Annual Report of the Board of Commissioners of the Central Park for the Year Ending December 31, 1867. Evening Post Steam Press 1868. See also: Accessed May 8, 2024, https://www.centralparknyc.org/articles/central-park-rustic -architecture

Kowky, Francis. *Country, Park, City: The Architecture of Calvert Vaux*. Oxford, 1998.

Major, Judith K. *To Live in the New World: A. J. Downing and American Landscape Gardening*. MIT, 1997.

Olmsted, Vaux, & Company, Report of the Landscape Architects. Sixth Annual Report of the Commissioners of Prospect Park. Brooklyn Park Commissioners, Annual Reports of the Brooklyn Park Commissioners, Brooklyn:1861-1873.

Olmsted, Vaux, & Company. 1870, January Brooklyn Park Commission. Tenth Annual Report. Eagle Print, 1870.

Schlett, James. *A Not Too Greatly Changed Eden: The Story of the Philosophers' Camp in the Adirondacks*. Cornell University Press, 2016.

Schuyler, David and Jane Turner Censer, eds. *Frederick Law Olmsted. The Papers of Frederick Law Olmsted: The years of Olmsted, Vaux & Company,* 1865-1874 Vol VI. John Hopkins, 1977.

The Adirondacks: William Durant, Grosvenor Atterbury, William Wicks and Augustus Shepard

"Adirondack," *New York Times*, August 9, 1864.

Applegate, Howard L. *The Story of Sagamore*. Syracuse University, 1962.

Bridger, Beverly. *Mrs. Vanderbilt's Sagamore*. Raquette Lake, N.Y.: Sagamore Institute of the Adirondacks, 2007.

Fernow, Bernhard. "Adirondack Forestry Problems." *The Forester* 6 (October 1900): 231.

Gilborn, Craig. *Adirondack Camps: Homes Away from Home,* 1850-1950. Adirondack Museum and Syracuse University Press, 2000.

Gilborn, Craig. *Durant: The Fortunes and Woodland Camps of a Family in the Adirondacks*. North Country Books, and Adirondack Museum, 1981.

Gilborn, Craig. et al., *Forever Wild: The Adirondack Experience*, Katonah Museum of Art, 1991.

Haynes, Wesley. "Sagamore Lodge," National Historic Landmark Nomination, National Park Service, 2000.

Haynes, Wesley. "Adirondack Camps National Historic Landmarks Theme Study," National Register of Historic Places, National Park Service, 2000.

Hotaling, Mary B. "W. L. Coulter, Adirondack Architect." M.S. Thesis, University of Vermont, 1995.

Jamieson, Paul F., ed., *The Adirondack Reader*. Adirondack Mountain Club, 1982.

Kirschenbaum, Howard. *The Story of Sagamore*. Sagamore Institute, 199

Kaiser, Harvey H. *Great Camps of the Adirondacks*. David R. Godine, 1982.

Kylloe, Ralph. *Rustic Style*. Henry N. Abrams, 1998.

McMartin, Barbara. The Great Forest of the Adirondacks. North Country Books, 1994.

Montgomery, Gladys. *An Elegant Wilderness: Great Camps and Grand Lodges of the Adirondacks*. Acanthus, 2011.

National Historic Landmark Nomination, Camp Pine Knot, United States Department of the Interior, National Park Service, 2004.

National Historic Landmark Nomination, Camp Uncas, United States Department of the Interior, National Park Service, 2008.

National Historic Landmark Nomination, Sagamore Lodge, United States Department of the Interior.

O'Leary, Ann Stillman. *Adirondack Style*. Clarkson Potter, 1998.

Pinchot, Gifford. *The Adirondack Spruce*. The Critic Co., 1898.

Pennoyer, Peter and Anne Walker. *The Architecture of Grosvenor Atterbury*. W. W. Norton & Co., 2009.

Schneider, Paul. *The Adirondacks: A History of America's First Wilderness*. Henry Holt, 1997.

Shepard, Augustus. *Camps in the Woods*. ed. R. W. Sexton. Architectural Book Publishing Co., 1931.

Terrie, Philip G. *Contested Terrain: A New History of Nature and People in the Adirondacks*. Syracuse University Press Adirondack Museum, 1997.

A Tribute to George & Jennie Goodsell. "Goodsell Musuem. Accessed May 8, 2024, https://www.webbhistory.org/Tribute_to_George_&_Jennie_Goodsell.htm

Wicks, William S. *Log Cabins and Cottages: How to Build and Furnish Them*. Forest And Stream Publishing Co., 1908.

Kirtland Cutter and the Chalet

Cieraad, Irene. "Bringing Nostalgia Home: Switzerland and the Swiss Chalet." *Architecture and Culture* 6, no. 2, (May 18, 2018): 265.

Dana, William. *The Swiss Chalet Book*. Comstock, 1913.

Gladbach, E. *Der Schweizer Holzstil in seinen cantonalen und constructiven Verschiedenheiten vergleichend dargestellt mit Holzbauten Deutschlands*. Köhler, 1868.

Mathews, Henry. *Kirtland Cutter: Architect in the Land of Promise*. University of Washington, 1998.

Rousseau, Jean-Jacques. *Julie or the New Heloise*. Marc-Michel Rey, 1761.

Ruskin, John. The Poetry of Architecture: or, The Architecture of the Nations of Europe. G. Allen, [1837] 1892.

Steelman, Louis. "The Swiss Chalet Type for America." *House and Garden* 20, (1911): 289.

Viollet-le-Duc, Eugène Emmanuel. *The Habitations of Man in All Ages*. Translated by B. Bucknall. Sampson Low Marston Searle & Rivington, 1876.

Railroads and National Parks

Haines, Aubrey L. *The Yellowstone Story-A History of Our First National Park. Vols. I and 2.* University Press of Colorado, 1996.

Langford, N. P. *Report of the Superintendent of the Yellowstone National Park for the year 1872*. Government Printing Office Office, 1873.

Lubetkin, M. John. *Jay Cooke's Gamble-The Northern Pacific Railroad, the Sioux and the Panic of 1873*. University of Oklahoma Press, 2006.

Mickelson, Sig. *The Northern Pacific Railroad and the Selling of the West*. Center for Western Studies, 1993.

Olson, Sherry. *The Depletion Myth: A History of Railroad Use of Timber*. Harvard, 1971.

Pinchot, Gifford and R. Kellogg. "The Timber Supply Of The United States." US Department of Agriculture. Forest Service Circular 66, Government Printing Office, 1909.

Winks, Robin W. *Frederick Billings: A Life*. Oxford University Press, 1991.

Yellowstone National Park

Annual Report of The Chief of Engineers United States Army to the Secretary of War for the Year 1892 in Four Parts and Atla; Appendixes to the report of the Chief of Engineers, United States Army.

Barringer, Mark. *Selling Yellowstone: Capitalism and the Construction of Nature*. University Press of Kansas, 2002.

Bartlett, Richard. *Yellowstone: A Wilderness Besieged*. University of Arizona Press, 1985.

Battle, D. G. and E. N. Thompson. *Fort Yellowstone Historic Structure Report*, US Dept. of the Interior, National Park Service. 1972.

Blust, Jr., Dick. "The President Arthur Expedition: The Fishing Trip That Helped Save Yellowstone." WyoHistory.org. April 29, 2019, Accessed May 8, 2024, https://www.wyohistory.org/encyclopedia /president -arthur expedition-fishing-trip-helped-xford University Press, 2007.

Culpin, Mary Shivers, *A History of Concession Development in Yellowstone National Park, 1872–1966.* National Park Service, Yellowstone Center for Resources Yellowstone National Park, Wyoming YCR-CR-2003-01, 2003.

Development in Yellowstone National Park, 1872–1966. National Park Service, Yellowstone Center for Resources, Yellowstone National Park, Wyoming YCR-CR-2003-01, 2003.

Hedren, Paul L. *After Custer: Loss and Transformation in Sioux Country*. University of Oklahoma, 2012.

"The History of the Construction of the Road System in Yellowstone National Park, 1872-1966." National Park Service, Accessed May 8, 2024. http://npshistory.com/publications/yell/hrs-roads/chap12.htm

Langford, Nathaniel. *Diary of the Washburn Expedition to the Yellowstone and Firehole Rivers in the Year 1870.* Published by the author, 1905.

Rydell, Kiki Leigh and Mary Shivers Culpin. Managing The "Matchless Wonders" A History of Administrative Development In Yellowstone National Park, 1872-1965. National Park Service, Yellowstone Center for Resources, 2006; See Appendix A Government-Built Buildings Constructed in Yellowstone National Park 1879–1973.

Sargent, Charles. *Report on the Forests of North America exclusive of Mexico.* US Government Printing Office, 1884.

Sellars, Richard West. "The Great Yellowstone Campfire Mystery." March 1992 *Courier* 37, no. 3 (March, 1992): 12-13.

United States Congressional Serial Set, Volume 2162, P. H. Conger Superintendent Department of the Interior Yellowstone National Park Office Superintendent Mammoth Hot Springs Wyoming November 3 1883, 20.

US Secretary of the Interior, Annual Report of the Department of the Interior, Government Printing Office, 1881.

Warhank, Josef. "Fort Keogh: Cutting Edge of a Culture." 1983 Thesis, California State University, Long Beach.

Williams, Michael. A*mericans and their Forests: A Historical Geography*. Cambridge University Press, 1989.

Joseph Sharp, William Cody and the Log Cabin

Boehme, Sarah. *Absarokee Hut: The Joseph Henry Sharp Cabin.* Cody: Buffalo Bill Historical Center, 1992.

Bonner, Robert. *William F. Cody's Wyoming Empire*. University of Oklahoma, 2016.

National Register of Historic Places Inventory-Nomination Form. Pahaska Tepee, United States Department of the Interior: National Park Service, 1973.

Sharp, Joseph Henry. "Home Department: A Real Lesson In House Building." *The Craftsman* 10, no. 3 (June 1906): 408.

"Three Craftsman Log Houses." *The Craftsman* 11, no. 6 (March 1907): 742.

The Old Faithful Inn

Curtis, William. "At Old Faithful Inn." *Washington Evening Star*, August 23, 1909.

Empson, William. *The Seven Types of Ambiguity*. New Directions, 1947.

Frost, Nedward M. National Register of Historic Places Inventory-Nomination Form, "Old Faithful Inn," Yellowstone National Park,. US Department of the Interior, National Park Service, 1973.

"Interview with W. H. Merriman." *Gardiner Wonderland*. March 23, 1905.

"Old Faithful Inn flooring restored in Cody." *Cody Enterprise*. Feb 24, 2014.

Quinn, Ruth. *Weaver of Dreams: The Life and Architecture of Robert C. Reamer.* Gardiner, Montana: Leslie & Ruth Quinn, 2004.

Raftery, J. H. *A Miracle in Hotel Building Being: The Story of the Building of the New Canyon Hotel In Yellowstone Park.* Yellowstone Park Hotel Company, 1911.

Reinhart, Karen. "Old Faithful Inn: Centennial of a Beloved Landmark" *Yellowstone Science* 12 2 (Spring 2004): 5."A Unique Plan: Tourists Will be Housed in Log Cottage at Upper Geyser Basin." *Livingston Enterprise*, November 22. 1902.

Venturi, Robert. *Complexity and Contradiction in Modern Architecture.* Museum of Modern Art,1966.

"Yellowstone National Park, R. C Reamer. Architect," The *Western Architect* III (Oct. 1904): 4-6.

The Longs Peak Inn and the Surreal

Cole, Thomas. "Thoughts & Occurrences: The journal of Thomas Cole kept from 1834 to1848." New York State Library, quoted in Barbara Novack, *Nature and Culture: American Landscape and Painting, 1825-1875.* Oxford University Press, 2007.

Mills, Enos A. *Trees That Twist,* ed. Elizabeth M. Mills and Eryn V. Mills ed., Temporal Mechanical Press. 2017.

Mills, Enos A. "A Home of Forest Fire Logs." *Sunset,* (May, 1921): 66.

Mills, Enos A. Esther Mills and Arthur Chapman, *The Story of Longs Peak Inn.* United States: Mrs. Enos A. Mills, n.d.

Read, Herbert. *The Philosophy of Modern Art.* Fawcett, [1953] 1967.

Wheeler, Olin D. *Wonderland.* St. Paul: Northern Pacific Railway, [1895] 1906.

Sacred Groves and The Portland Forestry Building

Allen, Alice Benson. Simon Benson: Northwest Lumber King. Binford & Mort, 1976.

"Architectural Splendors of Portland Excite Outspoken Admiration." *Oregon Daily Journal,* June 01, 1905, Section Two.

Craft, Mabel. "A Sermon in Church Building." *The House Beautiful IX* no. 3 (February 1901): 132.

Dudley, William. "Forest Reservations." *Sierra Club Bulletin* I, (January, 1896): 254-257.

"Forestry Club Revels in Outings at the Fair." *Sunday Oregonian*, October 01, 1905, Part 3.

Freudenheim, Leslie. *Building With Nature: Inspiration for the Arts and Crafts Home.* Salt Lake City: Gibbs Smith, 2005.

"A Glimpse in the Forestry Palace." *Sunday Oregonian*, July 09, 1905, Part Three.

Grant, J. D. *Saving California's Redwoods.* Save the Redwoods League, 1922.

"Hallie Erminie Rives' Impressions of the Fair." *Sunday Oregonian*, September 03, 1905, Part 4.

"In the Forestry Palace." *Sunday Oregonian*, July 09, 1905.

Kirkham, Stanton "The Forest," In The Open, 1908. See Accessed May 8, 2024, https://www.quotegarden.com/trees-redwoods.html#:~:text=Their%20immense%20trunks%20might%20be,only%20the%20forest%20cathedrals%20know.

"Lewis and Clark Centennial Exposition, Forestry Building, Portland, OR" Building History, Accessed May 8, 2024, https://pcad.lib.washington.edu/building/13170/.

"Lewis and Clark Exposition: Architecturally Originality of Design a Feature of the 1905 Worlds Fair." *Builder* 12, no. 4 April, 1906.

McClue, Elizabeth. "Oregon's Parthenon is 25 years Old." *Weekly Oregonian*, June 1, 1930.

Metcalfe, Gertrude. "The Indian as Revealed in the Curtis Pictures." *Lewis and Clark Journal*, 1 no.1 Jan, 1904.

Macrae, Marion. "Noted Indian Pictures on View at the Fair: Great Ethnological and Artistic Work Undertaken by E. S. Curtis." *Sunday Oregonian*, June 18, 1905.

"Organ will Peal Tones of Forest." *Morning Oregonian*, May 19, 1905.

"The Oregon Cathedral." *Lewis & Clark Journal,* 4 No 1, July, 1905.

Phillips, Blaine. "Lewis and Clark Exposition: Architecturally Originality of Design a Feature of the 1905 Worlds Fair." *Builder*, 12 no. 4 (April 1906): unpaginated.

Schama, Simon. *Landscape and Memory.* Alfred A. Knopf, 1995.

Siegel, Phillip and Nancy ed., *American Art and Culture.* Pennsylvania State University Press, 2005. Strother, French. "Saving the Big Trees: The Need of Further National, State, and Private Protection for the Remnants of the Groves that are Being Cut." *The World's Work* 18, (June 1909): 11607-11706.

Swedenborg, Emanuel. *Arcana Coelestia*, [1758], tr. by John Whitehead at sacred-texts.com Location 10504.

"Vast Cathedral of the Forests." *Oregon Daily Journal*, July 30, 1907.

White, Laura. "A Day in the Redwoods of Lagoon Creek." *Overland Monthly and Outwest Magazine* 18, no. 105 (Sept 1881): 257-280.

White, Richard. *It's Your Misfortune and None of My Own.* University of Oklahoma Press. Kindle Edition, 1991.

Bernard Maybeck

"Bohemians Will Soon Open Their New Forest Retreat," *San Francisco Call*, May 9 1904.

Caen, Herb. "Ten Second Interview," *San Francisco Chronicle*, Jan 18, 1953.

Cardwell, Kenneth H., *Bernard Maybeck: Artisan, Architect, Artist.* Santa Barbara, CA: Peregrine Smith, 1977.

Herny, Ed, Shelley Rideout and Katie Wadell. *Berkeley Bohemia: Artists and Visionaries of the Early 20th Century.* Gibbs Smith, 2008.

"House of Hoo Hoo," *The Bulletin A Monthly Journal Devoted To Hoo Hoo.* 21 no. 225 (November 9, 1914):14.

"House of Mrs. Phoebe A Hearst In Siskiyou Co. Cal," Maybeck & White. Architects, American Country Houses Bates and Gill, 1904.

Ives, Susan. "Elite Club Blocked from Logging Giant Redwoods." High Country News. April 1, 2011.

Maybeck, Bernard. "Hillside Building," 1906 Hillside Club papers, Bancroft library, UC Berkeley.

Maybeck, Jacomena. *Maybeck: The Family View.* Berkeley: The Berkeley Architectural Heritage Association, [1980] 1991.

"The Palace of Fine Arts." Transactions of The Commonwealth Club of California San Francisco 10, no. 10 (August 1915): 373.

Raymond, Maud Wotring et. al, *The Architecture and Landscape Gardening of The Exposition.* San Francisco: Paul Elder and Company, 1915.

"Save the Redwoods League: Mission and History," Accessed May 8, 2024, https://www.savetheredwoods.org/about-us/mission-history/#:~:text=Our%20History,the%20tallest%20trees%20on%20Earth.

Todd, Frank Morton. "Introduction" in Bernard R. Maybeck Palace of Fine Arts and Lagoon Panama-Pacific International Exposition, San Francisco, P. Elder and Co., 1915.

Weiss, Philip. "Masters of the Universe Go to Camp: Inside the Bohemian Grove."

Spy Magazine, November 1989, 58-76.

Wilson, Mark. *Bernard Maybeck Architect of Elegance.* Gibbs Smith, 2011.

Woodbridge, Sally B. *Bernard Maybeck: Visionary Architect.* Abbeville Press, 1992.

Louis Hill and The Great Northern Railroad

Funes, Yessenia. "The Forgotten Land Grab That Gave Us Glacier National Park." Gizmodo, Jan. 1 2018. Accessed May 8, 2024,:// gizmodo.com/the-forgotten-land-grab-that-gave-us-glacier -national-p-1821698.

Grinnell, George. "The Rock Climbers." *Forest and Stream* 29, nos 39-40 (December 29 1887): 448.

Jensen, Derrick and George Draffan, *Railroads and Clearcuts.* Keokee,1995.

Lange, Greg. "Frederick Weyerhaeuser makes one of the largest land purchases in United States history on January 3, 1900." Accessed May 8, 2024, https://www.historylink.org/file/5241 HistoryLink.org Essay 5241, Posted 2/19/2003.

"Louis Hill Didn't care for Railroad." *Fergus County Democrat.* (Lewistown, Montana), May 28, 1912.

Malone, Michael. *James J. Hill.* University of Oklahoma, 1996.

"Men of the West Gather at Lake." *Anaconda Standard*, Aug 29, 1912.

Puter, Stephen A. Douglas and Horace Stevens. Looters of the Public Domain Portland Priniting House, 1908. Accessed May 8, 2024, https://books.google.com/books?id=3I5D0nkOTdkC&printsec=frontcover&source=gbs_ge_summary_r&cad=0#v=onepage&q&f=false

"Radical Opponent of Pinchot-Roosevelt Reclamation Project won over by Pinchot." *Star Tribune Minneapolis*, June 12, 1910.

Rinehart, Mary Roberts. Through Glacier Park: Seeing America First with Howard Eaton. Houghton Mifflin, 1916.

Robinson, Bart. *Banff Springs: The Story of a Hotel.* Summerthougt, 1998.

"Suggestion for Uncle Sam to Enter See America First Campaign." The Post Office Clerk: Organ of the United National Post Office Clerks of the United States, The Association, Volumes 11-12, (1911): 105.

Taliaferro, John. Grinnell: America's Environmental Pioneer and His Restless Drive to Save the West. Liveright, 2019.

"Who's Who and Why? J. J.'s Son." The Saturday Evening Post 185, no. 2 (July 13, 1912): 19.

Young, Biloine W. with Eileen R. McCormack, *The Dutiful Son: Louis W. Hill.* RCHS, 2000.

Glacier National Park

"The 1914 Season at Glacier National Park." *See America First* 5, no. 3 (1914): 109.

Clayton, John. "Howard Eaton's Natural Hospitality." *Billings Magic City Magazine*, Jul 21, 2017.

Di Silvestro, Roger. *Theodore Roosevelt in the Badlands: A Young Politician's Quest for Recovery in the American West.* Walker & Company, 2012.

Djuff, Ray and Chris Morrison. *A View with a Room.* Far Country Press, 2001.

"Forestry Building in Glacier National Park." *Timberman.* (February 1912): 51.

Frobese, Frederic. Frederic Frobese to Louis Hill, Jan. 1913. Minnesota Historical Society.

Hill, Louis. L. W. Hill Telegram to Robert Reamer, March 2, 1912. Minnesota Historical Society.

Hill, Louis. Louis Hill to St. Paul Book & Stationary Co. date unknown. Minnesota Historical Society.

Hogeland, A. H. A. H. Hogeland to H. H. Parkhouse, March 14, 1912. Minnesota Historical Society.

"MacFarlane, Robert. *Mountains of the Mind.* New York: Vintage, 2003.

Many Glacier's 100th Birthday." The Inside Trail, Voice of the Glacier Park Foundation XIX no. 2. (Summer 2015): 1.

"Montana." *Timberman*, October, 1913.

National Register of Historic Places Inventory-Nomination Form. Historic Great Northern Railway Buildings and/or Many Glacier Hotel, Sperry and Granite Park Chalets, and the Two Medicine Store. Department of the Interior National Park Service, 1976.

"Northwest Honors Hill." *New York Sun*, September 17, 1912.

"Pacific Coast Hotelmen view Indian Equipped Hostelery." Aberdeen Herald, Nov 11, 1912.

Rinehart, Mary Roberts. *Through Glacier Park: Seeing America First with Howard Eaton with Howard Eaton.* Boston: Houghton Mifflin, 1916.

"Sacred Tepee Is Revered." *Pickens Sentinel* (Pickens, S.C.), May 7, 1914.

White, Richard. *The Republic for Which It Stands: The United States during Reconstruction.* New York: Oxford, 2017.

Yenne, Bill. Glacier National Park. Mt. Pleasant SC: Arcadia, 2006.

Kirtland Cutter in Montana

Renewable Technologies, Incorporated, "Cultural Landscape Report: Lake McDonald Lodge Historic District," Glacier National Park." Department of the Interior. National Park Service, 2006.

Logan, William. Report of the Superintendent of the Glacier National Park to the Secretary of the Interior. Washington DC: Government Printing Office,1911.

Bartos, Jeffrey Michael. "The Blight of the Federation: James McParland, The Pinkerton National Detective Agency and the Western Federation of Miners, 1892-1907."

Thesis Master of Arts in History, Montana State University. 2013.

Finn, Janet L. *Two Mining History: A Political Chronology.* University of California Press, 1998.

Hufstetler, Mark. "Renewable Technologies Cultural Landscape Report: Lake Mcdonald Lodge Historic District, Glacier National Park,

Dept. of the Interior, National Park Service, 2006. National Register of Historic Places Inventory/Nomination: Kootenai Lodge Historic District / Kelley-Evans "Camp." National Park Service, 1982.

Geology and Ruins

Doane, Gustavus. "The Report of Lieutenant Gustavus C. Doane upon the so called Yellowstone Expedition of 1870," Executive Documents The Senate of the United States for the Third Session of the Forty First Congress 1870-71, Volume 265. Government Printing Office, 1871.

Horan, James D. *Timothy O'Sullivan, America's Forgotten Photographer.* Doubleday & Company, 1966.

King, Clarence. *Mountaineering in the Sierra Nevada.* C. Scribner's Sons, 1902.

Langford, Nathaniel. *Diary of the Washburn Expedition to the Yellowstone and Firehole Rivers.* self-published, 1905.

Maximilian of Wied, Prince Alexander Philipp and Marsha V. Gallagher, *Travels in North America, 1832–1834: A Concise Edition of the Journals of Prince Maximilian of Wied,* 2017. Kindle.

Muir, John. "The Grand Cañon of the Colorado" [1902] 1893 in *The Complete works of John Muir.* Accessed May 8, 2024, https://read.amazon.com/?asin=B07QXZP382&ref_=kwl_kr_iv_rec_1

Muir, John. "The Treasures of the Yosemite." 1628 in *The Complete works of John Muir.* Accessed May 8, 2024, https://read.amazon.com /?asin=B07QXZP382&ref _=kwl_kr_iv_rec_1

Monson, Frederick. "Pueblos of the Painted Desert: The Hopi Build Their Dwellings on the Cliffs." *The Craftsman* 12 no. 1 (April 11907): 6.

Powell, John Wesley. *Canyons of the Colorado.* Library of Alexandria, [1891] 2020.

Rose, Ethel. "New Hopi Architecture on the Old Mesa Land." *The Craftsman* 30, no.4 (July 1916): 374.

The Santa Fe Railroad

Borneman, Walter. *Iron Horses.* Little Brown and Company. 2010.

Fried, Stephen. *Appetite for America: How Visionary Businessman Fred Harvey Built a Railroad Hospitality Empire That Civilized the Wild West.* New York: Banham Books, 2010.

James, George. "Aboriginal American Homes." *The Craftsman* 8, no. 5 (August 1905): 640-49.

James, George. *Through Ramona's Country.* Little, Brown and Co., 1909.

Lummis, Charles. "A Week of Wonders." *Out West* 16 (January 1902): 24.

National Register of Historic Places Multiple Property Documentation Form "Logging Railroad Resources of the Coconino and Kaibab National Forests, Arizona "United States Department of the Interior, National Park Service,1995.

Zega, Michael E. "Advertising the Southwest." *Journal of the Southwest* Vol. 43, No. 3 (Autumn, 2001): 281.

Mary Colter and Cultural Colonialism

Anderson, H. Allen. *The Chief: Ernest Thompson Seton and the Changing West.* Texas A&M University Press, 1986.

Berke, Arnold. *Mary Colter: Architect of the Southwest.* Princeton Architectural Press, 2002.

Brown, Michael F. "Who Owns Native Culture?" *New York Times,* Sept. 14, 2003.

Colter, Mary, Janet Balsom, and Grand Canyon Association. *Manual for Drivers and Guides: Descriptive of the Indian Watchtower at Desert View and Its Relation, Architecturally, to the Prehistoric Ruins of the Southwest.* Grand Canyon. Arizona: Grand Canyon Association, 2015.

Grattan, Virginia. Mary Colter: Builder Upon The Red Earth. Northland Press, 1980.

Hiller, Susan. *The Myth of Primitivism.* Routledge, 1991.

James, George Wharton. *Arizona, the Wonderland: The History of Its Ancient Cliff and Cave Dwellings.* The Page Company, 1917.

Kabotie, Fred. F*red Kabotie, Hopi Indian Artist.* Museum of Northern Arizona.1977.

Page and Turnbull, Inc., Historic Structure Report, Lookout Studio, Grand Canyon National Park. United States Department of the Interior, National Park Service 2009.

Rosaldo, Renato. "Imperialist Nostalgia." *Representations,* No. 26, Special Issue: Memory and Counter-Memory (University of California Press), Spring, 1989: 107-122.

Seton, Ernest Thompson. "Spirit of the Woods." The *Century Magazine* 103 December 1921.

Shaw, Fred. *False Architect: The Mary Colter Hoax.* Fred Shaw, 2018. Kindle Edition.

Simpson, W. H. and Fred Harvey. *El Tovar: A New Hotel Grand Canyon of Arizona.* Fred Harvey Co., 1905.

The University of Arizona, *Historic Structures Report, Hermit's Rest,* Grand Canyon National Park, US Dept. of the Interior, National Park Service, 2007.

Witt, David. *Ernest Thompson Seton, The Life and Legacy of an Artist and Conservationist.* Gibbs Smith, 2010.

Rationalists

Burroughs, John. "Roof-Tree" in *The Writings of John Burroughs: Signs and Seasons.* Houghton Mifflin Company, 1904.

London, Jack. "The House Beautiful" in *Revolution and other Essays.* London: Macmillan, 1906. Accessed May 8, 2024, https://www.marxists.org/archive/london/revolution/ch07.htm.

London, Jack. "What Life Means to Me" in *Revolution and other Essays* Macmillan, 1906, Unpaginated. Accessed May 8, 2024, https://www.bartleby.com/lit-hub/upton-sinclair/jack-london-8.

London, Jack, Jack London to George Sterling. May 28, 1905, in Gregory Hays and Matt Atkinson, *Jack London's Wolf House* Valley of the Moon Natural History Association.

Ruskin, John. *The Works of John Ruskin* E. T. Cook and Alexander Wedderburn ed., London: George Allen, 1903 *The Seven Lamps Of Architecture.*

Viollet-le-Duc, Eugene Emmanuel. *Discourses on Architecture Vol. 1.* Boston: Osgood, 1875.

Seton, Ernest Thompson. "The House that is Mine." *House and Garden* 43-44 (October 1923): 62.

Seton, Ernest Thompson. "The Story of Wyndygoul," *Country Life in America* 16, no. 5 (Sept 1909) 505.

The Paradise Inn

Kirk, Ruth. *Sunrise to Paradise: The Story if Mount Rainier National Park.* Seatle: University of Washington, 1999.

Sceva, Paul. Recollections by The Old Man of the Mountain. no publisher, 1972.

Snow, David E. *Historic Structure Report: Paradise Inn.* Mount Rainier National Park. Washington, Denver Service Center; National Park Service, 1976.

AHBL Civil Structure Engineers, 1996 Structural Assessment Report: The Paradise Inn. Archives Mt. Rainier National Park, 1996.

Albert Good, Stephen Mather and the Log Cabin

Baily, Diana ed. *Abraham Lincoln: A Living Legacy,* United States Department of the Interior. National Park Service. 2008.

"How A Conference in Berkeley in 1915 Helped Create the National Park Service." 100 Years: Panama-Pacific International Exposition. March 23, 2015 Accessed May 8, 2024, https://ppie100.org/how-a-conference-in-berkeley-in-1915-helped-create-the-national-park-service.

National Park Service. *Park Structures and Facilities,* United States Department of the Interior. National Park Service, Quinn & Boden Company, 1935.

Gilbert Underwood, Daniel Hull and Fred Willson

Albright, Horace, Horace Albright to Director National Park Service, July 7, 1926. Yellowstone Archives.

Albright, Horace, Horace Albright to D. H. Hull, August 8, 1924. Yellowstone Archives.

Albright, Horace. *Annual Report of the Director of the National Park Service to the Secretary of the Interior for 1926.* Government Printing Office, 1926.

Harrison, Laura Soullière." *Theme Study: Grand Canyon Lodge." Architecture in the Parks: A National Historic Landmark.* National Park Service.

Hausen, Jodi. "Fred Willson: A Modest Man who left a Big Mark." *Bozeman Daily Chronicle.* April 17, 2011.

Historic Structure Preservation Guide for the Bryce Canyon Lodge, Bryce Canyon National Park. National Park service, Denver, 1991.

Johns, J. S. "Discovery and Invention in the Yosemite. The Role of Railroads in Protecting, Promoting, and Selling Yellowstone and Yosemite National Parks." MA Thesis, University of Virginia. 1996.

Muir, John. *My First Summer in the Sierra.* Houghton Mifflin, 1911.

Tweed, William C. (May 5, 1978). "National Register of Historic Places Inventory-Nomination: Giant Forest Lodge Historic District, Camp Sierra." Sequoia National Park. National Park Service.

Thomas Vint and Ernest Davidson

Davidson, Ernest A., Landscape Work in Connection with Development of the Yakima Park Area including approach Highway within Mt. Rainier National Park a report to Thomas C. Vint, Chief Landscape Architect, no date or pagination, circa fall 1930. Archives, Mount Rainier National Park.

Historic Structure Report. South Rim Ranger Operations Building Grand Canyon National Park 2000. Accessed May 8, 2024, https://www.nps.gov/places/longmire-historic-tour-administration-building-exhibit panel.htm#:~:text=Park%20Superintendent%20Tomlinson%20called%20the,new%20facility%20opened%20in%20Ashford.

Thompson, Erwin N. *Historic Resource Study: Mount Rainier National Park* Denver: National Park Service, Denver Service Center, 1981, 168, quoting from Davidson, White River Inspection Trip, October 28-31, Park Development, Construction Programs, Archives, Mount Rainier National Park.

Tweed, William, Laura Soulliere and Henry Law, *Rustic Architecture: 1916–1942 III. The Formative Decade: 1918- 1927.* National Park Service Western Regional Office Division of Cultural Resource Management February, 1977 unpaginated, Accessed May 8, 2024, https://www.nps.gov/parkhistory/online_books/rusticarch/part3.htm

"Presenting Nature, The Historic Landscape Design of the National Park Service: A Policy And Process For Design," 1916 to 1927.

Herbert Maier

Hall, Ansel. "The Early Days in Yosemite." *California Historical Society Quarterly V* (Jan. 1923): 271-85.

Historic Structure Report, Yavapai Observation Station, Grand Canyon National Park. United States Department of the Interior, National Park Service. 2002.

Maier, Herbert, "Proceedings of National Park Service "Presenting" Conference of State Park Authorities, Washington, D.C., February 25, 1935." National Park Service, 1935, mimeo, quoted in Linda Flint McClelland, *Presenting Nature: The Historic Landscape Design of the National Park Service National Park Service 1993.*

Maier, Herbert and Albert H. Good, "Structures in State Parks: An Apologia." *American Planning and Civic Annual,* Harlean James, ed. American Planning and Civic Association,1935.

Maier, Herbert. "Inspector's Photographic Handbook," n.d. [1935], Photographs of Engineering Activities, Entry 127, RG 79, National Archives, Washington, DC.

Nason, George, "Architecture and its Relationship to the Design of Parks," *1940 Yearbook, Park and Recreaction Progress.* Government Printing Office, 1940.

Drawing Sources

Ramble Shelter Central Park
City of New York Municipal Archives, Department of Parks Collection, Central Park Summerhouse,1866 DPR-1004.

Uncas Lodge
https://my.matterport.com/show/?m=FbjYxesjw2u

Sagamore Lodge-
Adirondack Experience Collections Database MS 84-11 Karen Lux measured drawings of Sagamore main lodge, 1980.Sagamore Folio. Sagamore Institute of the Adirondacks, Drawings by Crawford and Sterns Architects.

Sagamore Casino-Adirondacks
Sagamore Folio. Sagamore Institute of the Adirondacks, Drawings by Crawford and Sterns Architects

Uncas Dining-Adirondacks
Adirondack Experience Collections Database, Camp Uncas materials19011966, Control Number 12065, Call Number MS 09-329.

Camp for Charles Huttig-Adirondacks
Adirondack Experience Collections Database, Augustus D. Shepard Architectural Drawing Collection.

Idaho Pavilion-Columbian Exposition
Joel E. Ferris Research Archives, Cheney Cowles Center of the Northwest Museum of Arts & Culture, Cutter & Malmgren Records. Item I84-207.275.

North Point-Adirondacks
Eastern Washington State Historical Society / Northwest Museum of Arts and Culture, Ferris Research Library and Archives.
Cutter & Malmgren Records. Item I84-207.159.

Old Faithful Inn-Yellowstone
Yellowstone National Park Archives. Collection of Maps and Drawings Series 1 Military Era Maps and Drawings sub series 01.04- folder 010.

Montana Historical Society. F. Jay Haynes Collection MC86 Folders16-18.

National Park Service Denver Service Center: Restoration Drawings, A&E Architects Missoula Montana: James McDonald Senior Preservation Architect.

Canyon Hotel-Yellowstone
Yellowstone National Park Archives. Collection of Maps and Drawings. Series 1 Military Era Maps and Drawings. sub series 01.04-folder 011.
Montana Historical Society. F. Jay Haynes Collection MC86 Folders1-8, 19-11.

Forestry Building, Portland Exhibition
Oregon State Archives Salem, National Register of Historic Places Portland.

Bohemian Club Lodge
Courtesy Abbeville Press

Parsons Lodge-Yosemite
Environmental Design Archives (EDA) College of Environmental Design at the University of California, Berkeley. Bernard Maybeck Collection, Project Records, 1897-1954 Box/Folder: 20 | 186, Drawings Oversize Folder: FF 213.

House of Hoo Hoo Exhibition Building
Environmental Design Archives (EDA) College of Environmental Design at the University of California, Berkeley. Bernard Maybeck Collection, Project Records, 1897-1954. Boxes 22, 31, Flat.

Glen Alpine Resort
Environmental Design Archives (EDA) College of Environmental Design at the University of California, Berkeley . Bernard Maybeck Collection, Project Records, 1897-1954. Box/Folder: 14 | 89-91, Drawings Oversize Folder: FF 77-78, Details Oversize Folder: FF 292.

Glacier Park Lodge-Glacier
Samuel Bartlett Drawings in the offices Glacier Park Incorporated.

Many Glacier Hotel, Many Glacier Hotel Dining-Glacier
Glacier Archive Series 01.10 File Unit 002 900-01, Buildings Great Northern Railway Folder 1.

Two Medicine Chalet-Glacier
Minnesota Historical Society Glacier Park Hotel Co. Two Medicine Camp, Log Dormitory, Drawings 6148-1 to 6148-4.

Sperry Chalet-Glacier
Glacier Archive, Series 01.10 File Unit 004 900-01 Buildings Chalets Folder 2.

Lake McDonald Lodge-Glacier
Eastern Washington State Historical Society / Northwest Museum of Arts and Culture, Ferris Research Library and Archives Cutter & Malmgren Records. Item I84-207.225.

Kootenai Lodge-Montana
Eastern Washington State Historical Society / Northwest Museum of Arts and Culture, Ferris Research Library and Archives.
Cutter & Malmgren Records. Item I84-207-119.

Lookout Studio-Grand Canyon
Denver Service Center/National Park Service. Page and Turnbull, Historic Structures Report, Lookout Studio Feb. 2009. Fred Harvey Company Drawing No.113-101773

Hermit's Rest-Grand Canyon
United States Department of the Interior, National Park Service, Historic Structure Report Hermit's Rest. 2007.
Kansas Historical Society. Atchison, Topeka and Santa Fe Railway Collection UID 57009, 56889.

Bryce Canyon Lodge and Cabins
Denver Service Center/National Park Service BRCA_129_60903A_[193385].
BRCA_129_60903A_[193385]

Grand Canyon Lodge at the North Rim
Denver Service Center/National Park Service GRCA_113_3148_[185142]
GRCA_113_9041_[151151]

Yavapai Museum-Grand Canyon
United States Department of the Interior, National Park Service. Historic Structure Report Yavapai Observation Station, 2002.

Desert Watchtower-Grand Canyon
United States Department of the Interior, National Park Service.
GRCA_113_D676_0033pg_Redacted.

GRCA_113_3302_[179072].
United States Department of the Interior, National Park Service. Historic Structures Report Desert View Watchtower 2008.

Paradise Inn, Mount Rainier
National Archives at Seattle.
Mount Rainier National Park Collection,
David E. Snow, Historic Structure Report: Paradise Inn. Mount Rainier National Park.
Washington, Denver Service Center; National Park Service, 1976. AHBL Civil Structure Engineers, 1996 Structural Assessment Report: The Paradise Inn. Archives Mt. Rainier National Park, 1996.

Logs Out Building
Fred Wllison, 1928 Comfort Station at OF Camp, Yellowstone Archive.

Old Faithful Lodge, Yellowstone
Yellowstone National Park Archives. National Park Service. Maps and Drawings Facilities and Maintenance Subseries 0501.405-407, United States Department of the Interior, National Park Service. Historic Structures Report. 1995

Bryce Canyon Lodge
Denver Service Center/National Park Service, BRCA_129_60090_[181798].

Geyser Hall, Yellowstone
Yellowstone National Park Archives. National Park Service. Maps and Drawings Facilities and Maintenance Subseries 0501.408-409.

Mt. Rainier Community Building
Mount Rainier National Park Collection,
Undated Set of drawings signed by Thomas Vint Mount Rainier National Park Collection.

Mt. Rainier Administration Building
Mount Rainier National Park Collection,
Set of drawings signed by Thomas Vint 5.21.28.

Grand Canyon Operations Building
United States Department of the Interior, National Park Service. Historic Structure Report South Rim Ranger Operations Building, 2000.

Madison Junction Trailside Museum
Denver Service Center/National Park Service, YELL_101_937A_[193561].

Norris Geyser Basin Trailside Museum
Denver Service Center/National Park Service, YELL_101_960_[195227]

Fishing Bridge Trailside Museum
Denver Service Center/National Park Service, YELL_101_8202_[201485].

Illustration Credits

Page	Source
5	Southern Appalachian Digital Collections.
7 Upper	Southern Appalachian Digital Collections.
7 Middle	WC Bikable.
7 Lower	Courtesy of Gilcrease Museum.
8	John Elk III ASP.
8	Courtesy of C. Russell Museum.
9	Dan Beard, *Shelters, Shacks and Shanties*
11	F. M. Piper, Royal Swedish Academy of Fine Arts .
13	Courtesy of the Soane Museum.
14	William Chambers, *A Treatise on Civil Architecture.*
15	*Some Designs of Mr. Inigo Jones and Mr. Wm. Kent* (Plate 32).
16	James Hall, *Essay on the Origin and Principles of Gothic Arch.*
17	John Serle, A Plan Of Mr. Pope's Garden: As It Was Left At His Death: (1745).
18	WC Willf.
20	F. M. Piper Royal Swedish Academy of Fine Arts.
22	WC Photochrom Print Collection.
25	Library of Congress Prints and Photographs Division LC-DIG-stereo-1s07111 E. & H.T.
27	*Harpers New Monthly Magazine* November 1855.
28	WC BotMultichillT.
29	WC Epicgenius.
29	WC Epicgenius.
29	New York Public Library Digital Collections. https://digitalcollections.nypl.org/items/510d47e1-0fdb-a3d9-e040-e00a18064a99.
32 Upper	Courtesy Central Park Conservancy.
32 Lower	Courtesy Central Park Conservancy.
33 Left	master-pnp-stereo-1s00000-1s07000-1s07100-1s07116u copy.tif Library of Congress Prints and Photographs Division LC-DIG-stereo-1s07116.
33 Right	Library of Congress Prints and Photographs Division LC-DIG-stereo-1s07115 Moulton J. W.
33 Lower	Eleventh Annual Report of the Board of Commissioners of the Central Park, For the Year Ending December 31, 1867. 1868.
33 Lower	Eleventh Annual Report of the Board of Commissioners of the Central Park, For the Year Ending December 31, 1867. 1868.
34 Right	Smithsonian Institution, Archives of American Gardens, Historic Gardens Stereograph Collection.AAG. STR, Item STR015027.
34 Left	Wallach Division of Art, Prints and Photographs: Photography Collection, TheNew York Public Library.' IMAGE DG91F218_113F.
35 Right	New York Public Library Digital Collections. https://digitalcollections.nypl.org/items/510d47e1-e490-a3d9-e040-e00a18064a99.
35 Left	Library Digital Collections. https://digitalcollections.nypl.org/items/510d47e1-e516-a3d9-e040-e00a18064a99.
36 Right	New York Public Library Digital Collections. https://digitalcollections.nypl.org/items/510d47e1-e488-a3d9-e040-e00a18064a99
36 Left	New York Public Library Digital Collections. https://digitalcollections.nypl.org/items/510d47e1-e486-a3d9-e040-e00a18064a99
37 Left	Public Library Digital Collections. https://digitalcollections.nypl.org/items/510d47e0-876d-a3d9-e040-e00a18064a99
37 Right	HistoricEchoPark.org [Photograph] Retrieved from the Library of Congress, https://www.loc.gov/item/2002722872/
39	Library of Congress
41	Adirondack Museum P020736_ADKX.
44 Left	Adirondack Museum 759. Camp Pine Knot, P001590_ADKX.
48 Lower	Library of Congress Matthews-Northrup Company. Call Number G3802.A19G5 1909.W6.
48	Adirondack History Museum P007026_ADKX
53	Adirondack Musuem 1984-060-0001_ADKX.
53 1st	Adirondack Musuem orig_354213526980_140557.jpg.
53 2nd	Adirondack Musuem P041039_ADKX.
53 3rd	Records of the National Park Service. orig_354213526980_204030.jpg.
53 4th	Adirondack Musuem P039541_ADKX.
65	Records of the National Park Service. orig_354213526980_671535.jpg.
65	Records of the National Park Service. orig_354213526980_271543.jpg.
71	*Log Cabins: How To Build And Furnish Them* by William S. Wicks.
72	*Log Cabins: How To Build And Furnish Them* by William S. Wicks.
72	*Log Cabins: How To Build And Furnish Them* by William S. Wicks.
74 Upper	Augustus Shepard, *Camps in the Woods* 1931. Architectural Book Publishing Company, Inc.
74 Lower	Augustus Shepard, *Camps in the Woods* 1931. Architectural Book Publishing Company, Inc.
78 Upper	Augustus Shepard, *Camps in the Woods* 1931 Architectural Book Publishing Company, Inc.
78 Lower	Augustus Shepard, *Camps in the Woods* 1931 Architectural Book Publishing Company, Inc.
81	*Vistas of the Fair* (Poole Bros., 1894).
82	Woodburyttype PBS.
83	*Sheppp's World's Fair Photographed.*
85	*The American Architect and Building News*, no. 962.
87	Cheney Cowles Center of the Northwest Museum of Arts & Culture. Cutter & Malmgren Records
87	DerSchweizer Holzstil in seinen kantonalen und konstruktiven Verschiedenheiten vergleichend dargestellt mit Holzbauten Deutschlands. Gladbach, Ernst,. Zürich, Schmidt, 1877.
91	Gladbach, *DerSchweizer Holzstil.*
92	Ashmolean Museum, University of Oxford.
92	Viollet-le-Duc *Habitations of Man in All Ages.*
93 Upper	Gladbach, *DerSchweizer Holzstil.*
93 Lower	Gladbach, *DerSchweizer Holzstil.*
94	WC Tony Grant.
94	Gladbach, *DerSchweizer Holzstil.*
96	Left: Gladbach, *DerSchweizer Holzstil.*
96	Right: Gladbach, *DerSchweizer Holzstil.*
99	WC Oregon Department of Transportation (Magnus Manske).
106 Left	Smithsonian American Art Museum Lent by the Depart ment of the Interior Museum.
106 Right	Yellowstone Photo Collection 14837.jpg Grand Canyon of the Yellowstone; k# 64,006; William H Jackson; 1871.

107 Oregon State University Special Collections & Archives: CC Oregon State University Special Collections and Archives.

109 EF Everit New York Public Library Digital Collections ID G90FF447_031ZF https://digitalcollections.nypl.org /items/510d47e0-948c-a3d9-e040-e00a18064a99.

109 *American Thresherman,* Jun 1907 pg 58.

110 Wesley Andrews Postcard c. 1915 (#365).

110 Montana Historical Society Library and Archives Haynes Foundation Photograph Collection Vintage negative number: 1615[A1.

112 https://www.yellowstonestereoviews.com.

112 Yellowstone Photo Collection 02819.jpg

113 Yellowstone Photo Collection 02917.jpg

113 Yellowstone Photo Collection 14836.jpg .

114 Yellowstone Photo Collection 14288.jpg.

114 [1901] Report Of The Acting Superintendent Of The Yellowstone National Park To The Secretary Of The Interior. 1901. P.27.

115 Yellowstone Photo Collection15339.jpg

115 Yellowstone Photo Collection 02959.jpg

116 WC Arcoterian

116 https://www.yellowstonestereoviews.com/stereolist.html 4 6246-Fort Yellowstone.

121 *Craftsman* June 1906 408.

122 *Craftsman* June 1906 408.

123 Left: Buffalo Bill Center of the West.

123 Right: WC Arcoterian.

124 Lee Foster / ASP.

125 Yellowstone Heritage and Research Center, From Thorn ton Waite, *Yellowstone by Train.*

128 Courtesy Yellowstone Archives # 161764.

126 https://www.yellowstonestereoviews.com/stereolist.html Depot & Park Entrance At Gardner, Mont. Y.N.P.

129 Corbin17 / ASP.

132 Yellowstone Stereoviews, F. J. Haynes.

133 Yellowstone Stereoviews, Norman A. Forsyth.

134 MontHS Sheet No. 2 May 1903.

134 MontHS Sheet No. 5 May 1903.

135 Yellowstone Park Archive Sheet No. 6 Partial May 1903.

140 Yellowstone History Center.

140 Library of Congress Prints and Photographs Division HABS -WY-WY0000-WY0093-PHOTOS-174606PV.

144 Gabbro / ASP.

147 Library of Congress Prints and Photographs Division HABS ARIZ,3-GRACAN,14A—9.

150 Steven Pavlov CC License.

151 Museum of the Rockies.

152 National Archive, Haynes Collection 71-6-31-76.

152 Copyright Doug Carr, courtesy of the Dana-Thomas House Foundation.

154 National Archive Haynes Collection.

156 Above Abraham Lincoln Presidential Library and Museum.

156 Below http://vintagemachinery.org.

157 Estes Park Museum 1984.094.005.

158 Denver library Z-8822 Image File: ZZR711008822.

159 Upper Estes Park Museum 1977.020.003 poor match.

159 Lower Estes Park Museum 1995.010.037.

160 Left Estes Park Museum 1990.006.005.

160 Right Estes Park Museum 1990.006.006.

161 Copyright (c) The Ansel Adams Publishing Rights Trust.

164 WC Vlas and Maria Buskey.

165 Adirondack Museum P062127_ADKX.

167 WC Haggin Museum Stockton California.

170 above WC Metropolitan Museum of Art.

170 lower WC Berkshire Museum, Pittsfield, MA.

173 Founds.org.

175 American Art Post card.

177 Oregon Historical Society, Library Reference code ba018894.

179 Oregon Historical Society, Library Reference code bb000443..

179 WC Source https://www.sandiegohistory.org/journal/ 98summer/photos.htm¿

182 OSU Special Collections & Archives Research Center. Lantern Slides Item Number: P217:set 049 slide 017.

183 Library of Congress Prints and Photographs Division LC-USZ62-57934.

185 Library of Congress LC-USZ62-57933.

187 Library of Congress Prints and Photographs Division LC-USZ62-64423.

187 Portland City Archives Record Number AP/354.

188 Library of Congress Prints and Photographs Divisi Call Number/LOT 12331.

188 University of Washington Libraries, Special Collections, UW11749.

190 University of Washington Libraries, Special Collections UW11750.

191 Postcard Pacific Novelty Company. San Francisco https://ppie100.org/tag/house-of-hoo-hoo/

193 Indiana University Digital Collections Charles W Cush man Series 25-64 P13792.

193 WC Staaliche Museen zu Berlin.

194 1906 February *American Homes and Gardens* (Munn and Co)

196 WC Amonroth.

199 Russ Bishop / ASP.

201 OpenSFHistory / wnp27.7932.

203 OpenSFHistory / wnp14.11371.

206 Upper Edward A. Rogers Collection, Bancroft Library, Univer sity of California, Berkeley.

206 Lower San Francisco Historical Photograph Collection SFPL AAE-0540.

209 Upper San Francisco Historical Photograph Collection SFPL AAE-0539.

209 Lower WC Rhododendrites.

210 Historical Preservation of Glen Alpine Springs Inc.

211 Left Historical Preservation of Glen Alpine Springs Inc.

211 Right Historical Preservation of Glen Alpine Springs Inc.

214 Historical Preservation of Glen Alpine Springs Inc.

215 California State Library, H.O.H. Shelley collection.

217 Glacier National Park Archives HPF_8072.

219 Glacier National Park Archives UM_t013117.

221 Glacier National Park Archive GLAC_10338_ HPF_3655_Hileman_5069.:

223 Ted's Great Northern Homepage. https://www.gnflyer.com/artwork.html

224 Minnesota Historical society.

226 Montana State Library HPF 4866.

228 Left Courtesy of the Gilcrease Museum.

228 Right USC Libraries Special Collections Filename: CHS-1207 George Fiske Photographer.

231 CC Warren Le May.

233 WC Acroterion.

235 Above Glacier National Park Archives DI_411.

235 Below Glacier National Park Archives HPF_9394.

236 Above Glacier National Park Archives HPF_8255a.

236 Below From Bridget Moylan *Glacier's Grandest*, Original not located.

243 MM3NFK Pictures Now / ASP.

249 RB47T Dan Leeth / ASP.

249 BRB4P3 Dan Leeth / ASP.

249 2K1W0R0 H. Mark Weidman Photography / ASP.

253 Dan Leeth / ASP.

257 Above Theodore Roosevelt Digital Library. Dickinson State University. libID=304688.

257 Below Glacier National Park Archives Photo Number GLAC 8256_Hileman 9606.

258 Glacier National Park Archives GLAC_8231_Hileman_10-26B.tif.

259 Glacier National Park Archives GLAC_729 (27511331896). George A Grant.

260 Top Glacier National Park ArchivesGLAC_6090_Marble_2834.tif.

260 Middle Glacier National Park Archives GLAC_11336_Grant_60.

260 Bottom Glacier National Park Archives GLAC_11814_Kiser.

261 "Glacier National Park: Hotels & Tours, 7," Minnesota HS.

264 WC Bill Heyden.

271 WC Warren LeMay

273 Dan Leeth / ASP.

274 Above WC Warren LeMay.

274 Below WC Warren LeMay.

283 Trevon Baker.

285 Trevon Baker.

293 Left "Maximilian, Prince of Wied *Travels in the Interior of North America*,

293 Right "Maximilian, Prince of Wied *ravels in the Interior of North America*,

295 Timothy O'Sullivan, Library of Congress Prints an Photographs Division LOT 3427-3, no. 14 [item] [P&P].

295 Timothy O'Sullivan Getty Institute 84.XM.484.4.

295 Upper Yellowstone Photo Collection 03094.

295 Lower Yellowstone Photo Collection 63092

297 WC Wmpearl.

298 Upper WC StellarD.

298 Lower WC Johnaragon1323.

299 Upper WC AlisonRuthHughes .

299 Lower WC Hasselblad500CM .

301 WC Bancroft Library.

303 Upper WC Jared.

303 Lower NP Gallery NPS F8D679CC-155D-451F-57F76AB95AE33CAF.

305 NPS Photo by Michael Quinn.

308 Upper NPGalleryNPS F8E51279-155D-451F-673E70ADBB3F99F2.

308 Lower NPGalleryNPS F8E51279-155D-451F-673E70ADBB3F99F2.

309 Middle WC NpsbPhoto by Michael Quinn.

311 GRCA 22646.

312 NP Gallery.nps F7544D58-155D-451F-67C67CA99943111B.

313 NP Gallery.nps F8C747AB-155D-451F-67B5B07261A18175.

320 Upper WC Jllm06..

321 Lower Union Pacific Museum UPC-1037

324 Upper WC King of Hearts.

324 Lower Union Pacific Museum UPB-0588.

327 Library of Congress Prints and Photographs Dision HABS ARIZ,3-GRACAN,14.

327 Nature Collection / ASP.

329 Upper Library of Congress Prints and Photographs Division HABS ARIZ,3-GRACAN,14A—9.

329 Middle Timothy Swope / ASP.

329 Lower Nature Collection / ASP.

331 Keystone-Mast Collection, UCR/California Museum of Photography, University of California at Riverside Identifier: 1996.0009.KU89396.

331 Keystone-Mast Collection, UCR/California Museum of Photography, University of California at Riverside Identifier: 1996.0009.ku89402.

333 Upper Keystone-Mast Collection, UCR/California Museum of Photography, University of California at Riverside Identifier:1996.0009.KU89389

333 Lower Natural History Archive / ASP.

340 Upper George Grant. NPgalleryNPS F73A9730-155D 451F 67D1A31A2B667B8A.

340 Lower Grand canyon National Park Archive Photo Number 5829.

343 Left Grand canyon National Park Archive Photo Number 5823.

343 Right Grand Canyon National Park: Geologic Fireplace 1199 NPS Photo by Erin Whittaker.

344 Union Pacific Museum UPB-0588.

345 NP. Gallery NPS Photo by Michael Quinn Desert View Watchtower 0058 Asset ID: 94B679C9-155D-451F-6744E8242B045DB2.

346 Albuquerque Museum, Postcard PA2014.007.753.

347 Indian Village, Postcard, San Diego History Center.

347 WC Cleveland Museum.

348 Right CC License NPS Photo by Michael Quinn Desert View Watchtower 06-230 (7395636476).jpg.

348 Left CC License 08430_Grand_Canyon_Historic_Desert View_Watchtower_Construction_c.1931 (5898099914).jpg.

349 WC Lacee Curtis.

352 Upper Nature and Science / ASP.

352 Lower CC License NPS Photo by Michael Quinn: Desert View Watchtower WTC02.

355 Middle Seton Legacy Project at the Academy for the Love of Learning in Santa Fe.

359	WC Bikeable ALTERED.
361	California State Parks: Jack London State Historic park.
362	California State Parks: Jack London State Historic park.
363 Left	*Architect and Engineer* p 41 July 1911 59.
364	Library Of Congress https://lccn.loc.gov /91784651LC-USZ62-103950 DLC.
365 Above	*Two Little Savages*, Ernest Thompson Seton.
367	CC Lee Coursey.
369	Mike Leakey CC Cropped.
371 Top	WC Holly Chena.
371 Bottom	WC Joe Mabel.
375	KBIN Graphics CC license 0114_acec_awards _paradise_inn.
375	WC Ashel Curtis University of Washington.
381	Good, *Park and Recreation Structures.*
382	Good, *Park and Recreation Structures.*
383	Open Parks Network YELL-93427-17.
384	San Francisco Public Library, Local identifier AAD-760Cardinell-Vincent Co Panama-Pacific International Exposition Company.
385 Left	WC Jamie: Toronto
385 Right	NPS.gov Digital Image Archive: ABLI4419.jpg.
386	WC Arcoterian.
387	Open Parks Network YELL-185334-1 YELL-20717 YELL-20717 YELL-185333-3 YELL-23295-31778 YELL-185327-368 YELL-22724 YELL24642.
388 Upper	WC Runner1928.
388 Lower	WC Runner1928.
389	Charles (Chuck) Peterson.
391	Yellowstone National Park Maps and Drawings.
392 Upper	Haynes Post card 28929.
392 Lower	Haynes Postcard Company 1920.
393 Upper	University of the Pacific, John Muir Drawings Collection.
393 Middle	Historic American Buildings Survey of California.
393 Lower	Haynes PC #22625.
394	National Park Service.
396 Upper	Open Parks Network YELL-12002-5.
396 Middle	Open Parks Network YELL-13022-1.
399	Corbin17 / ASP.
400 Upper	Chon Kit Leong / ASP.
400 Lower	WC Senapa.
406	WC Dhenbenn cropped.
408	RZUS Images ASP.
411	WC Acroterion.
416	WC George Showman
416	WC M. O. Stevens.
418	WC Acroterion
419	WC Acroterion.
421 Right	WC Steven Pavlov.
429	NP Gallery NPS `````F88A761B-155D-451F-67864F792E39C6E9.
434	NP Gallery NPS Asset ID 92e716986c9b41f3b 76319ce04f8e34e.
435	Allan Hartley/ ASP.
438	National Archive: Inspector's Photographic Handbook, 1930–1936 NAID: 520068Local ID: 79-HB.
440	Open Parks Network YELL-33650.
440	Good, *Park and Recreation Structures.*
441	WC Acroterion.
447 Left	Open Parks Network YELL38701.
447 Right	Open Parks Network YELL38701.
451	National Park Service: Jim Peaco; Catalog #20193d.
454	Open Parks Network YELL 33649 UC.
459	Courtesy Kengo Kuma and Associates.
464	© Andrea Zittel, Courtesy Regen Projects. Photo: Lance Brewer.
465	WC Clischm Modified.
465	BY ENCORE_RENDER_001.jpgoto' Courtesy of Sou Fujimoto Architects.

ASP	Alamy Stock Photo
CC	Creative Commons
MinnHS	Minnesota Historical Society
MontHS	Montana Historical Society
WC	Wikipedia Commons

All other photographs are the author's.

Index

A

Abbey, Edward, 471
Absaroka Crow tribe, 128–129
Absarokee Hut, 128–129, 488
Acadia National Park gate houses, 75
Acoma Pueblo, 302, 306–7
Adam, Robert, 20–21, 24, 26, 35, 94, 102, 104, 183, 277, 423, 476
Adams, Ansel, 168–169
Adams, Charles Francis, 137–138, 478
Addison, Joseph, 30–31, 476, 486
Adirondack Forest Preserve, 93
Adirondack Railroad, 47, 49, 51
Adirondacks, 8, 13–16, 31, 34–36, 39, 42–44, 47–49, 51, 53–54, 57, 67, 75, 77, 79, 85, 124, 134, 167, 171, 264, 376, 443–4, 477, 481, 487
Adirondack Spruce, The (Pinchot), 77
African art, 362
Agassiz, Louis, 34
Ahwahnee Hotel, 333, 345, 418, 424
Aislabie, William, 25
Albert, Prince and Queen Victoria, Swiss Cottage, 99, 102, 104, 232
Alberti Leon Batista, 24
Albright, Horace,159, 162, 393, 397–8, 484, 492
Alps, 28, 30, 99, 102, 231, 261, 265
American Association of Museums, 327
American Fur Company, 299
Ames Gate Lodge, 328, 464
Anderson, Archibald, 130
Anderson, Superintendent George, 132
Antlers Hotel, Colorado Springs, 127
appropriation, cultural, 468, 483
archetypes, 17, 362, 364, 469, 472
Architectural Record, 104, 479
Arikara Nation, Mandan, Hidatsa, and, 227
Arp, Jean, 171
arts and crafts architecture, 70, 391
Atchison, Topeka & Santa Fe Railway, See Santa Fe Railway
Atterbury, Grosvenor, 6, 57, 60, 64, 69, 72–75, 85, 124, 477, 487, 512. *See also* Camp Uncas, Camp Sagamore
authenticity, 469. *See also* structural honesty
Ayer, Everett, 306

B

Banff Springs Hotel, 134, 490
Bar Harbor, 127
Baronett Bridge, 120, 138–139
Bartlett, Samuel, 240, 242, 250, 290. *See also* Glacier Park Lodge
Bastrop State Park, 465
Beard, Dan, *Shelters, Shacks and Shanties*, 15–16
Bear Mountain State Park, 447
Bedford, Duchess of, Endsleigh Cottage, 28, 99, 232
Belton Chalet, 231, 248, 249
Benson, Simon, 186, 489
Benson raft, 186
Bergson, Henri, 171
Berkeley, California, 181, 200, 202–4, 217, 222, 326, 474, 480, 484, 489, 492
    1923 fire, 200, 217, 222
Berlin, Isiah, 15, 17, 85, 373, 469, 476, 486
Bierstadt, Albert, 176–177, 195, 242
Birch Moss Chapel, 467, 472
Blaise Hamlet, 100
Blockhouses, Mount Rainier, 440
Blockhouse, Yellowstone, 122
Bodmer, Karl, 299–300, 364, 470
Bohemian Club, 201, 202–3, 215, 222
Bohemian Club Lodge, 202–3
Bolton, Arthur, 20, 476–7
Boy Scouts, 15
Bread and Cheese Club, 175
Breton, Andre, 362
Bright Angel Lodge, 311, 351, 355
bristlecone pine, *Pinus longaeva*, 170–171, 191
Brookings, Oregon, 204
Brown, A. Page, 181, 440, 482, 485, 491
Bryce National Park, 111, 328–9, 331, 334, 346, 398–9, 407, 492
Bryce Lodge, 328–9, 331, 403, 405, 407–11, 418, 464,
Bryce Lodge, Deluxe Cabins, 328–32, 401
Bryant, William Cullen, 175–176, 178, 188, 477
Buffalo, destruction of, 108, 110
Buffalo Bill (William Cody) 127, 130–132, 134, 307, 474, 477, 488
Buffington, L. F., 119, 127
Bumpas, Hermon, 326, 443, 448, 464
Burke, Edmund, 30–31, 113, 176, 476, 486. *See also Philosophical Enquiry into the Origin of Our Ideas of the Sub-lime and Beautiful*
Burlington Railroad,(Chicago, Burlington, and Quincy Railroad), 130, 132
Burnham and Root, 305
Burroughs, John, 13–14, 16, 19, 78, 271, 367, 371–3, 375, 424, 476, 483, 486, 491
    as structural rationalist, 371–2
    Slabsides, 14, 367, 371–2
bus loop, Union Pacific, 328, 334, 399, 407
Butte, Montana, 110, 133, 167, 296, 479
    environmental damage, 110, 296

C

Camp, Huttig, Charles, 76, 82–84
Camp North Point, 67, 77, 249, 282
Camp Pine Knot, 15, 49, 51–54, 57–58, 60, 64, 67, 69, 72, 77, 79, 90, 99, 104, 157, 474, 477, 487
    construction types, 51–53
Camp Rabbit Wild, 57
Camp Sagamore, 64–71, 81, 85, 103–104, 379, 515
Camp Sagamore Dining Complex, 69
Camp Sagamore Lodge, 64, 67, 69, 103, 474, 477, 487
Camp Sagamore Playhouse, 70–71, 82
Camp Santanoni, 57, 77, 85
Camp Uncas, 15, 48, 53, 57–58, 60, 62–64, 67, 69, 72–74, 81, 85, 477, 487, 493, 498
Camp Uncas Lodge, 15, 48, 53, 56–64, 67, 69, 81, 85, 477, 487
Camp Uncas Dining Hall, 72–74
Camp, William Read, 57
Campbell, Reau, 134, 486
Campfire Girls, 15
Camping and Woodcraft, (Kephart), 15, 476, 486
Canadian Pacific Railroad, 134, 225
Canyon de Chelly, 300–301
Canyon Hotel, 121, 158–159, 238, 479, 488
Carr, Ethan, 474, 479, 484, 486
Carrère and Hastings, 183, 296
Castle Crater, 299
Castner, Captain Joseph, 123
cattle ranching, 108
Cedar Breaks National Monument, 328, 345, 407
Central Park, 33–36, 42–44, 47, 134, 474, 477, 487
    and Adirondacks, 34–36, 42–44
    Ramble, 35–36, 39, 42
    rustic structures, 34–41
chalet, 28, 31, 52–53, 60, 64, 89–90, 94, 99–102, 104, 158, 183–184, 204, 231–3, 240, 248, 250, 254, 260–61, 266–7, 268, 271, 275, 277–8, 282, 286, 309–10, 367, 375, 403, 483. *See also* Hill, Louis
chalets, backcountry, at Glacier National Park, 262, 266–75
Chambers, William, 20–22, 94, 104, 167, 183, 188, 367, 476, 486
Chapin, Frederick, 305
chateau, 134
Chicago, Burlington, and Quincy Railroad,130,132
Child, Harry, 133, 138, 162
Church of the New Jerusalem, 178–181
Cieraad, Irene, 99–100, 232, 477, 481–2, 487
Civilian Conservation Corps, CCC, 395, 465
Clark Fork River Basin, 296
Cody, Wyoming, 127, 130–132, 307, 391, 479, 488
Coeur d'Alene mine strikes, 296
Cole, Thomas, 127, 170, 479, 489
College of Indian Wisdom, 363
Colonial Williamsburg, 465, 469
Colter, Mary, 310–11, 316, 320, 328, 347–8, 350–51, 353–6, 359, 362, 469, 482–3, 491.
    See also Lookout Studio, Hermit's Rest, Desert Watchtower
    and cultural appropriation, 353–9
    called a hoax, 311
    criticism of, 354, 359
    geologic buildings, 353–9
Commissioner's House, Yellowstone,123
Conger, Patrick, 122, 127, 478
Cooke, Jay, 109, 113, 118, 478, 488
Cooper, James Fenimore, 175, 178, 479
Coronado Lodge at Palo Duro Canyon, 348
Corthell, Wendell, 102, 477
Cottage Hotel, 121
Coulter, William, 70–71, 85, 379, 487
Craft, Mabel Clare, 178, 181
Craftsman, The, 15, 102, 129, 170, 302, 305, 477–9, 482, 488, 491
Creative Evolution, (Bergson), 171
Cronin, William, 31
Crossley, Paul,175, 479
Crow Agency, 128, 129
cultural colonialism, 230, 362, 469
Curtis, Edward, 195, 488
Curtiss, Louis, 311, 355, 489
Cushing, Frank, 13, 14, 19, 305, 486
Cutter, Kirtland, 67, 89, 94–95, 188, 231, 249–50, 258, 266, 272, 276–8, 280, 282–3, 286, 290, 292, 296, 454, 464, 477, 480, 482, 487, 490. *See also* Idaho Pavilion, Kootenai Lodge, Lake McDonald Lodge

D

Dana, William, 102, 104, 159, 477, 487
Davenport Hotel, Spokane, 286, 290
Davidson, Ernest, 388, 422, 427–8, 432, 436, 438, 440–1, 447, 469, 484, 492. *See also* Longmire Community Building, Longmire Administration Building, Grand Canyon Administration Building
Deerslayer, The, 47, 175, 479
deforestation, 53–54, 77, 85, 119, 167, 226–7, 229–30
del Monte Hotel, San Diego, 127
Deluxe Cabins, Bryce, 329–31, 401
Department of the Interior, 121, 123, 140–141, 477–9, 482–8, 490–2
Department of War, 123
Desert Watchtower, 311, 355, 359, 361, 469–70, 483
    steel frame, 311, 355, 359, 361, 469–70, 483
d'Harnoncourt, Rene, 362, 483
Dillard, Annie, 175, 479
Diné (Navajo) Nation, 353–4, 356, 362, 483
Djuff, Ray, 250, 474, 481, 490
Doane, Gustavus Cheney, 108, 112, 194, 299, 478, 482, 491
Doran, Robert, 31, 113, 176, 234, 243, 476, 478, 481
Downing, Andrew Jackson, 31, 33–35, 39, 102, 134, 368, 476, 477, 487
Doyle, A. E., 183
Druids, 22–23, 44, 188, 264
Durand, Asher, *In the Wood*, 175–177
Durant, Thomas, 46–47, 49, 57, 113, 225, 477, 468, 512
Durant, William, 46, 49–54, 57, 60, 69–70, 72, 75, 77, 90, 94, 99, 130, 230, 412, 477, 487, 512. *See also* Camp Pine Knot, Camp Sagamore, Camp Uncas,
    as designer, 49, 477

E

Eaton, Howard, 264, 275, 481, 490
 tours at Glacier, 264–5
Echo Park, Los Angeles, 44
Eden, loss of, 17, 181, 472, 487
Elkhorn Cabin, 263, 264
Ellwood, Craig, 311
El Navajo Hotel, 356
Empson, William, 157
El Tovar, 16, 124, 307, 309–11, 347, 373, 397, 401, 412, 482, 491
Elwell, Farrington R., 126
Emerson, Ralph Waldo, 34, 48, 178, 326, 364
Ernst, Max, 362
Essay on Architecture (Laugier), 367
Essay on the Picturesque (Price), 27, 169, 476
Evans, Orvis, 286, 490

F

Farr, Albert, 369, 370
Farrel, Robert, 359, 483
Fernow, Bernhard, 77, 85, 487
Fewkes, J. W., 354
First Unitarian Church, Berkeley, 181
Fishing Bridge Museum, 389, 444, 447, 458, 460, 464–5, 469
 structure, 389, 444, 447, 458, 460, 465, 469
Fitzgerald, F. Scott, 225, 480
Follensby Pond, 34, 53
Forest and Stream, 250, 477, 481, 490
Forest Hymn, A, (Bryant), 175, 178
Forestry Building, 183–184, 194, 196–197, 208, 222, 230, 233, 235, 237, 240, 242, 250, 254, 261, 480–1, 489–90
Fort Custer, 115–116, 128
Fort Keough, 115
Fort Yellowstone, 123, 328, 488
Fountains Abbey, 25, 486
Frankl, Paul, 175, 479
Frick house, 296
Fried, Stephen, 307, 482–3, 491
Friedrich, Caspar David, 222, 470
Frobese, Frederick, 243, 481, 490

G

Gauguin, Paul, 13
Geyser Hall. 404, 418–49, 422–424, 484, 493
geology, 31, 107, 176, 234, 299–303, 306–7, 310–1, 318, 325–6, 328, 329, 331, 333–4, 336, 346–8, 350, 353, 452, 458
 as ruins, 176, 234, 299–300, 303, 306–7, 348, 350
 gridded, or vertical 31
 horizontal, 31, 107, 176, 234, 299–301, 302–3, 306–7, 310–1, 318, 325–6, 328–9, 331, 333–4, 336–8, 346, 350, 353, 452, 458
Giant Redwood Trees of California, (Bierstadt), 176, 242
Gilpin, William, 25, 364, 476, 482–3, 485–6
Girl Scouts, 15
Glacier National Park, 124, 157, 226–7, 229, 231, 233, 237, 248, 250, 261, 263–4, 266, 268, 272, 277–8, 282, 474–5, 481–2, 490. *See also* chalets, at Glacier National Park
Glacier Park Lodge (originally Glacier Park Hotel), 124–126, 230, 237–8, 240, 242–4, 246, 248, 250, 252, 254, 257–8, 260–1, 266, 268, 272, 277–8, 282–3, 290, 303, 364, 418, 468, 470
 and Native American exhibits, 124, 225
 classical elements in, 124, 225–6, 230
 Swiss elements in, 124, 225–6, 230
Glacier Point, Yosemite, 169, 194, 203, 235, 325–7
Gladbach, Ernest, *Der Schweizer Holzstil*, 52, 89, 99, 101–104, 184, 248, 261, 266, 375, 487
Glen Alpine Resort, 217–221
Going to the Sun Highway, 261, 275
Golden Gate Trestle, 120
Good, Albert, 19, 22, 44, 388–9, 395, 422, 427–8, 432, 435, 441, 443–5, 476, 483–5, 492
 and Maier, 443–4
Goodsell, George, 77, 477, 487
Gothic architecture, 8, 20, 22–23, 25–26, 30–31, 34, 82, 175, 181, 188, 201, 299–301, 373, 479, 486
Gottlieb, Adolph, 362
Grand Canyon, geology of, 301, 325, 328–9
Grand Canyon National Park,113, 123–124, 176, 234, 264, 300-2, 305–7, 360, 438, 447, 468–70, 482–4, 491–2, 306, 312, 316, 347, 355, 436. *See also* Lookout Studio, Hermit's Rest, Lodge at the North Rim, Yavapai museum, Desert Watchtower, Grand Canyon Administration Building
 and the Santa Fe Railroad, 16, 108, 111, 124
 Powerhouse, 424–5
Grand Canyon Administration Building (now the operations building), 436–9, 469–70
Grand Staircase, 328
Granite Park Chalet, 263, 267, 271, 275, 490
Grant, Madison, 222, 480
Grant, J. D., 176, 489
Great Basin National Park,199
Great Northern Railroad, 16, 111, 124, 134, 197, 225–7, 229–30, 233–4, 237, 242–3, 248, 250, 254, 258, 261, 264–6, 271, 277, 282, 296, 474, 480–1, 490, *See also* Yellowstone National Park
Greene brothers, 104
Grinnell, George Bird, 227, 232, 234, 250, 260, 264, 481, 490
Gropius, Walter, 267
Gros Ventre tribe, 227
grotesque, 36, 44, 167, 169
Gunsight Chalet, 267

H

Half Dome, 325
Hall, Ansel, 326, 348, 483–4, 486, 492
Haller, Nicholas T., 120–121
Hall, James, 23, 486
hammerbeam roof, 70, 203
Harriman E. H., 16, 107, 132–133
Harrison, Benjamin, 226
Harrison, William Henry, 33
Harvey Company, 305–7, 309–11, 316, 320, 353–6, 359, 467
Harvey, Fred, 307
Haupt, Herman, 117, 120, 478
Hayden, Ferdinand, 109
Haynes, F. Jay, 391, 487
Heath, Frederick, 375, 381, 423
Hedges, Cornelius, 109
Heidi, (Spyri), 99, 231–2
Hermit's Rest, 311, 312, 316, 318, 320–3, 347–8, 354–6, 359–60, 470, 482, 491
Heye, George, 356
Hidatsa, Arikara, Mandan Nation, 227
Higgins, C. A., 306
High House at Wolfenschiessen, 261
Hiller, Susan, 469
Hill, James J., 197, 225, 227, 230, 243, 261, 490
 and Piegans, 227
Hill, Louis, 16, 227, 229– 31, 233–4, 237, 240, 243, 248, 261, 265–6, 268, 272, 275, 277–8, 282–3, 286, 306–7, 423, 468, 481–2, 490
 and the chalet, 231, 233, 240, 248, 261, 267–8, 275, 277–8, 282, 286
 and Piegans, 226–7, 230, 233, 243, 268
Hillside Club, 200, 480, 489
Hiscoe, Charles, 172
Hoare, Henry, 26
Honnedaga Lake, 80, 82
hoodoos, 329, 331
Hopi Tribe, 302–3, 305, 310–1, 353–4, 356, 362, 364, 467, 410, 482–3, 491
Hopi House, 310–1, 315, 318, 347, 353–4, 356, 470
House and Garden, 102, 477, 483, 488, 491
House of Hoo Hoo, 199, 208, 210, 214–6, 222, 468, 480, 489
Huckel, J. F., 307
Huckel, Minnie Harvey, 307
Hull, Daniel, 328, 392–3, 398, 400, 424, 427, 483–4, 492
Huntington, Collis, 15
Hussey, Christopher, 19, 476, 486

I

Idaho Pavilion, 89–90, 95, 124, 277, 296,
imperialist nostalgia, 469, 485
"Indian Art of the United States," 362
Indigenous architecture, 467, 469
Inuit Shamanic masks, 362
Irving, Washington, 175–176, 178, 480
Isle of the Dead, Arnold Böcklin, 200, 222

J

Jackson, Helen Hunt, 305
Jackson, W. H., 113, 306
James, George, 305–6, 318, 320, 350, 364, 470, 482, 486, 491–2
Jeffrey pine, 169, 171
Jensen, Derrick, 226–7, 481, 490
Jewel Cave Ranger Station, 395
Johnson, Philip, 467–8
joints, 44, 67, 102, 117, 147, 169, 196, 207, 217, 242, 292, 299, 327, 331, 376, 378, 381, 445–6

K

Kabotie, Fred, 356, 362, 491
kachinas, 356, 362
Kaibab Limestone, 310, 315–6
Kaibab National Forest, 345
Kaiser, Harvey, 486–7
Kamp Kill Kare, 172
Kant Immanuel, 31, 176, 476, 478, 481, 486
Kazin, Alfred, 443, 465, 484, 486
Keith, William, 181, 474
Kelley, John Ryan A. Cornelius, 120, 286, 296, 490
Kendrick, J. W., 133
Kent, William, 23
Kephart, Horace, 8, 13–16, 19, 31, 78, 81, 229, 271, 467, 468, 475, 476, 486
King, Clarence, 19, 300, 303, 482, 489, 491
Kingman, Lieutenant Dan, 120–122, 127, 478
kivas, 354, 362–3, 467
Knight, Richard Payne, 28
Kolb Studio, 312
Kootenai Lodge, 276–7, 286, 290, 292, 294, 295–6, 418, 471, 474, 490,
 and structural frame, 277, 288, 290, 292
Kuma Kengo, 467, 472

L

La Fonda Hotel, 305
Lake Lodge, 162, 393, 401, 424, 479, 484
Lake McDonald Lodge (originally Lewis Glacier Hotel), 250, 277–8, 282, 290, 292, 470, 490
Lake Ranger Station, 393, 398, 427–8
Lake (Yellowstone) Hotel, 120–121, 123
 additions, 158
land grants to railroads, 49, 54, 108–109
Langford, Nathaniel, 108–110, 112, 122, 194, 234, 299–300, 303, 448, 478, 482, 488, 491
Last of the Mohicans, 57
Las Vegas, New Mexico, 305–6

Laugier, Marc–Antoine, 21, 181, 188, 367
lean tos, 34, 48, 53, 78, 232
Lears, T. J. Jackson, 13, 14, 232, 474, 476, 486
LeConte Memorial, 203, 327
Le Corbusier, 290
Levi–Strauss, Claude, 167
Lewis, Ion, 183
Lewis, John, 277–8
Lewis Meriwether, 234
Limerick, Jeffrey, 474
Limerick, Patricia, 474
Lincoln, Abraham, 23, 163, 392, 484, 492,
Birthplace Memorial, 23, 163, 392, 484, 492
Lincoln Logs, 392
lodgepole pine, 119, 138, 140, 142, 151, 155–156, 159, 169–170
Log Cabins and Cottages (Wicks), 78–90
log cabin, 13–14, 16, 33, 63–64, 78–79, 85–86, 89, 100–101, 104, 115, 117–118, 120–23, 132, 134, 138, 140, 156, 203–4, 232, 249, 267, 277, 286, 307, 368, 371–2, 375, 389, 397–9, 401–3, 418, 423, 427, 445, 454
as iconic object, 34, 127–131,163, 390–5, 441
log crib structures, 120, 162, 479
logs–out system, 400–1, 412, 415, 418, 422–4, 427, 441, 469
log railroad tie, 117
London, Jack, 202, 368–9, 371–3, 375, 424, 474, 483, 491
as structural rationalist, 368–9
Long Branch, 127
Longmire Administration Building, 328, 427, 432–6, 441, 469–70, 484
Longmire Village, 375–6, 388, 418, 427–8
Longmire Community Building, 388, 428–32, 435, 441
Longmire Springs Hotel, 375
Longs Peak Inn,165–167, 479, 489
Lookout Studio, 320, 347, 354–5, 359–60, 469, 470, 482, 491
Loos, Adolf, 367
Lummis, Charles, 306–7, 309, 482, 491
Lutyens, Edwin, 469

M

MacDowell, Edward,14–15
MacFarlane, Robert, 265, 482, 490
Madison Museum, 448–51
Madrone tree,178, 180
Maier, Herbert, 326–8, 331, 333, 347–8, 350–51, 359, 373, 381, 388–9, 395, 403, 424, 441, 443–5, 447–8, 450, 452, 454, 457–8, 461, 464–5, 469–70, 482–5, 492. *See also* Fishing Bridge Museum, Madison Muse um, Norris Museum, Yavapai Museum
and vernacular architecture, 441, 443–4, 447, 464–5, 469–70,482–5
his vision of primitive man, 373
Malaise, end of the century, 13, 476, 486
Mandan, Hidatsa, and Arikara Nation, 227
Many Glacier Hotel, 44, 108, 250, 254, 257–8, 260–61, 266, 277–8, 286, 292, 418, 468, 490
exposed structure, 258–9
Swiss elements in, 250, 254, 257–8, 260
Marent Gulch Trestle, 110, 117
Marias Massacre, 108
Mariposa grove, 169
Marsh, George Perkins, 113
Mather, Stephen, 275, 325–6, 328, 333, 375, 389, 391, 393, 395, 397–9, 427, 484, 492
Matisse, Henri, 362
Maybeck, Bernard, 14, 104, 181, 199, 200–4, 208, 210–11, 213, 216–7, 222, 327, 331, 468, 480, 489, 490. *See also* Glen Alpine Resort, House of Hoo Hoo
and Bohemian Club, 489
and ruins, 489
and Sierra Club, 489
and Palace of Fine Arts, 489
McMahon, Thomas, 250, 286, 292, 423. *See also* Many Glacier Hotel
Medicine Owl, 254
Mesa Verde, 299, 302, 305, 356
Mills, Enos, 65, 166–167, 326, 446, 478–9, 489. *See also* Longs Peak Inn
and mining, 89, 94–95, 108, 118, 167, 225, 296, 306, 424, 467
Monson, Frederick, 302–3, 482, 491
Montana Improvement Company, 110, 116, 119
monumentalization of the landscape, 176–177, 234–5, 237
Moore, Henry, 171
Moran, Thomas, 109, 113, 174, 176, 235, 302, 305–6, 486
Morgan J. P., 15–16, 48, 60, 72, 163, 373
Mount Rainier National Park, 107, 109, 226, 375–6, 381, 428, 440, 484, 491–2. *See also* Longmire Administration Build ing, Longmire Community Building, Nisqually Bridge, and Paradise Inn
Muir, John, 13, 107, 112, 165, 167, 170–172, 176, 178, 194, 203, 234, 300–303, 315, 325–6, 371, 397, 400, 476, 479, 481–2, 484, 491–2
Museum of Modern Art, 362, 479, 488

N

Nampeyo. 354, 483
Nash, Roderick, 28, 100, 227, 243, 481, 486
Nason, George, 465, 485, 492
National Hotel, 119–121, 127, 162
Native Americans, 89, 108, 110, 128, 170, 176, 195, 225, 227, 230, 233, 242, 254, 302, 305, 311, 354, 362–4, 372–3, 440. *See also* individual nations.
and cultural appropriation, 346, 348, 350, 362–3, 353–9, 467, 469
land taken by railroads, 108, 225–7, 230
Navajo Diné Nation, 128, 353, 356, 363
Nazi Völkisch movement, 465
Nessmuk,14
Nisqually River Suspension Bridge, 422, 441
Norris, Philetus, 122, 202, 440, 443, 445, 448, 452, 458
Norris Geyser basin, 445, 452
Norris Museum, 452–7
as exhibit narrative, 443, 452-4
structure, 443, 452
Northern Pacific Railroad, 107–113, 116–120, 124, 130, 132–135, 138,142, 170, 225–7, 230, 234, 238, 264, 296, 309, 478–9, 488. *See also* Yellowstone National Park

O

O'Keeffe, Georgia, 363
Old Faithful Camp, 393, 399, 401. *See also* Old faithful Lodge, Geyser Hall
Old Faithful Inn, 16, 108–111, 116–117, 124, 127, 131–134, 137–138, 140, 152, 155–159, 162, 166, 169, 170–171, 183, 197, 137–138, 140, 152, 155–159, 162, 166, 169, 170–171, 183, 197, 203, 242, 303, 309, 373, 378, 391, 393, 397, 400–01, 412, 418, 423, 441, 444, 454, 470–71, 479, 488
imitation at San Diego Fair, 354
Old faithful Lodge, 412–17. *See also* Geyser Hall
Old Faithful trailside museum, 448
Old Forge, 77–78
Olmsted, Frederick, 34–35, 39, 42–44, 47, 167, 476–7, 487. *See also* Central Park, Prospect Park
Oraibi, 310, 353, 356
Oregon Pavilion, Louisiana Purchase Exposition, 183
O'Sullivan, Timothy, 300–1
overcivilized, condition of being, 13, 476, 486

P

Palace of Fine Arts, 200–1, 208, 213, 215–6, 480, 489
Palo Duro Canyon State Park, 465
Panama California Exposition, 320, 354
Panama–Pacific International Exposition, 391, 480, 489, 492
Paradise Inn, 328, 375–6, 378–9, 381, 386, 418, 423, 428, 483, 491–2
snowfall at, 376–8
Park and Recreation Structures (Good),19, 388–9, 422, 427, 441, 443, 476, 484
Park Service, National, 16, 75, 108, 163, 250, 275, 292, 320, 325–6, 328, 333, 345, 348, 350, 359, 373, 375–6, 381, 388–9, 391–3, 395, 397, 398–400, 412, 418, 422, 424, 427–8, 438, 440–41,443–4, 447–8, 465, 467, 471, 474, 477–9, 482–8, 490–2
Parsons Lodge, 204
Passage to India, 243
Pawson, John, 472
Phantom Ranch, 355
Phillips, Frank and Waite, 14–15, 476, 480, 486, 489
Philosophical Enquiry into the Origin of Our Ideas of the Sublime *and Beautiful, A* (Burke), 30, 476, 486
Picasso, Pablo, 362
picturesque, 19–20, 27, 29–30, 33–35, 42, 72, 82, 102, 162, 169–171, 200, 307, 315, 326, 367, 486
Piegan Blackfeet Nation, 226–7, 230, 232–3, 243–54, 268
Pilley, Dorothy, 265
Pinchot, Gifford, 77, 85, 167, 230, 477–8, 481, 487–8, 490
Piper, F. M., 27
Piranesi, 200, 216, 222
Platonic view of the world, 169
Plaw, John, 26, 476
Plaza Hotel, Las Vegas,NM,, 305
Pollack, Jackson, 362
ponderosa pine, 309, 345
Pope, Alexander, 22, 24, 151, 181, 188, 350, 476, 486–7
Pope, John Russell, 172, 392
Portland Forestry Building, 183, 196, 230, 233, 235, 237, 250, 480, 489
Powell, John Wesley, 300, 305, 347, 482, 491
Price, Uvedale, 20, 26–27, 31, 113, 134, 169, 171, 367, 476, 479, 483, 486
primitive hut, 8, 21, 100, 167, 188, 216, 277,
primitive man, 303, 350, 364, 367–8, 371–3, 443, 465
"Primitivism in 20th Century Art," 362
Prince of Wales Hotel, 261, 475
Prospect Park, 42–43, 477, 487
Ptarmigan Wall, 229, 265
Pueblo Bonita, 306–7
Punchard, Charles, 391
Puter, Stephen, 226, 481, 490

Q

Queen Caroline, 23, 486
Quinn, Ruth, 133, 479, 483, 485, 488, 492

R

racism, in architectural theory, 100, 465
racism in relation to forest preservation, 222, 480
Rafferty, J. H., 158
Railroaded (White), 107, 477–8, 481, 486,
railroads, 132, 478, 481, 486, 488, 490, 492
and Native Americans, 108, 225–7, 230
and deforestation, 119, 226–7, 229–30
and mining, 110, 179
lack of need, 107–8, 225–6
Ramona (Jackson), 305, 482, 491
Raphael, 22
Read, Herbert, 57, 171, 479, 489
Reamer, Robert, 124, 133–134, 138, 140, 142, 156–159, 162–163, 171, 242, 250, 258, 277, 286, 292, 376, 393, 400, 403, 423, 446, 479, 481, 488, 490, 506, 514. *See also* Old Faithful Inn, Canyon Hotel
loss of interest in rustic architecture, 157–159, 162–163
Frank Lloyd Wright influence, 158–159
and Louis Hill, 242, 250

redwood, coastal, *Sequoia sempervirens*, 199 176–78, 181, 200–03, 210–11, 213–5, 222, 369, 400
habitat, 176
logging history, 176
preservation movement, 176
Reinhart, Karen, 474, 479, 488
Reitveld, Gerrit, 169
Reynolds, Samuel, 128
Richardson, H. H., 60
Ames Gate House, 328, 464
Rinehart, Mary Roberts, 231, 237, 264, 275, 481–2, 490
Robertson, R. H., 57, 85
Rockefeller, John D., 57, 75, 447–8
Rockefeller, Laura Spelman Memorial, 447
Rocky Mountain National Park, 167
Roosevelt, Theodore, 115, 263–5, 325, 401, 468, 478, 481, 490
Root House, 19, 25–27, 31, 33, 36, 157, 167
Rosaldo, Renato, 469, 485, 491
Rose, Ethel, 302, 482, 491
Round Tower house, Mesa Verde, 356
Rousseau Jean-Jacques 15, 28, 99–100, 102, 104, 231, 487
Julie: Or The New Eloise, 28, 487
ruins, 21, 29, 128, 176–7, 211, 254, 303,
two types, 25, 27, 350, 470
as memory, 200, 222, 234, 356,
as ruin of nature, 299–300, 306–7, 315, 346, 348, 364
Ruin The, (Simmel), 25,177, 222, 303, 315, 318, 359, 364, 470, 476, 482–3, 485–6
Runte, Alfred, 237, 474, 486
Rushing, W. Jackson, 362
Ruskin, John, 99–100, 102, 104, 303, 367–8, 372, 477, 483, 487, 491
Russell, Charles, 14–15, 264, 282, 392, 476, 486
rustic arbor, Boston Public garden, 44
rustic architecture, 8–9, 16–17, 19, 24, 27–28, 30–31, 33–34, 44, 47, 49, 53-54, 57, 69, 78, 85, 94, 111, 116, 120, 124, 134, 157, 159, 167, 181, 203, 230, 237, 242, 271, 309, 326, 328, 350, 372–3, 375, 381, 386, 389, 397, 407, 422–4, 440–1, 443, 465, 468–70, 474
rustic shelters, Golden Gate Park, 44
Rustic Summerhouse, Fairmount park, 44
Rykwert, Joseph,175, 479

S

sacred groves, 174–178
San Francisco Earthquake, 200, 217, 222
Santa Fe, New Mexico, 111, 124, 305–7, 309, 353, 356, 362–3, 372–4, 482, 491
Santa Fe Railroad, 304–7, 482, 491
spur line to south rim, 306
Sargent, Charles, 110, 478, 488
Save the Redwoods League, 176, 480, 489,
sawmills, 67, 110, 119, 122, 260, 267, 397, 400, 422–3
sawmills, portable, 115–116, 118, 120, 123, 127, 140, 159, 163, 441
S Bridge, Coeur d'Alene, 117
scenic nationalism, 177, 234
Schama, Simon, 176, 480, 489
Schiller, Friedrich, 15
Schweinfurth, A. C., 181
Scotia Pacific Lumber, Company, 204
Scotia Saving Bank, 204
See America First Movement,177, 231
Seneca, 14, 476
Sentinel Dome, 169
sequoia, giant, *Sequoiadendron giganteum*, 169, 175–176, 199
Sequoia National Park, 199, 400, 492
Seton, Ernest Thompson, 362–4, 372–3, 375, 424, 474, 483, 491
as structural rationalist, 372–3
Sharp, Joseph Henry, 127–129, 307, 478, 488
Shaw, Richard Norman, 60, 482, 491
Shelters, Shacks and Shanties (Beard) 15–16
Shenstone, William, 25, 200, 222, 364, 476, 486
Shepard, Augustus, 77, 81–82, 84–86, 412, 477, 487. *See also* Camp, Huttig, Charles
shingle style, 57, 127, 181
Sierra Club, 201, 203–4, 222, 480, 489
Sikyátki, 354
Silver Forest, 379, 428
Simmel, Georg, 25, 177, 222, 303, 315, 318, 350, 364, 470, 476, 482, 483, 485, 486
Slabsides, 14, 367, 371–2
Snowshoe cabins, 392
Somers, Montana, 226, 242
Speiltrieb, 15
Sperry Chalet, 266–7, 271–2, 274–5, 490
Spyri, Johanna, 99, 231
stair-step method of cutting log ends, 390, 393, 395
Stevens, Isaac, 112, 303, 478, 481, 490
Stewart, Dugald, 234, 481
Stickley, Gustav, 15, 102, 129, 131, 134, 391
stick-style, 127, 423
Stillman, William, 34, 53, 476–7, 487
St. Mary's Chalet, 261, 267, 272
Stonehenge, 22
Stott, Mary Clark, 67, 477
Stourhead, 19, 24, 26–27, 157, 487
structural expression, 81, 368, 372, 375, 388, 441, 444, 465, 469
structural "honesty," 80, 99, 312, 363, 368, 372–3, 375–6, 388, 424, 441, 444, 465, 468
structural rationalism, 75, 102, 373, 375–6, 389, 424
Studley Royal, 25, 29, 486
sublime, 29, 30, 31, 112–113, 176, 181, 188, 194, 197, 222, 231, 234–5, 237, 254, 264–7, 306
and age, 30, 176, 222
and immensity, 30–31,194
and imperialism, 29
as empowering, 112–113
in America, 31,113, 237
of height, 30, 231, 234, 235, 265, 266, 267
Sunrise Visitors Center, 440, 491
Surprise Valley Farm, 75
surreal, surrealism, 26–27, 36, 147, 151, 157, 159, 162, 166, 169, 171–172, 197, 329, 379, 446, 454, 458
Swan Lake, Montana, 276, 286
Swedenborg, Emanuel, 178, 181, 480, 489,
Swiftcurrent valley, 231, 250, 260, 267, 271
Swiss Alpine club huts, 266
Switzerland, 47, 101–102, 104, 169, 176, 230–2, 234, 260, 265–6, 464, 477, 481, 482, 487

T

Tacoma Eastern Railroad, 375
Taliesin West, 465
Taos Pueblo, 320, 354
tent camps, 16, 121, 133, 233, 266, 333, 399
Thoreau, Henry David, 326, 397
Three Bears, 264
Three Sisters Wilderness, 107
Thumb Ranger Station, 390, 394
Tibbel, Deborah, 354, 483
timber industry, 52–54, 77, 79, 89, 94, 102, 108, 110, 115– 118, 124, 137, 151, 183–184, 186, 188, 194–195, 197, 204, 208, 216, 225–6, 229, 242, 260, 267, 282–3, 296, 306, 375, 467
Timberman, 237, 272, 481–2, 490
Todd, Frank, 200, 474, 480, 489
Towards a New Architecture (Le Corbusier), 367
Tower Fall, 234–5, 302, 400
trailside museums, 450
transcendentalism, 175, 326
transcontinental railroad, 110, 113, 134, 225–6
Trees That Twist (Mills)165, 489
trial of the wilderness, 263–5, 267, 271–2, 356, 468
Turner, Frederick Jackson, 137–138, 163, 242, 424, 443, 465, 471, 477, 479, 484–5, 487
Turner Falls State Park, 465
Turner thesis, 137, 163
Tuttle, Merit, 393, 400
Tweed, William C., 440, 474, 484, 492
Two Medicine Chalet, 266–8, 270, 272, 274, 490

U

Uncle Tom's Cabin, 34, 392
Underwood, Gilbert, 326, 328–9, 331, 333–4, 338, 345–7, 350, 381, 391, 395, 398, 400–03, 407, 412, 418, 422–4, 427, 438, 441, 464–65, 469–70, 482–84, 486, 492. *See also* Bryce Canyon Lodge, Deluxe Cabin , Bryce Lodge, Grand Canyon Lodge at the North Rim, Geyser Hall.
and geology 329, 331
and Logs out system, 328, 400–3, 420
Union Pacific, bus loop tours, 328, 334, 399, 407
Union Pacific Dining Hall, West Yellowstone, 331
Union Pacific Railroad, 132, 328
Upper Geyser Basin, 123, 132–133, 138, 479, 488
US Forest Service, 77, 227, 230, 478, 481
Utah Parks Company, 328

V

Vanderbilt family, 15, 48, 70, 373, 487
Vanderbilt, Alfred, 16
Vanderbilt, Cornelius, 112
Van Horne, Cornelius, 225, 481
vaulted parallel leg truss, 338
Vaux, Calvert, 34–35, 39, 41–44, 134, 167, 328, 476–7, 487. *See also* Central Park, Prospect Park
Restawhile, 44
Venturi, Robert, 157
vernacular architecture, 44, 100–101, 117, 134, 216, 242, 355, 367–8, 395, 441, 443–4, 447, 464–65
Villard, Henry, 113
Vint, Thomas, 388, 427–28, 436, 438, 440, 447, 484, 492
Viollet-le-Duc, E. E., 85, 99–100, 231, 303, 367–8, 372–3, 477, 483, 488, 491
Virginia Water, Windsor Park, 29
Voth, Henry, 353

W

Warburg, Aby, 363
Warburton, William, 22, 41, 175, 181, 476, 487
Washburn-Doane expedition, 108
Watkins, Carlton, 169
Waugh, Dorothy, 388, 474
Webb, W. Seward, 77
Weyerhaeuser, Frederick, 226, 481, 490
Wheeler, Olin D., 170, 479, 489
Wheelwright Museum, 362
Whidden and Lewis, 183
White House Ruins, 301
White, John, 203
White, Mark, 204
White, Laura, 176, 201
White, Richard, 47, 107, 163, 225, 234, 237, 477, 478
Whittlesey, Charles, 309, 310, 353
Wicks, William, 77–81, 477, 487
Log Cabins and Cottages, 78–80
William Read Camp, 57
Williams, Michael,110, 478–9, 486, 488
Willson, Fred, 163, 397–8, 400, 422–5, 489, 492. *See also* Underwood, Gilbert
Winema Theater, 204
Wirth, Conrad, 443
Wölfflin, Heinrich, 242
Wolf House, 368–70, 483, 491
Worcester, Joseph, 178, 181, 184, 222
Wordsworth, William, 231

Worlds Columbian Exposition Chicago,1893, 16, 88–89, 167, 183, 208, 353
Wrighte, William, 21, 176, 476
Wright, Frank Lloyd, 158–159, 479
Wright, John Lloyd, 392
Wyatville, Jeffry, 28–29
Wyntoon, 201, 222

Y

Yavapai Museum, 347–8, 350, 359, 361, 364, 444, 447, 465, 469, 470, 492,
Yellowstone National Park, 16, 34, 107–113, 115–116, 118–120,122–124, 127, 130–134, 140, 147, 156, 158–59, 162–163, 166, 170, 176–177, 194, 234, 258, 264, 282, 299, 309, 326, 328, 331, 334–5, 376, 378, 391–3, 397–9, 400–03, 407, 412, 418, 422, 423–4, 440, 444–8, 452, 454, 458, 468, 474, 478, 479, 482–5, 488, 491–2. *See also* Fishing Bridge Museum, Geyser Hall, Great North ern Railroad, Madison Museum, Norris Museum, Old Faithful Camp, Old faithful Lodge, Old Faithful Inn, Robert Reamer
    and Northern Pacific Railroad, 107–113, 116, 118–120, 130–134, 170, 309
    construction of road system, 120–122, 127
    development of auto camp buildings, 390–405
    traditional log cabins, 390–4
    trailside museums, 440, 444–8, 452, 454, 458
Yellowstone Park Association, 120
Yellowstone Park Improvement Company, 118–120
Yosemite Falls, 234, 397
Yosemite Museum, 327
Yosemite National Park, 169, 204, 325, 333
Yosemite Village, 326

Z

Zion National Park, 111, 328, 331, 346, 399, 407, 418
Zion Lodge, 111, 328, 331, 346, 399, 407, 418
Zittel, Andrea, 471, 474, 485
Zuni Pueblo, 13